An Introduction to
MANAGEMENT
CONSULTANCY

An Introduction to

MANAGEMENT
CONSULTANCY

Marc G. Baaij

Los Angeles | London | New Delhi
Singapore | Washington DC

Los Angeles | London | New Delhi
Singapore | Washington DC

SAGE Publications Ltd
1 Oliver's Yard
55 City Road
London EC1Y 1SP

SAGE Publications Inc.
2455 Teller Road
Thousand Oaks, California 91320

SAGE Publications India Pvt Ltd
B 1/I 1 Mohan Cooperative Industrial Area
Mathura Road
New Delhi 110 044

SAGE Publications Asia-Pacific Pte Ltd
3 Church Street
#10-04 Samsung Hub
Singapore 049483

Editor: Matthew Waters
Editorial assistant: Nina Smith
Production editor: Sarah Cooke
Copyeditor: Gemma Marren
Proofreader: Audrey Scriven
Indexer: Silvia Benvenuto
Marketing manager: Alison Borg
Cover design: Francis Kenney
Typeset by: C&M Digitals (P) Ltd, Chennai, India
Printed and bound in Great Britain by Ashford
Colour Press Ltd

© Marc G.Baaij 2014

First published 2014

Apart from any fair dealing for the purposes of research or
private study, or criticism or review, as permitted under the
Copyright, Designs and Patents Act, 1988, this publication
may be reproduced, stored or transmitted in any form, or by
any means, only with the prior permission in writing of the
publishers, or in the case of reprographic reproduction, in
accordance with the terms of licences issued by the Copyright
Licensing Agency. Enquiries concerning reproduction outside
those terms should be sent to the publishers.

All material on the accompanying website can be printed off
and photocopied by the purchaser/user of the book. The web
material itself may not be reproduced in its entirety for use by
others without prior written permission from SAGE. The web
material may not be distributed or sold separately from the book
without the prior written permission of SAGE. Should anyone
wish to use the materials from the website for conference
purposes, they would require separate permission from us. All
material is © Marc G. Baaij, 2014

Library of Congress Control Number: 2013939740

British Library Cataloguing in Publication data

A catalogue record for this book is available from
the British Library

ISBN 978-1-4462-5612-1
ISBN 978-1-4462-5613-8 (pbk)

CONTENTS

PART 2: THE MANAGEMENT CONSULTANCY INDUSTRY 105

PART 3: THE MANAGEMENT CONSULTANCY FIRM 207

14 Structured communications 494

15 Structured implementation 533

ABOUT THE AUTHOR

MARC G. BAAIJ

Marc G. Baaij is an associate professor of strategic management at the Rotterdam School of Management (RSM), at the Erasmus University in the Netherlands. He graduated in economics and holds a PhD in strategic management. Prior to joining RSM, Marc has worked for IBM and the Boston Consulting Group (BCG). At IBM he held various positions in sales and marketing. At BCG Marc worked as a management consultant, and was later appointed as a manager of research. At RSM, Marc is involved in various activities; pre-experience and post-experience teaching; designing and managing educational programmes; and doing consultancy and scientific research projects. Marc's research has been published in leading international scientific and managerial journals and books.

Marc lives in Rotterdam, The Netherlands, with his wife Ellen and daughter Sophie. In his spare time he likes to spend time with his family, draw cartoons, read books, play tennis, and walk with his dog along the beach.

PREFACE

THE PERCEIVED ATTRACTIVENESS OF MANAGEMENT CONSULTANCY

Many outsiders, among which are business students, perceive management consultancy to be an attractive career. However, most of them have a very limited understanding of what management consultancy is really about. Students may see management consultancy as an attractive (start of a) career for several reasons. First, management consultancy provides a steep learning curve. Students may perceive consultancy as an extension to their (business) studies. Management consultancy is sometimes called the 'graduate graduate school of business'. Second, consultancy is popular because of the superior earnings compared to most other sectors. Third, consultancy also offers faster career opportunities. For instance, within ten years you may reach partnership of a management consultancy firm and earn as much as those at the top level of corporations, which typically takes much longer to attain. Fourth, management consultancy is a profession with a high status. Many consider it prestigious as consultants typically work with top management. Because management consultants may cure 'sick' organizations, they are sometimes even compared to doctors. Fifth, many may perceive management consultants as powerful. People may have good reasons to fear management consultants.

THE SECRETIVENESS AND AMBIGUITY OF MANAGEMENT CONSULTANCY

Management consultancy is not only seen as attractive. Many (outsiders) see consultancy as also relatively secretive and ambiguous. Management consultancy is difficult to understand for outsiders. A commonly accepted definition of management consultancy does not exist. You may ask: why is management consultancy so secretive and ambiguous? One reason is that the clients of management consultants do not like to make it publicly known that they need consultants. Therefore, management consultants have to be discrete to protect their clients' interests. As a consequence, management consultancy projects are (relatively) secret. Another reason concerns the fact that management consultancy firms tend to be relatively secretive about themselves. Most consultancies are private partnerships. Therefore they do not have a legal obligation to publish annual reports. Moreover, consultants do not even have a legal obligation to be listed in a professional register, like for instance accountants or lawyers. For all these reasons, outsiders, even professional researchers, find it difficult to develop an understanding of the management consultancy industry and its firms. Despite, or perhaps because of, this secrecy and ambiguity, management consultancy is seen as an attractive career. *This book aims to help outsiders with an interest in management consultancy to develop a better understanding of what management consultancy is in order to make an informed career decision and start their consultancy career with an advantage.*

A MULTI-LEVEL INTRODUCTION

This textbook provides a comprehensive introduction to management consultancy and supplies insights at four different levels to provide outsiders with a better understanding of management consultancy. It consists of four parts. Each part covers a level.

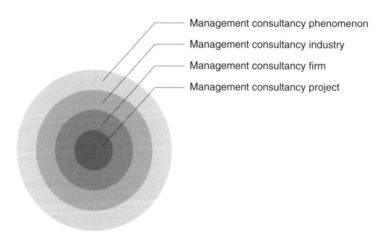

Management consultancy phenomenon

Management consultancy industry

Management consultancy firm

Management consultancy project

FIGURE 0.1 *Management consultancy at four different levels*

Level 1: the management consultancy phenomenon

The first part of the book is an introduction to the phenomenon of management consultancy. It consists of three chapters. The first chapter discusses different definitions of management consultancy in order to develop a synthesis. We also explore the boundaries of management consultancy. Moreover, we review the different roles of management consultants, both the formal and the informal – hidden – ones. Finally, we compare management consultancy with other knowledge-intensive professions. Chapter 2 explores the origins and the development of management consultancy over time. Thereby we explain the rise and decline of management consultancy firms during the industry's history. Moreover, we discuss the consequences of these historical patterns for today's consultancy firms. Chapter 3 investigates clients' reasons for hiring management consultants, both the formal – overt – reasons and the informal – covert – reasons. We also look critically at the impact of management consultancy on the client, on industries, and on the economy at large.

Level 2: the management consultancy industry

The second part of the book provides an overview of the management consultancy industry and its macro-environment. Chapter 4 provides an overview of the global management consultancy landscape. It investigates the range of consultancy services, the various client sectors, and the different client geographies. In Chapter 5 we analyse competitive strategies of consultancy firms, and the (dynamics of) competitive forces in the consultancy industry. Chapter 6 explores the relationship between management consultancy and the broader (macro) environment. We discuss how management consultants create and disseminate management knowledge in society, and we examine the impact of macro-economic (business) cycles, globalization, and technological developments on the management consultancy industry.

Level 3: the management consultancy firm

The third part looks inside the management consultancy firm. Chapter 7 focuses on the firm's activities. It presents the value chain of a management consultancy firm and discusses the various primary and support activities. Chapter 8 investigates the management of the consultancy firm. We explore the different types of organization, governance, and culture of the various consultancy firms. Chapter 9 is about people and careers in management consultancy. We discuss in detail how consultancy firms deal with recruitment, training, development, promotion, (involuntary) turnover, and alumni.

Level 4: the management consultancy project

The fourth part takes the reader through a typical management consultancy project. Chapter 10 takes an extensive look at client management and other stakeholders inside and outside the client organization. Chapter 11 provides a detailed look at how management consultants set up a client project. Chapter 12 shows how the world's top tier management consultancy firms approach complex client problems and opportunities. It provides a well-illustrated, step-by-step guide to structured problem diagnosis. Chapter 13 illustrates how top tier consultancies develop solutions for their clients. We outline in detail the process of structured solution development. Chapter 14 is about how top tier consultants communicate their recommended solutions to clients. We show a structured approach to the design of client presentations and reports. In the final chapter we show how consultants may assist clients with the implementation of solutions. We show a structured approach to implementation and we explore why implementations may fail to produce the expected results.

PRACTICAL GUIDE

The fourth part of the book gives a detailed and illustrated interpretation of the proven successful approach to structured problem solving by the world's top tier management consultancy firms, such as McKinsey & Company, Bain & Company, and the Boston Consulting Group. Access to this know-how used to be (almost) exclusively reserved for insiders. This structured approach to problem solving is highly valuable for students considering a career in management consultancy. However, this approach is also relevant for managers and entrepreneurs who work outside management consultancy. This book provides a guide, running cases, and exercises to develop the knowledge and skills in a proven problem solving approach, which is highly valued both inside and outside management consultancy.

CRITICAL REFLECTION

This book also takes a critical perspective on management consultancy. We critically reflect on the practices of management consultancy. Moreover, we broaden our perspective to include consultants' clients, client employees, consultancy firm employees, other stakeholders, and society in general. We consider the effects that management consultancy may have on all these groups. This book acknowledges various conflicts of interests between consultancy firms and these other actors. We are critical not only about consultants but also about clients. We emphasize that both parties may behave opportunistically and unethically. Such behaviour is not reserved for consultants. Clients may manipulate consultants as well.

INTENDED AUDIENCES

This introduction to management consultancy is designed for various audiences. *First*, the book addresses (business) students and graduates who are considering a career as an external or internal management consultant. *Second*, the book may be relevant to people employed in other lines of business, but are also considering a career switch to management consultancy. *Third*, the book may appeal to client managers and client employees who work with consultants and therefore have a need for better understanding management consultancy. *Fourth*, the book may be relevant to all others with an interest in management consultancy and a desire to deepen their understanding of management consultancy. This book may help aspirant consultants prepare for the selection process, in particular the case interviews. Finally, the structured approach to problem solving presented in this book is also valuable for people outside management consultancy.

AUTHOR

The book is written by an associate professor of strategic management who is an alumnus of the Boston Consulting Group. The author worked first as a management consultant and later as a manager of research at this top tier firm. Baaij works at the Rotterdam School of Management (RSM) of the Erasmus University Rotterdam in The Netherlands. He is an associate professor of strategic management and the academic director of RSM's Executive Master of Science in Management Consultancy programme. Baaij has designed various courses and workshops on management consultancy. He also trains managers and management consultants in the best practice problem solving method of the top tier consultancy firms.

An Introduction to Management Consultancy is written in a personal capacity and reflects his personal view on management consultancy. The book is based on his experience in management consultancy for BCG and RSM and on his experience in providing management consultancy courses and training at RSM. The book has also benefited from reviews and feedback by academic peers as well as practitioners, including senior consultants, alumni, and clients. It goes without saying that the book does not use any proprietary or confidential information of any management consultancy firm or its clients.

CHAPTER FORMAT

Each chapter begins with an introduction and an overview of the educational objectives. At the end of each chapter readers will find a summary, reflection questions, a mini case study for the application of acquired knowledge and skills, references, and suggestions for further reading. All chapters provide illustrations. The book offers a range of cases and mini cases on all kind of aspects of the management consultancy industry, the firms, and the projects. Moreover, the fourth part features two running cases which illustrate the process of structured problem diagnoses, solution development, communication, and implementation. All cases are based on real world examples, but they have been stylized for pedagogical reasons. Moreover, confidential information has been removed and, with the exception of the cases about Eden McCallum, Evalueserve, and McKinsey & Company, real names have been replaced by fictitious names to protect the interests of clients and their consultants.

COMPANION WEBSITE

The companion website of the book offers content for both students and lecturers. To cater to the needs of students, the site provides support materials, such as additional case studies, exercises, templates for structured problem solving, and web links to relevant websites and video materials. Additionally, the site offers, on an exclusive basis, specific materials and features for lecturers only.

ACKNOWLEDGEMENTS

I am grateful for the support provided by many people. I would like to thank the following people for their valuable feedback on cases and chapters: (in alphabetical order) Peter van Baalen, Fiona Czerniawska, Rob van Dale, Bas Giesberts, Ashish Gupta, Stefan Heusinkveld, Michel Olijslagers, James Parker, Flemming Poulfelt, Nathan Simon, Sebastiaan Vaessen, Marjon Wanders, Jaron Weishut, and Phebo Wibbens.

I am also indebted to the comments and suggestions provided by the book publisher's anonymous reviewers and by management consultants who wish not to be mentioned. The book also benefited from the questions and feedback that came from the students and managers who participated in my courses and workshops on management consultancy.

I also wish to acknowledge contributions from Sage: (in alphabetical order) Alison Borg, Sarah Cooke, Mark Kavanagh, Francis Kenney, Gemma Marren, Audrey Scriven, Nina Smith, Ruth Stitt, and Matthew Waters.

Last but not least, I would like to express my gratitude to my beloved wife Ellen and daughter Sophie who gave me the motivation and support to write this book and draw some cartoons (Sophie's idea).

PART 1
THE MANAGEMENT CONSULTANCY PHENOMENON

PART MAP

This part sets the scene by investigating what management consultancy is. Management consultancy is a popular term. But what do people actually mean when they speak of management consultancy? Each part of this book is designed to achieve a specific set of learning objectives. After studying the first part, you should be able to:

- Evaluate which professional services belong to the domain of management consultancy and which ones do not (Chapter 1).
- Explain the value propositions and market positions of management consultancy firms in terms of the historical development of the industry (Chapter 2).
- Critically evaluate when it is justified to hire management consultants (Chapters 1 and 3).
- Distinguish clients' informal reasons for hiring management consultants (Chapter 3).
- Critically reflect upon the impact of management consultants (Chapter 3).
- Determine which type of management consultancy project best fits a specific client's situation and need (Chapters 1 and 3).
- Critically reflect upon the question of whether or not management consultancy is a profession (Chapters 1 and 3).

CHAPTER 1: DEFINING MANAGEMENT CONSULTANCY

To develop a better understanding of management consultancy, this chapter investigates the distinguishing characteristics of management consultancy. Building on previous definitions of management consultancy, this book proposes a synthesis, which consists of a broad definition and a narrow definition of management consultancy. The chapter also investigates which professional services belong to the domain of management consultancy. Another important question you may ask is: who is responsible for a management consultancy project? This chapter shows how responsibilities between clients and their management consultants may be divided. It reviews the various roles – both the formal and the informal – that management consultants may realize. Finally, the chapter examines whether or not management consultancy is a profession.

CHAPTER 2: ORIGIN AND DEVELOPMENT OF MANAGEMENT CONSULTANCY

The second chapter deals with the history of the management consultancy industry. The key questions answered in this chapter are: where does management consultancy come from and how did the industry evolve over time? This review uncovers patterns in the history of the industry and explores the underlying causes, as well as the consequences. The chapter also explains why many management consultancy firms of the past were replaced by new entrants. The chapter might also have been named: 'The rise and decline of management consultancy firms'. Last but not least, it discusses the consequences of these historical patterns for today's management consultancy firms.

CHAPTER 3: REASONS, RISKS, AND RESULTS OF MANAGEMENT CONSULTANCY

The third chapter concentrates on the question: why do managers use consultants? The chapter identifies formal and informal reasons for using management consultants and then discusses whether or not management consultants meet clients' expectations. The chapter also critically explores the impact of management consultancy on clients, on the clients' industries, and on the broader, macro-environment. Furthermore, we compare internal and external management consultancy and discuss the main risks of external consultants. The chapter ends with explaining the impact of management consultancy in terms of its worldwide growth.

1

DEFINING MANAGEMENT CONSULTANCY

INTRODUCTION

The central question of this chapter is: what is management consultancy? There are different definitions of what constitutes management consultancy. The roles and effects of consultancy are subject to debate. The management consultancy industry is rather secretive. Its boundaries are ambiguous. Moreover, the industry is heterogeneous in type of firms. The best known management consultancy firms are large, globally operating organizations with strong brand names. However, there are only a few of those firms. Most management consultancy is done in (very) small firms that operate on a national or local scale. Many consultants are sole practitioners. Because most consultancy firms are not (well) known, outsiders may think that management consultancy is only about big global brands.

This chapter examines the key characteristics of management consultancy and reviews several definitions to arrive at a synthesis of definitions. Next, the chapter explores the boundaries between management consultancy and other business services. A case study gives an example of a management consultancy project. The chapter also provides an overview of the formal and informal roles of consultants. Furthermore, the chapter shows how these formal and informal roles are related. After an overview of management consultancy tasks, the chapter compares external management consultancy with the internal variant, and investigates the differences between internal and external consultancy as well as sketching the implications. Finally, for readers interested to develop a deeper understanding, the chapter considers the question whether or not management consultancy is a profession and identifies the benefits as well as barriers against management consultancy as a profession. It closes with a summary, reflective questions, a mini case study, suggestions for further reading, and references.

Main learning objectives

- Critically reflect upon the identity and boundaries of management consultancy.
- Distinguish the functionalist and the critical perspective on management consultancy.
- Understand the differences between existing definitions of management consultancy.
- Identify the distinctive characteristics of management consultancy.
- Distinguish client problems and opportunities that may require management consultancy.
- Understand the tensions in the division of responsibilities between consultants and clients, and the tensions that exist for a consultant who is serving clients in the same sector at the same time.
- Distinguish between different types of consultancy and business services.
- Identify and assess the different roles of management consultancy.
- Understand the differences in terms of roles and benefits between external and internal management consultancy.
- Critically reflect upon the question of whether or not management consultancy is a profession.

OPPOSING PERSPECTIVES ON MANAGEMENT CONSULTANCY

Functionalist perspective

You may ask: what is management consultancy about? Let's begin with a normative perspective on management consultancy. Management consultants are professional helpers. They create value for their clients, mostly managers of organizations, through providing independent advice. By advising managers on how to improve their organizations, management consultants may also create value for society. A popular analogy of management consultants is the medical doctor. Management consultants like to be compared with medical doctors. In the same way as doctors cure sick patients, management consultants cure 'sick' organizations. But management consultants do more than their medical counterparts. Management consultants can also make healthy organizations even better. The mission statements of global management consultancy firms illustrate management consultancies' ambitions to help clients create value. For instance: 'Our mission is to help our clients realize substantial and sustainable performance improvements'.

Critical perspective

In sharp contrast to this functionalist perspective on management consultancy, stands the perspective displayed in the critical academic literature (for an overview, see Clark and Fincham, 2002). This stream of research argues that management consultancy faces ambiguities over:

- the knowledge that management consultants claim
- what management consultants claim to do with that knowledge
- the claimed results of management consultants (Alvesson, 1993).

According to this critical research, part of management consultancy's knowledge consists of management fads and fashion that cater to the managerial need for reassurance in a world full of uncertainties (e.g. Kieser, 1997). Because of the difficulties of investigating the effectiveness of management consultancy projects, critical academic studies have not focused on the effect of management consultancy. Instead the critical literature concentrates on the rhetoric of management consultancy. The researchers claim management consultancies use their persuasive power to build legitimacy (e.g. Kieser, 1997; Legge, 2002). In contrast to the academic studies, popular criticism by some journalists and alumni of management consultancies does question the effectiveness of management consultancy. These articles and books typically seek out disastrous failures of consultancy projects to characterize management consultants as, for instance, witchdoctors and con men (e.g. O'Shea and Madigan, 1997; Pinault, 2000). It should be acknowledged that most – if not all – of these texts are anecdotal and are based on subjective interpretations of the authors' personal experiences.

Comparing perspectives

Which perspective is correct? Are management consultants like doctors, or are they masters of rhetoric, or maybe even witchdoctors? As in most cases, the real world picture is not black or white. Looking at the management consultancy industry does not provide an answer to this question. The spectrum of firms that call themselves management consultanties is rather broad. It includes the global top tier management consultancies, such as McKinsey & Company, which advise chief executive officers on strategy but it also includes the advisory services units of the big accountancy firms, such as Deloitte, and the consultancy arms of the big technology firms, such as Accenture. Furthermore, there are many small- and medium-sized management consultancy firms that operate locally or nationally. Some niche players with high-level expertise in a specific domain, for instance mergers and acquisitions, may even operate on a global scale. Finally, the number of sole practitioner management consultants is growing. This chapter explores the distinctive characteristics, roles, and responsibilities of management consultants. Chapter 3 looks at the effects of management consultancy on clients and the broader environment.

CHARACTERISTICS OF MANAGEMENT CONSULTANCY

Management consultancy is a service

To understand what management consultancy is, let's take a closer look at the distinctive characteristics of management consultancy. Management consultancy is a service. This has several implications. Being a service, management consultancy is intangible. There are no physical features that can be displayed or communicated. Typically the tangible outputs are the consultants' reports and PowerPoint presentations. The product of management consultancy is an intangible experience, which cannot be owned (Bowen and Schneider, 1988). However, in specific consultancy projects, such as cost reductions, the impact of consultancy is immediately measurable and therefore tangible. In fact, increasingly clients demand so-called contingent projects where (part of) the fees will be directly related to the achieved results. The fee may for instance be a percentage of the operational expense reduction.

Moreover, the creation and consumption of management consultancy take place simultaneously and are inseparable (Bowen and Cummings, 1990). The relationship between management consultants and clients is the medium of service delivery. The clients of the management consultant play an important role in both the consumption and creation of management consultancy (Argote, 1982). Management consultancy may be perceived as a form of 'co-creation'. Therefore, management consultants are heavily reliant on intimate access to their client's organization for knowledge. Moreover, as a service, management consultancy is perishable. It cannot be stored. Management consultancy is about utilization of the capacity of the consultancy staff. Although management consultancy is highly labour-intensive, there are opportunities for leverage and scalability. Procedures and software – for consultancy – enable leverage and make consultancy scalable. Moreover, among other things, knowledge management and marketing offer scale advantages.

Management consultancy is directed at managers

As the name indicates, management consultancy is a service directed at the managers of client organizations. These managers are responsible for (parts of) their organizations. These organizations can be commercial or not-for-profit. They may range from small to large. The managers may operate at different hierarchical levels, ranging from junior management to board level. The global top tier management consultancy firms advise chief executive officers of Fortune 500 corporations and presidents of countries. Managers and country leaders using management consultancies have in common that they are responsible for making decisions about the problems and opportunities of their organizations and countries.

Management consultancy is about decisions

The domain of the management decisions on which consultancy focuses is the positioning and functioning of organizations. This domain varies from strategic management and organization to the various business functions, such as operations and human resource management. Management consultancy is not about decisions on personal problems or the personal opportunities of individual managers. Personal effectiveness is the subject of training and coaching. Business effectiveness is the subject of management consultancy. However, we acknowledge that managers may hire consultants for their own benefits, for instance to rise in their organization's hierarchy. Management consultants may accept such projects. This type of hiring reason is informal. Chapter 3 will discuss all types of informal hiring reasons.

Management consultancy is knowledge-intensive

Management consultancy is about enabling or improving management's decision making on business problems or opportunities. Identifying and solving these problems or opportunities will put demands on the intellectual capability of the consultants. Management consultancy is, therefore, a knowledge-intensive service.

Management consultancy is based on independence

Management consultants need to be independent from their clients. This independence is a necessary, though not sufficient, condition for giving objective and impartial advice to managers. Management consultants should not have a hierarchical relationship with their clients. They should refrain from an equity relationship. Management consultants should not have an equity stake in their clients, nor vice versa.

Management consultancy is a business

A consultancy project is a business transaction between a client and a management consultancy. The client pays for the provision of the consultancy's services. In some cases the payment to the consultancy is based on the performance delivered by the consultancy. Because of the difficulty, or the impossibility, of measuring the effects of management consultancy, most clients pay their consultants on a time and material basis. Some consultancy firms also do some pro-bono projects for non-profit organizations. They may for instance give advice to a charity for free.

Management consultancy is about projects

Management consultancy is provided on a project basis. Clients engage management consultants not for an indefinite period of time but for a limited, specified period. Management consultancy is about providing particular deliverables, for instance, advice on a decision, or assistance with the implementation of a decision. After providing the service, the consultancy project is ended. Management consultancy is project-based and is, therefore, temporary. Nevertheless, many clients will have long-term relationships with the same management consultancy. Over time, the management consultancy may fulfil a series of projects for a client. You should, therefore, distinguish between the distinct transactions, which are the projects, and the on-going relationship between clients and consultants. Repeat business is very important for management consultancies. It is attractive to both parties as it saves on search costs for clients and acquisition costs for consultants. It gives consultants a flying start as they already know the ins and outs of a client organization. For many consultants the majority of clients will be existing clients. This is therefore repeat business.

Management consultancy can be full-time and part-time

Management consultancy does not have to be a full-time position. Some professionals provide management consultancy on a part-time basis. Business professors with a separate consulting practice on the side are an example of part-time management consultants.

DEFINITIONS OF MANAGEMENT CONSULTANCY

There are various definitions of management consultancy that character-ize it as a special professional service. As a result, no consensus exists about what constitutes management consultancy. Let's consider some of its definitions.

Definition 1: recommendation and implementation

The International Council of Management Consultants (ICMCI), a global professional association of management consultants, defines manage-ment consultancy as: 'Service provided to business, public and other undertakings by an independent and qualified person or persons in identifying and investigating problems concerned with policy, strategy, organization, effectiveness, procedures and methods, recommending appropriate action and helping to implement those recommendations' (ICMCI, 2012).

Definition 2: objectivity and independence

Another definition explicitly states that management consultancy is an advisory service and emphasizes the objectivity of management consult-ants: 'Management consultancy is an advisory service by specially trained and qualified persons who assist, in an objective and independent man-ner, the client organization to identify management problems, analyse such problems, recommend solutions to these problems, and help, when requested, in the implementation of solutions' (Greiner and Metzger, 1983: 7).

Definition 3: support decision making

A third definition is explicit about the situations that call for manage-ment consultancy. According to this definition, management consultancy is about helping clients make important decisions and take action in 'over complex' situations. In this type of situation, it is difficult to choose between alternative courses of action. At the same time, there is great significance attached to these actions (Hagenmeyer, 2007). According to the third definition: 'Management consultancy is thus a form of situation-specific assistance provided by an independent, external and professional intervention-expert who enables the management of a client's organization to take action in an over complex management situation' (Hagenmeyer, 2007: 110).

Definition 4: change implementation

An alternative definition explicitly mentions implementing change as a characteristic of management consultancy. This definition also elaborates on the potential benefits of consultancy, which include enhanced learning by clients. According to this definition: 'Management consultancy is an independent professional advisory service assisting managers and organizations to achieve organizational purpose and objectives by solving management and business problems, identifying and seizing new opportunities, enhancing learning and implementing changes' (Kubr, 2002: 10).

Definition 5: any form of help

The before-mentioned definitions are about management consultancy as a special professional service. Another approach is to define management consultancy as a broad function (Kubr, 2002). An example of a broad functional view is: management consultancy is 'any form of providing help on the content, process, or structure of a task or series of tasks, where the consultant is not actually responsible for doing the task itself but is helping those who are' (Steele, 1975: 3). However, this definition and similar definitions of management consultants as helpers or enablers are so broad that they can be applied to individuals who fulfil other positions than that of management consultancy.

A synthesis

This book aims to develop a synthesis of existing definitions. A common element in these definitions is providing assistance, or help, to managers. The question arises: what specific type of assistance may managers request from management consultants? Managers may turn to management consultants for assistance regarding problems and opportunities for their organizations. These organizations may face problems and opportunities that their managers need to address. Management must take decisions about courses of actions to solve these problems and seize these opportunities. Management may decide to solve these problems and seize these opportunities themselves. However, they may also decide to use management consultants to develop recommendations for solutions. Management consultants may provide advice on these managerial decisions. Consultants may identify and diagnose the organization's problem or opportunity. Subsequently, they may provide a recommendation for a particular action to solve the problem, or seize the opportunity. However, client management remains responsible for taking the actual decision about implementing the recommended solution.

AN INTRODUCTION TO MANAGEMENT CONSULTANCY

TABLE 1.1 *Some examples of a client organization's problems and opportunities*

Management level	Organization's problem or opportunity	Question to management consultant
Strategic level	The chief executive officer of a corporation sees an opportunity in an adjacent industry.	Should we enter this industry?
	The management team of a market leader is confronted with a stagnating market.	How should we grow the business?
	The executive vice-president of a business unit is confronted with a declining market share.	How should we regain competitiveness?
	The executive team of a corporation that faces a merger and acquisition wave sees an opportunity to acquire a competitor.	Should we acquire this competitor?
Operational level	The management team of a vertically integrated corporation has been approached by an outsourcing firm with an outsourcing offer that will increase their flexibility and reduce costs.	Should we outsource part of our activities?
	The chief operating officer of a manufacturing corporation has to recall his bestselling product because of quality problems.	How should we improve our product quality?
	The management team of a production plant is confronted with the entry of a low cost competitor in their market.	How should we reduce costs to match the low cost new entrant?
	The human resources officer of a professional services firm faces high staff turnover.	How should we retain our talents?

A NARROW DEFINITION

Table 1.1 presents some examples of a client's organization's problems and opportunities that management needs to address. The figure distinguishes two management levels: the strategic level and the operational level, as management consultants may offer advice at both levels. The first level is about improving the long-term performance of the client organization as a whole. The second level is about improving the performance of one or more of the organization's operational activities over a shorter term.

We may perceive the provision of advice on management's decisions for their clients as an essential service of management consultants. A narrow definition of management consultancy, therefore, concentrates on advice giving.

Management consultancy is a knowledge-intensive service which independent business professionals provide to managers of client organizations, and consists of objective advice on management's decisions regarding the solutions to the client organization's problems and opportunities (narrow definition).

A BROAD DEFINITION

The next step for management, after taking the decision regarding the solution to the problem or opportunity, is to implement the solution. A broader definition of management consultancy may include both advising on decisions and assisting clients on implementation of the solution. Only implementation, that is taking actions, will enable clients to solve their problems and seize opportunities and thereby achieve their organization's objectives. It should be noted that solutions are necessary but not sufficient to achieve results. Only the implementation of solutions may accomplish the achievement of results. Table 1.2 provides some examples of implementation tasks. The table distinguishes three categories of implementation tasks:

1. Tasks involving the organization units as a whole.
2. Tasks involving an individual primary activity of the organization.
3. Tasks involving an individual support activity of the organization.

TABLE 1.2 *Some examples of implementation tasks*

Tasks at the level of an organization unit	Tasks at the level of a primary activity	Tasks at the level of a support activity
Acquire an organization	Build a logistics system	Negotiate new terms and conditions with suppliers
Integrate an acquired organization	Introduce a process innovation in a plant	Develop new knowledge and skill through training
Divest an organization	Withdraw from a distribution channel	Set up an outplacement project for redundant staff

MANAGEMENT OF IMPLEMENTATION

Client managers may approach management consultants for assistance with the implementation of the recommended solutions. Just as advice provided by management consultants refers to management's decisions, the implementation assistance provided by management consultants should refer to the *management's* tasks regarding the implementation of the decisions (see Chapter 15). This is consulting to management, not working for its staff. The client management's tasks with respect to implementation are limited to:

- designing the implementation plan
- forming a team of client employees to execute the plan
- training the team members
- providing the communication of the plan
- coaching client management and team members
- advising management on an ongoing basis on the optimal approach throughout implementation
- monitoring the progress of implementation and suggesting adaptive and corrective actions when necessary
- evaluating the implementation.

Management consultants may assist client management with these tasks. A broad definition of management consultancy includes providing assistance with the management's tasks of implementation.

Management consultancy is a knowledge-intensive service which independent business professionals provide to managers of client organizations, and consists of objective advice on management's decisions regarding the solutions to the client organization's problems and opportunities (narrow definition), and may, in some cases, also consist of assistance with the management's tasks regarding the implementation of these solutions (broad definition).

Distinguishing management consultancy and business consultancy

Other implementation activities, which are not the tasks of client management, may be very important. Providing these non-management tasks may be essential to the success of implementation. However, they do not belong to the domain of management consultancy, according to this book's definition. Examples of such non-management tasks are the development of IT systems and training of personnel. This book interprets management consultancy as consultancy to management. The management consultant's services should always be at the client management level. Management consultancy, therefore, excludes doing the work of the professional staff that report to client management. Providing assistance for these non-management tasks regarding implementation may be termed 'business consultancy'.

To summarize, this book distinguishes two definitions of management consultancy and one definition of business consultancy. First, narrowly defined, management consultancy is about providing advice on client management's decisions on solutions for problems and opportunities for the organization of the client. Second, a broader definition of management consultancy combines advice on management's decisions with assistance on management's tasks with respect to implementing the recommended solutions. Third, combining advice to management with providing assistance on non-management tasks of implementing management's solutions may be termed business consultancy. Only providing assistance, without giving advice, should not be considered consultancy at all, but is a type of business services. Table 1.3 outlines the three categories of consultancy and business services as well.

TABLE 1.3 *Distinguishing types of consultancy and business services*

	No assistance with implementation	Assistance with managerial tasks regarding implementation	Assistance with non-managerial tasks regarding implementation
Advice on management decision	Management consultancy (narrow definition)	Management consultancy (broad definition)	Business consultancy
No advice on management decision		Business services	Business services

Firms and services offerings

Thus far, we have only examined 'what' constitutes management consultancy. We have not addressed the question: who is offering management consultancy services? When talking about management consultants, you will probably think of the (very) large management consultancy firms operating on a global scale, employing thousands of consultants. It is fully understandable if you equate management consultancy with the big firms because these firms are well known. Paradoxically, most management consultants do not work for the well-known, global firms. The majority of management consultants worldwide work in small firms or have a sole practice, and the latter means that they will work on their own as a one-man (or woman) consultancy firm.

Note that you cannot determine what management consultancy is by only considering the services providing firms because these firms are not necessarily limited to one type of service. Instead, firms may offer different types of services. For example, the very large firms may combine management consultancy with business consultancy and even with business services. Therefore, do not equate all the services offered by such a firm as management consultancy. The second part of this book will investigate in detail the different types of firms and the scope of the services they offer.

Seizing the real opportunity[1]

The following case study illustrates how management consultants may identify opportunities for their clients and develop solutions to seize these opportunities. This is a stylized case based on a synthesis of disguised real world situations. The case illustrates the importance of objective and impartial advice and shows management consultancy in a broad sense, that is, management advice combined with assistance with the management tasks of implementing the advice.

---

[1]All firms in the cases throughout the book are fictitious, with the exception of McKinsey & Company, Evalueserve, and Eden McCallum.

Perceiving opportunities

Winter 2012: Univers Bank is a relatively small bank that offers retail banking, commercial banking, and investment banking services. Its board wants to substantially increase the bank's return to shareholder value to join the league of the world's 20 best performing banks. To investigate opportunities for this performance improvement, the board has done a quick SWOT analysis (see Table 1.4). Based on these findings, Univers Bank's board perceives investment banking as a great opportunity to raise the bank's return. Investment banking is perceived as highly profitable and prestigious. Univers Bank is the market leader in investment banking in its (small) home country. Recently, one well-known international investment bank, Goldmine

TABLE 1.4 *SWOT analysis of Univers Bank*

SWOT confrontation matrix		Strengths			Weaknesses
		Leading investment bank in home country	Low exposure to bad debt	Global office network	Relatively high cost
Opportunities	Investment banking is an attractive sector	✓		✓	
	Investment bank Goldmine Bros is for sale	✓		✓	
Threats	Credit crisis		✓		

Bros, came up for sale. While most other banks cannot afford an acquisition due to the credit crisis, Univers Bank is well positioned as it has a low exposure to bad debt. Univers Bank operates a dense and expensive network of offices around the world. It mainly serves the retail and commercial banking activities. With the acquisition of Goldmine Bros, Univers Bank may leverage its worldwide network to become a global player in investment banking. The board thinks that such a position will certainly raise the bank's return to the desired level.

Univers Bank's board hires the management consultancy firm Acme & Company to devise a strategy for achieving the desired top position in global investment banking in order to gain within three years a position among the global top 20 of banks achieving the highest total shareholder return.

Debunking false opportunities

To understand the client's opportunity better, Acme & Company set out to do some preliminary fact finding. Based on their benchmark data of the global investment banking industry, they conclude that investment banking is a high return industry for the top players only. Moreover, Goldmine Bros was not part of the profitable top level in investment banking, even before the credit crisis forced the bank to give up its independence. The group of top investment banks is stable. Despite huge investments, no other bank outside this group has managed to conquer a top position in this seemingly attractive industry of global investment banking.

Acme & Company benchmarks the combination of the two banks, Univers Bank and Goldmine Bros, with the top investment banks. The management consultants discover that their client lacks the resources and the capabilities to compete with the top investment banks. Moreover, they find that the investment bank arm of Univers Bank, outside its small home market, has a weak position and earns a negligible return. To the surprise of the board, the bank's highest returns come from its retail division. The board had perceived retail banking as unattractive.

Identifying real opportunities

Moreover, Acme & Company identify Univers Bank's new internet-based business model for retail banking, which has been introduced highly successfully in the home market, as a very interesting opportunity to roll out internationally. Acme & Company, therefore, recommend that Univers Bank does not expand in global investment banking. Instead of building a global investment bank, the consultants point to the much higher return, and more feasible opportunity, of globally expanding the bank's internet retail business model. Moreover, building up an international internet retail bank will allow Univers Bank to thin out its expensive, dense, worldwide office network. The board of Univers Bank accepts the consultants' analysis.

Achieving effect

Next, Acme & Company develop a global competitive strategy for Univers Bank's internet retail bank. To assist management with implementation of the strategy, the consultants also formulate an action plan for the global rollout. The board responds positively to the recommended solution. They decide to give up their ambitions for a global investment bank. Instead, Univers Bank reallocates its resources to the global rollout of its internet retail bank, with a very positive effect on the bank's return to shareholders.

Discussion questions

1 What definition of management consultancy would best characterize the type of consultancy service provided by Acme & Company? Please choose between the narrow and the broad definitions provided in this chapter. Explain your answer.

2 Why did Univers Bank decide to hire a management consultant? Do you agree with the bank's decision to do so, or do you think that the bank should have refrained from hiring them? Please provide argumentation.

3 Which perspective on management consultancy is most applicable to this case? Please choose between the functionalist and the critical perspective. Explain your answer.

CATEGORIES OF PROFESSIONAL SERVICES

This book's definition of management consultancy may help to determine which professional services belong to the domain of management consultancy and which services do not. From our definitions we derive four main criteria for determining whether a service qualifies as management consultancy. Table 1.5 on the next page provides an overview of the outcomes.

Business process outsourcing

We may interpret hiring external management consultants as a form of outsourcing. However, if we define outsourcing in narrow terms as the externalization of business processes, such as operations, logistics, or administration, then outsourcing is not part of management consultancy. Such outsourcing is not the provision of advice on a management decision. Instead, this type of outsourcing is the outcome of a management decision. Outsourcing generally refers to non-management implementation tasks. Some management consulting firms may offer outsourcing on the side, or vice versa. In these situations you should distinguish between two types of professional services within the same firm. Such combinations of services may induce potential conflicts of interest between client and consultant. Professional services

TABLE 1.5 *Determining which professional services qualify as management consultancy*

	Criteria of management consultancy			
	Advice on management decision	Decision on management problem regarding the business	Assistance with managerial tasks of implementation	Independence of client management
Business process outsourcing	No			
Training	No			
Temporary work	No			
Venture capital investing				Not independent of client
Interim management	No, not advice but take decision			
Legal advice		Legal instead of business problem		
Accountancy		Financial instead of business problem		
Engineering		Technical instead of business problem		
Coaching		Personal instead of business problem		
Management guru	Only if guru provides advice			
Internal management consultancy	Yes	Yes	Can be	Only if independent

firms offering both consultancy and outsourcing services will need to balance the service firm's need for cross-selling consultancy and outsourcing with the client's need for independent management consultancy.

Training

Training does not belong to the domain of management consultancy either. Training is neither advice on management decisions, nor assistance on management's tasks regarding the implementation of solutions.

Some definitions of management consultancy will include the 'capability development' of clients as one of the benefits of management consultancy. Client management and staff may indeed learn from management consultants while working together during the consultancy project. However, this is a knowledge spill-over that is a positive side effect of the project. If clients decide to hire their management consultants only for the purpose of training their management and staff, then this service does not qualify as management consultancy.

Temporary work

Temporary work, or so-called 'body shopping', does not qualify as management consultancy if it is not about advice on management decisions, or assistance on management implementation tasks. Some clients may use management consultants for non-management implementation tasks. In such a case, the consultants will offer business services instead of management consultancy.

Venture capital investing

Venture capital investing does not belong to management consultancy. Venture capitalists may provide advice on management decisions. But venture capitalists are not independent as they have an equity stake in their 'clients'. Partners of one of the world's top management consultancy firms, Bain & Company, founded in 1984 a separate, and independent, venture capital firm named Bain Capital.

Interim management

Interim managers are not management consultants. Unlike management consultants they assume managerial responsibilities. Interim managers do not give advice on decisions, they take decisions.

Legal advice, accountancy and engineering

Legal advice is not management consultancy. Lawyers may provide advice to managers but not on business decisions. The domain of lawyers is legal problems and opportunities, rather than business ones. We acknowledge that business problems have legal aspects and therefore management consultants have to consider the legal side of their clients' business problems as well. Consultants may work together with legal advisors to investigate the legal side of the business problem. Legal advisors do not advise on business problems as a whole. Legal advice (in its pure form) is exclusively focused on the legal aspects of problems.

For the same reason, *accountancy* does not belong to management consultancy. Accountants may advise management on financial reporting. Of course business problems may have financial aspects. In such cases, management consultants should investigate the financial side of the business problems. However, accountancy in its pure form does not comprise advice to management on business problems or opportunities. It should be noted that all four of the world's largest accountancy firms have established separate management consultancy divisions.

Engineering is not part of management consultancy either. Engineers may provide advice but they must focus on technological problems and opportunities rather than business ones. Again, business problems may have technical aspects. Such problems require management consultants to consider these technical facets. They may hire engineers to analyse the technical side of the business problems. Engineers – in their pure form – will not advise on the business problem as a whole.

Personal effectiveness coaching

Personal effectiveness coaching is not management consultancy. Coaches may provide advice on the *personal* effectiveness of the individual manager. The problems and opportunities of an individual manager are not the domain of management consultancy. Management consultancy is about management decisions on the business problems and opportunities of the client organization.

Management gurus

Management gurus may be part of management consultancy. Some examples of management gurus are Jim Collins (bestselling author of, among others, *Good to Great*, 2001), Tom Peters (bestselling author of, among others, *In Search of Excellence*, Peters and Waterman, 1982), and one of the world's leading business scholars, Michael Porter (among others, the competitive forces framework, the value chain framework, and the generic competitive strategies). Communicating management ideas through articles, books, websites, and speeches is not management consultancy. Only if gurus also advise managers on business decisions, do they provide management consultancy. Michael Porter founded in 1983, together with colleagues of the Harvard Business School, the management consultancy firm Monitor Group (in 2012 acquired by Deloitte). As a partner of Monitor, Porter provides management advice to both leaders of corporations and national governments.

Internal management consultancy

Management consultancy is not reserved for *external* providers. Some large organizations have formed internal management consultancy units. These units serve managers in their own organization. As long as these internal consultants can operate independent of their clients, their work qualifies as management consultancy. In some cases, these internal consultancy units may also work for external clients. One of the world's top tier management consultancy firms evolved out of an internal consultancy. In 1963, The Boston Consultancy Group (BCG) was founded as the Management and Consultancy Division of the Boston Safe Deposit and Trust Company, which was a subsidiary of The Boston Company (BCG, 2013).

ROLES OF MANAGEMENT CONSULTANTS

This book distinguishes between the formal and informal roles of management consultants. In some client projects, management consultants may fulfil both roles. There might also be projects where the informal roles dominate. It is very difficult, or even impossible, to find out how often management consultants fulfil informal roles. Clients might be prepared to admit to outsiders that they use management consultants for the formal roles. However, most clients, and their management consultants as well, will most certainly be very reluctant to admit the use of the informal roles. This book distinguishes three formal roles: expert, doctor, and facilitator (based on Schein, 1988). Each of these roles is knowledge-based. Additionally, four informal roles are distinguished: hired hand, legitimator, political weapon, and scapegoat (see Table 1.6).

TABLE 1.6 *Roles of management consultants*

Role	Description
Expert	Provide knowledge to solve a problem defined by the client
Doctor	Identify and solve a problem for the client
Facilitator	Provide process which the client can use to identify and solve a problem
Hired hand	Provide temporary capacity for the client, not related to the specific client problem
Legitimator	Provide legitimacy to a client's solution against which other stakeholders are opposed
Political weapon	Provide arguments for a client's position in a political fight
Scapegoat	Take the blame for a client's solution that is not in the interests of other stakeholders

Management consultants as experts

The first formal role of the management consultant is the expert. Clients hire an expert to provide knowledge. These clients know, or think they know, that their organization has a problem or opportunity. Moreover, these clients are capable, or think they are capable, of defining their problem or opportunity. Then clients are in the position to purchase specific expertise from the management consultant to solve a problem or to seize an opportunity for their organization. This is called the *purchase of expertise* consultation model. Clients may also hire an expert management consultant if they have already found solutions for their problem or opportunity. If the stakeholders within or outside the client disagree about what is the best solution, then the expert management consultant may provide the required knowledge to evaluate the options. Management consultants may provide benchmark information and other external knowledge. They may also provide clients with contacts from their network. For instance, consultants may introduce a client to other, non-competing, relations of the consultant that represent best practices in other industries.

EXPERTS AS INNOVATORS OR BROKERS

The expert management consultant provides new knowledge to solve the client's problem, or seize the client's opportunity. The expert may develop or create this knowledge but the expert may also broker knowledge. Within the category of experts, we distinguish the knowledge innovator and the knowledge broker. The management consultant as knowledge broker disseminates knowledge across organizational borders and/or across industry borders. An example of knowledge brokering *within* one industry is when the management consultant transfers best practice manufacturing process from the leading automotive producers to a client automotive producer whose manufacturing process is trailing these best practices in automotive manufacturing. An example of knowledge brokering *across* industries borders is when the management consultant brokers knowledge about a business model from the consumer electronics industry to a client in the automotive industry. In the case of knowledge brokering, the knowledge may be new to the client but it may not be new to the client's industry. It is certainly not new to the world. Knowledge brokering needs to respect the interests and intellectual property rights of clients if it is not to become unethical or even illegal. A management consultant cannot broker sensitive knowledge from a particular firm, for instance a competitive strategy, to a direct competitor of that firm. For this reason, management consultancy firms that work for rival clients in an industry have to set up so-called 'Chinese walls' between the consultancy teams working for each client to prevent the leakage of sensitive knowledge. Some management consultancy firms may adopt a policy of only one client per industry to prevent the risk of leakage of sensitive knowledge to rivals.

Management consultants as doctors

The second formal role is that of the management consultant as a doctor. In this analogy, clients fulfil the role of the patient. These clients cannot define the problem, or opportunity, of their organizations. In their role of patients, clients may think they have a problem, or an opportunity. They have only vague ideas about this problem, or opportunity. For instance, an insurance company sees its profitability declining over time. The management of this insurer has no idea about the cause of this decline. This client hires a management consultant to diagnose, as a doctor, the client's situation in order to define the problem, or opportunity. Subsequently, as a medical doctor prescribes a treatment, the management consultant develops a solution for the client's problem, or opportunity. This model is named *doctor-patient consultation* (Schein, 1988). The consultant as doctor may diagnose and solve the client's problem. Next, they may provide an implementation plan for the solution. Finally, the doctor-consultant may assist client management in monitoring and controlling the implementation of the solution. Both the expert role and the doctor role are about management consultants providing content, or solutions, to their clients: this is called *content consultation*. These are 'content roles'.

Management consultants as facilitators

Another formal role of the consultant is not about content or solution provision but about providing a process by which clients may define and solve their problems themselves. The management consultant in a facilitator role helps clients to develop the content themselves. This is called *process consultation* and might also be called the 'do-it-yourself' version of consultancy (Schein, 1988). For instance, a retail company faces the entry of internet-based competitors into its market. This client wants to develop a new competitive strategy and hires a management consultancy firm to provide it with the method and techniques for strategy development. In process consultation, the client does the work under the guidance of the management consultant. Process consultation helps to get acceptance of solutions and eases the implementation of solutions because it is the client's own work. A benefit of process consultation is that clients may learn the consultant's methods and techniques for defining and solving problems and opportunities. Process consultation facilitates client capability development. To enhance capability development, client management needs to carefully select the employees to participate in the consultancy project on the basis of the need for capability development, not on the basis of availability for the project.

Management consultants as hired hands

The fourth role of the management consultant belongs to the informal category. This is the role of the management consultant as 'hired hand'. Clients may hire management consultants not for their expertise, or their problem solving skills, or for their process, but just because they are temporarily understaffed. The 'hired hand consultants' may be put to tasks that clients would generally do themselves, but for which they temporarily have capacity constraints (see for example, Sturdy et al., 2008). This consultancy role resembles (expensive) body shopping. For example, the newly appointed chief executive of a client corporation hires a partner from a management consultancy for three days per week for six months to assist this executive, without a specific problem or opportunity being identified.

Management consultants as legitimators

The fifth role is the management consultant as a legitimator. The authority of management consultants gives legitimacy to a solution. Clients might look for this legitimacy to be provided by a management consultant if stakeholders in and around the client organization – such as workers (unions), financial markets, and customers – oppose a particular solution that the client desires. For example, the board of a large corporation in a mature industry wants to enter another (but unrelated) industry. The corporation's shareholders and the financial analysts oppose such a move. The corporation, then, hires a prestigious management consultancy firm to develop a new corporate strategy that includes the desired diversification. Such a recommendation by a prestigious consultancy firm may provide a strong signal to these stakeholders. In such a case the client will publicly announce the recommendation by the consultants. They will even publicly announce the hiring of the consultants. The clients might be able to develop a solution themselves but acceptance by stakeholders may be lower than where a (prestigious) management consultancy develops the solution. Even worse is the situation where the management consultant is asked to rubber stamp a solution that the client has already developed. It goes without saying that the legitimator is an informal role for management consultants.

Management consultants as political weapons

The next role is also informal. This is the role of the management consultant as a political weapon, or a political ally, of the client management. The client management may use the management consultant to fight a political battle with actors inside or outside the client's organization. The consultant is supposed to provide arguments for the client's position. This may be an internal battle within the client organization, for instance, between rivalling managers or factions. It may also be an external battle between the client organization and external actors, for instance, national governments or suppliers. For example, two companies that were highly dependent on each other, an airport and an airline, came into conflict over an increase in airport tariffs. Each company hired its own management consultancy firm to provide arguments for (airport) and against (airline) the increase in tariffs.

Management consultants as scapegoats

The last informal role is the management consultant as scapegoat. The management consultants are used to taking the blame for a difficult, or unpopular, decision. For instance, a manufacturer of consumer electronics needs to cut its costs drastically to defend its market position against low cost competitors. The company wants to offshore part of its manufacturing activities from the manufacturer's home country to a cheaper overseas host country. The result of this offshoring will be the lay-off of a substantial part of its workforce. However, the company faces strong resistance from stakeholders, such as its workforce, the labour unions, and the home country's government. The company might hire a management consultancy, in particular one with a reputation for reducing costs and employment. These management consultants may do the dirty work of recommending the closure of plants and laying off the workforce in the client's home country. Client management then hides behind the back of the management consultants and keeps its hands clean.

Temptations and drawbacks of informal roles

TEMPTATIONS
The informal roles might offer a tempting perspective for management consultants. If clients ask the consultant to fulfil an informal role, then the offer may look like easy money. In particular, if the demand for the management consultancy's services is weak, then the consultancy firm might be inclined to accept the client's offer. However, informal roles come at a price. Besides the ethical issues of the informal roles, these roles have negative commercial effects as well for the management consultancy. The informal roles, in particular legitimator, political weapon, and scapegoat, depend to a large extent on the consultancy's reputation as developed through its formal roles.

DRAWBACKS
However, the informal roles erode the consultancy's reputation. If it becomes known that the consultancy accepts informal roles, then other clients looking for formal roles will avoid the particular consultancy firm. Without sufficient new projects that require formal roles and with the spreading of the word that the firm fulfils informal roles, the reputation

of the involved consultancy firm will deteriorate. If their reputation has deteriorated than the usefulness of the consultancy firm for clients looking for informal roles will dry up as well. Eventually, the consultancy firm will run out of formal and informal business. To wrap up: accepting informal roles may set in motion a vicious cycle for the management consultancy. However, it should be noted that management consultants need not always be aware – upfront – of informal reasons. It may happen that the client hides the informal reason (see Chapter 10). Alternatively, a consultancy project may begin for a formal reason, but during the project the client may add an informal agenda.

DIVISIONS OF RESPONSIBILITIES

The management consultancy process consists of five sub-processes:

1. Identifying the problem (opportunity).
2. Diagnosing of the problem.
3. Developing one or more alternative solutions.
4. Making a decision.
5. Implementing the decision.

The division of responsibilities between clients and management consultants for the sub-processes may be seen as a spectrum.

Management consultants as management substitute

On one end of the spectrum, management consultants take, or are given by their clients, responsibility for all five sub-processes. Management consultants make decisions and implement them. In this extreme situation, management consultants have become a substitute for client management. There is no responsibility left for the client. Clients may choose this position for several reasons:

1. The client is in a hurry and the time opportunity costs are high (then the relatively high costs of consultants are justifiable).
2. The client is a start-up and lacks the staff. For example, a firm wants to establish a new subsidiary in a foreign country and hires a team of consultants to set up that subsidiary, while the client searches for permanent staff.
3. The client management feels incapable of critically monitoring the management consultants and defending its position. Such incapability, however, erodes the reason for the existence of client management.

Bogus consultancy

At the other end of the spectrum, management consultants will do exactly what the client says. In this extreme situation, the client takes too much responsibility and is not prepared to share any responsibility with the management consultants. The consultant does not carry responsibility for any of the five sub-processes. This is what is sometimes called 'bogus consultancy' (Hagenmeyer, 2007). Management consultants face reputation risks when they accept such a position. Table 1.7 outlines the division of responsibilities between client and management consultant for the different models of management consultancy.

TABLE 1.7 *Different divisions of responsibilities between client and consultant*

Sub-processes	Problem identification	Problem diagnosis	Developing a solution	Decision making	Implementation
Models	**Responsibility for sub-process**	**Responsibility for sub-process**	**Responsibility for sub-process**	**Responsibility for sub-process**	**Responsibility for sub-process**
Management substitute	Consultant	Consultant	Consultant	Consultant	Consultant
Doctor-patient consultation	Consultant	Consultant	Consultant	Client	Client (consultant may assist when requested)
Purchase of expertise	Client	Consultant	Consultant	Client	Client (consultant may assist when requested)
Process consultation	Client and consultant (facilitator)	Client and consultant (facilitator)	Client and consultant (facilitator)	Client	Client and consultant (facilitator)
Bogus consultation	Client	Client	Client	Client	Client

EXTERNAL VERSUS INTERNAL MANAGEMENT CONSULTANCY

This book defines management consultants as independent business professionals. This definition does not suggest that only external professionals can be a management consultant. That would be too narrow a view of management consultancy. This book distinguishes between internal and external management consultants. Internal management consultants are permanent employees of an organization and they will typically only consult for this single 'client'. External management consultants are the owners or permanent employees of an independent consultancy firm. They have temporary consultancy engagements with varying client organizations. Internal management consultants may provide the same services as external consultants. Some internal management consultants are former external consultants, and vice versa. Table 1.8 outlines the main differences between internal and external management consultants and infers implications. Chapter 3 will discuss the reasons why organizations may establish internal management consultancy departments instead of hiring external consultants.

TABLE 1.8 *Main differences between internal and external management consultants*

Area	Differences	Implications
Knowledge	Internal consultants will generally focus on one organization.	Internal consultants will have better client understanding, which may benefit in particular expert consultation on implementation, and process consultation.
	External consultants will generally work for a broader group of clients, that may span different sectors.	External consultants will have broader, more varied knowledge, and skills which may benefit expert consultation and doctor consultation that requires new-to-the-client knowledge and skills.
Relation to client	Internal consultants are subject to the client's hierarchy, whereas external consultants operate at arm's length.	External consultants are more suited to provide impartial, independent consultancy. However, external consultants may also better be used as a political ally and scapegoat.
Reputation	Internal consultants may develop an internal reputation but not a public reputation. External consultants may develop a strong public reputation.	If external consultants have a strong public reputation, they may be used as legitimators.
Cost	Internal consultants generally have lower fees than external consultants.	Internal consultants' cost advantage may be particularly decisive if clients need hired hands and large-scale, long-term consultation on implementation.

MANAGEMENT CONSULTANCY AS A PROFESSION

This book's narrow and broad definitions assume management consultants to be professionals. However, is management consultancy a profession or not? This question is still up for debate. Certain stakeholders claim the professional status of management consultancies. But other stakeholders reject this idea. Let's first ask ourselves: what is a profession?

Characteristics of a profession

When talking about a profession, examples of doctors and lawyers come to mind. A profession may be defined as a business activity that is accompanied by a formal, legally enforced institution that protects the interests of the public and the professionals involved, by designing qualification standards, accrediting educational institutes, compulsorily registering members, monitoring and controlling the activities of members, and when necessary, taking sanctions. Essential components of a profession are an accepted and authoritative body of knowledge and skills, combined with a code of conduct.

Doctors versus consultants

One flaw in the analogy of the medical doctor is a lack of legal enforcement of the profession. Unlike the medical profession, management consultancy is not protected by law. Doctors, lawyers, engineers, and accountants are examples of legally enforced professions. You cannot call yourself a medical doctor without the required education. However, anybody may call themselves a management consultant. In fact, many people do.

Protecting the interest of clients

You may ask: who would have an interest in whether management consultancy is a profession and why? Clients may benefit from quality assurance provided by a profession to protect them against bad practice by some management consultants. A professional institute may protect clients against management consultants who are incompetent, or act unethically. Protection of client interests by a professional institution is particularly relevant for management consultancy. Management consultancy is a service that is difficult to assess, even afterwards. Professional standards may to some extent reduce uncertainty for clients.

Protecting the public interest

The general public may also benefit from professional standards for management consultancy. If bad management consultancy leads to bad business decisions and results, which in their turn may cause the bankruptcy of client organizations, then there will be a negative impact on the economy and society. If public sector clients underperform because of bad consultancy practices, then society also suffers. Since legal protection of the profession does not exist, it is all about reputation. A consultant's reputation is a key reference point for potential clients. Moreover, that reputation is a disciplining mechanism for consultants. Because of its importance, consultants will consider the risk of unethical behaviour for their reputation.

Protecting the interests of peers

Management consultants themselves may also benefit from professional standards. The bona fide and competent management consultant may find in the professional institute an ally against dishonest and incompetent peers. Professional standards and compulsory registration regulate entry into the management consultancy sector. These standards also signal quality which in its turn may promote management consultancy in both the market for its services as well as the market for professional labour. Management consultants may, therefore, find it easier to sell their services and attract talent.

Professional institutes

Various institutes attempt to support management consultancy. There are professional institutes for individual consultants as well as institutes for consultancy firms. These aim to increase credibility, quality, and ethical standards for management consultancy. They also provide voluntary accreditations for consultancy firms and individual consultants. However, no institute or accreditation is legally enforced. An example of a professional institute is the worldwide umbrella organization, the International Council of Management Consulting Institutes (ICMCI). ICMCI has a voluntary certification and registration. According to membership statistics in 2010 about 8,080 consultants worldwide were certified and registered by the ICMCI as a certified management consultant (CMC). This number amounts to less than 1 per cent of the global population of management consultants (Greiner and Ennsfellner, 2010).

Trade associations

There are also trade associations that serve the interests of the consultancy industry as a whole. They may lobby, do research, and seek positive publicity for management consultancy. Some examples are the Association of Management Consultancy Firms (AMCF) for the United States, and the European Federation of Management Consultancies (FEACO) for Europe.

Evaluation difficulties

The question arises: why is management consultancy not a legally enforced profession if there are clear benefits for clients, for the public, and for consultants, as stated before? We discuss three reasons: evaluation difficulties, domain ambiguity, and diverging interests. First, even for clients, the work of management consultants is very difficult if not impossible to evaluate. For a professional institute, as an outsider to the client–consultant relationship, it will be even more difficult to monitor the quality of management consultancy services. For governments the case for a legally enforced profession as protection of the public interest will be weak, given the difficulty or impossibility of identifying the negative influence of management consultancy on society. Chapter 3 will take a closer look at the effects of management consultancy. If monitoring the output of consultancy is not feasible, then the professional institute may monitor the input of consultancy. An institute may monitor the knowledge, skills, and values of management consultants.

Domain ambiguity

Second, management consultancy is too ambiguous and diffuse for a common standard of knowledge, skills, and values. The ICMCI has developed a body of knowledge and skills (see Table 1.9 on the next page). This systematic stocktaking of the required knowledge and skills serves as the basis for their certification, which is the CMC. Unfortunately, there is no industry-wide agreement on what constitutes the body of knowledge and skills. This may not come as a surprise. If a *shared* definition of management consultancy is lacking, how can we expect a *shared* body of knowledge and skills? Conflicting interests between management consultants make it difficult to arrive at a shared definition of management consultancy. If a broad definition of management consultancy is adopted, then the pure advisors, often the high profile management consultancy firms, will not participate. If a narrow definition is accepted then many firms that do implementation work will be left out of the profession.

Diverging interests

Third, not all consultancy professionals are interested in being subjected to professional standards and compulsory registration. Obviously the incompetent, unethical, and fraudulent professionals will oppose the implementation of standards. However, professionals that regard their competences as superior will have no interest in a standardization of inputs, i.e. knowledge, skills, and values. Average and below-average competent consultants will benefit from the legitimating effect of input standards and certificates. Above-average consultants will oppose such certification as it will level the playing field. The top consultancy firms do not need public standards for legitimacy because they have their own private means for legitimacy, which is their reputation, including their brand.

TABLE 1.9   *The certified management consultancy core competency framework of the ICMCI*

Categories	Sub-categories	Components
Values and behaviour	Beliefs	Values, ethics and professionalism
	Analytical skills	• Observations and analysis • Conceptualization and problem solving
	Relationships	• Complexity, change and diversity • Communication and presentation • Responsibility and accountability • Influencing
	Personal development	• Focus and time management • Self development
Technical competence	Specialization	• Knowledge and skill
	Consultative	• Client focus • Project management • Consultative process • Knowledge • Partnering and networking • Tools and methodologies • Risk and quality management
Business acumen	Consultant business	• Consultancy environment • Commercial aspects of assignment
	Client business	• External awareness • Business knowledge • Understanding the client • Client's project imperative

Source: ICMCI[2]

SUMMARY

Narrow and broad definitions

This book distinguishes between a narrow and a broad definition of management consultancy. *Management consultancy is a knowledge-intensive service which independent business professionals provide to managers*

---

[2] www.icmci.org/?page=6972393 (accessed 10 November 2012).

of organizations, and consists of objective advice on management's decisions regarding the solutions to the client organization's problems and opportunities [narrow definition], and may, in some cases, also consist of assistance with the management's tasks regarding the implementation of these solutions [broad definition].

Roles

Management consultants fulfil one or more roles for their clients. Formal roles are expert, doctor, and process facilitator. Management consultants may also fulfil informal roles, such as hired hand, legitimator, political weapon, and scapegoat. The informal roles will depend on the formal roles and they will also undermine the formal roles.

Division of responsibilities

The division of responsibilities between management consultants and their clients may cover a spectrum. On one side, consultants as substitute management assume all responsibilities for the client. On the other side resides 'bogus consultancy' where clients take all the responsibilities.

External versus internal consultancy

Management consultancy does not necessarily have to be done by external market agents. Clients may also establish internal management consultancies. Despite commonalities, internal and external consultants have differences that have important implications for their roles.

Profession

Unlike the medical doctor with whom management consultants like to compare, management consultancy is not a legally enforced profession. This chapter discussed the motivations for professionalization, but it also revealed some important reasons why management consultancy is not a legal profession.

REFLECTIVE QUESTIONS

1. Do we really need a definition of management consultancy? Why should we care about a definition? Explain your answer.

2. To what extent can management consultants provide truly independent advice? Critically reflect upon the relation between consultant and client. Explain your answer.

3. Should the professionalization of management consultancy be left to the practitioners, which are the management consultants? Or should governmental regulators take a role in the professionalization of management consultancy? Explain your answer.

4. What role may business schools play in the professionalization of management consultancy? Explain your answer.

5. How will an equity investment of a management consultancy in a client organization influence the division of roles and responsibilities between the management consultancy and its client? Explain your answer.

MINI CASE STUDY

To certify or not to certify

The management consultancy firm Acme & Company typically sends promising young consultants that lack a business educational background after about two years of work to a prestigious international business school for an MBA programme. Three young management consultants of Acme & Company are about to complete their MBA study at the leading Jobs School of Business. The inspiring curriculum has led the three consultants to develop an idea for a new business model for management consultancy. The consultants are so convinced of the value of their model that they want to implement it. Instead of returning to their employer, Acme & Company, which will promote them to project leader on their return to the firm, they decide to establish their own management consultancy firm, which is named 'Management Consulting 2.0!' One of the decisions they have to make is whether they should certify themselves as CMC with a professional institute of management consultancy.

Questions

1 Reflect upon the costs and benefits of accreditation for management consultants. What costs and benefits may accreditation provide to management consultants? Explain your answer.

2 Who benefits from accreditation? Identify the stakeholders that benefit most. Provide argumentation.

3 Should the partners of 'Management Consulting 2.0!' consider accreditation? Identify the pros and cons of accreditation for this firm. Explain your answer.

FURTHER READING

Handbooks of management consultancy

Greiner, L. and Poulfelt, F. (eds) (2005) *Management Consulting Today and Tomorrow*. New York: Routledge.

Kipping, M. and Clark, T. (eds) (2012) *The Oxford Handbook of Management Consulting*. Oxford: Oxford University Press.

Kubr, M. (ed.) (2002) *Management Consulting: A Guide to the Profession* (4th edn). Geneva: International Labour Office.

Critical academic perspective

Clark, T. and Fincham, R. (eds) (2002) *Critical Consulting: New Perspectives on the Management Advice Industry*. Oxford: Blackwell.

Popular journalistic criticism

O'Shea, J. and Madigan, C. (1997) *Dangerous Company: The Consulting Powerhouses and the Businesses They Save and Ruin*. London: Nicholas Brealy.

Pinault, L. (2000) *Consulting Demons: Inside the Unscrupulous World of Global Consulting Corporations*. New York: HarperCollins.

REFERENCES

Alvesson, M. (1993) 'Management fashion', *Academy of Management Review*, 21 (1): 254–285.

Argote, L. (1982) 'Input uncertainty and organizational coordination in hospital emergency units', *Administrative Science Quarterly*, 27: 420–434.

BCG (Boston Consulting Group) (2013) www.bcg.com (accessed 13 June 2013).

Bowen, D.E. and Cummings, T.G. (1990) 'Suppose we took service seriously?', in D.E. Bowen, R.B. Chase and T.G. Cummings (eds), *Service Management Effectiveness*. San Francisco, CA: Jossey-Bass, 1–12.

Bowen, D.E. and Schneider, B. (1988) *Services Marketing and Management: Implications for Behaviour*. Greenwich, CT: JAI Press.

Clark, T. and Fincham, R. (eds) (2002) *Critical Consulting. New Perspectives on the Management Advice Industry*. Oxford: Blackwell.

Collins, J. (2001) *Good to Great. Why Some Companies Make the Leap … and Others Don't*. New York: HarperCollins.

Greiner, L. and Ennsfellner, I. (2010) 'Management consultants as professionals, or are they?', *Organizational Dynamics*, 39 (1): 72–83.

Greiner, L.E. and Metzger, R.O. (1983) *Consultancy to Management*. Englewood Cliffs, NJ: Prentice-Hall.

Hagenmeyer, U. (2007) 'Integrity in management consulting: a contradiction in terms?', *Business Ethics: A European Review*, 16 (2): 107–113.

ICMCI (International Council of Management Consultants) (2012) www.globalcmc.com (accessed 11 January 2012).

Kieser, A. (1997) 'Rhetoric and myth in management fashion', *Organization*, 4 (1): 49–73.

Kubr, M. (ed.) (2002) *Management Consulting: A Guide to the Profession* (4th edn). Geneva: International Labour Office.

Legge, K. (2002) 'On knowledge, business consultants and the selling of total quality management', in T. Clark and R. Fincham (eds), *Critical Consulting: New Perspectives on the Management Advice Industry*. Oxford: Blackwell, 74–92.

O'Shea, J. and Madigan, C. (1997) *Dangerous Company: The Consulting Powerhouses and the Businesses They Save and Ruin*. London: Nicholas Brealy.

Peters, T.J. and Waterman, R.H. (1982) *In Search of Excellence. Lessons from America's Best-Run Companies*. New York: Harper & Row.

Pinault, L. (2000) *Consulting Demons: Inside the Unscrupulous World of Global Consulting Corporations*. New York: HarperCollins.

Schein, E.H. (1988) *Process Consultation: Its Role in Organization Development*. Reading, MA: Addison-Wesley.

Steele, F. (1975) *Consultancy for Organizational Change*. Amherst, MA: University of Massachusetts Press.

Sturdy, A., Clark, T., Fincham, R. and Handley, K. (2008) 'Re-thinking the role of management consultants as disseminators of business knowledge: knowledge flows, directions and conditions in consultancy projects', in H. Scarborough (ed.), *The Evolution of Business Knowledge*. Oxford: Oxford University Press, 239–258.

AN INTRODUCTION TO MANAGEMENT CONSULTANCY

2

ORIGIN AND DEVELOPMENT OF MANAGEMENT CONSULTANCY

INTRODUCTION

The previous chapter concluded that management consultancy is not a profession enforced by legislation. Although management consultancy is not legally enforced, it has benefited at several moments in its history from legislation. This chapter shows how regulatory changes together with technological and institutional changes have shaped the history of the management consultancy industry. You will also learn that some of the largest successes in the history of management consultancy depended on knowledge developed by clients. Furthermore, this chapter identifies which management consultancy created the first bestselling management book. The history of management consultancy reveals the rise and decline of consultancy firms. We discuss the causes of these dynamics.

This chapter sets the scene by investigating the advisor throughout the history of humankind. It subsequently addresses the question: when and where did management consultancy emerge? The chapter closes with a summary, reflective questions, a mini case study, suggestions for further reading, and references.

Main learning objectives

- Put the management consultancy industry in its historical perspective.
- Explain the structure of the industry as the outcome of historical forces.

- Critically reflect upon the historical changes of the industry.
- Understand the reason for the existence of the advisor through the ages.
- Explain the emergence of the management consultancy industry during the second industrial revolution.
- Distinguish the emergence of different fields of management consultancy during the history of the industry.
- Understand the influence of regulatory changes on the development of management consultancy fields and firms.
- Understand the influence of technological changes on the development of management consultancy fields and firms.
- Understand the influence of institutional changes on the development of management consultancy fields and firms.
- Understand the geographic expansion of management consultancy.
- Explain the rise and (relative) decline of individual management consultancy firms.

THE ADVISOR THROUGH THE AGES

The previous chapter defined management consultancy as essentially an advisory service to management (the narrow definition). Assistance to managers regarding the implementation of the advice may also be included (broad definition). But advice remains the essence of management consultancy. Management consultancy defined as advising to management cannot, by definition, be older than management. The next paragraph will explore the rise of management in the United States and in Europe, which took place during the second industrial revolution in the second half of the nineteenth century.

The origin of the advisor

The origin of the advisor, however, lies much further back in history than the second industrial revolution. Our focus is on the professional advisor. By this we mean an individual who is paid for providing advice. The advisor is compensated by the receiver of the advice. Giving paid advice to someone, not necessarily to a manager, can be considered an activity of all times. However, before the second industrial revolution, the receivers of the advice were not managers. These clients of the earlier advisors, though, shared some characteristics with the clients of management consultants. Paid advice has always rested on two conditions.

High-value decisions

First, the need for advice is based on high-value decision making in highly complex situations. The advice receivers need to make decisions that represent high value to these receivers. Moreover, the decision making is highly complex for the receivers. Value and complexity are both essential conditions for paid advice. If the particular decisions are not complex, the persons faced with the decisions may be able to make these without help from others. The decision makers may not need advice to solve their problems. If the decisions do not have high value for the decision makers, then the problems are not worth the request for paid advice.

Wealth and power

The second condition of paid advice is the ability of the advice receivers to be able to afford to pay for the advice, or otherwise assure the cooperation of an advisor. This ability of the advice receivers rests on their wealth and power. Before the second industrial revolution, the most important economic production factor was land. In the agricultural society, the (large) landowners fulfilled the condition of wealth and power to afford paid advice. Emperors and kings were the most important landowners in that era. They also had to make many high value decisions on highly complex situations. Think about politics and the military. Emperors and kings thus satisfied both conditions for advice receiving.

Changes that shaped the development of consultancy fields

The history of management consultancy is presented in terms of the development of different fields of management consultancy services (see also Kipping, 2002). The chapter concentrates on three types of changes that shaped the development of consultancy fields and also shaped the demand for management consultancy: technological change, regulatory change, and institutional change. Figure 2.1 provides an overview of the emergence of consultancy fields. In this section, our focus is on the United States because it represents the largest market for management consultancy and has fulfilled an important role in the historic development of the industry (see for example McKenna, 2006). In the subsequent section, we look at the development of management consultancy on a global scale.

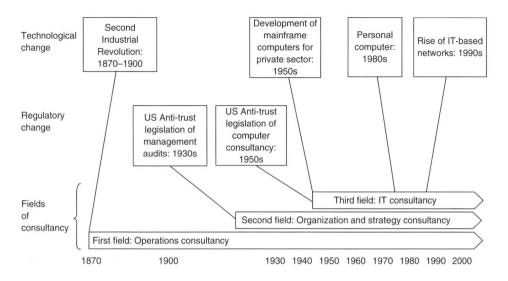

FIGURE 2.1 *The emergence of management consultancy fields*

Note: Con refers to consultancy

THE EMERGENCE OF THE FIRST FIELD OF MANAGEMENT CONSULTANCY: OPERATIONS CONSULTANCY

The rise of the manager

From the 1870s onwards, the industrial revolution introduced capital-intensive ways of mass production. The agricultural society of the prior era had not allowed mass production. However, in the industrial era mass production became increasingly important. The volume and capital-intensity of the new form of production implied large organizations and high capital needs. The capital needs of these organizations typically exceeded the funds of their founders. Therefore, the need for capital drove these organizations to financial markets. At the financial markets, investors bought shares in these organizations. The shareholders became the new owners of the organizations. In contrast to the founders, these shareholders were not involved in the daily running of the organizations. As a result, ownership and management of these organizations became separated and the modern corporation was born (Chandler, 1990). In these shareholder organizations, the founders gave way to a new class of professional managers. These professional managers were neither entrepreneurs nor owners. They got paid to run the organizations for the shareholders.

Seeking advice

The professional managers faced large challenges in coordinating these large new organizations, with revolutionary production technologies and operating at a scale that was unprecedented in history. The second industrial revolution brought large benefits but it also confronted management with big challenges. Efficiency of factory operations was one the major concerns for management. These managers were paid to make high value decisions on complex problems. Recall that high value decisions and complex problems are the conditions for paid advice. Moreover, because of the separation of management and ownership, managers did not have to use their own money to pay for advice. Managers used the money that was entrusted to them by the owners, or shareholders. It was, therefore, no surprise that these managers sought advice from others in order to make their high value decisions on the complex problems of their organizations. Thus the question arises: to whom did the first managers turn for advice?

First actors giving management advice

At that time, the modern management consultant, as we know today, did not yet exist. Managers turned to various types of actors. The choice of actor depended on the nature of the problem and the type of knowledge that managers needed. Auditors, bankers and engineers are examples of these first consultants to management. Because of the complexities of operations, operations developed into the first large field requiring management consultancy. Most of the first management consultants focused on operations, in particular, improving the efficiency of those operations.

The oldest management consultancy firm was founded in 1886: Arthur D. Little. Its founder, Arthur D. Little, was an American engineer who started a research laboratory. At that time, the firm provided engineering consultancy to factory managers. Improving factory operations became the first field of management consultancy.

Scientific management

The first successful service of management consultancy was developed at the end of the nineteenth century. It was based on a method for improving the efficiency of operations by studying and optimizing each individual part of an operations task. At that time, shirking by factory workers, or purposefully slowing the work pace of the industrial assembly line, was a significant problem for management. To eliminate this practice of factory workers, this consultancy method included wage incentive systems for such workers. This method became known as 'scientific management'.

The principles of scientific management

How does scientific management work? The principles are twofold:

- Disaggregate the production work into increasingly small parts.
- Measure and compare productivity per part to optimize the organization of production work.

Scientific management used time and motion studies to measure productivity. Modern management consultancy still uses these principles, not just for operations efficiency but for other purposes as well. The structured problem solving method, as presented in Part 4, borrows from the scientific management principles.

Adam Smith

Disaggregating work goes back to much earlier times than scientific management. A well-known earlier application of disaggregation of work is provided in 1776 by the economist Adam Smith in his book *An Inquiry into the Nature and Causes of the Wealth of Nations*. He emphasized the benefits of labour specialization. This division of labour is based on the disaggregation of work into parts. Smith used the famous example of a pin factory to show the benefits of specialization. Disaggregating the production of pins into a number of tasks led to increased labour productivity.

Frederick W. Taylor

The intellectual father of scientific management was the American engineer Frederick W. Taylor (1856–1915). He is often called the grandfather of management consultancy (Kipping, 2002), although at that time the term 'management consultant' was not used. In the early decades of management consultancy, the management consultants on operations were named 'industrial engineers' or 'efficiency experts'. It may be noteworthy to indicate that Taylor did not develop the method while acting as a management consultant. He discovered the principles of scientific management while working as an engineer and manager in the American steel and paper industry.

Codification of knowledge

Only later, in 1893, did Taylor set up a management consultancy practice. As a consultant, he installed his system of scientific management in client organizations for a fee. After 1901, Taylor codified his method and wrote several books about it. His most influential book was titled *The Principles of Scientific Management* (1911). Taylor's publications represented the first codification of management consultancy knowledge. This is an important practice that continued throughout the history of management consultancy and influenced the dissemination of knowledge among management consultancies, clients, and other stakeholders.

Bedaux Consultancy

Taylor developed a following of other management consultants. These management consultants were experienced in practice. They typically came from industry and had an engineering background. Their services were based on experience. The most successful firm in providing a scientific management based consultancy for operations was the Bedaux Consultancy (Kipping, 2002). This American firm was founded in 1916 by the French immigrant Charles E. Bedaux. Bedaux opened offices around the United States. In the second half of the 1920s, the firm expanded into Europe, opening an office in London in 1926, and then in other parts of the world. In 1931, the Bedaux Consultancy operated with over 200 consulting engineers in ten offices (Kipping, 2002). During the 1980s and 1990s, the firm disappeared as a result of a merger and a subsequent acquisition. Why did such a successful pioneer disappear from the scene? In this chapter's section on the rise and decline of management consultancies we explore the answer.

Scientific management in the United States

Scientific management first became popular in the United States. Managers increasingly turned to efficiency experts, such as Bedaux, for implementing scientific management in their factories to improve the speed of operations through motion studies and wage incentive systems. The heydays of scientific management in the United States were in the first decades of the twentieth century. Towards the end of the 1920s, the demand for scientific management services was saturated in the United States. A backlash against scientific management even arose as managers' and workers' attitudes against the method grew increasingly negative.

Scientific management in Europe and Russia

At the same time however demand in Europe and Russia arose. Scientific management, and the management consultancies offering the system, crossed the Atlantic. By the 1950s, demand for operations management consultancy based on scientific management had also dried up in Europe and Russia. Most management consultancies diversified their services but kept a focus on operations efficiency. In the 1960s, most of these consultancies had disappeared. When scientific management as a management consultancy service became saturated in the United States in the 1920s, a new field of management consultancy arose there.

THE EMERGENCE OF THE SECOND FIELD OF MANAGEMENT CONSULTANCY: ORGANIZATION AND STRATEGY CONSULTANCY

Bankers

The second industrial revolution resulted in the emergence of big corporations. Corporations increased their scale and scope (Chandler, 1962; 1990). This development induced the demand for consultancy on corporate-wide and organizational problems to corporate (top) management. While consultants advised shopfloor management on operations efficiency, bankers provided corporate management with advice on corporate-wide and organizational problems. However, in the 1930s, during the Depression Era, the United States introduced regulatory reforms that would influence management consultancy (McKenna, 2006).

REGULATORY CHANGE AND THE WITHDRAWAL OF BANKERS
The first US regulatory reform was the Glass-Steagall Banking Act of 1933, which separated investment and commercial banking and forbade the consultative and reorganizational activities conducted by banks, in order to restrict flows of collusive information between companies. As a result of this legislation, the banks lost control of the market for this field of management consultancy. This act stimulated demand for independent management consultants, who were not part of a bank. The second reform was the Securities Act of 1933 which demanded that any financing should be preceded by a due diligence (the investigation of the subject firm) by competent management consultants (McKenna, 2006). This act stimulated demand for due diligence by independent management consultants.

Accountants

While factory management used scientific management to improve the efficiency of their operations, executive management struggled with cost control for their corporations. The increasing size and complexity of corporations increased the need for new systems of cost accounting. In the

1920s, cost accounting provided a new opportunity for executive management to improve the results of their corporations. To meet this demand, accountancy firms specialized in 'industrial and financial investigations', or management audits, for executive management. Accountancy firms offered both financial audits and management audits, the latter representing management consultancy. However, in 1936, the American Securities and Exchange Commission (SEC) required accountancies to restructure their practices around corporate audits to maintain their professional independence and avoid potential conflict of interest. The SEC decided that the accountancies' management audits represented a conflict of interest with corporate auditing.

REGULATORY CHANGE AND THE WITHDRAWAL OF LARGE ACCOUNTANCIES

The SEC regulations of 1936 forbade accountants to combine financial audits with management audits on the quality of corporate executive decisions. Large accountancy firms, such as Arthur Andersen, withdrew from management consultancy, as their financial auditing work was more important than their management auditing (consultancy) business. Small and more specialized cost accounting firms decided to focus on management audits. These firms shifted their services from monitoring costs as accountants, to lowering costs as management consultants.

Management engineers

It was these small cost accountants, rather than the industrial engineers, that dominated the management consultancy field of operations efficiency, which seized the opportunity of a new management consultancy sub-field: management audits. These cost accounting firms became known as 'management engineering' firms. While the industrial engineers worked for factory management and focused on blue collar productivity, the management engineers worked for executive management and focused on white collar productivity. Whereas the industrial engineers were self-trained engineers, the management engineers were university-trained accountants and lawyers.

GROWTH OF MANAGEMENT ENGINEERING

The 1930s was a decade when the industry achieved fast growth of 15 per cent annually (McKenna, 2006). The 1940s also meant fast growth although at a lower rate: 10 per cent annually (McKenna, 2006). The number of management engineering firms in the United States grew from 100 in 1930 to 400 by 1940, and 1,000 in 1950 (ACME, 1964). Booz Allen Hamilton and McKinsey & Company are the best known examples of these cost accounting firms that transformed into management engineering firms. The growth of these firms after the regulatory changes illustrates the impact of the new demand for management audits. In 1926, which was twelve years after its foundation, Booz employed only one other consultant. But in 1936, the firm, now renamed Booz Allen & Hamilton, employed eleven consultants (McKenna, 2006). McKinsey & Company, founded in 1926, had expanded to over 26 employees (McKenna, 2006). Moreover, the firm had opened a second office in New York in addition to its first office in Chicago.

The emergence of the sub-field 'organization consultancy'

The management engineers' main consultancy tool was the general survey, which is an integral assessment of a company's organization, including the management, the organizational structure, the procedures, budgets, and quotas. These general surveys required the cooperation of executive management. The subject of the survey – administration and organization – was also the responsibility of executive management. As a result, the management engineering firms provided consultancy to executive management.

These management engineering firms also profited from the demand by investment bankers for evaluating possible mergers and acquisitions (due diligence) and for restructuring ailing companies. Moreover, the management engineers benefited from the demand for management audits by both executive management and banks.

THE RISE OF THE CORPORATE FORM

In the 1920s, in large US corporations (DuPont, General Motors, Sears, and Standard Oil (Exxon)) a new type of organization was developed. These corporations had become so large in scale and scope that the traditional centralized type of organization was no longer effective. In response to the ineffectiveness of the centralized model, these large corporations developed the decentralized, multi-divisional organization, or abbreviated, the 'M-form' (Chandler, 1962). Executive managers of other large US corporations also wanted to adopt the M-form. The question was: how to implement such an organization form? Management consultancies recognized the newly emerging demand for the M-form. They began to offer services on organization implementation. This development stimulated the sub-field of consultancy named organization consultancy. During the 1940s and 1950s, the management consultancies implemented the M-form in many large US corporations. The management consultants that embraced this new consultancy field of improving organizations were not the industrial engineers that dominated the consultancy field of improving operations, such as the Bedaux Consultancy. Rather, it was the management engineers from the second field, such as McKinsey & Company and Booz Allen & Hamilton, who seized the new opportunity of organization consultancy.

US CONSULTANTS GO TO EUROPE

After the US demand for these (M-form) organization studies declined due to market maturity, European corporations started to hire the US management consultancies in the 1960s to implement this M-form organization. Similar to the scientific management method in the 1920s, the market shifted from the United States to Europe. In the late 1950s and the 1960s, the US management consultancies, such as Booz Allen & Hamilton, McKinsey & Company, and Arthur D. Little, expanded into Europe, opening new offices. These consultancies first worked for the European subsidiaries of US corporations. Later, from the mid-1960s, they also worked for European companies and subsequently for European government institutions.

The emergence of the sub-field 'strategy consultancy'

Operations consultancy and organization consultancy were based on knowledge developed in client organizations, respectively scientific management and the M-form. The same corporations that had improved the effectiveness of their organization by implementing the M-form, with the help of organization consultants, struggled with the management of their divisions.

The rise of the diversified corporation confronted executives with the challenge of managing a portfolio of divisions and businesses that were more or less related to each other. As a result, the need for advice on corporate portfolios arose. In the 1960s in the United States a newly established management consultancy firm developed the knowledge that led to a new sub-field: strategy consultancy (Kiechel, 2010).

THE BOSTON CONSULTING GROUP

The consultancy that developed the sub-field of strategy consultancy is the Boston Consulting Group. BCG was founded in 1963 by Bruce Henderson. He had worked before for Arthur D. Little, the oldest consultancy. BCG was the first consultancy to develop services to meet the demand of executive management for advice on corporate strategy. The Boston Consulting Group developed new concepts such as the experience curve and the growth/share matrix, or BCG matrix, for effective management of a portfolio of businesses. Strategy became a new growth field for management consultancy. The M-form (first sub-field) induced portfolio management, or corporate strategy (second sub-field). Like the organization studies of the 1940s and 1950s, corporate strategy studies in the 1960s were commissioned by executive management.

The Boston Consulting Group dominated the sub-field of strategy consultancy, at least for some time. Also in geographical terms, BCG was a first mover. In 1966 (five years ahead of the competition), the firm opened an office in Tokyo. In response to the recession of the early 1970s, BCG began to promote organizational models from Japan. In 1967,

Roland Berger, a former BCG consultant, founded his own firm – Roland Berger Strategy Consultants. In 1973, another alumnus from the Boston Consulting Group, Bill Bain, set up his firm – Bain & Company. It looked like BCG and its spinoffs would dominate the field of strategy consultancy in the 1960s and early 1970s.

THE EMERGENCE OF THE THIRD FIELD OF MANAGEMENT CONSULTANCY: INFORMATION TECHNOLOGY CONSULTANCY

In the 1950s, a new field of consultancy emerged. This field would become a very large one. Neither the management consultancies that dominated the field of organization consultancy, nor the consultants that dominated the field of operations consultancy, entered this new field. Instead, new entrants seized the opportunity provided by it. What was this field, which firms came to dominate it, and why did the organization and strategy consultancy firms not seize this new opportunity?

Development of mainframe computers for the private sector

In the 1950s, mainframe computer usage started to spread in the private sector. The first mainframe computers were developed during the Second World War. Their usage was mostly limited to the military and to governments. Technological developments made the mainframe computers feasible for more widespread use. It was IBM that dominated the (mainframe) computer industry at that time. The firm was nicknamed 'Big Blue' because it was such a large firm and dominant force in the industry and because its computers were blue. The spread of mainframe computers in the private sector, mostly large corporations, led to increasing demand for consultancy services related to the computers. Computers were new and complex. The corporations that bought computers needed expertise on various topics, such as installing and using computers, and the development and maintenance of software. Computer manufacturers were natural candidates to become the consultants to provide such expertise.

Prohibition of IBM and other computer manufacturers

However, in the 1950s, US anti-trust regulation prohibited IBM and other computer manufacturers from enter the emerging field of information technology (IT) consultancy. Similar to the regulatory changes in the 1930s that cleared the field of management audits for the management engineering firms, regulatory changes in the 1950s cleared the new field of consultancy (McKenna, 2006). Again US anti-trust regulation fulfilled an important role in the history of management consultancy.

Information technology consultancy

IT consultancy consisted of providing advice on installing and using 'electronic computer systems'. According to this book's definition of management consultancy, most IT consultancy services would qualify as business consultancy (non-managerial tasks of implementation) rather than management consultancy in a broad sense that is advice plus the managerial tasks of implementation. The US Department of Justice prohibited IBM from providing consultancy services. In 1956, IBM settled the anti-trust suit by the federal government. The firm accepted a consent decree that meant that it would not enter IT consultancy.

New entrants

Neither the industrial engineers of the first field, nor the management engineers of the second field seized the new opportunity of the field of IT consultancy. While IBM was forbidden to enter IT consultancy, one employee decided to leave IBM to set up his own IT services firm to offer skilled IT professionals and computing capacity. The firm was Electronic Data Systems (EDS) and the former IBM employee was the American Ross Perot. Perot was an IBM salesman before he founded his firm in 1962. The big accountancy firms that were forced out of management consultancy in the 1930s because of regulatory changes seized the opportunity offered by new regulatory action in the 1950s to re-enter management consultancy, although in a different field. The accountants entered IT consultancy instead of management audits.

Re-entry of accountancies

An example of an accountancy firm that started to offer services for the implementation of computer systems in the 1950s is Arthur Andersen.[1] By 1955, management consultancy had grown into a US$1 billion business (Gross and Poor, 2008). In the 1960s, the eight largest accountancy firms in the world, the Big Eight, had entered IT consultancy.

---

[1]Arthur Andersen was one of the big accountancy firms until 2002 when the firm voluntarily gave up its accountancy licences after having been found guilty of criminal charges related to its auditing of the energy company Enron.

Other entrants

The field was not limited to accountancies or to US firms. In the 1960s, firms on other continents also entered IT consultancy. For instance, in 1967 in France the precursor of the IT consultancy Capgemini was founded. A year later in India, the Tata Consultancy was founded. These and other IT consultancies specialized in the installation and integration of computer systems. In 1982, the US Department of Justice dropped its anti-trust suit against IBM. In 1991 the firm's 1956 consent decree was lifted. Subsequently, IBM entered the IT consultancy market. This entry was very successful. In 1996, the IBM Consulting Group already had annual revenues of US$ 11 billion dollars (IBM, 1997).

INSTITUTIONAL CHANGES DRIVING THE GROWTH OF MANAGEMENT CONSULTANCY

The previous section showed the expansion of management consultancy over time in terms of the accumulation of fields (operations, organization and strategy, information technology). Our explanation concentrated on technological changes (the second industrial revolution and the development of information and communication technologies) and regulatory changes (in particular the US anti-trust regulation). However, during the industry's history, a number of institutional changes also took place that contributed to the demand for management consultancy (David, 2012). Figure 2.2 visualizes these changes for the US market.

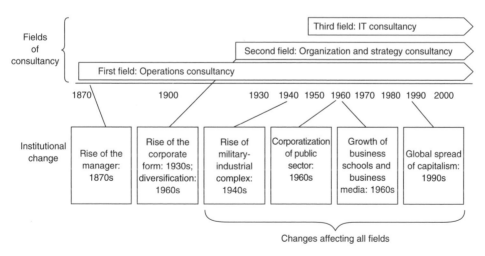

FIGURE 2.2 *Key institutional changes in the US management consultancy industry*

Note: Con refers to consultancy

The professional manager

As discussed in the section about the first field of management consultancy, that is operations consultancy, the emergence of the modern corporation with separation of ownership and control led to the rise of the professional manager. It was this manager from which management consultants derive their reason for existence.

The corporate form

The development of the corporate form in the 1930s induced the second field (organization and strategy consultancy), in particular the sub-field of organization consultancy. The arrival of the large diversified corporation during the 1960s created a need for the sub-field of strategy consultancy. Figure 2.2 distinguishes four additional institutional changes in the US that stimulated demand for consultancy in each of the three fields.

The rise of the military-industrial complex

During the 1940s, the rise of the military-industrial complex (the network of armed forces, the defence contractors or corporations that supply products and services to the armed forces, and legislators) in the US and some other countries created a demand for management consultancy. At first, management consultants were hired to provide their services to address the challenges put forward by the Second World War. But after the war, new defence programmes by the military-industrial complex induced the continued demand for consultants.

The corporatization of the public sector

During the 1960s, two institutional changes took place in the US that had positive effects on the demand for management consultancy. At later stages, these changes spread from the US to other regions of the world. One change was the corporatization of non-corporate sectors, most importantly the government and health care. Many organizations in the non-profit sectors attempted to adopt the values and practices of profit-oriented corporations. In their efforts to resemble corporations, these non-profit organizations turned to management consultants to provide advice.

The growth of business schools and business media

The other change during the 1960s concerned the growth of business schools and business media in the US. Business schools and business media are important partners for management consultants in the creation and dissemination of management knowledge (see Chapter 6). Business schools helped management consultancy in three ways:

- Supplying graduates to the consultancy firms.
- Facilitating the creation and dissemination of management knowledge.
- Providing legitimacy to management and management consultancy (David, 2012).

Management consultancy benefited in two ways from the growth of the business media: through publicity, the business press increased awareness of management consultancy and also helped to create management fashion, which stimulated consultancy demand (David, 2012).

The global spread of capitalism

MARKET REFORMS

In the 1990s, capitalism became more important in the economy worldwide. In that decade, the former state socialist economies came under increasing pressure. Towards the end of the 1980s and in the 1990s, former state socialist economies transformed into a market capitalist system. Eastern Europe (the fall of the Iron Curtain in 1989), the former Soviet Union (the collapse of the USSR in 1991), China (reforms started in 1978, privatization took off after 1992) and India (reforms started in 1991) are some important examples of such economies adopting (elements of) the capitalist system.

In the 1990s, both in the Western world and in the former state socialist economies, governments began to deregulate industries and privatize organizations. Examples of such industries are aviation, health care, railways, and utilities such as electricity, mail, and telecommunications. These changes implied large challenges for client management in these industries, which induced the demand for management consultancy.

GLOBALIZATION OF MARKETS

These transformations had significant implications, not only for the organizations within those countries, but also for organizations all over the world. For client management the geographic playing field became much larger and much more complex. These changes induced a demand for management consultancy on an increasing international scale. Western firms needed management consultants to help them enter new international markets. In the 1980s, markets became increasingly global. This globalization not only applied to product markets, but also to capital markets and labour markets. Organizations moved production and other value-adding activities offshore. The result was the rise of global value chains. In response to the increasing competition, the 1980s witnessed two merger and acquisition (M&A) waves.

These waves created a demand for management consultancy to develop M&A strategies and to assist in post-merger integration processes.

In the 1990s, Western companies expanded into newly opened markets in former socialist countries. In the 2000s, companies from emerging markets also entered the Western markets. As a result of these movements, competition became increasingly global. Managers involved in global competition turned to management consultants for advice.

TRANSFORMATION FROM MANAGERIAL TO INVESTOR CAPITALISM

Within the Western, capitalist world, the 1980s saw the growing influence of so-called 'investor capitalism' at the expense of the previous 'managerial capitalism' (Fligstein, 1990). As a consequence, power shifted from corporate managers to investors, most prominently the activist shareholders. Management came under increasing pressure from (activist) shareholders to create shareholder value. However, client management also received incentives, stock options, and other results-based compensation, to deliver the required results. As a result, the need for, and the desire to produce, shareholder value increased substantially in the 1980s. These pressures stimulated the demand for management consultancy.

RISING COMPLEXITY, AND INCREASING TIME AND PERFORMANCE PRESSURE

Since the 1980s, the environment for client organizations has undergone significant change. Besides the afore-mentioned political changes, client management also witnessed important technological changes. The most important changes concerned information and telecommunications technologies, which enabled new forms of organization; induced a trend towards more networked organizational models and further decentralization; enabled the geographic dispersion of activities, implying the emergence of global value chains; and gave rise to the knowledge economy, with its new products, services, and business models. In the 1990s, the internet gave rise to the so-called 'new economy'. These technological changes enabled innovations in products and production processes. Moreover, the speed of product and process innovations increased which led to a shortening of product life cycles.

The result of all these changes was increasing challenges for client management. The complexity of management challenges, in terms of problems and opportunities, surged. The pressure from financial markets on management to create (shareholder) value also increased. Moreover, the time available for management to address these challenges diminished. As a result, the need for speed grew. Together, these challenges for management fuelled the demand for management consultancy.

INTERNATIONALIZATION OF US MANAGEMENT CONSULTANCIES

To Europe   The United States was the most prominent country in the development of the management consultancy industry. All three fields of management consultancy (operations, organization and strategy, information technology) emerged in that country. US management consultancy firms first disseminated their knowledge to Europe. In the 1920s, they spread scientific management to there. In the 1960s, the US consultancy firms spread the M-form organization into Europe. At that time, the US management consultancy firms also began building office networks in Europe.

Moving East   With the fall of the Iron Curtain in Eastern Europe in 1989 and the collapse of the Soviet Union in 1991 new geographical areas for (Western) management consultancy firms emerged. US and (mostly) European management consultancy firms expanded their office networks into Eastern Europe and Russia during the 1990s. In the 2000s, the rise of emerging markets, most prominently the so-called BRIC countries (Brazil, Russia, India, and China), opened new geographical opportunities for the management consultancies.

Moreover, in the Middle East new opportunities for management consultancy arose. Because of the massive growth of wealth as a result of rising oil prices, governments and (national) companies had the funds to hire management consultants to transform their organizations into best practices. Governments needed management consultants to help them identify investment opportunities in Western markets in which to invest a part of their increasing cash flow. Western management consultancy firms expanded their office networks into all of these new territories – BRIC and the Middle East – and increasingly became global firms.

CASE STUDY

McKinsey & Company

The following case study provides a brief overview of the history of one of the icons of management consultancy: McKinsey & Company. The history of this firm mirrors some important aspects of the history of the management consultancy industry.

James O. McKinsey

McKinsey & Company is named after a professor of business policy at the University of Chicago. In 1926, James O. McKinsey founded a firm in finance and budgeting services. The Chicago-based firm focused on the important business problems of senior management. McKinsey had developed a common problem solving approach. It was an integrative approach from a top management perspective. As management consultants at that time were called management engineers, McKinsey & Company was said to be an accounting and engineering firm. In 1933, McKinsey's firm profited from regulatory reforms in the United States that forbade banks to engage in consultative activities, and forced accountancy firms

▶

to choose between financial and management auditing service. Whereas banks and large accountancy firms withdrew, new firms such as McKinsey & Company captured the opportunity of management auditing/engineering.

Marvin Bower

In 1935, James O. McKinsey temporarily left his firm to lead and turn around one of the firm's clients, the retailer Marshall Field's. Two years earlier, in 1933, a man had joined McKinsey & Company who would be of critical importance to the firm's further development during his fifty-nine year term of service. His name was Marvin Bower. After the unexpected death of James O. McKinsey in 1937, the firm, which comprised a Chicago office and a New York office, was split in two. The Chicago office became A.T. Kearney & Company, after its office director, Andrew Thomas Kearney, a managing director who had joined the firm in 1929. The New York office acquired the rights to the name McKinsey & Company, and was led by Bower and two colleagues. It was Marvin Bower who introduced the term 'management consulting'. Recognizing the need for a professionalization of consulting, Bower, who had been a corporate lawyer, modelled McKinsey & Company on the most prestigious law firms. He introduced 'professional language'. For instance, instead of company, projects, and customers he spoke of firm, engagements, and clients. He also attempted to make the appearance of consultants more professional and insisted on a dress code.

Values

Most important was Bower's introduction of values in the 1930s that would guide professional conduct and bind the firm. Some examples are: 'Put the client's interest first and separate yourself from the job' (Haas Edersheim, 2004: 39): only undertake engagements when the expected value for the client exceeds the firm's fees (McKinsey, 2012): 'Center problem solving on the facts and on the frontline [of the client personnel]' (Haas Edersheim, 2004: 40). In the 1930s, Bower also complemented James McKinsey's problem solving approach with an orientation towards action. Getting clients to take action, that is adopt the consultant's recommended solution, required client ownership. The need for client ownership led to the notion of working in partnership with clients: the 'engagement'. In contrast with the dominant principle of billing on a per-diem basis, Bower introduced value-based fees for clients: McKinsey & Company began to bill for the value received by the clients. Following the law firms, Bower also introduced the promotion practice of 'up or out'; employees were either promoted, or asked to leave the firm. Instead of hiring experienced managers from industry, Bower shifted recruitment to the smartest graduates from the best business schools. In the 1950s, McKinsey & Company started MBA-recruiting from the Harvard Business School.

Expansion and stagnation

Being an advisor to chief executive officers made it natural step to expand the portfolio of services with an organization-type of consultancy. In the 1940s, McKinsey

& Company became successful in implementing the multi-divisional form in US corporations. Whereas in the 1950s Arthur Andersen started to provide advice on installing and using 'electronic computer systems', McKinsey & Company was a highly successful organization consultancy. Towards the end of the 1950s, the firm opened its first international office in London. Whereas McKinsey & Company was expanding fast with its organization consultancy, first in the United States and later, in the 1960s, internationally, in the US a new entrant, the Boston Consulting Group, pioneered strategy consultancy. In the 1970s, McKinsey & Company faced a declining demand for organization consultancy. The firm heavily invested in knowledge development to successfully enter strategy consultancy.

Regaining momentum

In the 1980s, the investments paid off. One of the knowledge development studies led to the management bestseller *In Search of Excellence* (1982). In the 1980s, the firm regained fast (international) growth. In the 1990s, when information technology moved to the management board agenda, McKinsey & Company decided to enter information (technology) consultancy. To catch up with established competitors, it acquired in 1989 the Information Consulting Group (ICG). Although the majority of ICG staff left within a few years, McKinsey & Company managed to build a business technology practice. This practice took a top management approach that focused on the relation between strategy and information technology. The firm's information technology practice focused on advice. It refrained from designing, implementing, or running (that is outsourcing) technology systems.

Worldwide impact

By the 2000s, McKinsey & Company had grown into a broad player, active in the major fields of management consultancy, from operations, to organization, strategy, and information technology. The firm operated on a global basis and had a large, worldwide impact, not only through its engagements and the continuous stream of management publications from its global office network (98 offices and 17,000 employees, of which 9,000 were consultants according to Forbes, 2011) but also through its alumni-network of 24,000 registered alumni in 120 countries, including over 230 chief executive officers of companies with annual revenues exceeding US$1 billion (McKinsey, 2012).

Discussion questions

1 Explain the rise of McKinsey & Company during the 1930s and 1940s.

2 Why did Marvin Bower model McKinsey & Company on a law firm? Explain your answer.

3 Reflect upon how McKinsey & Company responded to the emergence of new (sub-) fields of consultancy, that is the rise of strategy consultancy and the rise of information technology consultancy. Why was the firm, in both cases, a late mover? Explain your answer.

4 What lessons for management consultants can be drawn from the history of McKinsey & Company? Elaborate on your answer.

THE RISE AND DECLINE OF MANAGEMENT CONSULTANCIES

The history of management consultancy shows the rise and decline of individual consultancy firms. Typically, the rise in firms is explained by the emergence of new consultancy fields. New fields provide opportunities for new entrants. Incumbent firms may decline. Some incumbents disappear, that is they left the industry or lost their independence due to an acquisition. Other management consultancy firms fall back only in relative terms, that is, losing their market share.

An example is the management consultancy firm the Bedaux Consultancy that focused on scientific management to improve operations efficiency. From the late 1950s onwards, the organization and strategy consultancy firms increasingly displaced the operations oriented consultancies, such as Bedaux (Kipping, 2002). Some operations oriented consultancy firms disappeared. In the 1980s, the consultancies focused on organization and strategy were surpassed by consultancies that concentrated on information technology. Not all of the IT consultancies' revenues qualify as real management consultancy in the sense of advice to management and assistance with managerial implementation tasks. But even the pure management consultancy revenues of the big IT firms may surpass the revenues of some pure management consultancy firms. Figure 2.3 provides for each of the three

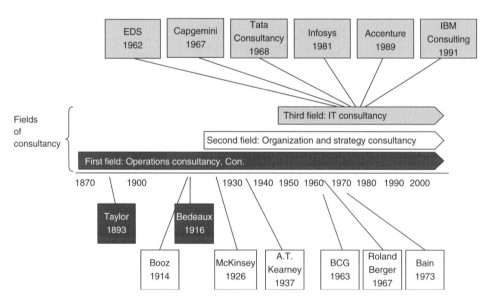

FIGURE 2.3 *Examples of leading firms for each of the three fields*

Note: Year refers to the year of foundation. Con refers to consultancy fields some examples of consultancies that are leading firms in their field, or in the case of the first field, firms that were leading their field.

Entering a new field

You may ask yourself: why did management consultancy firms which were first movers in the development of a new consultancy field, and which dominated the consultancy industry as a whole, eventually lose their leading position? Management consultancy firms which were leaders in one field of management consultancy found it difficult to establish a similar position in a new field (Kipping, 2002). When the second field (organization and strategy) emerged, the leading firms in the first field (operations consultancy) lost their dominant position in the management consultancy industry (as a whole) to the leading firms in the new field of organization and strategy consultancy. The leading operations consultants did not succeed in achieving a similar position in the new field of organization and strategy consultancy. History then repeats itself: when the third field (IT consultancy) emerged, the leaders in the second field lost their dominant position in the management consultancy industry (as a whole) to leading firms in the new field of IT consultancy. The leading organization and strategy consultants did not succeed in achieving a similar position in the new field of IT consultancy.

Business models

Apparently, for incumbent management consultancy firms, entry into a new consultancy field is difficult. Not only does the consultancy product vary by field, but so do business models. We discuss how fields differ in some key aspects of the business model:

- Client relations.
- Consultancy resources.
- Consultancy economics.
- Consultancy reputations.

The business models vary by field. Each field targets another group of clients. This means that client relations vary by field; compare for instance the target clients for operations consultancy, which are factory management, with the target clients for organization and strategy consultancy, which are executive management. Different target groups lead to a different client value proposition by field. For example, organization and strategy consultancies may develop a new corporate strategy to enable the corporation to achieve its growth objectives, while IT consultants may advise about a new computer system for an administrative process. These differences in value proposition have implications for the required resources, the economics, as well as the reputation of the consultancy.

CLIENT RELATIONS

Relations with clients may also explain the decline of management consultancy firms. The efficiency experts worked for factory management. Management audits and organization studies were directed towards executive management. This difference in management level may help explain why efficiency experts were not the most suited to benefit from the demand for management audits and organization studies. The small cost accountants benefited from the regulatory changes in the 1930s to grow in the field of management audits. These audits provided management engineers with contact with executive management. This relationship with executives put the management engineers in the right position for organization studies. Strategy consultancy was also directed towards executive management. The common client may explain why many organization consultancies (eventually) successfully entered the strategy field. In contrast, information consultancy was initially directed at lower client management (managers in the electronic data processing department), and did not receive executive management attention until the 1990s. This difference in client relations may help explain why organization and strategy consultants did not focus on information consultancy, at least not before 1990. They may not even have considered it as relevant, because their client, executive management, did not focus on IT.

CONSULTANCY RESOURCES

Resources also vary by field of consultancy. The efficiency experts of the first field were often sole practitioners. Organization and strategy consultancy is done in relatively small teams made up of a senior partner and a number of junior consultants. Information consultancy involves large teams of juniors. In addition to the number of consultants on a project, the type of consultants also varies by field. Efficiency experts are experienced individuals with a background in the industry. Organization and strategy consultancies typically recruit the smartest graduates from the most prestigious business schools. These people are hired for their intelligence, not for their industry experience. IT consultancy firms which rely – to a large extent – on standardized procedures and other forms of knowledge management are less dependent on the high intelligence quotient of their recruits.

CONSULTANCY ECONOMICS

Within consultancy economics, we may distinguish differences in the fee structures and differences in the capital intensity of management consultancy in different fields of management consultancy. Differences in client value proposition lead to differences in fee structure. Hourly fees (the fee charged per hour of consultancy) in organization and strategy consultancy are typically significantly higher than in IT consultancy. Such a difference in fees discourages organization and strategy consultancy firms from entering

IT. It is difficult to combine, in one organization, consultants who work at significantly different fee levels.

Higher capital intensity may also inhibit consultancy firms from entering a new field. Information technology consultancy firms have a (very) high capital intensity compared to firms operating in the other fields. Information technology consultancies typically combine management consultancy with other professional services. Because of these other services, in particular outsourcing services, they need huge investments in physical capital – ICT infrastructure. Because of the importance of physical assets, the IT firms have large opportunities for scale economies. Compared to organization and strategy consultancy firms, the information consultancies therefore have to be (very) large. Information consultancies may employ tens of thousands of consultants. Because of the scale economies, entering IT consultancy requires large – financial – investments. To finance these investments, information consultancies have become publicly listed firms. Strategy and organization consultancy firms are typically professional partnerships.

CONSULTANCY REPUTATIONS

Reputation is highly important in management consultancy, as consultancy is an intangible product. The reputation of a management consultancy firm signals quality and is also crucial for the informal role of providing legitimacy to clients. The reputation of an operations efficiency expert can turn from an asset into a liability if the firm enters organization and strategy consultancy. Executive management probably perceives the consultant as an efficiency expert, not as an expert on organization and strategy. The consultancy firm will have a credibility problem. Building a new reputation typically requires significant efforts (including investments in marketing) and a lot of patience.

The unattractiveness of embryonic fields

A new consultancy field in an embryonic stage is not attractive for large, established consultancy firms in well-developed fields. The new field is too small for them. However, by the time the consultancy field has grown large enough for the big firms, it will already be occupied by other consultancy firms and by then those other firms will be well entrenched.

The curse of success for established consultancies

Management consultancy firms established in a particular field are so occupied with their currently successful product that they do not look for new opportunities. Their opportunity costs are too high as they can earn lots of money with their traditional service. Moreover, entering new fields carries risk compared to further exploiting a proven field.

The rise of organization and strategy consultancies and the relative decline of operations consultancies

This new field of management consultancy differed in some important aspects from operations improvement, the first field of consultancy (see also Kipping, 2002). The business model of operations consultancy differed from organization and strategy consultancy. Both the target client groups and the value proposition differed. Operations consultancy was about the productivity of blue collar workers, whereas organization and strategy consultancy was about the financial performance of the whole corporation, including both blue collar and white collar workers.

DIFFERENT CLIENT RELATIONS
The clients varied by field. Operations consultants worked for operations or factory management, whereas the organization consultants worked for executive management. The management engineers already worked for executive management. The management audits they provided had the broad scope of covering the whole client organization, not just the operations. Therefore, management engineers were in a good position for organization and strategy consultancy.

DIFFERENT CONSULTANCY RESOURCES
The type of consultant differed as well between operations consultancy and organization and strategy consultancy. The operations consultants were self-taught, experienced experts. The organization consultants were university-trained accountants and lawyers. Whereas in operations consultancy all consultants were seniors, the organization consultants introduced the partnership model, whereby the senior partners worked with groups of junior consultants. For the junior positions, the organization consultants would recruit fresh graduates from prestigious business schools, most prominently the Harvard Business School.

REPUTATIONS
Reputations played a role. The industrial engineers had a reputation for operations efficiency, not for organization and executive management consultancy. Moreover, they suffered from the backlash in the United States against scientific management. Finally, operations consultants who were successful with scientific management may have fallen victim to the 'curse of success'.

INTO DECLINE
In the 1950s, after the demand for scientific management in Europe had dried up, the efficiency experts diversified their consultancy activities, but kept their focus on efficiency improvement. From the 1960s onwards, these consultancies went into decline and eventually disappeared. These firms went out of business, or they were acquired and integrated into other consultancy firms.

The rise of IT consultancies and the relative decline of organization and strategy consultancies

The reasons why the organization and strategy consultants did not enter the new field of information consultancy may resemble those of the industrial engineers. Differences between, on the one hand, the business models of organization and strategy consultancy, and on the other hand, information consultancy, may have prohibited organization and strategy consultancies from entering information consultancy. These differences included the subject of consultancy, the nature and the scope of projects, the client management level, the type of consultants, the ratio of junior consultants to partners, and the reputation. The second part of this book will discuss these differences in further detail. In addition, the organization consultancies may have faced the curse of success, like the industrial engineers before them. In the case of the organization consultancy firms it was not only the success of their traditional field of organization consultancy that kept these firms from exploring information consultancy, it was also the emergence in the 1960s of a new sub-field that was more tempting and more relevant for these firms: strategy consultancy.

CURSE OF SUCCESS

The differences between information consultancy and strategy consultancy were relatively difficult to bridge. However, corporate organizational structure and strategy are intertwined. Organization and strategy consultancy are related fields. But the organization consultancies were not the first movers in strategy consultancy. BCG 'invented' strategy consultancy. Why did the organization consultancies not develop the emerging field of strategy? An important explanation may be the curse of success. Around 1960, the organization consultants, most prominently Booz Allen & Hamilton (300 consultants and 12 million dollar revenue) and McKinsey & Company (165 consultants and 6.7 million dollar revenue), reached the peak of their power (McKenna, 2006). They were unchallenged at that time. The firms enjoyed high growth in demand. Booz handled 500 individual clients in 1967, whereas McKinsey & Company worked for 300 clients in 1962 (McKenna, 2006). By the end of the 1960s, Booz Allen & Hamilton employed more than 1,200 consultants, which made it the largest US management consultancy (Higdon, 1969).

CHANGING FORTUNES

Whereas in the 1960s, new entrants explored the strategy field, the organization consultants exploited the success of their field. The 1960s were a decade of fast growth for management consultancy (McKenna, 2006). In contrast, the 1970s were a period of slow growth for both the organization and the strategy sub-fields. In the 1970s, the organization consultants in particular faced an increasingly difficult situation. Their traditional business of organization studies was under threat when the demand for organization studies also declined in Europe. Organization was no longer the primary problem for executive management. Moreover, in the new sub-field of strategy, the organization consultants faced first movers and thought leaders, which were the Boston Consulting Group and Bain & Company.

FIGHTING BACK

In the second half of the 1970s, McKinsey & Company invested heavily in order to fight its way into the sub-field of strategy consultancy (Kiechel, 2010). The firm funded research on strategy, Japan, and corporate culture. McKinsey & Company introduced, in the early 1980s, its 7-S framework for analysing strategy in response to the success of BCG's concepts. This framework was presented in the first management bestseller, *In Search of Excellence*. This book was written by McKinsey partners Peters and Waterman (1982). With the 7-S framework McKinsey & Company achieved a top ranking as an innovative strategy consultancy during the 1980s. In that decade the firm emphasized organizational culture. The heart of the 7-S model was the shared values of the organization, which referred to culture. With this emphasis on culture, McKinsey & Company built on its heritage in organization consultancy.

THE GROWING DIVIDE

While McKinsey & Company in the 1980s caught up in the sub-field of strategy, management consultancy's third field, information technology consultancy, had taken off. After the slow growth of the 1970s, the management consultancy market increased growth during the 1980s (McKenna, 2006). Already during the 1970s, a divide had emerged between the consultancies focused on organization and strategy on the one side, and the consultancies focused on information technology on the other side. During subsequent decades, several attempts were made from both sides to cross the divide. However, the differences between the two fields of consultancy proved to be (too) large. IT consultancies entered organization and strategy consultancy either through organic development or via acquisition. An example of the latter was the acquisition in 1995 of A.T. Kearney by EDS. Organization and strategy consultancy firms attempted to enter IT consultancy. Some firms, such as the Boston Consulting Group, set up their own IT group, while others, such as McKinsey & Company, acquired (small) IT consultancies.

The entries and exits of accountancies

In 1936, many large accountancy firms withdrew from management consultancy – management audits – due to requirements by the US SEC. In the 1950s large consultancies entered IT consultancy. In the 1980s, the Big Six accountancy firms led by Arthur Andersen expanded their consultancy divisions, either through internal growth or through acquisitions. In 1989, Arthur Andersen separated its accounting and consulting divisions. The accountancy business continued to operate under the name of Arthur Andersen, whereas the consultancy business took the name Andersen Consulting. In the 1990s, the world's six largest accountancies saw their revenues from non-audit services surpass their audit revenues. In 1989, the revenues of Andersen Consulting amounted to just over US$1 billion. In 1998, the consultancy business had grown revenues to US$8.3 billion, whereas the accountancy business' revenues were US$6.1 billion (Kipping, 2002). The 1990s were a decade of fast growth for management consultancy (McKenna, 2006). For instance, McKinsey & Company's revenues grew from US$1.1 billion in 1991 to US$2.5 billion in 1998 (*Financial Times*, 1999).

ACCOUNTANCIES WITHDRAW

However, the consultancy business of the accountancies created a conflict of interest with their accountancy business. In the late 1990s, the chairman of the US SEC concluded that the leading accountancies were no longer truly independent because of their heavy reliance on consultancy business. Under pressure from the SEC, the accountancies divested themselves of their consultancy divisions. This is similar to the SEC's 1936 requirement for accountancies to choose between financial auditing and management auditing.

In 2001, Andersen Consulting became Accenture. By 2002 all the big accountancies had sold their consultancy divisions. For instance, Ernst & Young Consulting was sold to Capgemini, and PriceWaterhouseCoopers Consulting was acquired by IBM Consulting. The exit of the accountancies from management consultancy was another stimulus to the demand for other management consultancy firms.

ACCOUNTANCIES RE-ENTER

In the early 2000s, corporate scandals – most prominently, Enron, Parmalat and WorldCom – led to new legislation. Enron led to the fall of the accountancy firm Arthur Andersen, but the reputations of some management consultancies which served these corporations also suffered. In 2002, the US Sarbanes-Oxley Act formally forbade accountants from offering management consultancy to their accounting clients. Similar to the 1930s, regulatory changes played out in favour of management consultancies. However, the bursting of the dotcom bubble in 2000 and the 9/11 attacks in 2001 led to an economic downturn which caused a decline in the management consultancy market.

In the second half of the 2000s, the accountancies returned to management consultancy. After an absence of a couple of years (because their contracts with the firms that bought their consultancy divisions in the late 1990s and early 2000s did not allow the accountancies to set up a consultancy business in a defined period after the sale), they started to rebuild their management consultancy practices. The credit crisis of 2008 caused another economic downturn and a declining demand for management consultancy.

SUMMARY

Institutional changes

The management consultancy industry benefited several times from a tail wind in the form of regulatory actions in the United States that cleared the field of competitors from other industries. The US anti-trust legislation of the 1930s drove bankers and large accountancy firms from the field of management audits. Small cost accountants, such as Booz Allen & Hamilton, and McKinsey & Company, turned into management engineers.

US anti-trust legislation in the 1950s prevented computer vendors (among which was IBM) from entering the emerging field of information consultancy. This legislation gave the market to the large accountancy firms, such as Arthur Andersen. When the ban on computer vendors was lifted in the early 1990s, IBM and other computer firms entered information consultancy.

The management consultancy industry also benefited from several other institutional changes, including the rise of the manager, the rise of the corporate form, the corporatization of the non-corporate sector, the rise of business schools and business media, and the global spread of capitalism.

Emergence of new fields

The history of the industry shows the opening of new fields of consultancy over time. Initially, operations were the most important field. In the 1930s the rise of the corporate form stimulated the second field: organization and strategy consultancy. The third field, information technology consultancy, is rooted in the 1950s. The history of management consultancy shows that each field was dominated by different firms. Leading firms in one field found it difficult to establish leading positions in fields that emerged at a later stage. The emergence of new fields induced the rise of new firms. The difficulties of moving from one field into another led to the decline (in absolute or relative terms) of firms.

REFLECTIVE QUESTIONS

1. Why did the industrial engineering firms that once dominated management consultancy disappear? Explain your answer.

2. Why, in the 1930s, did one accountancy firm, McKinsey & Company, decide to focus on management audits (management consultancy), whereas another accountancy firm, Arthur Andersen, decided to withdraw from management audits, in order to focus exclusively on financial audits? Explain your answer.

3. Should the management consultancy firms that focused on organization studies have entered the field of IT consultancy in the 1950s, when that new field emerged? Why, or why not? Explain your answer.

4. What lessons, if any, can you draw for management consultancy firms from the history of the management consultancy industry? Explain your answer.

5. To what extent do you expect that historical forces (technology, regulatory, and institutional) will continue to influence the management consultancy industry? Explain your answer.

MINI CASE STUDY

The return of an accountancy firm

During the history of management consultancy, accountancy firms several times entered and exited the management consultancy industry. Debit & Credit is a very large international accountancy firm. In the 1990s, Debit & Credit operated with a management consultancy division. In the early 2000s, under pressure from the US SEC, the accountancy firm sold its management consultancy division to a large information consultancy firm. Ten years later, some partners of Debit & Credit think the firm should re-enter management consultancy because competitors are also setting up consultancy divisions. Consultancy seems to offer more attractive opportunities than accountancies. Other partners have doubts about re-entering consultancy. Should Debit & Credit re-enter the management consultancy industry?

Questions

1 What are the reasons for Debit & Credit to re-enter the management consultancy industry? What field(s) of consultancy would be most suitable? Elaborate on your answer.

2 What are the reasons for the firm not to re-enter management consultancy? Elaborate on your answer.

3 What should Debit & Credit do and why? Explain your answer.

FURTHER READING

Academic perspective

Kipping, M. (2002) 'Trapped in their wave: the evolution of management consultancies', in T. Clark and R. Fincham (eds), *Critical Consulting: New Perspectives on the Management Advice Industry*. Oxford: Blackwell, 28–49.

Kipping, M. and Clark, T. (eds) (2012) *The Oxford Handbook of Management Consulting*. Oxford: Oxford University Press.

Kipping, M. and Engwall, L. (2002) *Management Consulting: Emergence and Dynamics of a Knowledge Industry*. Oxford: Oxford University Press.

McKenna, C.D. (2006) *The World's Newest Profession: Management Consulting in the Twentieth Century*. New York: Cambridge University Press.

Journalistic perspective

Haas Edersheim, E. (2004) *McKinsey's Marvin Bower: Vision, Leadership & the Creation of Management Consulting*. Hoboken, NJ: John Wiley & Sons.

Kiechel, W. III (2010) *The Lords of Strategy: The Secret Intellectual History of the New Corporate World*. Boston, MA: Harvard Business Press.

McDonald, D. (2013) *The Firm: The Story of McKinsey and Its Secret Influence on American Business*. New York: Simon & Schuster.

REFERENCES

ACME (Association of Consulting Management Engineers) (1964) *Numerical Data on the Present Dimensions, Growth, and Other Trends in Management Consulting in the United States*. New York: Association of Consulting Management Engineers.

Chandler, A.D. Jr. (1962) *Strategy and Structure: Chapters in the History of the American Industrial Enterprise*. Cambridge, MA: MIT Press.

Chandler, A.D. Jr. (1990) *Scale and Scope: The Dynamics of Industrial Capitalism*. Cambridge, MA: The Belknap Press of Harvard University Press.

David, R.J. (2012) 'Institutional change and the growth of strategy consulting in the United States', in M. Kipping and T. Clark (eds), *The Oxford Handbook of Management Consulting*. Oxford: Oxford University Press, 71–92.

Financial Times (1999) 'Consultants face future of change and uncertainty', *Financial Times* (FT Director), 17 March, I–II.

Fligstein, N. (1990) *The Transformation of Corporate Control*. Cambridge, MA: Harvard University Press.

Forbes (2011) List of Americas largest private companies, www.forbes.com (accessed 2 March 2012).

Gross, A.C. and Poor, J. (2008) 'The global management consulting sector', *Business Economics*, 43 (4): 59–68.

Haas Edersheim, E. (2004) *McKinsey's Marvin Bower: Vision, Leadership & the Creation of Management Consulting*. Hoboken, NJ: John Wiley & Sons.

Higdon, H. (1969) *The Business Healers*. New York: Random House.

Kiechel, W. III (2010) *The Lords of Strategy: The Secret Intellectual History of the New Corporate World*. Boston, MA: Harvard Business Press.

Kipping, M. (2002) 'Trapped in their wave: the evolution of management consultancies', in T. Clark and R. Fincham (eds), *Critical Consulting: New Perspectives on the Management Advice Industry*. Oxford: Blackwell, 28–49.

McKenna, C.D. (2006) *The World's Newest Profession: Management Consulting in the Twentieth Century*. New York: Cambridge University Press.

McKinsey & Company (2012) www.mckinsey.com (accessed 2 March 2012).

Peters, T.J. and Waterman, R.H. (1982) *In Search of Excellence: Lessons from America's Best-Run Companies*. New York: Harper & Row.

Smith, A. (1776) *An Inquiry into the Nature and Causes of the Wealth of Nations*. London: W. Strahan and T. Cadell.

Taylor, F.W. (1911) *The Principles of Scientific Management*. New York: Harper & Brothers.

3

REASONS, RISKS, AND RESULTS OF MANAGEMENT CONSULTANCY

INTRODUCTION

This chapter provides a critical perspective on:

1. The reasons for hiring management consultants.
2. The risks of using consultants.
3. The results that management consultants may achieve.

We begin with a discussion of the difficulties in measuring the effect of management consultancy. Next, we relate these effects to the different fee setting strategies of consultants. Subsequently, we look at the benefits sought by clients and their hiring reasons. We compare the reasons for hiring external consultants with those for employing internal consultants. Additionally, we explore the risks of using external consultants. The chapter closes with a summary, reflective questions, a mini case, suggestions for further reading, and references.

Main learning objectives

- Understand the difficulties of measuring the effects of management consultancy projects and explain the consequences for consultancy fees.

- Distinguish formal and informal reasons for hiring management consultants and corresponding effects sought by clients.
- Compare the effects of external and internal management consultancy on clients.
- Identify the risks of unethical behaviour by management consultants.
- Understand resistance to management consultancy.

DIFFICULTIES IN MEASURING THE EFFECT OF MANAGEMENT CONSULTANCY

Critical view

Critical academic literature (for an overview, see Clark and Fincham, 2002) argues that management consultancy faces ambiguities over the claimed results (Alvesson, 1993). Because of the difficulties of investigating the effectiveness, critical academic studies have not focused on the effect of management consultancy. Popular criticism by some journalists and alumni of management consultancies questions the effect of management consultancy (see for example, Ashford, 1998; O'Shea and Madigan, 1997; Pinault, 2000).

Growth in demand

Nevertheless, the demand for consultancy has grown rapidly, in particular since the 1980s. In 1886 the oldest management consultancy firm was founded: Arthur D. Little. In 1955 worldwide revenues reached US$1 billion. By 1980 revenues amounted to US$3 billion. In 1999, management consultancy accounted for 60 billion. Six years later in 2005, industry revenues had grown to US$150 billion.[1] How to explain this growth for management consultancy services if their effect is ambiguous?

The impact

The impact of management consultancy can be separated into, on the one hand, the effect of individual consultancy projects, and on the other hand, the number of projects.

---

[1]Source of 1955 and 2005 data is Gross and Poor (2008). Source of 1980 and 1999 data is Clark and Fincham (2002). Gross and Poor refer to various sources, including Kennedy Information. Clark and Fincham only refer to Kennedy Information.

Methodological problems

No academic study has (as yet) measured the effect of management consultancy in terms of client performance. Measuring this effect is difficult for various reasons, including three methodological issues (Engwall and Kipping, 2002):

1. Difficulties in isolating the effect.
2. Lack of comparison.
3. Bias

DIFFICULTIES IN ISOLATING THE EFFECT First, there is the problem of isolating the effect of management consultancy on client performance. The advice, and implementation assistance, of management consultants are among several factors that will influence the performance of clients. Moreover, the effects of consultancy may only materialize some time after the completion of the consultancy project. The causality between management consultancy and client performance is, therefore, difficult to measure (see Figure 3.1).

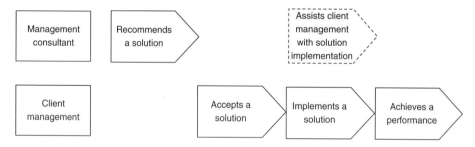

FIGURE 3.1 *The chain of causality from advice and assistance to client performance*

Note: Dotted line indicates that assistance is optional (only applicable if broad management consultancy)

Reasons for a deviating performance The client may implement the consultants' solution wrongly or with a delay. The client may also lack sufficient resources and capabilities to implement the solution correctly. Actors within the client organization may shirk. Even worse, actors within the client organization who oppose the solution may sabotage the implementation. In particular, if the management consultants do not assist client management with the implementation of a solution, the management consultants will have no influence on that implementation. For the management consultants it is difficult to monitor the implementation, in particular if the consultants' role was restricted to advice giving. Moreover, even if the clients implement the consultants' solution flawlessly, the realized client performance may deviate from the intended outcome. As stated before, various factors inside and outside the client organization may also influence client performance, such as overall economic downturns or industry specific downturns. The solution is one among several factors that may have an effect on client performance.

LACK OF COMPARISON

Second, there is the problem of a lack of comparison. It is not possible to measure what would have happened to client performance without management consultancy. Identical twins, with one organization using management consultancy and the other refraining from consultancy, do not exist.

BIAS

Third, there is the problem of bias. The stakeholders, clients and consultants have an interest in justifying the consultancy project and will, therefore, overrate the effectiveness of the project. Objective measurement will be difficult to achieve.

Data and disclosure problems

Besides methodological problems, there are problems with data. Data on management consultancy are hard, if not impossible, to get for outsiders, that is, those others besides clients and consultants. Clients have no interest in disclosing their usage of management consultancy, let alone share information about the effect of that management consultancy, and they will certainly not provide data on management consultancy projects that failed. In the case of successful projects, clients may have an incentive to claim the success for themselves and hide their usage of consultants. Management consultants have an interest in communicating their successful consultancy projects. When consultants have to pitch a new project to a prospective client, they usually like to show the results of similar types of projects. From a prospective client's point of view, the strongest credentials are those with a client name and a contact person, or a reference letter from the client executive. However, clients may require that consultants sign non-disclosure agreements. Even in the absence of such non-disclosure contracts, consultants may be reluctant to communicate data about client projects because of client sensitivities. As a result, management consultancy is a relatively closed industry.

FEES FOR EXTERNAL MANAGEMENT CONSULTANCY

Even for clients and consultants with their superior access to information about the consultancy assignment it is difficult to evaluate the effect of management consultancy. The afore-mentioned methodological reasons make any evaluation of the effect difficult if not impossible. This lack of measurement of the effect has consequences for the pricing of management consultancy, that is the fee that management consultants can ask of their clients.

Principles of pricing

In general, the prices of products, projects or services, can be conceptualized as a spectrum (see Figure 3.2). The lower limit of the pricing spectrum is the cost of a product. On the one hand, there are the direct costs of the salaries, the travel, and other project-related expenses of the consultants staffing the project. On the other hand, there are the indirect costs of the management consultancy firm, including the supporting functions. Suppliers cannot afford to offer their product at a price that is below cost, at least not in the long term. The cost sets the floor for the pricing. The upper limit of the pricing spectrum is the client's willingness to pay for the product. What determines this 'willingness to pay'? The maximum amount that a client is willing to hand over for a product or project is the value they attach to – or the perceived effect of – the particular product or project.

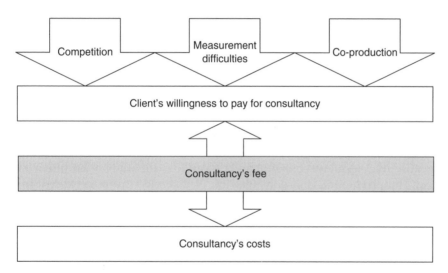

FIGURE 3.2   *The spectrum of a management consultancy fee*

Fees based on effects

Therefore, it is highly relevant for management consultancies to measure this effect, provided that the effect is large. This willingness to pay for management consultancy increases with the effect of management consultancy. A management consultancy could claim a share of the created worth if they could prove the worth of their advice. Management consultancy fees could then be based on a share of the created worth. For instance, a management consultancy develops a corporate restructuring strategy for a large corporation. Assume this strategy is worth US$500 million in terms of reduced costs. A percentage for the management consultancy might then be justifiable. Let's hypothetically assume a 0.5 per cent fee. In this fictitious example, the management consultancy would then earn US$2.5 million from the project.

Factors affecting fees

Three factors push management consultancy fees (far) below the upper price limit of willingness to pay.

MEASUREMENT DIFFICULTIES

First, the effect of a management consultancy project is often not possible, or at least very difficult, to measure. However, in some cases this may also be advantageous for management consultants. If the effect is below client requirements or even negative, then the consultants will benefit from the measurement difficulties.

As a result of such difficulties, management consultancy fees are generally based on time and materials. Those fees are probably significantly below the US$2.5 million mentioned in the example. At the management consultancy Bain & Company they say: 'We sell profit at a discount' (Kiechel, 2010).

CO-PRODUCTION

A second factor pushing down fees below the upper limit is the fact that management consultancy is often a co-production by client and consultant. Because management consultancy is a service, clients play an important role. The production and consumption of a service are intertwined. In a management consultancy project, clients have a (important) role, not only in the development of the advice but also in the implementation of that advice. For the advice development, the knowledge of the client is often essential. Implementation cannot be done without client effort. Therefore, a management consultancy project is a co-production by consultants and clients. This leads to another issue regarding the effect of management consultancy. Not only is the effect of the project hard to measure, one also needs to distinguish the individual contributions of consultants and clients. The effect of the consultancy project should be divided among both parties.

Dividing the effect Let's take the example of a corporate restructuring project because the effects are relatively easy to quantify. Consultants and clients together will identify the restructuring opportunity and the consultants will assist the client with implementing of the restructuring programme. We have assumed that the cost savings from this project are US$500 million. How much of this effect is attributable to the management consultants? Theoretically, a marginal analysis may provide some insight. Such an analysis would be based on the effect that the client may be able to achieve without the help of management consultants. In our example, the client might be able to achieve on its own a cost saving of US$300 million. The additional US$200 million is due to the hiring of management consultants. But again, it is a co-production. The additional savings of US$200 million are not only attributable to consultants. This effect should be divided among client and consultants. The bargaining power of the client determines how the effect is divided. Chapter 5 will elaborate on this bargaining between client and consultant. Moreover, consultants may be willing to offer a project for a lower fee if they see opportunities for further work. By selling the project at a relatively low fee, they hope to move into a better position to land a large future project (Chapter 10 discusses in more detail the pricing strategies of consultants).

COMPETITION

The third factor pushing down consultancy fees below the upper limit is competition. We may distinguish three competitive forces with a downward impact on consultancy fees: (a) competition among incumbent management consultancies; (b) the threat of new entrants into the management consultancy industry; and (c) competition from substitutes for management consultancy. Chapter 5 will explore these competitive forces in detail.

Rewards and risks

If project fees are based on time and materials, then management consultants will not encounter (a large) risk on their projects. If the expected results of the project fail to materialize, then the consultants still receive their fees. Their client fully absorbs the risk of a failed project. Result-based fees for consultants would shift some part of this risk onto the consultants. However, the downward potential for consultants remains limited. Whereas a client may go bankrupt in the worst case, the consultants may lose the variable part of their fees. Management consultants typically cannot be held accountable for the client's negative results for two reasons: measurement and responsibility.

MEASUREMENT

First of all, the relationship between management consultancy services and client performance is hard to measure. The measurability relationship may vary between projects. In general, the effect of top-line (growth) projects is harder to measure, and to assign to a consultant's contribution, than bottom-line (cost reduction) projects. Projects on strategic sourcing or process efficiency lend themselves relatively well to the measurement of effects and are more often linked to consultancy fees. Especially during times of budget issues, clients may opt for risk-reward projects.

RESPONSIBILITY

Second, management consultants are never responsible for management decisions. Even in the case of consultants as a management substitute (see Chapter 1), client management remains responsible for any decision. Consultants only provide advice. It is the client's responsibility whether to follow this advice and make particular decisions, or to reject it. Some consultants will add legal clauses to their contracts that will exclude all accountabilities for any negative effect that may arise in the context of the consultancy project. Even though management consultants may not have their fees at stake, a failed consultancy project will negatively affect their reputation when word gets out.

REASONS FOR HIRING MANAGEMENT CONSULTANTS

Measuring the effect of management consultancy in terms of client performance assumes that clients hire management consultants to improve the effectiveness and/or efficiency of their organization. However, this chapter shows that the reasons for hiring management consultants do vary. Not all reasons are (directly) related to the performance of the organization. There is no single effect from management consultancy, but several effects. These cannot be measured only in terms of the performance of client organizations (Ernst and Kieser, 2002). The question arises: for what reasons do client managers hire management consultants?

Different effects sought

We explore what effects client management seeks from management consultants. According to this book's (narrow) definition, clients hire management consultants to provide advice on decisions to solve problems. However, clients may also hire these consultants to provide assistance with managing the implementation of the solution (broad definition). These definitions reflect formal reasons for hiring consultants. Client management uses consultancy for other reasons as well. Clients will seek various effects from consultants. We analyse the effect of management consultancy by clients' reasons for using consultants. Figure 3.3 provides an overview of these reasons and the effects clients seek.

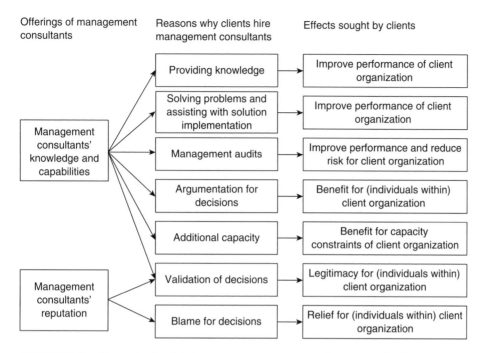

Offerings of management consultants

Reasons why clients hire management consultants

Effects sought by clients

Management consultants' knowledge and capabilities	Providing knowledge	Improve performance of client organization
	Solving problems and assisting with solution implementation	Improve performance of client organization
	Management audits	Improve performance and reduce risk for client organization
	Argumentation for decisions	Benefit for (individuals within) client organization
	Additional capacity	Benefit for capacity constraints of client organization
Management consultants' reputation	Validation of decisions	Legitimacy for (individuals within) client organization
	Blame for decisions	Relief for (individuals within) client organization

FIGURE 3.3 *Reasons for hiring management consultancy and effects sought*

Reasons and roles

These hiring reasons mirror the roles of management consultants, as described in Chapter 1. Chapter 1 distinguished formal roles (expert, doctor, and facilitator), and informal roles (hired hand, legitimator, political weapon, and scapegoat). Providing knowledge mirrors the expert role. Solving problems is the doctor role or the facilitator role. As a doctor, the consultant provides the solution. As a facilitator, the consultant provides the process of problem solving.

The functionalist perspective

Chapter 1 discussed two opposing perspectives on management consultancy. We distinguished between the functionalist perspective and the critical perspective (Armbrüster, 2006). In the functionalist perspective, management consultants are the developers and carriers of management knowledge. According to this perspective, management hires management consultants to provide knowledge and capabilities to solve problems in an objective and independent way. These hiring reasons relate to the formal roles of management consultants: the management consultant as an expert;

the management consultant as a doctor; and the consultant as a facilitator (providing a process for problem solving).

The critical perspective

The critical perspective acknowledges that management consultants solve problems. In addition, this view distinguishes various informal roles. Clients may hire management consultants to provide temporary capacity (hired hand), to legitimize clients' solutions which other stakeholders oppose (legitimator), to support clients in political fights (political weapon), and to take the blame for clients' solutions that are not in the interests of some other stakeholders (scapegoat). These reasons differ in terms of the effect of management consultancy. Management consultancy is defined as providing *independent* advice (see Chapter 1); however, the consultant depends on the client for their payment. Therefore, the consultant may be vulnerable to opportunistic clients who hire a consultant as a legitimator, political weapon, or scapegoat. In each of these situations, we can no longer qualify the consultant's advice as independent.

CASE STUDY

The effect of advice

The following case study illustrates how management consultants may have a positive effect on their clients' performance. This is a stylized case based on a synthesis of disguised real world situations. The case also illustrates the importance of independent advice.

In search of synergies

Blivet Corporation is a vertically integrated company. The company has positions in the manufacturing of components and final products (based on these components). Blivet was originally a component manufacturer. Ten years ago the company decided to enter into manufacturing of final products. The management of Blivet regarded manufacturing as an attractive industry. Moreover, that management saw substantial synergies between components and final products. When the final product manufacturer, Target Corporation, one of its main customers, came up for sale, Blivet acquired it. The integrated company, however, did not perform as was expected. On the contrary, its revenues diminished and its profitability declined even more. The stock market responded negatively: the company's stock halved. At that time, five years ago, the management of Blivet decided to hire one of the world's top management consultancy firms, Brain

& Company, to help Blivet improve its shareholder value.

The advice

Based on three months of rigorous research, Brain & Company came to the conclusion that Blivet should exit the component business and focus its resources on the final product manufacturing. This advice came as a shock to Blivet's management as the company had been founded as a component producer. Moreover, the component business represented 80 per cent of Blivet's revenues. Divesting the component business implied shrinking the company to a fifth of its original size. However, when Blivet publicly announced its retreat from component manufacturing, its stock price soared. After the divestiture of the component division, the remaining final product division was renamed Focus Corporation. In the following five years, Focus has tripled the revenues of its final product business while increasing its already high profitability. Although the company is currently about 60 per cent of its original size, its stock market value has increased fivefold since the announcement of its withdrawal from components.

The logic

The consultancy project by Brain & Company revealed that the component industry was no longer attractive for Blivet. Moreover, the expected positive synergies between components and final products did not exist. In contrast, the synergies proved to be negative. Other customers from Blivet's component business withdrew their orders when it took over Target, which was one of their competitors. Moreover, Target could no longer buy components from competitors of Blivet, but was forced to source all its components from its new owner. However, Blivet was not the most competitive provider. Brain & Company showed that final product manufacturing was an attractive industry. Economies of scale were decisive in final product manufacturing. Blivet's scale was too small and the company lacked the capital to invest in its scale. By selling the unattractive component activities and reinvesting the receipts of the sale in the final product manufacturing business, Focus Corporation could reach a competitive scale. Moreover, by breaking up the relationship with components, Focus could purchase components from the best sources available. Finally, by pruning the company's portfolio to final products only, management could focus their attention on a single core business. The rise of Focus Corporation's stock price reflected investors' expectations about the new strategy developed by Brain & Company.

Discussion questions

1 What was/were the main reason(s) why Blivet hired an external management consultancy? Elaborate on your answer.

2 Should Brain & Company have based its consultancy fee on the performance effect that its advice generated? Why, or why not? Explain your answer.

3 If you were the chief executive officer of Blivet, would you have accepted a performance-based consultancy fee for Brain & Company? What are the pros and cons of performance-based fees for clients? Explain your answer.

THE EFFECTS OF KNOWLEDGE

Knowledge plays an important role in most of the offerings of management consultants (see Figure 3.3). The newness of this knowledge determines the width of the effect (see Figure 3.4).

If management consultants are innovators in the sense that they develop knowledge that is new to society, they have the largest and widest effect. In other situations, management consultants act as carriers of knowledge from one industry to another. They have gained knowledge in one industry that is new to another industry. In some cases, the knowledge may not even be new to the client. The knowledge on which the advice is based may have already resided in the client organization. Even in such a case, however, management consultants could have an effect. The knowledge may have tacitly existed in the client organization, or it may have been fragmented. In such situations, the added value of management consultancies may be based on extracting, structuring, and synthesizing the existing knowledge within the client organization (Armbrüster, 2006).

The effect of management consultancy does not always have to be positive. Management consultancy projects may have a negative effect on clients. The advice may be flawed or wrongly implemented. The project may be done for informal reasons that are in the interests of the individual client manager but not in the interests of the client organization. Furthermore, as a result of unethical advice given by the management consultant to the client, other organizations in the client's industry or society at large may suffer.

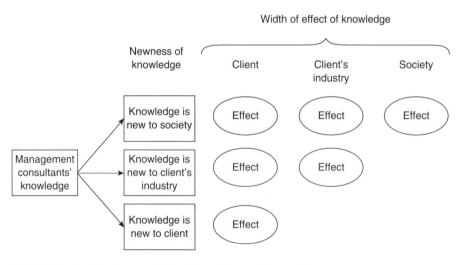

FIGURE 3.4 *Varying width of the effect of knowledge*

Effect mechanisms

Management consultants have knowledge about the client's problem and about problem solving processes. They also have the capabilities to solve problems. What is the effect of the knowledge and capabilities of management consultants? Figure 3.5 shows that client projects are not the only mechanism through which management consultants' knowledge and capabilities have an effect for clients as well as society.

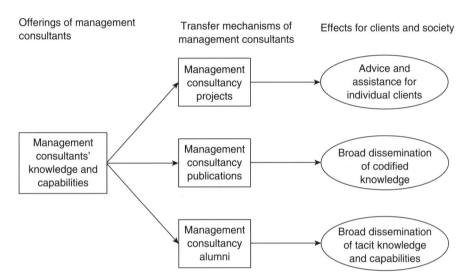

FIGURE 3.5 *Three mechanisms through which management consultancy effects clients and society*

PROJECTS
Clients may benefit from the advice and assistance that management consultants provide in projects. However, advice and assistance are not the only channels through which clients may benefit. Clients may also learn from management consultants. The more client employees are involved in the consultancy project, the better the opportunity for client learning. During the projects, clients may absorb knowledge from consultants and they may also develop new capabilities by learning from these consultants.

PUBLICATIONS
Clients, other (non-client) organizations, and society at large may benefit from the publications of management consultancies. Consultancies may codify their knowledge and distribute it in the form of publications, either in print (articles, books, and reports) or in electronic form on the internet (firm website and other websites). McKinsey & Company's *In Search of*

Excellence is probably the best-known publication by a management consultancy. It has sold over 5 million copies.

ALUMNI
Finally, clients, other organizations, and society may benefit from the talent development within management consultancies. Through their projects, the individual consultants develop knowledge and capabilities. Management consultancies typically have a relatively high turnover of staff (see Chapter 9). The result is a stream of knowledgeable and skilled alumni flowing out of the management consultancies into society. Alumni may join clients or other organizations. They may also become entrepreneurs. In any case, they disseminate the knowledge and capabilities of the management consultancies to the benefit of the hiring organizations and society at large. This effect is relatively large as the number of alumni is a multiple of the number of employees within the management consultancy firms. Alumni, in particular those of the global top management consultancy firms, may achieve senior management positions in corporations and other organizations. An example is McKinsey & Company, which has more than 230 alumni that, as chief executive officers, lead large (more than US$1 billion revenue) organizations. Moreover, more than a fifth of its 24,000 alumni have started their own business (McKinsey, 2012).

THE EFFECTS OF PROBLEM SOLVING AND MANAGEMENT AUDITS: THREE FIELDS OF MANAGEMENT CONSULTANCY

Given these difficulties, we explore the effects of management consultancy for the three fields of management consultancy that were identified in Chapter 2. We acknowledge that Table 3.1 on the next page represents a functionalist view on the effects of management consultancy. The figure shows the overtly desired results of consultancy projects, that is the formal hiring reasons of clients (not the covertly desired results which reflect the informal hiring reasons).

The scope of the effect

If management consultants develop new knowledge for whatever consultancy field, they may have an effect at three levels: client, industry, and society. If the knowledge applied by the management consultants is new and superior for the client's industry, then that client may become the best practice firm in its industry. If the knowledge is new and superior to society, then society as a whole may benefit from the new best practices.

TABLE 3.1 *The effect of different fields of consultancy on client performance*

Consultancy field	Effect on client performance
Operations	Improvement of client's operational efficiency and effectiveness
Organization and strategy	• Improvement of client organizational efficiency and effectiveness • Improvement of the client organization's competitiveness • Improvement of the client's business portfolio (only applicable if multiple businesses)
Information technology	Improvement of the efficiency and effectiveness of the client's information systems and processes

However, if the management consultants broker the knowledge about best practices from one industry to another industry, then they only enable an industry to improve.

Negative effects

Improving the performance of a client organization may come at the expense of employment and job satisfaction. Even if the client organization as a whole benefits, individual actors inside or outside the client organization may suffer. In the case that management consultants broker the knowledge about best practice in the client's industry, then they only enable the client to catch up with the best practice competitors. In this situation, management consultants contribute to levelling the playing field of an industry. Even if the overall effect of management consultancy on an industry is positive, not everyone in the industry may benefit. In the situation of levelling the playing field in an industry, management consultants may erode the competitive advantage of best practice firms.

Operations consultancy

Management consultancy in the first field, operations, has the objective to improve the operations in terms of, for instance, costs, speed and quality. These improvements are measurable. If the advice is well implemented and other factors do not intervene, then the effect of management consultancy should be visible. This effect on the client's operations can be quantified and can even be translated in financial terms.

Organization and strategy consultancy

ORGANIZATION CONSULTANCY

The second field is organization and strategy consultancy. In organization consultancy, management consultants use their knowledge and capabilities to improve the client's organizational structure. The improvement of the organization structure may be measured in terms of the intra-organizational processes and interactions with outside stakeholders. The performance improvement of processes and interactions is measurable. As in the case of operations improvement, the effect for the client's industry and society depends on the newness of the management consultants' knowledge. Do management consultants introduce revolutionary new knowledge, or are they brokering existing knowledge about organizations across industries, or even within industries?

STRATEGY CONSULTANCY

Strategy consultancy is probably the most difficult consultancy field to measure. Strategy is about the fit between the organization and its environment. As a result the influence of environmental factors is significant. Moreover, strategy solutions are broad in scope; they cover the whole client organization including all functions. As a result, implementation is complex. Furthermore, the effects of strategy implementation need time to materialize. Given the combination of relatively long time interval and the relatively large number of intervening factors (because of the broad organizational scope and the significant role of the environment), the chances of influence by other factors are relatively strong.

Information technology consultancy

The third field, information technology consultancy, is mainly about developing and implementing information systems for client organizations. These systems typically have performance specifications that are measurable. Clients and consultants may measure whether the IT systems are implemented on time and whether they function according to specifications. Again, the newness of knowledge determines the width of the effect, from client to society.

THE EFFECTS OF INFORMAL ROLES

Besides the formal roles of solving problems and conducting management audits, we distinguish four informal roles for management consultants: the hired hand, the legitimator, the political weapon, and the scapegoat.

Hired hand

The effect of the hired hand is relatively limited if the management consultants conduct tasks that could be done by client employees. If the work does not require distinctive knowledge and capabilities, management consultants as hired hands cannot differentiate themselves from client employees. Management consultants hired as temporary capacity may be perceived as relatively expensive temps. They only temporarily relieve the capacity constraints of their clients. By relieving these temporary capacity constraints, consultants enable clients to avoid having to hire permanent staff. This is relevant in countries with strict labour regulations on hiring temporary labour and firing employees.

Legitimator

The role of the legitimator is to validate client management decisions. This validation may enable client management to overcome the opposition of internal and external stakeholders. If the decision holds value potential then validating these decisions may release this value. If the opposition is overcome, the client organization will benefit. The effect of validation on client performance is, therefore, indirect.

Political weapon

The role of the political weapon is to provide arguments for client management decisions. If the management consultant is used in a political fight between the client organization and an external party, then the client organization may benefit. In the case of a micro-political fight, between factions or individuals within the client organization, the factions or individuals that use management consultants may benefit. As in the case of validation, the provision of arguments does not directly affect client performance. However, in an indirect way, the argumentation may enable the client to improve its performance. In the case of micro-political fights, the effect of the political weapon for individual managers is direct.

Scapegoat

The scapegoat takes the blame for client management decisions. Management consultants as scapegoats help the implementation of decisions against which opposition exists. If these decisions have value potential for the client organization, the scapegoat enables the client organization to realize this value. This is an indirect effect. Management consultants as scapegoats always provide relief for the management of the client organization. This is a direct effect at the level of the individual client manager.

THE EFFECTS OF THE GROWTH IN DEMAND FOR MANAGEMENT CONSULTANCY

Finally, the total impact of management consultancy not only depends on the effect of the individual consultancy project but also on the number of projects. Revenues from management consultancy took off in the 1980s. Political and technological developments and related changes in the competitive landscape since the 1980s had important consequences for client management as they increased the complexity of problems, reduced the time required for problem solving, and increased the pressure to improve organization performance. These challenges for management stimulated the demand for management consultancy. The number (and size) of projects grew, and induced a growing impact for management consultancy on client sectors and society at large. Chapter 6 will discuss the growth of management consultancy in more detail.

EXTERNAL VERSUS INTERNAL MANAGEMENT CONSULTANCY

The previous section listed the effects of management consultancy as problem solvers and auditors. If these effects are substantial, why don't clients develop these knowledge and capabilities in-house, instead of hiring outside agents? This is the classic 'make-or-buy' decision, which is the subject of transaction cost economics (Coase, 1937; Williamson, 1975). This decision is driven by a combination of production arguments and governance arguments (see Table 3.2 on the next page). Production is about the development of advice and the delivery of assistance. Governance is about coordinating the relationship between the client and the consultant. One coordination mechanism is the price system. The market is based on the price system. This is the option of external management consultancy. An alternative coordination mechanism is the hierarchy. The client organization is based on the hierarchy. This is the option of internal management consultancy.

Preference for external management consultants

PRODUCTION ARGUMENTS
Scope   As Chapter 1 indicated, external management consultants have some advantages relative to in-house consultants, or the in-house solution. First, external management consultants have the advantage of working on

TABLE 3.2 *Arguments for external and internal consultants*

	Preference for internal consultants	Preference for external consultants
Production arguments	• In-depth knowledge of client organization is critical • Strong resistance against outsiders • Price/performance ratio of external management consultants is high compared to internal consultancy	If external management consultants: • achieve economies of scope • achieve economies of scale If independence is important
Governance arguments	• Required client-specificity of knowledge and capabilities is high • Uncertainty about opportunistic behaviour of external management consultants is high • Frequency of projects is high	
Informal agenda		If client wants: • legitimation of decisions • arguments for political conflicts • to shift the blame for decisions

a broader scope, one of organizations and sectors. Although some internal management consultancies also offer their services to other organizations besides their own, generally, external management consultants work for a broader set of organizations, geographies and industries then their internal counterparts. As a result, external consultants enjoy economies of scope that internal consultants cannot match. These scope economies consist of the potential to offer fresh perspectives, to accumulate more knowledge and experience, and to broker knowledge across organizations, geographies, and industries. Organizations may hire external consultants for their experience in other industries and their ability to apply that knowledge in the client organization. This is knowledge that the client cannot develop, or only at a higher cost (Armbrüster, 2006).

Clients may also employ former consultants (alumni) to strengthen their internal consultancy units. In this way, clients can leverage the individual consultant's own experience, although not the consultancy firm's collective experience as manifested in its network of experts and knowledge management system. However, external consultants may have less knowledge about the client organization than internal consultants.

Scale External management consultants have the advantage of working on a broader scale. External management consultants can be larger than internal consultants because their market is not limited to one organization. The larger size of operations may enable external management consultants to achieve economies of scale that internal consultants cannot match. As a result, external consultants may be more efficient than internal ones.

Independence Another advantage to external management consultants is their independence. This allows them to provide an impartial perspective and advice. Internal management consultants cannot match this independence, at least not when they work in their own organizations. Being an outsider has advantages. We previously discussed the economies of scope. However, internal provision of management audits is in some cases no option, regardless of levels of specificity, uncertainty and frequency. For instance, management audits require independence. Internal management consultants often lack this. Therefore, clients can use only external management consultants if they want a management audit. Another example is the validation of management decisions.

INFORMAL AGENDA ARGUMENTS External management consultants are better equipped than internal consultants to provide legitimacy for management decisions. Clients use the reputation of the external consultancy to add legitimacy to their decisions. The reputation and independence of external consultants can be an advantage if client management hires consultants to provide argumentation for political fights. Finally, external management consultants as outsiders are better positioned to take the blame for management decisions.

Preference for internal management consultants

PRODUCTION ARGUMENTS

The outsider position of external management consultants may also be a disadvantage. External management consultants may face resistance from stakeholders within or outside the client. Moreover, if the project requires in-depth knowledge about the client, internal consultants may have an advantage. Of course, clients need to compare the production advantages of external management consultants with their costs. In general, the fees of external consultants will exceed those of internal ones. However, if the price–performance ratio of external consultants becomes uncompetitive compared with that of internal consultants, than the latter will have an advantage.

GOVERNANCE ARGUMENTS

Specificity   Whereas production arguments (scale, scope, and independence) favour the usage of external management consultants over internal consultants, governance arguments may induce the opposite. Transaction cost arguments indicate that high asset specificity, high uncertainty, and high frequency favour internal solutions over external ones.

First, we must address asset specificity. In the case of management consultancy, the relevant assets are knowledge and capabilities. If the knowledge and capabilities required to offer management consultancy to a particular client are highly specific to that client, then external management consultants will be reluctant to invest in developing that knowledge and capabilities. The reason for this reluctance is that the management consultants cannot deploy, at least not sufficiently, that specific knowledge and capabilities with other client organizations. Therefore, the management consultants cannot achieve sufficient scale to earn back their investment in knowledge and capabilities without becoming too dependent on that client. This dependence may bring with it the risk of opportunism, or hazard, on the part of that client. That particular client may use their power to take advantage of the management consultants via a hold-up. Because of the risk of such a hold-up, external management consultants will not invest in the specific knowledge and capabilities the client needs. Such clients will be forced to develop the client-specific knowledge and capabilities in-house.

Uncertainty   The second governance argument for internal management consultancy is uncertainty about the opportunistic behaviour of external management consultants. If clients expect opportunistic behaviour from external consultants, they may favour internal consultancy. Uncertainty is based on information asymmetry between clients and external management consultants. Clients do not have the same information as management consultants. As a result, they cannot completely monitor the behaviour of management consultants. Management consultants might take advantage of the information asymmetry by behaving opportunistically. With an increasing probability of opportunistic behaviour by external consultants, clients are better off building the knowledge and capabilities in-house, rather than using external management consultants. Another factor is how critical the knowledge to be developed, or to be shared with consultants in the project, is for the client. This determines client risk. Figure 3.6 visualizes how specificity and uncertainty influence the decision between external and internal management consultancy.

Frequency   Frequency is also a factor in the governance decision. Whereas external management consultancy is a variable cost for the client, setting up an internal management consultancy generates fixed costs for the client. To recover these fixed costs, the client needs a minimum volume of services,

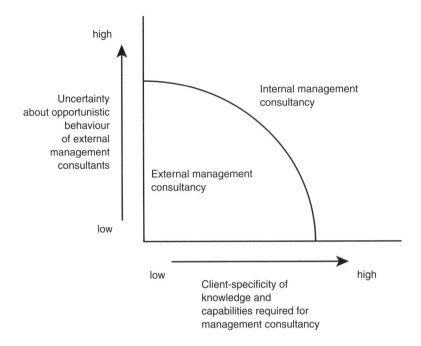

Uncertainty
about opportunistic
behaviour
of external
management
consultants

Internal management
consultancy

External management
consultancy

low

low   high

Client-specificity of
knowledge and
capabilities required for
management consultancy

FIGURE 3.6 *The frontier of external management consultancy for client problem solving*

or frequency of consultancy projects per period. This is the so-called break-even volume of consultancy projects. Only if the frequency of management consultancy projects exceeds the break-even threshold, will an internal management consultancy be a viable option, at least in economic terms. This is why only large corporations and large non-profit organizations have their own internal consultancy units. For problems that occur infrequently, it is economically not feasible to set up an internal management consultancy.

RISKS OF USING EXTERNAL MANAGEMENT CONSULTANCY

The use of external management consultants may carry risks for clients. We focus on three such risks: overdependence, isomorphism, and opportunism.

Overdependence

First, clients may risk becoming overly dependent on external consultants. For instance, if clients rely too much on external consultants to solve their problems, they will not develop internally the resources and capabilities for solving such problems. These clients may even lose these problem solving resources and capabilities. For instance, if the chief executive officer of a corporation decides to bypass its own management and staff and hires external management consultants for problem solving, then management and staff will not accumulate experience. They may become frustrated and might even leave the corporation. With a loss of internal resources and capabilities for problem solving, the client will be forced to hire external management consultants. Such organizations run the risk of entering a vicious cycle. Over time internal resources and capabilities will be eroded and eventually the client becomes overly dependent on external management consultants. These consultants may eventually become a management substitute (see Chapter 1). Moreover, overly dependent clients run the risk of becoming the victims of opportunistic consultants.

Isomorphism

Second, if more organizations in the same sector rely on management consultants, the sector may run the risk of isomorphism, or similarity of organizations (DiMaggio and Powell, 1983). If the advice of management consultants for the different organizations is similar, then implementation of this advice will imply that these organizations come to resemble each other more. This is termed 'isomorphism'. These organizations adopt the same practices and structures as other organizations in their sector. We distinguish four situations that bring about this isomorphism.

STANDARDIZED ADVICE   Isomorphism may be due to the behaviour of an individual management consultancy firm. The same management consultancy firm gives similar, or even identical, advice to multiple organizations in the same sector. This consultancy offers a standardized solution to its clients.

HERD BEHAVIOUR OF CONSULTANTS   In another situation, isomorphism among client organizations may also reflect isomorphism on the side of the management consultancy firms. The client organizations within a sector hire different management consultancy firms. However, these consultancy firms provide similar or identical advice to their clients.

HERD BEHAVIOUR OF CLIENTS   In a third situation, isomorphism in the client sector may be due to the herd behaviour of these client organizations. Clients may ask for the same advice from management consultancy firms. Clients choose the same solutions as the other organizations in their sector for reasons of legitimacy and risk reduction. Isn't it better to be collectively wrong, than individually right?

CATCH UP   Finally, clients may ask for the same solution as their best practice competitors have implemented in order to catch up with these rivals. If particular organizations are successful with a certain solution, competitors may want to implement this solution as well. External management consultants that have experience with this solution, or may even have developed this solution in the first place, may be an attractive source for implementing such a solution in the client organization. It is like a prisoner's dilemma. The client knows that imitating a best practice competitor, with the help of management consultants, will only get their organization closer to that best practice or – in the case of excellent implementation – at a par. Catching up with best practice will by definition not bring the client a competitive advantage. However, the alternative of not trying to catch up with best practice is worse.

Opportunism

Third, clients using external management consultants may face uncertainty about the behaviour of their consultants. Consultancy projects are by definition temporary. After shorter or longer periods, projects come to an end. However, consultancy firms are not temporary organizations. They strive for continuity. Therefore, these firms need new projects. What are the most probable new clients for the management consultancy firm? For which clients will the management consultant be most valuable? Competitors of the client may be interested in the services of the management consultancy firm because the firm has accumulated industry expertise. They have learned about the industry. In particular if the first client of the management consultancy achieves success with the consultants' advice, competitors may be interested in hiring this consultancy. If the management consultancy uses knowledge from the original project, or even builds on this knowledge, then the original client runs a risk. The knowledge spill-over from the original client to competitors may imply an erosion of the original client's competitive advantage.

Reducing the risk of knowledge spill-overs

SAFEGUARDS Management consultancy firms may offer safeguards against knowledge spill-overs from one client to another. These consultancy firms may assign different consultancy teams to competing clients. These teams are separated by so-called 'Chinese walls', which prevent knowledge flowing from one team to the other and thus from one client to another. The teams do not communicate with each other about their projects. They do not share information. Management consultancy firms may also offer exclusivity to their clients. They may offer not to accept projects that may conflict with their client, like giving advice to any industry competitor in the same geographical area, for instance the country. Of course, such an exclusivity offering comes at a price for the client because the management consultancy has to be compensated for the loss of future business in the sector. Bain & Company used to have a policy of no more than one client per sector.

REPUTATION AND REPEAT BUSINESS The risk of knowledge spill-overs by management consultants diminishes if reputation and repeat business become more important to the management consultants. Brokering of knowledge to competing clients may negatively affect the consultancy firm's reputation in the marketplace. A deteriorating reputation may negatively affect the consultancy firm's potential to acquire new projects. In particular if the original client offers the potential for future projects, then it is in the interests of the consultancy firm not to spill over knowledge to competitors. To maintain the relationship with the original client, and to secure future projects with that client, the consultancy firm will voluntarily refrain from any practice of knowledge spill-over in the client's sector. Finally, the risk of knowledge spill-overs in a sector will be low if clients hire external consultancies for fresh new insights. In these situations, consultancy firms may still broker knowledge, but this brokerage will be across sectors instead of within the same sector.

RESISTANCE TO MANAGEMENT CONSULTANCY

We can distinguish two sources of resistance on the part of some stakeholders in the client organization to management consultancy projects (see also Part 4). First, there is resistance to management consultants because they are outsiders; they are not one of us. Stakeholders may not like to be told by outsiders what to do. Second, there is the stakeholders' resistance to change. Stakeholders may not like change at all, irrespective of the question of who initiates that change: client managers or consultants. Management consultants are mostly hired by client managers to create change. Therefore, consultants will face resistance to change.

FRUSTRATION Not everyone will necessarily benefit from the advice and assistance of management consultants. The client organization as a whole may benefit. But factions and individuals within the client organization may feel bypassed. Hiring external management consultants instead of letting employees solve the organization's problems may create the impression that management does not trust the capabilities of its own employees. These employees may feel overlooked by their management and may even become frustrated. As a result, they may resist the consultant's solution.

LOSS OF POWER, RESOURCES, AND JOBS Furthermore, the consultant's advice may also lead to negative consequences for factions and individuals in the client organization. Reorganizations may shift the balance of power within the client organization. New strategies may shift the allocation of resources in the client organization. Factions and individuals in the client organization may lose power and resources, such as capital and people. Individuals may even lose their job as a result of consultancy advice. In particular such lay-offs induce a fear of management consultancy. Some management consultancy firms have developed a reputation for restructuring with massive layoffs. There are clients that exploit this reputation and use such consultancy firms as scapegoats. Of course, such client actions will add to resistance from stakeholders within the client organization.

ENVY   The fees, income, and prestige of external management consultants may also arouse negative emotions and resistance among client employees, in particular, if client management uses management consultants as a relief for internal capacity constraints. The management consultant as a 'hired hand' is an expensive temporary worker. The high costs of these temps may arouse negative sentiments among client staff. Moreover, young consultants, fresh from business school, expensively dressed, and driving premium brand company cars, may arouse the envy of client employees who cannot afford such luxuries.

CONFLICTS   Finally, if client management hires a management consultancy as an ally in a micro-political conflict, that is, a political conflict within the client organization, then opposing factions and individuals in the client organization will resist these management consultants.

MANAGEMENT CONSULTANTS' PRACTICES FOR GENERATING DEMAND

CONSULTANTS' RHETORIC   As the effect of management consultancy is difficult to assess, convincing clients to hire management consultants may demand a great deal from the marketing and sales capabilities of management consultants. Management consultants may revert to rhetoric and impression management to persuade clients to hire them (Clark and Salaman, 1998). Creating or emphasizing uncertainty may also contribute to the demand for management consultancy. Management consultants also disseminate management fashion, that is, management concepts and tools. Some examples are business process re-engineering (BPR), total quality management, and 'lean six sigma'. Such management fashion induces the demand for management consultancy.

Client management cannot keep up with the stream of new management concepts and tools and therefore hires consultants. Moreover, fashion contributes to the perceived uncertainty of client management, which in its turn induces additional demand (Ernst and Kieser, 2002). Management consultants sometimes create their own market. In the 1980s, management consultants helped their clients to downsize and outsource headquarters activities. Lean headquarters meant less internal resources for problem solving. Thus, lean clients had to hire management consultants more often.

CLIENTS' EXPERIENCE   However, clients are becoming increasingly experienced and sophisticated. They have learned from previous experiences with management consultants. Moreover, clients have been hiring former consultants (alumni). As a result the rhetoric of management consultants will lose its effectiveness with increasing client experience and sophistication. Moreover, to a growing extent, clients are no longer satisfied with impressive PowerPoint presentations and thick reports. Instead of (empty) words, they want deeds from their consultants. Clients demand results instead of reports. Therefore, such clients no longer let management consultants get away with a report, and demand that their consultants implement what they advise. Large clients increasingly use purchase departments for hiring management consultants. Such professional purchasers typically focus on the costs and benefits of management consultancy. Consultants, therefore, come under increasing pressure to prove their positive effect.

SUMMARY

MEASURING EFFECTS   This chapter discussed the impact of management consultancy. The total impact of management consultancy depends on the effect of an individual consultancy project and the number of projects. No study has been able to measure the effect of a management consultancy project because of the various difficulties regarding method and data.

TYPES OF EFFECT   This chapter argues that management consultancy creates effects through three mechanisms:

- Projects.
- Publications
- Alumni.

We can distinguish several effects of management consultancy:

- Performance effects for the client, but possibly also for the client sector, and for society at large.
- Legitimacy for the client.
- Relief of the client's capacity constraints.
- Personal benefits for individuals within the client organization.

The effects vary by reasons for hiring consultants. We distinguish various hiring reasons, which mirror the formal roles (expert, doctor, and facilitator), and the informal roles (hired hand, legitimator, political weapon, and scape-goat) of management consultants. The effects of the informal roles on client performance are mostly indirect. However, individual managers within the client organization may directly benefit from these informal roles.

EXTERNAL VERSUS INTERNAL CONSULTANCY

How should clients grasp the effects of management consultancy: through external or internal consultants? There are production arguments in terms of knowledge, capabilities, reputation, and costs. Moreover, there are governance arguments in terms of client-specificity of knowledge and capabilities; uncertainty about the behaviour of consultants; and the frequency of consultancy projects. External management consultancy may not only create benefits but may also carry risks. The main risks are:

- Clients becoming overly dependent on management consultancy.
- Client sectors becoming isomorphic.
- Knowledge spill-overs from the client to other (competing) organizations.

As the effect of management consultancy is not always positive for every actor within the client organization, management consultants may face resistance from actors.

REFLECTIVE QUESTIONS

1. To what extent may we expect a management consultant to be independent? Provide argumentation.
2. In what field of management consultancy (operations, organization and strategy, information technology) do you think it is most difficult to measure the effect of management consultancy? What is your explanation for this?
3. Reflect upon the effects of management consultancy on society. When does management consultancy have a positive effect on society, and when a negative effect? Explain your answer.
4. What do you consider to be the most important effect on clients of the ambiguity of the effects of management consultancy? Argue why this is so.
5. How does the sector specialization of a management consultancy firm influence the risks for this firm? Explain your answer.
6. When will internal management consultancy have a larger positive effect on the client's performance than external consultancy? And when is the opposite true? Argue why this is so.

MINI CASE STUDY

Claiming impact

The management consultancy True Value Providers or TVP specializes in corporate transformation, that is, large-scale change processes. TVP has formulated its mission as: to help clients create value by offering the highest quality advice and implementation assistance. TVP's slogan is: 'We provide true value'. The clients of this consultancy firm are significantly more successful than their industry peers. TVP has carried out a study of the total shareholder return (stock price increase plus dividend) of their 300 publicly listed clients. These clients outperformed their peers by a ratio of three to one. TVP's board is considering using this finding in an advertisement as proof of their superior impact on client performance.

Questions

1 Why is this advertising approach attractive for TVP? Why not? Provide argumentation.

2 What are the strengths and weaknesses of this study? Critically reflect upon the study's method. Explain your answer.

3 Should TVP make this claim based on this study's findings? Provide arguments.

4 How might prospective clients interpret this claim? Explain your answer.

FURTHER READING

Critical academic perspective

Armbrüster, T. (2006) *The Economics and Sociology of Management Consulting*. Cambridge: Cambridge University Press.

Clark, T. and Fincham, R. (eds) (2002) *Critical Consulting: New Perspectives on the Management Advice Industry*. Oxford: Blackwell.

Kipping, M. and Clark, T. (eds) (2012) *The Oxford Handbook of Management Consulting*. Oxford: Oxford University Press.

Kipping, M. and L. Engwall (eds) (2002) *Management Consulting: Emergence and Dynamics of a Knowledge Industry*. Oxford: Oxford University Press.

Sturdy, A., Handley, K., Clark, T. and Fincham, R. (2009) *Management Consultancy: Boundaries and Knowledge in Action*. Oxford: Oxford University Press.

Sturdy, A. (2011) 'Consultancy's consequences? A critical assessment of management consultancy's impact on management,' *British Journal of Management*, 22(3): 517–530.

Popular journalistic criticism

Ashford, M. (1998) *Con Tricks: The Shadowy World of Management Consultancy and How to Make it Work for You*. London: Simon & Schuster.

O'Shea, J. and Madigan, C. (1997) *Dangerous Company: The Consulting Powerhouses and the Businesses They Save and Ruin*. London: Nicholas Brealy.

Pinault, L. (2000) *Consulting Demons: Inside the Unscrupulous World of Global Consulting Corporations*. New York: HarperCollins.

Sturdy, A., Handley, K., Clark, T. and Fincham, R. (2009) *Management Consultancy: Boundaries and Knowledge in Action*. Oxford: Oxford University Press.

REFERENCES

Alvesson, M. (1993) 'Management fashion', *Academy of Management Review*, 21 (1): 254–285.

Armbrüster, T. (2006) *The Economics and Sociology of Management Consulting*. Cambridge: Cambridge University Press.

Ashford, M. (1998) *Con Tricks: The Shadowy World of Management Consultancy and How to Make it Work for You*. London: Simon & Schuster.

Clark, T. and Fincham, R. (eds) (2002) *Critical Consulting: New Perspectives on the Management Advice Industry*. Oxford: Blackwell.

Clark, T. and Salaman, G. (1998) 'Creating the right impression: towards a dramaturgy of management consultancy', *Service Industry Journal*, 18: 18–38.

Coase, R. (1937) 'The nature of the firm', *Economica* (New Series), 4 (4): 386–405.

DiMaggio, P. and Powell, W. (1983) 'The iron cage revisited: institutional isomorphism and collective rationality in organizational field', *American Sociological Review*, 48: 147–160.

Engwall, L. and Kipping, M. (2002) 'Introduction: management consulting as a knowledge industry', in M. Kipping and L. Engwall (eds), *Management Consulting: Emergence and Dynamics of a Knowledge Industry*. Oxford: Oxford University Press, 1–18.

Ernst, B. and Kieser, A. (2002) 'In search of explanations for the consulting explosion', in K. Sahlin-Andersson and L. Enwall (eds), *The Expansion of Management Knowledge: Carriers, Ideas and Circulation*. Stanford: Stanford University Press, 146–163.

Gross, A.C. and Poor, J. (2008) 'The global management consulting sector', *Business Economics*, 43 (4): 59–68.

Kiechel, W. III (2010) *The Lords of Strategy: The Secret Intellectual History of the New Corporate World*. Boston, MA: Harvard Business Press.

McKinsey & Company (2012) www.mckinsey.com (accessed 5 March 2012).

O'Shea, J. and Madigan, C. (1997) *Dangerous Company: The Consulting Powerhouses and the Businesses They Save and Ruin*. London: Nicholas Brealy.

Pinault, L. (2000) *Consulting Demons: Inside the Unscrupulous World of Global Consulting Corporations*. New York: HarperCollins.

Williamson, O. (1975) *Markets and Hierarchies: Analysis and Antitrust Implications*. New York: Free Press.

PART 2
THE MANAGEMENT CONSULTANCY INDUSTRY

The previous part set the scene by defining management consultancy. It showed the industry development over time. It also explored the industry's impact on clients, industries, and society. The current part investigates management consultancy at the industry level. First, we define the management consultancy industry. We explore its various dimensions. Second, we investigate the (competitive) relationships between key actors in the management consultancy industry. We also analyse the main competitive forces in this industry. Third, we research the relationship between the management consultancy industry and the management knowledge cluster of industries. Additionally, we examine the relationship between the management consultancy industry and macro-economics. Each chapter in this part is designed to achieve a specific set of learning objectives. After studying this part you will be able to:

- Analyse the three key dimensions of the global management consultancy industry in terms of services, client sectors, and geographies (Chapter 4).
- Understand the differences between management consultancy firms in terms of scale and scope (Chapter 4).
- Identify the key actors in the management consultancy industry (Chapter 5).
- Evaluate the attractiveness of the industry in terms of the competitive forces (Chapter 5).
- Critically reflect upon the implications of key industry developments for the competitive forces in the industry (Chapter 5).
- Critically reflect upon the role of management consultants in the management knowledge cluster of industries (Chapter 6).

- Explain the implications for management consultancy of the macro-development towards a knowledge society (Chapter 6).
- Explain the implications for management consultancy of macro-economic trends (Chapter 6).

CHAPTER 4: OVERVIEW OF THE MANAGEMENT CONSULTANCY INDUSTRY LANDSCAPE

This chapter first discusses the difficulties in analysing the industry. Second, we investigate three key dimensions of the industry: the services offered by management consultants, the client sectors served, and the geographies where consultants operate. Third, we discuss some key differences between management consultancy firms. We compare firms with widely differing scales and scopes. We also examine how client size varies by consultancy firm.

CHAPTER 5: THE COMPETITIVE LANDSCAPE OF THE MANAGEMENT CONSULTANCY INDUSTRY

In this chapter we identify the key actors within the management consultancy industry: incumbent management consultancy firms, clients, suppliers, new entrants, and substitute providers. We use Porter's competitive forces framework to analyse the attractiveness of the management consultancy industry. We assess each of these forces: the rivalry between incumbent management consultancy firms; the power of clients; the power of suppliers; the threat of new entrants into management consultancy; and the threat of substitutes for management consultancy. We also interpret the impact of key industry developments on these competitive forces. These developments include the convergence of industries and the rise of new business models based on information and communications technologies (ICT).

CHAPTER 6: MACRO-DEVELOPMENTS AND THE MANAGEMENT CONSULTANCY INDUSTRY

This chapter considers the impact of management consultancy on the macro-environment. We investigate the impact of the macro-environment on the management consultancy industry. First, we explore the impact of the trend towards a knowledge society. What does it mean for management consultancy? We argue that the management consultancy industry contributes to the development and dissemination of management knowledge in the macro-environment. Second, we examine the impact of macro-economic (business) cycles on the management consultancy industry. Finally, we investigate how the globalization of product markets, factor markets, and capital markets, in combination with the geographic spreading of capitalism and shareholder value management in the 1980s and 1990s, affected the management consultancy industry.

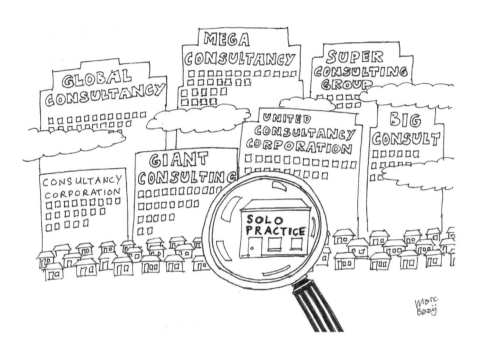

4

OVERVIEW OF THE MANAGEMENT CONSULTANCY INDUSTRY LANDSCAPE

INTRODUCTION

This chapter sketches the global landscape of the management consultancy industry. But before we investigate this landscape, we first discuss why analysing this industry is difficult. Next, we investigate key dimensions of the management consultancy industry. We identify the main services offered by management consultants. We also distinguish client sectors and geographies. Subsequently, we discuss some key differences between management consultancy firms. The chapter investigates the differences between large and small consultancy firms. We also compare the scope of firms in terms of services, client sectors, and client geographies. Furthermore, the chapter studies differences in the clients for management consultants. We investigate differences in the size and geography of clients. The chapter ends with a summary, reflective questions, a mini case study, suggested further reading, and references.

Main learning objectives

- Understand the difficulties in analysing the management consultancy industry.

- Understand three key dimensions of the management consultancy industry:

  o The services that management consultancy firms offer.
  o The sectors in which the clients of management consultancy firms operate
  o The geography of clients.

- Understand the heterogeneous composition of the management consultancy industry.
- Explain the key differences between management consultancy firms.
- Critically reflect upon the rise of big global consultancy firms.

ANALYSING THE MANAGEMENT CONSULTANCY INDUSTRY

As stated in the first part of the book, it is difficult to study the management consultancy industry. In the third chapter we concluded that it is difficult if not impossible to measure the *impact* of management consultancy. In the current chapter, we find that it is even difficult to measure the *size* of the management consultancy industry. Numbers regarding management consultancy revenues are hard to get. Even the number of management consultancy firms and the number of individual consultants are difficult to assess. Information about profits generated by management consultancy firms is even more complicated if not impossible to obtain. In general, industry statistics are difficult to find. In particular information about the global industry is hard to find. Compared to industries like automobiles, beverages, or computers, the management consultancy industry provides challenges for researchers. The question arises: why is the management consultancy industry so difficult to analyse?

No definition

First of all, we do not have a commonly accepted definition of what constitutes management consultancy. The first chapter already indicated that definitions of management consultancy vary. We distinguished between the different definitions that co-exist in both the literature and practice. When you have to assess a particular industry study, you always have to look at the definition applied in that particular study. What definition of management consultancy did the researchers use for their study? What services were included and which ones were excluded? Not only do management consultancy definitions vary, we also have to take into account variations in the categorization of management consultancy. Most studies distinguish categories of management consultancy. Examples of this are strategy consultancy, IT consultancy, and operations consultancy. However, the definitions of categories also vary. Therefore, in order to interpret industry studies correctly, we have to know these studies' definitions of consultancy and its categories.

No obligation

Second, the first chapter concluded that management consultancy is not a legally enforced profession. As a result, there is no obligation for management consultants to register themselves. Researchers in management consultancy have no registers as sources of industry data. However, there is a voluntary registration for management consultants. Professional associations provide such registration. But a large share, if not the majority, of management consultants, are not registered. Therefore, such registration does not provide a complete picture of the industry. Professional associations do not have comprehensive industry statistics.

Publically listed management consultancy firms have extensive publication obligations. Their annual reports provide information about their financial results. However, only a small number of management consultancies are listed on the financial markets. Most consultancies are private firms. As a result they are not obliged to publish such information.

No interest

Third, clients of management consultancy have no interest to provide information. Most clients are reluctant to make it public that they use management consultants. Some clients, in particular the large ones, may not even know how much they spend on consultancy. These organizations may lack oversight of consultancy expenditures by their various divisions and the various departments within these divisions. Most clients are unlikely to inform researchers how much they spend on management consultancy. Therefore, customers of consultancy are not a source of industry data. Because of their clients' interests, and because of the considerations of competition, management consultancies will be reluctant to voluntarily disclose information about their clients and revenues.

Diverging industry estimates

Despite these issues, some statistics about the management consultancy industry do exist. On the one hand, government statistical bureaus collect industry data. These government agencies typically cover the industry on a country-wide basis. On the other hand, some private sector institutions report management consultancy industry statistics on a regional or global scale. One important private source is Kennedy Information (see Figure 4.1). No academic research on the global management consultancy industry exists. An exception is an academic meta study (Gross and Poor, 2008) of various private sector industry studies.

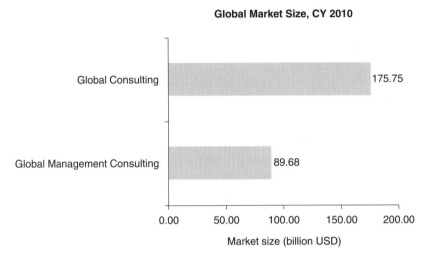

Global Market Size, CY 2010

FIGURE 4.1 *The global management consultancy industry (2010)*

Note: CY: calendar year
Source: Courtesy of Kennedy Information (2013)

Conceptual framework

To understand the volume of demand for management consultancy, we would propose a conceptual framework. Figure 4.2 visualizes a framework of three key drivers of demand for a particular management consultancy service, such as strategy advice. We emphasize that this framework is only conceptual. It has not been empirically verified, given the lack of data on the industry.

CLIENT ORGANIZATION   The first driver we can distinguish is the client organization. With regard to management consultancy services, we would acknowledge other roles but we focus on the problem solving role of management consultants. All other things being equal, the need for problem solving increases with the level of change and the complexity of the client's scale and scope. Changes at the client organization may induce a demand for management consultancy. Examples of such changes are: mergers and

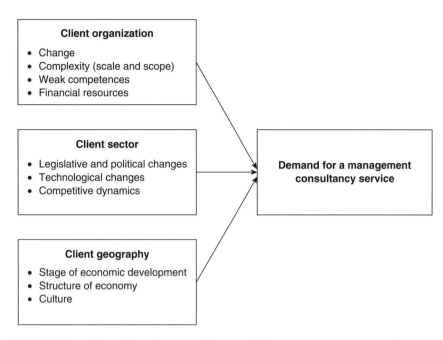

FIGURE 4.2   *Three key drivers of demand for management consultancy*

acquisitions, divestitures, joint ventures, offshoring, outsourcing, changes in leadership and ownership, going public or private, privatization, the entry or exit of markets, internationalization. The larger the scale and the wider the scope of the client organization, the more complex the client's problems will be. Opportunities will also be more complex to seize. The need for help increases inversely with client competences for problem solving. The weaker the client's problem solving competences, the stronger the demand for help by management consultancies. Finally, the hiring of management consultants depends on the financial resources available to clients. Clients should have sufficient financial resources to afford to hire management consultants.

CLIENT SECTOR   The demand for management consultancy is also influenced by the sector the client operates in. All other things being equal, the demand for management consultancy in a sector increases with the amount of change in a sector. Sector dynamics generally pose challenges to the organizations operating in that particular sector. These dynamics lead to problems to be solved (or opportunities to be seized). We can distinguish three types of sector dynamics. First, legislative and political changes may lead to problems (or opportunities) that may require the services of management consultancies. Regulation, deregulation, privatization, changing political systems, and the opening up of countries, are some examples of legislative and political changes. Second, technological changes, for instance in the area of ICT, may pose problems (and opportunities) for organizations. Third, dynamics in terms of sector competition may generate problems (or opportunities) for organizations. In particular, merger and acquisition waves in a sector induce consultancy demand.

CLIENT GEOGRAPHY   The third driver is the geography where the client operates. By geography we mean the country of a national organization, or the group of countries in the case of multinational organizations. Demand for management consultancy varies by country. Several explanations for the differences in demand can be distinguished: the stage of economic development of a country, the structure of the economy, and the culture of the country.

Stage of economic development. First, management consultancy targets managers. Without (professional) management, there is no management consultancy. The question arises: to what extent does the national economy rely on (professional) management? The number of organizations with professional management varies with the stage of the national economic development. Developed economies with many organizations led by professional management will have a larger demand for management consultancy services than economies with few management-led organizations. However, countries that are going through strong economic development may require external expertise to build their industries and companies. In particular, countries with sufficient natural resources, such as oil and gas, can afford to hire (foreign) management consultants. The Middle East is an example.

Structure of the economy. Second, the structure of the national economy influences demand. Structure refers to the economy's composition in various sectors. It also refers to the size distribution of the organizations in the national economy. This argumentation is linked to the driver 'client sector' and the driver 'client organization' (see Figure 4.2). Because management consultancy demand varies by client sector, the composition of the national economy in terms of sectors influences the demand for management consultancy in a particular country. Countries where a high share of the national economy consists of sectors with a large management consultancy demand will need more management consultancy than countries where that share is low. The scale of organizations in a country matters as well. The presence of large organizations in a country increases demand for management consultancy. Countries with a high number of large-scale organizations will have a greater demand for management consultancy than countries with a low number.

Culture. Last but not least, the culture of a country influences the demand for management consultancy. Norms, values, and practices have an effect on management's willingness to hire management consultants. Cultural differences between countries may raise a barrier against hiring management consultants if management consultants are predominantly foreigners. Some national cultures may prefer to develop solutions in-house rather than search for outside help in the form of external management consultants. In certain other cultures however, management is eager to hire management consultants from (Western) countries, as they specifically seek best practices for Western markets. This chapter presents a case about South Korea that illustrates the influence of national culture on the demand for consultancy.

THE MANAGEMENT CONSULTANCY INDUSTRY IN THREE DIMENSIONS

Management consultancy is not a homogeneous industry. The conceptual framework (see Figure 4.2) indicates how three key drivers influence the demand for management consultancy services. First of all, management consultancy services vary. Management consultants may offer a spectrum of differing services. As a result, we may segment the management consultancy industry by services offered. Second, there are differences between the sectors that clients operate in. The characteristics of the client sector influence the demand for consultancy. Consequently, segmenting the management consultancy industry by client sector makes sense. Third, geography still matters in a globalizing world. A *global* management consultancy industry does not exist. National differences continue to play an important role in the use of management consultancy (see case study). Therefore, geographic segmentation is relevant to the management consultancy industry. In this part we research three dimensions of the management consultancy industry. Figure 4.3 visualizes these dimensions.

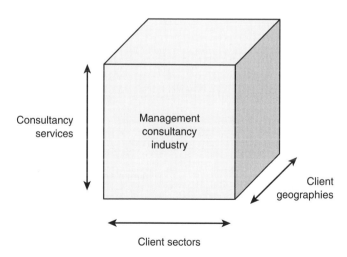

FIGURE 4.3 *Three dimensions of the management consultancy industry*

Services offered

CATEGORIZATIONS   The first dimension of the management consultancy industry consists of the services offered by management consultants. However, the categorizations of management consultancy services vary according to the source of the research. Different researchers apply different categorizations. Kennedy Information distinguishes five main categories of consultancy services: financial consulting, operations management, information technology, human resources (HR), and strategy (see Figure 4.4). Financial consulting and HR consulting belong to the field of strategy and organization consultancy (Chapter 2).

BUYING AND DELIVERING CONSULTANCY   A breakdown of the industry into services may be useful for understanding that industry. However, it is not the way in which management consultancy is bought and delivered. Clients (formally) hire management consultants to solve a problem, or to provide an approach to seize an opportunity. Services are a means to that end. Clients of management consultants do not buy an IT project; they buy a solution to a profitability problem. For instance, the problem solving may require a change in the client's strategy, a redesign of operations, and a new IT system. Very few consultancy projects will fit with the narrow categories as defined in Figure 4.4.

What comes to mind when looking at Figure 4.4? Change management is missing. This may come as a surprise because management consultants are

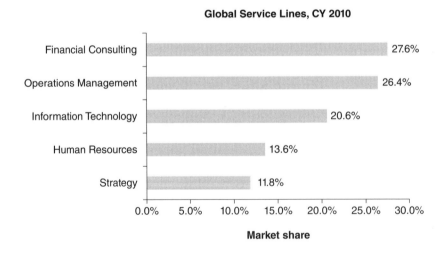

FIGURE 4.4   *The global management consultancy industry by services (2010)*

Note: CY: calendar year

Source: Courtesy of Kennedy Information (2013)

often seen as agents of change. More than half of consultancy projects are about change management. It does not appear in the taxonomy of Figure 4.4 because change management is inherent within each category. Change management can be applied to each of the services, for instance a change of strategy and a change of operations.

EXPLAINING DIFFERENCES ACROSS SERVICES   How can we explain differences in industry revenues per service? These services offered by management consultants mirror the business functions that client organizations need to perform. For instance, operations management consultancy mirrors the operations function of clients. Differences in the sizes of client functions may explain differences in the sizes of the related management consultancy services. For clients, strategy is a smaller function than operations management and so the consultancy revenues for strategy are smaller than those for operations management. Strategy is typically a small part of many projects, but may have large implications for the fulfilment of the other parts of the project. Strategy implementation typically involves operations, HR, and IT.

IT is becoming increasingly integrated with other consultancy services. In the past pure IT projects used to be the norm, for instance the implementation of a big enterprise resource planning (ERP) system. More and more, IT is integrated with strategy, operations, and other services. The breakdown of Figure 4.4 suggests a division into separate services. However, in practice these services are interwoven.

Sectors of clients served

The second dimension of the management consultancy industry consists of the sectors in which clients of management consultants operate. We may categorize management consultancy by the sectors of their clients. The categorizations of client sectors vary by researchers. Figure 4.5 on the next page visualizes Kennedy Information's categorization of the nine largest industries in terms of consultancy revenues, and a category termed 'other industries'.

EXPLAINING DIFFERENCES ACROSS CLIENT SECTORS
How to explain the shares of the various client sectors? We can distinguish various possible explanations for differences between sector shares. First, client sectors vary in size which refers to the number of organizations operating in a sector and the size of those organizations. All other things being equal, large client sectors will have a greater need for management consultancy than small sectors. Management consultancy will generate larger revenues in large client sectors than in small ones.

Second, the need for management consultancy may differ by client sector. We may distinguish three reasons why some client sectors may make more use of management consultants than other sectors.

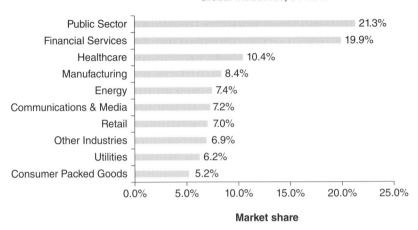

Global Industries, CY 2010

Sector	Market share
Public Sector	21.3%
Financial Services	19.9%
Healthcare	10.4%
Manufacturing	8.4%
Energy	7.4%
Communications & Media	7.2%
Retail	7.0%
Other Industries	6.9%
Utilities	6.2%
Consumer Packed Goods	5.2%

Market share

FIGURE 4.5   *The global management consultancy industry by client sectors (2010)*

Note: CY: calendar year

Source: Courtesy of Kennedy Information (2013)

Complexity. First, the occurrence of high value and complex decision making may vary across sectors. Organizations with a large scale and scope will face more high value and complex decisions than organizations with a small scale and scope. Industries where organizations have a larger scale and scope tend to have a greater need for consultancy than industries where organizations have a small scale and scope. Moreover, organizations in sectors that experience high levels of volatility and change may face more high value and complex decisions than counterparts in stable sectors. Some examples of sources of sector dynamics are deregulation, technological development, and industry consolidation in terms of merger and acquisition waves.

Competences. Second, all other things being equal, organizations with weak competences for problem solving have a higher need for management consultancy than organizations that possess strong competences. If organizations cannot solve their problems, they have to rely on outside help, such as management consultants. Sectors with many organizations that have weak competences will have a greater need for management consultancy than sectors with more competent organizations. An example of a sector with relatively weak organizations is a recently deregulated sector. The organizations in such a sector have to make a significant transition from non-profit organization to a profit organization. They typically lack the competences for solving the new types of problems they face. Therefore, they may hire consultants to help them make that transition.

Financial resources. Third, the wealth of organizations may vary by sector. To afford management consultancy, organizations need financial resources. Rich organizations can better afford management consultancy than poor ones. Sectors with relatively cash-rich organizations will be able to buy more management consultancy services than poor sectors.

Geographies of clients served

The third dimension of the management consultancy industry consists of the geographies of clients. We categorize management consultancy by the geographic region of their clients. The categorizations of regions vary by researchers. Kennedy Information distinguishes four main categories of client geographies: North America, Europe/Middle East/Africa (EMEA), Asia Pacific, and Latin America. Figure 4.6 visualizes their findings.

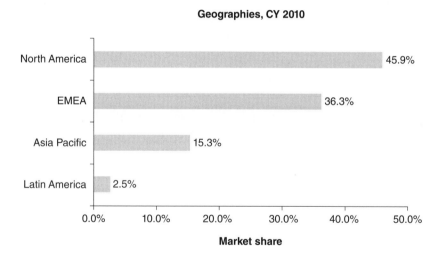

FIGURE 4.6 *The global management consultancy industry by client geographies (2010)*

Note: CY: calendar year

Source: Courtesy of Kennedy Information (2013)

EXPLAINING DIFFERENCES ACROSS GEOGRAPHIES   How to explain differences across geographies? We consider some of the possible explanations: stage of economic development, structure of the economy, and culture.

Stage of economic development. One possible reason for differences among countries is the stage of economic development of countries. The demand for management consultancy increases with the stage of economic development. Management consultancy emerged in the Western world during the second industrial revolution. Related to the stage of development is the reliance on professional management in a country. Countries vary in their reliance on professional management. Management consultancies work for (professional) management.

Structure of the economy. Furthermore, the structure or composition of the national economy in terms of sectors influences the demand for management consultancy. The demand for management consultancy varies by sector. Countries with a relatively large share of sectors will demand more management consultancy than countries that have a small share of such sectors. What also matters is the presence of large firms in a country. All other things being equal, countries with many large organizations will have more demand for management consultancy.

Culture. Last but not least, the demand for management consultancy varies with the willingness to hire outsiders. The culture of a country may influence this willingness. The culture may affect the trust of clients in external management consultants. This willingness to hire external consultants relates to the make-or-buy decision, which concerns governance costs. The cultural context of the client may affect governance costs and thus influence the decision to hire an external management consultant.

CASE STUDY

Management consultancy across borders[1]

This case study about Western management consultancy in South Korea illustrates that a *global* management consultancy industry does not exist. The industry is

[1] This case study draws to a large extent on Wright and Kwon (2006).

not global in the sense that national markets resemble each other and that the services are uniform across national borders. Although management knowledge may have a wide appeal, this case study shows there are limits to the applicability of management knowledge across national borders.

A tough market for Western management consultancies

Until the 1990s, South Korean managers made little use of the services of Western management consultants. The Korean economy was perceived as a leading example of the Asian economic miracle. The chaebols – large, family-owned and highly diversified conglomerates – were seen as the engine of the South Korean model. Chaebols focused on the internal generation of knowledge. They only selectively used external management consulting services. The success of the chaebols further reduced their demand for management consultancy. The weak role of foreign direct investment in South Korea also limited the opportunities for Western consultancies to gain a beachhead in this country, whereas in Europe, foreign direct investment by US corporations had facilitated the expansion of US management consultancies in Europe. Furthermore, the South Korean government forbade the establishment of local offices by foreign business services providers, including management consultancies. This implied that Western consultancies had to fly in teams from other offices. However, in the early 1990s the South Korean government relaxed its regulations on the establishment of local offices by foreign service providers. Various Western management consultancies responded by opening offices. Nevertheless, South Korea remained a tough market for Western management consultancies.

The boom of Western management consultancy

All this changed in 1997. At that time the South Korean economy entered into a severe economic crisis. The South Korean currency went into freefall. In December, the government had to seek financial assistance from the International Monetary Fund (IMF). The business press and Western management consultancies blamed the crisis on fundamental structural weaknesses in the Korean economy. In particular the chaebol came under attack. Government officials also began to criticize the chaebols. Furthermore, as part of the financial bailout the IMF demanded that South Korea should fundamentally change its markets and restructure its chaebols. Under pressure from the South Korean government, the chaebols sought the advice of the Western management consultancies to restructure themselves. These Western consultancy firms positioned themselves as key agents for implementing best (Western) practices in the South Korean economy. The consultancies benefited from a massive growth in demand for their services. The restructuring of the complex diversified chaebols involved debt reduction, downsizing, delayering, and attempts to reduce diversification.

Recovery and resistance

Within a few years, the demand for Western management consultancy plummeted. This caused the closure of many Western consultancies' offices. From late 1998, the Korean economy had sharply recovered and the renewed success of South Korean corporations undercut criticism of the South Korean (business) model. The large South Korean companies continued their focus on the internalization of management knowledge. They only selectively and pragmatically adopted Western management advice, adapting it to fit their own model. Moreover, the rush of Western consultancies had resulted in poor levels of services in many instances. Disappointment about the low level of services and the high costs further reduced demand. South Korean management perceived Western management consultancies as outsiders promoting Western solutions to South Korean business. The Western solutions, in particular those that impacted employment and pay, induced strong resistance from both trade unions and managers.

Localization

For Western consultants it was highly difficult if not impossible to tap into the Korean business networks, given the strong emphasis on family and kinship ties, and shared educational and military backgrounds. Most Western management consultancy firms had not succeeded in adapting to the South Korean market. Only the management consultancy firms that had localized their South Korean operations survived the shake-out among Western consultancies. These surviving firms operated with a predominantly Korean staff that spoke the language and understood the culture.

Discussion questions

1   What differences between the South Korean market and Western markets for management consultancy can you identify? What do these markets have in common? Explain your answer.

2   What role(s) in management consultancy did the South Korean companies look for when they started to hire consultancies after 1997? Explain your answer.

3   How do you evaluate the practices of most Western management consultancy firms in South Korea during the booming demand for their services?

SCALE OF FIRMS IN THE MANAGEMENT CONSULTANCY INDUSTRY

The management consultant is a heterogeneous concept. There are many different types of management consultants. The firms in the management consultancy industry vary substantially. In this section, we examine differences in the scale of consultancy firms. We define scale in terms of revenues and (consulting) staff.

Scale

Management consultancy firms vary in scale. The well-known management consultancies are (very) large. Examples of such large firms are McKinsey & Company, Booz Allen Hamilton, and the Boston Consulting Group. Very large firms include the consultancy arms of the big accounting firms Deloitte, PwC, Ernst & Young, and KPMG. But the consultancy arms of Accenture and IBM also rank among the world's largest consultancies (see Figure 4.7).

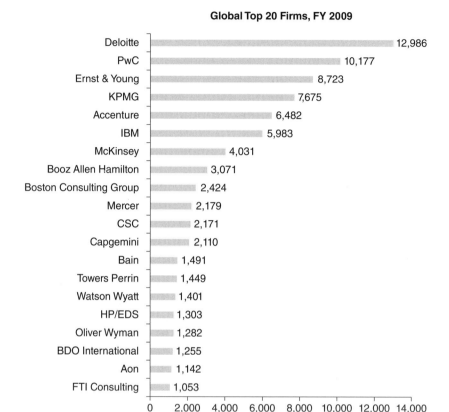

Global Top 20 Firms, FY 2009

Firm	Revenues (millions USD)
Deloitte	12,986
PwC	10,177
Ernst & Young	8,723
KPMG	7,675
Accenture	6,482
IBM	5,983
McKinsey	4,031
Booz Allen Hamilton	3,071
Boston Consulting Group	2,424
Mercer	2,179
CSC	2,171
Capgemini	2,110
Bain	1,491
Towers Perrin	1,449
Watson Wyatt	1,401
HP/EDS	1,303
Oliver Wyman	1,282
BDO International	1,255
Aon	1,142
FTI Consulting	1,053

FIGURE 4.7   *Revenues for the top 20 firms (2009)*

Note: FY: Fiscal Year

Source: Courtesy of Kennedy Information (2013)

Due to our familiarity with the (very) large firms we may be tempted to think that most management consultancy firms are large. However, in reality most management consultancies are (very) small scale. Two thirds of all management consultants work in firms of less than ten employees. Moreover, many consultants operate as sole practitioners. Whereas large management consultancies employ one third of all consultants worldwide, they generate half of all management consultancy revenues. As a result, large firms have revenues per consultant that are twice that of small firms. Figure 4.8 visualizes these findings.

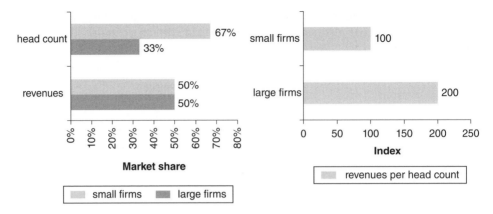

FIGURE 4.8 *Comparison of consultancy staff and revenues (2003)*

Source: Curnow and Reuvid (2003)

Comparing large and small consultancies

VOLUME AND FEE   How can we explain the large difference in revenues per consultant between small and large consultancy firms? Revenues consist of volume and price. The volume is the number of hours billed to clients. The volume of work per consultant may differ between large and small consultancy firms. In the category of small firms we find many sole practitioners, and among the sole practitioners we find part-timers. The higher the share of part-timers, the lower the volume per consultant.

The price of management consultancy is the fee, or the billing rate per hour (or per day). Large consultancy firms are generally able to charge higher billing rates than small firms. The rate difference may be explained by several factors, including the type of clients, the type of work, and the consultancy firm's reputation.

LARGE VERSUS SMALL CLIENTS   Large consultancy firms tend to work for larger client firms than small consultancies. Large client organizations typically prefer to work with large consultancy firms. The scale, scope, and complexity of the problems of large client organizations may demand services and capacity that only large consultancy firms can offer. For instance, a small consultancy firm cannot offer the large team of consultants necessary to diagnose a large-scale and complex problem, to support a large-scale implementation process for a client, or to define a new organization structure for a client's operations across three continents. Because of the higher value at stake in such problem solving and solution implementation, large client organizations may be willing to pay higher rates than small client organizations. Large client organizations may also prefer the well-known reputations of the large consultancies. Choosing the big reputation consultancy firms may reduce uncertainty for clients. Consultancies' reputations are also important for informal roles, such as the legitimation of client decisions.

Not only do large clients prefer large consultancies, it is the other way around as well. Large consultancies prefer large clients. Because small clients typically cannot afford the fees of large consultancies, the large consultancies prefer to work for large clients. Large, well-known clients typically serve as a better reference for the consultancy firm during their business development activities at other clients. Serving a small client may not be profitable for large consultancy firms. In contrast, small consultancy firms with lower costs may find small clients attractive to work for.

SCOPE OF FIRMS IN THE MANAGEMENT CONSULTANCY INDUSTRY

Advice and assistance

Management consultancy firms differ in scope. The first chapter distinguished narrow and broad management consultancy. Management consultancy in a narrow sense is providing advice to management. Management consultancy in a broad sense combines providing advice with providing assistance with the managerial tasks regarding the implementation of the recommended solutions. Business consultancy is defined as advice combined with provision of assistance with non-managerial implementation tasks.

Firms may provide management consultancy in a narrow sense or in a broad sense. Some firms offer both management consultancy and business consultancy. Other firms combine management and business consultancy with business services, such as outsourcing.

We cannot equate management consultancy and the firms offering these services. Management consultancy services may only be part of their offerings. We do not speak of management consultancy firms but of firms operating *in* the management consultancy industry. They offer management consultancy services, but not all their services may be management consultancy. Therefore, not all firms operating in the management consultancy industry are purely management consultancies.

Roles

The first chapter also distinguished the various roles of management consultancy. Formal roles of management consultants are the expert, the doctor, and the facilitator. Management consultants may also fulfil informal roles. We discussed the hired hand, the legitimator, the political weapon, and the scapegoat. The width of the spectrum of roles may vary and so may the weight of individual roles. Some firms may specialize in the expert role, whereas others may opt for the doctor or facilitator role. Firms may also differ in terms of their mix of formal and informal roles.

Services

The previous section emphasized three dimensions of the industry: services, client sectors, and client geographies. Management consultancy firms may differ on each dimension and offer different services. The number of services may also vary. We may perceive a spectrum of the scope of management consultancy services. At one end of this spectrum, we will find firms solely focusing on a single service. This represents a very narrow scope. The specialist firms may focus on, for instance, operations or strategy. The advantage of this focus is the faster build-up of knowledge and capabilities. Specialist consultants benefit from learning effects. An example of such a specialist management consultancy firm is Simon-Kucher. This consultancy specializes in pricing.

At the other end of the services spectrum, we will find firms offering a very broad scope of management consultancy services. An example of a broad firm is Accenture. This firm combines a broad range of management consultancy services with business consultancy and outsourcing. The advantage of a broad offering of services is economies of scale and scope. Moreover, it offers convenience to the client: one-stop shopping, and one transaction partner who is responsible for a whole bundle of services. Figure 4.9 visualizes examples of the differing scope of services.

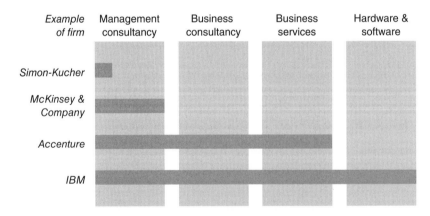

FIGURE 4.9 *Examples of the differing scope of services*

Source: corporate websites, 2012

AN INTRODUCTION TO MANAGEMENT CONSULTANCY

MULTIPLE SPECIALIZATIONS   We like to emphasize that management consultancy firms offering a broad scope of services are not necessarily generalist consultants. Typically, broad firms are organized into so-called 'practice areas'. These practice areas are (to a certain extent) staffed with specialists, in particular at the higher level: managers and partners (in the large firms, junior staff are typically not specialized). Offering multiple services at the specialist level assumes a certain scale. Only large-scale firms have sufficient consultancy staff to allow for specialization in different services or practice areas. Figure 4.10 gives an example of a management consultancy firm offering multiple specializations. McKinsey & Company covers eight services.

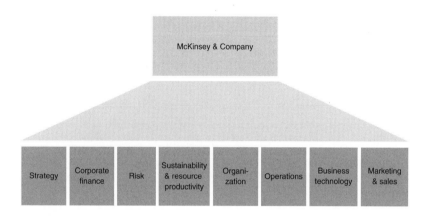

FIGURE 4.10   *Multiple specializations within one firm*

Source: McKinsey & Company (2012)

Client sectors

EXPERIENCE EFFECTS   Firms may also differ in terms of the number of client sectors they serve. Again, we may perceive a spectrum in the scope of client sectors. Some firms focus solely on one single client sector. This constitutes a very narrow scope. An example is consultants that focus on airports. These consultants know everything there is to know about airports. They may provide all kinds of consultancy services to airports, ranging from strategy to organization and operations. As stated before, the advantage of such a focus is the faster build-up of knowledge and capabilities. Client sector specialist consultants enjoy experience effects. Specialists can ride the learning curve faster than generalists. They know their sector better than generalist consultants that work in multiple sectors.

ECONOMIES OF SCOPE   However, generalist consultants may enjoy economies of scope. They may have a broader perspective, at least in terms of sectors, than sector specialists. Generalists may be able to broker best practice knowledge from one client sector to another. Large management consultancies that have multiple sector specializations combine the best of both worlds. They have in-depth sector knowledge similar to sector specialist firms. For instance, their knowledge of airports matches the knowledge of specialist airport consultants. However, they can also offer a broad perspective because they have specialist consultants for different client sectors. As an illustration of the scope in terms of services and client sectors, Figure 4.11 visualizes the offerings of Bain & Company. Compare these service offerings with McKinsey & Company (Figure 4.10). Can you note any differences?

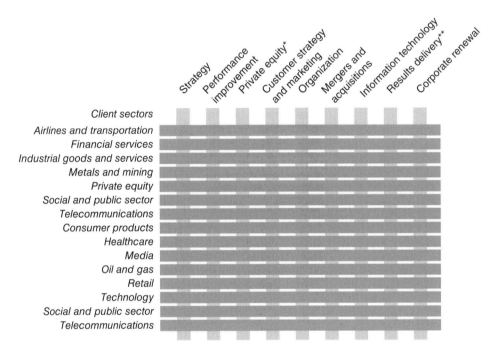

FIGURE 4.11 *An example of client sectors and services*

Notes: * 'private equity' refers to consultancy to private equity clients; ** 'results delivery' refers to change management.
Source: Bain & Company (2012)

THE DOMINANT DIMENSION   Firms distinguish between consultancy services and client sectors and may be organized as a matrix of services and sectors (see, for example, Figure 4.11). However, the two dimensions of the matrix, services and sectors, are not equally important to the firm. The client sectors are leading. Clients buy services, not the other way around. A client of a consultancy firm typically interacts with the consultancy partner who is responsible for the client sector to which that client belongs. Assume the client is a bank. The partner for the banking sector 'owns' this client.

Depending on the demands of the client, the partner may involve a colleague who specializes in the service demanded, for instance strategy.

Geographies

The majority of management consultancies are small. Two thirds of all management consultants work in firms with less than ten consultants (see Figure 4.8). These small consultancy firms typically serve small clients. As a result, small consultancy firms will most likely be confined to national markets, or even to local markets. However, the consultancy industry also contains a number of (very) large firms. These firms generally operate nationally or even across national borders.

GLOBAL PRESENCE AND LOCAL RESPONSIVENESS   As management consultancy is a service, it cannot be exported from the home country of the consultancy firm. An automotive firm may ships its cars from its manufacturing plant in the home country to customer markets all over the world. A management consultancy firm with one office may send consultants from its office in the home country to clients all over the world. However, travel time, costs, and the personal burden for consultants, such as jet lag and time away from home, make such a policy inefficient and inconvenient. Moreover, differences across geographies make local customized approaches necessary (see, for example, the case study about South Korea). To improve local responsiveness, international consultancy firms may (also) want to work with consultants who are natives of the countries in which they serve clients. Native consultants have some advantages over non-native consultants: they speak the language of the local client and they better understand the local culture. Probably, they will be more sensitive to local needs and customs.

BUILDING GLOBAL PRESENCE   Management consultancy firms that expand internationally will typically open offices abroad.

The chapter on the history of the industry indicated that in the 1960s US-based consultancies expanded their office networks to cover Europe. Since then, office networks have become increasingly international. Globalization of management consultancy firms is usually no different from that of other firms. Consultancies follow their clients into new geographies. For instance, if a client of a Western consultancy firm decides to enter Asian markets, then that client may ask their consultant to provide advice and assistance on this internationalization strategy. Western consultancy firms earn the majority of their revenues in emerging markets from the emerging market subsidiaries of their existing Western clients. The local management consultancy firms do the majority of the consultancy work for local clients in emerging markets.

At present, many large consultancy firms have world-spanning networks of offices. As an example of a global office network, Figure 4.12 visualizes how McKinsey & Company's offices are distributed across regions.

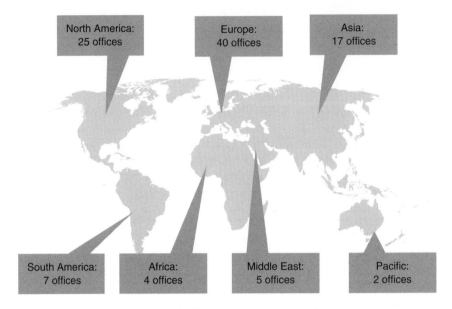

FIGURE 4.12 *An example of offices across geographies*

Source: McKinsey & Company (2012)

ADVANTAGES OF A GLOBAL PRESENCE   Globalization becomes increasingly important for management consultancy firms. As clients become more international, their consultancy firms will be induced to follow them. To an increasing extent, small domestic clients may also consider internationalization. As a result, the demand for management consultancy to help clients to internationalize and the demand for consultancy on an international basis (consultancy projects covering multiple countries) will increase. Management consultancy firms that operate on an international scale have four important advantages over local rivals.

1. International consultancies can match the geographic scope of their international clients. International consultancies can serve clients consistently in all the countries clients operate in. With local offices, the consultants can work with client employees in all countries.

2. Through their international office networks, international consultancies possess (in-depth and tacit) knowledge of the host countries of their clients. They can offer knowledge of the host country to those clients who consider entering that country.

3. International consultancies can broker best practices across countries. They can identify the best practices in country A and apply that knowledge for the benefit of a client in country B. Of course, consultancies should still pay attention to the differences in local

circumstances. There are limits to the transferability of knowledge across national borders (see the case study about South Korea).

4. Having operations around the world allows management consultancy firms to better manage the utilization of their consultancy staff. If a certain country or region faces a (temporary) economic downturn, and therefore experiences a reduction in consultancy demand, then a global firm may use its consultants from that country to work on projects in other countries, where that demand is not impacted. This makes global firms more flexible in terms of capacity management.

SUMMARY

The management consultancy industry is difficult to analyse. There is no common definition of management consultancy. As management consultancy is not a formal profession, there is no (legal) obligation to register. Furthermore, stakeholders have little or no interest in providing data voluntarily. As a result, industry statistics are scarce.

THREE KEY DIMENSIONS OF THE INDUSTRY   This chapter characterizes the management consultancy industry using three dimensions:

1. Services provided.
2. Client sectors served.
3. Client geographies.

We show that a homogeneous management consultancy industry does not exist. The industry is too heterogeneous. Differences between services, sectors, and geographies are large. Financial consulting and operations management dominate the global revenues (together, over 50 per cent). The public sector and financial services are the most important client sectors (together, over 40 per cent). Worldwide industry revenues are also geographically skewed. North America accounts for almost half of the worldwide revenues (about 45 per cent).

DIFFERENCES BETWEEN FIRMS   This chapter investigates firms operating in the management consultancy industry. Just as a standard management consultancy industry does not exist, there is no typical management consultancy firm. Not all firms in the management consultancy industry are pure management consultants. We find firms that not only offer management consultancy services but also business consultancy, business services, and other products and services. The population of firms operating in the management consultancy industry is heterogeneous. Our analysis reveals a variety of firms. First, we can distinguish small and large firms. The majority of firms are (very) small i.e. less than ten consultants. Besides the majority of small and unknown firms, there are a small number of very large and well-known firms. The large firms have a revenue per consultant that is twice the amount of small firms. Second, we can distinguish differences in terms of services, client sectors, and client geographies. In general, a large scope requires a large scale. The large firms can combine specialization and breadth. Small firms are forced to specialize in a narrow domain.

REFLECTIVE QUESTIONS

1. What are the main challenges in measuring the size of the global management consultancy market? Explain your answer.

2. What are the implications of the difficulties in measuring the management consultancy market? Why does it matter and for whom?

3. How would you measure the size of the management consultancy market in terms of revenues in your country? Provide two alternative approaches. Explain your choices.

4. The public sector is the largest client sector worldwide (see Figure 4.5). Is it the largest client sector everywhere? Use the key drivers of demand for management consultancy (see Figure 4.2) to frame your answer.

5. Is the client base for small management consultancy firms typically limited to small client organizations? Explain why or why not.

6. How do you evaluate the rise of global firms in the management consultancy industry? What are the causes and what are the consequences of this development? Elaborate on your answer.

MINI CASE STUDY

From Australia to Africa

Rooted in Australia

MineCons is an Australian management consultancy firm that specializes in the mining industry. This is a subset of the 'manufacturing and natural resources' sector. MineCons was founded in 2002 by two former senior managers of a large mining corporation: Peter Pit and Brad Blast. Currently, the consultancy firm employs seven consultants, including the two founder-owners. All consultants are native Australians with rich experience in the mining industry. The firm operates with a single office that is located in Australia. Most of the consultancy work is based in MineCons' home country.

African business

However, for the last three years the consultancy has received an increasing stream of work from mining corporations on the African continent. In the first year, MineCons conducted one small consultancy project for a client in Africa. The second year, the consultancy firm was asked to do two small projects for African corporations. Last year MineCons did three small projects and one medium-sized project in Africa.

It is April. The firm has already done two small projects. Last month, the founders were approached by Lion Mining Corporation, an African mining corporation. They have hired MineCons three times already during the past three years for small projects.

The opportunity

Lion Mining has approached MineCons for a very large consultancy project. This project will require four consultants to work for eighteen months on the client's sites in Africa. MineCons' founders consider whether they should accept this commission of Lion Mining. There are a couple of issues. First, to staff this consultancy project, the consultancy firm needs to hire two additional consultants. With the current level of domestic work MineCons cannot afford to have more than two consultants working abroad.

Second, another issue concerns travelling. Until now MineCons' founder-owners Peter and Brad used to fly in their consultants to the African projects. As long as these projects were relatively short, that is maximally a couple of weeks, expatriating the Australian consultants was still acceptable. However, eighteen months is too long as the consultants have families at home.

Third, a final issue concerns the nature of the new project. In contrast to previous projects in Africa, this new project for Lion Mining will involve working together intensively with local, African employees of this client. Client interaction and communication will be an important success factor in this project. Will MineCons' Australian consultants be able to succeed?

Questions

1 What should Peter and Brad do? Should they accept Lion Mining's new commission or not? Give Peter and Brad your advice. Provide arguments for your advice.

2 If you think MineCons should accept the project, how should the firm deal with the three issues of the new commission as outlined above? Give Peter and Brad your advice. Provide arguments.

3 Now switch to the perspective of the client. Should Lion Mining consider hiring MineCons? Why, or why not? Critically reflect upon the scale of MineCons.

FURTHER READING

Curnow, B. and Reuvid, J. (2003) *International Guide to Management Consultancy: The Evolution, Practice and Structure of Management Consultancy Worldwide*. London: Kogan Page.

Faulconbridge, J. and Jones, A. (2012) 'The geographies of management consultancy firms', in M. Kipping and T. Clark (eds), *The Oxford Handbook of Management Consulting*. Oxford: Oxford University Press, 225–243.

REFERENCES

Bain & Company (2012) www.bain.com (accessed 25 March 2012).

Curnow, B. and Reuvid, J. (2003) *International Guide to Management Consultancy: The Evolution, Practice and Structure of Management Consultancy Worldwide*. London: Kogan Page.

Gross, A.C. and Poor, J. (2008) 'The global management consulting sector', *Business Economics*, 43 (4): 59–68.

McKinsey & Company (2012) www.mckinsey.com (accessed 25 March 2012).

Wright, C. and Kwon, S.-H. (2006) 'Business crisis and management fashion: Korean restructuring and consulting advice', *Asia Pacific Business Review*, 12 (3): 355–373.

5

THE COMPETITIVE LANDSCAPE OF THE MANAGEMENT CONSULTANCY INDUSTRY

INTRODUCTION

This chapter sketches the competitive landscape of the management consultancy industry. The chapter is divided into three parts. First, we outline the different competitive strategies of management consultancy firms. We emphasize the importance of knowledge about management problems and solutions. We show how the exploration and exploitation of this knowledge influence the competitive strategies of consultancies. Second, we explore the five competitive forces in the consultancy industry. We interpret each of these forces in the specific context of the management consultancy industry. This allows you to develop insight into the competitive dynamics of this industry. Third, we investigate key developments that affect the management consultancy industry: globalization, market maturation, the development of information technology, and the convergence of the management consultancy industry with other industries. The chapter presents a case study of the network-based consultancy firm EdenMcAllum to illustrate a new business model in management consultancy, and ends with a summary, reflective questions, a mini case study, suggested further reading, and references.

Main learning objectives

- Understand the differences in the competitive strategies of firms in the management consultancy industry.

- Relate knowledge exploitation and exploration to competitive strategy.
- Evaluate the attractiveness of the management consultancy industry in terms of the competitive forces.
- Understand key developments affecting the management consultancy industry.
- Critically reflect upon the implications of these key industry developments for the competitive forces in the industry.

COMPETITIVE STRATEGIES

Exploration and exploitation of knowledge

Management consultancy is a knowledge-intensive service. Knowledge about management problems and solutions plays a crucial role in the competitive strategies of management consultancy firms. Management consultancy is about knowledge exploration and knowledge exploitation, respectively, the development of new knowledge and the application of existing knowledge.

KNOWLEDGE EXPLORATION   The earliest management consultants at the end of the nineteenth century and in the early twentieth century needed to develop new knowledge because management (consultancy) was a new field. Client management hired them to solve new problems for which no solutions existed at that time. Consultants needed to develop new solutions. When client management hired them to assist with the management's tasks of implementing these new solutions, consultants also had to develop new knowledge about implementation.

BRAIN CONSULTANCY   Solving new client problems requires large effort. Management consultants have to invent the wheel. This puts large requirements on consultants. They have to be smart and creative to come up with new solutions. They have to explore knowledge. The consultants focusing on new problems have to compete on the basis of their brain power. They claim: we can help you best because we are smartest. What matters most in the competition between consultants for new problems is a consultant's ability to solve the newest (and most complex) client problems. Consultancy based on knowledge exploration is called the 'brain' type of consultancy (Maister, 1982).

KNOWLEDGE EXPLOITATION   When a second client approaches the management consultant with a problem that the particular consultant has already solved for another client, then the management consultant can use the same knowledge, or at least build on the already developed solution. The more often management consultants face the same, or similar, client problems, the more they can rely on their previous knowledge or experience. They do not have to reinvent the wheel every time a new client approaches them with the same or a similar problem. By exploiting their knowledge, management consultants become more efficient.

KNOWLEDGE ACCUMULATION Figure 5.1 visualizes the accumulation of knowledge of a consultancy. Assume the consultants work in project teams of four. Consultants on average do four projects per year. As a consequence, the number of projects that a firm conducts equals the number of consultants. Assume two firms with a stable number of consultants. A has 500 consultants, whereas B employs 1,000 consultants. Every year, firm A does 500 projects, whereas B does 1,000 projects. Figure 5.1 shows how the firms accumulate knowledge at different speed (assuming knowledge accumulation per project is the same for both firms). Over a period of ten years, firm A will have accumulated 5,000 projects in its knowledge base, whereas firm B will have added 10,000 projects to its knowledge base. This example illustrates economies of scale in knowledge development in management consultancy.

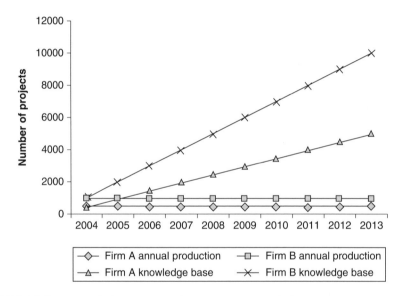

FIGURE 5.1 *Knowledge accumulation varies with firm size*

Note: 'annual production' refers to the number of projects conducted annually. The 'knowledge base' is the accumulated number of projects over time.

GREY HAIR CONSULTANCY Consultants may exploit their experience to solve client problems. They claim: we can help you best because we have solved similar problems before. Consultancy based on knowledge exploitation is called 'grey hair' consultancy (Maister, 1982). The emphasis in grey hair consultancy is on experience rather than brain power. The consultants should have experience. Grey hair consultancy is only appropriate for client problems that have been solved before. It is not suitable for new problems.

PROCEDURE CONSULTANCY To increase efficiency further, management consultancies strive to codify their experience into procedures. Procedures take the form of methods, tools, and techniques. Examples are: frameworks, models, road maps, checklists, and step plans. If consultants can codify their knowledge in procedures, they no longer have to rely on experienced, grey hair consultants. They may hire inexperienced or at least less experienced individuals. They are cheaper and they may be more easily moulded to the firm's requirements. These inexperienced consultants need to be trained in the firm's procedures. With the help of these procedures, they can solve the known problems of clients. Because the procedures are essential to the consultancy project's value creation, and because the owners of the consultancy firm own these procedures, these owners can seize the lion's share of the project fees.

EFFICIENCY AND LEVERAGE Procedure consultancy (Maister, 1982) provides two significant benefits for the consultancy firm. The first is cost saving and efficiency gains. The procedures allow the consultancy firm to hire inexperienced consultants. Inexperienced consultants are cheaper to hire than experienced ones. Moreover, procedures allow consultants to work more efficiently on projects. Second, procedures provide 'leverage'. Procedures enable consultancy firms to leverage their experience. With procedures the firm can more easily expand its scale of operations. The consultancy firm is no longer limited by the availability of experienced people. The pool of inexperienced individuals is larger than that of experienced ones. To develop a grey hair consultant may take a substantial period of time. To hire and train a procedure consultant is much less time consuming. The consultancy business becomes more scalable as a result.

CODIFIED VERSUS TACIT KNOWLEDGE Of course, not all consultancy knowledge can be codified. Tacit knowledge in the heads of grey hair consultants is difficult, if not impossible, to codify. Moreover, procedures are less demanding to imitate than tacit experience. Codified knowledge is easier to observe and, therefore, to imitate. Moreover, management consultancy procedures often cannot be protected by intellectual property protection rights. A well-known example is the BCG matrix. Basically every consultancy firm uses its own variant of this matrix. Codified knowledge of brain consultancies gives (small) procedure consultancy firms the chance to catch up and offer the best practices (developed by brain consultants) to their clients. This imitation induces the need for innovation. If followers catch up with the thought leader, then the leader has to come up with the next big idea to stay ahead.

SOFTWARE-BASED CONSULTANCY Procedure consultancy is delivered as a service. Although the procedure consultancy firms no longer need experienced staff, they still need people to provide advice and assistance to clients. Therefore, procedure consultancy remains a labour-intensive, and thus relatively costly, activity. To reduce costs further, management consultancies may attempt to codify their knowledge into software. Management consultancy is 'productized': services become (software) products.

An example of such a product is 'analytics' software to diagnose client problems. The software may be used in two ways. One way is that consultants use it to make them more efficient and effective. As a result, the productivity of consultants increases. Microsoft Excel is the basic analytics product that every consultant uses. Consultants may use macros and standardized templates for business cases and valuations. Another way is that the consultancy firm sells the software to clients. For instance, consultants may develop a route optimization tool for a client in logistics. Next time, these consultants can sell this tool – with some minor adjustments – to other logistics companies. Clients may then use the software without the help of consultants. Software is more scalable than procedures. Once developed, the marginal cost of software is close to zero. The efforts required to produce additional copies of software are very small.

An example is McKinsey Solutions.[1] McKinsey & Company has added web-based services to its portfolio of client services. McKinsey Solutions offers a portfolio of web-based knowledge (including proprietary benchmark data and publications), tools (such as analytical algorithms), and expert support for clients to help them identify opportunities for performance improvement and design solutions for performance improvement, and then implement these solutions.

Comparing four types of management consultancy

Figure 5.2 visualizes four different types of consultancy based on the familiarity of problems and the codifiability of knowledge. Because of the efficiency potential of codification, management consultancies will strive for codification of their knowledge. Besides efficiency, codification also helps to retain the knowledge inside the firm. The firm becomes less dependent on knowledgeable consultants who may retire or leave the firm for other reasons. Consultancy knowledge typically follows a pattern of increasing codification over its life cycle. When brain consultancy leads to the development of new knowledge, the level of codification will typically be (very) low. Over time, consultancies will attempt to codify their knowledge. Experience will be translated into procedures. And finally, procedures may be programmed into software. Not all consultancy knowledge will follow this pattern. Only specific sorts of knowledge will lend themselves for codification. Management problems that require tacit knowledge will not evolve beyond grey hair consultancy whereas some new (codifiable) knowledge may directly be programmed into procedures or software.

---

[1]http://solutions.mckinsey.com/catalog/ (accessed 20 April 2013).

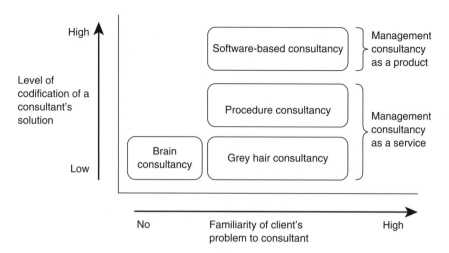

FIGURE 5.2 *Comparing the four types of management consultancy*

CLIENT VALUE PROPOSITIONS

Figure 5.3 outlines how these four types of consultancy may be related to types of value propositions for clients. In the previous section, we discussed software as the final form of knowledge codification. Software can be programmed procedures which support operational excellence but software can also be based on brain-type of knowledge and contribute to product leadership (see Figure 5.3).

Treacy and Wiersema (1993) distinguish between three generic value propositions: product leadership, operational excellence, and customer intimacy. We translate these propositions into management consultancy.

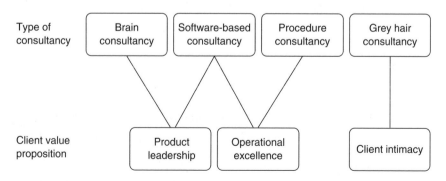

FIGURE 5.3 *Relating types of consultancy and client value propositions*

Product leadership. Product leadership is about innovation and based on knowledge exploration. Product leadership of a management consultancy firm means innovative solutions for client problems. This is about the management consultant as a thought leader. This value proposition may fit with brain consultancy and software-based consultancy based on brain knowledge (see Figure 5.3).

Operational excellence. Management consultancy firms that offer an operational excellence value proposition focus on the cost side of their offering. They strive for the lowest cost. This does not necessarily mean that consultancy firms with operational excellence compete on price. Wherever possible they will keep prices (project fees) as high as possible and earn an additional margin because of their lower costs. Operational excellence is based on knowledge exploitation. Because their solutions are not as innovative as the product leadership offerings, the operational excellence propositions have to be cheaper. The lower costs of the operational excellence proposition fit best with the efficiency of the procedure consultancy and software-based consultancy based on procedures (see Figure 5.3).

Client intimacy. The third value proposition is neither innovative (product leadership) nor low cost (operational excellence). The client intimacy value proposition is based on an intimate relationship between consultants and their clients. Consultants using the client intimacy proposition differentiate themselves from competitors by means of a superior relationship with their clients and a superior responsiveness to client needs. This value proposition may be associated with a grey hair consultancy. Grey hair consultancy is not as innovative as brain consultancy and not as low cost as procedure consultancy. Grey hair consultancy may derive its distinctive value from the intimate client relationship (see Figure 5.3). A focus on another value discipline, such as product leadership of operational excellence, does not mean that the consultancy firm can forego client intimacy. Client intimacy is – to a varying extent – important to all consultancy firms. Most consultancy firms obtain the majority of their revenues from existing clients. All consultancy firms need some degree of client intimacy, but some firms may decide that client intimacy is their main focus.

Cost versus differentiation strategies

We relate the client value propositions to Porter's (1985) competitive forces framework. Porter distinguishes between two bases of competition: lower cost and differentiation. We relate the value propositions to the competitive strategies.

Product leadership propositions are based on product innovation. Innovation is a manner of product differentiation. Product leadership propositions suit a *differentiation strategy*. If product innovation means high value to clients, than clients are willing to pay premium fees for product leadership propositions. Premium fees are the main profit driver of product leadership propositions.

Regarding differentiation strategy, product leadership is not the only differentiator. Another important differentiator is the quality of consultancy services provided. This quality of services provision depends to a large extent on the knowledge and skills of the individual consultants. Within a (large) consultancy firm, the knowledge and skills of consultants may vary due to differences in talent and experience. It makes a difference whether a client is served by a so-called 'A-team' consisting of the firm's top performers or by a 'B-team' consisting of inexperienced and less-qualified consultants (see Chapter 9). In fact, the A-team of a second tier consultancy firm might be better than the B-team of a top tier firm.

Operational excellence propositions are about low costs. They imply cost-based competition. *Cost leadership and cost focus strategies* fit operational excellence value propositions. Low costs are the main profit driver of operational excellence propositions. We emphasize that management consultants typically do not compete on price. Lowering prices may send the wrong message to prospective clients. In general, prospective clients find it difficult to interpret the quality of consultancy services. They may therefore perceive price to be a signal of quality. Consultancy firms want to signal that they are the best. As a consequence, they should ask high prices. Asking high prices is not always possible. To an increasing extent (large) clients will organize tenders where multiple consultancy firms may bid for the same project. Typically, the lowest bidder gets the project (see Chapter 10).

Client intimacy propositions are not based on low costs. An intimate relationship with the client is a way for the management consultant to differentiate themself from the competition. Therefore, client intimacy propositions are a form of *differentiation strategy*. Because client intimacy is relatively labour-intensive, it cannot compete on cost. The relationship-based differentiation allows higher fees than operational excellence consultancy, though not as high as product leadership consultancy. Premium fees are the main profit driver of client intimacy propositions.

Competitive advantage

What competitive strategy best fits a management consultancy firm? Should the firm pursue cost or differentiation? If the consultancy decides on a differentiation strategy, what should be its basis of differentiation? The choice of competitive strategy depends on several factors. We focus on three important ones: clients, competitors, and the consultancy firm itself.

Clients. The competitive strategy is influenced by the choice of clients. What clients will the consultancy firm target? As outlined in the previous chapter, the scoping options for consultancy firms present a spectrum, with on one hand, a very narrow scope of specialization in one client sector on a local scale, and on the other hand, a very broad scope of many client sectors on a global scale. Next, the choice of client problems drives the competitive strategy.

Does the consultancy firm focus on new problems or familiar problems? Finally, the codifiability of the consultancy's knowledge affects the strategy. New problems with low codifiability suggest a brain type of consultancy, whereas familiar and highly codifiable problems indicate a procedure type of consultancy.

Competitors. The previous section hinted at a direct relationship between type of consultancy and value proposition. However, the competitive situation may influence that relationship. If competition is weak, than a management consultancy firm may get away with one strong value proposition only. For instance, a brain type of consultancy, BrainCon (fictitious firm), may focus on the product leadership proposition, and relatedly a differentiation strategy. But if competition is strong than a management consultancy firm may have to combine multiple strong value propositions. In the example of BrainCon, if the firm faces strong competition from other brain consultancy firms, than product leadership differentiation may not be enough to win business from its rivals. In such a competitive situation, the consultancy firm may have to combine product leadership differentiation, to some extent, with other value propositions, such as client intimacy differentiation. BrainCon may have to invest in the client relationship to get the brain business.

Consultancy firm. Competitive strategy is not only driven by clients and competitors. The resources and capabilities of the consultancy firm also influence the choice of strategy. Compare outside-in thinking (the environment guides the strategy development) and inside-out thinking (the organization's resources and capabilities guide the strategy development) about strategy. Large management consultancy firms have a greater potential for scale economies that enable cost strategies than small firms. Firms with a consultancy staff of highly talented professionals will be better equipped for a differentiation strategy based on product leadership. A strong client network is a good basis for a differentiation strategy based on client intimacy.

TRADE-OFFS Decisions about the basis of competitive advantage for management consultancy firms are influenced by trade-offs between the different competitive advantages. In Figure 5.4 we distinguish three bases of competitive advantage. Porter distinguishes cost and differentiation. Based on the client value propositions of Treacy and Wiersema, we decompose differentiation into product differentiation and client relationship differentiation. We postulate increasing marginal costs for a particular competitive advantage. By this we mean that the marginal costs of a consultancy firm's competitive advantage increase when the consultancy strengthens the particular advantage. The increasing costs to competitive advantages imply a convex relationship between two competitive advantages. The curve implies a trade-off between competitive advantages. With a given set of resources, a management consultancy firm cannot strengthen multiple competitive advantages

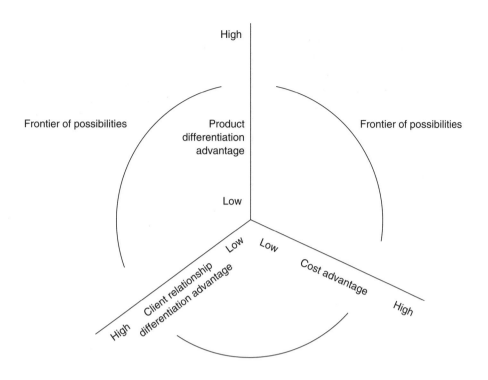

FIGURE 5.4 *Trade-offs between competitive advantages for management consultancy firms*

Source: based on the work of Porter (1985), and Treacy and Wiersema (1993)

simultaneously. Strategy is making decisions. For the sake of simplicity, Figure 5.4 only shows bilateral trade-offs. In real life, management consultancy firms face *trilateral* trade-offs between the three bases of competitive advantage. The leaders of the consultancy have to decide simultaneously how to position their firm along the three axes. Large firms operating in multiple markets may make different trade-offs in different markets, depending on several factors, such as the maturity of markets and the firm's willingness to expand in a market. Over time, as conditions evolve, consultants may change their trade-off decisions. It is a dynamic decision.

Competitive scope

Typically the decisions 'how to compete' (competitive advantage) and 'where to compete' (competitive scope) are interwoven. For the purpose of simplicity we discuss the two decisions one after another. We frame the 'where decision' in three dimensions: services, client sectors, and geography (see also Chapter 4).

Services. Regarding the first dimension, this chapter focuses on management consultancy services, that is, advice to management and assistance with the managerial tasks of implementing advice. However, firms may combine management consultancy with business consultancy, business services, and other services. We may conceptualize the services scope on a spectrum that ranges from specialist management consultancy firms to conglomerates offering a broad range of services. An example of a firm specializing in management consultancy is McKinsey & Company. IBM Consulting is an example of a very broad player.

Client sectors. The second dimension is about the number of client sectors served. Some firms specialize in a single client sector, while others are generalists who work in a large range of sectors (see Chapter 4).

Geography. The third dimension is the geographic scope of the firm. We acknowledge that the majority of management consultancy firms is (very) small and focuses on the national or local market. For these firms competition is contained within the local environment, or a national scale. However, there are also a number of (very) large firms, such as the consultancy arms of Deloitte and PwC, that operate on a global scale.

SCALE AND SCOPE   Figure 5.5 visualizes three different groups of firms operating in the management consultancy industry. The horizontal axis combines the scale and scope of firms. We distinguish three groups. On the left, the figure positions firms with a small scope. These are typically the small specialist consultancy firms. On the right, the figure positions firms that combine a large scale with a broad scope. Here you find the big global conglomerates, combining management consultancy with other professional services.

In the middle we find firms that are medium-sized and have a relatively wide scope. They are, for instance, generalist consultancy firms that offer a wide range of services to a wide range of client sectors in various countries. The vertical axis measures the profitability of the firms. Figure 5.5 shows a

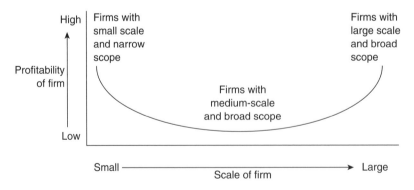

FIGURE 5.5   *The combination of a firm's scale and scope affects its profitability*

so-called 'smiley curve'. Firms at both ends of the spectrum have high profitability, while the players in the middle have low profitability. They are literally stuck in the middle.

Small specialists may achieve high profitability due to specialization advantages and experience effects. Moreover they may operate in relatively uncontested niche markets that are not attractive to the large consultancy firms. The big broad players in the consultancy industry may seize economies of scale and scope. The mid-sized players with a relatively broad scope do not enjoy economies of scale while they have to cope with the complexity of managing a broad scope operation. The broad scope in combination with small scale typically implies little opportunity for achieving experience effects.

CASE STUDY

A network-based management consultancy firm[1]

The opportunity of the alumni

There are much more alumni in the top tier management consultancy firms, such as McKinsey & Company, Bain & Company, and the Boston Consulting Group, than consultants currently employed by these firms. Moreover, the number is increasing. A substantial number of alumni become independent freelance consultants. Two alumni from one of the top tier firms invented a business model that capitalized on the growing alumni pool.

---

[1]Based on various sources, including the company, company website, and various newspaper and journal articles, including Birkinshaw (2006) and *Business Strategy Review* (2007).

A new business model in management consultancy

Liann Eden and Dena McCallum once worked for McKinsey & Company. Eden left on becoming a mother because she wanted a change of lifestyle. McCallum joined a corporate firm. In her new position as a client of consultancy, she began looking for a more tailored and less costly alternative for the traditional offering of the top tier consultancies. Clients do not always have the need, and the budget, to hire a complete team from a traditional top tier firm.

Eden and McCallum joined forces and founded a business to couple freelance alumni from the top tier consultancies to clients. Some alumni want a different life style. Some clients want top tier level consultancy, but do not have the need, or the budget, for the traditional fully leaded team-based offerings of the top tier consultancy firms. Some clients don't want a consultant to 'own' their issue and present a report, but want to develop the answer themselves – with help.

▶

How it works

Eden and McCallum built a network of freelance alumni from the top tier consultancies. They invest in getting to know these consultants well, and work on multiple projects with many of them but none of the consultants is on their payroll. Eden McCallum employs them on a contract basis, when a project opportunity arises for which they are suitable. Eden McCallum works with clients to decide the right level of resourcing and experience for the project at hand without being constrained by the economics of traditional firms. Typically this results in a smaller and more tailored team (two or three people from Eden McCallum working closely with the client).

In an Eden McCallum setting these alumni now offer a different value proposition from their previous employer. For one thing, these alumni do not have access to the resources of their former firms. They do not have access to the expertise of the worldwide staff, the knowledge management systems, and the proprietary methods and techniques. However, these consultants have been trained in many approaches and techniques and are selected for projects specifically for the experience and skills that they bring. Moreover, much of what used to be proprietary research these days is available on-line. The Eden McCallum value proposition therefore provides top-calibre consultants with relevant experience at about half the rates of the traditional top tier firms.

Everybody happy?

Freelance alumni-consultants may find the business model of Eden McCallum attractive. It provides sole practitioners with a brand and the opportunity to work on more diverse projects in more diverse team-settings. Moreover, the firm relieves them of the need to find clients themselves. Eden McCallum provides alumni with the opportunity of having a regular supply of work. They can decide to accept work or not. This flexibility allows for a more balanced lifestyle. Eden McCallum maintains good relationships with the top tier consultancy firms. So far, Eden McCallum doesn't typically compete with the traditional firms. Whereas McKinsey or BCG typically work for the CEOs of the largest corporations, Eden McCallum serves these clients mostly at the level of BU/division leaders. Eden McCallum also serves smaller clients who would not have hired the top consultancies anyway. However, if this business model of mediating top tier alumni spreads and cannibalizes the core business of the top tier firms, the relationship of Eden McCallum with these consultancies may change.

Discussion questions

1 What, if any, competitive force(s) in the consultancy industry does Eden McCallum illustrate? Explain your answer.

2 How do you assess the competitive advantages and disadvantages of Eden McCallum compared to the traditional top tier consultancy firms? Explain your answer.

3 Characterize and evaluate the present relationship between Eden McCallum and the alumni. Explain your answer.

4 Does Eden McCallum have a sustainable competitive advantage? What, if any, are the key threats to the firm? Explain your answer.

COMPETITIVE FORCES

In this section we provide an overview of the main elements of the management consultancy industry. For this purpose, we use Porter's competitive forces framework (see Figure 5.6). We discuss each of the five groups of industry actors: competitors, buyers, suppliers, substitutes, and new entrants. Competitors are the established, incumbent management consultancy firms. The buyers are the clients of these management consultancies. As management consultancy is a people business, the main suppliers are individuals who are willing to work for management consultancy firms. Substitutes for management consultancy refer to alternatives such as client management solving problems and implementing solutions without the help of management consultancies. Other substitutes include research firms, advertising agencies, and charity organizations of retired experts that advise some managers for free (for instance, managers of non-profit organizations or managers in developing countries). New entrants consist of newly founded consultancy firms as well as established firms from other industries that set up a management consultancy subsidiary. For each group of industry actors, we examine the main determinants of the competitive force related to that particular group (see Figure 5.6).

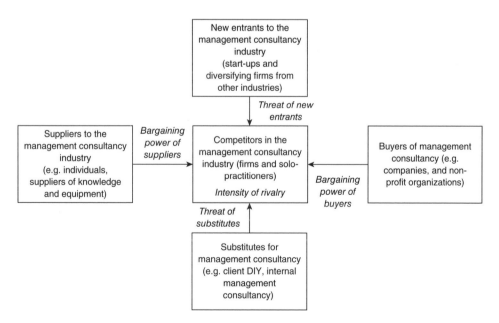

FIGURE 5.6 *Elements of industry structure*

Source: based on Porter (1985: 6), DIY refers to Do-It-Yourself

Industry competitors or internal rivalry

The archetypal management consultancy industry competitor does not exist. The industry encompasses a heterogeneous population of providers of management consultancy services. We distinguish between pure players and the hybrids. In this chapter, we adopt the perspective of the pure players; these are firms and sole practitioners that solely focus on management consultancy services. As the geographic scope is global, we focus on pure players with international presence.

TABLE 5.1 *Rivalry determinants*

Rivalry determinant	Comment	Dampens rivalry	Enforces rivalry
Industry growth	Consultancy revenue growth	High growth	Slow growth or decline
Ratio of fixed costs to value added	Fixed costs is mostly wages	Low ratio	High ratio
Intermittent overcapacity	Capacity of consultancy staff	No intermittent overcapacity	High intermittent overcapacity
Product differences	Differentiation through client relations, quality, and people	Large differences	Small or no differences
Brand identity	Brand of the consultancy firm	Strong brands	Weak or no brands
Switching costs	Switching between consultancy firms	High switching costs	Low or no switching costs
Concentration and balance	Market share of top 4 consultancies. Balance of shares	High concentration, large size differences between firms	Low concentration, equal-size firms
Informational complexity	Transparency for buyers of consultancy services	High informational complexity	Low informational complexity
Diversity of competitors	Differences between consultancy firms	Low diversity	High diversity
Corporate stakes	Corporate owners of consultancy firms	Low corporate stakes	High corporate stakes
Exit barriers	Ease of exiting the consultancy industry	Low exit barriers	High exit barriers

Source: based on Porter (1985)

DETERMINANTS OF RIVALRY   Porter distinguishes between 11 determinants of the intensity of rivalry among industry competitors (see Table 5.1). The higher the intensity of rivalry, the larger the pressure on competitor profitability.

Industry growth   Industry growth lowers the intensity of rivalry. During its history the industry has expanded its scope in terms of services and geographies. During the second half of the twentieth century, growth was primarily driven by the expansion of consultancy services: information technology and strategy. However, in the first decade of the twenty-first century it is primarily geographic expansion that drives industry growth. Emerging markets, such as Brazil, Russia, India, and China (the so-called 'BRIC countries'), provide a new impetus to the management consultancy industry. However, the geographic expansion cannot mask that management consultancy, at least in the developed countries, has turned into a mature industry.

Fixed costs to value added   The ratio of fixed costs to value added of the consultancy is another determinant of rivalry. If this ratio is high then competitors will have a larger inclination to reduce prices in order to gain business than when this ratio is low. High fixed costs imply low variable costs, which in turn make additional sales profitable at low price levels. Management consultancy is a people business. It is not capital intensive. The capital costs are minimal. However, if the consultancy employees have permanent contracts then labour costs are fixed. This means a high ratio of fixed costs to value added. Management consultancy firms are less inclined to reduce fees to win business, as lowering fees gives out a negative signal. In particular, because the impact of management consultancy on client performance is hard or impossible to measure, management consultancy firms use all other means to signal quality. Buyers may associate high fees with high quality. Instead of lowering the billing rate, management consultancies will charge less time to the client. If a consultancy project is sold for a lower amount of official time, then the consultants assigned to the project will have to work overtime to get the work done in the period agreed. Management consultancy firms do not give a rebate on the billing rate but on the billed hours. The economic effect for the client is the same as a price discount but in the case of a reduction in billed hours, the consulting staff pay the price (discount).

Intermittent overcapacity   Intermittent overcapacity is a third determinant of rivalry. Overcapacity adds to rivalry. The utilization of its consultancy staff is a key performance driver for a management consultancy firm. Overcapacity implies lower utilization and thus lower performance and so lower profit. Management consultancy firms will avoid overcapacity, that is consultants being idle or, euphemistically termed, consultants being 'on the beach'. Therefore, consultancy firms will be inclined to give rebates. As stated before, these rebates will not be given on the billing rate but on the official hours charged to the client. If overcapacity is expected to reach a permanent status, then consultancy firms will cut the overcapacity by taking leave of redundant staff.

Product differences A fourth rivalry determinant is product differences between firms. If the product differentiation is large, then the rivalry will be less intense than when the product differentiation is small. In the absence of product differences, the competitors offer identical products. This is the case of commodity industries. In commodity industries, the rivalry is fierce. Price is the only competitive weapon if competitors cannot differentiate their products.

Client relationship differentiation. In the management consultancy industry, the product is a service. Services are intangible. Moreover, they are inseparable from the service providers. Service provision and consumption take place simultaneously. The service is also inseparable from the service consumer. The variability is typically higher for services than for products. In most cases of management consultancy, the quality of service depends not only on the service provider but also on the consumer or client. The latter is a co-creator of the consultancy service. Clients need to provide information. They may also be used as a sounding board. Moreover, clients implement the advice, in some cases with the assistance of management consultants. The role of the client suggests that the relationship between client and consultant is essential. Differences in relationship with clients, for instance stronger ties with a client, may reduce the rivalry between consultancies.

Quality differentiation. The advice and assistance provided by management consultancy firms may be another source of differences between firms. The quality of the advice and implementation assistance may differ. A complicating factor is that the impact of management consultancy is hard or impossible to measure. Clients may assess the project, including the methods, techniques, and knowledge that management consultants use. They may also assess the inputs into the project, that is the individual consultants.

People differentiation. The quality of the individual management consultants depends on their individual skills, knowledge, and attitude. Clients may consider the professional qualifications, educational background, and professional track record of individual consultants. The consultants draw on the organizational resources of their firm. These resources include firm-wide knowledge management systems, peer networks, support staff, methodologies, tools, and techniques. Both differences in quality of individuals and differences in the quality of firm resources may create differences in the services delivered between management consultancy firms.

Brand identity The previous determinant, product differences, may be interpreted as objective or subjective. Brand identity is only about subjective differences. Brands are means of differentiation. Differentiation reduces the intensity of internal rivalry. The large management consultancy firms all have well-known brands. Strategies for brand development vary by firms. Some firms that want to establish a brand of a thought leader invest in research and development. But they also invest in promotion to show their R&D findings. Other firms sponsor sport and cultural events. Another strategy is advertising. However, probably the most important determinant of consultancy brands is the work of the consultancy firms. Consultants develop a reputation by their work for clients. Client experiences and referrals help to build, or destroy, brands.

Switching costs If clients can easily, without any cost, switch from one supplier to another, than rivalry among suppliers will be higher than when switching is costly. We may find several types of switching costs in the case of management consultancy. There is the cost of building a relationship between client and consultant. Relationships enable trust. Clients need to spend time and effort to teach the new management consultant. The consultant needs to learn the details of the client. Additionally, clients need to learn about the approach of the new consultant. If the consultant uses different methods and techniques, client employees that work with the consultant need to learn these methods and techniques. However, if the approaches of consultants are similar, then these costs to clients are minimal.

Concentration and balance In a full competition all competitors are of equal size. Concentration is very low and competition is balanced. In management consultancy, most firms are small and only a small share are (very) large. Management consultancy has a low concentration, but competition is unbalanced.

Informational complexity Informational complexity reduces the intensity of rivalry. The informational complexity of management consultancy from a buyer perspective is relatively high. Management consultancy is not a transparent industry. The industry lacks standards. There is no obligatory registration. It is hard or impossible to measure impact.

Diversity of competitors Differences between consultancy firms add to the intensity of rivalry. The population of management consultancy firms is rather diverse. On the one hand, we have the (very) small firms that operate on a local or national level. On the other hand, we find the (very) large firms that operate on a global level. The strategic group of large, international firms used to be dominated by firms from the United States.

Corporate stakes Corporate ownership heightens the intensity of rivalry. If competitors are part of larger corporations than rivalry will increase. Management consultancy used to be an industry made up of relatively small firms, that is without the presence of large corporations and their subsidiaries. Before the arrival of the corporations, the firms in the management consultancy industry were professional partnerships. However, with the development of IT consultancy, corporations have entered the industry: the so-called managed professional businesses (see Part 3). Large IT hardware or IT services corporations have added management consultancy divisions. Examples are IBM, Accenture, and Capgemini. Moreover, the big accountancy firms, among which are Deloitte, Ernst & Young, KPMG, and PwC, have set up advisory arms.

Exit barriers   If exit barriers are high then the internal rivalry will be more intense than when barriers are low. Management consultancy firms do not face high exit barriers. These organizations do not have large, industry-specific asset bases. They are not characterized by long-term liabilities towards customers or suppliers. As a result, management consultancy firms can exit at a relatively low cost.

Buyers

The buyers of management consultancy services are a heterogeneous group. They may differ in size and operate in different industries and countries. The type of consultancy services they seek may vary across buyers. Also reasons for buying consultancy may vary. Porter distinguishes between two determinants of buyer power: buyer bargaining leverage and buyer price sensitivity.

DETERMINANTS OF BUYER BARGAINING LEVERAGE   Table 5.2 outlines the determinants of buyer bargaining leverage.

Buyer concentration versus firm concentration. Buyer concentration increases the leverage of buyers, which in turn increases buyer power over management consultancy firms, thereby reducing the profitability for consultancies. Regarding management consultancy, buyer concentration varies by sector. Firm concentration in management consultancy is rather low. Most consultancies are (very) small. Moreover, large consultancies work for large buyers and small consultancies work for small buyers.

Buyer volume. The size of the buyer budget influences bargaining leverage. Large buyer organizations tend to have larger budgets for management consultancy services than small buyers. The large organizations, therefore, have more bargaining leverage. Large buyers often have larger agreements with consultancy firms. For instance, these buyers may commit to X million dollars per year but at a Y per cent discount on the daily billing rate of consultants.

Buyer switching costs relative to firm switching costs. If the buyer switching costs are relatively low, then bargaining leverage will be relatively higher than when these costs are relatively high. The more similar the approaches of management consultancy firms, the lower the buyer switching costs. The same applies to buyers. A high similarity of buyers lowers switching costs for consultancy firms.

TABLE 5.2 *Determinants of buyer bargaining leverage*

Buyer power determinant	Comment	Reduces buyer bargaining leverage	Increases buyer bargaining leverage
Buyer concentration relative to firm concentration	Dominance of consultancy buyers versus dominance of consultancy firms	Buyer concentration is smaller than consultancy firm concentration	Buyer concentration is larger than consultancy firm concentration
Buyer volume	Size of buyer budget for consultancy	Small buyer volume	Large buyer volume
Buyer switching costs relative to firm switching costs	Flexibility of buyers and consultancy firms	Buyer switching costs exceed consultancy firm switching costs	Consultancy firm switching costs exceed buyer switching costs
Buyer information	Information about management consultancy	Shortage of information for buyer	Abundance of information for buyer
Ability to integrate backwards	Ability of buyers to set up an internal consultancy department	Weak ability to integrate backwards	Strong ability to integrate backwards
Substitute products	Ability of buyers to solve problems themselves	Low availability of substitute products	High availability of substitute products
Pull through	Buyer bypasses consultancy firms to access talent	Low pull through potential	High pull through potential

Source: based on Porter (1985)

Buyer information. Information about management consultancy augments bargaining leverage. Because management consultancy is a service, it is more difficult for buyers to obtain information compared to products. The lack of transparency of the management consultancy lowers the opportunities for buyers to collect information. Moreover, buyers may lose information about consultants. The people who buy management consultancy services may leave the buyer's (procurement) department or leave the buyer organization altogether. Even large buyer organizations find it difficult to keep the (soft, tacit) knowledge about management consultancy (firms) inside.

Ability to integrate backwards. Backward integration enlarges bargaining leverage. In terms of management consultancy, backward integration by buyers means that these organizations establish their own (internal) management consultancy units. Because of (breakeven) economics (minimum efficient scale), large buyers are in a better position to set up internal consultancy units than small buyers.

Substitute products. Substitute products also improve bargaining leverage. A substitute for management consultancy is that buyers solve their problems themselves and implement their solutions without the help of external management consultants. If buyers have strong competences and sufficient time, than the competitiveness of substitute products in relation to management consultancy will be better than when buyers lack the competences and time.

Pull-through. Pull-through raises bargaining leverage. If buyers can bypass consultancy firms and deal with the consultancy firms' suppliers directly, they have more leverage than when they cannot bypass consultancy firms. The key suppliers to consultancies are the individual talents. Clients may compete in the labour market with management consultancy firms for these talents.

DETERMINANTS OF BUYER PRICE SENSITIVITY   Table 5.3 outlines the determinants of buyer price sensitivity.

TABLE 5.3   *Determinants of buyer price sensitivity*

Buyer power determinant	Comment	Reduces buyer price sensitivity	Increases buyer price sensitivity
Ratio of price to total purchases	Share of consultancy purchases in buyer's total purchases	Low ratio of price to total purchases	High ratio of price to total purchases
Product differences and brand identity	Differentiation of consultancy firms	Large product differences and strong brand identity	Small product differences and weak brand identity
Impact on quality and performance of buyers	Effect of management consultancy services on quality and performance of buyers	Large impact on quality and performance of buyers	Small impact on quality and performance of buyers
Buyer profits	Room for consultancy purchases	High buyer profits	Low buyer profits
Decision makers' incentives	Incentives of buyers for keeping budget for consultancy purchases	Weak decision makers' incentives	Strong decision makers' incentives

Source: based on Porter (1985)

The ratio of price to total purchases raises the price sensitivity of buyers. The ratio of management consultancy fees to the total purchases of buyers will generally be relatively low. Large buyers may in absolute terms buy large amounts of management consultancy, but the ratio to their total purchases may be similar to small buyers.

Product differences and the brand identity of management consultancy firms reduce price sensitivity. For a discussion about product differences and brand identity in management consultancy, see the section on rivalry determinants.

The impact on quality and the performance of buyers diminishes price sensitivity. The impact of management consultancy services on the buyer's performance and quality is difficult, if not impossible, to determine. The absence of measurable impact, all other things being equal, induces price sensitivity.

Buyer profits lower price sensitivity. Profits vary by buyer and by buyer sector. Buyers and sectors with high profitability are more attractive for consultancies than buyers and sectors with low profitability.

Decision makers' incentives influence buyers' price sensitivity. If decision makers, such as (top) management at the buyer organization, have incentives for keeping to consultancy budgets or for achieving certain financial results, then they will be more price sensitive to management consultancy fees than when they don't have such incentives.

Suppliers

Management consultancy is a knowledge-intensive service. The most important inputs for this industry are individuals with knowledge and knowledge-processing competences for solving problems and implementing solutions. The precise people requirements vary by type of consultancy; compare brain consultancy, grey hair consultancy, and procedure consultancy. The most important suppliers to management consultancy firms are individuals who seek employment. Of course, there are other suppliers. For instance, consultancy firms typically rent offices, buy computers and other office equipment, lease company cars, purchase air travel tickets, and use hotels and restaurants. Moreover, they may outsource activities, such as (market) research and administrative services. In this section, however, we focus on people.

DETERMINANTS OF SUPPLIER POWER   Table 5.4 outlines the determinants of supplier power.

Differentiation of inputs increases the power of suppliers – in the case of consultancy, the individual consultants. The knowledge and

TABLE 5.4 *Determinants of supplier power*

Determinants of supplier power	Comment	Dampens supplier power	Enforces supplier power
Differentiation of inputs	Quality differences between consultancy staff	Small differentiation of inputs	Large differentiation of inputs
Supplier switching costs relative to firm switching costs	Flexibility of suppliers and consultancy firms	Supplier switching costs exceed consultancy firm switching costs	Consultancy firm switching costs exceed supplier switching costs
Presence of substitute products	Alternatives for (talented) consultancy staff, e.g., procedures and software	High availability of substitute products	Low availability of substitute products
Supplier concentration relative to firm concentration	Dominance of consultancy suppliers versus dominance of consultancy firms	Supplier concentration is smaller than consultancy firm concentration	Supplier concentration is larger than consultancy firm concentration
Importance of volume to supplier	Need for suppliers to sell large volumes	High importance of volume to supplier	Low importance of volume to supplier
Cost relative to total purchases	Share of supplier cost in total purchases of management consultancy firms	High cost relative to total purchases	Low cost relative to total purchases
Impact of inputs on cost or differentiation	Effect of supplies on cost or differentiation of management consultancy firms	Small impact on cost or differentiation of management consultancy firms	Large impact on cost or differentiation of management consultancy firms
Threat of forward integration	Ability of suppliers to enter management consultancy	Low threat of forward integration	High threat of forward integration

Source: based on Porter (1985)

competences of human resources vary. Moreover, the hiring needs of consultancies differ as well. For instance, brain type consultancies want to hire only the smartest graduates from the top business schools. Such candidates have more supplier power than candidates with lower grades or those from less prestigious schools. Procedure consultancies have lower requirements for recruiting consultancy staff.

Supplier switching costs relative to firm switching costs. If the supplier switching costs are relatively low, than supplier power will be higher than when the costs are high. Consultancy firms invest in their recruits, in particular if those recruits are graduates. Switching junior consultants from one consultancy to another raises costs for the firms that trained these consultants. If the differences between consultancy firms are large, then switching costs for consultants will be higher than when differences are small. If the differences are large then switching costs for firms will also be higher. They have to invest more in new candidates from different firms than from similar firms. Typically, there is a turnover of talent across consultancy firms. Consultancy firms may hire each other's (top) talent. This has a lot to do with client relationships. As client relationships are often personal, hiring an individual consultant implies acquiring that individual's client base.

The presence of substitute inputs lowers supplier power. The rise of information and communications technology has made the labour market more international. Management consultancy firms may offshore part of the work to overseas staff. Overseas staffing has become a substitute for onshore staff in management consultancy firms. However, firms may also bring offshore staff to onshore markets. Substitute input may also mean an alternative to human resources. The meaning of substitute input varies by type of consultancy. In procedure consultancy, procedures and software are a substitute for consultants. Over time, procedures may become a substitute for experience if the experience can be codified. This example shows that over time new substitutes may arise.

Supplier concentration relative to firm concentration raises supplier power. The people working for management consultancy firms are not concentrated. Management consultants do not have unions. There are professional associations of consultants, but most consultants are not members of such organizations. There are no intermediaries who control the supply of consultants to consultancy firms, similar to what Eden McCallum does for alumni.

Importance of volume to supplier reduces supplier power. As suppliers to management consultancy firms mainly consist of individuals that sell their hours, volume potential is limited. Individuals can only sell their own available hours. Most individuals want a full-time employment contract. There are no economies of scale to be reaped for suppliers.

Cost relative to total purchases by firms in the industry. If input cost relative to total purchases by management consultancy firms is low, then supplier power will be higher than when input costs are high. The costs of human resources are (very) high relative to the total purchases of management consultancy firms. Management consultancy is a people business. The firms have very little physical capital (for example, office equipment, and perhaps office buildings, if they do not rent their office space). They mainly rely on human capital. Management consultancy will, therefore, be sensitive to labour costs.

Impact of inputs on the cost or differentiation of management consultancy firms will raise supplier power. As already indicated, human resources bear a large impact on the cost of management consultancy firms. Management consultancy is a service. The quality of the service providers, that is the individual consultants, has a high impact on the quality of the service delivered. As discussed earlier, the impact of management consultancy services is hard, if not impossible, to measure. If output quality is hard to measure, clients may consider input quality, that is the quality of individual consultants, as a signal of output quality. Management consultancy firms signal the quality of their work with the quality of their consultants. This reliance on inputs raises the power of suppliers, that is the individual consultants. The reliance on the quality of the individual consultants varies by type of consultancy. It will be relatively high in brain and grey hair consultancy. However, in procedure consultancy it will be relatively low. It will be even lower when consultancies codify their knowledge into software.

The threat of forward integration relative to the threat of backward integration by firms in the industry raises supplier power. Backward integration by firms is not applicable to management consultancy, unless consultancies set up their own (business) schools. However, individuals may integrate forward by founding their own consultancy firm. This is a real threat. Individuals may decide not to join a firm but set up their own consultancy business. There are various examples of consultants leaving a firm to establish their own firm. This threat of setting up firms raises the power of suppliers. Individuals may also develop a virtual consultancy firm, a flexible network organization of independent individuals that share knowledge and other resources.

New entrants

New entrants to the management consultancy industry may have different forms. One form is alumni from established management consultancies who found their own practice. Such people may become sole practitioners, or they may build a new management consultancy firm. Bain & Company as well as Roland Berger Strategy Consultants were founded by alumni from BCG. Another form of new entrants is established firms from other industries that set up a management consultancy subsidiary. An example is IBM. As described in Chapter 2, this IT firm entered the management consultancy industry in 1991 after the firm's 1956 consent decree was lifted (the US Department of Justice dropped its anti-trust suit in 1982).

DETERMINANTS OF THE THREAT OF ENTRY   Table 5.5 presents the determinants of threat of entry.

TABLE 5.5 *Determinants of threat of entry*

Determinants of threat of new entrants	Comment	Reduces threat of new entrants	Increases threat of new entrants
Economies of scale	Investments of management consultancy firms in knowledge management and advertising, among others	Large economies of scale	Small economies of scale
Proprietary product differences	Intellectual ownership rights for consultancy firms	Large proprietary product differences	Small proprietary product differences
Brand identity	Brand identity of incumbent management consultancy firms	Strong brand identity	Weak brand identity
Switching costs	Switching costs for the buyers of consultancy services	High switching costs	Low or no switching costs
Capital requirements	Capital required for setting up a management consultancy firm	High capital requirements	Low capital requirements
Access to buyers	Relationship between buyers and incumbent management consultancy firms	Weak access to buyers	Strong access to buyers
Proprietary learning curve & low-cost design	Access to knowledge developed by incumbent management consultancy firms	Learning curve and design are proprietary	Learning curve and design are public
Access to necessary inputs	Access to talent for management consultancy	No or limited access to necessary inputs	Easy access to necessary inputs
Government policy	Government policy as barrier to new entrants	High entry barrier	Low entry barrier
Expected retaliation	Retaliaton by incumbent fims against new entrants	High expected retaliation	Low expected retaliation

Source: based on Porter (1985)

Economies of scale raise barriers to new entrants. Economies of scale in management consultancy are primarily limited to knowledge management and advertising and promotion. The investments in knowledge management systems refer to scale economies. But also the accumulation of knowledge via consultancy projects is related to scale (see Figure 5.1). Expenditure on advertising and promotion is also sensitive to scale.

Proprietary product differences imply entry barriers. If a management consultancy can acquire intellectual ownership rights to its knowledge, then it has a barrier against new entrants and incumbent competition.

The brand identity of incumbent, established, management consultancy firms represents an entry barrier. The large management consultancy firms typically have well-known brands. New entrants without strong brands have to overcome this disadvantage.

Switching costs for buyers (clients) serve as an entry barrier. If the switching costs are high, it will be more difficult to enter the management consultancy industry than when switching costs are low. Switching costs in management consultancy are relatively low in the sense that clients can switch consultancies at low or no cost. However, most consultancies invest in long-standing relationships with their clients. Long-standing relations may raise the switching costs for clients.

Capital requirements may represent a barrier to entry. Management consultancy is a service industry. It is labour intensive rather than capital intensive. However, building an international office network, developing a knowledge management system, and developing a brand will require substantial investments.

Access to buyers (clients) is another entry barrier. Buyer relations are very important in management consultancy. Most management consultancy firms aim for long-standing relations with clients. Repeat business is more profitable than continuously having to develop new business. If established consultancy firms invest heavily in their client relations, then it will be more difficult for new entrants to acquire these clients.

A proprietary learning curve represents an entry barrier. Management consultancy is a knowledge-intensive business. Knowledge development can serve as a competitive advantage. The most important source of knowledge for management consultants is their client projects. When established consultancy firms can develop proprietary new knowledge through their work for clients, then they have a competitive advantage over new entrants.

Proprietary low-cost design may be an entry barrier. Knowledge in management consultancy is typically not proprietary. It is difficult, if not impossible, to obtain patents for management knowledge.

Access to necessary inputs is another entry barrier. For management consultancy the most important input is people. If established management consultants have preferential access to (the most talented) people, then they have a barrier against new entrants that lack such access.

Government policy may raise entry barriers. The case study about South Korea provides an example of entry barriers by government policy. Until the 1990s, the South Korean government forbade the establishment of offices by foreign management consultancy firms. If management consultancy were a legally enforced profession, than admission criteria would constitute an entry barrier. Only entrants that would meet the required knowledge and skills standards would be allow to practice as management consultants. Because management consultancy is not a (legally enforced) profession, anyone may call themselves a management consultant. An increasing number of people are deciding to become sole practitioners. Calling yourself a management consultant, developing a website, and creating a business card are relatively easy. The proof of the pudding is in the eating: acquiring and retaining clients is the real challenge.

Expected retaliation by incumbent firms represents another entry barrier. If established management consultancy firms can signal to new entrants that they can and will effectively protect their turf from the new entrants by lowering fees (often in a disguised form of lowering the amount of billed hours, or offering free services to clients), then new entrants may be discouraged.

Substitutes

One substitute for management consultancy is that the buyer (client) does the problem solving and solution implementation themselves. This is the make-or-buy decision: do-it-yourself or hire an external management consultant. The buyer may do the consultancy work themselves. An alternative is that the buyer establishes an internal consultancy unit. Another substitute for management consultancy is staffing companies, such as Eden McCallum. Instead of hiring a management consultancy firm, the buyer puts together a team of alumni.

DETERMINANTS OF SUBSTITUTION THREAT   Table 5.6 outlines the determinants of a substitution threat.

Relative price performance of substitutes. The relative price of the buyer's do-it-yourself alternatives does not only refer to the production costs but also to transaction costs. External management consultancy may carry high transaction costs for buyers (see Chapter 3). The relative performance of client management do-it-yourself alternatives depends on the knowledge and skills of the buyer (management and professional staff).

Switching costs. If switching costs are low for the buyer then the substitution threat will be higher than when these costs are high. If clients

TABLE 5.6 *Determinants of substitution threat*

Determinants of substitution threat	Comment	Reduces substitution threat	Increases substitution threat
Relative price performance of substitutes	Ratio of price to performance of substitutes relative to management consultancy	Inferior ratio of price to performance of substitutes	Superior ratio of price to performance of substitutes
Switching costs	Cost of switching from management consultancy to substitute	High switching costs	Low switching costs
Buyer propensity to substitute	Likelihood of buyers to switch from management consultancy to substitutes	Weak buyer propensity to substitute	Strong buyer propensity to substitute

Source: based on Porter (1985)

do not have long-term obligations with external management consultancy firms, then they can stop hiring them without incurring costs.

Buyer propensity to substitute raises the substitution threat. If buyers of management consultancy have a high propensity to switch to substitutes, then the threat of these substitutes will be higher than when the propensity is low. This propensity will vary by buyer.

KEY DEVELOPMENTS

In this section we sketch four developments that have (had) a significant influence on the competitive forces in the management consultancy industry (see Figure 5.7). The first is the convergence of management consultancy with other related industries; second is the globalization of supply and demand; third is the development of information and communication technology; and fourth is the maturation of demand (in particular geographies).

Industry convergence

The history of the management consultancy industry shows firms from other industries entering the management consultancy industry. Until the 1930s, when new legislation was introduced, accountants and banks used to be active in US management consultancy. In the 1950s, accountancy firms returned to management consultancy. This time, they focused on IT consultancy rather than management auditing. In the 1990s, the management

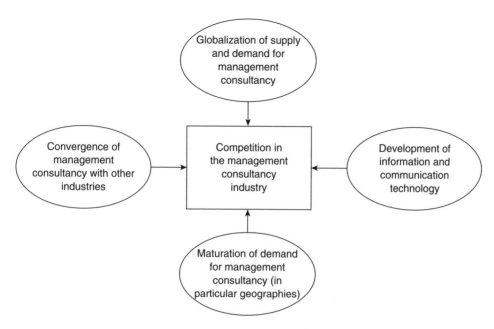

FIGURE 5.7 *Four key developments impacting competition in management consultancy*

consultancy industry witnessed the entry of large computer firms. These computer firms expanded their offerings of hardware, software, and IT services with management consultancy. As some firms succeeded in carving out consultancy staffing as a separate offering, the staffing industry enters the management consultancy industry.

We also found management consultancy firms expanding in other industries. An example is the IT consultancy firms that entered the outsourcing industry. Another example is strategy and organization consultancy firms, such as Bain & Company, entering the private equity industry.

Globalization

Regarding the globalization of management consultancy, we may distinguish three consequences: the opening up of new geographic markets, outsourcing and offshoring, and the emergence of global networks.

OPENING UP OF NEW GEOGRAPHIC MARKETS   Towards the end of the 1980s and in the 1990s, former state socialist economies, such as the Soviet Union, China, and Eastern European countries, transformed towards becoming a market capitalist system. This transformation was accompanied by market liberalization, industry deregulation, and the privatization of former state-owned companies. These developments stimulated the demand for (Western) management consultancy firms. This growth in demand reduced the rivalry among management consultancy firms.

OUTSOURCING AND OFFSHORING   The increasing integration in the 1990s of product, factor, and capital markets across national borders led to shifting patterns of trade and production. Outsourcing and foreign direct investment, including the offshoring of production and other value-adding activities, became common practices. Management consultancy firms benefited from the associated demand for advice on these practices. Again, the growth in demand reduced internal rivalry. The management consultancy industry also embraced the opportunities of outsourcing and offshoring. Some management consultancy firms outsourced non-core activities such as administrative services and graphics (presentation) production to third party services providers. Some Western IT consultancies moved part of their administrative and production activities off-shore to lower-cost locations.

GLOBAL NETWORKS   To serve global clients and seize opportunities in the emerging markets, management consultancy firms needed to operate on a global scale. Opening offices around the world was one approach to building a global presence. Management consultancy firms that did not have the resources for setting up offices abroad had the option of establishing alliances with foreign consultancies. Together national consultancy firms had the option to form international networks which could compete with the global consultancy firms.

Development of information technology

The 1950s witnessed the spread of computers as organizations, outside the defence sector, adopted computers. The use of computers led to new buyer problems and opportunities. In response to these new buyer needs, a new management consultancy service emerged: IT consultancy. Information and communications technologies contributed to the knowledge economy. The knowledge economy implied new products, services, and business models for buyers, as well as management consultancy firms. Information technology stimulated the demand for management consultancy. Technological developments continued to create new buyer problems and opportunities. For instance, in the 2000s, many buyers went on-line. Growth in the demand for consultancy implied a reduction of internal rivalry. However, the opportunity of IT consultancy also induced new entries into the management consultancy industry.

NEW ENTRANTS   Chapter 2 discussed why new consultancy firms, rather than the traditional strategy, organization, and operations consultancy firms, seized the opportunity of entering IT consultancy. The size of demand

and the nature of the services induced a larger scale for consultancy firms. Therefore, IT consultancy firms were typically much larger than the traditional consultancy firms. For some time, IT consultancy firms and the traditional consultancy firms co-existed as separate strategic groups in the consultancy industry. However, in many cases, IT, organization, strategy, and operations problems cannot be separated. When buyers increasingly demanded integrated solutions to their intertwined IT, organization, strategy, and operations problems, the consultancy firms had to respond. IT consultancy firms strived to add organization, strategy, and operations to their offerings. Traditional strategy and organization consultancies attempted to expand their offerings with IT services. Both groups faced (considerable) difficulties entering the new domains because of the large differences in elements of the business models, such as client relations, consultancy resources, consultancy economics, and consultancy reputations (please refer to the discussion in Chapter 2). As the two groups of consultancy firms entered their respective domains, the internal rivalry increased. Because of the differences between the firms, the diversity of competition also increased. This increased diversity then aggravated the rivalry among consultancy firms.

OUTSOURCING Some large IT consultancies also added services beyond the domain of management consultancy. These firms crossed the boundaries of management consultancy and expanded into outsourcing. The IT consultancies' offerings expanded from advice and implementation assistance, to running client IT operations. In particular, IT operations outsourcing is relatively capital intensive. The entry into outsourcing therefore meant a substantial rise in the capital needs of these firms. These funding needs exceeded the resources of private firms. The combined consultancy and outsourcing firms turned to the capital markets to fund their outsourcing business. Consultancy and outsourcing firms are typically publicly owned, listed corporations. Traditional strategy and organization consultancies are typically privately owned firms with partnership structures.

BUSINESS MODEL INNOVATION Information and communication technologies also affected the offerings of management consultancy firms and the way they operate. We have already discussed how management consultancy firms codified their knowledge into procedures and software products. IT thus enabled the expansion of consultancy offerings with software. The internet enabled new opportunities for the web-based delivery of management consultancy services to clients. Technological developments allowed for new business models in the management consultancy industry. The traditional delivery of consultancy services is through the personal interaction of consultants and clients. However, some client problems may also be solved online. The suitability of online models of consultancy depends, among other things, on the codifiability of the knowledge and on the client's need for trust. If understanding and solving the client problem involves tacit knowledge, then human interaction is necessary. Online communication is less suited to exchanging tacit knowledge. If trust plays an important role for clients, then online consultancy is less suitable here.

ONLINE CONSULTANCY   Online consultancy may take two forms. First, management consultants in remote locations interact via the internet with the client to solve the client's problem. This type of online consultancy is based on the offshoring of management consultancy. Offshoring management consultancy allows management consultancy firms to tap into an expanded, international labour pool. Second, software may solve the client's problem. In this option, the human delivery of services is substituted by a software-based delivery. Clients may use the consultancy firm's online software products to diagnose and solve their problems. Such an offering resembles an automated version of the facilitator's role of management consultants. An example is McKinsey Solutions.

Market maturation

Management consultancy emerged in the United States during the late nineteenth century. In the early twenty-first century, the market for management consultancy was maturing, at least in some geographies, including the United States, Japan, and Western Europe. In the maturing geographies, we distinguish several consequences for competition among consultancy firms. In this section we outline the consequences of market maturation for:

1. management consultancy practices
2. buyers
3. the alumni of management consultancy firms
4. the products of management consultancy.

MATURATION AND MANAGEMENT CONSULTANCY PRACTICES

Need for marketing. New geographies and IT consultancy, as described in Chapter 2, fuelled the growth of management consultancy. However, demand from traditional geographies (mainly Western markets) for traditional services (operations, organization, and strategy) witnessed stagnating growth. Stagnating growth led to increasing competition. Because of stagnating growth, management consultancy firms needed to (aggressively) market their services. In the past, most consultancy firms only used advertising to fill vacancies. Nowadays, some firms engage (heavily) in advertising and promotion to stimulate sales.

Deepening client relations. Because developing new clients in a stagnating market is becoming increasingly difficult, management consultancy firms seek to maintain relations with their current clients. Instead of acquiring new clients and working on a single project basis, management consultancy firms strive to develop long-term relations with their current clients and do projects on a continuous basis. Management consultancy firms focus on a smaller client basis for which they do more work. Repeat business is a growing share of management consultancies' work. Relatedly, client intimacy is becoming an increasingly important client value proposition for consultancies.

MATURATION AND BUYER BEHAVIOUR

Buyer experience. A mature management consultancy market means that (most) buyers have (substantial) experience with management consultancy services. This experience leads to buyer information. Repeat buyers are therefore better informed about what management consultancies do. Moreover, some buyers have employed former consultants, that is the alumni from the management consultancy firms. These alumni have switched from the supply side to the buy side of consultancy. The buyers who employ alumni benefit from the knowledge of these professionals. Experience from prior consultancy projects and employing alumni enable buyers to better assess consultancy services and consultancy firms. Experienced buyers know what to demand from consultants and how to manage their relationship with consultants. This buyer information in its turn raises buyer power. Some buyers have formalized their procurement of management consultancy services. They have specialist procurement professionals who select and negotiate with management consultancy firms.

Diminishing demand for doctors. Experienced buyers need different management consultants roles from those of inexperienced buyers. Inexperienced buyers may need the doctor consultant who has to identify the problem for the buyer. Experienced buyers may be able to identify the problems themselves. They may hire consultants to provide specific expertise. Demand shifts from the doctor to the expert role. Moreover, experienced clients may decide to solve their problems themselves and hire management consultants to facilitate the problem solving process. This implies the management consultant as facilitator.

From reports to results. Buyer experience has also contributed to buyers becoming more sensitive to the impact of management consultancy on their performance. This sensitivity to consultancy impact also adds to buyer power. In the past, it was common that management consultancy was limited to providing advice. The management consultants produced a report for the client and left. The consultancy report was the final product supplied by the management consultancy. Clients had to implement the consultants' recommendations themselves. Clients have become more focused on performance. As a result, they focus more on the impact of consultancy on their performance. They are not satisfied with reports, they want results. Recommendations are no longer sufficient. Clients demand from consultants that they implement their recommendations. As a consequence, management consultancy has evolved from advice to advice and assistance with management's tasks of implementation. The industry is moving away from our narrow definition of management consultancy (advice only) towards a broad definition (advice and assistance).

MATURATION AND ALUMNI

Rising alumni pool. Most management consultancy firms have a so-called 'up-or-out' career policy for consultants. Consultants are evaluated on a regular basis. Based on these evaluations, and the consultancy firm's vacancies, consultants either get promotion to a higher level or they have to leave the consultancy firm (Chapter 9 will elaborate on this human resource policy). At regular intervals, consultants have to face the up-or-out decision. Because of the pyramidal organization structure of most consultancy firms, the up-or-out policy implies a relatively high turnover of consultancy personnel and a steady stream of alumni. Management consultancies with an up-or-out policy typically have (much) more alumni than consultants. The growing pool of alumni may affect competitive forces in several ways. One example is the Eden McCallum case. If alumni establish rival management consultancy firms, than the internal rivalry among management consultancy firms will increase. Alumni contribute to new entries into the industry. If alumni join the buyers of management consultancy services, then two consequences for competitive forces may be distinguished.

Alumni as advocates. Alumni may become advocates for their previous employers, the management consultancies. Depending on their hierarchical position, these advocate alumni may hire, or stimulate the hiring of, their former employer for consultancy projects at their new employer. Such behaviour may lower the buyer's price sensitivity and hence lower the buyer's power. For this reason, management consultancy firms spend substantial time and effort in maintaining (strong) relations with their alumni.

Alumni as demanding clients. Alumni may also turn into the most critical and demanding clients of management consultancies. Alumni have more knowledge of how management consultancy firms operate than buyers without experience inside consultancies. Alumni therefore know better how to get the most value from the consultancy firms. Alumni contribute to buyer information and thus buyer power. Buyers may employ alumni to professionalize the procurement of management consultancy services and to better manage the relationship with management consultancy firms.

MATURATION AND PRODUCTS

Commoditization. Mature industries have lower product innovation rates than young industries. Over the life cycle of an industry, the rate of product innovation typically diminishes. When management consultancy emerged as an industry, all client problems were new. The need for innovation was therefore high. Management consultants had to innovate.

They had to explore solutions for new client problems. This corresponds with the brain type of consultancy. Over time the share of problems that are new to consultants diminishes. Of course, new developments inside and outside client organizations may lead to new problems and opportunities. An example is the rise of the internet during the 1990s and the emergence of a so-called 'new economy'. This new economy presented problems and opportunities that were new to clients and consultants alike. However, overall the tendency is that the share of new problems in the total set of annual consultancy projects declines. As a result the balance in the consultancy industry shifts from knowledge exploration to knowledge exploitation. As management consultants strive to codify their knowledge into software in order to better exploit their intellectual property then the consultancy industry moves to software-based consultancy. Codification may contribute to the commoditization of consultancy. Codified knowledge is more vulnerable to imitation. Imitation by rival consultancies will turn the procedure into a commodity product. Price will become increasingly important. Commoditization means that product differences between consultancy firms diminish. As a result, the internal rivalry between firms increases proportionally. Moreover, decreasing product differences mean increasing buyer power. As a result, the price pressure will increase.

Disaggregation and specialization. Another development concerns the disaggregation of the management consultancy's activities. In the past, management consultancy firms offered complete packages of activities. They sold consultancy projects to clients, they designed these projects, they staffed the projects with their own consultants, and these consultants executed all necessary tasks of the projects. In the 2000s, new offerings became increasingly visible. New entrants competed with specialized, modular offerings. As a result, the industry witnessed an increasing specialization in offerings, for example, consultancy firms that focused on selling and designing consultancy projects while outsourcing their execution to contractors. Such contractors may include consultancy firms that specialize in data collection and analysis. Another example is firms that concentrate on staffing projects. Eden McAllum is an example of such a staffing specialist. There are even consultancy firms that specialize in offering clients to select and manage other consultancy firms. New entrants and the resulting increase in diversity of competition lead to an increase in the intensity of competition in the consultancy industry.

SUMMARY

This chapter provided a brief introduction to the competitive strategies that are common in the management consultancy industry. In this knowledge-intensive industry, knowledge exploration and exploitation fulfil an important role in competitive strategy. Knowledge exploration allows for differentiation strategies.

Cost competition increases with knowledge commodification. Besides product differentiation and cost competition, we can distinguish client intimacy as a value proposition for management consultancies.

To deepen understanding of the competitive forces in management consultancy, we investigated the underlying determinants of each individual force. For each of the determinants, we made an interpretation of the specific context of the management consultancy industry. We showed how the determinant may reduce or increase the competitive force in the management consultancy industry. Students may use these interpretations to conduct a competitive forces analysis for a specific strategic group of consultancy firms, or a specific geography.

The chapter outlines the impact of four key developments in competitive forces.

First, the *convergence* of management consultancy and some other industries, such as accountancy, computers, and private equity, induced blurred boundaries for management consultancy.

Second, *globalization* not only led to the opening up of new geographic markets but also induced outsourcing and offshoring. Consultancy firms responded to globalization by, among others, building global networks.

Third, the development of *information technology* created a new area of consultancy and induced new entries into the industry. IT induced new business models in management consultancy.

Fourth, *market maturation*, at least in some geographies, affects the practices of consultancy firms and the behaviour of buyers. Market maturation is accompanied by the rise of alumni pools and the commoditization of management consultancy products.

REFLECTIVE QUESTIONS

1. Take the example of one of the top tier management consultants, such as McKinsey & Company, Bain & Company, or the Boston Consulting Group. How do you evaluate the attractiveness of the management consultancy industry from the perspective of this individual firm? Do the key developments described in this chapter make the management consultancy industry more or less attractive for this firm? Argue why or why not.

2. Explain how increasing buyer price sensitivity may influence the competitive strategy of a management consultancy firm.

3. Describe the relationship between market maturation in certain geographies and the power of suppliers in these geographies. Explain your answer.

4. How can a management consultancy firm curb buyer power? Give three suggestions.

The invasion of foreign firms

The business model

Visor Partners is the leading management consultancy boutique in ResourceCountry. ResourceCountry is a country that is very rich in natural resources. A few state-controlled and state-owned corporations that exploit these resources dominate the national economy. Visor Partners has very strong relationships with the executive management of these corporations. The consultancy boutique also has strong ties with the powerful ResourceCountry's government and governmental institutions. The firm could develop such a strong network because of its specific human resource strategy. The boutique offers partnerships to retired executives of ResourceCountry's corporations and governmental institutions. Visor relies on the networks that these executives bring with them. All partners of Visor have strong client networks, are very senior, and have rich experience in management. When advising clients, they rely on their managerial experience.

New entrants

Until two years ago, Visor Partners was highly successful. The firm all but monopolized the domestic market for giving advice to the general management of the leading corporations and governmental institutions of ResourceCountry. Two years ago, most of Visor's corporate clients shifted their focus from domestic business to international business. The international ambitions and the huge financial resources to fund their ambitions made these corporations attractive for international management consultancy firms. At that time, the first foreign management consultancy firms began to approach Visor Partners' client base. None of the international consultancies had an office in ResourceCountry. Most firms had, until then, not worked for ResourceCountry's organizations. During the previous two years, the big three international consultancies started to make inroads into Visor Partners' business.

New approach

These foreign consultancy firms applied a radically different approach from that of Visor. The firms offered young consultants, often business school graduates, who worked strictly according to their firm's globally standardized approach. The disciplined approach guaranteed high-quality, high-consistency services. To make things worse for Visor Partners, the fees for which the international firms were prepared to work, were significantly below Visor's going rates. It had already lost a couple of prestigious consultancy projects to the foreign firms. How could they turn the tide?

▶

Questions

1 How would you describe Visor Partners in terms of: a) the type of consultancy, b) the client value proposition, and c) the competitive strategy? Explain your answer.

2 How would you describe the big three international management consultancy firms that target Visor Partners' clients in terms of: a) the type of consultancy, b) the value proposition, and c) the competitive strategy? Compare, on the one hand, Visor Partners, and on the other hand, the big three international management consultancy firms. What are the implications of these differences for Visor Partners?

3 Assume Visor Partners asks you for advice about what to do. Can Visor Partners respond to these foreign consultancy firms? If so, how should they respond? If not, what is the alternative for Visor Partners? Provide argumentation.

FURTHER READING

Armbrüster, T. (2006) *The Economics and Sociology of Management Consulting*. Cambridge: Cambridge University Press.

Christensen, C.M., Wang, D. and van Bever, D. (2013) 'Consulting on the cusp of disruption', *Harvard Business Review*, 91(10): 106–114.

McKenna, C.D. (2006) *The World's Newest Profession: Management Consulting in the Twentieth Century*. New York: Cambridge University Press.

REFERENCES

Birkinshaw, J. (2006) 'A balanced approach: Eden McCallum puts the word "networking" to a different use', *Financial Times*, 20 November.

Business Strategy Review (2007) 'Making the firm flexible', Spring, 72–75.

Maister, D.H. (1982) 'Balancing the professional firm', *Sloan Management Review*, 24 (1): 15–29.

Porter, M. (1985) *Competitive Advantage: Creating and Sustaining Superior Performance*. New York: Free Press.

Treacy, M. and Wiersema, F. (1993) 'Customer intimacy and other value disciplines', *Harvard Business Review*, January–February, 84–93.

6

MACRO-DEVELOPMENTS AND THE MANAGEMENT CONSULTANCY INDUSTRY

INTRODUCTION

The previous chapter explored the industry environment. This chapter moves beyond the industry boundaries, to research the *macro*-environment. First, we examine the impact of macro-economic (business) cycles on the management consultancy industry. Second, we explore how technological developments influence the consultancy industry, in particular the technological developments that induce the transformation to a knowledge society. As an example, the chapter offers a case study about the impact of ICT-driven disruption on management consultancy. Third, we investigate the cluster of industries that create and disseminate management knowledge, of which management consultancy is a part. Finally, we investigate how the globalization of markets (product, factor, and capital markets) and the geographic spreading of capitalism in the 1980s and 1990s affected the management consultancy industry. The chapter ends with a summary, reflective questions, a mini case study, suggested further reading, and references.

Main learning objectives

- Analyse the implications for management consultancy of macro-economic trends, in particular the business cycle.

- Analyse the implications for management consultancy of the macro-development towards a knowledge society.
- Explain why management consultancy revenues accelerated in the 1980s.
- Critically reflect upon the cluster of industries that create and disseminate management knowledge.
- Relate the different industries and actors within these industries in the management knowledge cluster.
- Evaluate the effect of management fashion on the different actors in the management knowledge cluster.
- Understand the impact of macro-political developments on management consultancy, in particular the geographical spreading of capitalism in the 1980s and 1990s.
- Critically reflect upon the statement that management consultants are 'carriers of US management models'.

THE IMPACT OF BUSINESS CYCLES ON MANAGEMENT CONSULTANCY

Demand during the cycle

The first chapter presented the popular analogy of management consultants as medical doctors. Management consultants like to be compared with medical doctors. Just as doctors cure sick patients, management consultants cure 'sick' organizations. The more serious the problems of organizations, the more they will need the help of consultants. The more frequently organizations have problems, the more they will need the help of management consultants. Economies typically display cycles which consist of upturns of economic growth or expansion and downturns of stagnation and decline. In the downturn of the business cycle, the number of troubled companies will peak. Because troubled companies are potential clients for consultants, we expect the demand for consultants to peak in the downturn of the business cycle. In the upturn of the cycle the number of troubled companies will reach a low and we may expect the demand for consultancy to bottom out. Demand for management consultancy is expected to be countercyclical to the business cycles of the economy.

Medical doctor metaphor

Several researchers have investigated the relationship between the development of the economy and the development of the demand for management consultancy (see Armbrüster, 2006). The findings of these studies do not support the countercyclical pattern that the medical doctor metaphor suggests. To the contrary, management consultancy demand develops pro-cyclically to the business cycle (Armbrüster, 2006). The cycles of management consultancy demand are more pronounced than the business cycles. In the business cycle upturns, the growth of demand for consultancy outpaces economic growth. In the downturn of the business cycle, the consultancy demand declines faster than the economy. How may we explain these counter-intuitive results?

Hiring reasons

Demand for management consultancy may be explained in terms of the reasons for hiring consultants. Chapter 3 outlined the main hiring reasons, including knowledge provision, solving problems and seizing opportunities, argumentation for client decisions, validation of client decisions, and finally, taking the blame for client decisions. As we can see, the role of management consultants is not limited to curing sick patients, it is also about helping clients seize opportunities. Except for the reason of problem solving, all other reasons are formulated in neutral terms: they may apply to client problems but also to opportunities.

Business cycles

Let us assume that the number of problems and opportunities of clients balance out on average. In economic downturns, we may expect the number of cost problems to reach a peak and the number of growth opportunities to reach a low, whereas in upturns the pattern is expected to be the opposite. If we assume that the number of problems and opportunities will balance out over business cycles, than we may expect a flat demand for management consultancy. However, demand is pro-cyclical. Empirical evidence indicates that during the move from downturn to upturn the demand for consultancy accelerates. This coincides with the assumed shift in the composition of client issues from problems to opportunities. During the shift to a downturn, when client issues switch from opportunities to problems, the opposite occurs. These developments raise the questions: is it the nature of client issues that counts? How does the nature of client issues influence the demand for management consultancy?

The nature of client issues and the demand for consultancy

Let us assume that client problems in economic downturns are about losses. Solving the problems of client companies in an economic downturn

AN INTRODUCTION TO MANAGEMENT CONSULTANCY

implies reducing costs. The other route to profit improvement, that is revenue growth, is less probable in a downturn. Reducing costs is mostly a grey hair problem, or even more likely a procedural problem. Most problems concerning high costs are not new to consultants. Consultants will probably have experience and procedures for cost reduction. The same may also apply to the client organization. Therefore cost problems represent less demand for the *formal* roles of management consultants: providing knowledge, developing solutions for problems and opportunities, and facilitating clients' solution development. Clients may do this themselves. They may only need management consultants for *informal* roles: in particular, for taking the blame, and providing legitimation for unpopular decisions to reduce costs. Prior research concluded that management consultancy is more opportunity-driven than problem-driven (Armbrüster, 2006). To sum up, we hypothesize that the ratio of opportunities to problems influences the demand for (the formal roles of) management consultancy. We expect that the demand for consultancy increases with the ratio of opportunities to problems (see the horizontal axis of Figure 6.1).

Discretionary financial resources

Not only do clients with (cost) problems in economic downturns have less need for the formal roles of management consultants, due to their (cost) problems, they also cannot afford management consultants, or at least, they will have less to spend on consultancy. In a downturn, the typical first reaction of organizations is to lower expenditure in areas that can be cut easily. Consultancy is one of them. Clients can shorten consultancy projects, defer them or cancel them.

These two hypothesized factors, less need for (formal) management consultancy in a downturn and less discretionary financial resources to spend on consultancy during a downturn, might explain the pronounced downturn in consultancy demand during the downturn of the economy (see 'trough' in Figure 6.1 on the next page).

Economic upturn

In an economic upturn, the two hypothesized factors, the clients' opportunity-to-problems ratio and the amount of discretionary financial resources of the clients, explain the pattern of management consultancy demand. In an upturn in the business cycle, the number of opportunities for client companies rises. Let us assume the opportunities in upturns are typically about revenue growth. Compared to reducing costs in a downturn, finding new revenue growth in an upturn requires more new knowledge. Identifying and seizing new opportunities requires innovative thinking. These are brain types of client issues. Therefore, it is more

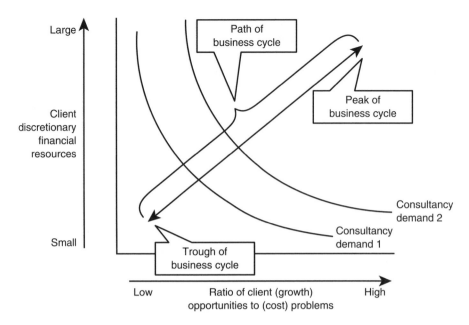

FIGURE 6.1 *Hypothesized demand for management consultancy during a business cycle*

Note: 'Consultancy demand 1' is an isoquant representing all combinations of discretionary financial resources and ratios of opportunities and costs that generate the same level of demand. The level of demand of 'Consultancy demand 2' exceeds that of 'Consultancy demand 1'.

probable that clients will look for specialists in a brain type of solution development. The need for management consultancy will grow. Moreover, during an upturn, clients will have more financial resources to spend on management consultancy than in a downturn. These two factors, the high opportunity-to-problems ratio and the large amount of resources to spend, may explain the pronounced upturn in consultancy demand during the upturn in the economy (see 'peak' in Figure 6.1).

Demand for management consultancy moves from trough to peak and back to trough during a single business cycle (see 'path' in Figure 6.1). To conclude, in Figure 6.1, the demand for management consultancy oscillates between the peak and trough point. The figure presents a hypothetical explanation for the pro-cyclical nature of consultancy. The more recent economic crises – that is the crisis as a result of the 2000–2001 dotcom crash, the 2007–2009 global financial crisis as a result of the US subprime mortgages, and the European sovereign-debt crisis which broke out in 2010 and is still ongoing – confirm the pro-cyclical nature of demand for management consultancy. These crises severely hit management consultancy revenues.

THE IMPACT OF TECHNOLOGICAL WAVES ON MANAGEMENT CONSULTANCY

The history of management consultancy shows the role of technology developments and the related opportunities as drivers of the demand for management consultancy. Technological developments follow a wave-like pattern. Whereas business cycles take periods of around ten years, these technological waves may last for decades. We outline below the most important technological waves since the mid-nineteenth century, which marked the beginning of the second industrial revolution.

The second industrial revolution

Chapter 2 describes how management consultancy emerged in response to the management challenges of the second industrial revolution, which took place in the second half of the nineteenth century. New technological developments, such as the steam engine and the railroad, opened up new opportunities for firms. The management of these firms needed specialist help to achieve the full potential of the new production technologies. This opportunity led to scientific management and related operations consultancy.

Steel, electricity and the internal combustion engine

From the late nineteenth century until the beginning of the Second World War, another cycle of technological developments took place, which included steel production, the use of electricity, the internal combustion engine, pharmaceutical discoveries (penicillin), and mass production techniques. These developments led to the rise of big corporations. The increasing scale and scope of these corporations induced the development of the multi-divisional form. That development then stimulated organization consultancy (see Chapter 2).

Oil, semi-conductors, plastics

From the Second World War to the early 1980s, the most important technological developments concerned oil, plastics, commercial aviation, new pharmaceutical drugs, and semi-conductors, and the latter enabled consumer electronics and business computers. These technological innovations created new opportunities for business, which in turn stimulated the demand for management consultancy. The diversification of companies in different businesses created the need for corporate portfolio management, which in its turn stimulated the rise of strategy consultancy. One innovation, the business computer, induced information technology (IT) consultancy.

Information and telecommunications, and biotechnology

Since the early 1980s, the most important technological developments have concentrated on information processing and telecommunications, biotechnology, and robots. The early 1980s saw the introduction of the IBM personal computer (PC). In the 1990s, the internet was commercialized. These technological developments stimulated the demand for management consultancy, and in particular, IT consultancy.

Towards a knowledge society

These technological developments induced the transformation of society. The industrial revolutions transformed the agricultural society into an industrial one. The information and telecommunications revolutions of the 1980s and 1990s marked the transformation into a post-industrial society. That transformation however does not comprise all countries. Countries vary in their stage of technological and economic development. Today, some still resemble agricultural societies, whereas others have an industrial profile. However, the most advanced countries have already transformed into knowledge societies. These are typically innovation-driven economies (World Economic Forum, 2013). In agricultural societies, natural resources and labour constitute the most important production factors. In an industrial society, capital is the most important factor.

Management knowledge

The most important production factor in the post-industrial society is knowledge. In a post-industrial society, companies and countries increasingly compete on the basis of knowledge. Knowledge and innovation favour management consultancy. We have seen that management consultancy benefits from (technological) opportunities. Moreover, management consultancy is a highly knowledge-intensive service. Management consultants know how to explore and exploit knowledge. This becomes increasingly relevant as knowledge becomes more important in a society. Management consultants may play an important role in the development and dissemination of knowledge, and in particular one type of knowledge: management knowledge.

Management consultancy and ICT-driven disruption

ICT-driven disruption of client industries

The spread of computers in the 1960s led to a new area of management consultancy: information technology (IT) consultancy. New developments in information and (tele) communications technologies (ICT) during the 1990s resulted in a boom in demand for management consultancy, and a subsequent bust, during the early 2000s.

In the mid-1990s, the internet and in particular the World Wide Web was commercialized. The internet enhanced the potential for connectivity between computers, irrespectively where they were located on the world. This connectivity potential created many and large opportunities for both profit and non-profit organisations. Internet allowed new business models to compete more effectively and more efficiently. 'E-business' was born. New internet-based firms, known as 'dot-coms', disrupted many industries. In some industries, such as insurance, e-business disrupted the distribution channel through disintermediation. In other industries, like music and newspapers, it digitalized the product. In retail, the sales channel was digitalized as web shops substituted for brick-and-mortar stores.

Boom and bust of demand for management consultancy

TManagement of organizations in many industries were confronted with the challenges of the internet. Solving these challenges seemed to require truly new knowledge because the internet was thought to lead to a 'new economy' where the laws of the 'old economy' no longer seemed valid. Therefore these managers massively hired consultants to help them respond to the internet. Internet-projects meant brain type of consultancy as consultants' experience and existing procedures could not be used for these new challenges. The internet-revolution also stimulated the foundation of many new firms. These 'start-ups' often lacked the financial funds to afford management consultancy fees. Management consultants therefore adapted their remuneration model according to the needs of these new clients. Consultants introduced 'equity pay': they accepted payment in client equity. Some consultancies went further, and invested their own capital in these dot-coms, for example via a venture capital division. As not all consultancies were willing to go the direction of taking equity, quite a large number of consultants, including partners, set up their own (internet) firms.

The stocks of dot-coms and other firms with e-business activities benefited from the expectations-driven boom in demand by investors during the second half of the 1990s, which caused the dot-com bubble. However, in the 2000–2001 period dot-com stocks collapsed as it became clear that many expectations of the new economy were unrealistic. The burst of the bubble caused a slump in demand for internet-related management consultancy projects. Consultancies that had invested in dot-com start-ups were in particular hit, as they had to write-off their investments.

ICT-driven disruption of the management consultancy industry[1]

During the second half of the 2000s, ICT started to disrupt the management consultancy industry. The established management consultancy firms with their traditional business model of consultancy projects delivered by a team of a manager and a couple of junior consultants, faced the entry of new firms with modular – web-based – consultancy offerings based on software and data assets. This disruption was driven by three forces. *First*, during the 2000s, the ICT-driven growth of data in organizations and sectors led to the rise of 'big data', which are very large and complex data sets that are difficult if not impossible to analyse with traditional tools and techniques. Moreover, while the collection of data was a major part of the consultancy job in the previous decades, the access to data was democratized in the 2000s. *Second*, the challenge of big data led to

the development of predictive technology – e.g. artificial intelligence algorithms – and other big data analytics. This automation of knowledge work allowed more efficient, faster and more complex data analysis then traditional consultancy teams could achieve. *Three*, the 2000s witnessed increasing sophistication of clients with management consultancy as a result of:

- Their accumulated experience with consultancy.
- Their hiring of alumni of – top tier – consultancy firms.
- The increased level of – business – education of client management.

Sophistication increased clients' cost consciousness and reduced their reliance on the consultancies' brand names, reputations and legitimacy, which are the traditional strengths of the established firms. The sophisticated clients know what analyses are required to solve their issues, and realize that not every issue requires a consultancy project manager plus two junior consultants three months to solve it[2].

The alternative business models for consultancy include the value-added process business and the facilitated network. These models do not cover the entire value proposition of the established consultancy firms but focus on specific parts.

---

[1] The section on disruption of management consultancy draws heavily on Christensen, Wang and van Bever (2013).

[2] Dominique Barton, Global Managing Director of McKinsey and Company in an interview on Harvard Business Review Blog Network with Clayton Christensen, professor of business administration at Harvard Business School. http://blogs.hbr.org/2013/09/clay-christensen-and-dominic-barton-on-consultings-disruption/ (accessed 7 October, 2013)

The value-added process business can be internet-based consultancy products to solve problems of defined scope with standard processes. Motista, Salesforce.com and McKinsey Solutions are some examples of this model. Facilitated networks model enable the exchange of consultancy services, for instance assembling leaner project teams of alumni of the top tier management consultancy firms who have become freelance consultants. Eden McCallum is an example of a network model. The new firms with their alternative business models typically focus first on smaller clients and less complex issues that are not the traditional target markets of the established consultancy firms. However, it is a characteristic of disruptive innovation that disruptors trade-up over time.

Discussion questions

1 How do you evaluate the role of management consultancy firms in the boom and bust in the 1990s and early 2000s as result of the 'new economy'? Explain your answer.

2 Evaluate the 'equity pay' for management consultancies. What are the advantages and disadvantages? Elaborate on your answer.

3 How should established management consultancy firms with a traditional business model respond to the disruption of their industry? Explain your answer.

THE IMPACT OF MANAGEMENT KNOWLEDGE ON MANAGEMENT CONSULTANCY

Knowledge plays an increasingly important role in societies, in particular, in post-industrial societies. One type of knowledge is management knowledge. This is knowledge that is relevant for management. Management knowledge includes knowledge about business leadership and general management, strategy, organization, and the functional disciplines, such as accounting, finance, human resource management, information management, marketing management, operations management, and technology management.

Management knowledge is crucial for management consultants. Knowledge plays an important role in the clients' reasons for hiring management consultants and in the roles fulfilled by consultants. Management consultants use new knowledge, concepts, and techniques to sell their services to clients. Innovative knowledge gives the consultants legitimacy; it makes them credible in the eyes of the client (e.g. Alvesson, 1993). According to a more critical view, consultants talk clients into problems to sell their new solutions (Kieser, 2002). Examples of important knowledge for consultants throughout the history of the consultancy industry are: scientific management, the multi-divisional form of organization, the portfolio matrix, total quality management, business process re-engineering, and shareholder value management.

Management fashion

In the field of management knowledge, fashion plays an important role. Fashion may be defined as a change in tastes and convictions as a reaction to previous tastes and convictions (Blumer, 1969). Fashion is generally driven by the individual's need to demonstrate their uniqueness. This need is dominant for the innovators and early adopters (see Figure 6.2). Fashion also satisfies the need for general acceptance by the majority of customers. Adoption by the majority erodes the uniqueness of the innovators and early adopters, which fuels the need for a new fashion. As a result of the conflicting needs of different customer segments, we face a continuing succession of fashions.

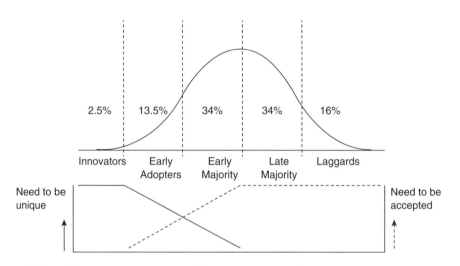

FIGURE 6.2 *Adoption curve of a management fashion*

Notes: The percentages in the upper graph refer to adoption curves in general, not to management consultancy in particular. In the lower graph, the solid line indicates the need for clients to be unique. The dotted line indicates the need for clients to be accepted.

Cycles of management fashion

Management knowledge may also follow a cyclical pattern. The field of management knowledge has seen many cycles of management fashion. One example of a management fashion is the technique of business process re-engineering. This management technique became popular in the 1990s. In 1990, a Massachusetts Institute of Technology (MIT) professor named Hammer published a breakthrough idea about BPR in the *Harvard Business Review*. In 1993, Hammer and a management consultant named Champy published a bestselling book about BPR, *Reengineering the Corporation*, and in 1995 Champy published another BPR bestseller, *Reengineering Management*. In the 2000s however, interest in BPR waned.

Another example is the balanced score card. In the early 1990s, a Harvard Business School professor named Kaplan, and a management consultant named Norton, together published a couple of articles about the balanced score card in leading professional magazines, among which was the *Harvard Business Review* (e.g. Kaplan and Norton, 1992). In 1996, Kaplan and Norton published a book, *The Balanced Score Card*, which became a bestseller. In the 1990s, this technique was widely adopted in the Western world. In the next decade, the technique diffused globally.

Concept development

Academic research on the development of new concepts by management consultants distinguishes three phases (Heusinkveld and Benders, 2002). The first phase comprises activities related to the set-up of innovative ventures by individual consultants within the consultancy firm who received their inspiration from client work. In the second phase, the consultancy firm forms and facilitates a group of people who do the concept development. The third phase consists of activities related to the dissemination of the concept throughout the firm and the concept's commercialization and implementation in client organizations. Another form of concept development is 'top down', that is the leadership of the consultancy firm decides to systematically develop new knowledge as part of the firm's strategy (Heusinkveld and Benders, 2002). The alternative is 'bottom up' concept development, which is by individual consultants and based on client work.

Decline of a fashion

Management fashion may be characterized as a relatively transitory collective belief by managers that a particular management technique will improve the performance of an organization (Abrahamson, 1996). The technique then receives a lot of attention in the management media (management sites, magazines, and books) for some years. Attention from managers also increases until a saturation point is reached, as shown in the adoption curve in Figure 6.2. Around the saturation point, the media lose interest. The focus of attention shifts to a new management technique. Why do management and the management media lose interest in a management technique? First, the technique has been widely adopted and success-fully implemented in practice. It has delivered on its performance claims, solved the management problem, or enabled management to seize an opportunity. As a result, the problem and opportunity move off the management agenda.

Second, the technique has been widely adopted, but its implementation in practice was not as successful as promised, or in the extreme case, the technique turned out to be a complete flop and has failed to deliver on its performance claims. Management starts searching for a new technique. This second pattern resembles the diet phenomenon. Diets also follow a fashion pattern of cycles. Because (most) consumers are not successful with a particular diet, the demand for diets is insatiable. On a regular basis, new diets are launched. Every failed diet creates the appetite for a new diet.

Success of management fashions

In management fashion, we (often) do not even know whether or not the new management technique is successful. Attention from management, and attention in the management media, do not necessarily mean that the management technique is also implemented in practice (Clark and Greatbatch, 2004; Nijholt and Benders, 2007). Even if managers (with the assistance of consultants) implemented the new technique in their practice, we may still lack knowledge about the performance impact of the new technique. A systematic evaluation is not possible because too many factors simultaneously influence the performance of organizations, and because the time lag between the implementation of a new management technique and the impact on the organization's performance may be relatively long (Jung and Kieser, 2012). Management fashions are typically introduced without empirical proof or evidence. Therefore, management fashions are defined as 'beliefs'. Because management cannot empirically verify whether a management technique was really successful, management remains uncertain about the technique's effects. This uncertainty creates the opportunity for new management fashions with new performance promises.

A critique on management consultants is that they reinforce recurrent cycles of management knowledge that do not lead to an accumulation of knowledge (Lammers, 1988). According to this critical view, consultants reinvent the wheel, or put old wine in new bottles. This view suggests that the introduction of 'new' knowledge by consultants primarily serves a marketing purpose.

Reinforcing loops

Figure 6.3 visualizes the mechanisms that fuel management fashion. First, the promise or claim that a new management technique will increase performance induces a demand by managers for the new management technique (relation 'a' in Figure 6.3). The competition will respond positively to the performance claim and, therefore, adopt the new management fashion ('b' in Figure 6.3). Adoption by the competition induces the demand for the new management fashion ('c' in Figure 6.3) for two alternative reasons. Innovators will face the need for the next management fashion when other organizations 'catch up' by adopting the management fashion. Non-leading organizations will be induced to adopt the management fashion once other firms have adopted this fashion. The non-leading organizations are motivated by imitating others. They prefer to follow the herd. Demand for the new fashion induces implementation of the fashion ('d' in Figure 6.3). If the effect of the management fashion is unclear, or even negative, then management will be open to another management fashion that promises better performance results ('e' in Figure 6.3).

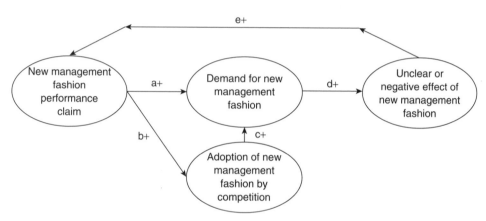

FIGURE 6.3 *Reinforcing loops in management fashion*

Motivations for buying management fashion

Why do managers adopt management fashion? There are several reasons.

A need for control. Many managers perceive that their organizations and the environment of their organizations have become increasingly complex and dynamic. This complexity and uncertainty create a (perceived) loss of control by managers (Ernst and Kieser, 2002). The need to secure and enhance control leads to a demand for management techniques. Management techniques may simplify complex management problems and thereby suggest the controllability of these problems. An example of such a technique is the growth-share matrix of the Boston Consulting Group. Some techniques provide a new frame of reference and a language that create the perception of control (Kieser, 2002). Take, for instance, business process re-engineering.

Need to innovate. Management fashions are often purposely vague so that the implementation process is not well covered and managers may interpret it in a way that fits them best (Benders and Van Veen, 2001). Moreover, managers are constantly in a tough competition for careers (Kieser, 2002). They are expected to innovate. Adopting a management fashion enables ambitious managers to innovate, without the investments and risks that are normally associated with innovation.

Need for legitimacy. In contrast, follower-managers adopt management fashions to gain legitimacy. They jump on the bandwagon of a management fashion, even if they doubt its effectiveness, because it is better to be collectively wrong than individually right. Moreover, in the case that the implementation of the fashion fails, management can blame others: 'We selected the right approach/model because it has been proven at company A and B, but it failed here because the management consultants did a bad job' (scapegoat). Furthermore, management fashions provide managers with legitimation for the decisions they would like to make. Management fashion may provide ideological framing and argumentation for a restructuring decision or an acquisition (Jung and Kieser, 2012).

THE MANAGEMENT KNOWLEDGE CLUSTER

The creation and dissemination of management knowledge

The substantial demand for management fashion makes it a lucrative business opportunity for various agents. Several industries are involved in the exploration and exploitation of management fashion and management knowledge in general. Management knowledge is a business. Both the exploration and exploitation of management knowledge can be viable businesses. Like pharmaceuticals, the agents in the cluster look for blockbusters. The next big management idea will be a great hit. Unlike pharmaceuticals, the developers of new management knowledge cannot get patent protection. Intellectual property is weakly protected against imitation by other agents in the management knowledge cluster. The 'management knowledge cluster' is the label for four connected industries involved in the creation and dissemination of management knowledge (Engwall and Kipping, 2002): management, management consultants, management education, and the management media. Figure 6.4 visualizes the four industries and their connections.

FIGURE 6.4 *Main knowledge flows in the management knowledge cluster*

Source: based on Engwall and Kipping (2002)

FLOWS OF KNOWLEDGE AND PEOPLE

We will first elaborate on the knowledge and people flows visualised in Figure 6.4. Subsequently, we will discuss the four industries in more detail.

Knowledge flows. Figure 6.4 shows the flows of knowledge in terms of research activities, publications, and consultancy and teaching by the agents in the different management knowledge industries. Research is about developing knowledge. Publications and teaching are about distributing knowledge. Consultancy can be both developing and distributing knowledge.

People flows. Besides research, publications, and services, knowledge also flows in terms of people. People may move from one management knowledge industry to another. For instance, former management consultants (the so-called alumni of the management consultancy firms) may become managers, or they may join business schools. Managers and business school professors may become management consultants. People are carriers of codified and tacit knowledge. For the readability of the figure, the people flows have been omitted.

Boundaries. The boundaries between the four industries are not as clear cut as Figure 6.4 suggests. Management consultants may be involved in education. For instance, part of the implementation of a recommendation may involve the training of client management. Some management consultants are part-time professors. Management scholars may be involved in management consultancy. Business school professors may combine education, research, and consultancy. They may be part-time consultants. They may have even founded their own management consultancy firm. For instance, a group of Harvard Business School professors established the management consultancy firm Monitor (acquired by Deloitte in 2012). Managers may be part-time professors, or they may give guest lectures at business schools.

MANAGEMENT GURUS   One very visible agent of management fashion is missing in Figure 6.4: the management guru. Management gurus do not constitute a separate category of agents, besides managers, management consultants, and management scholars. It is a role that can be found in each category. Management gurus are management thinkers who develop and promote new management knowledge. The guru role is different from management consulting. Management consultants provide advice and assistance with the management tasks of implementing advice. Management gurus develop and disseminate management knowledge. They disseminate their ideas through publications and live presentations. Whereas the business model of management consultants is based on client projects, the business model of management gurus is based on books and seminars. Management gurus are usually sole practitioners.

Three types of management gurus may be distinguished: academic gurus, consultant gurus, and hero managers (Huczynski, 1993). Michael Porter is an example of an academic guru. Porter is not only a management scholar and a management guru, but he is also a management consultant. He is co-founder of Monitor. An example of a consultant guru is Norton. This consultant created, together with Kaplan, the balanced score card. The first management hero was Lee Iacocca, a president of the Ford Motor Company in the 1970s, and a chief executive officer of the Chrysler Corporation from the late 1970s to 1980s. The emergence of the management hero, or 'celebrity CEO' (chief executive officer), in the 1980s may be attributed to the tendency to personalize the success of (big) corporations. Top management of these corporations got credited for the corporate successes. Remuneration for top management took off at that time. Managers became interested in learning from these stars of business. The rescue of automotive giant Chrysler in the 1980s is attributed to Iacocca. His 1984 book, *Iacocca:*

An Autobiography, became a bestseller. In the 1980s, more managers began to publish their management knowledge for the general public.

Management

The first industry of the management knowledge cluster is management.

USERS OF MANAGEMENT KNOWLEDGE   Managers are users, or consumers, of management knowledge. We have already discussed several motivations for using management fashion. An additional motivation is based on publicity. Previous research (Staw and Epstein, 2000) found that companies which were reported to have adopted management fashion were *perceived* to be better managed and more innovative than their peers, which were not reported to have implemented management fashion. Implementation of management fashion may also positively influence the perception of financial analysts and investors (Jung and Kieser, 2012).

PRODUCERS OF MANAGEMENT KNOWLEDGE   Managers can also be sources, or producers, of management knowledge. Various management innovations have been developed by managers. For instance, scientific management was developed by Taylor, while he was a manager, which is before he became a consultant. The multi-divisional form is another example of new management knowledge that was developed by managers. Both techniques have been subsequently adopted and diffused by management consultants.

Management consultants

The second industry of the management knowledge cluster is management consultants.

PRODUCERS AND USERS OF MANAGEMENT KNOWLEDGE   Management consultancy is about management knowledge. Management consultancies are knowledge-intensive firms and management consultants are knowledge workers. Management consultants can be both producers and users of management knowledge. Management consultants explore new knowledge through the brain type of consultancy. They learn from the brain type of client projects. Management consultancies may also develop new knowledge through 'internal' studies, which are studies without a client.

KNOWLEDGE BROKERS   In most consultancy areas, over time the balance tilts from knowledge exploration to knowledge exploitation. New client problems require knowledge exploration by means of the brain type of consultancy. Familiar problems can be solved by exploiting existing knowledge. Grey hair and procedural consultancy qualify as knowledge exploitation. Management consultants may also function as carriers, or brokers, of management innovations (e.g. Sahlin-Andersson and Engwall, 2002). In this role, consultants are the distributors of management knowledge. They exploit existing knowledge across organizational borders, industry borders, and geographic borders. Knowledge developed in one organization is exploited in another organization within the same industry. The same applies to industries and countries. Knowledge developed in one industry (country), is exploited in another industry (country). In many instances this knowledge is not copied exactly. Instead, consultants may modify the knowledge to the specific client situation at hand. The main vehicle for management consultants to develop and distribute knowledge is a consultancy project for a client. However, management consultants also distribute management knowledge through media, among which are, reports, books, press clippings, magazine and newspaper articles, websites, conferences, advertisements, guest lectures, personal meetings, and interviews.

CREATORS OF FASHION   Management consultants may create management fashion themselves. However, they may also jump on a bandwagon created by others (Benders et al., 1998). For instance, the management consultancy CSC Index (Champy was a chief executive at that firm) introduced business process re-engineering. But other management consultancies jumped on the bandwagon and developed their own version of BPR, or in some cases only changed the labels.

RHETORICIANS   Management consultants have an interest in management fashion. Management fashion stimulates the demand for management consultancy (Abrahamson, 1996). Clients may need assistance to evaluate whether a new management technique is suitable for their organization, and subsequently, advice (and assistance) on how to implement the technique in their specific situation. The functional vagueness of management fashion increases the need for management consultancy. Management consultancies may use rhetoric to promote a new management fashion. They address client insecurity and fear, and hope to get the client to adopt the new technique and hire the consultancy to advise and assist the client on implementation of the particular technique. Over the product life cycle of a management fashion, management consultants may subsequently create, codify, and commoditize management knowledge.

A continuous stream of management fashion creates the need for client management to orient. Whereas each individual management fashion is supposed to simplify management issues, a stream of management techniques may lead to confusion and a need for orientation. This need then fuels the demand for consultancy.

CONSULTANTS AND GURUS   Figure 6.5 visualizes the division of roles between management gurus and management consultants in the production and adoption of a management fashion. Management gurus create a new

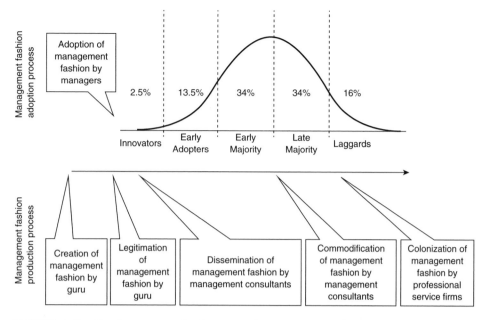

FIGURE 6.5 *Production and adoption of management fashion*

Source: author's interpretation of Suddaby and Greenwood (2001)

management fashion. Recall that management consultants and scholars can be gurus. After the legitimation of a fashion, management consultants will disseminate it via their clients. Over time, consultants will commoditize the fashion to increase efficiency. Once the fashion has been turned into a commodity, then professional service firms will attempt to take over the business by competing on cost.

Management media and business schools are not part of Figure 6.5, to keep the figure simple. However, they also play a role in management fashion production and dissemination. Management gurus may be business school professors and management journalists. Management media and business schools help to legitimate and disseminate a new management fashion. Conference organizers may also play a role. Conferences provide a podium for live presentations. Management gurus use such live presentations to communicate and legitimate their management fashion.

Management education

The third industry of the management knowledge cluster is management education. Business schools as educational institutions are distributors of management knowledge. Business schools became (in the United States) increasingly important in the 1960s. Business school professors teach management knowledge to business students. Professors use books, articles, case studies, websites, their own (consultancy or managerial) experience, and their own research. Business school professors may combine education with academic research. Academic research at business schools creates new management knowledge. Professors produce new management knowledge through their academic research. They may distribute their own or others' management knowledge through its publication in books and articles and websites, through presentations at academic and professional conferences, through management education, and through management consultancy.

Management media

The fourth industry of the management knowledge cluster is management media. The relevant media from a management knowledge perspective consist of, on the one hand, the management publishers and, on the other hand, the management journalists. Regarding publishers of management knowledge we distinguish between publishers of various media, including newspapers, management magazines, management books, radio programmes, television programmes, internet, and social media. Management media became (in the United States) increasingly important in the 1960s. The market for management books took off in the 1980s, with the publication in 1982 of the management bestseller *In Search of Excellence* by Peters and Waterman, then partners at McKinsey & Company. Internet and social media accelerate the distribution of management knowledge. These media may shorten the cycle of a management fashion.

Related to the publishers are the organizers of conferences on management knowledge. They also play an important role as distributors. In particular, management gurus rely on conferences and seminars.

In addition to publishers, we have the journalists that specialize in managerial subjects. Their products, including articles, books, website content, and programmes for radio and television, contribute to the distribution of management knowledge. Journalists, to a larger or a smaller extent, do research. Their research may lead to the production of new management knowledge.

Producers of management fashion

Where does the management knowledge come from? Which of the four industries of the management knowledge cluster is responsible for what share of new management knowledge? We point to a study that investigated the influence of management thinkers, or management gurus (Davenport and Prusak, 2003). This study measured the business impact on several criteria, including web hits and media mentions. Figure 6.6 presents the ranking of the 100 most influential management thinkers. Half of them are academics or business school professors. According to this study, the large management consultancies are not the largest source of management thinkers. A lot of management fashion is produced by niche firms. Mainstream consultancy firms adopt it later and integrate the new management concepts into their services. Unlike the knowledge innovators, these mainstream firms are not evangelical about new ideas. They take a pragmatic approach: if a new idea becomes big then they will pick it up. They have a strategy of knowledge imitation and exploitation, rather than knowledge exploration.

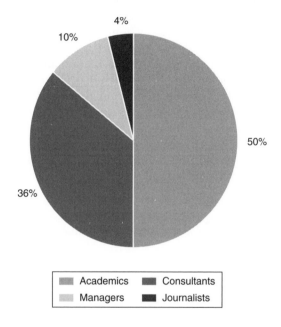

FIGURE 6.6   *Top 100 management gurus*

Source: Davenport and Prusak (2003)

Backlash against management fashion?

FLAWED METHODOLOGY   Since the introduction of *In Search of Excellence*, a stream of (similar) management books has appeared. These books all attempt to discover the holy grail of excellence, preferably persistent excellence. Many books gained bestseller status, among others, *Built to Last* (Collins and Porras, 1994) and *From Good to Great* (Collins, 2001). Academics (e.g. Rosenzweig, 2007) critiqued the methodology of these books to discover management recipes. A key flaw is that the success books make use of retrospective sense making to uncover the 'secrets of success'. Despite the results of the methodological critique, and despite the failure of various firms that were previously identified as 'excellent', there continues to be a demand for this type of management literature.

SOPHISTICATED CLIENTS The critical literature on management consultancy portrays clients as the victims of management fashion and the marionettes of management consultants (e.g. Clark, 1995; Kieser, 2002). But client sophistication is increasing. Clients are becoming better educated and their experience with management consultancy is growing. Some clients are also former consultants. Client sophistication induces a more critical attitude towards management consultancy and management fashion (Jung and Kieser, 2012). Sophisticated clients have a results orientation. They are not just interested in just ideas, they also look for a positive impact on performance. Client sophistication may lead to a more critical attitude towards management fashion. Research indicates that management consultants tend to focus on tangible reference projects and empirical evidence to support the claims of management fashion (Nikolova et al., 2009). These results seem to indicate that consultants are adapting their approach to sophisticated clients. Other management scholars doubt whether clients really have changed their approach to management fashion. These authors conclude that there continue to be clients who do not demand that management fashion has to deliver what it promises (Jung and Kieser, 2012).

GLOBALIZATION AND THE SPREAD OF CAPITALISM

Management consultants are not only creators and carriers of management fashion between organizations and industries. Consultants are also perceived as agents of globalization and Americanization (Kipping and Wright, 2012). In the twentieth century, the US managerial model rose to prominence in the (Western) world. Management consultancy firms, predominantly US firms, supported the diffusion of this managerial model. As carriers of this management model, they induced the international dissemination of the US model. US management consultancies also followed their US clients abroad (Kipping, 1999). The typical next step for these consultancies was to work for foreign clients. The opening up of foreign markets, and the promotion of free trade and foreign direct investment in the post Second World War period, presented new geographic opportunities for (US) management consultants as carriers of the US managerial model. Globalization also allowed new practices, such as off-shoring and outsourcing across borders. Emerging global value chains provided new opportunities for management fashion and management consultancy.

Neo-liberalism

The 1980s witnessed the rise of neo-liberalism and its faith in free markets. The most prominent examples were the economic reforms in China (starting in 1979), the Reagan administration in the United States (1981–1989), and Thatcher in the United Kingdom (1979–1990). Milestones were the collapse of communism in the Eastern European block in 1989 and the collapse of the Soviet Union in 1991. We may distinguish a three-fold impact of the rising prominence of neo-liberalism. On each occasion (US) management consultancies played a role as carriers of knowledge. These consultancies were, therefore, nicknamed 'agents of capitalism' (Kipping and Wright, 2012).

First, neo-liberalism transformed the *private sector in the Western economies*. Management consultancy helped to spread the predominantly Anglo-Saxon, shareholder value management in Anglo-Saxon economies, and later in non-Anglo-Saxon economies. As a result, management consultants stimulated the transformation from managerial capitalism to shareholder capitalism in many economies.

Second, neo-liberalism induced the spread of capitalism to *former state socialist economies*. In China, India, the Soviet Union, and the Eastern European countries the market ideology became more important. The economic transformation led to a deregulation of industries and privatization and the restructuring of firms. Shortly after former planned economies introduced the market mechanism, Western management consultancies arrived in these countries (Kipping and Wright, 2012). International financial institutions, such as the IMF and the World Bank, used management consultancies to reform national economies. Some management consultancy firms actively shaped the capitalism system (Kipping and Wright, 2012). An example is the McKinsey Global Institute, a think tank of McKinsey & Company that develops country reports, which have stimulated macro-economic reforms in various countries (Engwall, 2012).

Third, neo-liberalism induced the spread of a free market ideology in the *public sector in Western countries* (e.g. Saint-Martin, 2000). Western economies deregulated specific industries, among others utilities. State firms were privatized and needed to be restructured. Management consultancies supported the application of private sector knowledge to the public sector. Again management consultancy firms acted as carriers of management knowledge.

Management consultancy benefited from all three developments of a free market ideology. In all three instances, management consultancies seized the opportunity of political reform and helped policy makers and managers to realize the desired transformations of economies and organizations.

SUMMARY

Whereas the previous chapter dealt with the industry of management consultancy, this chapter explored the macro-environment of management consultancy. We discussed the relationships between various aspects of the macro-environment and management consultancy.

Macro-economic development

The macro-economy develops in cycles. We may expect management consultancy to be counter-cyclical to the business cycle. But empirical research reveals a pro-cyclical behaviour. This chapter conceptually explained this behaviour in terms of two factors: the ratio of (growth) opportunities to (cost) problems of clients, and the amount of discretionary financial resources of clients.

Development of a knowledge society

As part of the transformation to a knowledge society, a cluster of management knowledge has emerged. We may distinguish four connected industries involved in the production, distribution, and consumption of management knowledge: management, management consultancy, management media, and management education. Management consultancy can be both the producers and distributors of management knowledge. We focused on a particular type of management knowledge: management fashion.

Macro-political development

Management consultants as carriers of management knowledge have benefited from the macro-political development towards capitalist models in both public and private sectors in countries worldwide. The chapter described how Western management consultancy firms helped to diffuse shareholder capitalist models in many parts of the world.

REFLECTIVE QUESTIONS

1. The demand for management consultancy is pro-cyclical to the business cycle. How may a particular management consultancy firm combat the decline in its revenues during the downturn of the business cycle? Explain your answer.

2. The twentieth century witnessed the emergence of the management knowledge cluster. This cluster is responsible for the phenomenon of management fashion. What are the consequences of the management fashion phenomenon for the macro-economy? Does management fashion have a positive influence, a negative influence, or is it neutral? Elaborate your answer.

3. Why do management consultants spread management fashion? Is this a valuable role for consultants and for which stakeholders is it valuable? Argue why, or why not. Elaborate on your answer.

4. Some management scholars portrayed Western management consultancy firms as 'agents of capitalism'. What is the argumentation of these scholars? Is the consultancy firms' role of agent politically motivated, or do you perceive other motivations for management consultancy firms? Explain your answer.

MINI CASE STUDY

In search of the next big idea

Price competition

Jacques Hermes is the founder and managing partner of the medium-sized management consultancy Pyramid Advisory (PA). PA operates as a private partnership with fifteen partners. The firm employs thirty-five consultants and twelve support staff, including two information and research professionals. Two thirds of PA's client projects can be categorized as grey hair consultancy. The remaining one third qualify as procedure work. PA is facing increasingly intense competition. Besides traditional rival consultancies, PA faces a rising number of freelance consultants. The freelancers are willing to work at half the rate of the traditional consultancy firms. Various rivals of PA have already cut their fees. Clients do not perceive sufficient differences between PA's services and those provided by freelancers and rival firms. Therefore, these clients are no longer willing to pay a premium for PA. The utilization rate of PA's consulting staff has dropped far below the firm's breakeven level. Jacques struggles with the question: how to respond to the price pressure?

Thought leadership

During the last partner meeting, some partners suggested adopting a strategy of differentiation through thought leadership. PA cannot lower wages without losing or demotivating its talented staff. The firm cannot lower other costs any further. Therefore, differentiation through thought leadership seems a better option. A small group of PA consultants studied a number of successful management innovations. The group proposed that PA invest in research and development: the firm should set up an internal study to develop a new management concept.

Questions

1 What are the two main ways in which management consultancy firms explore new management knowledge? Explain your answer.

2 Evaluate whether these two ways may be appropriate for Pyramid Advisory. Elaborate on your answer.

3 What alternative strategies for Pyramid Advisory should Jacques consider? Elaborate on your answer.

FURTHER READING

Heusinkveld, S. (2013) *The Management Idea Factory: Innovation and Commodification in Management Consulting*. Oxon: Routledge.

Heusinkveld, S. and Benders, J. (2012) 'Consultants and organization concepts', in M. Kipping and T. Clark (eds), *The Oxford Handbook of Management Consulting*. Oxford: Oxford University Press, 267–284.

Kipping, M. and Engwall, L. (2002) (eds) *Management Consulting: Emergence and Dynamics of a Knowledge Industry*. Oxford: Oxford University Press.

Sturdy, A., Handley, K., Clark, T. and Fincham, R. (2009) *Management Consultancy: Boundaries and Knowledge in Action*. Oxford: Oxford University Press.

REFERENCES

Abrahamson, E. (1996) 'Management fashion', *Academy of Management Review*, 5 (1): 254–285.

Alvesson, M. (1993) 'Organizations as rhetoric: knowledge-intensive firms and the struggle with ambiguity', *Journal of Management Studies*, 30 (6): 997–1015.

Armbrüster, T. (2006) *The Economics and Sociology of Management Consulting*. Cambridge: Cambridge University Press.

Benders, J. and Van Veen, K. (2001) 'What's in a fashion: interpretative viability and management fashions', *Organization*, 8: 33–53.

Benders, J., van den Berg, R.-J. and van Bijsterveld, M. (1998) 'Hitch-hiking on a hype: Dutch consultants engineering re-engineering', *Journal of Organizational Change Management*, 11 (3): 201–215.

Blumer, H. (1969) 'Fashion: from class differentiation to collective selection', *Sociological Quarterly*, 10: 275–291.

Champy, J. (1995) *Reengineering Management: The Mandate for New Leadership*. New York: HarperBusiness.

Clark, T. (1995) *Managing Consultants: Consultancy as the Management of Impressions*. Buckingham: Open University Press.

Clark, T. and Greatbatch, D. (2004) 'Management fashion as image-spectacle: the production of best-selling books', *Management Communication Quarterly*, 17: 396–424.

Collins, J. (2001) *From Good to Great: Why Some Companies Make the Leap … and Others Don't*. New York: HarperCollins.

Collins, J. and Porras, J. (1994) *Built to Last: Successful Habits of Visionary Companies*. New York: HarperCollins.

Davenport, T. and Prusak, L. (2003) *What's the Big Idea? Creating and Capitalizing on the Best Management Approaches*. Boston, MA: Harvard Business School Press.

Engwall, L. (2012) 'Business schools and consultancies: the blurring of boundaries', in M. Kipping and T. Clark (eds), *The Oxford Handbook of Management Consulting*. Oxford: Oxford University Press, 365–388.

Engwall, L. and Kipping, M. (2002) 'Introduction: management consulting as a knowledge industry', in M. Kipping and L. Engwall (eds), *Management*

Consulting: Emergence and Dynamics of a Knowledge Industry. Oxford: Oxford University Press, 1–18.

Ernst, B. and Kieser, A. (2002) 'In search of explanations for the consulting explosion', in L. Engwall and K. Sahlin-Andersson (eds), *The Expansion of Management Knowledge: Carriers, Ideas and Circulation*. Stanford, CA: Stanford University Press, 47–73.

Hammer, M. (1990) 'Reengineering work: don't automate, obliterate', *Harvard Business Review*, July/August, 68 (4): 104–112.

Hammer, M. and Champy, J. (1993) *Reengineering the Corporation: A Manifesto for Business Revolution*. Boston: Nicholas Brealey Publishing.

Heusinkveld, S. and Benders, J. (2002) 'Between professional dedication and corporate design: exploring forms of new concept development in consultancies', *International Studies of Management & Organization*, 32 (4): 104–122.

Huczynski, A. (1993) *Management Gurus*. New York: Routledge.

Iacocca, L. with Novak, W. (1984) *Iacocca: An Autobiography*. New York: Bantam.

Jung, N. and Kieser, A. (2012) 'Consultants in the management fashion arena', in M. Kipping and T. Clark (eds), *The Oxford Handbook of Management Consulting*. Oxford: Oxford University Press, 327–346.

Kaplan, R. and Norton, D. (1992) 'The balanced score card – measures that drive performance', *Harvard Business Review*, January/February, 70 (1): 71–79.

Kaplan, R. and Norton, D. (1996) *The Balanced Score Card: Translating Strategy into Action*. Boston, MA: Harvard Business Review Press.

Kieser, A. (2002) 'Managers as marionettes? Using fashion theories to explain the success of consultancies', in M. Kipping and L. Engwall (eds), *Management Consulting: Emergence and Dynamics of a Knowledge Industry*. Oxford: Oxford University Press, 167–183.

Kipping, M. (1999) 'American management consulting companies in Western Europe, 1910s to 1990s: products, reputation, and relationships', *Business History Review*, 73 (2): 190–220.

Kipping, M. and Wright, C. (2012) 'Consultants in context: global dominance, societal effect, and the capitalist system', in M. Kipping and T. Clark (eds), *The Oxford Handbook of Management Consulting*. Oxford: Oxford University Press, 165–185.

Lammers, C. (1988) 'Transcience and persistence of ideal types of organization theory', in N. DiTomaso and S. Bacharach (eds), *Research in Sociology of Organizations*. Greenwich: JAI Press, 203–224.

Nijholt, J.J. and Benders, J. (2007) 'Coevolution in management fashions', *Group & Organization Management*, 32 (6): 628–652.

Nikolova, N., Reihlen, M. and Schlapfner, J.-F. (2009) 'Client–consultant interaction: capturing social practices of professional service production', *Scandinavian Journal of Management*, 25 (3): 289–298.

Rosenzweig, P. (2007) *The Halo Effect ... and the Eight Other Business Delusions that Deceive Managers*. New York: Free Press.

Sahlin-Andersson, K. and Engwall, L. (2002) 'Carriers, flows, and sources of management knowledge', in K. Sahlin-Andersson and L. Engwall (eds), *The Expansion of Management Knowledge*. Stanford, CA: Stanford University Press, 74–95.

Saint-Martin, D. (2000) *Building the New Managerialist State: Consultants and the Politics of Public Sector Reform in Comparative Perspective*. Oxford: Oxford University Press.

Staw, B.M. and Epstein, L.D. (2000) 'What bandwagons bring: effects of popular management techniques on corporate performance, reputation, and CEO pay', *Administrative Science Quarterly*, 45: 523–556.

Suddaby, R. and Greenwood, R. (2001) 'Colonizing knowledge: commodification as a dynamic or jurisdictional expansion in professional service firms', *Human Relations*, 54: 933–964.

World Economic Forum (2013) www.weforum.org (accessed 25 June 2013).

PART 3
THE MANAGEMENT CONSULTANCY FIRM

PART MAP

This part concentrates on the management consultancy firm. We acknowledge that a typical management consultancy firm does not exist. As discussed in Part 2, there is a large variety of firms. In this part we focus on commonalities of the various firms in terms of their activities, management, organization, and career policies. In case of important differences between types of firms, we will differentiate between these firms.

Each chapter in this part is designed to achieve a specific set of learning objectives. After studying this part you will be able to:

- Analyse the primary and support activities in the value chain of a management consultancy firm (Chapter 7).

- Evaluate the different configurations of value chains of management consultancy firms (Chapter 7).

- Relate value chain activities to the competitive advantages of management consultancy firms (Chapter 7).

- Identify the main elements of business models for management consultancy and understand the interdependencies between these elements (Chapter 8).

- Evaluate the appropriateness of different business models for a specific management consultancy firm (Chapter 8).

- Conduct a quantitative analysis of the economics of a management consultancy firm (Chapter 8).

- Analyse the hiring practices of management consultancy firms (Chapter 9).

- Understand what it takes to make a career in a management consultancy firm (Chapter 9).

- Explain the implications of the up-or-out policies of management consultancy firms (Chapter 9).

CHAPTER 7: THE VALUE CHAIN OF THE MANAGEMENT CONSULTANCY FIRM

This chapter begins with exploring the value chain of a management consultancy firm. We provide an overview of the primary and support activities of a consultancy. First, we discuss the primary activities in more detail. In particular, we will pay attention to marketing and sales activities. Regarding the management consultancy's support activities, we concentrate on the knowledge management activities. We examine the internal relationships between the individual activities in the consultancy value chain. We also investigate the relationship between the value-adding activities and the competitive advantage of a consultancy firm. Finally, we explore options for the disaggregation of the management consultancy value chain, and the resulting new business models.

CHAPTER 8: MANAGING THE MANAGEMENT CONSULTANCY FIRM

This chapter is structured in four parts. First, we discuss the business models that management consultancy firms may use. In particular we pay attention to the interdependencies between a model's elements. Moreover, we outline the main strategic decisions that managers of management consultancy firms may have to take. Second, we investigate the various governance structures, leadership, and legal forms of consultancy firms. Third, we explore the organization structures of management consultancy firms, and the micro-structures of project teams. Fourth, we examine the economics of the consultancy. We show the different ways that consultancy firms may earn money, and we explain why some firms are forced to grow.

CHAPTER 9: PEOPLE AND CAREERS IN MANAGEMENT CONSULTANCY

This chapter is structured in three parts. First, we discuss what job applicants look for in a management consultancy, and vice versa, what consultancy firms look for in applicants. Second, we explore the career structures and the career development activities in management consultancy firms. Third, we look critically at the so-called up-or-out model which many consultancies use. We also investigate the performance appraisal system and identify what it takes to be promoted to manager and eventually make partnership. Finally, we reflect on the price of consultancy for the individual consultants.

7

THE VALUE CHAIN OF THE MANAGEMENT CONSULTANCY FIRM

INTRODUCTION

This chapter provides a tour of the value-adding activities of the management consultancy firm. We state that a typical management consultancy firm does not exist. The management consultancy industry consists of a variety of firms. While acknowledging the differences, we focus on the commonalities between consultancy firms. This chapter begins with a visualization of the value chain of a management consultancy firm. We discuss the primary activities of the consultancy firm whereby we emphasize the marketing and sales activities. The other primary activities will be discussed in Part 4. Next, we discuss the consultancy firm's support activities. This chapter's focus is on knowledge management while the firm's leadership and HRM are the subjects of Chapters 8 and 9. We also examine the internal linkages between the consultancy's value chain activities. Next, we discuss how the consulting firm's value-adding activities relate to its competitive advantage. We look at new developments that will lead to the disaggregation or breakup of the consultancy value chain. We discuss how new types of outsourcing and off-shoring of consultancy value activities lead to new configurations of value activities for consultancy firms. The chapter ends with a summary, reflective questions, a mini case study, suggested further reading, and references.

Main learning objectives

- Identify the main differences between the management consultancy firm's value chain and the textbook example of a value chain.
- Understand the primary and support activities in the consultancy value chain.
- Identify the main linkages between the consultancy's value-adding activities.
- Identify key relationships between the consultancy's value-adding activities and its competitive advantage.
- Understand the motivations for disaggregating the consultancy's value chain.
- Identify different configurations of the value chains of management consultancy firms.

UNDERSTANDING THE VALUE CHAIN

The textbook value chain

The value chain is a popular framework for analysing the activities of an organization (Porter, 1985). Most textbooks show only the value chain of a manufacturing firm as an example (see Figure 7.1). However, the value chain of a management consultancy firm differs from that of a manufacturer. Both the primary and the support activities vary.

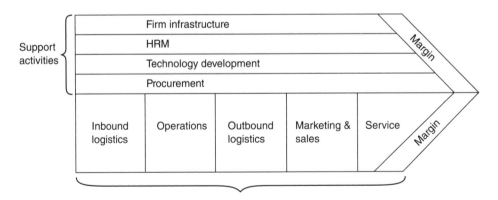

FIGURE 7.1   *The textbook example of a value chain*

Source: Porter (1985)

A management consultancy firm value chain

Figure 7.2 presents the specific value chain of a management consultancy firm. The primary activities begin with marketing, and client relationship management is the last primary activity. Client relationship management is not only an after-sales service but may also serve a marketing function as it may lead to follow-up projects and other repeat business from prior clients. In the following section, we will elaborate on the main differences between the manufacturing (textbook) value chain and the specific management consultancy firm's value chain.

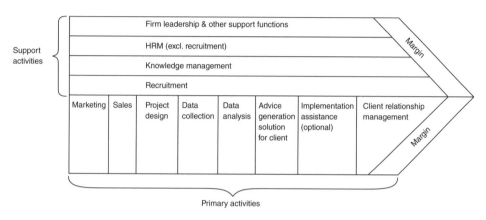

FIGURE 7.2   *The value chain of a management consultancy firm*

Source: author's interpretation of Porter (1985)

The main differences between the management consultancy value chain and the manufacturer's value chain

DIFFERENCES IN THE OPERATIONS–SALES SEQUENCE   First, the sequence of primary activities differs. A manufacturing firm typically first produces its products and then sells them to the clients. An exception is build-to-order products. A management consultancy firm does not first 'produce' a product and then sell it. A consultancy firm begins with selling its services to the client. Only after the sale will the firm deliver its service to the client.

DIFFERENCES IN OPERATIONS   Second, the operations or production activities differ between manufacturers and consultancies. A management consultancy firm delivers a service instead of a physical product. A manufacturer transforms raw materials (inputs) into a physical product for the client. A management consultancy firm transforms raw data into advice for the client. Some consultants only generate advice/solutions, whereas others also provide assistance with implementation, respectively the narrow and the broad definitions of management consultancy. The operations of consultants do not involve the creation of a tangible product but rather their work is a service. Consultancy is an intangible product.

DIFFERENCE IN DISTRIBUTION Third, the distribution activities are another area of difference. The manufacturing of physical products requires inbound and outbound distribution. Raw materials have to be distributed to the operations site and stored there. Moreover, the final products are stored and then distributed from the operations site to clients or distributors. Management consultancy neither uses raw materials nor creates physical products. Therefore, the consultancy value chain lacks inbound and outbound logistics.

DIFFERENCE IN R&D The support activities of a management consultancy firm also differ in various respects from those of a manufacturing firm. Consultants may undertake R&D activities; however, unlike in manufacturing, these are not about physical products. Typically, management consultants develop new knowledge during projects for client. They learn from their projects. Management consultants may also conduct so-called 'internal studies' – not commissioned by clients – for the special purpose of developing new knowledge. These internal studies are closer to the traditional concept of R&D. Management consultancies are knowledge-intensive firms which provide services. Management consultants' R&D is about the development of new knowledge about solutions and consultancy processes. This knowledge is to be used in subsequent client projects.

DIFFERENCE IN PROCUREMENT In manufacturing firms the procurement of raw materials and manufacturing equipment is an important support activity. In management consultancy firms, the procurement of materials and equipment plays a relatively minor role compared to manufacturing firms. The main equipment of management consultancy firms consists of computers, copiers, and telecommunication equipment. Rather than office equipment, the most important resources for a management consultancy are its employees. In the consultancy chain we therefore have recruitment instead of procurement. Recruitment is particularly important in management consultancy firms with an up-or-out policy because such an HRM policy typically creates a high outflow and inflow of personnel. The importance of recruitment for consultancy firms justifies a dedicated place in the value chain, separate from the other HRM activities.

THE PRIMARY ACTIVITIES OF THE MANAGEMENT CONSULTANCY FIRM[1]

The primary activities in consultancy literature are often conceptualized as a cycle. This management consultancy cycle is the subject of Chapter 11. Chapter 7 uses the value chain concept instead of the cycle because the value chain integrates primary and support activities. Moreover, the value chain is a general concept, which is also used beyond management consultancy. Therefore, the value chain allows for a comparison of management consultancy and other businesses.

Marketing

TARGET AUDIENCES   The marketing of consultancy is not about selling projects to clients but about making clients and prospects aware and interested in the consultancy firm's offerings. Prospects are potential clients for the firm's services. The objective of marketing is to competitively position the consultancy firm and create opportunities for contact with the firm's target audiences. We can distinguish between two types of audiences for management consultancy firms. One audience consists of current clients and prospects. The other audience consists of the firm's potential employees. Consultancies have to identify the target audiences of both (potential) clients and (potential) employees. Firms also have to decide what value proposition to offer to these target clients and employees.

TECHNIQUES   The management consultancy's people, the website, the office building, and publications are the tangible aspects of the consultancy firm, while the service itself is intangible. Consultancies use these various tangible aspects to contribute to the desired image and to market the firm to the target audiences. To market their firm, consultants use various techniques, which include networking, communications, advertising, and promotion.

NETWORKING   Management consultants – in particular the most senior consultants within the firm – may participate in professional and social activities to promote their firm. They may join all types of network organizations to increase their exposure to clients and prospects, as well as stakeholders, which may influence the clients' and prospects' decision on hiring consultants. Examples of such network organizations are business clubs, industry associations, charity organizations, sport clubs, and the boards of public sector institutes, such as museums, music halls, hospitals,

---

[1]This section on primary activities heavily draws on Kubr (2002).

or other places where consultants have the opportunity to meet clients and prospects. Consultants may also do voluntary, unpaid work – so-called 'pro-bono' projects – to promote their consultancy firm and meet clients and prospects.

COMMUNICATING   Consultants communicate their knowledge in many ways. The internet fulfils an increasingly important role in consultants' communication. Consultancy firms have websites, with webinars and videos, addressing clients, prospects, job seekers, alumni, and other interested stakeholders. Consultants may use their websites for various purposes, including the promotion of services, sharing knowledge, and communicating – via discussion groups – with stakeholders. In addition to websites, consultancy firms may also have apps. Consultants also use more traditional communication mechanisms. They may deliver presentations at seminars and conferences (public or organized by the consultancies themselves). Consultants may also give a customized presentation for an individual client or prospect. Moreover, consultants may write magazine articles, blogs, and books. Consultancy firms may use direct mailing to distribute their publications – for instance, the firm's own management magazine (such as the *McKinsey Quarterly*) – to target audiences. Furthermore, management consultants may use free publicity to reach their audiences. Interviews with consultants, or articles about consultants and their firm, are examples of such publicity.

ADVERTISING AND PROMOTION   Consultants may use advertising to market their firm. Advertisements may appear in the print media and on the internet as well as on radio and television. Consultancy firms may use sponsoring to promote their services. The object of the consultancy firm's sponsoring can be an event or an individual, for example, Accenture sponsors a Formula One racing team. Consultancy firms may also sponsor a classical concert or a golf tournament.

Sales

Consultants – in most large firms only the senior ones (partners) – are responsible for selling their firm's services to clients and prospects. We distinguish between the consultancy firm's sales to existing clients and to new clients. Because experience with a consultancy firm is an important criterion for clients to select a particular firm, consultants should first look at their existing clients, assuming that these clients present attractive opportunities for the consultancy. The consultancy firm has a competitive advantage when selling a proposal to an existing client: so-called repeat sales.

SELLING TO EXISTING CLIENTS   During an ongoing consultancy project, the consultants may identify an opportunity for new work beyond the scope of the current project. Consultants may also make follow-up visits to existing clients after a project has finished, to identify new selling opportunities. Therefore, consultants have an information advantage over competitors who do not have such privileged access to information about the client organization. Consultants have a preference for focusing their sales efforts on existing or previous clients because this is more efficient than trying to convert prospects, which they have not served before, into clients (see Chapter 10). Most consultancy firms sell the majority of their projects to existing clients. However, if the existing client base does not offer sufficient business potential, then consultants have to approach prospects.

APPROACHING PROSPECTIVE CLIENTS   We can distinguish three alternative ways for consultants to approach prospective clients. First, the best way is to contact a prospect via a referral. After direct experience with a particular consultancy firm (which only applies to clients), the referral is the second best driver for organizations to hire a management consultancy firm. Consultants should, therefore, induce their clients to make referrals to prospects.

Second, consultants may approach prospective clients via a marketing lead. The marketing efforts of the consultancy firm may generate so-called 'leads' for follow-up contact. Leads are organizations which have responded positively to marketing efforts and have expressed an interest in the consultancy firm's services.

Third, consultants may 'cold-call' prospective clients. Cold calling is contacting prospects without a client referral or marketing lead. This approach has the lowest chance of success and should only be used if referrals and leads are not available or feasible.

MEETING THE PROSPECTIVE CLIENT   If the consultant succeeds in getting an initial appointment with the prospect, then the consultant will use this first meeting to gain the prospective client's confidence. The prospect needs to have confidence in the consultant before they are prepared to discuss their needs with the consultant. After having gained their confidence, the consultant needs to develop an understanding of the prospect's needs for using a consultant. The consultant has to conduct a preliminary diagnosis of the prospect's problem/opportunity. The consultant has to demonstrate their understanding of the prospect's problem or opportunity. Next, the prospect may ask the consultant to develop a proposal for a consultancy project. Traditionally, consultants sold services directly to the client who used their services. To an increasing extent (sophisticated, large) organizations use their procurement departments to manage the hiring of consultancy firms. This means that consultancy firms have to follow the formal (bureaucratic) process of such procurement organizations instead of the informal process of directly dealing with clients. The sales process will be described in further detail in Chapter 11.

Project design

THE APPROACH   The consultants will design the project based on their understanding of the client or prospect's problem or opportunity. The project design outlines the objectives of the project and the approach to achieve these objectives. Typically the more senior consultants in the firm design the projects. The objectives determine the deliverables of the project. The project design also needs a definition of the scope: what is included in the project and what is not? In addition, consultants need to specify the performance criteria: how to evaluate the project results? Next, the consultants design the approach to achieve the objectives. The consultants select the appropriate methods and techniques for data collection, analysis, and interventions. They plan a schedule of all required activities of the project.

RESOURCES   Based on these activities, the consultants determine what resources they require for the project. The most important resource for the project is people. The consultancy firm plans for how many consultants, what knowledge and skills they need, and for how long. The project may also involve people from the client and external stakeholders. Data are also an important resource for the project. Consultants should specify what data they need for their activities. Moreover, the consultant and the client should agree on the division of roles and responsibilities in the project. Next, the consultants should budget the project's costs. Chapter 11 describes the project design in further detail. The consultants also need to set up a management structure for the project. The project team reports to the steering committee, which should include (a representative of) the client. The consultants should also plan the communication of progress and final results to the client.

Data collection

DESK AND FIELD RESEARCH   Data are required for analyses. They are the fuel for analysis. Data can be quantitative and qualitative. The data needs of the project are derived from the intended analyses. Consultants first decide what to do with the data before they start collecting the data. We can distinguish between various data sources and data collection methods. There are two general methods for data collection: desk and field research.

DESK RESEARCH   Consultants start with desk research: what data are already available? The first source of data for consultants is their knowledge from previous projects, which may be stored in the consultancy firm's knowledge management system. The client is another key source of desk research data. The consultants may also use data that are published in the public domain sources, such as articles, books, databases, magazines, newspapers, reports, and the internet.

FIELD RESEARCH   If the required data are not available via desk research, then consultants will use field research to collect the data. Sources for field research can be client employees, the client's suppliers, the client's clients, and the client's competitors, governments, NGOs, and the general public. We can identify some important field research methods for consultants. Consultants may conduct interviews. They may interview individuals, but they may also have focus group interviews. Furthermore, they may use observations to collect data. Finally, consultants may use questionnaires for data collection. All collected data need to be evaluated for reliability and quality. In some cases, data are needed from several sources to increase reliability. Chapters 12 and 13 will describe data collection in more detail.

Data analysis

ORGANIZING THE DATA   Data analysis begins with organizing the data. Consultants group the data by place, time, responsible person, and other criteria. Organizing the data makes it easier to understand the data, and to process the data. The next step is to investigate the organized data. We distinguish between two different types of investigation: investigating the relationships between existing data and predicting future data.

ANALYSING RELATIONSHIPS Consultants may compare variables or objects, such as revenues, costs, investments, productivity, and quality. Benchmarking is a form of comparison which is popular with consultants. Consultants may also investigate the ratios of variables. An example is the Pareto Principle, or the '80/20 rule'. Consultants may also investigate the causality between variables. For example: what drives profit? Finally, consultants may investigate the correlation between variables. Popular frameworks for investigating relationships between variables are the 7-S framework of McKinsey & Company, the BCG matrix (and other two-by-two matrices), Porter's competitive forces framework, and the value chain framework.

PREDICTING THE FUTURE   The second type of investigation is about predicting future developments of variables. The simplest approach is to extrapolate the past. We assume that the future will be as the past. A more sophisticated approach to predicting future values of variables combines a causal model with scenario analysis. For the critical drivers of the causal model, consultants develop alternative scenarios of the future. Consultants use these scenarios to run the models.

CHECKING THE QUALITY   After every type of investigation, consultants do a so-called 'sanity check', which is a quality check. Project managers and steering committees may also take a critical look at the results of the consultants' analysis and ask themselves: can this be true? Complete and transparent documentation of the analytical approach is essential for evaluating the quality of analysis. Chapters 12 and 13 describe the data analysis in more detail.

Advice generation

ANALYSIS AND CREATIVITY   Consultants generate advice for clients to support decision making to solve problems or seize opportunities. Advice generation is not only based on data analysis, it also requires creativity. Consultants have to create possible solutions for the client. We can distinguish between two alternative approaches for solution creation. First, consultants start with generating possible solutions or possible advice. The possible solution is formulated as a hypothesis that needs to be tested through data analysis. Data collection and analysis follow after the generation of the hypothesis. Chapters 12 and 13 describe this approach in more detail. Second, an alternative approach is to collect and analyse the data and synthesize the results of the analyses. Then advice generation follows the synthesis. Synthesis is about putting the pieces – the results of individual analyses – together in order to develop insights and draw conclusions on the decisions that client should take. Synthesizing the analysis results is also a creative process.

UNCERTAINTY   Often, consultants do not have one, single best solution for their client because there is too much uncertainty. Recommendations are about the future, which is by definition uncertain. Consultants may involve clients in the advice generation as sounding boards. They may work out various possible solutions, or options, for their client and may help clients to evaluate these possible solutions. Consultants may model the impact of options under various scenarios to help the client choose a solution. They will present their advice to the client often in the form of a PowerPoint presentation. The presentation may be combined with a discussion about the advice and the next steps. The consultants may also write a text report for the client. Advice generation will be further described in Chapter 13.

Implementation assistance

THE MANAGERIAL TASKS   Consultants may assist client management with the managerial tasks of implementation. Management consultancy firms may also be hired to do the actual implementation work (execution) but that work does not qualify as management consultancy. Implementation work is a business service, while assisting management with managing the quality, costs, and time of implementation is a consultancy service. Consultants have to agree with the client about the division of roles and responsibilities for the implementation. The consultant can assume varying responsibilities for implementation. However, the client ultimately remains responsible for the implementation.

RECOMMENDATIONS VERSUS DECISIONS The consultants only advise and assist their client. Consultants recommend, but only clients take decisions. Consultants may develop a plan of the implementation, including what actions are necessary to achieve the desired results. They may design the implementation processes and create a resource plan. Consultants may form and manage the implementation project team and develop a schedule. Consultants may also develop a contingency plan – a 'plan B' – for deviating circumstances. Consultants may develop the communication plan for the implementation process. During the implementation, consultants may monitor the progress of implementation and develop corrective and adaptive actions. Chapter 15 describes the consultants' implementation assistance in more detail.

Client relationship management

EVALUATION After the implementation – or after advice giving if the consultants did not assist in implementation – an evaluation of the project may take place. According to predetermined criteria, the consultants, or the client, may evaluate the effect of the project. Evaluation may generate follow-up work. Consultants may write a final – closing – report, which summarizes the benefits of the assignment and may provide suggestions for future work. Consultants debrief clients about the project. They may develop documentation of the project to hand over to the client.

FUTURE PROJECTS Termination of the project does not imply the end of the relationship between client and consultant. Consultants disengage in such a way as to keep doors open for future projects.

To show their commitment, consultants may return to their clients after a defined period to quickly assess the progress made and the results achieved by executing their advice or implementation plan. These return visits are a so-called 'win-win' situation: the client receives 'free' advice on where they are standing and, if applicable, what needs to be done; the consultants may learn whether their work is being used successfully. Moreover, the consultants may identify new opportunities to support their client, which may lead to new projects for the consultants.

FOLLOW-UP VISITS As stated before, existing clients are the most attractive source of new projects. Consultants may periodically visit clients to review progress in implementation of the advice. Consultants may also make follow-up visits to former clients to identify new selling opportunities.

Client relationship management comprises marketing activities targeted at existing clients. Consultants use various formal and informal activities to maintain the relationship with their clients, such as lunches, dinners, and seminars. In addition, consultants may send copies of articles, books, and reports of the consultancy firm's internal studies to keep clients informed about their offerings.

THE SUPPORT ACTIVITIES OF THE MANAGEMENT CONSULTANCY FIRM

Recruiting

CONSULTANCY IS A PEOPLE BUSINESS Recruiting is positioned in the value chain as a support activity. However, that should not be interpreted as recruiting being unimportant for management consulting. Recruiting is very important to management consultancy firms for several reasons. First, consultancy is a service, which means it is a people business. Second, because the quality of consultancy outputs is difficult to assess, clients also look at the quality of the inputs, that is, the people within the consultancy. Third, in many consultancy firms the turnover of staff is relatively high, which puts high demands on the firm's recruiting function.

MARKETING AND SCREENING Recruitment starts with marketing to the consultancy firm's target audience of potential employees. The objective of this marketing is to create awareness and interest among the ideal candidates and make them apply to the firm. Consultancy firms may use various methods to reach their audience, such as advertising, the company website, and recruitment events for students. The next step in the recruiting process is the screening of applications. The application letters, forms, and CVs are evaluated using several criteria. If an application meets the criteria, then the consultancy invites the candidate for an interview, typically at the consultancy firm's office.

INTERVIEWING The consultancy firm uses the interview to further evaluate the candidate. Many firms will use a case interview to test the problem solving skills of the candidate. Firms may also use other forms of testing. The selection process typically comprises several interview rounds, and one or more tests. Every interview and test is a hurdle that the candidate should pass. If the candidate fails on any occasion, the selection process stops for this candidate and the candidate will be rejected. Candidates that succeed through each interview round and test will receive a job offer from the firm. The final step is the negotiation of the terms and conditions of the employment contract. Chapter 9 describes recruiting in more detail.

Knowledge management[2]

EXPLICIT AND TACIT KNOWLEDGE   Management consultancies are an archetype knowledge-intensive firm. Knowledge is an essential ingredient in all management consultancy roles. But what is knowledge? There are two views of this: knowledge as a possession versus knowledge as something socially embedded (Newell, 2005).

CODIFICATION STRATEGY   In the first view, knowledge is explicit and generic. It can be codified, stored, and transferred from one location to another. This type of knowledge fits the procedural type of consultancy and lends itself to a codification strategy (Hansen et al., 1999). In a codification strategy consultancy firms commodify knowledge by codifying it and subsequently sharing the codified knowledge among the consultancy staff (Hansen et al., 1999). ICT systems play an essential role in a codification strategy.

PERSONALIZATION STRATEGY   In contrast, socially embedded knowledge is tacit, situation specific, and difficult to transfer. This type of knowledge fits the grey hair type of consulting and requires a personalization strategy. The tacit knowledge cannot be codified and stored in IT systems. Socially embedded knowledge can only be transferred through personal interactions between individuals. The personalization strategy rests on the personal networks of consultants.

EXPLORING KNOWLEDGE   Knowledge management comprises various activities, the balance of which may vary by consultancy firm. The first activity is the exploration or development of knowledge that is new to the consultancy firm. Please note that the knowledge does not have to be new to the world. Firms may develop new knowledge in three ways: through client projects, internal studies, and absorbing knowledge from external sources.

> *Client projects.* Consultants develop knowledge as a spin-off of their projects for clients. After the termination of client projects, consultants evaluate the projects for their knowledge potential, that is what has been learnt from the project. Chapter 5 shows the relationship between the size of the firm and the accumulation of knowledge from client projects. The larger the firm, the faster it accumulates knowledge.
>
> *Internal studies.* Next to client projects, consultancy firms may undertake projects for the specific purpose of developing new knowledge. In contrast to client projects, these projects are not

---

[2]The section on knowledge management heavily draws on Werr (2012).

commissioned by clients. The so-called 'internal studies' are the equivalent of R&D projects.

External sources. Rather than developing knowledge themselves, either through a client project or internal studies, management consultancy firms may also absorb knowledge that is new to them from external sources, such as academic researchers, management gurus, and other consultancies.

STORING KNOWLEDGE   The second activity after knowledge development is the filing or storing of the new knowledge.

Explicit knowledge. If the knowledge is explicit, then management consultancy firms will codify the knowledge. The codified knowledge is transformed in electronic files or paper documents, to be stored in a computer or library.

Tacit knowledge. If the knowledge is tacit, then it is in the heads of individuals within the consultancy firm. Firms may create a database or catalogue which provides information about what knowledge is held by which individual in the firm.

Control. If the knowledge is in the heads of individual consultants, then the consultancy firm is vulnerable. Firms may own the knowledge but they cannot control it; every day that knowledge walks out of the door. The 'experts' of the consultancy firm may set up a new business to exploit their knowledge or they may join a rival consultancy. If the knowledge is codifiable, then the firm is in a strong position as that knowledge is stored in the IT systems which are owned and controlled by the firm.

DISTRIBUTING KNOWLEDGE   The third activity of knowledge management is the distribution of knowledge. This is about the transfer of the stored knowledge to the firm's consultants for exploitation in client projects.

Knowledge management systems. Explicit knowledge can be codified and stored in IT systems. The consultants may access this knowledge through computer networks, such as an intranet. The knowledge is then easily and immediately accessible at any time on a worldwide scale. In contrast, tacit knowledge is much harder to distribute.

The master–apprentice model. Tacit knowledge is a kind of knowledge which because of its nature is difficult to transfer to another person by writing it down. An important part of the knowledge required for consultancy is tacit. It can only be acquired by observation of a role model, for instance a partner or another senior consultant, imitating their behaviour and practicing that behaviour. This is the master–apprentice model of learning which is common in management consultancy firms.

Functional and industry experts. Within a management consultancy firm there may be experts in a field, a functional practice, or an industry practice. Consultants who need the tacit knowledge of these experts can only obtain it via personal interaction with the expert. Consultants looking for the knowledge may contact the experts. Depending on the extent of knowledge, a few phone calls or personal meetings may be sufficient to transfer that knowledge. If the client project heavily depends on the tacit knowledge of the expert, then this expert may be assigned part-time or full-time to the project.

The need to specialize. Many consultancy firms bring their consultants together on a regular basis to share the tacit knowledge gained on consultancy projects. Firms, in particular the large ones, are organized by fields, the so-called functional practices like 'strategy' and industry practices like 'financial services'. After the first few years, consultants are supposed to specialize in one or more practices and become a member of the practice group. Each practice group organizes regular meetings for an exchange of knowledge.

Human resource management

A PEOPLE BUSINESS   As mentioned before, management consultancy is a people business. The consultancy firm's people are its most important asset. The consultants are the carriers of the consultancy firm's competences. Therefore it is essential for consultancy firms to develop and keep their talent (and to take leave of those employees who fail to meet the firm's requirements). This is the objective of the HRM function. HRM begins where recruitment ends.

DEVELOPING TALENT   The newly hired consultant typically receives training. Training comprises of formal training courses as well as on-the-job training (the master–apprentice model). Many firms have an introduction programme for new consultants, a so-called 'boot camp' which not only focuses on technical competences but also on socialization in the firm, that is understanding the firm's values and norms. Consultancy is an experience business and therefore consultants predominantly learn by doing. Projects are a crucial source of development for consultants. Therefore, the staffing of consultants – determining which consultancy projects a consultant will work on – is very important for the development of the consultant's competencies. However, the staffing of consultants on projects is a power reserved for the firm's leadership.

EVALUATING PERFORMANCE   Another important HRM activity is the performance evaluation of consultants. Consultants are frequently evaluated. Many firms evaluate their consulting staff after each project. Evaluation determines the compensation – remuneration and other perks and awards – as well as the promotion of consultants to new hierarchical levels of the consultancy organization. One or more bad evaluations may bring about the end of a consultant's career at a firm. HRM is also responsible for the outplacement of consultants who do not meet the performance criteria, or who no longer want to work for the firm.

MANAGING THE ALUMNI NETWORK   The work of HRM does not stop there. Even after people have left, many consultancy firms will invest in the relationship with their former employees, or alumni as they are called. HRM functions maintain relations with these alumni because these former employees may remain valuable to the firm as clients and advocates of the firm. Chapter 9 will describe HRM in more detail.

Firm leadership and other support functions

LEADERSHIP   The leadership function of the management consultancy firm comprises several activities.

1. The leaders are responsible for policy making. They develop the firm's strategy and tactics.
2. The leaders allocate the firm's resources, in particular the staffing of consultants is a leadership activity.
3. The leaders make the decisions for major investments.
4. The leaders appoint the senior managers in the firm.
5. The firm's leaders maintain relations with external stakeholders, such as governments, media, and shareholders (if the consultancy firm has external shareholders).

If the consultancy firm is a professional partnership, then the partners lead the firm. These individuals own the firm. Some consultancy firms that are listed on the stock market are led by managers who are not the owners. External shareholders own these so-called 'managed professional businesses'. Chapter 8 describes leadership in more detail.

SUPPORT FUNCTIONS   Several other support functions – besides recruitment, knowledge management, and HRM – may be distinguished. The level of differentiation of such functions depends on the size of the firm. Large firms will distinguish more support functions then small firms. Almost all firms will have some kind of administrative support, that is secretaries who support the partners and consultants. Accounting is also a common support function among consultancy firms. As computers and intranets play an important role in most consultancy firms, ICT is another support function frequently found in consultancy firms. Large firms may also have a separate PR function for interfacing with the media and other stakeholders. Other support functions of large firms include legal and fiscal matters. Large firms often have a support function – typically named 'graphics' or 'production' – that is responsible for the production of PowerPoint presentations and reports, which are the most important physical outputs that consultancies produce. Consultants remain responsible for the content of presentations and reports, but they may delegate the design of the layout and graphs, as well as the actual creation of PowerPoint presentations, to specialists.

LINKAGES BETWEEN ACTIVITIES

Client services and knowledge management

The management consultancy firm's value-adding activities are linked to each other and form a system. We emphasize some important internal linkages between these activities. First, we look at the linkages between client services and knowledge management. Client services comprise project design, data collection, data analysis, advice generation, and implement assistance (see Figure 7.3). Client projects can be a source of new knowledge for the management consultancy firm. In the client service activities, the consultancy firm develops new knowledge. The firm may exploit this new knowledge in similar new client projects. The knowledge exploitation allows the firm to increase both the quality and the efficiency of their client projects. Clients may choose consultancy firms which can exploit the required knowledge because of the higher quality and efficiency of such firms. Knowledge management may therefore allow the firm to acquire more projects.

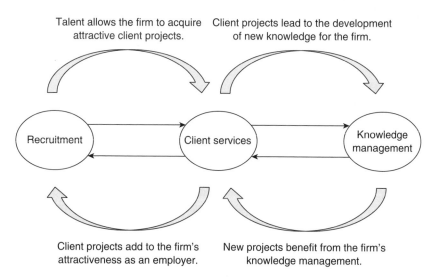

FIGURE 7.3 *Internal linkages between recruitment, client services and knowledge management*

Client services activities and recruitment

Second, we consider the link between the client services activities and the recruitment activities. Recruitment attracts the new talent that can be assigned to client projects. The quality of recruit adds to the (perceived) quality of client services. The client services also have an effect on recruitment. The more attractive the client projects, the more attractive the consultancy firm will be for talent. Firms with the most prestigious clients and projects have the first pick of the talent.

Reinforcing feedback loops

The internal linkages as depicted in Figure 7.3 show reinforcing feedback loops. The client services fulfil a key role in these loops. Better client projects lead to better talent and better knowledge which in turn allow the firm to undertake better client projects. Strong firms therefore become stronger. Such firms have entered a virtuous loop. This positive loop will make the firm increasingly strong. The reverse is unfortunately also true. Weak firms that do not succeed in acquiring attractive projects will find it difficult to develop knowledge and recruit talent. Such firms will enter a vicious circle. This negative loop will make them increasingly weak.

CASE STUDY

Evalueserve and the outsourcing of high-end parts of the consultancy value chain[1]

Management consultancy firms used to outsource only the relatively low-end back-office services, such as administration. The management consultancy firms' high-end knowledge activities, such as data collection and analysis, were deemed to be exempt from outsourcing. However, nowadays consultancy firms may even outsource these high-end knowledge activities to external specialist firms. Knowledge process outsourcing (KPO) is a relatively new type of outsourcing which refers to the high-end knowledge activities of management consulting firms as well as other knowledge-intensive organizations.

The term KPO was coined by Evalueserve, which is one of the first and largest KPO firms. In December

[1]Based on information from the company and from the company website. Available at www.evalueserve.com/site/en.html (accessed 4 September 2012).

2000, a former McKinsey partner, Marc Vollenweider, and a former IBM research director, Dr. Alok Aggarwal, founded Evalueserve (which stands for 'evaluation services'). They offered knowledge services to management consulting firms and other clients worldwide. The firm's services nowadays include knowledge management support, quick turnaround data research, market and competitive intelligence, and customer insights through data analytics and market research.

The firm at present runs four research centres spread over the world – India, China, Chile and Romania – which conduct various activities, such as mining and the sourcing of both internal and external data of clients, cleansing data (identifying and repairing incomplete and incorrect parts of data), combining data from different sources, analysing data, visualizing data, and reporting data (creating various types of output customized to the client). Most of the firm's employees have double degrees in business, finance, IT, engineering, science, and law. In addition to the research centres, the firm has client relationship offices spread across the world, while Evalueserve's executive team resides in the United States and Europe. At present, the firm employs over 2,600 employees from over forty nationalities, and provides over four million hours of services annually to its more than 500 clients, which are not limited to management consultancies.

Discussion questions

1 What is the difference for management consultancy firms between outsourcing low-end activities and high-end activities? Elaborate on your answer.

2 Why should management consultancy firms outsource their high-end (knowledge) activities to firms like Evalueserve? Why not? Elaborate on your answer.

3 What, if any, implications does the provision of high-end knowledge activities by outsourcing firms have for the management consultancy industry? Explain your answer.

VALUE CHAIN AND COMPETITIVE ADVANTAGE

Chapter 5 discussed alternative competitive strategies. In this section, we examine how the sources of competitive advantages are related to the firm's value chain. Table 7.1 on the next page translates competitive advantages and client value propositions to value chain activities. We only show the most relevant value activity per proposition.

Compete on intangibles

Management consultancy firms primarily compete on intangible resources; reputation, relations, knowledge, and consultancy staff. Reputation and

TABLE 7.1 *Relations between competitive advantage and value activities*

Competitive advantage	Cost leadership	Differentiation	
Client value proposition	Operational excellence	Client intimacy	Product leadership (Thought leadership)
Most relevant primary value activities	Efficiency of: • project design • data collection • data analysis • advice generation • implementation	• marketing • sales • client relationship management	Creativity of: • project design • data collection • data analysis • advice generation • implementation
Most relevant support activities	Knowledge management: re-using codified knowledge	Knowledge management: re-using tacit knowledge	Recruitment of creative talent

Sources: competitive advantage: Porter (1985); client value propositions: Treacy and Wiersema (1993)

relations are based on the quality of prior client projects. We interpret the quality of work in terms of meeting the client's expectations. If the quality of work or the price–quality ratio is not competitive then the consultancy will face a deterioration of its reputation and relations. Quality of work depends on the consulting firm's knowledge and staff. Knowledge is an essential ingredient, but it is not a likely source of sustainable competitive advantage for a management consultancy firm. A knowledge-based advantage cannot protect a consultancy firm against imitation by competitors. The consultancy industry does not have property rights like the pharmaceutical industry. Competitors can imitate by making slight variations in the knowledge.

The ultimate competitive advantage

Consultancy staff are therefore the ultimate source of a sustainable competitive advantage for management consultancy firms. Success in management consultancy is a matter of getting and keeping the best people. Which people are 'best' for a firm depends on the firm's client value proposition. Management consultancy is a people business. The staff underlie all three different client value propositions. For an operational excellence proposition the firm needs cheap staff. A client intimacy proposition primarily rests on the quality of the firm's people that are responsible for selling projects and maintaining client relationships. A product or thought leadership proposition requires creative people.

DISAGGREGATION OF THE VALUE CHAIN[3]

Traditional value chain

Traditionally, management consultancy firms are fully integrated. They conduct all value-adding activities in-house. Their value chain is complete and comprises all primary and support activities. Historically, all management activities were conducted within one organization. However, new more focused value chains are emerging as traditional, full value chains are being disaggregated or broken-up.

Drivers of value chain disaggregation

CLIENT SOPHISTICATION   The first driver of value chain disaggregation is increasing client sophistication. Clients are becoming more sophisticated for several reasons.

Education and experience. They become better educated. Most client management has also obtained an MBA. Furthermore, during previous projects clients develop more and more experience with consultants. Some clients will even have had experience as a consultant. Some client organizations will hire alumni from (top) consultancy firms.

Changing demand. Client sophistication changes the demand for consultancy. Sophisticated clients no longer want full services from consultants (from project design to implementation assistance) or at least they do not want to have the full package at the traditional fee level. Clients may hire consultants for specific, specialist activities and integrate these activities with their own work. For instance, sophisticated clients can do the project design themselves. These clients only need the capacity to perform the activities of data collection, analysis, advice, and implementation. Such clients may hire hands from specialist temp agencies like Eden McAllum. Alternatively, the clients may outsource specific activities, such as data collection and analysis, to specialist firms such as Evalueserve. This brings us to the second driver.

---

[3]This section on disaggregation heavily draws on Schmidt et al. (2005).

INFORMATION AND COMMUNICATION TECHNOLOGIES The second driver of value chain disaggregation is developments in information and communication technologies.

> *Specialists.* ICT enables the outsourcing of certain activities to specialist low-cost providers anywhere in the world. Inputs and outputs of activities can be transmitted via intranet or internet. For instance, ICT facilitates data collection and analysis for client projects by specialist offshore firms such as Evalueserve. Moreover, ICT enables electronic marketplaces where clients can contact specialist providers of particular services. ICT gives rise to new specialist players in the management consultancy industry. Such specialists do not offer the full spectrum of client services but focus on one or a few services, such as data collection and analysis.

> *Integrators.* In response to the rise of specialist service providers, we may also see the emergence of integrator firms. Specialization of service providers in one or a few value-adding activities of the management consultancy value chain leads to the need for bundling or integrating the distinct complementary services of the various specialist firms. Either clients do the integration themselves, or they hire integrator firms. On behalf of their clients, these integrators bundle the services of various specialist service providers. For instance, integrators do the project design for their clients and source people or services from multiple specialist providers.

New value chain configurations

FULLY INTEGRATED VALUE CHAIN As a result of these two drivers (client sophistication and ICT), some traditional full-service management consultancies no longer operate a fully integrated value chain. The traditional full-service consultancy firms may choose to offer a smaller range of services/ activities if that is what their clients want. Or the traditional firm may continue to offer the full services, but outsource those activities where the firm does not have a competitive advantage. In both cases, the consultancy firm will adapt its value chain.

PARTIAL VALUE CHAIN A partial value chain is a value chain that has some 'empty' slots (see Figure 7.4 on the next page). Figure 7.4 visualizes the value chain of a management consultancy that has a competitive advantage in terms of its client reputation and client network. The consultancy exploits this advantage and sub-contracts as many value chain activities as possible to external specialist service providers. The firm keeps project design in-house because it is based on deep client understanding, which is part of the firm's competitive advantage. The consultancy outsources data collection, analysis, advice generation, and implementation assistance to various external specialist service providers. Finally, client relationship management is kept within the firm because it is fundamental to its competitive advantage.

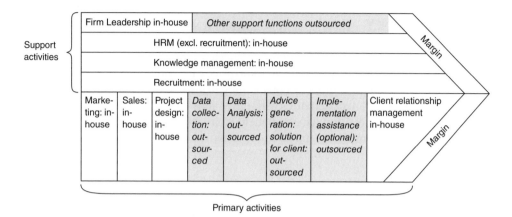

FIGURE 7.4 *An example of a partial value chain*

Note: The shaded activities are out-sourced to external services providers

INTERNATIONAL VALUE CHAIN   Traditional management consultancy firms may keep their value-adding activities in-house, but relocate them off-shore, that is to locations with a better supply of talent, lower wages, lower office rent, lower tax burden, and other cost advantages. Most major global management consultancies have captive (in-house) off-shore activities. To summarize: management consultancy firms may disaggregate their value chain by outsourcing (disaggregating across organizational boundaries), and by offshoring (disaggregating across geographic boundaries).

Consequences of value chain disaggregation

INCUMBENT FIRMS AND NEW ENTRANTS   We can see two different groups of consultancies which create new (disaggregated) configurations of value chains. On the one hand, we have the new entrants which have designed disaggregated value chains, that is the specialists and the integrators. On the other hand, we have the traditional, incumbent consultancies that have redesigned their full value chain to be competitive in the new industry landscape of value disaggregation.

INTENSITY OF COMPETITION   Disaggregation of the consultancy value chain has a number of consequences for consultancy firms and their clients. Value chain disaggregation increases the intensity of competition because it lowers the barriers of entry to consultancy. It is easier to set up a consultancy with a disaggregated value chain than it is to set up a full value chain. Moreover, ICT lowers the costs of distance. New entrants from distant lower-cost countries can compete if they can use the internet to transfer inputs and outputs for their consultancy activities.

TRANSPARENCY   Value chain disaggregation also induces a greater transparency in consultancy offerings and fees. Value chain disaggregation allows the unbundling of consultancy offerings. Specialist providers that offer only one step of the value chain create market prices for individual consultancy services. Traditional, incumbent consultancy firms can no longer afford to cross-subsidize less efficient activities with other activities. Because of the increasing intensity of competition, clients benefit from value chain disaggregation. They benefit from more choice, more transparency, and lower fees for consultancy.

SUMMARY

The management consultancy's value chain differs in important respects from the textbook value chain. Operations and logistics are different, as well as the sequence of primary activities. This chapter explains the main differences and discusses each of the value-adding activities of the management consultancy firm. We emphasize the linkages between the client service activities on the one hand, and the recruitment and knowledge management activities on the other hand. Management consultancies primarily compete on intangibles: reputation, relations, knowledge, and staff. Consultancy staff are the ultimate source of a sustainable competitive advantage. We show that different competitive advantages and client value propositions are based on the different strengths of consultancy staff. Finally, we illustrate how client sophistication and ICT developments drive the disaggregation of the management consultancy value chain. Besides the traditional fully integrated value chain we distinguish between two emerging partial value chains, the specialist firm and the integrator firm.

REFLECTIVE QUESTIONS

1. The book relates different types of knowledge management strategies to different types of consultancy: the codification strategy fits procedural consultancy, while the personalization strategy fits grey hair consultancy. What knowledge management strategy would best fit the brain type of consultancy? Explain your answer.

2. If recruitment is critical for management consultancy, why is recruitment not considered a primary activity in the consultancy's value chain? Explain your answer.

3. This chapter discusses the drivers of the disaggregation of the management consultancy value chain. Which management consultancy firms will probably maintain a full value chain? Please provide arguments.

Outsourcing the consultancy's activities?

Avoid a loss

OV&A is a small consultancy firm. It consists of three founding partners, Olsen, Veblen and Andersen, and twelve consultants. The firm faces a rising intensity in competition. Consultancy fees are therefore under pressure. To avoid a loss, OV&A needs to reduce its costs. To identify opportunities for cost reduction, a task force of managing partner Olsen and two senior consultants conducts a cost analysis. The firm has decided not to touch consultancy staff salaries and benefits. Instead, they will focus on opportunities to cut overhead costs.

The PowerPoint production department

One candidate for cost savings is the firm's PowerPoint production department. At present, four part-time management assistants (two full-time equivalents) are dedicated to the production of PowerPoint presentations for the consultants. These assistants are not responsible for the content of slides but only undertake the data entry into the computer. The production assistants occupy two rooms in the office, which is located in an expensive part of a metropole.

India

One of the senior consultants in the taskforce has suggested: why not outsource our PowerPoint production to an external supplier in India? Various India-based PowerPoint producer firms advertise their services on the web. Their offerings look professional and attractive to the task force members. What should Olsen do?

Questions

1 Is PowerPoint production a primary or a support activity of OV&A? Provide arguments for your answer.

2 What are the advantages for OV&A and what are the disadvantages of outsourcing the PowerPoint production to an offshore supplier? Explain your answer.

3 What would you advise Olsen to do with the suggestion to outsource PowerPoint production to an offshore supplier? Provide arguments for your answer.

FURTHER READING

Kipping, M. and Clark, T. (eds) (2012) *The Oxford Handbook of Management Consulting*. Oxford: Oxford University Press.

Kubr, M. (ed.) (2002) *Management Consulting: A Guide to the Profession* (4th edn). Geneva: International Labour Organization.

REFERENCES

Hansen, M., Nohria, N. and Tierney, T. (1999) 'What's your strategy for managing knowledge', *Harvard Business Review*, 77 (2): 106–116.

Kubr, M. (ed.) (2002) *Management Consulting: A Guide to the Profession* (4th edn). Geneva: International Labour Organization.

Newell, S. (2005) 'The fallacy of simplistic notions of the transfer of "best practices"', in A. Buono and F. Poulfelt (eds), *Challenges and Issues in Knowledge Management*. Greenwich, CT: Information Age Publishing, 51–68.

Porter, M. (1985) *Competitive Advantage: Creating and Sustaining Superior Performance*. New York: Free Press.

Schmidt, S., Vogt, P. and Richter, A. (2005) 'Good news and bad news: the strategy consulting value chain is breaking up', *Consulting to Management*, 16 (1): 39–44.

Treacy, M. and Wiersema, F. (1993) 'Client intimacy and other value disciplines', *Harvard Business Review*, January–February: 84–93.

Werr, A. (2012) 'Knowledge management and management consulting', in M. Kipping and T. Clark (eds), *The Oxford Handbook of Management Consulting*. Oxford: Oxford University Press, 247–266.

8

MANAGING THE MANAGEMENT CONSULTANCY FIRM

INTRODUCTION

This chapter takes a look at the management consultancy firm from the perspective of leadership. The central question addressed in this chapter is: how to manage a management consultancy firm? We start with the strategic choice of the firm's business model. We subsequently pay attention to the control function. We also outline different ways of structuring firms. Finally, we provide insight into the economics of a management consultancy firm. The chapter ends with a summary, reflective questions, a mini case study, suggested further reading, and references.

Main learning objectives

- Critically reflect upon the leadership of management consultancy firms.
- Identify the main elements of a management consultancy business model and their interdependencies.
- Distinguish between the strategic decisions the managers of consultancy firms may take about their firm's business model.
- Understand the differences between the management consultancy firm as a professional partnership and as a managed professional business.
- Understand the organizational challenges of managing a management consultancy firm.

- Compare the various mechanisms used to manage consultants.
- Identify the main elements of the organizational structure of a management consultancy firm.
- Understand the micro-structure of a consultancy project team.
- Conduct a quantitative analysis of the economics of a management consultancy firm.
- Critically reflect upon the way management consultancy firms make a profit.

BUSINESS MODELS

A management consultancy is a business operation. It sells its services to clients at a profit. A management consultancy should therefore be managed as a business. As a management consultancy relies heavily on its people, the business model of a management consultancy emphasizes not only target clients but also target employees. Figure 8.1 visualizes the business model of a management consultancy.

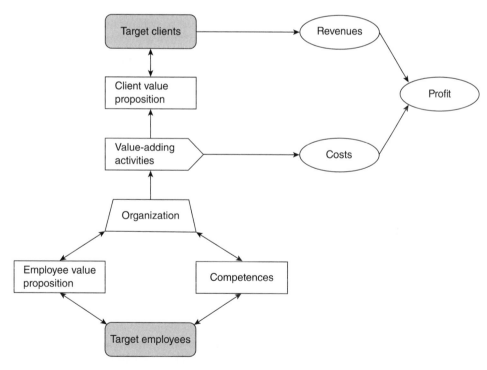

FIGURE 8.1   *The main elements of a business model of a management consultancy firm*

Strategic decisions

To manage a management consultancy its leaders have to make decisions about the elements of the business model, such as the selection of target clients and target employees, development of the client value proposition, and the employee value proposition. The most important questions where the leadership have to make decisions are:

1. How to position the firm on the market for consultancy services?

   o Which clients to target? Typical decisions will include: the selection of which type of industries and geographies, client size (in terms of full-time equivalents, sales, or assets), managerial level (top management, middle management, or lower-level management).

   o What value proposition to offer to these target clients? What is the focal dimension of the value proposition: operational excellence, client intimacy, or product leadership? What type(s) of consultancy will the firm offer: brain, grey hair, procedure or software-based consultancy? Is the firm prepared to deliver informal propositions such as legitimacy, political weapon, and scapegoat?

2. How to develop and deploy the competences to create the client value proposition?

   o What value-adding activities are required to deliver the client value proposition?

   o What competences are required to conduct the value-adding activities?

   o What organization is required to develop and deploy the required competences?

3. How to position the firm on the labour market?

   o Which employees to target for the required competences?

   o What value proposition to offer to these target employees?

Interdependencies between elements

We emphasize the relationships between the elements of the business model (Figure 8.1). These elements are interdependent. The implication of the interdependencies is that the leadership cannot change one element of the model without adjusting the interdependent elements (cf. Maister, 1993). For instance, if the leaders decide to shift their focus to another client group with different needs, then they cannot leave their client value proposition unchanged. However, changing the value propositions will have implications for the activities of the firm. A change of client may cascade down to the selection of employees. Without such adjustments the business model becomes unbalanced and it will lose its effectiveness. The required integrated approach to business model change makes it difficult for management consultancy firms to switch to another type of consultancy (Kipping, 2002).

Business model development

OUTSIDE-IN PERSPECTIVE   The sequence of these questions and related decisions reflects an 'outside-in' perspective on business model development. The starting point lies outside the consultancy firm and this is the market for consultancy services. The leadership identify the most attractive clients to target. All subsequent decisions are derived from this client selection. The hidden assumption underlying the outside-in perspective is that the management consultancy is flexible enough to develop and deploy the required competences.

INSIDE-OUT PERSPECTIVE   An alternative sequence is the so-called 'inside-out' perspective. In this perspective the point of departure lies inside the management consultancy. It is the firm's existing competences. What is the most attractive client value proposition that may be created with the available competences? What are the most attractive clients that may be targeted with such a proposition? What value proposition may be created for employees? Which employees may be targeted with this value proposition? The hidden assumption of the inside-out perspective is the inflexibility of the firm's competences. Instead of adapting the competences to suit the most attractive clients, the management consultancy adapts its client focus to suit its competences.

The scope of the business

In the previous paragraph we focused on the identification of clients and the client value proposition. The client identification includes the identification of client sectors or client industries, such as banking, energy, government, retail, and transportation. The leadership of the management consultancy also has to make strategic decisions about the type of consultancy services to offer to the clients in the identified sectors, among which are operations, IT, corporate strategy, and HR. Finally, the leaders need to decide on the client geographies served. Which regions and countries should the management consultancy operate in? To decide on which clients sectors to serve, what services to offer, and in which geographies to operate, the firm's leaders may analyse the attractiveness of the sectors, services, and geographies. Clients may demand a broad scope. However, a broad scope may increase the complexity, and therefore the costs, of the consultancy organization.

Exploitation and exploration

EXPLOITATION   If the leadership have defined an attractive business model, then the consultancy firm can exploit that model. However, there are limits to this exploitation of the firm's existing business model. Several changes may erode the attractiveness of the existing model. For example, client demand for the existing client value proposition may become exhausted. Moreover, changes in competition, such as a commoditization of knowledge, may undermine the firm's competitive advantage (Suddaby and Greenwood, 2001). For these reasons, the management consulting firm needs an exploration of its business model.

EXPLORATION   Firms need to seek new clients in new sectors and new geographies. Firms also need to develop new client value propositions. This implies the development of new practice groups, new functional practices, and new industry practices (Morris et al., 2012). If exploration flows from current client projects – which are exploitation – then the firm does not have a trade-off between exploration and exploitation. Exploitation allows exploration. However, if business model exploration requires the firm to allocate resources, in particular consultancy staff, from paid client projects to unpaid internal research projects, then the firm faces a trade-off between exploitation and exploration. The leadership may be tempted to put their best people on paid projects for their best clients, instead of staffing their talents on internal studies. Short-term orientation may win from long-term interests.

The size of the business

COSTS AND BENEFITS   Related to the decision about the consultancy firm's scope in terms of the number of sectors, services, and geographies, the leadership also needs to make decisions about the desired size of the firm in terms of revenues. What is the optimal size of a consultancy firm? A larger size may bring benefits but also (overhead) complexity costs. Size may generate benefits if there are scale economies. The more capital intensive the management consultancy firm, the larger the scale economies. Scale economies for consultancies can typically be found in ICT systems, knowledge management, and advertising and promotion.

CLIENTS   Large clients in general will prefer large consultancies over small ones. Large, complex and international client projects demand large, international consultancy firms. To be able to offer a broad spectrum of services, a consultancy needs to have a larger size than when a firm specializes in one or a few services. Size also leads to costs for a consultancy. Size normally increases the complexity of the organization and induces growth in overheads with, as probable consequences, greater bureaucracy and indirect costs. Size may therefore come at the expense of flexibility. Finally, an expanding size may come at the expense of the cohesion, culture, and identify of the firm. However, as the section on economics will point out, some organization models cannot be sustained without continuous growth.

ORGANIZATIONAL STRUCTURES

Professional partnership

We distinguish between two archetypal consultancy firms: the consultancy partnership and the managed professional business, or MPB (Richter et al., 2007). Professional partnerships are common in organization and strategy consultancy. MPBs are most often found in IT consultancy. Consultancy partnerships are a professional bureaucracy. They are called a professional partnership, or P2-architecture (Greenwood et al., 1990). Figure 8.2 visualizes the structure of a P2-type consultancy firm. The *strategic apex* of the professional partnership is the partner group. The partners are the leaders and owners of the firm. The *middle line* of professional partnership consists of the project managers (or project leaders). The project managers delegate the work to the consultants in the operating core, in line with the policy defined by the partners. The consultancy firm's *operating core* consists of all employees that work directly for clients (cf. Mintzberg, 1993). In a P2-type of consultancy, the project managers as well as the partners participate in the operating core. The operating core is the dominant element of the P2-structure.

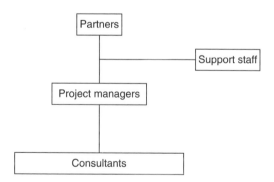

FIGURE 8.2 *The structure of the professional partnership*

ELEMENTS OF THE STRUCTURE   The operating core of the consultancy firm may be organized into groups. This grouping may be based on consultancy services, client sectors, or geographies. Consultants may be part of more than one group, that is overlapping groups. The *techno-structure* of the consultancy firm comprises the committees of partners and possibly project managers and consultants that are responsible for the design of methods, techniques, and other procedures for the operating core. The consultancy's *support staff* consists of several groups – among which are HRM, information systems (IS), administrative staff, and an information and research department – which support the consulting staff of the firm.

PARTNERSHIPS AND SOLE PROPRIETORSHIP   The brain type and grey hair type of consultancies in general use a P2-type of form. Professional bureaucracies primarily rely on a standardization of skills. The work of the professionals is too complex to fully understand and control by leaders who do not participate in the operations, that is consulting to clients.

In a sole proprietorship or a small start-up we will not find a differentiation of structural elements. The sole practitioners fulfil all the roles in the structure.

In the small start-up (with employees) the organization structure is also relatively simple, with on the one hand the founder/leader, and on the other hand everyone else. The founder/leader controls the organization.

CONSULTANCY FIRMS WITH MULTIPLE OFFICES   When consultancy firms increase their geographical scope, they may open additional offices in other locations. As a result the 'multiple office consultancy firms' will emerge. We may distinguish between two opposite management philosophies for the multiple office consultancy firms.

> *One-firm model.* On the one hand, the offices may be managed as one firm: the so-called 'one-firm' principle (Maister, 1985). In this collectivist approach, headquarters maintains high standards of consistency across offices. The offices are loyal to the firm and cooperate closely. The offices also have a shared profit-and-loss account. Therefore the results are shared.

> *Warlord model.* On the other hand, the divisional form may be led as a so-called 'warlord' or 'star-based' model (Maister, 1985). This is an individualistic approach where each office has a lot of autonomy and acts – relatively speaking – on its own. Headquarters encourages internal competition between the offices. Of course, each office has its own profit-and-loss account.

Managed professional business

MANAGEMENT AND OWNERSHIP   Management consultancy firms that have the structure of the MPB are typically large firms which operate in IT consultancy, such as Accenture and IBM Consulting. In contrast to the professional partnership, the MPB is managed by administrators with little or no involvement with the primary process of actually conducting management consultancy. Unlike the partners in the P2-type of management consultancy firms, the administrators of the MPB do not own the consultancy. They are professional managers who are employed by the MPB. The MPB is typically a publically listed corporation. The MPB is owned by shareholders, who are represented by external directors (see Figure 8.3).

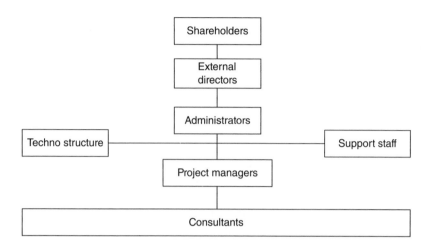

FIGURE 8.3 *The managed professional business*

PROCEDURE TYPE   In general, MPBs offer a procedure type of consultancy. The main control instrument is the standardization of procedures, that is a standardization of how consultants work. Such organizations may adopt the structure of a machine bureaucracy. In this type of structure, the techno-structure and the support staff are relatively large. The techno-structure designs the procedures. The support staff will typically include a large information and research department which controls the central knowledge management system with the codified knowledge base of the firm. The middle line of project managers is also elaborated to control the many consultants in the operating core who do relatively low skilled work, in comparison to the consultants in brain and grey hair types of consultancy.

DIVERSIFIED CONSULTANCY FIRMS   The organization structure of a large consultancy firm with multiple services may turn into a divisional form. Such firms may combine pure management consultancy (advice as well as assistance with the management of the implementation of advice) with business consultancy (that is implementation work, not assistance with the management of implementation) and professional services (that is services unrelated to advice, such as outsourcing and information systems development). Each individual division within the firm has its own structure (see Figure 8.4). However, it is also part of a loose administrative structure. The divisional form is managed by a central headquarters.

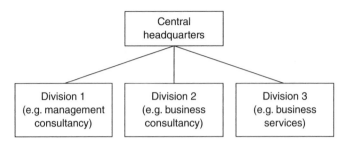

FIGURE 8.4 *The diversified consultancy firm*

LEADERSHIP AND CONTROL

Managing management consultants is 'to manage the unmanage-able' according to the founder of the Boston Consulting Group, Bruce Henderson (Hagerdorn, 1982). Consultants often value independence highly and they need to be independent in order to function as consult-ants. Moreover, they are often intrinsically motivated. To control the con-sultancy staff, the leaders of management consulting firms have several mechanisms at their disposal:

1. Organization structuring.
2. Monitoring.
3. Rewarding.
4. Standardization.

ORGANIZATION STRUCTURING   The leadership may control the consult-ants by means of the organization structure.

Job definition. First, leaders have to define the jobs of each member of the organization. The leadership influence employee behaviour by setting the tasks, responsibilities, authorities.

Reporting structure. Second, leaders have to develop a reporting structure. Hierarchical reporting is a crucial control instrument. Reporting lines are fundamental to monitoring and rewarding.

Job grouping. Third, leaders control the organization by grouping jobs. Jobs in consultancy firms are typically grouped by function: consultants versus support staff. The consultancy staff are grouped by service, client sector, and geography: the so-called practice groups (Kubr, 2002). Large management consultancy firms may combine service groups (functional practices) and client sectors (industry practices) in a matrix structure (Greenwood et al., 2010). Geography is organized by office, that is each office serves its own geographic territory.

MONITORING   Another control mechanism for the management consultancy firm's leadership is monitoring its consultants. We may distinguish between monitoring consultants' behaviour and monitoring their performance.

Behaviour. The leaders may monitor the behaviour of consultants. Leaders watch what consultants are doing, such as interviewing client personnel, analysing data, and writing plans. This requires observation of consultants' activities on a regular basis.

Performance. Monitoring the consultants' performance does not require (regular) observation of the consultants' activities. One aspect of consultants' performance is the output of their work. Examples of consultants' output are interview notes, the outcome of an analysis, and a PowerPoint presentation.

Output quality. Leaders may monitor the quality of the consultants' output. Monitoring quality poses challenges for leaders. Although the quality of some consultancy products, such as analyses and reports, may be evaluated, the quality in terms of the value of consultancy work for clients remains difficult to assess. In previous chapters we discussed the difficulties of assessing the effects of management consultancy on client performance. Because the value for the client is difficult to evaluate, the consultancy leadership may delegate the monitoring of the quality of the consultants' work to their clients. They may ask clients to fill in evaluation forms or evaluate the consultants' work in other ways.

Output quantity. Instead of monitoring the quality of consultants' output, leaders of the consultancy firm may also monitor the quantity of output. Typically the consultancy firm's leaders will monitor the number of hours billed to clients, or the amount of billings (revenues) to clients by a consultant. Of course, non-client work by a consultant – such as interviewing job applicants, administrative work, and knowledge development – has to be taken into account as well. Not only may the leaders of the management consultancy firm and its clients monitor the behaviour of consultants, professional organizations may also monitor consultants, in particular consultants who are members of the organization. These organizations may have ethical codes of conduct that members will need to follow.

REWARDING   An alternative control mechanism of the leadership is rewarding the consultants. Rewarding is related to monitoring. Behaviour and performance that meet the leaders' objectives get rewarded.

Rewards. Rewards can be monetary as well as non-monetary. Monetary rewards include a higher variable salary, salary raise, presents – from a dinner voucher to a holiday – and bonuses on top of a fixed salary. Promotion to a higher hierarchical level – for instance from consultant to manager – is a monetary reward, but also has non-monetary aspects such as power and prestige. The ultimate reward in a professional partnership is the promotion to partner. The individual becomes part of the circle of partners that lead the firm and share its profits. Non-monetary rewards comprise compliments, awards, outings, membership of a club of high-performance employees, and other forms of recognition.

Sanctions. The opposite of rewarding is sanctioning consultants' undesired behaviour and performance. Underperformance leads to negative attention and 'punishment'. There is the anecdote of a management consultancy firm that created a weekly list of the top performers, and a list of the underperformers in terms of billability, that is the number of billed hours a consultant achieved in a week. By putting the lists in the elevator of the firm's office, the leaders made sure that those lists would not escape anybody's attention. The ultimate punishment of course is firing people – or whatever veiled term leaders may use – who fail to meet the firm's objectives in terms of behaviour and performance. Consultants who violate the ethical code of professional organizations may lose their registration and membership of those organizations.

STANDARDIZATION   The consultancy firm's leadership may also revert to standardization to control its consultancy staff. We can distinguish between three types of standardization.

Knowledge, skills, and attitude. First, leaders may strive to standardize consultants' knowledge, skills, and attitude. Training programmes may, partly, achieve this goal. However, selective recruitment – from one or a small set of business schools – may also help to standardize the workforce.

Behaviour. Second, the consultancy firm's leadership may attempt to standardize the behaviour of consultants. The leaders may prescribe how consultants must do their job. Consultancy firms may have databases, or handbooks, filled with methods and techniques for every activity of consultancy. A centralized knowledge management system is also a tool for the leadership to control the consultancy staff. Standardization of how consultants work fits the procedure type of consultancy (e.g. Hansen et al., 1999).

Outputs. Third, the leaders may standardize the consultants' outputs. They may stipulate what the products of their consultants should look like. Examples of standardized outputs are fixed format charts, PowerPoint slides, presentations, and reports.

ORGANIZATIONAL CULTURE

Leadership and culture

LEADERSHIP   Leaders have more responsibilities then the development of the firm's strategy and business model. Leadership is also essential for developing the firm's culture. Leaders define and communicate values.

They set an example by acting as role models. For management consulting firms in particular, the culture is important. Management consultants are professionals who value independence and operate most of the time at clients' premises. Culture keeps the consultants aligned and provides identity and direction. It is not enough for the leaders of management consultancy to be good at developing a business model and a culture, and administrative tasks.

PROFESSIONALISM   A leader needs to be – or to have been – an excellent professional in order to lead professionals. The leaders of the management consultancy firm have to prove superior professional achievements to be trusted by the professionals and to earn credibility. Moreover, experience in consultancy helps leaders to understand the business they have to lead. The double demands of management consultancy firms on their leaders – leadership and professionalism – may cause problems. This combination of excellent leadership and excellent professionalism in one person is rare.

P2-type versus MPB-type

The organizational culture of the management consultancy firm consists of the collective values, beliefs, norms, systems, and symbols that drive consultants' behaviour, and that provide shared meanings that the consultants attach to their behaviour. Professional partnerships and managed professional businesses typically have different cultures. The culture of P2-type consultancy firms is typically characterized by values emphasizing craftsmanship, apprenticeship, professionalism, and independence. Such firms are usually a meritocracy and have an up-or-out policy. The culture is open and can be elitist. As P2-type consultancies are run by the partners and the decision making is decentralized, communication in the P2 is informal. In contrast, MPB-type consultancies are typically run as a business. Decision making is centralized and communication is formal. MPBs follow an industrial model with a focus on efficiency. There is a clear hierarchy and the culture is more formal and business-like

Three roles of culture

The culture fulfils various roles:

1. The firm's leaders may use the culture to control the consultants.
2. The culture may be used to differentiate the firm in the eyes of clients and job seekers.
3. The culture may provide a sense of belonging for the consultants.

CONTROL BY CULTURE   The firm's leadership may use the culture to control its consultants' behaviour in two ways: professionalism and performance.

Stimulate professional, ethical behaviour. First, the leaders may use the culture to stimulate professional, ethical behaviour. The firm wants its consultants to behave professionally. It is essential that consultants behave with integrity. They should have the clients' trust. They should also respect the clients' interests. The leaders may emphasize that the consultants should put clients' interests above the consultancy firm's interests. Moreover, consultants should not violate the confidentiality of client information.

Stimulate performance. Second, the culture is used to stimulate performance. The firm's leaders want the consultants to work hard. The culture may emphasize the importance of performance. An example is a firm's value that consultants should always exceed client expectations. It is not just about working hard – putting in more hours – it is also about achieving an impact or results for clients.

Stimulate cooperation. The firm's leaders may also use the culture to stimulate consultants to cooperate. Such cooperation may refer to working together as a project team, working together as an office, or even the cooperation of different offices as one firm. The leaders may emphasize an individual consultant's contribution to the team, the office, or the firm.

Communication. The desired behaviour is communicated through various ways, including training programmes, speeches, meetings, and role model behaviour. Performance appraisals are also a way to exercise cultural control: desired behaviour is rewarded while undesired behaviour is punished. The up-or-out system is an example of a cultural control system of consultancy firms that want to stimulate performance.

DIFFERENTIATION BY CULTURE   Management consultancy is an intangible product. Compared to tangible products, such as automobiles, management consultancy services are difficult to assess for (potential) clients as well as for job applicants. The people in a consultancy firm are among the most tangible parts. Consultancy firms may use the culture to differentiate themselves in the eyes of clients and job applicants. The culture is used to influence the behaviour of the consultants which in its turn should influence the perception of clients and job seekers. For instance, the leaders of a particular firm may want to establish the shared belief that their consultants are superior to those of the competition: we are smarter, we are the best of the best. Such an elitist attitude may attract clients and talent. However, other consultancy firms may want to instil other beliefs, for instance, we are more creative, we are friendlier, we are more fun to work with. Differentiation through culture is communicated through various mechanisms, such as the attitude and behaviour of consultants, the way they dress, the type of cars they drive, the type of offices they occupy, and the type of websites they have. There is, for example, the case of the consultant from a large, international consultancy firm. He said: 'When I am at an international airport somewhere in the world, I can spot from a large distance who are consultants from my firm, even if I do not know them. I recognize them by their looks, their clothing, and their valises'.[1]

CULTURE AS IDENTITY Unlike many other professions, consultants do not spend most of their time at the office. In contrast, most days of the week consultants are out of the office. They work at the client's premises or somewhere else in 'the field'. Because of their heavy involvement with the client, consultants may risk identifying more with their client than with their own firm. They may feel part of the client organization. This risk increases with the duration of the consultancy project. It is a risk because part of the reason for the existence of consultants is to be independent and provide a fresh, objective perspective. Consultancy firms may use the culture to create a sense of belonging for the consultants. The consultancy firm's leaders may want to create the feeling of a kind of family. Consultants belong to the family (of the firm): you are one of us. The culture provides the consultants with a (professional) identity, separate from that of the client. Such an identity may be based on beliefs: we are different, we think differently, we work differently. Consultants may also have a different jargon. They may use other expressions and terms from those of their clients. The identification with the consultancy firm is reinforced through socialization events, such as introduction programmes, office outings, drinks, dinners, parties, and other informal events. There is the example of the management consultant that spent too long at a particular client's. The consultant had been so long at the client's that the client's employees thought the consultant was one of them. When, during the consultant's stay, a new problem arose at the client's, a meeting was set up to discuss this problem. During the meeting, it was proposed to hire a consultant – while the consultant was sitting at the table.

LEGAL FORMS

Legal liabilities

An important decision for leaders of consultancies is their choice of legal form. Consultancy organizations may be natural persons or legal persons. A legal person is a legal entity that exists independent of the owners. It is a way to limit legal liabilities for the owners. The owners are protected from any liability incurred by the organization, with the exception of abuse of the legal form to commit fraud. It may also offer fiscal advantages. Moreover, a legal entity enhances the consultancy's ability to attract external financial funding.

---

[1]Personal communication.

SOLE PROPRIETORSHIP   A consultancy organization consisting of a single person is a sole proprietorship. This individual is the only consultant in the organization. There are no other professionals in the organization. However, the sole practitioner may have alliances with other, independent practitioners. If the sole proprietorship is a natural person, the sole practitioner is personally liable for any debt, obligation, or legal claims that may be charged against this person. Sole practitioners may establish a legal person for their operations.

PARTNERSHIP   Another popular form of consultancy organization is the professional partnership. A partnership consists of two partners at a minimum. Together the partners run their consultancy organization. The partners own the business. They are personally liable for any legal charges made against their organization and may set up a legal person for their partnership to reduce legal liabilities. Moreover, they may establish a legal person for each partner individually.

PUBLIC CORPORATION   A third form of consultancy organization is the public corporation.

> *Funding*. Consultancy firms, whose capital needs exceed the funding possibilities of the partners and even external financiers, may have to access the financial markets to sell stocks and/or bonds. Examples are IT management consultancy firms that want to expand into related business services, such as outsourcing, so their capital needs increase significantly. To list stocks and bonds on the financial markets, the consultancy has to become a public corporation. Selling the shares on the stock market may also be an option for partners to make cash. The partners no longer own the consultancy. The firm transforms from a professional partnership into a managed professional business.

> *Legal obligations*. Consultancies as public corporations have to comply with financial reporting legislation. They also face requirements with regard to corporate governance. For instance, they need a board of directors and they need to organize shareholders' meetings.

> *Financial obligations*. Listed MPB-type consultancy firms face pressure from shareholders and financial markets in general. The administrators of these firms have to take into account their stock price when making (policy) decisions. While professional partnerships may decide to focus on other objectives besides profit, managers of a public corporation have to maximize shareholders' value. While a partnership may decide to re-invest all of its profits in a long-term project, the managers of a public consultancy corporation have to regularly pay out dividends to shareholders, and therefore cannot sacrifice a short-term profit for an uncertain, long-term return.

INTERNAL CONSULTANCY   Internal consultancy organizations are part of a larger organization. This larger organization may be a public corporation. The internal consultancy typically is a department within the larger organization. It has no separate legal identity. The larger organization assumes all liabilities.

Transition of a management consultancy firm

Facing the challenge

Prestige

BMD & Company is a very small but highly prestigious general management consultancy firm. The five partners who run BMD prefer not to call themselves management consultants but favour the term 'board counsellors'. BMD exclusively works with the C-level, which is the board level, comprising the chief executive officer, the chief financial officer, the chief strategy officer, and other chief officers. BMD likes to distinguish itself from the big strategy consultancy firms. The partners like to say: 'While the strategy firms provide strategy advice to every level, we provide everything for the C-level'.

The partners

The five partners are very creative and unorthodox personalities. The way they behave and dress may even be called a bit eccentric, totally different from that of the chief executives they advise. All BMD partners are conceptually very strong, good at developing big pictures. Their ideas are unusual, surprising, counter-intuitive, and always valuable. However, their advice is relatively weak on (implementation) details.

The future

The partners are very good at relationship development. Clients love to work with BMD. However, the small geographic scope of the boutique firm – they only work in the home country, which is rather small – is increasingly a problem as the clients are becoming more internationally oriented. Moreover, the firm is very small: five partners, seven consultants, and four support staff members. They currently serve half of the boards of the top forty largest companies in the home country. However, given the internationalization trend of their clients, the future for BMD is becoming increasingly bleak.

Making the decision

International expansion

The partners have considered opening offices abroad, however, they have arrived at the conclusion that such an expansion is not feasible. The firm lacks the capital and the management capacity to handle such growth. As an alternative, BMD has explored options to set up a network of international alliances. Unfortunately, the attempt failed as the network did not work. However, recently the firm was approached by Universal Consultancy, one of the big strategy consulting firms. While its arch-rival, Bluenote, has been well established in BMD's home market, Universal has not entered this market.

Acquisition

Universal wants to establish a market position fast and therefore prefers the acquisition of a local player over build-ing a new office from scratch in BMD's home country. Universal has offered the partner-owners of BMD to buy their firm with shares in Universal. All BMD partners will become partners in the Universal firm. With Universal's international network of more than fifty offices, the BMD partners will finally have the international pres-ence that their clients demand. Two BMD partners want to sell their shares and exit the firm. Universal buys their shares with cash, while the other three partners join the Universal partnership. All seven BMD con-sultants and four support staff members join Universal as employees.

Facing the consequences

Growth

Two Universal partners who are natives of BMD's home country join the remaining three BMD partners in BMD's office. One of the Universal partners becomes the director of the office. After the acquisition

by Universal, the office grows fast. Within two years the partner group has expanded from five to seven. However, the growth of the consultancy staff is even more impres-sive: the staff have grown from seven to forty-two people. Moreover, Universal introduced a new layer in the consultancy staff. The firm appointed fourteen project leaders to manage the twenty-eight con-sultants in the office. Out of the original seven consultants from the BMD firm, two were promoted to project leader while the other five left the firm.

The Universal way

Universal introduced the formal manage-ment approach that the firm uses world-wide. At Universal's training academy all consultants, project leaders, and also part-ners receive intensive training in all facets of the Universal way of consultancy. Universal has a highly formalized and standardized approach to consultancy. For each type of client problem, Universal has proven, well-structured methods and techniques. The firm exploits a global knowledge manage-ment system with an enormous amount of case studies from previous client pro-jects. Universal has seen all possible cli-ent problems before. The organization structure is very hierarchical. The culture is hard driven. Client impact comes first. Everybody is expected to exceed client expectations. However, whoever meets expectations gets rewarded generously in salary, bonuses, and other perks.

Alienation

The three former BMD partners have much higher incomes than even in the best years of BMD. However, they are unhappy as they miss the old BMD culture. The former BMD partners cannot get used to the Universal way of consultancy. They feel alienated in the big Universal organization. They have kept their clients, but they have lost their firm.

Discussion questions

1 Why can the former BMD partners not get used to the Universal way of consulting? Do they have a reason for feeling alienated? Explain your answer.

2 How would you characterize the former BMD firm in terms of the type of consultancy and in terms of Mintzberg's typology (strategic apex, middle line, techno-structure, support staff, and operating core)? Explain your answer.

3 Compare the two firms, Universal and BMD, before the merger. To what extent does Universal differ from BMD? Explain your answer.

4 What should the former BMD partners who stayed in the Universal organization do? Provide argumentation.

MICRO-STRUCTURE OF A PROJECT TEAM

Team composition

With the exception of the sole practitioner, consultancy projects are executed by a project team. Such a team typically consists of a partner, a manager, and a couple of consultants. While the manager and the consultants are usually assigned full time to a single project, a partner runs two or more projects simultaneously. The project team has a clear division of roles and responsibilities. Partners are responsible for project acquisition and client relationship management. Moreover, they have the final responsibility for the project. They supervise the managers. However, partners may also participate in the project execution. Managers are responsible for project management. They supervise the consultants, but they may also participate in the execution of the project. Consultants do only the professional tasks of project execution.

Partner leverage

CONSULTANCY STAFF An important characteristic of project teams is the so-called 'leverage' (Maister, 1993). The leverage refers to the partner. Leverage is the ratio of non-partner consultancy staff to partners, or how many consultancy staff a partner has to work with. We emphasize that only the consultancy staff are counted. Non-consulting staff – support staff – are not included in the leverage. In the next section on economics we will explain why. Figure 8.5 presents an example of a micro-structure where a partner has two managers who each manage three consultants. Each manager may work on a different project. The total non-partner staff of the partner amounts to eight. The leverage is therefore eight. The leverage may be lower or higher in practice. The managers may be assigned to one single project but also to two different projects with each manager running one project.

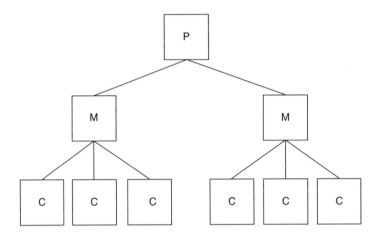

FIGURE 8.5 *A partner with a leverage of eight*

Notes: P = Partner, M = Manager; C = Consultant

In Figure 8.6 we see a partner with a much larger consultancy staff. This partner works with three instead of two managers. Each manager has five instead of three consultants. In total the partner has a group of eighteen

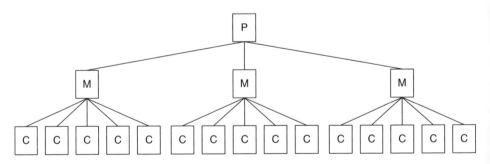

FIGURE 8.6 *A partner with a leverage of eighteen*

Notes: P = Partner, M = Manager; C = Consultant

consultancy staff members to work with. The three managers and fifteen consultants may be assigned to one single project but also to three different projects with each manager running one project.

TYPES OF CONSULTANCY   The leverage varies by type of consultancy (Maister, 1993). The brain type of consultancy typically has the lowest leverage, while the procedure type of consultancy is characterized by the highest leverage. Grey hair consultancy occupies an in-between position. Maister (1993) found a ratio of 1:6 for brain consultancy. Kipping (2002) mentioned a leverage of 1:20 for procedure consultancy.

ECONOMICS[2]

Revenues

THE PROJECT   The product of the management consultancy firm is the project. Consultancy firms sell projects to clients. The consulting staff deliver the project (with the support of the support staff). The project team structure is based on the type of project. The type of project determines what consultancy functions – partner, manager, and consultant – are needed and how many people per function.

PROJECT TEAM STRUCTURE   Table 8.1 provides an example of a fictitious management consultancy firm named the Pyramid Practice (PP). The numbers used in this example are fictitious. The goal of this simple and stylized example is to give an initial insight into the basic economics of a consultancy.

Assume PP specializes in one particular type of consultancy project which requires half of the time of a partner, a full-time manager, and six full-time consultants. This is the project team structure. Table 8.1 shows how many staff PP needs in order to conduct twelve projects at the same time.

TABLE 8.1 *Staffing for twelve projects*

Functions	Average requirement per project	Target utilization	Required for 12 projects
Partners	0.5	0.75	8
Managers	1	0.75	16
Consultants	6	0.9	80

Note: requirement for 12 projects = (12 × average requirement per project) / target utilization

―――――――――

[2]This section heavily draws on Maister (1993).

TARGET UTILIZATION   The functions are not 100 per cent of the time available for projects. They have also other obligations, such as training, administrative services, and internal studies for knowledge development. Partners have 75 per cent of their time available for projects. Their target utilization, that is time available for projects divided by total available time, is 75 per cent. In this example, the partners and the managers have the same target utilization. In practice, the partners probably have a lower target utilization because of other responsibilities. Consultants have a target utilization of 90 per cent in the example. We can calculate the required staff for a project, based on the average requirement per project, and the target utilization per function.

BILLINGS FOR ONE PROJECT   The economics of a management consultancy firm are based on revenues and costs. Revenues are received billings from clients in return for delivering services. Firms may use different methods of billing for a project. One method is the fixed amount of money. For instance, PP budgets a project that is expected to take three months or 480 hours of calendar time. Table 8.2 provides, for each of the three functions, how many hours need to be billed. The partner has to spend half of the time on the project, which is 240 hours (average requirement per project: 0.5). The manager is required full time, thus 480 hours. The six consultants are assigned full time: 6 times 480 equals 2,880 hours. Next, we multiply the billed hours by the billing rate per hour. Note that the billing rate varies by function. The partner has the highest billing rate, while the consultants have the lowest. Total billings for this particular project are expected to amount to $420,000.

ANNUAL TARGET BILLINGS   PP can also assess the target billings for a whole year. Assume that a year comprises 2,000 working hours for the consultancy staff. Furthermore, assume that the firm has a capacity of 40 partners, 80 managers, and 240 consultants. Table 8.3 presents the calculation of the annual target billings for the firm.

TABLE 8.2   *Billings for one project*

Functions	Average requirement per project	Duration of project (hours)	Billed hours	Billing rate per hour ($)	Billings (* 1,000 $)
Partner	0.5	480	240	250	60
Manager	1	480	480	150	72
Consultants	6	480	2,880	100	288
Total			3,600		420

Note: billed hours = average requirement per project × duration of project

TABLE 8.3 *Annual target billings for the firm*

Functions	Capacity per function	Target utilization per person	Target billed hours per person	Target billed hours per function	Billing rate per hour($)	Target billings (*1,000 $)
Partners	40	0.75	1500	60,000	250	15,000
Managers	80	0.75	1500	120,000	150	18,000
Consultants	240	0.9	1800	432,000	100	43,200
Total	360			612,000		76,200

Notes: target billed hours per person = 2,000 × target utilization per person; target billed hours per function = target billed hours per person × capacity per function (number of persons in that particular function)

Profit

COSTS   The costs of the management consultancy firm the Pyramid Practice primarily consist of wages. The wages can be divided between consultancy staff and support staff. The consultancy staff comprise the consultants, the managers, and the partners. Table 8.4 presents the annual compensation for the consultancy staff, which is assumed to be $28 million.

TABLE 8.4 *Calculating the profit per partner*

Functions	Target billings per function (*1,000 $)	Annual compensation per function (* 1,000$)	Billing multiple	Target billings minus compensation per function (* 1,000$)
40 Partners	15,000	8,000	1.9	7,000
80 Managers	18,000	8,000	2.3	10,000
240 Consultants	43,200	12,000	3.6	31,200
Total target billings minus compensation				48,200
Overhead				25,146
Profit				23,054
Profit per partner				576

PP budgets the overhead at 33 per cent of target billings (see Table 8.3). The percentage for overheads may be different in real life. Overheads include the wages for support staff, office rent, leases for office equipment and company cars, and other expenses.

TARGET PROFIT   Subtracting the consultancy compensations and the charge for overheads from the target billings gives us the target profit for PP: around 23 million. PP has forty partners who share the profit. Dividing the profit by forty generates the profit per partner: 576,000. We assume here that each one of PP's partners receives an equal share. In real life, there may be differences between partners. Firms may distinguish between junior partners and senior partners.

BILLING MULTIPLE   Firms make profits because the billings minus compensation for consultancy staff exceed the overheads. Table 8.4 shows both the billings and the compensation for each of the three functions. Based on the billings and the compensation, we calculate the billing multiple. This is the billing divided by the compensation. The higher the multiple for a consultancy function, the more profitable the function is. Typically, the billing multiple is highest for the consultants (3.6 for PP's consultants). In our example, the consultants contribute most to the firm's profit. A consultant earns $50,000 per year, while his or her target billings are $180,000 (1,800 billed hours at a rate of $100 per hour).

Profit per partner

KEY PERFORMANCE INDICATOR   The profit per partner is a key performance indicator of the (P2-type of) consultancy firm. To analyse the profit per partner, we must use a formula (see Table 8.5). We need to unpack the ratio of profit per partner into three factors: profit per partner is margin multiplied by productivity multiplied by leverage (Maister, 1993).

TABLE 8.5   *Profit per partner formula*

Factor	Description	Value
Margin	= Profit / revenues	30%
Productivity	= Revenues / non-partners	238
Leverage	= Non-partners / partners	8
Profit per partner	= Margin × Productivity × Leverage	576

Margin. The first factor is the firm's margin which is the ratio of profit and billings. We express profit as a percentage of billings.

Productivity. The second factor is the productivity of the non-partner consultancy staff: consultants and managers. Please note that we must exclude the support staff as well as the partners. Productivity of the non-partner consultancy staff is the average amount of billings per person. If we multiply margin by productivity we get the average profit per non-partner consultancy staff person.

Leverage. To calculate the profit per partner we need a third factor. This is the leverage, which is the number of non-partner consultancy staff per partner. The average profit per non-partner consultancy staff multiplied by the number of non-partner consultancy staff per partner generates the profit per partner.

The Pyramid Practice's partners receive their profit on top of their compensation. The annual compensation per partner amounts to $200,000 (see Table 8.4). The profit per partner is $576,000 (see Table 8.4). Each PP partner therefore earns $200,000 plus $576,000: in total $776,000. A more sophisticated system would differentiate the partner bonus by seniority of partners.

DIFFERENT TYPES OF CONSULTANCY The Pyramid Practice is a procedure type of consultancy. Other types of consultancy, such as the brain and the grey hair consultancies, operate with different economics. In Figure 8.7 we compare the profit per partner for the three types of consultancy: brain, grey hair, and procedure (cf. Maister, 1993). We unpack the profit per partner into the three factors: margin, productivity, and leverage.

You will see that the factors for the three types of consultancies are very different. Despite these differences in factors, the profit per partner in this example is the same for the three types. The differences in factors balance out. The procedure type has the highest leverage but the lowest productivity and margin. The brain type of consultancy shows the opposite profile: highest productivity and margin but the lowest leverage. The grey hair type occupies an in-between position.

Planning the projects

PRODUCTIVITY Productivity is one of the factors driving the profit per partner. Productivity is based on billable hours multiplied by the billing rate per hour. Firms will strive to maximize the amount of billed hours and the hourly billing rate. The amount of billed hours per person is capped by the billable hours. In our example the billable hours were 2,000 per year.

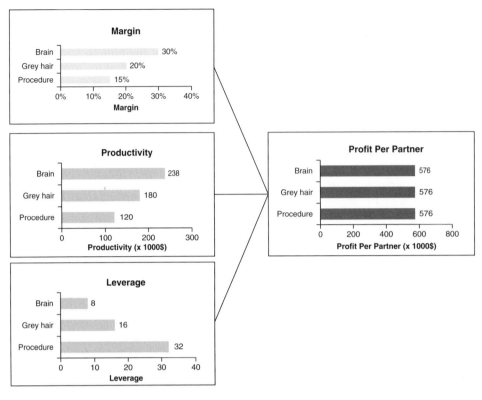

FIGURE 8.7 *Unpacking profit per partner for different types of consultancy*

Source of profit per partner (PPP) formula: Maister (1993)

The firm wants to maximize the utilization of billable hours. As mentioned earlier, consultants cannot be assigned 100 per cent of their time on billed projects. They have other obligations, such as training, administrative services, and internal studies. Firms strive for maximum utilization of billable hours within these constraints. Utilization drives productivity, which in its turn drives profit per partner.

CAPACITY PLANNING   Capacity planning aims at maximizing the utilization of the consultancy staff. In addition, capacity planning is the main input for a consultancy firm's recruitment targets and efforts. Because it is of such importance for the profit, capacity planning is the responsibility of the (senior) partners.

We use a new example to illustrate capacity planning. Assume another fictitious management consultancy firm, Minor & Company, can handle three projects simultaneously. Assume all its projects are of equal size. Three projects imply target level utilization of the firm's consultancy staff.

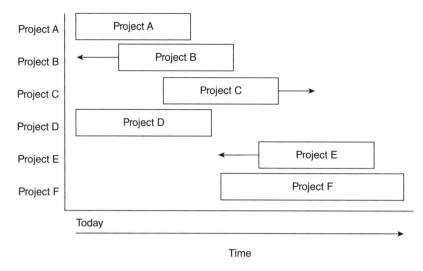

FIGURE 8.8 *Managing the project pipeline for utilization*

The partners of the firm need to acquire projects to keep capacity utilization at the target level. Figure 8.8 visualizes the timing of different projects for Minor & Company.

Today the utilization is only 67 per cent. The firm has only two projects – A and D – while it has capacity for three. However, it expects to start a new project soon. This is project B. The partner responsible for the particular client should try to convince this client to start this project B at an earlier time in order to increase Minor's utilization to the desired level. Of course the partner will use another argument that is more in the client's interest.

Looking further ahead in the pipeline of expected projects, we see that project C comes too early. If C begins on the date planned, the firm will have to handle four projects simultaneously. Minor's capacity is insufficient for this number of projects. Therefore, the partner responsible for the client who ordered project C will try to persuade this client that it is better to postpone this project a bit. To prevent a drop in utilization, the client for project E should be encouraged to start the project a bit sooner.

Growth of the firm

CONSULTANCY STAFF GROWTH Our fictitious firm the Pyramid Practice shows substantial growth. In the period of ten years the total for consultancy staff, including partners, has grown from 360 to 2,434 people

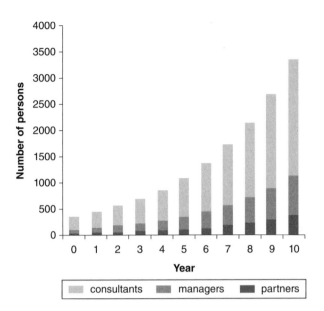

FIGURE 8.9 *The growth of the firm's staff*

(see Figure 8.9). The number of partners has grown as well, from 40 to 305 partners.

GROWTH AND PROFIT   Figure 8.10 visualizes the growth of PP's profit. Whereas the profit of the firm grows (left-side graph), the profit per partner

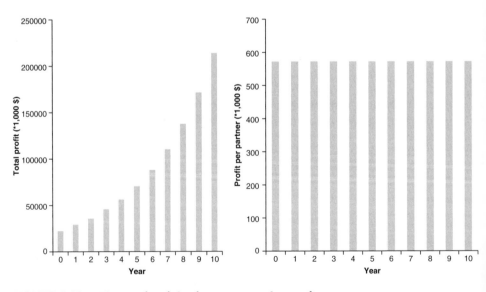

FIGURE 8.10 *The profit of the firm versus the profit per partner*

stays at the same level (right-side graph). How can we explain the stable profit per partner? Profit per partner is driven by margin, productivity, and leverage. Let us assume that margin and productivity are stable. How about leverage? Both the number of non-partner staff and the partner staff show growth (see Figure 8.9).

LEVERAGE If we look at the ratio of non-partner staff to partner staff, that is the leverage, we will find this ratio to be stable (see Figure 8.11). Leverage has not improved because of the firm's growth. The increase in the firm's profit has been fully absorbed by the increase in the number of partners. All profit drivers remained stable. Therefore, the profit per partner remains stable. Unless the firm improves its margin, productivity, or leverage, the growth in the firm's profit does not contribute to the profit per partner. You may ask yourself: why does a management consultancy bother to grow if this does not lead to a higher profit per partner? This is an important question that we will answer in the next chapter.

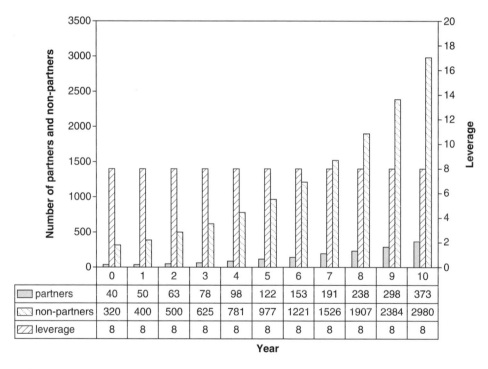

	0	1	2	3	4	5	6	7	8	9	10
partners	40	50	63	78	98	122	153	191	238	298	373
non-partners	320	400	500	625	781	977	1221	1526	1907	2384	2980
leverage	8	8	8	8	8	8	8	8	8	8	8

FIGURE 8.11 *The development of the firm's size and leverage*

Notes: FTE = Full-Time Equivalent; non-partners = consultants and managers

Inflow and outflow of staff

The Pyramid Practice has hired a substantial number of consultants: the so-called 'new hires' (see Figure 8.12). However, the firm also takes leave of consultants and managers. PP has a career policy of 'up or out'. Either staff get promoted to the next hierarchical level or they have to leave the firm, respectively up or out. The next chapter will elaborate on this policy. The net growth of the consultancy staff is the new hiring minus the staff going out. In Figure 8.12 we can see both inflow (new hiring) and outflow (staff leaving) increase over time. Because new hiring exceeds the numbers of staff leaving, the firm continues to grow.

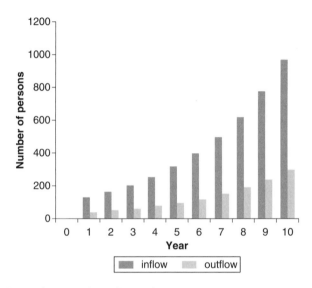

FIGURE 8.12 *Inflow and outflow of non-partner consultancy staff*

SUMMARY

This chapter outlines the different facets of managing a management consultancy firm. We began with the business model of the firm, which is a system of interdependent elements. When the leaders of the firm adapt the business model, they should maintain a balance between the model's elements. Managing consultants is a challenge. However, the firm's leaders have several control mechanisms at their proposal. We briefly discussed the most important ones: structuring, monitoring, rewarding, standardizing, and cultural control. Management consultancy firms may adopt different legal forms. We discussed natural and legal persons, private and public-listed consultancy firms. Organization structures may vary by firm and we distinguished between the different structures: the operating core, the middle line, the techno-structure, the support staff, and the strategic apex of the firm (Mintzberg, 1993). Furthermore, we indicated the key elements of the project team structure, in particular the leverage: the number of non-consulting staff per partner. Three drivers determine profit per partner: margin, productivity, and leverage.

REFLECTIVE QUESTIONS

1. Compare the effectiveness of the different control mechanisms that leaders of management consultancy firms may use. Explain your answer.
2. If leaders adapt the type of consultancy project, then they need to adapt the type of organization structure of the consultancy firm. Do you agree? Provide arguments for your answer.
3. What, if any, is the optimal leverage for a consultancy firm? Provide argumentation.
4. What, if any, is the relationship between the three factors that drive profit per partner? Explain your answer.

MINI CASE STUDY

Downsizing the consultancy firm

Growth

Brain Boutique (BB) is a management consultancy firm with a partnership structure. The firm was founded fifteen years ago by Peter and Patrick. The two founders chose to provide a brain type of consultancy and started with four managers and twelve consultants. During the years, BB has grown to six partners, twelve managers, and thirty-six consultants. The four new partners obtained shares, but the two founding partners still hold the majority of shares.

Decline

Three years ago, after twelve years of uninterrupted revenue growth, the firm faced stagnation in its revenue. Last year revenues even declined, and during this year this decline continued. The prospects for

▶

revenue growth are dim. The current professional staff level of fifty-four members (partners, managers, and consultants altogether) is no longer attainable with the current revenue development. The two founders decide to downsize the firm's staff. How should Peter and Patrick do this?

Questions

1 What was BB's leverage when starting the firm and how large is it at present?

2 What options for downsizing their staff do the founders have? Explain your answer.

3 What strategic alternatives do the founders have to respond to the revenue decline? Explain your answer.

4 What would you advise Peter and Patrick to do? Provide arguments for your answer.

FURTHER READING

Armbrüster, T. (2006) *The Economics and Sociology of Management Consulting*. Cambridge: Cambridge University Press.

Greiner, L. and Poulfelt, F. (eds) (2010) *Management Consulting Today and Tomorrow*. New York: Routledge.

Haas Edersheim, E. (2004) *McKinsey's Marvin Bower: Vision, Leadership & the Creation of Management Consulting*. Hoboken, NJ: John Wiley & Sons.

Kubr, M. (ed.) (2002) *Management Consulting: A Guide to the Profession* (4th edn). Geneva: International Labour Organization.

Maister, D. (1993) *Managing the Professional Services Firm*. New York: The Free Press.

Mandele, M. and Parker, J. (2009) *Changing the Leopard's Spots: Renewal of the Professional Firm*. Amsterdam: FT Prentice Hall.

Morris, T., Gardner, H. and Anand, N. (2012) 'Structuring consulting firms', in M. Kipping and T. Clark (eds), *The Oxford Handbook of Management Consulting*. Oxford: Oxford University Press, 285–302.

REFERENCES

Greenwood, R., Hinings, C. and Brown, J. (1990) 'P2-form strategic management: corporate practices in professional partnership', *Academy of Management Journal*, 33 (4): 725–755.

Greenwood, R., Morris, T., Fairclough, S. and Boussebaa, M. (2010) 'The organizational design of transnational professional service firms', *Organization Dynamics*, 39 (2): 173–183.

Hagerdorn, H.J. (1982) 'The anatomy of ideas behind a successful consulting firm', *Journal of Management Consulting*, 1 (1): 49–59.

Hansen, M., Nohria, N. and Tierney, T. (1999) 'What's your strategy for managing knowledge?', *Harvard Business Review*, 77 (2): 106–116.

Kipping, M. (2002) 'Trapped in their wave: the evolution of management consultancies', in T. Clark and R. Fincham (eds), *Critical Consulting. New Perspectives on the Management Advice Industry*. Oxford: Blackwell, 28–49.

Kubr, M. (ed.) (2002) *Management Consulting: A Guide to the Profession* (4th edn). Geneva: International Labour Organization.

Maister, D. (1985) 'The one-firm firm: what makes it successful?', *MIT Sloan Management Review*, 27 (1): 3–14.

Maister, D. (1993) *Managing the Professional Services Firm*. New York: The Free Press.

Mintzberg, H. (1993) *Structures in Fives: Designing Effective Organizations*. Englewood Cliffs, NJ: Prentice-Hall.

Morris, T., Gardner, H. and Anand, N. (2012) 'Structuring consulting firms', in M. Kipping and T. Clark (eds), *The Oxford Handbook of Management Consulting*. Oxford: Oxford University Press, 285–302.

Richter, A., Dickmann, M. and Graubner, M. (2007) 'Patterns of human resource management in consulting firms', *Personnel Review*, 37 (2): 184–202.

Suddaby, R. and Greenwood, R. (2001) 'Colonizing knowledge: commodification as a dynamic of jurisdictional expansion in professional service firms', *Human Relations*, 54: 933–953.

PEOPLE AND CAREERS IN MANAGEMENT CONSULTANCY

INTRODUCTION

The chapter begins with a discussion of the reasons for applying to a management consultancy firm. Next, we outline the recruitment process. What is more, we examine what consultancy firms look for in job candidates. Then, we sketch the career structure of management consultancy firms. Subsequently, we take a look at the mechanisms for career development. We also pay attention to performance appraisals. The chapter provides insight into the criteria for becoming a manager and a partner. We describe the process of partner promotion evaluation and decision making. The chapter provides a critical review of the up-or-out policy. We look at voluntary and involuntary turnover of consultancy staff. The chapter also pays attention to the price that individual consultants may have to pay. Finally, we consider the relationship between the firm and its alumni. The chapter ends with a summary, reflective questions, a mini case study, suggested further reading, and references.

Main learning objectives

- Critically reflect upon life as a management consultant.
- Understand why management consultancy is popular with many students.
- Understand the recruitment process and what it takes to get a job offer.

- Identify the roles and responsibilities at different levels of the consultancy career structure.
- Identify the main activities in the daily life of management consultants.
- Understand the career development system: what it takes to be promoted to manager and partner.
- Evaluate the benefits and costs of careers in management consultancy.
- Understand gender issues in management consultancy.
- Understand the (in)voluntary turnover of management consultancy staff.
- Understand how consultancy experience can further career opportunities outside consultancy.
- Critically reflect upon the career policies of management consultancy firms.

REASONS FOR APPLYING

If you consider applying for a position at a (top tier) management consultancy firm, you will not be the only one. Management consultancy is very popular among MBA and other business students, as well as more experienced people from industry, that is non-consultancy sectors. The prestigious management consulting firms in particular are seen as attractive employers. Why do so many business students look for a position in management consultancy? This section explores the common reasons for applying for a job as a management consultant. We distinguish between three categories of motives for joining a (top tier) management consultancy firm: to learn, to earn, and to gain status.

Steep learning curve

The first reason for applying is to develop yourself. Joining a management consultancy firm will typically put you on a steep learning curve. From day one you will get considerable, intellectual challenges. You will work on challenging management issues for big name clients. As you move from project to project, you will work on a variety of management issues. You will have the opportunity to experience a range of different organizations from the inside. You will gain experience in different industries and countries.

INTERNATIONAL EXPERIENCE   The global consultancy firms offer rich international experience. Consultancy firms are often very diverse in terms of nationalities. Consultants therefore get the chance to work in international teams. Moreover, the international consultancies typically work for international clients. Consultants get the opportunity to work with client managers and employees with different nationalities. Moreover, international consultancies stimulate short-term and long-term transfers of consultants to other offices around the world, to broaden the consultant's international experience.

THE 'GRADUATE GRADUATE SCHOOL OF BUSINESS'   The variation and the breadth of experience will speed up your learning. In addition to projects, you may follow all kinds of workshops, courses, and other training programmes for your personal development. Management consultancy helps you to further develop your knowledge, skills, and attitude. You develop knowledge about management issues, people, business functions, and industries, among others. Through the projects you develop skills in different areas, including problem solving, presentation, and project management. As a result of your experience you develop the self-confidence and presence to advise clients and lead project teams. A couple of years of consultancy experience provides a good extension to your business education. Because management consultancy is such a good training ground, it is nicknamed the 'graduate graduate school of business'.

CAREER SPRINGBOARD   Consultancy can be a springboard for your career. Moreover, management consultancy can be fun. It is inspiring to work with a diverse group of highly talented and motivated – young – people. What is more, consultancy can be entertaining. After periods of hard work, management consultancy firms often organize events to relax and enjoy, such as dinners, parties, and office outings, including skiing and sailing trips abroad. Consultancy firms have a culture of 'work hard – play hard'. This is a very important aspect of these firms.

Superior earnings

HIGH STARTING SALARIES   The (top tier) management consultancy firms typically pay much better than the industry. An exception to the rule are the (top tier) investment banks and private equity firms. As a management consultant you will have a higher salary then most of your peers in other sectors. On top of the high salaries, consulting firms may offer attractive bonuses if you meet the job requirements. Even though consultants' salaries are high, the real pay-off is at the top of the consultancy career ladder. If you make partner you will share in the firm's profits, which can be substantial.

FAST PROMOTION   To make the financial outlook even more attractive, you can get promoted in management consultancy faster than in most other sectors. Most management consultancies are run as meritocracies; performance rather than tenure counts. If you are an outperformer you will be promoted quickly, regardless of your age or tenure.

Some people joining a management consultancy firm do not have the ambition to become a partner, although they do not admit it during the application process as it would damage their chances of getting an offer. These people just want the steepest possible learning curve in order to have a jump start in industry (non-consultancy sectors) or in their own company. For example, many children of large family-owned companies are sent to management consultancy firms for a couple of years to get the best possible 'graduate graduate' training to bring back the knowledge and competences to the family company.

OTHER BENEFITS   Furthermore, there may be all kind of other benefits to the job. Consultancy firms may give you, among others, a (premium) company car, the newest smart phone, PDA, and a fancy laptop computer. Furthermore, there may be generous reimbursement rules for all kinds of expenses, including travel, dinners, and MBA tuition.

Status

WORKING WITH TOP MANAGEMENT   Working for a (top tier) management consultancy may enhance your status considerably. As a management consultant you will work for the (top) management of clients. You will work with hierarchical levels that your peers who joined other sectors will take many years – if ever – to reach. While your non-consulting peers are working in operations, you will work on the (strategic) management issues of these organizations. A very important aspect of management consultancy – even at the entry level – is that as a management consultant you have the opportunity to have a real impact on the important, strategic decisions of a client. This high impact is very rewarding and satisfactory. Because of your ties with top management, and because of the mandate given you by the top of the client organization, many people in the client organization may look up to you or even be scared of you. But also outside the client premises, consultancy may enhance your status.

ELITIST IMAGE   At a party it probably cannot hurt to drop into the conversation that you are a management consultant with a prestigious, boutique consultancy firm. Many people will be impressed by the elitist image of such consultancy firms. Finally, the image of these firms may help you even beyond your consultancy career. If you eventually decide to turn your attention to other career opportunities outside consultancy, then a couple of years with a prestigious consultancy firm will enhance the status of your CV substantially.

A PEOPLE BUSINESS

Talent

Management consultancy is a knowledge-intensive service business. People are essential to this business. In fact, it is a people business. Management consultancy firms not only compete for clients but also for talent (Maister, 1993). The dependence of consultancy firms on people varies by type of management consultancy. In a procedure type of consultancy, firms codify and centralize knowledge. They reduce their dependence on the knowledge and skills of their people. But procedure type consultancies need large numbers of people, given the dependence on high leverage. In a brain type consultancy, such codification is not feasible. Firms providing a brain type of consultancy will be most dependent on the qualities of their people. Because of the low leverage, this type of firm needs relatively low numbers of people.

Competing for the best people?

BRAIN CONSULTANTS   Consultancy firms that operate in the brain consultancy business, or firms that aspire to an elite positioning in the client market, will aim to hire the best people. Such firms will go after the best graduates of the top business schools. To get the best talent, these consultancy firms are willing to pay premium salaries and (sign on) bonuses. Brain consultancy firms compete with investment banks, private equity firms, the big name corporates, and universities for the most talented graduates.

PROCEDURE CONSULTANTS   However, firms with a procedure consultancy business model will target a different type of candidate. Because of their codified knowledge, they do not need to hire the best graduates. They can afford to work with less talented people. By focusing on less qualified employees, such consultancy firms can pay significantly lower wages. Not all consultancy firms are interested in hiring graduates straight out of the classroom.

GREY HAIR CONSULTANTS   Grey hair consultancy will look for experienced candidates. They may look for experienced managers and professionals from the industry, that is non-consultancy sectors. In addition, the importance of experience increases with the extent of implementation work. The more implementation work, the more experience matters. Management consultancy firms that do much implementation work may therefore prefer experienced candidates.

People as a sign of quality

As the quality of the output of consultancy is often hard to assess, clients may look at the quality of the inputs, that is the consultancy people. Recruiting only the best and the brightest may provide a signal to (potential) clients (Armbrüster, 2006). The more difficult it becomes to get a job offer from a consultancy firm, the more prestigious the firm becomes for clients who look at input factors as indicators of output quality. However, the hard-to-get-an-offer-from consultancy firm may also become more wanted by talent who also equate input quality with output quality, and who are attracted by the firm's elitist image.

THE RECRUITMENT PROCESS

Recruitment is a very important function in management consultancy firms for three reasons:

1. Consultancy is a people business and therefore recruiting people is crucial.
2. Consultancy firms typically have a relatively high turnover of consultancy staff, which puts a rather heavy demand on the firms' recruitment function.
3. Consultancy firms prefer to promote internal people rather than hire external candidates for the higher level (partner) positions. Recruitment has to provide sufficient numbers of talented people with the potential for partnership.

The stage gate process

The selection of candidates for positions with the consultancy firm is a kind of funnel process. Because of the popularity of management consultancy, the firms receive large amounts of applications each year. To filter out the right people, consultancy firms have developed a funnel approach. The firms have set up a sequence of stage gates to select the people that fit the consultancy firm's requirements (see Figure 9.1). At each stage of the process, applications may be rejected.

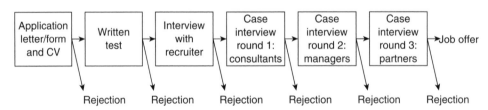

FIGURE 9.1   *The stage gate process of recruitment*

Application assessment

MOTIVATION   The selection process starts with the assessment of the candidates' applications. An application consists of an application letter and a CV. Some consultancy firms have automated the application process and offer the option of online application. Candidates no longer submit a letter but fill in the firm's online application form.

The recruiters want to know why candidates want to become a management consultant. Do the applicants' letters provide any indicator that the applicants understand what consultancy is about, or are they just attracted by the image and remuneration of management consultancy?

QUALIFICATIONS   Moreover, are there any signs that the candidates have thought about what would make them attractive for the consultancy firm? Do candidates know what it takes to be successful in management consultancy? Do candidates demonstrate an interest in the specific consultancy firm? Recruiters may look at study grades for indicators of analytical skills. Recruiters will be interested in high school grades for mathematics because they are a good benchmark (national exams). Besides analytical skills, candidates will also have to convince the recruiters that they have social skills. The letter and CV should provide evidence of good interpersonal skills; for instance, have candidates been active, besides their studies, in organizational activities?

INVITATION   Recruiters usually apply a list of assessment criteria. If the applications are positively evaluated on these criteria, then recruiters will invite candidates for a personal, face-to-face, interview. The interview will typically be with a management consultant of the firm. It will take place at an office of the firm. The opportunity (time) costs of having consultants conduct application interviews are high. Therefore, in case of doubt about the candidate's suitability, a recruiting team member – support staff – will have an interview with the candidate for further assessment.

CASE WORKSHOPS   Some firms organize case workshops to test candidates. Candidates are invited to the firm's office for a workshop. Recruiters will divide the candidates into groups of four or five people to work on a business problem. Consultants of the firm will observe how the candidates as a group solve the problem and present their solution. The consultants will also evaluate the performance of the individual candidates. Successful candidates will be invited for a round of personal case interviews. Because of the group work, the firm will save consultants' time. Moreover, the group work will allow the consultants to assess how the candidates interact with their peers. During workshops, during interviews with recruiters, and during subsequent interviews with consultants, the fit between the candidate and the consultancy firm is one of the key criteria. The interviewers have to assess how well a candidate would fit within the firm. Does that candidate have the specific attributes that the firm is looking for? Some consultancy firms require candidates to take a written test. Such tests may investigate the candidates' analytical skills and personality. Candidates who pass the written test are invited for a face-to-face case interview.

Case interviews

THE AGENDA   A case interview is a selection interview in which the candidate has to solve a case, a business problem. This selection technique originated from the case teaching at Harvard Business School and other business schools (Armbrüster, 2006). The interview consists of four parts.

1. In the first part the interviewer will put questions to the candidate.
2. In the second part the interviewer will ask the candidate to solve a case.
3. In the third part, the interviewer will ask the candidate to present his or her findings, conclusions, and recommendations, similar to a real client-consultant setting.
4. In the fourth part of the interview, the candidate may ask questions of the interviewer.

The problem solving part typically takes between 25 and 30 minutes and forms the largest part of the interview. The case is a business problem that the candidate needs to solve. For instance, computer manufacturer X is entering computer manufacturer Y's core market. Firm Y has hired the management consultancy firm for advice.

CASE STUDY

A case interview with a management consultancy firm

The preparation

Within a couple of days of sending his online application to the management consultancy firm Acme & Company, John was invited to come to Acme's local office in his home country. John knew he would have to solve cases during the application interviews. He knew such interviews would be though. Therefore he had prepared himself thoroughly for these case interviews. He had studied the examples on Acme's website and those of rival firms. He had also practiced some cases with friends who already had positions at other management consultancies.

The interview

When John entered the Acme office, he was impressed by the modern and luxurious interior. A recruitment assistant led John to the interview room. His interviewer was a young woman who introduced herself as Jennifer. After taking their seats, Jennifer briefly explained that she was a senior consultant. She provided a short introduction about herself. Then she outlined the structure of the interview. Jennifer explained that first she would like to ask some questions about John's CV. After the CV review, she would like to discuss a case with John. This would take up the majority of the interview time. But after the case interview there would be ample opportunity for John to put questions to Jennifer.

The case[1]

After a brief discussion about the CV, Jennifer introduced the case:

Jennifer: Your client is StyleCo. This is a retailer of women's fashion, mainly blouses, jackets, gowns, skirts, suits, and trousers. StyleCo has been a market leader for many decades. However, three years ago a new fashion retailer named SiggyCo entered the market. SiggyCo is rapidly increasing its share of the market while StyleCo is losing its share. The share loss has become so serious that StyleCo has asked Acme & Company to develop a new strategy. How would you approach this problem?

John: Please let me check if I understand the problem correctly. StyleCo faces a competitive threat. New entrant SiggyCo wins market share, while StyleCo loses share. Therefore, StyleCo is looking for opportunities to regain its share.

Jennifer: That is correct. How would you proceed?

John: I would like to use the following structure to address StyleCo's problem. First, I would like to understand how consumers make purchasing decisions for women's fashion. Second, I would like to know why StyleCo loses share and SiggyCo wins. Third, I would like to take a closer look at StyleCo to get a better idea of how it may respond to SiggyCo.

Jennifer: That sounds like a solid approach. So what would you like to know?

John: First, I would look to develop a sense of what criteria consumers use when buying women's fashion. I would start with looking for available market research.

Jennifer: Good. That is what we did during the project. Our data revealed the following: over the past years price has become the most important purchasing criterion. Moreover, consumers now demand more frequent collection renewal than in the past. Trendiness has become the second-most important buying criterion. In contrast, the willingness of consumers to pay a price premium for superior quality has dropped significantly and has fallen out of the top three of key criteria.

John: Thank you for this interesting information. It seems that client demands have changed over time. I would like to know how StyleCo and SiggyCo perform on these purchasing criteria.

---

[1]The firms in this case are fictitious.

Jennifer: We benchmarked the competitors. We found that StyleCo continues to lead on quality. SiggyCo achieves a significantly lower score on quality, but it outperforms StyleCo on both price and trendiness.

John: This information suggests that StyleCo's value proposition no longer fits consumer preferences. I would like to explore opportunities for StyleCo to align its value proposition to the changed consumer demand.

Jennifer: How would you proceed?

John: I would like to explore StyleCo's competences for improving its product trendiness. Furthermore, I would like to investigate opportunities for cost reduction which will allow StyleCo to become more price competitive.

Jennifer: Assume that StyleCo has the competences to become the most trendy women's fashion producer. However, it will come at a price. Investments in design and increasing frequency of collection renewal are costly.

John: I conclude that StyleCo needs to find even larger cost reduction opportunities to pay for the investments in trendiness. You mentioned earlier that StyleCo continues to lead in quality while consumers are no longer willing to pay a premium for superior quality. I would like to investigate what cost savings StyleCo may achieve by bringing its quality level in line with consumer preferences.

Jennifer: Good thinking. You may assume that the cost savings on quality will be substantial enough to allow StyleCo to invest in collection renewal and make its prices more competitive. What would you recommend StyleCo to do?

John: I recommend that StyleCo adapts its value proposition to align better with consumer preferences in order to outcompete SiggyCo. StyleCo should invest in trendiness, which is design and collection renewal, to outperform SiggyCo. Furthermore, StyleCo needs to reduce the price gap with SiggyCo just enough to win back its clients. The room for the design and renewal investments and for the price reduction should be found in the cost savings that will be realized by aligning the product quality with consumer preferences.

Jennifer: That is a very interesting conclusion. Thank you.

Discussion questions

1 How well did John do the case interview? Provide argumentation.

2 Do you think case interviews are a good way to test your fit for management consultancy? What are the strengths and weaknesses of this technique? Elaborate on your answer.

3 What other techniques may management consultancy firms use to test candidates for a management consultancy position? Elaborate on your answer.

INVESTIGATING THE CASE   So what do interviewers look for during a case interview? First, consultants want to test the candidate's analytical skills.

Not just cracking the case. A case interview is not just about cracking the case. To put it even stronger, it is not about the solution at all. Consultancy firms use cases for two reasons. First, they want to test the candidate's problem solving skills. How good are the candidate's listening, analytical, and creative skills? The interviewer wants to find out *how* candidates approach the case. Part 4 covers the structured problem solving that the top tier management consultancy firms look for. Typically, there is not one single best solution to the case. Candidates should therefore not just say that the answer is, for example, $250 million.

Show the line of thought. Candidates have to show their line of thought. Interviewers do not like candidates to base the solution on their experience or whatever prior knowledge candidates may have about the case. Interviewers want to assess the candidates' ability for thinking logically. Interviewers are interested in candidates who can use logic to reduce the complexity of the case. Consequently, candidates should not make the case more complex by force fitting all kind of theories and frameworks they were taught at business school. For example, candidates may artificially force Porter's competitive forces framework into their analysis where it is not appropriate. Interviewers do not appreciate this and candidates typically get stuck.

Respond to feedback. If a candidate goes a bit off-track, then the interviewer will usually give hints and feedback. An important assessment factor is whether the candidate picks up these hints and feedback and acts upon them or stubbornly continues on the wrong course without incorporating the hints and feedback. The extent of being willing and able to be coached is very important. What is more, candidates should never guess the solution. They should always have (fact-based) argumentation for their solution.

INTERACTING WITH THE INTERVIEWER   Second, consultants want to test the candidate's interpersonal performance. What impression does the candidate make? This is not only about the appearance, such as clothing and body language, but also about behaviour. How does the candidate interact with the interviewer? The case is not about spending 30 minutes in splendid isolation to return with a brilliant solution. It is an interview. Candidates have to interact with the interviewer.

Extracting hidden information. Almost always the candidate is not given upfront all the information that is needed to solve the case. Candidates have to put the right questions to the interviewers to extract the hidden information. Interviewers will pay close attention to how candidates try to extract the data and how they explain their train of thought. Can the candidate create a conversation? Is the candidate friendly, confident, and a pleasure to work with?

Dealing with stress. How does the candidate act under stress? How does the candidate behave if they get stuck in their attempt to solve the problem, or how do they respond if the interviewer becomes unfriendly or puts pressure on the candidate? Some consultancy firms include one interview during which the interviewer acts rather impolite, uninterested, or even aggressive. This is done on purpose: to test each applicant's reactions. It is relevant because consultants may face this behaviour in real life client–consultant interaction. Does the candidate remain calm and confident in stressful situations? The interviewers try to answer the question of whether they could send the candidate to a client.

THREE ROUNDS OF INTERVIEWS   Candidates are usually invited to three rounds of case interviews. The number of interviews may vary from firm to firm and may depend on how convincing the candidate was during previous interviews. Each interview will be done by a different interviewer from the consultancy firm.

First round. The first round of interviews usually consists of two or three interviews, each one with a different consultant. After the interviews, the interviewers will together evaluate the interviews. They will follow a structured process to evaluate a candidate's performance during the interviews. If the interviewers unanimously conclude that the candidate meets the firm's requirements, then the candidate passes the first round. All candidates will be called by one of the interviewers. If a candidate is rejected then the interviewer will outline the main arguments for the decision and answer any questions the candidate may have.

Next rounds. If the candidate has passed the first round, then he or she will be invited for a second round of three interviews. This time the candidate will be interviewed by three managers. The successful candidates who pass the manager interviews will continue to the third and final interview round. Then three of the firm's partners – often including the managing partner of the office – will put the candidate to the test. After a successful completion of the third round, the candidate will receive a job offer from the firm.

Types of interviews

In most case interviews, the interviewer will use a business problem case to test the candidates. However, in some interviews, candidates will be confronted with other types of tests, such as the data analysis case, the estimation question, the brain teaser, and the behavioural/fit interview.

BUSINESS PROBLEM CASE   The business problem case is the most common case for an interview. The candidates have to answer a question about a business problem. An example: firm A considers acquiring firm B. Firm A asks the consultancy firm to help them make the decision. Another example: firm C's profits dropped significantly during the past few years. Firm C cannot understand the cause(s) of this decline, and approaches the consultancy firm to identify the cause(s) and develop recommendations to regain prior profits. A final example: firm D thinks there is a new market opportunity, but they cannot figure out what the opportunity is exactly and how to seize it. Firm D hires the consultancy firm to assess the opportunity and come up with a strategy to exploit it.

Candidates have to structure the problem first. Then they have to develop a hypothesis about a possible solution. Subsequently, they need to analyse facts to test the hypothesis. Candidates have to extract the facts from the interviewer. A verified hypothesis is a possible solution to the problem. Candidates have to defend their solution to the problem. However, candidates should remember that the interview is not just about the solution. Interviewers are primarily interested in *how* candidates approach the business problem. Part 4 of this book elaborates on the problem solving method of the top tier management consultancy firms.

DATA ANALYSIS CASE   An alternative to the business problem is the data analysis case. The purpose is to test how candidates work with data. Candidates receive a data pack in the form of text, figures, and graphs. Together with the data pack, the candidates receive some specific questions about the data. An example: you are presented with a chart. The interviewer may ask you what you conclude from the presented data. Alternatively, the interviewer may show you a couple of conclusions and ask you to select one. Another example: the interviewer shows you a data figure. You are asked to make an analysis of something, for instance the profitability of a product, a market share, or unit cost. Candidates need to answer these questions with use of the data. They should base their answers only on the data given. Based on their answers, candidates will should develop a recommendation. Subsequently, candidates will have to present and defend their answers and recommendation to an interviewer.

ESTIMATION QUESTION   Candidates have to estimate an answer to a question. You may have to answer the question: how many kilograms of beef will a fast food restaurant chain use worldwide this year? Another example of a question is: how many new cars will be bought worldwide this year? The challenge is not to guess the answer, but to develop a structured approach. Candidates should break the complex question down into smaller and simpler ones. Moreover, candidates will need to do some mental maths to arrive at a concrete number.

BRAIN TEASER   Interviewers use brain teasers to test a candidate's creativity. Candidates have to solve a puzzle, or answer a question that requires creative or so-called 'out-of-the-box' thinking. For example, the candidate is allowed to move one digit to make the following equation correct: $42 - 14 = 2$ (answer in footnote[1]). Another example of a brain teaser is the following question: why are covers for manholes round (answer in footnote[2])? This type of interview is frequently used at the start to break the ice before a larger business problem case interview.

FIT INTERVIEW   The fit interview is used to assess how the candidate would fit with the culture of the firm. Does the candidate embody the values that the firm is looking for? Is the interviewer convinced that they want to spend many hours on projects together with the candidate? Is the interviewer convinced that it would be fun to have a team dinner with the candidate, or to visit a bar together at the end of the week? How would sitting next to the candidate be in an airport terminal if a flight is delayed for several hours, followed by sitting next to each other in a plane for a long intercontinental flight? Although these fit questions to assess the chemistry between both parties are always part of all interviews, even at entry level, they are used even more for experienced hires, that is candidates who want to join the firm from industry or another consultancy firm. Experienced candidates are typically moulded by previous employers. Such people may have more difficulty fitting in with the culture of the hiring consultancy firm.

Assessment centres

Some management consultancy firms may use assessment centres to appraise candidates. An assessment centre may take one or two days. It could comprise a mixture of interviews, exercises, and tests. Additionally, candidates may have a couple of interviews with recruiters and consultancy staff, typically managers and partners. Furthermore, candidates may have to undertake exercises, both group and individual ones. Simulations and role plays may also form a part of these exercises. Finally, candidates may have to take psychological and intelligence tests.

Application preparation

The combination of, on the one hand, the popularity of management consultancy among graduates, and on the other hand, the toughness of the consultancy firms' recruitment process, has led to an industry of job

---

[1]Move the digit '4' in a diagonal direction so it becomes the exponent of '2'. 2 to the power of 4 equals 16. $16 - 14 = 12$.
[2]A round cover cannot fall into the manhole.

application preparation products and services. For instance, there is a variety of books and websites with tips and techniques for case interviews. Various business schools have consultancy clubs that may help candidates prepare for applications. There are also specialized firms that train candidates in all steps of the recruitment process, from writing an application letter to handling the most difficult case interviews. Candidates may also find guidance on applications, as well as tips and exercises for case interviews on the websites of various management consultancy firms, under the heading 'Careers'.

WHAT ARE MANAGEMENT CONSULTANCY FIRMS LOOKING FOR?

Management consultancy firms search for candidates that combine different qualities. Broadly speaking the sought after qualities fall into six categories (see Figure 9.2). The required strength of the qualities and the assigned importance of qualities may vary between the different types of management consultancy.

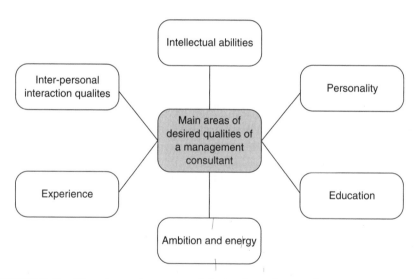

FIGURE 9.2 *The six main areas of desired qualities of a management consultant*

Intellectual abilities

Problem solving is an important role for management consultants. Management consultants should therefore have strong intellectual abilities. They must be able to diagnose and solve (complex) client problems.

Consultants therefore need to be analytical. They also have be original thinkers because clients look for fresh views. Consultants ought to be creative. They should be able to think outside-the-box. Moreover, they have to be able to synthesize large amounts of information. Finally, consultants need to have good business judgement.

Inter-personal interaction qualities

Management consultancy is a people business. Consultants have to develop relationships with their clients and with other stakeholders. During projects, consultants often need to work in teams made up of colleagues and client employees. Consultants must therefore be team players. Because of the people side of consultancy, analytical intelligence is not enough for management consultants. They also have to possess emotional intelligence. Consultants need to understand people and quickly sense psychological and political situations. Consultants may face resistance from client employees and other stakeholders. They may get involved in conflicts and need to resolve such conflicts. Consultants have to gain the trust of clients and other stakeholders. They also need to exercise leadership. Consultants must influence clients and other stakeholders. They therefore need to have persuasive powers. Consultants should be able to motivate people to cooperate.

Personality

Consultants may need to withstand high levels of frustration. It is essential for consultants to have a high tolerance for ambiguity and uncertainty. Consultants have to be flexible. They must also withstand pressure and stress. They have to possess a high level of self-control. Management consultants need to be emotionally mature. They need self-confidence and self-awareness. Consultants benefit from a strong presence or charisma. They need the courage to defend their position. Consultants have to preserve their independence. Authority gains respect and is a basis for influence. But consultants also need to be friendly. They should be a pleasure to work with. A sense of humour is a benefit. Consultants need to be honest and have integrity. They need to be responsive to feedback and humble when required.

Ambition and energy

Consultants need to be ambitious. They should have a strong drive and dedication to their job. Someone may have a tick in the box along all dimensions but lack ambition and energy. Such a person may be an onlooker on the sidelines but not a 'mover'. Management consultancy is a demanding function. Consultants often have to work long weeks and long days. They may frequently have to travel internationally. Moreover, consultants have to be flexible regarding their working hours. They have to be prepared to cancel social obligations in order to work unexpected hours. The client – and the consultancy firm – may override the social agenda of the consultant. Consultants should have the stamina to keep up with the high demands that the function puts on them. Only consultants with drive and energy can withstand the burden of long hours, restaurant food, the frequent travel including time zone differences, and the stress of management consultancy in general. Consultants should try to find time for exercise to stay fit.

Education

Management consultants should have at least the basic knowledge and skills with respect to the main business disciplines, such as accounting, HRM, organization, IT, marketing, logistics, finance, and strategy. MBA and other business studies are natural training backgrounds for management consultants. However, a business degree is not always necessary. Management consultancy firms also recruit people with other advanced professional degrees, as long as their educational background includes a strong component of analytical training. Engineers and medical doctors are examples of other analytical professions that are sought by management consultancy firms.

Experience

GRADUATE HIRING VERSUS INDUSTRY HIRING   Until the 1950s, management consultancies used to hire experienced managers and professionals from the industry, that is non-consultancy sectors. After that time, an increasing number of consultancy firms switched to hiring MBA graduates from the best business schools. However, in the 2000s, consultancies progressively reconsidered experienced hires. Sophisticated clients increasingly demand industry and functional expertise from their consultants. These clients do not want just-graduated consultants who need to gain industry/functional experience while being paid (substantial) fees by them. Because sophisticated clients demand experienced consultants, the consultancy firms need to hire experienced staff. Experienced hires will probably become increasingly important for management consultancy.

THE CHALLENGE OF EXPERIENCED HIRES   However, experienced industry hires present a challenge to consultancy firms. For a firm it is much easier to hire graduates fresh from business school or university because these inexperienced juniors can be more easily moulded into the desired form. Integrating experienced hires into the consultancy firm is much more challenging as they will enter the firm with their own way of doing things. They are the product of other firms' cultures. Moreover, while experienced industry hires may have been successful in their industry, and may even have led large groups of people, they will lack consultancy experience. These industry hires have to learn the basics – such as structured problem solving (Chapter 12 and 13) and structured communication (Chapter 14) – and may have to work for much younger project managers who have already mastered these skills. It is a challenge both for the industry hires and the consultancy firms. As a result, the career success rate for industry hires is lower than that for graduate hires.

HOW TO ENHANCE YOUR HIRING CHANCES   What can you do to enhance the chances of being hired by your preferred management consultancy firm? We take the six categories of sought after qualities and identify some success tactics (See Table 9.1). For each category we provide a key indicator, which is what recruiters look for to assess the applicant's quality. Knowledge of these indicators may help you improve your chances of being hired.

TABLE 9.1   *Tactics to enhance hiring chances*

Sought after qualities	Key indicator	Success tactics
Intellectual abilities	Problem solving in the case interview	Prepare for case interview. Learn the structured problem solving method.
Inter-personal interaction qualities	(case) Interview: interaction with the interviewer	Build a conversation and gain trust. Be assertive and friendly.
Personality	(case) Interview	Remain calm and confident under stress.
Ambition and energy	Appearance and behavior	Be energetic.
Education	Analytical training	Emphasize the analytical components of your education.
Experience	Relevant industry and functional experience	Emphasize your extracurricular activities.

CAREER STRUCTURES

The pyramid structure

MAINTAIN LEVERAGE   Most management consultancy firms have a pyramid type of organization structure. Figure 9.3 visualizes the pyramid structure. The pyramid's form reflects the leverage of the partners and the project team structure. Managing the firm's pyramid – maintaining the leverage structure – is of great importance for the business model. Partners will therefore spend considerable time forecasting the future amount of project work (or the project pipeline), expected promotion, and expected council-out cases (where the employee is 'advised' to seek a position outside the consultancy firm) in order to maintain the right balance across all hierarchical ranks within the pyramid, that is maintain the leverage.

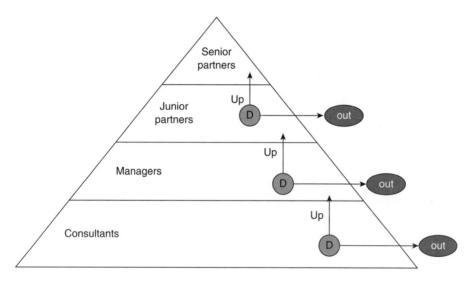

FIGURE 9.3   *The pyramid structure of the professional partnership-type of consultancy*

Note: D stands for the up-or-out decision

VARYING FORMS AND TITLES   The exact form of the pyramid therefore varies by type of consultancy. The number of levels in the pyramid may also vary across firms. To complicate things further, firms may use different job titles for the same functions. The bottom of the pyramid consists of the consultants. They may also be called associates or analysts (the terminology may vary by firm). The consultant level may be differentiated in junior and senior positions. For the sake of simplicity Figure 9.3 does not show this differentiation. The level above the consultant is the manager. Another term for manager is project leader. Some firms distinguish between junior and senior level managers.

THE TOP OF THE PYRAMID The top of the pyramid is occupied by the firm's partners. If the firm is a professional partnership, then the partners are the leaders and the owners. Many professional partnership consultancy firms differentiate between junior and senior partners. Figure 9.3 distinguishes between senior and junior partners because of important differences. The next section will pay attention to these differences. Finally, in a publicly listed consultancy firm (the managed professional business or MPB-type of consultancy) the leaders do not own the firm. The administrators of the MPB are employees of the firm, although they may hold shares in the firm.

The functions in the pyramid

Table 9.2 outlines some key characteristics for each of the four functions at different levels of the pyramid. For each level, we identify the firm's value-adding activity that is most closely related to the function. For the partner we distinguish multiple value-adding activities. However, most consulting staff, from consultants to partners, will to a smaller or larger extent be involved in various supporting value-adding activities, such as knowledge management

TABLE 9.2 *Functions, activities, responsibilities, time, and promotion odds*

Function	Main value-adding activity	Main responsibilities	Maximal time in function	Average percentage promotion
Senior partner	Leadership of the firm, marketing & sales	Leading the firm, developing the firm's strategy and organization. Promoting the firm.	No predetermined time	Not applicable
Junior partner	Marketing & sales	Developing client relations, selling projects, carrying the final responsibility for projects.	4 years	50%
Manager	Operations management	Project management, supervising consultants, providing training	4 years	50%
Consultant	Operations execution	Data gathering, data analysis, assisting with implementation of advice	4 years	50%

Note: Maximal time in position and promotion percentage may vary by firm and recruiting. Table 9.2 summarizes the main responsibilities for each function. Please note the differences between junior and senior partners.

TIME IN FUNCTION We give an example of the average time in a specific position. In real life, time spent in a position may be higher or lower. Many consultancy firms have an up-or-out career system. There are norms for time spent at a hierarchical level. After that time, consultants are promoted, or they leave the firm. The tenure may vary by firm. The number of levels may also be different across firms. Typically the career development to the partner level takes between six and twelve years (Kubr, 2002).

PROMOTION CHANCES We provide an example of the odds of being promoted to the pyramid's next level. The odds are the percentage of staff that are promoted. In practice, the odds of promotion may vary. Various factors will influence the promotion chances of staff. Besides individual performance, the leverage and team project structure of the firm affect the odds. Moreover, the growth rate of the firm determines how much room – or 'space' as consultants often refer to this – is available at the various levels of the firm.

THE NEED FOR GROWTH To provide career development chances to the consulting staff, firms have to grow. Without growth, the firm cannot promote staff, unless they want to change the leverage. The previous chapter showed how growth of a firm did not lead to growth of the profit per partner. Firms nevertheless strive for growth because growth allows firms to promote talented staff while keeping the leverage intact. Without sufficient promotion opportunities, the most talented staff will leave for other opportunities outside the consultancy firm. If people are critical for the success of the firm, then the firm cannot afford to lose its talent. As a consequence, the consultancy firm must grow.

THE MIX OF ACTIVITIES Table 9.2 shows per function what the *main* value-adding activities are. However, a particular function in the firm, for instance a consultant, is typically involved in multiple value-adding activities, although to different extents. Figure 9.4 visualizes how the mix of value-adding activities changes when an individual rises through the ranks of the consultancy firm. As discussed in the previous chapter, managers and partners of the (P2-type of) consultancy firm remain involved in the consultancy work, although to a lower extent. Consultants, even at the junior level, are supposed to participate in idea generation. Consultants may also receive some project management responsibilities, to test and prepare for their promotion to manager. Consultants and managers do not have sales targets like partners do. But consultants and managers are supposed to support the marketing and sales activities of the firm. Often current projects will provide opportunities for business development. As consultants and managers on the project are on the frontline, they may be in a good position to spot opportunities for new work and generate leads for the firm's partners.

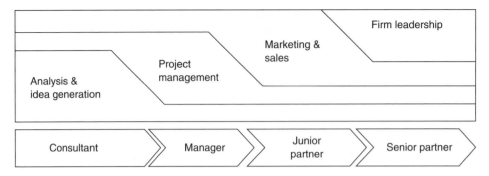

FIGURE 9.4 *The mix of value-adding activities of the different consultancy functions*

Career development

We can distinguish three main mechanisms through which consultants develop competences:

1. Staffing.
2. Training.
3. Evaluation.

STAFFING   The most important mechanism for development is staffing. By staffing we mean the allocation of consultants to projects.

> *Learning by doing.* Projects can be work for clients. However, consultants may also be assigned to internal studies, that is projects not related to a particular client. Because consultants learn most by doing (consultancy as a craft), projects provide opportunities to develop new knowledge and skills.

> *Learning by observing.* Consultants may learn by observing more senior colleagues and other people in higher level positions, such as the manager or partner on a project. This is the idea of the apprenticeship model. The junior learns their craft from the senior. The apprenticeship model lends itself very well to the transfer of tacit knowledge. In the brain type of consultancy and grey hair consultancy, apprenticeship is a common model for development. Consultants learn from their superiors, that is they learn by observing and subsequently practicing.

> *Formal training.* In a procedure type of consultancy, formal training takes a more important role in a consultant's development. Formal training is sufficient because a procedure type of consultancy relies (to a large extent) on codified or explicit knowledge.

Repetition of projects. Staffing may represent a dilemma to the consultancy firm. From the firm's perspective it may be efficient to staff consultants on similar types of project. Repeatability leads to efficiency and reduces uncertainty for the firm. Repetition may also enable consultants to develop competences. However, with an increasing number of similar projects the learning curve for consultants flattens while they may become increasingly bored. Eventually the (best) consultants may decide to leave.

Variation in projects. To retain talent, consultancy firms should ensure sufficient variation in staffing experiences. Moreover, variation in projects adds to the development of the consultants, which is also in the interests of the firm. Clearly, the role of staffing is one of the most important ones within a consultancy firm. To a large extent, it manages the trade-off between short-term profitability and the long-term performance of a firm. Moreover, it has to ensure that the right team of consultants, in terms of that team's composition of skills, knowledge, and experience, is assigned to the projects.

TRAINING   Another important development mechanism is training.

Internal offerings. Consultancy firms may have internal offerings. Such offerings may vary from an internal course to integral training programmes for all levels. Large firms will have training departments. For the new hires, firms will usually offer an introduction programme, sometimes called 'boot camp'. The new consultants are trained in important consultancy knowledge and skills and also learn about professional standards, including ethics. Procedure type of consultancies need to teach the new hires the (proprietary) knowledge and skills as embodied in the firm's procedures.

The (mini) MBA. If recruits do not have a business studies background, firms may offer business training, sometimes nicknamed a 'mini-MBA'. Introduction programmes are not only about knowledge and skills, but also about socialization of new consultants. New hires are introduced to the values of the firm and other cultural aspects. Consultancy firms may also use external training for their staff. Some management consultancy firms have a policy of sending consultants that do not have a business studies background to a (top) business school for an MBA, usually after about two years with the firm.

Networks. Partners may have personal coaches for personal (psychological) development as the transformation from manager to partner is, in psychological terms, a big step. Besides developing consultants' capabilities, training for consultants of large firms with international office networks is an important mechanism to let consultants from different offices and geographic regions meet together. Such training also serves the important purpose of building (informal) networks, which facilitate the (international) sharing of knowledge.

Opportunity cost. Training carries an opportunity cost. Time spent on training cannot be used for client projects. While hours on client projects can be billed, hours spent training cost money. For the consultant's development and for the long-term interest of the consultancy firm it is important that the consultant receives sufficient training. However, if there is scarcity of consultancy staff, the short-term interests of the firm may prevail over those of the individual consultant, and the firm may staff the consultant on the project instead of letting them attend training.

EVALUATION   The third mechanism of competence development is evaluation.

Project evaluation. Typically firms will evaluate their staff after each individual project. However, even during projects, the firms may evaluate their staff. Evaluation is not only an important tool for the development of consultancy staff, it is also used to control the quality of the consultancy work. Furthermore, evaluation is used to manage the performance of individuals, as well as the firm as a whole.

Mentors. Consultants may have been assigned a mentor. The mentors guide the consultants. They may also be role models for their consultants. They act as sounding boards and they provide developmental feedback. However, self-reflection is also an important technique for developing oneself.

Performance appraisals. Last but not least, firms will have periodic performance appraisals. These appraisals may also provide important developmental feedback. What is more, they are critical for career development. Appraisals provide the necessary information for up-or-out decisions. The promotion decisions will be elaborated on in a following section.

THE BUDDY SYSTEM   Besides mentoring, some management consultancy firms offer a 'buddy' system. A new hire is assigned a buddy. A buddy is a consultant who is of the same rank as the new hire but has been with the consultancy firm for one or two years. The buddy can informally help the new hire get accustomed to the firm. The informal nature of the buddy relationship is important. A new hire can ask their buddy all the questions that they may not ask their mentor because of the formal relationship and the hierarchical difference.

HOW TO IMPROVE YOUR DEVELOPMENT   There are various ways to improve your personal development as a management consultant.

Challenging projects. Strive to get assigned to the most challenging projects for the best clients of the consultancy firm. Not all clients are the same. There are best clients and not so good clients from the perspective of the consultancy firm. Some clients are more important than others to the consultancy. Although consultancy firms will be reluctant to admit it, the best clients get preferential treatment in terms of attention from the consultancy firm's best people. Not all consultancy staff are equal. Even though firms may use the up-or-out model, there will still be differences in the quality of people. Make sure you work for the clients that are most important to your superiors. Moreover, not all projects are alike. Projects may range from routine to new-to-the-world challenges. The latter category of projects is more exciting and offers better development potential.

Performance counts. How do you enhance your chances of being assigned to the best projects and clients? Most consultancy firms are meritocracies. This means that performance counts. Your past performance on projects will determine your future staffing chances. However, other factors also influence staffing. Staffing is a people business.

Building relationships. Therefore you should invest in building relationships with the people who influence the staffing. This is not only the partner who is responsible for staffing. Other partners and managers may also have a say in staffing decisions. They may give their preferences for certain consultants and they may also veto some proposals from the staffing partner. You have to be on the radar of these people.

Be flexible. It helps if you are not only a star performer but also a pleasure to work with. Moreover, it helps if you are flexible. Be prepared to travel, to work long hours, and cancel social obligations when a project requires it. Moreover, do not refuse staffing proposals too often.

Impression management. In general, career development is to some extent self-managed and therefore you have to be pro-active and assertive (Kumra and Vinnicombe, 2008). Impression management is important for career development. A substantial part of career development occurs in informal networking outside normal working hours (Rudolph, 2004).

Life as a management consultant

What does the (working) life of a management consultant look like? Projects should take the largest share of the consultant's time. Consultants are assigned to client projects or internal projects. When they are not assigned, they are euphemistically said to be 'on the beach'. Consultants should not be too long on the beach because a consultant's utilization is essential for the economics of the management consultancy and thus also essential for the career prospects of the individual consultant. When not assigned to projects, consultants may be involved in developing proposals for prospects. Business travel may take up a substantial part of a consultant's time. Consultants also spent time on training and internal meetings. Last but not least, management consultancy firms provide opportunities for relaxation, including dinners, outings, and sometimes even holidays. Table 9.3 sketches a week in the life of a management consultant.

TABLE 9.3 *A week in the life of a management consultant*

Hours	Monday	Tuesday	Wednesday	Thursday	Friday	Saturday	Sunday
07:00	Flight to client site	Preparation project kick-off (from 7:30)	Working breakfast with client (from 8:00)	Preparation presentation for client (from 7:30)	Data analysis (from 7:30)		
09:00	Project team meeting	Project kick-off with client	Client interviews	Client interviews	Data analysis	Data analysis	
12:00	Team lunch	Lunch with client team members	Lunch with colleagues	Conference call	Office lunch		
13:00	Preparation of project planning	Data collection	Data analysis	Stakeholder interviews offsite	Practice area meeting		Read professional literature
18:00	Preparation project kick-off	Dinner with client team members	Team dinner	Client meeting	Happy hour in the office		
20:00	Dinner with colleagues	Data analysis (till 22:00)	Data analysis (till 21:00)	Flight to home			Prepare for interviews (till 21:00)

PERFORMANCE APPRAISALS

At periodic intervals, all consultancy staff and partners will be subjected to performance appraisals. Consultants are appraised by managers. Managers are appraised by junior partners. Junior partners are appraised by senior partners. Senior partners are appraised by their peers. Performance appraisals are structured processes. The appraisal uses criteria that reflect the qualities that consultancy firms look for: intellectual, inter-personal, and personal qualities (also see Figure 9.2). Table 9.4 provides an example of a performance appraisal for a management consultant. It is a relatively high-level overview of the criteria. In real world performance appraisal forms you will find much more detailed criteria.

Grading

The assessor will grade the consultant for each criterion on a scale. The example in Table 9.4 uses a five-point scale. The grades range from 1 (excellent performance) to 5 (poor performance). Repeated 1 grades increase the probability of promotion before the standard time of your current position is over. A grade 3 performance means that the consultant meets the firm's expectations. Just meeting the requirements of your current level will not be sufficient for promotion. You need to exceed the requirements of your current level.

Remaining a grade 3 will mean that the firm will keep you on board until the expiration of your term. At the up-or-out moment the grade 3 performers are asked to leave. Firms will not explicitly communicate this to their grade 3 performers in order to keep morale high. A grade 4 means that the consultant has to improve their performance. Otherwise they will have to leave the firm before the expiration of the standard term. The risks of an early-out are very high with a grade 5.

TABLE 9.4 *Performance evaluation of a management consultant*

		Grade 1: excellent	Grade 2: above expectations	Grade 3: meets expectations	Grade 4: below expectations	Grade 5: poor
Intellectual abilities	Problem-solving: execution	√				
Interpersonal interaction qualities	Client interaction			√		
	Team work		√			
Personality	Credibility & confidence				√	

QUALITY DIFFERENCES Within a consultancy firm you will find differences in quality, or more precisely, the quality (in the eyes of the firm) range between grades 1 and 5. Both grade 1 performers and grade 5 performers will be assigned to client projects. The appraisal will be accompanied by developmental feedback. The firm will help the consultant to improve their performance, for instance by providing additional training and through mentoring.

Promotion to manager

INCREASING REQUIREMENTS   A high grade during the performance appraisal does not guarantee that the consultant will be promoted to manager. To qualify for manager, the consultant should not only master the work of a consultant, they should also have demonstrated their potential to succeed as a manager. The requirements for managers vary considerably from those of consultants. Table 9.5 shows how the requirements accumulate for the various levels in the consultancy firm. Managers are not only (very good) in the execution of problem solving, that is data collection and data analysis, they also have to excel at the design of the problem solving approach. Managers also need to evaluate, and when necessary to improve, the quality of the work of consultants in their project team. Moreover, managers have to synthesize the results of the consultants' analyses into insightful solutions for clients. While consultants need to be good team members, managers should be able to lead teams and develop the individual consultants in their team. The requirements in relation to the clients also increase. While consultants need to have a good interaction with a client, the managers need to build and manage the relationship with the client. They have to manage the dialogue with the client and they need to lead them during the project.

TABLE 9.5   *Performance evaluation criteria for different levels*

	Consultant	Manager	Partner
Intellectual abilities	Problem solving: execution	Problem solving: design & control; insight creation	Thought leadership
Inter-personal interaction qualities	Client interaction	Client relationship management	New business development
	Team work	Team leadership	Firm leadership
		Team development	Firm development
Personality	Credibility & confidence	Role model	Leadership

DEMONSTRATE QUALIFICATIONS   Consultants that are considered for promotion to manager will be given opportunities to demonstrate that they qualify for manager. Although formally they are still consultants, these candidates for promotion will be given managerial tasks as a test. Such tests are very important because a consultant needs to prove that they are able to operate successfully at the next level of the pyramid before actually being promoted to that level.

Finally, even candidates that qualify for promotion may not always get a promotion. The odds of promotion are not only determined by individual performance but also by other factors, which include the growth of the firm. For instance, during a downturn the firm may have to let go even high potential staff.

Promotion to partner

An even bigger step than promotion from consultant to manager is the promotion from manager to (junior) partner. The distinction between manager and partner is a ceiling in the pyramid of the consultancy firm. This ceiling is reflected in the important economic metric of the leverage. Leverage is defined in terms of the number of non-partners – consultants and managers – per partner. Consultants and managers work for the partners. The billings – fees charged to clients – of consultants and managers exceed their salaries and associated costs. This is the so-called billing multiple: that is fees divided by the costs of a consultant. The profit belongs to the partners.

OWNERSHIP   Partners own the consultancy firm and are the employers while consultants and managers are employees. In a publicly owned/listed firm the leaders are employees, like the consultants and managers. Leaders of public consultancies may have a share of the profit but it will be less than the profit share of partners in a private firm. However, a new partner needs to buy into the firm. They have to invest private capital to become a partner. The partner also runs a financial risk. If the firm gets into financial trouble, partners may receive a so-called capital call, which means that they have to provide additional capital from their own means to help resolve their firm's financial difficulties.

PERMANENCE   Besides remuneration there is another big difference between partners and the rest. Consultants and managers are temporary staff in the (up-or-out) firm. They stay only for a certain period of time in a consultant or managerial position. After that time they will be promoted or leave. There is no maximum tenure for partners. Only when an employee has achieved the highest level, may they stay in the firm. However, this does not mean that partners are always permanent. Even partners are subject to evaluation. Partners have to keep performing at the highest level. Whoever fails to meet the requirements of partnership has to leave.

RESPONSIBILITIES   Not only the benefits increase substantially when promoted to partner, so do the responsibilities. The responsibilities of a partner exceed those of a manager. Partners have to be able to advise at the highest client level, including the chief executives of large organizations. Partners bear the final responsibility for the projects. If projects fail, the partner is to blame. Moreover, partners have to sell. They need to develop new clients and acquire new projects. The partner needs to be an authority. Partners have to influence, motivate, and lead both clients and consultancy staff.

PSYCHOLOGICAL TRANSFORMATION   These new requirements can only be met if the individual undergoes a deep, psychological transformation (Ibarra, 2000). To be successful in the new role, the fresh partner has to develop their self-image and develop a new style and behaviour. Confidence and presence have to be developed to new, higher levels. To successfully make this leap, partners benefit from mentors and other role models.

SENIOR PARTNER   The final promotion is from junior partner to senior partner. Senior partners have the same responsibilities as the juniors. However, on top of those they carry some additional responsibilities, such as leadership of the firm. Moreover, the senior partners are responsible for the evaluation and promotion of partners. Senior partners form the so-called partner evaluation and promotion committee.

EVALUATION AND PROMOTION PROCESS   The process of evaluating and promoting candidates to partnership is structured in three steps (see Figure 9.5).

Nomination. The process begins with nominations by the partner group of the local office where the candidate works and/or the partner group of the functional/industry practice to which the candidate belongs. These partners should recommend the candidate for partnership. The partner group has to prepare an information package to provide argumentation for the nomination. The firm has structured what information is required to back up the nomination.

Evaluation. The nomination package is sent to the partner evaluation and promotion committee. The chair of the partner evaluation and promotion committee will do a desk review of the nomination packages. If the nomination passes this first screening then the chair of the partner evaluation and promotion committee will select one of the members to conduct a so-called due diligence study of the candidate. This member will visit the local office of the candidate to conduct a series of personal interviews with people in the candidate's environment to develop a 360 degree perspective on that candidate. The number of interviews will range between ten and twenty, and includes superiors (partners), subordinates (consultants), peers (managers), support staff members, and other relevant people. However, the partner evaluation and promotion committee may also talk directly to clients. If the outcome of the due diligence report is positive, then the nomination moves into the final stage, which is the review by the complete partner evaluation and promotion committee.

Decision. Before their meeting, all members will review the information package and the due diligence report of each candidate. During the meeting, the members will discuss and review each of the individual candidates. The candidates fall into three categories.

1. The first category comprises the strong candidates who clearly meet the partnership requirements. The committee will decide to promote them.

2. In the second category you find the weak candidates who are not yet ready for partnership but are perceived to have the potential for making partner. These candidates will be given a chance to be nominated again at a later stage. Some candidates can be nominated several times before they are promoted. If the partner evaluation and promotion committee does not see (sufficient) improvement potential then the candidate enters the third category.

3. The third category comprises the weak candidates who are clearly not fit for partnership. They will be irreversibly rejected. As a result of the firm's up-or-out policy, these candidates will be asked to leave the firm.

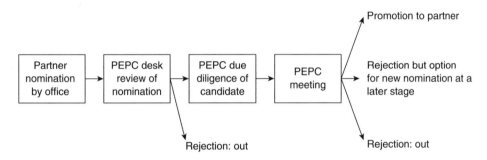

FIGURE 9.5 *Evaluation and promotion of candidates to partnership*

Note: PEPC stands for Partner Evaluation and Promotion Committee

TURNOVER

The up-or-out policy

Many management consultancy firms have an up-or-out policy. 'Up' refers to promotion of an individual to a higher level in the consultancy firm's hierarchy (see Figure 9.6). An 'out' decision means that the individual must leave the consultancy firm. The firm offers only two options. Either you move up the firm's hierarchy – within a predetermined period – or you have to go. Figure 9.6 only shows promotion after the *maximum* time allowed for a promotion. Some individuals may get promoted faster. Most firms are very reluctant to use the term 'firing'. They may not even like to use the wording 'up or out', instead they will speak of 'grow or go'. The consultancy firm will have all kinds of disguising jargon, but it comes down to a dismissal of those employees who do not meet the firm's expectations. The policy means that if you are not considered for promotion, you cannot stay with the firm. The up-or-out system is the ultimate consequence of a meritocracy. It is not seniority but performance that matters.

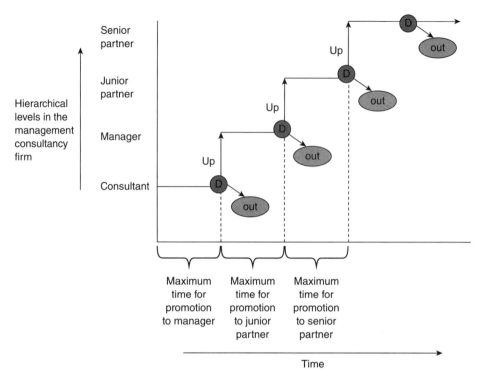

FIGURE 9.6 *The up-or-out policy of the professional partnership consultancy firm*

Note: D refers to the up-or-out decision

Survival of the fittest

DARWINIAN SELECTION The up-or-out policy may be interpreted as a Darwinian selection mechanism; only the fittest (fit between the individual's performance and the firm's demands) survive (reach the level of the partnership). This is very effective from the firm's perspective. All the weak performers are weeded out. The firm ends up with the best people in the partnership (best as defined by the firm) and with potential partners in the lower ranks of consultants and managers. The policy also keeps everybody below the rank of partner on their toes. The selection mechanisms force all aspirants for partnership to give their best. The up-or-out system is therefore highly motivating. It is a carrot-and-stick model. You either get a carrot (promotion) or you get the stick (exit the firm). Both ambition and fear will drive the people in the race for partnership to give their best to the firm.

SURVIVORS As a result of the weeding out of the weak performers, there remain only those people in the organization who are still 'in the race' for partnership. Some people are on track to achieving partnership, while others who just meet their current level's requirements will only be kept on until the next up-or-out moment. Because the latter group are often unaware of their fate, everyone still has the hope that they can make partner. However, we would like to add that not everyone who joins a management consultancy is in it for the long run (partnership). Some consultants will just want to get the experience for a few years, to learn as much as possible, and then leave the firm. Even people whose performance within the firm would enable them to make partner may leave the firm to pursue other opportunities.

MORALE   The benefit to dismissing people who lack potential is that the organization is cleared of people who run the risk of becoming frustrated, losing motivation, and becoming jealous at their more successful peers. With the so-called losers of the up-or-out game gone, the firm ends up with winners (partners) and potential winners (managers and consultants who have survived so far and who are still in the race for partnership). The morale among these survivors will be high, which is good for productivity.

Involuntary turnover

The up-or-out policy is generally the biggest contributor to the involuntary turnover of consultancy staff. However, failing to meet the firm's performance expectations is not the only reason why consultants are dismissed. There are other sources for involuntary turnover: downsizing the firm, crime, and unethical behaviour.

DOWNSIZING THE FIRM   The first source is downsizing the consultancy firm. In previous chapters, we discussed the cyclical nature of the management consultancy industry. The demand for management consultancy typically fluctuates over time.

Temporary underutilization. Capacity utilization is the essence of management consultancy's economic model. Capacity refers to the consultancy staff of the firm. Fluctuations in demand mean fluctuations in consultancy staff utilization. Declining utilization rates directly affect profit, that is profit per partner. Partners may be prepared to accept temporary below-target utilization for a certain period of time only if they expect a recovery in utilization afterwards. Then they can keep capacity in place even though demand is too small to keep that capacity fully utilized. Dismissing large numbers of consultants is bad for morale in the firm. Moreover, when the economy recovers and the number of projects sold increases, it may prove difficult to ramp up again as talent is scarce during economic upturns, and candidates are reluctant to join firms that only recently – during the economic downturn – fired large numbers of consultants.

Structural underutilization. If the longer term outlook of the demand for the firm's services does not look promising, then partners will adjust their capacity to the lower level of demand. Adjusting capacity downward is a euphemistic expression for downsizing the consultancy staff. It means that the firm will dismiss consultants. The firm may sharpen its selection process and raise the bar for its staff. The result is involuntary turnover. When firing people, the firm should take into account that the leverage structure is preserved. The ratios between partners, managers, and consultants should be maintained because they reflect the project team structure. If the ratios are changed then the firm is no longer able to efficiently staff project teams that fit with the firm's type of consultancy. To summarize, during down-cycles in the consultancy industry, firms will seek refuge in downsizing their staff. In the up-cycle, or in anticipation of an upturn, firms will step up their recruitment efforts.

CRIME AND UNETHICAL BEHAVIOUR   Crime and the violation of ethical standards may be another source of involuntary turnover. It goes without saying that consultancy staff who act illegally will be fired. Some examples of the illegal acts of consultants are:

1. Stealing information from clients and the consultancy firm to sell to competitors.
2. Leaking sensitive information to competitors and the media.
3. Using foreknowledge about clients or the consultancy to trade on stock markets.
4. Manipulating data or creating false data.
5. Blackmailing clients or other stakeholders with information.
6. Bribing clients or other people to obtain information.

Unethical behaviour includes using critical insights developed in prior projects to advise competitors of the original client, or abuse of a position of power against lower-ranked consultancy staff or against clients.

New opportunities after dismissal

Involuntary turnover in management consultancy has, in comparison to other industries, less negative effects for the individual concerned. The exception is dismissal because of crime and unethical behaviour. The least affected are consultants who are dismissed because of a down-cycle. Their performance track record was not the reason for their dismissal. If they have developed sufficient competences during their tenure with the consultancy firm, and if their former employer is a prestigious consultancy, these individuals will have good credentials on the job market. Even consultants who became victims of the up-or-out policy may find good jobs. Failing to meet the (high) expectations of some top tier management consultancy firms does not mean that the dismissed consultants are not good. Their competences may be highly valued by other, less prestigious consultancy firms or other industries. Because of the relatively good job market chances of former consultants, the downside of the up-or-out policy for individual consultants is less severe.

Voluntary turnover

Not all consultants and managers that leave the consultancy firm are forced out. Some staff turnover is voluntary. People may leave a management consultancy firm for various reasons. One reason is a change in lifestyle. These individuals will probably leave the consultancy industry altogether. The next section will elaborate on the lifestyle issues of consultants. Other voluntary leavers may join a rival consultancy firm or they may want to set up their own consultancy firm. Regarding the group that intends to establish its own consultancy, it is important to distinguish between consultants, managers, and partners. Consultants and managers who leave the firm have not yet developed all the competencies that are required to lead a firm. Leading the firm is the domain of the senior partners. Partners that leave can set up their own firm more easily than managers and consultants.

THE PRICE OF CONSULTANCY

LONG HOURS AND STRESS   Management consultancy typically pays (substantially) more than other industries, but also demands (substantially) more from staff. Working weeks of sixty to seventy hours on average are not unusual. If you include the business travel, the number of hours may easily reach eighty or more. Moreover, when consultancy projects approach their deadlines, the days tend to become even longer. Consultants not only have a large amount of work, they also face great pressure. This pressure comes from two sides. First, clients will exercise pressure on consultants. Because clients have to pay high fees, they have high expectations and demands. Second, the consultancy firm's up-or-out policy adds to the pressure on consultants.

LITTLE CONTROL   Consultants not only have to be able to function under stress, they also have to be very flexible. They have little control over their agenda because consultancy is highly unpredictable. For consultants it is difficult to plan social activities in the evenings or even during the weekends. They may have to cancel their social obligations when new, unexpected work turns up. Data may be delivered later than expected. Analyses may go wrong. Clients may reschedule a meeting or come up with new, unexpected demands. A new project may have to start earlier than expected, or arrive unexpectedly. Always last-minute things may arise that will have priority over private activities, at whatever time they may occur. Consultants may even have to return earlier from holidays, or may even need to cancel their holiday plans, if the firm requires them to do so. Of course the firm pays the expenses. Management consultancy is for these reasons labelled as an 'extreme job' (Hewlett et al., 2007).

LIFESTYLE AND LIFE CYCLE   For young people the consultancy lifestyle may not be such an issue. For consultants who are early in their career, the work is new. It is exciting to move from one client to another, from one industry to another, from one city to another, or even from one country to another. Young people may find it fun to travel. For the young consultants there is much to learn. Moreover, younger people in general have more energy. They may cope better with the long hours. Furthermore, young people may be more flexible. They may have fewer social obligations, such as partners and families. Therefore, young people have lower opportunity costs. Such people may enjoy staying in a luxury hotel with the project team and having dinners together.

When people become older, their opportunity costs increase. If consultants become older they are either promoted to manager or they are asked to leave (up or out). As managers are older, the probability increases that they have developed relationships and have families with young kids. These managers face increasing social obligations – from their partners and families – that may be difficult to combine with the demands of the consultancy firm. While their costs of work rise, they do not (yet) receive the (large) financial benefits that the partners have. The category of manager is therefore most vulnerable to voluntary turnover.

GENDER AND CONSULTANCY

THE 'GLASS CEILING'   The number of women and men that enter management consultancy firms is about equal. However, research reveals that more women drop out as they progress up the hierarchy of the firm (Rudolph, 2004). This phenomenon is nicknamed the 'glass ceiling' or the 'leaky pipeline' and it is not unique to management consultancy. There are three specific reasons for the higher drop-out for women in management consultancy.

THE UP-OR-OUT POLICY   The first reason is the up-or-out policy of the consultancy firms. This 'rat race' for making partner discriminates against women (Kumra and Vinnicombe, 2008). The extreme job and the specific promotion criteria better fit men than women. An important fact is that female consultants may become mothers. It is possible but certainly not easy to combine motherhood with consultancy. Most consultancy firms have special programmes to cater for female consultants with young children, but they cannot compensate fully. For a female partner in a consultancy firm, it is easier to raise children because partners have more control over their agenda. For consultants up to manager, the demands of being at the client site are often too much.

THE CLIENT FOCUSED NATURE OF CONSULTANCY   The second reason concerns the client focused nature of management consultancy. Client contact increases when promoted to higher levels on the consultancy pyramid. Male dominance in the top management of client organizations favours men in the higher levels of the consultancy firm.

MASCULINE STEREOTYPES   The third reason for the higher drop-out for women is the still dominant idea that men rather than women are suited to consultancy (Kelan, 2012). The ideal template for consultants is based on masculine characteristics. Women have to 'fit in' to succeed in management consultancy, which makes it a problem (Rudolph, 2004).

LIFE AFTER THE FIRM: ALUMNI

THE OUT-CONSULTANT   When consultancy staff have to leave (as a result of the up-or-out policy), the consultancy firm may help these individuals to identify and find new job opportunities. Typically, the consultants are given a certain amount of time, for example three months, to search for a new job outside the firm. The firm may decide not to staff the 'out-consultant' any longer on projects, but to let them work on internal studies so this consultant has a better opportunity to focus on finding a new job. Consultancy firms may put considerable time into counselling consultants out. They may even use their network of client contacts to help the consultant find a job. After all these consultants become the alumni of the firm.

THE WIN-WIN DEAL   Helping alumni to land good jobs is beneficial to both the alumni and the consultancy firm. Outplacement help by the firm softens the consequences of the out-decision for the affected individuals. The management consultancy does not want the alumni to carry bad feelings and complain about their former employer. Reputations are crucial for consultancies. Consultancy firms do not want to turn their alumni into adversaries. On the contrary, the outplacement service and other alumni services are directed towards developing positive relationships with alumni and creating advocates and ambassadors for the firm.

NEW BUSINESS DEVELOPMENT   If the alumni get a job at a client or a prospective client, they can become a valuable source for the consultancy firm. Alumni that reach high positions at other organizations may become clients of the consultancy firm or they may refer their former consultancy firm to other organizations that intend to hire consultants. A top tier firm like McKinsey & Company has hundreds of chief executive officers of large firms in its alumni network. Alumni may also be sources of industry knowledge for the consultancy firm. Consultancy firms therefore try to keep warm relationships with their alumni. Firms may organize conferences, dinners, and other events in order to network.

THE ALUMNI NETWORK   The number for a consultancy firm's alumni can be many times that of the number of consultancy staff (consultants, managers, and partners) active within the consultancy firm. A simplified, fictitious example may show how this works (see Figure 9.7).

Assume that at the outset, the firm employs 100 consultants. Furthermore, assume that because of the up-or-out policy the *average* tenure of consultancy staff at a firm is five years, that is a turnover of 20 per cent. Presume that the firm recruits people at an average age of twenty-three. This implies that *on average* people will leave at the age of twenty-eight. Furthermore, suppose that the firm grows by 5 per cent each year.

The total number of alumni accumulates with the annual inflow of alumni. In the sixth year, the total number of alumni surpasses the number of consultants within the firm. Eventually, alumni will retire, thereby creating an outflow of alumni. Assume people retire at the age of sixty-five. This implies that retirement will begin to eat into the number of alumni from year 38 onwards. Figure 9.7 shows that the number of consultancy staff in the firm reaches 704 by year 40. However, the total number of alumni reaches 2,353 at that time, which is more than triple the firm's staff at that time.

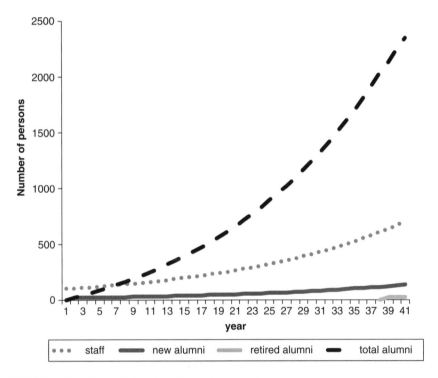

FIGURE 9.7 *Growth in the alumni network of a management consultancy firm*

AN INTRODUCTION TO MANAGEMENT CONSULTANCY

The alumni network can be a powerful tool for the consultancy firm if they succeed in turning their alumni into ambassadors for the firm. Of course, not all alumni may wish to maintain relations with their former employer. They may decide not to join the firm's alumni network. Therefore, the alumni networks are usually smaller than the total number of alumni.

SUMMARY

Application and selection

The most important reasons for applying for management consultancy positions are the steep learning curve, the superior earnings, and the status of the job. Management consultancy firms use a stage gate process for their recruitment which comprises several rounds of case interviews and assessment centres. The case interviews are a selection tool to assess each job candidate's performance with regard to problem solving and personal interaction. Consultancy firms look for intellectual abilities, interpersonal qualities, and personality, health, education, and experience.

Career

The typical career structure of a private consultancy firm distinguishes four functions at increasing levels, which are consultant, manager, junior partner, and senior partner or firm leader. Roles and responsibilities vary across levels. The up-or-out policy dictates the maximum time at a particular level and the promotion chances at each level. In performance appraisals staff are graded on a five point scale from 1 (excellent) to 5 (poor). This chapter discussed the requirements for promotion to manager. The biggest step is promotion to partner. We investigated the difference between partners and the other consultancy staff. Evaluation of candidates for partnership is a structured process that is reserved for committees of senior partners.

The up-or-out policy

This chapter elaborated on how the up-or-out policy works and the benefits it creates for the consultancy firm. An up-or-out system leads to involuntary turnover but it is not the only reason for that involuntary turnover. Downsizing the firm also causes involuntary turnover, and so do crime and unethical behaviour by individual consultants.

The price of consultancy

However, not all turnovers are involuntary. Some consultants may leave their firms by exercising free will. Voluntary turnover may be motivated by the (high) price of consultancy for individuals. Management consultancy is a so-called 'extreme job', which means a heavy workload, a high level of stress, and little control over your personal life. Finally, we explored the most important reasons why women are dropping out more frequently than men: the up-or-out policy of consultancy firms, the client-focused nature of consultancy work, and the masculine stereotype of a management consultant.

REFLECTIVE QUESTIONS

1. What are the advantages and disadvantages for management consultancy firms of hiring graduates straight out of business school, compared to hiring experienced professionals? Take into account the different types of consultancy. Explain your answer.

2. Evaluate the attractiveness of a career in management consultancy for a business graduate straight out of business school. What are the pros and cons? How do they compare? What is your personal view?

3. Do you consider the up-or-out policy to be ethical? Please provide arguments.

4. How could a management consulting firm stimulate a more balanced gender distribution, in particular in its higher ranks? What policies could it put in place? Explain your answer.

MINI CASE STUDY

Promotion to partner?

Twice a year, the five senior partners of the World Consultancy Group (WCG) that form the firm's so-called Partner Evaluation and Promotion Committee (PEPC) will meet somewhere in the world to review the firm's candidates for partnership. WCG's process of evaluating and promoting candidates to partnership is structured using three steps. The process begins with nominations by the partner group of the local office where the candidate works. These partners prepare an information package for the PEPC. The chair of the PEPC will do a desk review of the nomination packages. If the nomination passes this first screening then one of the PEPC members conducts a so-called due diligence study of the candidate. If the outcome of the due diligence report is positive, then the nomination moves into the final stage, which is a review by the complete PEPC.

Three categories of candidates

Before their meeting, all members will review the information package and the due diligence report of each candidate. During the meeting, the members will discuss and review each of the individual candidates. The candidates fall into three categories. First, the strong candidates who clearly meet the partnership requirements. The committee will decide to promote them. Second, the weak candidates who clearly are not (yet) ready for partnership. These candidates will be rejected. If the PEPC perceives potential, then a candidate will get a chance to be nominated at later stage. However, if the PEPC does not see improvement potential, then the rejection decision is irreversible. The first two categories of candidates take up the least time for the PEPC. It is the third category that consumes most of the time in the PEPC meetings. This is the category of the so-called 'in-between' candidates. They are not clear accepts, but they are not clear rejects either.

The last candidate

Top performer

It is the end of a long day. The committee has only one candidate in the in-between category to discuss before they will go out for dinner in town. The candidate's name is Hans. Hans joined WCG as a consultant, directly after his graduation in business studies. Hans excelled in problem solving. Moreover, he worked extremely hard. WCG sent Hans to a top business school to get an MBA degree, after two years in consultancy. Two years later WCG promoted Hans to manager. As a manager Hans also excelled. He made his projects hugely successful. Hans consequently exceeded client and partner expectations. His project teams always went the extra mile. Clients and partners were very pleased with the great results that his project teams achieved.

Not everybody is happy

However, not everybody was happy with Hans. The due diligence study about Hans by one of the PEPC members revealed that most of the consultants that had worked on his projects were very unhappy about the way he Hans treated them. According to them, he was only focused on the results for the client. He did not have an eye for the interests of the consultants that were entrusted to him. Hans had a reputation for creating exhaustive projects. Even by the standards of WCG, which had the reputation of being a tough firm, Hans was exceptional. He was never satisfied but always wanted more data and more analyses. Working weeks of seventy to eighty hours were normal for Hans and he demanded that his consultants work just as long. Consultants complained that Hans drained his teams. There had been incidents were consultants had spontaneously burst into tears because of the strain and exhaustion. There had even been a few consultants who had become overworked while working for Hans. In contrast, Hans was always full of energy. He never looked tired and did not seem to suffer from working the long hours. Because he was always at work, Hans did not have time for his family.

His spouse felt neglected and they had divorced two years previously. Since then Hans has worked even harder than before. What should the PEPC do?

Questions

1 What are the most important criteria that the PEPC should use to decide whether or not Hans should become partner? Provide arguments.

2 Provide reasons why Hans should become partner, and why he should not become partner. What would you recommend to the PEPC? Provide arguments.

3 How do you evaluate the role of WCG regarding protecting the interests of the consultants whom the firm entrusted to Hans? Elaborate on your answer.

FURTHER READING

Kubr, M. (ed.) (2002) *Management Consulting: A Guide to the Profession* (4th edn). Geneva: International Labour Organization.
O'Shea, J. and Madigan, C. (1997) *Dangerous Company: The Consulting Powerhouses and the Businesses They Save and Ruin.* London: Nicholas Brealy.
Pinault, L. (2000) *Consulting Demons. Inside the Unscrupulous World of Global Consulting Corporations.* New York: HarperCollins.

REFERENCES

Armbrüster, T. (2006) *The Economics and Sociology of Management Consulting.* Cambridge: Cambridge University Press.
Hewlett, S., Luce, C., Southwell, S. Bernstein, L. (2007) *Seduction and Risk: The Emergence of Extreme Jobs.* New York: Centre for Work-Life Policy. Available at: www.worklifepolicy.org/index.php/action/PurchasePage/item/201 (accessed 2 November 2012).
Ibarra, H. (2000) 'Making partner: a mentor's guide to the psychological journey', *Harvard Business Review*, March–April: 147–155.
Kelan, E. (2012) 'Gender in consulting: a review and research agenda', in M. Kipping and T. Clark (eds), *The Oxford Handbook of Management Consulting.* Oxford: Oxford University Press, 499–508.
Kubr, M. (ed.) (2002) *Management Consulting: A Guide to the Profession* (4th edn). Geneva: International Labour Organization.
Kumra, S. and Vinnicombe, S. (2008) 'A study of promotion to partner process in a professional services firm: how women are disadvantaged', *British Journal of Management*, 19 (S1): S65–S74.
Maister, D. (1993) *Managing the Professional Service Firm.* New York: Free Press.
Rudolph, H. (2004) 'Beyond the token status: women in business consultancies in Germany'. Available at: www.econstor.eu/dspace/bitstream/10419/48948/1/3939 9645X.pdf (accessed 2 November 2012).

PART 4
THE MANAGEMENT CONSULTANCY PROJECT

PART MAP

This part concentrates on the management consultancy project.

After studying this part you will be able to:

- Understand the needs of clients and other stakeholders (Chapter 10).
- Understand the client-consultant relationship (Chapter 10).
- Understand project management approaches (Chapter 11).
- Understand project team dynamics (Chapter 11).
- Diagnose an ambiguous problem, or opportunity, for a client (Chapter 12).
- Formulate hypotheses about possible causes and solutions in relation to a client's problem or opportunity (Chapters 12 and 13).
- Design custom analyses for hypothesis testing of these possible causes and solutions (Chapters 12 and 13).
- Select appropriate research methods for the data that are required for these analyses (Chapter 12).
- Translate a solution into an implementation plan for achieving the desired results (Chapters 12 and 15).
- Identify and understand the causes of a client's and other stakeholders' resistance, and select appropriate approaches for anticipating and handling this resistance (Chapters 12 and 15).
- Design a well-structured report or presentation to communicate the solution and the implementation plan to a client and other stakeholders (Chapter 14).
- Identify and understand the challenges of implementation, and select appropriate approaches for anticipating and handling these challenges (Chapter 15).

CHAPTER 10: CLIENTS AND OTHER STAKEHOLDERS

This chapter is about the development of the client-consultant relationship. We elaborate on how clients may perceive consultants and how they may feel when hiring consultants. We give attention to hidden hiring reasons and client manipulation of consultants. The chapter outlines the development of a project proposal by consultants. We distinguish between different models for the procurement of consultancy services. Finally, we discuss the consultants' contractual and moral obligations to clients.

CHAPTER 11: MANAGEMENT OF A CONSULTANCY PROJECT

This chapter is about the management and organization of a consultancy project. We outline the roles and responsibilities of the steering committee and the project manager. The chapter provides an overview of the phases of a project: initiation, design, execution, control, and closure. We also discuss the selection of the project team and the stages of team development. Finally, the chapter takes a look at the work of the junior consultant on the project.

CHAPTER 12: STRUCTURED PROBLEM DIAGNOSIS

Structured problem solving is the hallmark of the world's top tier management consultancy firms, such as McKinsey & Company, Bain & Company, and the Boston Consulting Group. Chapters 12 and 13 are indicative of the problem solving approach as used by these firms. Chapter 12 provides a step-by-step guide to a structured diagnosis of a client's problem, as well as an opportunity. We use running cases to illustrate the method and techniques.

CHAPTER 13: STRUCTURED SOLUTION DEVELOPMENT

Chapter 13 shows how top tier management consultants develop solutions for their clients' problems and opportunities. We provide a step-by-step guide to a structured development of solutions. We also pay particular attention to the challenges of uncertainty in solution development. The chapter uses running cases to illustrate the method and techniques.

CHAPTER 14: STRUCTURED COMMUNICATIONS

Structured communication is another hallmark of the world's top tier management consultancy firms. Chapter 14 is indicative of the communication approach as used by these firms. Chapter 14 provides a step-by-step guide to a structured presentation of the consultant's solution. We also pay attention to the structured design of presentation slides. We use running cases to illustrate the method and techniques.

CHAPTER 15: STRUCTURED IMPLEMENTATION

This chapter is about how consultants may implement the recommended solutions. We analyse the relationship between solution development and implementation and present a structured approach to implementation. In addition, we discuss possible roles for clients and consultants in the implementation process. The chapter adds to understanding implementation by considering the main challenges that consultants face during implementation. Finally, we discuss the evaluation of implementation projects and the consultants' contribution to the projects.

10

CLIENTS AND OTHER STAKEHOLDERS

INTRODUCTION

This chapter is about clients and their stakeholders. It concentrates on the development of the client–consultant relationship. This relationship usually begins with the marketing and sales activities of the consultant. The chapter considers the perspective of both the client and the consultant on the relationship. We focus on the role that the feelings and perceptions of clients may play in the client–consultant interaction. This chapter considers both the overt and covert hiring reasons of clients. Additionally, we investigate the positions and power of different stakeholders over the consultancy project. We compare different consultancy procurement models and we outline the consultant's proposal and contract with the client. Furthermore, we discuss the ethics and responsibilities of consultants with respect to clients. The chapter ends with a summary, reflective questions, a mini case study, suggested further reading, and references.

Main learning objectives

- Understand how clients may feel when hiring consultants.
- Understand how clients may critically perceive consultants.
- Analyse the different needs of clients, as well as the overt and covert hiring reasons of clients.

- Identify the challenges for consultants when trying to sell projects.
- Critically reflect upon the rational and emotional side of the client–consultant relationship.
- Analyse the positions and power of different stakeholders over consultancy projects.
- Identify the main elements of a project proposal and contract.
- Compare different procurement models.
- Reflect upon ethics and responsibilities of the consultant.

THE MANAGEMENT CONSULTANCY CYCLE

The value chain

Chapter 7 presented the activities of a management consultancy firm as a value chain. Figure 10.1 on the next page visualizes the primary activities of the value chain as a cycle. Management consultants go through cycles of activities. A consultancy project may be conceptualized as a single cycle. After completing a project, management consultants move to their next project. They may do another project for the same client or they may start working for another client. Each new consultancy project means a new cycle.

Marketing

A cycle usually begins with marketing activities by the management consultant. Marketing consists of various activities by the consultant to arouse the interest of a prospect. Prospect is the term used for a potential client. Consultants may use advertising and promotion to market their services. Typically, management consultants prefer to 'pull' the prospect to the consultant, instead of 'pushing' the consultancy service to the prospect. By 'pull marketing' we mean: making the prospect want to talk with the consultant about their services.

Sales

The next activity in the cycle is sales. Sales are about selling a consultancy project to a prospect. In a nutshell, sales are transforming an initial contact with a prospect into a contract. In practice, selling is a difficult process where the consultant first needs to build a relationship with the prospect, before they can explore the prospect's problem. Based on an understanding of the prospect's problem, the consultant develops a proposal for a project. After the sale of the consultancy project, the execution of the contract starts.

Execution of the contract

The execution of the contract begins with *design*: the consultant needs to design the project. Next the consultant executes the project design. Figure 10.1 follows the classic sequence of project execution: *collect the data* through desk and/or field research; *analyse the data*, synthesize the analysis results and draw conclusions; develop a recommendation for the client, that is *generate advice*. After the client has decided to implement the advice, the consultant may be asked to assist management with this implementation. Such *implementation assistance* typically implies that the consultant provides advice on how to implement the solution. After the project has been implemented, the results may be evaluated. The final step in project execution is the termination or closure of the project. After this termination, the consultant has to continue to manage the relationship with the client. This *client relationship management* may allow the consultant to identify or develop opportunities for further projects. In this chapter, we emphasize marketing, sales, and client relationship management: the highlighted activities in Figure 10.1.

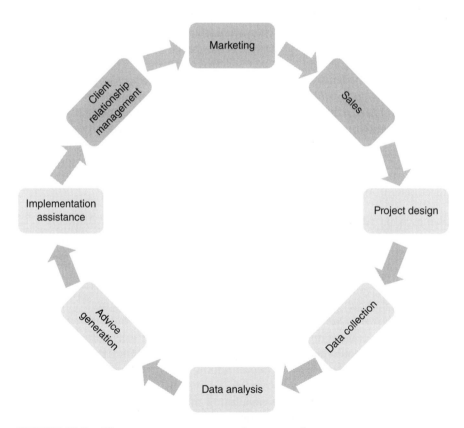

FIGURE 10.1   *The management consultancy cycle*

THE CONSULTANT'S PERSPECTIVE

The consultant's motivations

Although this chapter is about the client, we begin with a question about the motivation of a management consultant. Why is a consultant interested in undertaking projects for clients? We distinguish between the various motivations of consultants for carrying out projects.

ECONOMICS   The first motivation concerns the economics of the management consultant. Consultants sell projects to earn money. Projects by definition have a finite duration. Although the project duration may range from a couple of days to more than a year, projects have in common that they are not permanent. Because all projects end, management consultants – more or less frequently – need to acquire new projects to keep their consultancy staff utilized. They move from project to project. Moreover, firms using the up-or-out model have to grow. Replacement of old projects is not sufficient. Up-or-out consultancy firms need more projects or bigger projects.

KNOWLEDGE DEVELOPMENT   The second motivation for performing projects is to develop knowledge. Consultants – in particular brain type of consultants – may be triggered by the intellectual challenge of a project. The prospect's issue may be new to the consultant. It may be new to the prospect's industry. It may even be new to the world. These new issues provide an opportunity for consultants to develop new knowledge. We should note that management consultants do not develop knowledge for the sake of knowledge. Management consultancy is a business. Therefore, this new knowledge should be relevant to exploit it in future client projects. A project is the way for consultants to earn money. This brings us back to the economics of the consultant. Ultimately the knowledge development motivation is an economic motivation.

REPUTATION DEVELOPMENT   The third motivation for consultants to do a project is to develop – or keep – a reputation. Projects may influence the reputation of the consultant. Prestigious projects may build up the consultant's reputation. Projects are prestigious for various reasons, for instance because they offer a strategically important opportunity for the client and preferably also for external stakeholders. In general, projects for prestigious clients – large, leading, well-known organizations – may strengthen the consultant's reputation. Of course the consultant should be able to refer to these clients. To benefit, the consultant should have the right to make known that they have worked for these clients. Even better, these clients should refer to the consultant.

WEAKENING COMPETITORS   Consultants may also be motivated to carry out a project for competitive reasons. Acquiring a project may help the consultant to weaken an established rival. If the project is important to the rival consultancy, than preventing this competitor from getting the project may undermine them. Consultants may also acquire projects to pre-empt a new entrant. If there is the threat of a new entry, then established consultants may want to leave no space for the new entrant. The incumbent consultancies will target all projects to prevent the new entrant from building a beach head in the incumbent consultancies' market.

DOING GOOD   Finally, consultants may want to perform a project out of altruistic motivations. In addition to commercial projects, consultants may do so-called 'pro bono' projects. These are unpaid projects for charities or other non-profit organizations to do something good for society. Of course, such pro bono projects may contribute to the reputation of the consultancy firm. Pro bono projects may give consultants a good feeling, thereby motivating – and retaining – consultancy staff.

The consultant's road to projects

A CONSULTANT-SPECIFIC SEQUENCE   To acquire a project, the consultant needs to approach clients. Thinking from the consultant's perspective we can discover a consultant-specific sequence of the activities that led to a project. Figure 10.2 begins with the development of the value proposition. Then the consultant identifies a target market based on the proposition. However, the consultant may also begin with the identification of the target market and subsequently develop a value proposition that fits this market.

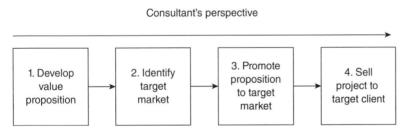

FIGURE 10.2   *The consultant's sequence of activities leading to a project*

MARKETING   Figure 10.3 visualizes the process of marketing and selling a consultancy project. Marketing makes prospects aware of the consultancy firm's value proposition and may stimulate the prospect's interest in this proposition. Such an interest may create a sales lead. Sales leads are opportunities to contact prospects. Assume that a prospect has some interest in the offerings of the consultant and therefore might be interested in meeting the consultant. Figure 10.3 breaks down the sales process into four steps. The horizontal axis shows the time sequence. The vertical axis indicates the probability of sales leads as a result of various marketing mechanisms (based on Glückler and Armbrüster, 2003).

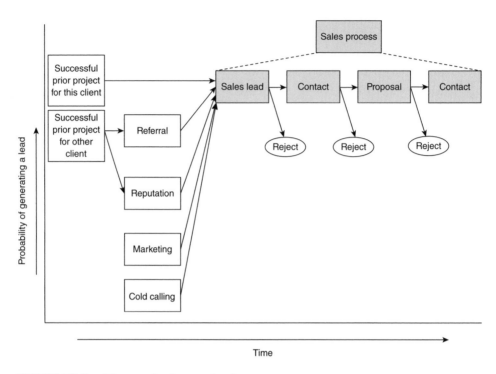

FIGURE 10.3 *The marketing and sales process*

GENERATING SALES LEADS   Marketing is not the only way to generate sales leads. We may distinguish between the different mechanisms to create sales leads.

Repeat business. The most effective way, which has the highest probability of generating a lead for a consultant, is having done a successful project for that particular client in the past. This is called 'repeat business' and those clients are named 'repeating clients'.

Referral. The second best way for a consultant to develop a lead is referral by another client of the consultant. Because the consultant has done a successful project for this client in the past, the client may refer the consultant to a prospect. Therefore, successful prior projects create opportunities for acquiring new projects: success breeds success. This reinforcing cycle benefits the established management consultancy firms. At the same time, it makes it difficult for new entrants to build a consultancy practice.

Reputation. Reputation is also an essential mechanism to generate sales leads. Prospects may invite consultants based on their reputation.

Consultancy firms develop a reputation, primarily through their client work. However, marketing may also help to create a reputation. Reputation benefits the established consultancy firms.

Marketing. Marketing is important in management consultancy. There is no legal obligation to use management consultancy. Consultants therefore have to promote their services. Advertising, PR, and publications are some examples of the marketing instruments of management consultants. Some firms, such as Accenture, may adopt a marketing strategy that resembles a fast moving consumer goods company: large-scale advertising and (sports) sponsoring. Consultants may also use informal networking activities to promote their services. They may join network clubs, sports clubs, and charity organizations in order to set up informal contacts. The idea is to transform informal contacts into formal contacts.

Cold calling. Some consultants may use so-called 'cold calling' to develop sales leads. They will make telephone calls to prospects. The consultants use these calls to make the prospects aware of an issue and to create interest in the consultant's value proposition. Cold-calling is an example of a 'push strategy'; the consultants push their propositions.

FOLLOWING UP LEADS Consultants have to follow up on sales leads. In consultancy firms, this is the task of the partners and possibly others with sales responsibilities. They have to convert the sales lead into a contact, that is secure an appointment to meet the prospect. However, partners may also fail to get an appointment. In such a case, they have to turn to the next sales lead. The purpose of the contact with the prospect is to receive a request to make a proposal for a project. Of course, not all initial contacts will lead to requests for proposals. Moreover, the consultant may not be the only one who is asked to develop a proposal. The prospect may invite several consultants. If the prospect accepts the consultancy firm's project proposal, then a contract can be made. After the contract has been signed, the project can begin.

REFUSING TO SELL Thus far, we have assumed that consultants approach prospects. However, this may also be the other way around. Prospects may approach consultants. This seems attractive but may carry risks for the consultant.

Selectivity. Consultants should avoid any temptation to sell outside their defined target market. They should not pick up everything that goes by. If the consultant is being approached by a prospect, they should be selective. Rejecting a prospect that falls outside the target market may be interpreted as arrogance on behalf of the consultant, but it is just good business sense. Consultants must dare to refuse projects that do not fit their target market and value proposition.

Competence development. The question arises: why should consultants stick to their defined business model, including target market and proposition? Executing projects that fit the consultant's value proposition provides the fastest learning curve. This fit allows a consultant the best means to develop competences. It is better to focus on one single learning curve where one can progress quickly and go far, than being fragmented over various learning curves, where one progresses slowly and does not go far. A sales strategy focused on a defined target market and value proposition not only enhances competence building but also generates a sharp profile and reputation for the consultant. The focused consultant will be more recognizable for prospects.

SELLING TO REPEATING CLIENTS   Repeating clients are clients that have commissioned projects from the consultant before. When selling to an existing client, a consultant has an advantage over competitors.

Competitive advantage. The consultant has experience with the client, they have insight into the client organization and have developed trust. Consultants should exploit that competitive advantage. By selling to existing clients, the consultant increases sales to these clients and deepens the relationship, which in its turn facilitates future repeat business. There is a reinforcing loop in selling to existing clients. Eventually the consultant may become the preferred supplier or house-consultant. Moreover, repeating client sales is more efficient than trying to create new clients.

Cost savings. Assume that developing a proposal in response to a prospect's request costs the consultancy firm $150,000 in time and expenses. Further assume that the consultancy firm's success ratio for requests for proposals by prospects – not existing clients – is 20 per cent. This ratio implies that one out of five proposals leads to a contract for a consultancy project. The acquisition cost per contract is $750,000. Developing new business is relatively expensive when compared to repeat business. A consultant may save on marketing and sales costs by focusing on existing clients, assuming that these clients provide sufficient business opportunities. By focusing on repeating clients, a consultant shifts the strategy from continuously hunting for new – single – transactions to developing a long-term, on-going relationship.

CLIENT RELATIONSHIP MANAGEMENT   As stated before, it is easier for consultants to sell projects to current clients than to new prospects. Nonetheless, consultants often neglect their existing clients and prefer hunting for new clients. New business development seems more attractive than nurturing existing business. Of course there are situations where new business development is a must, for instance, when existing clients do not provide sufficient growth opportunities. But in general, it is important for a consultant to maintain a good relationship with their current clients. Consultants need to visit them, especially if there is no new project foreseeable (Maister, 1993). Consultants should entertain their existing clients, provide them with the intellectual capital to build loyalty, and cultivate a lasting relationship. Consultants should consider this as sowing before harvesting. When a new issue – a problem or an opportunity that needs investigation – arises in existing clients, they will think of their consultant. The next step is that they will call their consultant to discuss the issue.

FEWER CLIENTS, MORE SALES   A key account principle for management consultants is to focus on the most attractive clients. The maxim is to sell more to the best clients and to sell not one particular service but bundles of different services. An example illustrates the maxim. Twenty years ago a leading management consultancy – let's call them Acme & Partners – worked for 450 out of the top 500 firms in its home country. Since then Acme has doubled its revenues. The question may arise: how many of the top 500 do they serve at present? You would expect that Acme has increased its share of the top 500. In contrast, Acme has pruned its client base. It currently works for only 300 clients. Selling more services to fewer clients is the explanation for their growth.

BROKERING AND ETHICS   Figure 10.3 shows that prior projects may make a consultant more attractive in the eyes of clients and prospects. Some firms like to hire a consultant after that consultant has completed a project for a leading competitor in the prospect's industry. These prospects want to benefit from the experience of the consultant.

Efficiency. It may be tempting for consultants to sell projects to organizations that are similar to the consultant's existing clients, or to organizations with issues that are similar to the consultant's existing clients. Selling projects to similar organizations, or about similar issues, is not only efficient in terms of project sales but also in terms of project delivery. Such repeating projects are efficient to deliver because the consultant can broker the solution that was developed for the prior project. This is the so-called 'copy-paste' solution.

Ethics. Brokering solutions may be efficient but using sensitive knowledge about previous clients to help new clients is also unethical. If the prior client's knowledge is confidential, then such brokering practice is illegal. Clients can protect themselves against such leakage of knowledge to competitors by including an exclusivity clause in the consultant's contract; that is the consultant may not work for any other firm in the client's industry for a certain period of time. Large consultancy firms cannot permit working for only one client per industry. This would limit their scale. Consultancy firms will have taken measures to prevent the leakage of sensitive, confidential knowledge.

For instance, they will have different consultants working for different clients in the same industry. Consultants that work for competing clients are separated by so-called Chinese walls. These walls prevent the involved consultants from exchanging sensitive and confidential information about their clients. The separate consultancy teams in combination with Chinese walls allow the firm to simultaneously serve clients that are direct competitors.

THE CLIENT'S PERSPECTIVE

Understanding the client

So far we have only looked through the eyes of a management consultant. Now we switch our perspective to the client. Being able to switch perspectives is a critical success factor for consultants. To get the client's business, the consultant needs to understand the client. This sounds obvious, but its practice is stubborn.

The client's road to a project

In the previous section we outlined the sequence that is logical from the consultant's point of view. Figure 10.4 presents the logical sequence for clients.

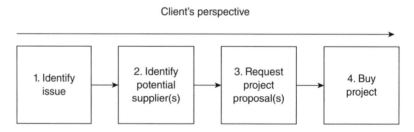

FIGURE 10.4 *The client's sequence of activities leading to a project*

IDENTIFY THE ISSUE   First, the client becomes aware of an issue that needs to be addressed. The issue can be a problem or an opportunity that needs to be investigated. However, it can also be an informal hiring reason. In case of a problem or an opportunity, the client has to take a make-or-buy decision. For informal hiring reasons, the client always needs an external management consultant.

IDENTIFY THE SUPPLIER   If the client decides to look for outside help, then they will approach one or more external management consultants to submit a project proposal. After evaluating the proposals, the client may select one.

What does it feel like to be a client?

Imagine how you may feel when you are the client of a management consultant. We outline some common feelings that clients may have (based on Kubr, 2002).

1. Clients are worried about the problems they are confronted with. They are under pressure to solve these problems.

2. Clients may believe they are incompetent because they have failed to solve the problem themselves. Client managers may be disappointed about their own staff for being unable to solve the problem.

3. Clients may be afraid to become dependent on an outsider, that is the management consultant. Clients may fear a loss of control. They may be terrified of turning over intellectual control to a consultant. Clients may also worry about the moral hazards of working with a consultant. Will the consultant behave opportunistically and leak sensitive information to competitors? Clients may feel vulnerable and exposed when they invite a stranger – a management consultant – into their organization at a time when it is in a weak position.

4. Another fear that clients may have is that of choosing the wrong consultant for their project. What if the consultant is incapable? Clients may also be anxious they will pay too much for the services offered. They may also be afraid that they will not be able to justify the high fee to stakeholders.

5. Regarding stakeholders, clients may fear the reactions of superiors, subordinates, and colleagues about hiring consultants. Clients may be anxious that stakeholders will say that the client should be capable and should have solved the problem itself. Shareholders do not pay managers to hire consultants to solve problems.

6. By hiring a consultant, the client takes a personal risk. If the consultancy project fails, the client may be held accountable by the stakeholders.

7. Finally, the client may be sceptical about the consultant. The client may be suspicious and doubt that the consultant will deliver what is promised and what is paid for.

The client may not have all of the above-mentioned feelings in every consultancy project. Clients' feelings may vary with the situation at hand. For example, compare the situation where the client needs a consultant to solve an urgent and serious problem with the situation where a client hires a consultant to legitimate an intended decision of that client.

How clients may perceive consultants

We can distinguish between the functional perspective and the critical perspective on management consultants.

THE FUNCTIONAL PERSPECTIVE In the functional perspective, management consultants are regarded as experts, as doctors that cure sick patients (clients), or they are regarded as facilitators (process consultants).

THE CRITICAL PERSPECTIVE The critical perspective assumes that management consultants are opportunistic and lack sufficient capabilities. We may distinguish several critical perspectives on consultants.

Rhetoric. Clients may think that management consultants create demand for their services. As stated before, not all clients have the same perceptions of consultants in all situations. Perceptions may vary by client and the situation at hand. Consultants use rhetoric, or so-called 'consultancy speak', which is a mystic vocabulary mixed with jargon, to increase the client's perception of uncertainties. Consultants may use esoteric language to portray the client's environment as fast-changing and uncertain. Through rhetoric, management consultants stimulate client anxiety and hence the demand for consultancy services.

Management fashion. Consultants also create demand through developing management fashion (Abrahamson, 1991). These new management concepts create the need for clients to catch up. In the process of catching up, consultants make clients dependent on them: the consultants create a golden jail for clients (Kakabadse and Louchart, 2006).

Sell more. Clients may also believe that management consultants will try to sell more than the current consultancy contract or the current consultancy project. Clients can suspect that consultants will try to extend current projects. Clients may perceive that once the contract is secured, consultants will start thinking about a new one (Bloch, 1999). Clients may also think that consultants must please the people who sign the consultancy contracts ('his master's voice').

Push solutions. Clients may be convinced that consultants push solutions. Consultants resemble missionaries: they convert clients. Clients may believe that consultants will try to convince them that they have the solutions to all client problems (Kakabadse and Louchart, 2006). In this perception, consultants sell snake oil.

Old wine in new bottles. Consultants may be seen as salesmen who sell old ideas as new ones. According to this critical view, consultants repackage old wine in new bottles. This new labelling may be related to creating management fashion.

Flawed services. Clients may think that management consultants sell flawed services (De Burgundy, 1998). The consultant's services may be perceived as ineffective. Clients may perceive the consultant's services as cosmetic or quick fixes that lack long-term value for the client.

Standardized solutions. Clients may believe that consultants sell standardized solutions: that is one size fits all. In this critical perception, consultants mystify their product through so-called 'consultobabble'. Through vague jargon they try to hide the inadequacies of their services (Williams, 2003).

Sell partner – deliver junior. Clients may also negatively perceive the consultancy practice of leverage. Clients may feel disappointment when the senior partner sells the project and subsequently sends juniors to execute the project. After the juniors have done the job, then the partner returns for the final presentation. Clients may have expected more face time with the senior partner. In particular, if the juniors have insufficient experience and skills, the client may get a negative perception. The client may look at the leverage model as senior partners sending the school bus – with juniors – to the client site to learn the job at the client's cost.

Steal your watch. Clients may think that consultants use the clients' own knowledge instead of the consultants' presumed expertise. This perception can be summarized with the phrase: consultants borrow – or even worse, steal – your watch to tell you the time for a fee.

Distinguishing between different types of clients

It may sound obvious to say that not all clients are alike, but this may easily be overlooked. Clients may vary on several dimensions. The differences along these dimensions will influence the relationship between client and consultant. Consultants should be aware of these differences when they try to develop a relationship with a client.

VARYING EXPERIENCE   First, clients may have varying experience. There is a spectrum ranging from inexperienced, first-time clients to highly experienced, seasoned clients. An increasing number of clients will have held prior positions in management consultancy. These people not only have experience dealing with consultants, they also have experience acting as consultants. The experience of the client influences the client–consultant relationship. Among other things it influences the balance of power between client and consultant.

VARYING POWER   Second, the power of clients versus consultants may vary. The balance of power between client and consultant may differ for various reasons, such as the relative size of the client and the consultant (see Chapter 4 for a discussion about the different sources of buyer power). It should be noted that power asymmetry is not reserved for one side: client or consultant. You may have relations between powerful clients and weak consultants. There may also be situations with powerful consultants and weak clients. But we may also distinguish between balanced relations where client and consultant work as partners.

VARYING KNOWLEDGE AND CAPABILITIES   Third, the knowledge and capabilities of clients may vary. Some sophisticated clients will have almost no knowledge and capability gap with their consultants. Such clients may have no need for inexperienced juniors. These clients may prefer to work only with the most senior consultants on an equal basis. The client and the consultant work as co-makers of the solution to the client's problem.

VARYING HIRING REASONS   Fourth, the hiring reasons may vary across clients. As stated before, different clients may hire consultants for different reasons. We may distinguish various formal and informal reasons for hiring management consultants.

Developing the relationship with a prospect

PROSPECTS AND CLIENTS   In the previous section we discussed that selling consultancy services to existing clients or prior clients may be more efficient and effective than developing new client relationships. However, we would also acknowledge situations when there is a need to develop new client relations. We have already described how consultants make contact with the prospect. This section starts when the consultant receives an invitation for an initial contact with the prospect (see Figure 10.5).

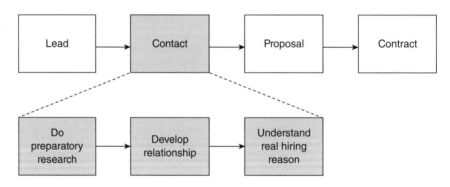

FIGURE 10.5 *Establishing contact with the prospect*

PRE-CONTACT   Management consultants should thoroughly prepare for the initial meeting with the prospect. The consultant should have at least a basic knowledge of the prospect. This knowledge includes the prospect's products, its value-adding activities, and how the prospect is organized. The consultant should also have some understanding of the prospect's industry.

In addition, the consultant needs information about the people, both the prospect and other important stakeholders. Large consultancy firms may have knowledge management systems holding this type of information. Otherwise, the consultant will have to do some (desk) research. The consultant should not use the initial meeting with the prospect to ask questions which the consultant could have answered through a little preparatory research. The consultant should not only do their homework about the prospect, they should also prepare to prove this claimed value proposition to the prospect. What evidence can they share of their expertise and experience in solving problems for clients?

INITIAL CONTACT   The initial contact is in the first place an orientation for both the prospect and the consultant. The consultant should try to form a bond with the prospect. Before discussing the hiring reason, the consultant needs to build a relationship with the prospect. A sound relationship is a prerequisite to make a client gain trust and feel comfortable with the consultant and the consultancy process (Pellegrinelli, 2002). Prospects want to assess the consultant first before they are ready to discuss their issue. Prospects will in particular look for indicators of the consultant's trustworthiness, competences, and empathy or sensitivity to the prospect's situation (Sadler, 2001).

BUILD CREDIBILITY   During the first meeting(s) the consultant needs to build credibility. The consultant may use references from prior clients and may also demonstrate their thought leadership (in particular if they are in a brain type of consultancy). This credibility building is a necessity because management consultancy is not a profession. Anyone can call themselves a management consultant. The spectrum of people who call themselves consultants runs from principled and competent people to charlatans. The absence of professional qualifications is not only a problem for principled and competent consultants who also have to prove their credibility, it also poses a problem for prospects. The absence of professional standards makes the hiring of consultants more difficult. Prospects have a higher risk of hiring the wrong person (a charlatan or an incompetent consultant).

INTERPERSONAL FIT   A critical success factor for a consultancy project is the interpersonal fit between client and consultant (Covin and Fisher, 1991). Similarity in client and consultant – for instance shared backgrounds – may help to create a climate of trust. Thinking on the same wavelength and having the same reference frames may stimulate the development of the relationship. However, in the problem solving stage of the consultancy project, it may be beneficial if the consultant thinks differently and introduces new reference frames to the client. Consultants who succeed in changing a client's outdated dominant logic create significant value for their client.

RATIONAL VERSUS EMOTIONAL VIEW OF CONSULTANCY Management consultancy projects may seem only rational. In the rational view, consultants are the experts and clients hire them for problem solving. The problem solving is rooted in facts and analysis. According to the rational view, consultants only use logical argumentation. Recommendations are implemented according to plan. Consultancy projects are about improving business results for the client. This rational view is one-sided.

The emotional side. Consultancy projects also have an emotional side. Because of the emotional aspects in consultancy projects, consultants need to develop the emotional depth of the relationship with the prospect (Kakabadse and Louchart, 2006). We concentrate on the client's emotions. However, we acknowledge that consultants also have their anxieties, frustrations, and uncertainties. Consultants' emotions may emerge in particular when clients try to manipulate them.

Anxieties and uncertainties. What is the emotional side of the client–consultant relationship? We provide some examples. Clients have their anxieties and uncertainties. Clients may have a more or less vague awareness of an organizational situation that needs to be improved and that justifies an intervention by management consultants (Arnaud, 1998). Clients may sense that they have an issue, but they may be uncertain about the specific nature of the problem (Wittreich, 1966).

Emotional support. Clients may hire consultants not only for pragmatic advice – solutions to business problems – but they may also implicitly hire consultants for emotional support (Lundberg and Young, 2001). Consultants can act as sounding boards. Top managers in particular may hire a management consultant as a sounding board. In most organizations it is lonely at the top. Top managers typically cannot share their uncertainties with peers or subordinates (Johanson, 2003).

Perceived loss of control. Clients' uncertainties are to a large extent associated with the fast-changing environment in which they have to operate. This fast-changing environment leads to a (perceived) loss of control by client managers. Clients who are top managers are in particular under pressure from their organization's shareholders, supervisory boards, and other stakeholders to do something. These top managers have to show that they are creating change (Kakabadse and Louchart, 2006).

Rhetoric. The rhetoric of management consultants may reinforce client uncertainty. Management fashion fulfils an important role in such rhetoric. However, consultants may also provide reassurance of a sense of control for clients. In this role, consultants aim at reducing the uncertainties that clients have (Sturdy, 1997).

WHO IS THE CLIENT? During the initial meeting(s) the consultant needs to assess the prospect. A key question that needs to be answered is: who is the real client?

> *The user client.* The contact person may not necessarily be the real client. He may be a gatekeeper. We define the real client as the problem-owner. This is typically the manager who is responsible for the problem area and has an interest in solving it (Kubr, 2002). This is the so-called *user* client.
>
> *The economic client.* Consultancy has to be paid for by the client. The person who holds the authority – and the budget – to make the hiring decision is called the *economic* client. The user client and the economic client can be the same person. However, in some (large) organizations the user client and economic client may be different people. The user client may be the manager of a particular department, while the economic client is the general director of the organization.
>
> *Stakeholders.* If the two client roles are divided between two people, the consultant needs to reach agreement with both the user client and the economic client to sell a project. Sometimes the client is not a manager of the organization but a stakeholder. This can be an internal stakeholder, such as the supervisory board, and the work council. However, external stakeholders can be clients as well. Think of banks, private equity funds, and (major) shareholders.

THE TRAP OF THE INDEPENDENT ARBITER It is crucial for consultants to know who the real client is. Consultants should never serve more than one master at the same time (Kakabadse and Louchart, 2006). They should give exclusive and sole attention to the client. Consultancy is defined as independent advice. However, the consultant should not think and act as if they are an independent arbiter in the field of – stakeholder – forces that may characterize the client organization. They should realize who has hired them. To avoid the penalty of being never hired or recommended again, consultants should focus solely on solving their client's problems and remain far from any action that will conflict with that client's interest. We would acknowledge this is a purely economic perspective. There is also the ethical perspective. If serving the client's interests will lead to unethical practices, than consultants should decide whether they want to be part of such a scheme. Such decisions are about values. Ethics refer to the distinction between what you have the right to do and what is right to do.

CHECKING THE CLIENT Consultants should not only check the position and status of the client, they should also find out how much experience the prospect has with consultants. This is important when deciding on the division of roles and responsibilities. But it is also useful information for the negotiation of the consultancy fee. Additionally, consultants should determine what the chances are that the contact will result in a consultancy project for them. They should test how open the prospect is to the consultant. Consultants should find out whether the prospect is ready to explore the issue with the consultant. Another important success factor for consultancy projects is motivation. Is the prospect motivated to have the issue solved by a consultant in general? And if so, is the prospect motivated to have the issue solved by this specific consultant? The consultant should also assess the knowledge and competences of the prospect. What, if any, contribution can the prospect make to the consultancy project?

CASE STUDY

Understanding the client

Meeting the client

Ronald has recently been promoted to partner of Acme Consulting. The consulting firm has given him responsibility for the Transnational Corporation, a medium-sized client of Acme. Ronald's predecessor at Transnational is another partner, Heinrich, who is going to retire. In a transfer call, Heinrich warned Ronald about the chief executive officer of Transnational, Dennis. Ronald should be careful when dealing with Dennis. Heinrich introduced Ronald to Dennis during a visit. During this meeting Dennis largely ignored Ronald and focused his attention on the retiring Heinrich.

Lunch with the client

Three months after the transfer of the client from Heinrich to Ronald, Ronald receives a call from Dennis. Dennis invites Ronald for a lunch at an expensive restaurant to get to know each other a bit better. During this lunch Dennis takes the floor. He extensively lectures Ronald about Transnational and about how important he has been as the leader, and still is, for the success of his company. Ronald hardly gets an opportunity to speak as Dennis continuously dominates the conversation. Ronald decides to listen politely to his client. After coffee has been served, Dennis suddenly changes the conversation.

The business proposition

After one and a half hour of storytelling, Transnational's CEO gets down to business. The reason why he has invited Acme Consulting is that he has a job for the consultancy. He has determined that Transnational needs to change its organization from a geographic structure to a product structure. Transnational is organized into three geographic divisions: Americas, Asia-Pacific, and Europe, Middle East and

Africa (EMEA). The new organization should be structured around Transnational's four product categories. Acme's consultants may work out the details of this reorganization and implement it.

Anxiety

Ronald is surprised by the sudden turn in the discussion, but he feels flattered by the request. However, when he carefully enquires how Dennis has determined that this reorganization is necessary, the CEO responds indignantly. How did this young partner dare to question the judgment of one of the biggest names in the industry! Did the newcomer not know how important trust is in a client–consultant relationship?

The ultimatum

After making his displeasure visible, Dennis half-rises and says that Acme's arch-rival, the consultancy firm Brain & Company, is eager to start doing work for Transnational. Before he leaves, the CEO lets Ronald know that he expects a project proposal from Acme within a week. Ronald is scared. As a partner he needs to sell projects. He cannot afford to lose this client, in particular not to arch-rival Brain & Company. Such a loss of business, and loss of face, would be the worst imaginable start to his career as a partner.

Discussion questions

1 What went wrong in the meeting? Explain your answer.

2 Is Ronald to blame? What, if any, mistakes did he make? Explain your answer.

3 What should Ronald do? What options do you see? Compare the advantages and disadvantages of these options. Elaborate on your answer.

UNDERSTANDING THE PROSPECT'S REAL HIRING REASON

Understanding the prospect's issue

The next step for consultants after having developed an initial relationship is trying to understand the prospect's real hiring reason. Consultants naturally feel the urge to promote their services. They may be under pressure to sell a project. However, pushing their services will be counterproductive. Consultants should develop the discipline to try to understand the prospect's issue before offering anything. They should not be tempted by the prospect to talk about solutions before they have a sound understanding of the prospect's issue. Only after fully understanding the hiring reason may consultants begin to discuss their services. Consultants need to listen to the prospect before they speak.

Understanding the prospect's needs and expectations

The consultant needs to understand the needs and expectations of the prospect. What is the prospect looking for? Why do you think you should be hired? The consultant should discover what purpose the prospect has in mind with the consultancy project. How can the consultant develop an understanding of the prospect's needs? Before the initial meeting with the prospect, the consultant may tap their network to gather intelligence about the prospect. If the consultant has network contacts who know the prospect, then they may provide valuable insights on the prospect's personality, motivations, and past behaviour. During the meetings with the prospect, the client should listen carefully, and subtly verify the prospect's real reason for hiring the consultant. We can distinguish between the overt and covert reasons that prospects may have.

Overt hiring reasons

The consultant should find out why the prospect is considering hiring a management consultant. The prospect may have a problem that they want to solve. The prospect may lack the competences to solve this problem. There are also situations where the prospect has skilled staff to solve the problem, but they are occupied with other tasks. The client does not have time to solve the problem.

TASKS OR PEOPLE PROBLEM?   Consultants should find out whether the problem is about tasks (technical problem solving) or about people (people and relationships). A technical problem may be a people problem in disguise. For instance, technical problems may be the result of dysfunctional relationships between people or dysfunctional individuals.

WHAT ROLE IS REQUIRED?   After learning about the problem, the consultant should find out what role(s) the prospect seeks. The prospect may seek an *expert*: the consultant is expected to provide expertise to solve the prospect's problem. If the problem is vague, then the prospect may look for a doctor–patient relationship: the *doctor* (consultant) diagnoses and solves the problem of the patient (client). In contrast, the prospect may only want a process for problem solving: the consultant should then be a process *facilitator*. Finally, the prospect may seek a *hired hand* (or brain): the consultant is then only expected to provide a temporary capacity. We would emphasize that this phase is about understanding the prospect's needs and expectations. Understanding needs does not automatically equal a delivery of services to fulfil these needs. We do not want to create the impression that the consultant subsequently should do everything that the client initially expected.

WHAT WILL BE THE DIVISION OF TASKS?   The consultant should also investigate what division of tasks the prospect expects. What ideas does the prospect have about who will do what in the consultancy project? What is the prospect prepared to contribute to the project in terms of time, information and skills? Some prospects will prefer a joint project in which client and consultant work as co-makers. Other prospects may not want to be involved at all in the project. Some may expect a high degree of contact with the consultant, while others will have no such need. Furthermore, some prospects may want consultants to be present on site and visible to the stakeholders. On the contrary, other prospects may prefer consultants to be invisible.

SELECTION OF A MANAGEMENT CONSULTANT   The consultant also needs to understand how the prospect selects a management consultant. What selection criteria does the prospect have: price, competences, speed or something else? How does the prospect rank the different criteria? What is most important to the prospect? Furthermore, consultants should always try to find out whether other consultancy firms have been invited as well. If other firms compete for the project, then the consultant should try to discover with which firms the consultant is in competition. Competitive intelligence will inform the consultant on how to approach the prospect in order to win the project.

Covert hiring reasons

HIDDEN AGENDAS   We have explored the critical view of management consultants, whereby clients are presented as the victims of opportunistic and/or incompetent consultants. However, we may also take a critical look at clients. Consultant can be the victims of clients. Clients may manipulate consultants. They may use consultants as a tool to achieve a purpose, or as an alibi to cover their deeds. For consultants it is therefore essential to find out whether clients have a hidden agenda. What, if applicable, are the prospect's covert reasons for hiring consultants?

PROSPECT'S DEFINITION OF THE PROBLEM VERSUS THE REAL PROBLEM   If the prospect has already defined the problem, the consultant needs to clarify and check this (see Figure 10.6). If the problem definition is unclear then the consultant should attempt to clarify it. Next, the consultant should check whether the prospect's definition of the problem is valid.

> *Check the problem definition.* The consultant should not take the prospect's problem definition for granted but should check it. They need to do some fact checking and conduct some (quick) analyses to verify the underlying assumptions of the prospect's problem

definition. Checking the prospect's definition is necessary because it may be wrong.

Wrong definitions. The definition may be wrong for two reasons. First, the prospect may not be able to develop a correct interpretation of the problem. This is a case of the prospect's lack of knowledge and skills. Second, the prospect may have a covert reason for hiring. The prospect's problem definition is covering the real, hidden reason. Consultants have to understand the *real* reason which is not necessarily overt (Kakabadse and Louchart, 2006).

Implications. If the consultant's check reveals that the prospect's definition is not valid, then the consultant should propose further analysis to identify the prospect's problem. If the consultant finds that the prospect has intentionally given a wrong definition of the problem in order to cover a hidden reason, then the consultant should consider withdrawal. The consultant's decision – to withdraw or to accept the project anyway – depends on the consultant's values.

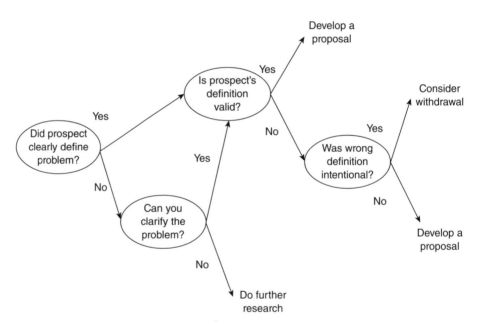

FIGURE 10.6 *Clarifying and checking the prospect's definition of the problem*

THE CONSULTANT'S DILEMMA What should a consultant do when the client has intentionally presented a wrong picture of the problem? The defined problem is not a problem at all, or it is not the real problem but a symptom. Should the consultant accept the client's definition and sell the project that the prospect wants for their own covert reasons?

Redefine the problem? Should the consultant demand a redefinition of the problem? Redefining the problem may interfere with the prospect's covert interests and hiring reasons. In this case, the consultant runs the risk that the prospect will approach the consultant's competitors to conduct the project. Moreover, a redefinition of the problem by the consultant may be interpreted as a trick to sell a bigger project. The prospect may not like that either. In particular, if the consultant has no alternative prospects, it may be tempting to give in to the manipulative prospect.

Accept the wrong definition? Should the consultant – who does not have the luxury of alternative projects – accept the wrong problem definition? Becoming 'his master's voice' – certainly in the case of a manipulative client – is a dangerous route for management consultants. The consultant risks getting involved in unethical practices and they also risk damaging their reputation. The challenge for the consultant is therefore to disagree with the prospect's problem definition without being disagreeable (Stumpf and Tymon, 2001).

COVERT REASONS AND INFORMAL ROLES   What are the issues that the prospect wants to cover with their official problem definition? The covert hiring reasons relate to the informal roles of consultants. We can distinguish between four main covert reasons why clients may hire consultants.

1. Clients may use consultants to legitimate their decisions. They will use consultants as a rubber stamp. Clients already know the decision they would like to make but they need legitimation. They thus hire a consultant to rubber stamp the decision.

2. Clients may hire consultants as political weapons. Consultants are hired to provide argumentation for a client who is entangled in a political fight to redistribute power. This fight may be with internal factions in the organization, but it may also concern external parties. Besides providing argumentation in the form of facts and analyses, management consultants may also help their clients by creating fear, uncertainty, and doubt among a client's adversaries and other stakeholders (Kakabadse and Louchart, 2006).

3. Clients may use consultants as scapegoats. The client may hire the consultant to take the blame for unpopular decisions. This may fit the client's 'good guy – bad guy' role play. The consultant gets the role of the bad guy, which allows the client to play the good guy.

4. Clients may hire consultants to act as brokers of sensitive – competitive – knowledge. This is different from the overt reasons where clients may also hire consultants to play the role of knowledge brokers. The covert reason points to unethically obtained knowledge.

For example, some clients might hire a consultant because they have recently advised a leading competitor of the client. The client wants to learn from the consultant's experience with the competitor and get valuable inside knowledge. Alternatively, some clients might hire consultants to spy – a covert way of collecting competitive intelligence.

A BALANCED APPROACH   Management consultants should listen to the prospect and try to understand the real problem and hiring reason before offering anything. Consultant and client need to develop a mutual understanding of the problem. There should be agreement on the problem definition. Consultants need to close the gap between clients' expectations and the consultants' views about what should and can be done. Consultants have to withstand the temptation to sell a solution – an approach to the prospect's problem – that they do not expect to work (only to please the client). Moreover, they should withstand the temptation to sell a project that they cannot reasonably expect to deliver. When offering a proposition for a project to the prospect, consultants should keep it as simple as possible (Kakabadse and Louchart, 2006). Buying a management consultancy project is already – both rationally and emotionally – difficult enough, therefore, consultants should not burden prospects with unnecessary details and side-tracks.

THE ROLE OF THE CLIENT'S STAKEHOLDERS

NOT A ONE-ON-ONE RELATIONSHIP   The client does not operate in a vacuum, but has to deal with various types of stakeholders, both within the client's organization and outside this organization (see Figure 10.7 on the next page). The consultant, therefore, should not take a narrow perspective of the client–consultant relationship. It is not simply the one-on-one relation between client and consultant. The management consultant only works for the client. But the client's stakeholders may affect the work of the consultant. Therefore, the consultant will intentionally or unintentionally enter in relations with these stakeholders. Consequently, the consultant has to take into account their relations with these stakeholders.

INVESTIGATE STAKEHOLDERS   The consultant needs to investigate the various stakeholders.

Client relationships. First, the consultant needs to look at the relationship with the client. Stakeholders' interests may be aligned with the client, but there may also be conflicts of interest. As stated before, the client may be involved in a political battle with internal peers, such as rival managers and rival divisions. In addition, the client may be involved in battles with external stakeholders, such as governments, shareholders, and business partners. We would emphasize

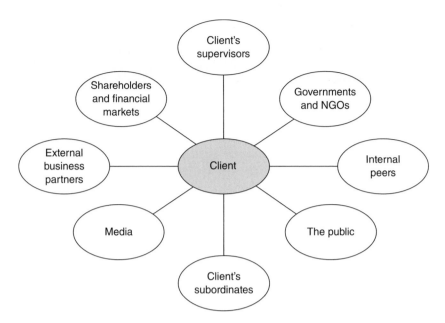

FIGURE 10.7 *The client and their stakeholders*

that a consultant should never assume they can be an independent arbiter. The consultant works for the client, is paid by the client and is therefore a party in the political fight. The consultant needs to take into account these internal and external stakeholders and develop a better understanding of them.

Position with regard to the problem. Second, the consultant has to consider the position of the different stakeholders with regard to the client's problem. How are the stakeholders affected by the client's problem? Do they suffer from the problem, or do they benefit from the problem? If a stakeholder has an interest in a solution to the problem, what does their ideal solution look like?

Position with regard to the project. Third, the consultant has to assess the position of the various stakeholders regarding the consultancy project. The consultant has to find out whether they need the stakeholders' support for the project. For instance, the consultants may need information and skills from stakeholders to successfully execute the project. Are there stakeholders that are critical to the success of the project? Furthermore, the consultant needs to identify stakeholders who have the potential to negatively influence the project, that is the power to sabotage the problem solving and/or the implementation of the solution. Table 10.1 presents a structured approach to identifying the relationships of the various stakeholders to the consultancy project. For each stakeholder, the consultant analyses how the stakeholder is likely to be affected by the project and is likely to affect the project.

TABLE 10.1 *Assessment of stakeholders' relationship with the consultancy project*

Name	Affected by project		Required for project		Potential for negatively influencing the project	
	Nature	Extent	Yes or no	Extent	Yes or no	Extent
Stakeholder A	Positive	Large	Yes	Large	Yes	Large (can sabotage)
Stakeholder B	Negative	Large	Yes	Small	Yes	Small
...						

ACTIONS REGARDING THE STAKEHOLDERS   The assessment of the stakeholders' relations with the project may guide the consultant's actions regarding the stakeholders. To decide on required actions, the consultant needs to consider the three dimensions of Table 10.1. The first dimension – affected by project – determines the motivation of stakeholders. This motivation is either positive or negative, depending on how they (expect) to be affected by the project. The second and third dimensions – respectively 'required for project' and 'potential for negatively influencing the project' – determine the capabilities of stakeholders. These capabilities are either (potentially) positive or negative for the project. The assessment of the motivations and capabilities of stakeholders enables the consultant to make predictions about what actions these stakeholders may take regarding the consultancy project (see Figure 10.8).

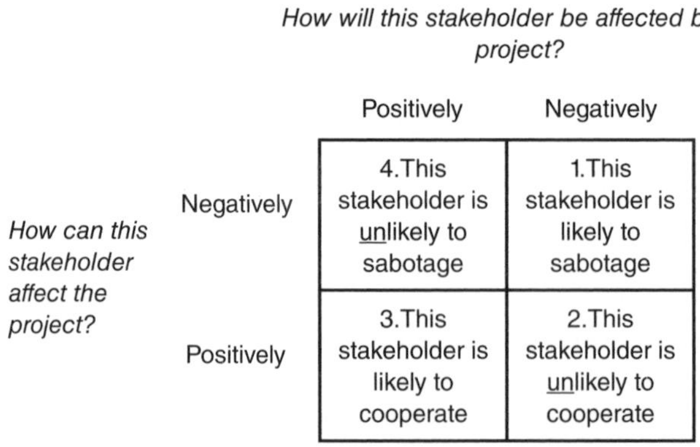

How will this stakeholder be affected by the project?

		Positively	Negatively
How can this stakeholder affect the project?	Negatively	4. This stakeholder is unlikely to sabotage	1. This stakeholder is likely to sabotage
	Positively	3. This stakeholder is likely to cooperate	2. This stakeholder is unlikely to cooperate

FIGURE 10.8 *Predicting stakeholders' actions regarding the consultancy project*

Stakeholder–consultant relationships

THE NATURE OF THE RELATIONSHIP The two dimensions – horizontal and vertical axes – of Figure 10.8 together determine the nature of the relationship between stakeholder and between consultant. Figure 10.8 distinguishes between four different types of relationship. Within a single consultancy project, different stakeholders may have different types of relationships with the consultant. Different types of relations call for different types of actions from the consultant.

THE LARGEST NEGATIVE POTENTIAL The first quadrant represents the top priority for the consultant to take action. This type of relationship represents a large negative risk for the consultancy project. The consultant has to take action to prevent the involved stakeholder from sabotaging the project. The consultant needs to find a way to align this stakeholder with the interests of the project, or disarm this potentially destructive stakeholder. Alignment means a move from quadrant one to four. The client may compensate the stakeholder or – in the case of an internal stakeholder – provide a better position for that stakeholder. Disarmament implies that the stakeholder is no longer able to sabotage the project. The client may move internal stakeholders to other positions where they can do no harm. The ultimate act of a client would be to fire internal stakeholders before they can sabotage.

THE LARGEST POSITIVE POTENTIAL The third quadrant represents the largest positive potential for the consultancy project. Here the consultant finds potential allies and has to invest in relationships with these stakeholders. These stakeholders should become active supporters of the project.

MIXED CASES The fourth quadrant is a mixed case. The stakeholder has the capability to negatively affect the project but has no motivation to do so. This stakeholder may become dangerous. The consultant should pay attention to changes in the stakeholder's motivation or perception. Even if this stakeholder perceives (wrongly) that they will be negatively affected, they may become motivated to sabotage the project. The consultant should manage the expectations of this stakeholder with great care.

The second quadrant presents a potentially positive contribution to the project. The stakeholders can help but they will not do so. The stakeholder has a negative motivation. If this stakeholder's support is important for the success of the project, then the consultant has to attempt to align the stakeholder.

DEVELOPING THE PROPOSAL

Parts of the proposal

With a sound understanding of the client, the stakeholders, the problem, and possibly other hiring reasons, the management consultant develops a proposal for the client. A proposal typically consists of three parts (see Figure 10.9). The first part of the proposal is a project description. Here the consultant describes the client's problem and presents the suggested approach for solving it. The second part serves the purpose of convincing the client that the consultant can deliver what is promised in the first part. In this part, the consultant portrays their profile as proof of their experience and competence. This profile should make it plausible that the consultant is capable of successfully executing the proposed approach to the problem. In the third part, the consultant outlines the terms and conditions, which will include the project fee.

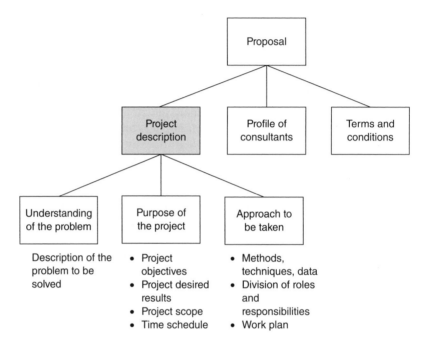

FIGURE 10.9 *The composing parts of the proposal*

Project description

UNDERSTANDING OF THE PROBLEM First, the consultant shows their understanding of the project: what they think is the problem. During previous meetings, the client and consultant should have developed a shared definition of the problem. The consultant describes the problem to be solved. This problem description is important because it defines the boundaries of the consultancy project. In addition, the consultant may sketch out the background to the problem, as well as the context.

PURPOSE OF THE PROJECT Next, the consultant describes what is to be accomplished by the project and present its objectives. The proposal also indicates the scope of the project. It specifies what is included in the project and what is not. The proposal acknowledges the desired results for the client, for instance, an organizational transformation and/or a performance improvement. The proposal also provides indicators of results. With the help of these indicators it can be determined whether the desired results have been achieved. An example of a performance indicator is profit. The consultant also describes the deliverables that they intend to provide to the client. Examples of consultancy deliverables are a recommended solution for the problem and detailed planning for the implementation of the solution. The consultant should also state when, at what time, the deliverables will be realized. Typically the proposal will including a timing schedule. The schedule provides sufficient detail: not only the deadlines of final deliverables but also milestone planning, including the timing of the intermediate deliverables, interim reports, and progress review meetings.

APPROACH TO BE TAKEN   After having defined the client's problem and the consultant's expected deliverables, the proposal describes how the consultant intends to generate this output. The consultant explains what methods and techniques will be used, for instance, for diagnosing the client's problem, or for transforming the client's organization. The proposal also indicates what data will be required for the analyses and what sources of data will be used. Moreover, the proposal makes clear who does what. It proposes a division of roles and responsibilities between client and consultant. The proposal explains what the consultant will bring in, such as time, skills, information, and other possible resources. The consultant also specifies what they require from the client to successfully complete the project. These requirements are the dependencies of the consultant. Clients may be required to deliver, among other things, liaison services, data, the time and skills of management and staff, office facilities, secretarial support, and an ICT infrastructure. Moreover, the proposal provides information about the project organization, including the project team structure and the project board. The proposal also includes a work plan which states the intended activities, the scheduling of these activities, and the people responsible for each of these.

Profile of the consultant

The consultant not only describes the project and its desired results, they also aim to convince the prospect that they are capable of executing the project and achieving the desired results. To assure the prospect, the consultant provides information about his or her competencies and experience. If the consultant is part of a management consultancy firm, then the proposal may distinguish between, on the one hand, the competencies and experience of the individual members of the (proposed) project team, and on the other hand, the competencies and experience of the consultancy firm as a whole (see Figure 10.10).

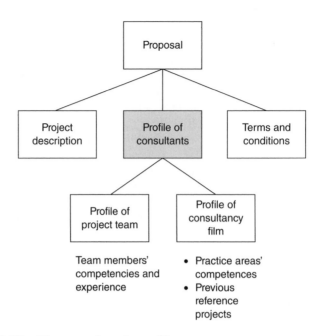

FIGURE 10.10 *The consultant's profile*

The profile of the project team usually includes the CVs of the proposed individual members of the project team, which will generally include the partner, the manager, and the consultants. The profile of the consultancy firm comprises the competences and reference projects of the relevant practice areas within the firm. For instance, if the proposal is about a takeover in the banking industry, then consultancy firms may provide a profile of their strategy practice and their financial services practice.

Terms and conditions

In this section of the proposal, the consultant presents the fee for the project (see Figure 10.11). How much does the client have to pay for the project? The proposal also indicates the schedule of payments. Besides the financial terms and conditions, this section of the proposal contains how the consultant intends to deal with contingencies and disputes. Contingencies refer to (unforeseen) changes in the project that are not accounted for in the proposed project approach and fee. For instance, changing environmental conditions or changing client demands may lead to additional work for the consultant, for which that consultant needs to be paid. The disputes stand for possible conflicts between client and consultant. For instance, the client may not deliver the promised data and skills (in the form of participation of client employees in the project). Alternatively, the client may not be satisfied with the quality of the consultant's work. The consultant proposes how disputes are settled, for instance, via arbitrage or court ordering. Finally, the consultant provides the general, legal and ethical terms and conditions. The ethical terms and conditions denote the ethical code of the consultant, or the code of the professional trade organization of which the consultant is a member.

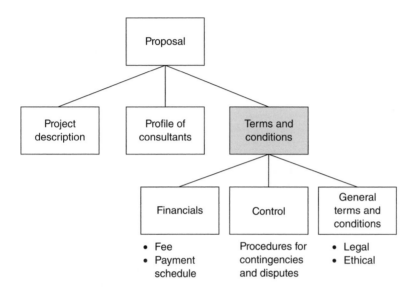

FIGURE 10.11 *The consultant's terms and conditions*

SETTING THE FEE

Range of fees

What should be the fee for the consultancy project? Figure 10.12 shows the range of probable fees. The value of the project perceived by the prospect determines the maximum that the prospect is willing to pay for the consultancy project. The prospect will not be prepared to pay more for the project than they expect the project to be worth. The minimum economically rational fee for which the consultancy is willing to offer the project is the marginal cost to the consultancy. The marginal cost of a project is the increase in the total cost of the consultant for delivering that project. The consultant will not be prepared to offer the project if they would lose money on it.

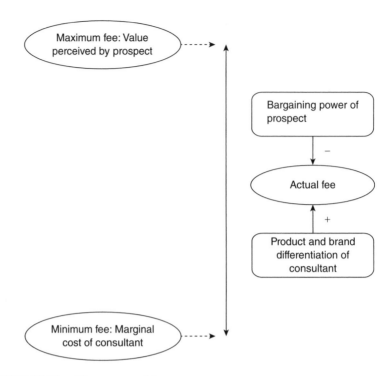

FIGURE 10.12 *The range of fees*

MAXIMUM FEE   The prospect's perception of the project's value sets the maximum fee for the project. We have already discussed the difficulties in assessing the value impact of a consultancy project. Prospects may therefore – partially – base their value assessment on the inputs of the consultancy project.

Willingness to pay. The brand name and the prestige of the consultant may influence the prospect's value perception and hence their willingness to pay for the consultant's services. The project fee may influence the prospect's perception of the project's value. Prospects will expect that the project fee reflects the strength of the consultant's competences and the value they will create. For instance, no prospect expects a project by a top tier consultancy firm to be cheap. A low price may even raise the prospect's suspicions: 'If it is that cheap, it cannot be good'.

Ability to pay. Consultants should not only look at the prospect's willingness to pay, they should also consider their ability to pay for the project. The prospect may attach a high value to the project, but how much can they afford to pay? Price sensitivity is one of the drivers of the prospect's bargaining power. Highly profitable prospects are less price sensitive than prospects with a low profitability or even a negative financial performance. Some prospect firms and sectors are – structurally – more profitable than others. Consultants have to adjust their fees accordingly. They should charge what the traffic can bear.

MINIMUM FEE The marginal cost to the consultancy is the minimum – economically rational – fee. However, in two situations, consultancies may be willing to accept a project at a lower fee, thus subsidizing the project.

First, the consultant may accept a fee below the marginal cost if this project is a so-called 'loss leader'. By accepting this loss-making project, the consultancy expects to acquire profitable projects in the future. The loss leader is treated as an investment in the acquisition of future – profitable – projects. The loss leader argument makes sense for consultants who approach a new prospect, or enter a new market or customer segment.

Second, the consultant may accept a fee below the marginal cost if the consultancy can prevent a competitive move by accepting this project. By accepting a loss-making project the consultant may, for instance, pre-empt the entry of a new competitor into the consultant's market, which may have a stronger negative impact on the consultant's financial results.

ACTUAL FEE The actual fee will typically be lower than the maximum fee (prospect's value perception) and higher than the minimum fee (consultant's marginal cost). The interplay between prospect and consultant determines the fee. As described in Chapter 4, the bargaining power of the prospect will exercise a downward pressure on the consultant's fee. The consultant has two options to respond to the bargaining power of a prospect. First, the consultant may use their differentiation, if any, to strengthen their bargaining position. The stronger their product and brand differentiation, the better the consultant can defend a high fee. Second, the consultant may shift their focus to prospects with low bargaining leverage and/or low price sensitivity. Prospects that are relatively small, that do not have the in-house capability to solve problems, that lack experience with consultants, and that lack access to (top) talent, have a low bargaining leverage. Prospects that are highly profitable are typically less price sensitive.

ALTERNATIVE FEE-SETTING MECHANISMS There are four mechanisms that determine fee-setting, variously based on value, cost or time.

> *Contingency fees.* Corresponding to the bases of the maximum and minimum fees, the consultant can set their fee by the prospect's valuation of the project, or their cost of delivering the project. Fees based on valuation are called contingency fees. Contingency fees may be a way for the consultancy to capture a (much) bigger remuneration. This type of fee-setting is possible if the results of the consultancy project can be measured. The fee is made dependent on the realized impact of the consultancy project on the client's performance. After

the closure of the project, its performance impact is measured. Not all projects lend themselves to contingency fees. For example, cost reduction projects lend themselves better to contingency fees than projects for developing a growth strategy because the impact of a cost reduction is easier to measure than a growth strategy. Clients with financial difficulties may like contingency fees. The consultancy project gets paid out of the results that the project generates. Because of the 'no-cure-no-pay' principle, there is no strain on the client's cash flow. A special form of contingency fee is the equity payment. The client pays the consultant in equity, or a mix of equity and cash. This may be an appropriate route for start-up firms who lack cash. The downside to this form of fees is that equity payments bring the independence of the consultant into jeopardy.

Cost-based fees. Most consultancy project fees are based on costs. The majority of consultants bill for projects on a time and expenses basis. Time is the number of billable hours (or days) of the consultant. These hours are multiplied by the consultant's hourly billing rate. The consultant's reimbursable expenses for the project may include travel, hotels, and meals. In addition, the consultant may invoice the expenses related to third party services for the project, such as legal, fiscal, and technical advice, as well as market research by external suppliers. These services were necessary inputs to the client project, which the consultant could not or would not generate alone.

Flat fees. A consultant who uses a time basis for the project fee has two options. One option is the flat fee. This is based on the budgeted hours and expenses. If the actual hours and expenses exceed the budgeted amount, then the profitability of the project will diminish. The consultant takes an economic risk. A contingency provision may protect the consultant: if the amount of work increased due to unforeseen external events or client's changes to the project requirements, then consultant and client must renegotiate the amount of budgeted hours and expenses.

Variable fee. The second time-based option is a variable fee. This is based on the actual hours spent on the project. The more hours the consultant spends on the project, the more the client needs to pay. Therefore, the economic risk rests solely with the client. The client may hedge themselves by specifying a maximum number of hours that the consultant may spend on the project.

PRESENTING THE PROPOSAL

PROSPECT'S EXPECTATIONS
Often the prospect invites the consultant to present the proposal and to explain it where necessary. When invited, the consultant should find out before the presentation what the prospect's

expectations of the proposal presentation are. Does the prospect expect a formal or an informal presentation? The consultant needs to know who will be the audience: who will attend and what will be their interests? Furthermore it is important to know how much time is available for the presentation and how much room needs to be reserved for questions and discussions.

MESSAGE AND ARGUMENTATION   Developing effective presentations is very important for consultants. Therefore, we will spend a whole chapter on presentations (Chapter 14). The consultants should make the presentation orient towards the prospect and other eventual attendees. The prospect forms the point of departure for the presentation. The message and the supporting argumentation need to be relevant to the prospect and other eventual attendees. The consultant should also make the presentation attractive for the audience. It should never be boring. The consultant needs to keep the attention of the prospect and other attendees. The consultant must also build in flexibility in the presentation: the attendees may interrupt the presentation if they want to question or criticize some of its aspects, or if they intend to discuss issues.

The consultant should be prepared for critical questions and negative comments. They also need to have back-up slides with answers to anticipated questions. The consultant should encourage some discussion at the end. To prepare for this discussion, the consultant needs to consider: what are the likely issues that will come up? Obviously the presentation should not exceed the allotted time. If the prospect requests a fifteen minute presentation, then the consultant should carefully plan that the proposal can be presented within exactly that time frame. The audience may perceive a presentation that exceeded the time limit as annoying and disrespectful. Finally, the consultant needs to rehearse and rehearse the presentation repeatedly, as they will only get one chance to do it right. Proposals can therefore be costly – in terms of time spent – for consultants.

THE CONTRACT

THE AGREEMENT   After the presentation and subsequent meetings, the prospect and consultant may negotiate the project approach and the (financial) terms and conditions. If these negotiations are successfully completed, then the prospect and consultant can draw up the contract. This is the legal document that confirms the agreement between the prospect and consultant. Table 10.2 presents a high-level overview of the typical content of a contract for a consultancy project. Most of the content has already been discussed in the section about the proposal. Here we concentrate on the legal items. The contract specifies how the consultant should handle with the client's confidential information. This is a critical clause for the client because any leakage of confidential knowledge to the client's competitors, suppliers, or other external actors may seriously damage that client's competitive position.

TABLE 10.2 *The items in a contract for a consultancy project*

Contract item	Brief description of item
Contracting partners	Client and consultant
Scope	Objectives of project, description of work, time schedule
Outputs	Expected results, deliverables to be generated by consultant, e.g. reports and (intervention) activities
Inputs	To be delivered by client and consultant: e.g. time, skills, resources, and information
Financials	Fees and expenses, billing and payment procedures
Legal	Handling of confidential client information
	Liability of consultant for damages caused, limitiation of liability
	Protection of intellectual property of consultant
	Termination and revision
	Dispute resolution

LIABILITY   Liability is another important item. By definition consultants are not responsible for the results of their advice. The client is solely responsible for making any decisions on the basis of the consultant's advice. Therefore the client carries sole responsibility for the consequences of implementing the consultant's advice. However, the client may hold the consultant accountable if that consultant has made mistakes, for instance, if their advice is based on flawed analyses or faulty data.

INTELLECTUAL PROPERTY   We discussed the how confidential knowledge client's has to be protected. Additionally, the consultant's intellectual property, such as methods, techniques, and data, also needs protection. The client has no right to use the consultant's intellectual assets outside the project without the consultant's prior permission. Finally, the contract should regulate the termination and revision of that contract. Who and when – under what conditions – has the right to terminate and/or revise the contract?

PROCUREMENT MODELS

Direct procurement

So far, we have discussed clients' hiring reasons. The next question is: how do clients actually hire a management consultant, or procure (buy) management consultancy projects? We can distinguish between two procurement models (see Figure 10.13). Traditionally, the problem-owner hired the consultant. This is what we call the 'direct procurement' model. Procurement takes place within a personal relationship between the client and the consultant. The client contacts one or more consultants who they know from their own experience, or are recommended to them by their network. Alternatively, the clients may be approached by one or more consultants. Client and consultant meet and they try to develop a relationship, as described in this chapter. If there have been multiple consultants, then the client has to choose one consultant. Direct procurement may be characterized as a personal process of procurement.

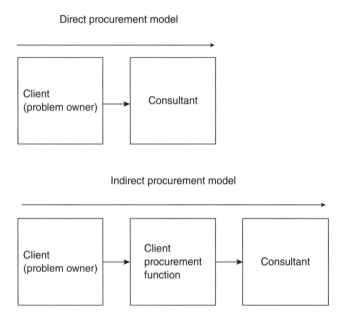

FIGURE 10.13 *Direct versus indirect procurement*

Indirect procurement

To an increasing extent, large and sophisticated clients are switching from the direct procurement model to a different model. These clients differentiate the procurement process. They separate the usage and the procurement of consultancy services. These clients introduce the so-called *technical* buyer. These buyers are procurement professionals who are not involved in the problem that the consultants have to solve. Recall that the *user* client is the problem-owner and the *economic* client is the person who holds the authority – and the budget – to make the hiring decision. The procurement professional may be both the technical buyer and the economic client. However, the technical buyer and the economic client may be separate roles. This alternative method for procurement is named the indirect model of professional procurement. You may ask why an increasing number of clients move to the indirect model.

Professional procurement

The key difference between direct and indirect procurement is the professional procurement function. This function manages a systematic and rational process. In consultation with the problem-owner the procurement function defines the problem and the related project requirements. In addition they define the selection criteria for the suppliers (consultancy firms). Professional procurement typically works with a long list of potential suppliers, that is the consultancy firms.

> *Request for information.* The procurement function sends to the firms on the long list a request for information (mostly abbreviated as RFI). This means that the invited consultancy firms have to provide information about how they would approach the prospect's problem (a description of this problem is provided by the procurement function). Next, the procurement function screens the received information provided by the consultancy firms.
>
> *Request for proposal.* The procurement function then sends out to selected consultancy firms a request for proposals (mostly abbreviated as RFP). Inviting multiple consultancies to submit proposals implies an organized competition between consultancies: a so-called beauty contest.

Comparing direct and indirect procurement

The direct model offers some clear advantages over the indirect one. It is a relatively simple and short process because it has no intermediary procurement function. Therefore, it is relatively easy and fast to implement. However, direct procurement also suffers from some disadvantages, in particular for large clients. These disadvantages concern accountability, scale economies, and bargaining tactics.

ACCOUNTABILITY   First we shall discuss accountability. In small organizations, the client is the owner of the organization. This client does not need be accountable to others. They do not have to justify the decision to hire a management consultant. Large organizations typically have a separation of management and ownership: professional managers versus shareholders. The client – the professional manager – needs to be accountable to the shareholders. Shareholders do not want managers to hire some consultants just because they are part of an old boys' network. Even worse, is the risk of corruption by professional managers. The shareholders want to avoid the possibility that professional managers will take kick-backs from consultants; that is 'if you hire our consultancy firm we will – of course discretely – transfer a percentage of our project fee to an untraceable bank account of yours anywhere in the world'. Large organizations need a professional procurement process that is systematic and transparent with clear procurement criteria. Each purchase of a consultancy service should be accounted for: why is the consultancy hired? Public sector organizations in particular have a need for accountability. After all it is tax payers' money that is spent on consultancy projects. Clients in the public domain may have the legal requirement to follow a (highly) regulated procurement process for management consultancy services.

SCALE ECONOMIES   Second, indirect procurement is motivated by scale economies. This applies in particular to large organizations. Large clients may benefit from scale economies in the procurement of management consultancy services. If a client is willing to buy more consultancy (larger projects and/or a series of projects on a regular basis) then the marketing and sales cost of the consultant may decrease compared to the situation where the consultant has to sell small projects to different clients. Clients may skim the consultant's cost savings by negotiating better terms. To achieve these economies of scale, large clients should avoid the fragmentation of consultancy procurement. A centralized procurement function may achieve scale economies by bundling the demand of the individual problem-owners. All individual problem-owners within the client should buy directly from the same consultancy firm. The central procurement function has more bargaining power than the individual problem-owners. The procurement function may design a framework contract to capture scale economies.

BARGAINING TACTICS   Third, indirect procurement may enable better usage of bargaining tactics. The individual problem-owner may be too caught up in their daily work to give sufficient time and attention to bargaining tactics. Moreover, such managers are typically not professional buyers and thus lack the skills and experience of bargaining. A professional procurement function will consider a broader scope of potential consultancy firms then a problem-owner who is occupied with their business responsibilities. The procurement function will use, and reinforce, the competition between consultancy firms. RFIs and RFPs are used to broaden the arena and intensify the battle among consultants for the client's project. The consultancy firms have to compete with each other. Through this competition, the procurement function aims to achieve better quality and/or lower prices. However, such beauty contests may also cause negative reactions from consultancy firms. Some consultants may not want to compete in such formal processes, in particular the open tender procedures. In particular the best consultancies may be able to afford to ignore these tenders.

COMPLEXITY   We already pointed out that indirect procurement is more complex than direct procurement. Indirect procurement may be bureaucratic, that is it creates red tape. Moreover, a centralization of procurement not only creates benefits it may also carry costs.

First, there is a possible conflict of interest between the problem-owner and the procurement function. The problem-owner is focused the best solution for their problem. The procurement function will be focused on getting the lowest price.

Second, there is the issue of the procurement function's capacity to judge the quality of the proposals of the management consultancy firms. The central procurement function will be at some distance from the operations, where the problems exist that consultants need to solve. If the procurement professional is not involved with the problem, and lacks experience in working with consultants, how can they evaluate the proposals of the various consultancy firms? The weaker the procurement professional's capability to judge the consultancy proposals, the stronger the temptation to select proposals on the basis of price. This raises a conflict of interest between problem-owner and procurement. The client may partly overcome the problem of evaluating consultancy proposals by hiring former consultants as procurement professionals.

ETHICS AND SOCIAL RESPONSIBILITY

Ethical codes are part of the terms and conditions. Both client and consultant should behave ethically and responsibly. In this chapter we paid attention to possible unethical behaviour by both clients and consultants. Clients may manipulate consultants, while consultants may behave opportunistically.

Responsibility towards the client

It is obvious that consultants have a responsibility towards clients. There are contractual obligations towards clients. Consultants should not violate client confidentiality. They should not broker sensitive client knowledge to the client's competitors. Moreover, they should refrain from insider (stock) trading using sensitive client information.

In addition to contractual obligations, consultants have moral obligations towards their clients. They should not overcharge. Consultants are not supposed to bill more hours than were delivered. They must not bill expenses twice, such as invoicing to two different clients the same research report bought from a third party. Moreover, consultants should not send inexperienced junior consultants to gain experience at the cost of the client. Consultants ought not to create expectations they cannot deliver. For instance, partners in consultancy firms should not make clients believe they will get the time of a partner when that partner intends to use only juniors.

Obligation towards other stakeholders

Besides a moral obligation towards the client, consultants have a moral obligation towards other stakeholders. The characteristics of a client's problem may force a consultant to develop a solution that has negative consequences for some stakeholders. However, the consultant should not recommend actions that will harm stakeholders while these are not necessary for solving the client's problem. Unnecessary – from a problem perspective – damage to stakeholders may take place if the client hires the consultant for informal reasons. Consultants should be cautious to accept a project – for informal reasons – where their actions will lead to unnecessary damage to other stakeholders.

SUMMARY

Understanding the prospect's perspective

Selling consultancy projects is challenging, in particular for new clients. Repeat sales to existing clients are usually more efficient then acquiring new clients. To sell to new clients, the consultant first needs to build a relationship with the prospect. Understanding the prospect's perspective is a critical success factor for building this relationship. Prospects considering consultancy may have negative feelings of failure, fear, and uncertainty. Moreover, prospects may have critical, negative perceptions of management consultants. Therefore, a consultant first needs to gain a prospect's trust before the prospect's issue can be discussed.

The hiring reason

It is important that the consultant understands the prospect's hiring reason before discussing the consultancy services. The discussion between consultant and prospect will first address the overt hiring reasons, which will typically concern problem solving. However, the consultant should probe for covert reasons. The prospect may also have a hidden agenda. To avoid being manipulated by the prospect, the consultant should discover the real hiring reason.

The stakeholders

The consultant also needs to investigate the stakeholders around the prospect. The consultant should identify the position and power of each stakeholder and define their actions accordingly. Based on their understanding of the prospect, the hiring reason(s), and the stakeholders, the consultant prepares a proposal for a project. The project fee can be based on the prospect's perceived value as well as on the consultant's cost. Most consultants will calculate their fee on a cost basis, in particular their time and expenses. Procurement used to be direct between client – problem-owner – and consultant, but large and sophisticated clients will increasingly turn to an indirect model, in which a professional procurement function intermediates between problem-owner and consultant.

REFLECTIVE QUESTIONS

1. The sales approach of management consultancy firms – in which their most-expensive people, the partners, build a relationship with prospects in order to sell projects – seems inefficient. Can you think of more efficient sales approaches for consultancy firms? Explain your answer.

2. Should consultants always withdraw if they find out that the prospect has a hidden agenda? Explain your answer. If you think there are examples of hidden agendas where consultants should not withdraw, explain how they should respond to the prospect's covert hiring reason.

3. The consultant should understand the prospect's problem which needs to be solved. What should the consultant do if they discover that the prospect's definition of the problem is flawed, and that the prospect is, in fact, the problem? Take the case of a prospect who is a dysfunctional top manager, who quarrels with all of their peers and subordinates, and makes bad decisions. Explain your answer.

MINI CASE STUDY

The alumnus

Presenting a proposal

Ronald, a partner at Acme Consulting, needs to present a proposal for a problem solving project to LargeConglomerate Inc. Ronald and his team have been working on this proposal for a month. The chief executive officer of LargeConglomerate has invited Ronald to give a short PowerPoint presentation to the whole executive management team of LargeConglomerate.

The newly appointed executive

Last week, the CEO informed Ronald that the firm had expanded the executive team with a new position. The newly appointed executive will be present in the meeting. As part of the preparation, Ronald had conducted interviews with all four existing executives. There was no opportunity for Ronald to meet the new executive, Martin, in person before the meeting.

The alumnus

However, Ronald already knows Martin. Martin is an alumnus of the top consultancy firm Elite Consulting. Elite Consulting considers itself to be superior to all other consultancy firms. Ronald has heard about Martin. Martin has a reputation for being arrogant and aggressive. He was a senior partner at Elite. The CEO has told Ronald that Martin will become the new CEO when he retires in two years. The CEO thinks it is a good idea to have Martin in the steering committee of the new consultancy project for Acme. This will allow LargeConglomerate to benefit from the expertise of two big names in consultancy: Elite and Acme.

The meeting

Ronald does not dare to openly disagree, but he is not assured that the cooperation between Martin and himself will work. He fears that Martin will certainly have the last word.

Before the meeting, the CEO introduces Ronald and Martin to each other. Martin acts in a reserved and patronizing manner. This approach confirms Ronald's fears. After the CEO formally opens the meeting and welcomes Acme, Ronald starts to present.

The confrontation

When Ronald wants to introduce his third PowerPoint slide, Martin interrupts the presentation. He expresses very harsh criticism of Acme's proposed approach to solving LargeConglomerate's problem. Even though Ronald has not yet finished his presentation, Martin has drawn his conclusions already. He smashes Acme's approach to smithereens. In a five minute lecture, Martin systematically criticizes in a detailed way all the supposed weaknesses in Acme's proposal. The other client executives of LargeConglomerate are dumbstruck. The CEO visibly feels embarrassed by the situation, but had not dared to intervene in Martin's monologue. After silence falls, all heads turn towards Ronald. Martin shows unconcealed contempt for him. Ronald had not expected a warm welcome from Martin, but this reaction is a very unpleasant surprise. What should Ronald do?

Questions

1 What explanations for Martin's behaviour can you think of? Explain your answer.

2 Could the harsh and open critique on Ronald's presentation have been prevented? If yes, how? If not, why not? Elaborate on your answer.

3 What would you advise Ronald to do? Explain your answer.

FURTHER READING

Maister, D. (1993) *Managing the Professional Services Firm*. New York: The Free Press.

REFERENCES

Abrahamson, E. (1991) 'Managerial fads and fashions: the diffusion and rejection of innovations', *Academy of Management Review*, 16 (3): 586–612.

Arnaud, G. (1998) 'The obscure object of demand in management consultancy: a psychoanalytical perspective', *Journal of Managerial Psychology*, 13 (7): 469–484.

Bloch, B. (1999) 'How they put the con in consulting', *Managerial Auditing Journal*, 14 (3): 115–117.

Covin, T. and Fisher, T. (1991) 'Consultant and client must work together', *Journal of Management Consulting*, 6 (4): 11–20.

De Burgundy, J. (1998) 'Management consultancy: a modern folly?' *Management Decision*, 36 (3): 204–205.

Glückler, J. and Armbrüster, T. (2003) 'Bridging uncertainty in management consulting: the mechanisms of trust and networked reputation', *Organization Studies*, 24 (2): 269–297.

Johanson, A. (2003) 'Consulting as story-making', *Journal of Management Development*, 23 (4): 339–354.

Kakabadse, N. and Louchart, E. (2006) 'Consultant's role: a qualitative inquiry from the consultant's perspective', *Journal of Management Development*, 25 (5): 416–500.

Kubr, M. (ed.) (2002) *Management Consulting: A Guide to the Profession*. Geneva: International Labour Organization.

Lundberg, C. and Young, C. (2001) 'A note on emotions and consultancy', *Journal of Organizational Change*, 14 (6): 530–538.

Maister, D. (1993) *Managing the Professional Services Firm*. New York: The Free Press.

Pellegrinelli, S. (2002) 'Managing the interplay and tensions of consulting interventions: the consultant–client relationship as meditation and reconciliation', *Journal of Management Development*, 21 (5): 343–365.

Sadler, P. (2001) *Management Consultancy: A Handbook for Best Practice* (2nd edn). London: Kogan Page.

Stumpf, S. and Tymon, W. Jr (2001) 'Consultant or entrepreneur? Demystifying the war for talent', *Career Development International*, 6 (1): 48–55.

Sturdy, A. (1997) 'The consultancy process – an insecure business', *Journal of Management Studies*, 34 (3): 389–413.

Williams, R. (2003) 'Consultobabble and the client–consultants relationship', *Managerial Auditing Journal*, 18 (2): 134–139.

Wittreich, H.F. (1966) 'How to buy/sell professional services', *Harvard Business Review*, March–April: 127–138.

11

MANAGEMENT OF A CONSULTANCY PROJECT

INTRODUCTION

This chapter is about a structured approach to managing a management consultancy project. It describes the five phases of a project. Additionally, we give attention to the organization structure of a project. The chapter describes the division of roles, responsibilities, and authority between the steering committee and the project manager. We also discuss the composition of project teams and we look at the dynamics of team development. In particular, we consider the role of the junior consultant on the project. The chapter ends with a summary, reflective questions, a mini case study, suggested further reading, and references.

Main learning objectives

- Understand the need for a structured approach to the management of a consultancy project.
- Know each of the five phases of a project.
- Know what a project work breakdown structure is.
- Relate the roles of stakeholders to the phases of a project.
- Understand the organization structure of a project.

- Know the five stages of project team development.
- Understand the work of a junior consultant in a project.

DEFINING THE MANAGEMENT CONSULTANCY PROJECT

Definition

A successful proposal leads to a contract for a management consultancy project (see Chapter 10). But what precisely is a management consultancy project? A project is a temporary structure to execute a predefined set of interrelated activities directed at achieving a predefined objective for the client with a predefined set of resources within a predefined time frame.

Regarding management consultancy projects, we can distinguish between two different objectives. In the *narrow* definition of management consultancy, the project objective is to deliver a recommendation to achieve a specified business result for a client. To achieve this result, the recommended solution should be feasible to implement. The client organization needs to be willing and able to implement this solution. The client organization's willingness to implement refers to acceptance of the solution and support for the solution by stakeholders inside and outside the client organization. In the *broad* definition of management consultancy, the project objective is both to deliver a recommendation that is feasible to implement and to assist with the managerial tasks of implementing that recommendation.

The activities of management consultancy projects are problem solving and solution implementation. The main project resources are the consultants' skills, knowledge, and time.

Different types and scopes of management consultancy projects

DIFFERENT TYPES   A typical management consultancy project does not exist. We already described the different types of consultancy: brain, grey hair, and procedural consultancy (Maister, 1993). We also covered the different roles for management consultants. We distinguished between the formal roles, such as expert, doctor, and process facilitator (Schein, 1987), and the informal roles, political weapon, legitimator, hired hand, and scapegoat. Management consultancy projects vary with the type of consultancy and the consultant role. Moreover, different management consultancy projects may cover different functional practices, such as operations, strategy and organization, and IT.

DIFFERENT SCOPES   Furthermore, the scope of management consultancy projects may vary. Examples of questions about the project scope are:

1. Is the project only about problem solving, or does it also, or only, cover solution implementation?
2. How complex is the scope of the client's problem?
3. Does the client have a mono-disciplinary problem or is it a multi-disciplinary problem? Multi-disciplinarity points to the number of functional practices that the consultant needs to cover in the project. For example, compare a project that is only about IT with a project that covers IT, strategy, organization, and finance.

The scope of a management consultancy project typically increases with the scope of the client. The higher the number of client products and markets, the larger the scope of the project. Moreover, the scope of the project typically grows with the number of countries that the client's problem applies to. For example, compare a national project for a domestic client and an international project for a global client.

Related to the scope of the project is the duration of the project. The time from initiation to closure of a management consultancy project may range from a couple of days to more than a year. Moreover, the number of consultants involved in the project may vary as well. Projects may range from one individual consultant to large teams of more than a hundred consultants.

STRUCTURING THE MANAGEMENT CONSULTANCY PROJECT

Level of formality

The scope – and the related complexity – of the consultancy project determine the project management approach. The larger the scope, the more formal and elaborate the approach should be. Figure 11.1 presents a formal approach to a management consultancy project. We would acknowledge there are less formal and more formal approaches to project management. The approach in Figure 11.1 is systematic and requires a large amount of discipline from the consultants. It comprises five main phases: initiation, design, execution, control, and closure. The approach may have an iterative element, as visualized by the control cycle in Figure 11.1. The execution may deviate from the project plan, which may require corrective and adaptive measures to meet that plan. However, developments inside or outside the client organization may necessitate a change to the original project plan.

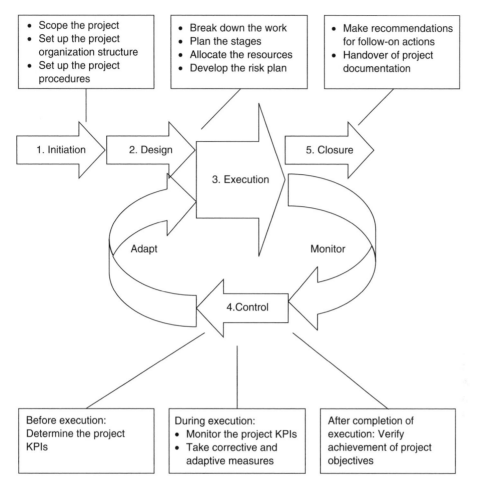

FIGURE 11.1 *A structured approach to project management*

Note: KPI refers to key performance indicators

The discipline to prepare

Before the consultants can really start to execute the project, they will have to do a lot of preparatory work in the initiation and design phases. In some cases, initiation and design are part of the project proposal. The consultants will have already done (most of) the initiation and design work before the client has signed the contract. The client makes the decision to hire the consultants partly based on their evaluation of the quality of the proposed initiation and design.

THE ADVANTAGES OF A STRUCTURED APPROACH   You may ask yourself: why do consultants need a project management approach? Figure 11.1 gives the impression of a lot of bureaucracy. However, such an approach may bring several advantages to the consultant, in particular if the project is complex. For instance, defining and controlling the scope of the project will help the consultant to avoid doing too much work (that is not included in the project fee!) or too little work (forgetting important activities!). Carefully designing the project execution and the control phases helps the consultant to produce the right quality of services within the time frame agreed. Moreover, the project design and control help the consultant to complete the project within budget (and make a profit).

In this chapter we assume that the project is commissioned to a consultancy firm with three hierarchical layers: partner, manager, and consultants. We would also acknowledge that many consultants are sole practitioners. But we chose a more complex organization form in order to show the division of roles and responsibilities in a consultancy project.

PHASE 1: INITIATION

Set up the project organization structure

THE STEERING COMMITTEE   The client and the consultant together establish the steering committee (abbreviated as 'steerco' and may also be called the 'project board'). The steering committee consists minimally of two people. One of them is the client decision maker, or the problem-owner. Typically this is an executive. This person is the sponsor of the project. The other person on the steering committee is the representative of the consultancy. If the consultancy is a partnership, then the representative is typically one of the firm's partners. If the economic client (the buyer) and the technical client (the problem-owner) are two different individuals, then the steering committee may also include the technical client. In addition, the client may recruit one or more experts to the steering committee.

QUALITY ASSURANCE   Formally, the steering committee is responsible for quality assurance, which implies checking appointments and procedures, reviewing quality, and monitoring decreases and increases in the project's scope. In a management consultancy project the responsibility for the quality assurance typically lies with the consultancy partner.

ACCOUNTABILITY   The steering committee is accountable for the project. If the project fails, the client will be held accountable by superiors or stakeholders, such as shareholders and external (non-executive) directors. The client will in turn hold the consultancy partner accountable.

SOUNDING BOARD   The steering committee may decide to set up a separate sounding board. This group of individuals does not have a mandate but may give advice to the project manager. The project manager should keep the steering committee and the sounding board informed about the progress of the project. Often, the client appoints some sounding board members that do not function as a separate forum. They participate in meetings of the steering committee where they fulfil a sounding board function.

THE PROJECT MANAGER   The steering committee has the mandate for the consultancy project. Formally, the steering committee appoints the project manager. However, in the case of a management consultancy project, the consultancy partner will nominate the manager. Often the nomination of the project manager is part of the consultant's proposal. The client has the right to reject the nomination.

The project manager runs the project on behalf of the steering committee and reports to the steering committee. Because the manager is a function within the management consultancy firm, they also report to the firm's partner on the project (see Chapter 9). Formally, the steering committee defines and distributes the roles between the steering committee and the project manager, in terms of tasks, responsibilities, and authorities. Informally, the project manager (commissioned by the consulting partner) takes the lead. In practice, the project manager does the work of initiation and design. The project manager therefore takes the initiative. The client in the steering committee needs to approve the project manager's proposal.

Set the scope of the project

THE CONTRACT   Typically, the scope of the project is defined in the contract. If the contract does not define the project's scope, then the steering committee needs to define the (major) project deliverables and desired outcomes for the client in terms of results. The steering committee should make both the quantity and the quality dimensions of the deliverables explicit. In practice, the project manager, commissioned by the consultancy partner, takes the lead. They make a proposal, but the steering committee needs to approve it.

THE PROJECT DELIVERABLES   The project manager makes suggestions regarding, among others, the extent of the consultancy project deliverables: how much growth should the consultants' recommendation generate? How much cost should be saved by implementing the recommended solution? An example of specifying the required quality is the accuracy level of the estimates that the consultants will make, and the breadth and depth of the consultants' analyses in terms of, for example, the number of interviews and the number of benchmarks. To avoid client dissatisfaction on the one hand and cost-overruns for the consultancy firm on the other hand, the contract, or otherwise the steering committee, should define upfront what deliverables are included and what is excluded from the consultancy project.

THE DEPENDENCIES   Moreover, the steering committee should identify the interfaces for the project. These interfaces are the dependencies or other type of linkages with other projects. An example of dependencies is the timely availability of data for the analyses. Another example is the availability of people for interviews and other project-related activities.

RISKS AND CONSTRAINTS   Additionally, any known risks of the project should be identified as soon as possible. To identify these risks, the project manager may set up a brainstorming session with knowledgeable stakeholders. For each identified risk, the project manager needs to assess the likelihood as well as the impact on the project.

The project manager also has to identify the project's constraints. What are the boundary conditions of this project? For instance, the client may want to reduce the manufacturing costs and so sets as a constraint that they do not want to offshore manufacturing to a country with unethical labour practices.

THE ACCEPTANCE CRITERIA   The steering committee also has to decide upon the acceptance criteria for the project. The client may have unrealistic requirements. Then the consultancy partner has to 'educate' that client about what is realistic. Furthermore, the steering committee should prioritize the acceptance criteria. They should distinguish between 'must have' and 'nice to have' project results. In addition, the steering committee has to agree upon the project evaluation criteria. Next, the steering committee has to decide upon the project schedule. The steering committee members should set the completion dates for the major deliverables of the project. These are the so-called milestones.

RESOURCES   Finally, the steering committee needs to determine what resources will be made available for the project to achieve the project objectives. The project resources include time and the skills of individuals and a budget for expenses. Often, the project proposal includes requirements for the client, such as the supply of data to the consultants and the making available of client employees to contribute to the project.

Set the project procedures

COMMUNICATION   Next, the steering committee formally, and the project manager informally, should set the operational procedures for the project. As stated before, the consultants may have already defined these procedures in their project proposal. Such procedures cover various aspects of the project. One aspect is project communications. Several questions arise about communications.

1. At what time intervals should the project manager report information to the steering committee? What information should be reported?
2. When should the steering committee meet with the project manager?
3. When should stakeholder groups inside or outside the client organization be informed? Which stakeholder groups should be informed?
4. What is the appropriate level of formality for meetings?

Besides communications procedures, the project also needs procedures for recording or logging developments within the project. Typically the recordings are stored in the so-called project file.

ISSUE MANAGEMENT   Another important area for procedures is the management of issues. Issue management includes the procedures for dealing with disagreement, conflict, and escalation. Procedures are in particular required for dealing with changes to the project scope. Changes in the project scope may arise because of altering the external circumstances – for instance, unexpected changes in the economy or the client's industry – or because the client changes their mind.

PROJECT DEFINITION DOCUMENT   The results of the project initiation stage are collected in a project definition document. This document contains the project objective statement, as well as the major deliverables and their deadlines. The project definition document also holds a description of the project organization structure and the operational procedures. The project definition document serves as a reference point for the project manager and the steering committee. Often, the project proposal serves as the project definition document.

PHASE 2: DESIGN

Break down the project work

REDUCE COMPLEXITY   Before the project manager can plan the project and allocate the work to consultants in the project team, they need to reduce the complexity of the project work. If the project is about problem solving, then the consultancy firm (the partner, the project manager, and possibly the consultants) typically develops an initial hypothesis about the solution (see Chapter 13). The project work consists of testing the assumptions underlying this hypothesis. Hypothesis testing consists of data collection and data analysis. The hypothesis is typically too abstract to allow any delegation to individual consultants. In (large) consultancy firms the consultants are often juniors with little or no experience. The project manager breaks down project work into increasingly smaller project activities. Figure 11.2 provides a simplified example of a project work breakdown.

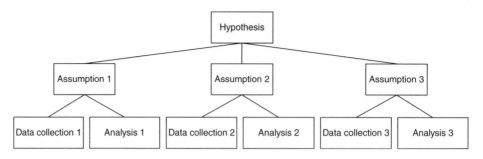

FIGURE 11.2 *A work breakdown structure for a management consultancy problem solving project*

DELEGATION OF WORK   The figure shows how the project manager breaks down the project work of testing the hypothesis into three pieces. Each piece is about testing an assumption in that hypothesis. Next, the project manager breaks down each assumption test into smaller tasks: data collection and data analysis. Figure 11.2 does not have a breakdown into a third level. In real life projects, the project manager typically continues breaking down project activities into increasingly smaller pieces. They continue the breakdown process until they arrive at a sufficiently low level of project activities that allows for project planning, as well as for allocating project pieces to (junior) consultants. The project activities at the lowest level of the work breakdown structure should be small and concrete enough to delegate to individual consultants.

Rules for breakdown

NO DUPLICATIONS   The breakdown of the project work is based on two rules (see also Minto, 1987). First, the tasks should not overlap each other, which means no duplications. Second, the tasks put together should be complete, which means that no task necessary to complete the project is missing from the breakdown. When breaking down the project work, it is necessary that the resulting tasks do not overlap each other. Overlapping is undesirable because the breakdown into tasks serves as a basis for dividing the project work among consultants. A division of work among consultants is only necessary if the project work requires more than one consultant. If the breakdown leads to overlapping tasks, then allocation of the overlapping tasks to different consultants will imply the duplication of work. Duplication means inefficiency and a delay for the project.

COMPLETENESS   The breakdown should be complete. This means that the consultants will not miss out any task that is necessary for the project. It is embarrassing for the project manager when the client or other stakeholders during a steering committee meeting, or even worse during a final presentation, point to omissions in the consultants' analyses:

- Why did you not investigate this?
- Have you not considered this?
- Have you not thought about this?

In the next chapter – about structured problem diagnosis – we will elaborate on these rules for breaking down structures.

Communications

ROLES OF COMMUNICATION   The project work does not only include the tasks required for problem solving and solution implementation, it also comprises communications tasks. Communication supports various roles, among which are project control, gathering intelligence, sound boarding, and ensuring stakeholders' support.

Communication for project control is about providing the steering committee with information about the progress of the project. Consultants may also communicate with stakeholders inside and outside the client organization to gather information, not only data but also insights regarding the problem and potential solutions. Furthermore, consultants will communicate their findings and preliminary recommendations to the steering board to solicit feedback. Finally, communications to stakeholders inside and outside the client organization during the project may help to get a buy-in and support from these stakeholders. Chapter 14 elaborates on communications.

PROCEDURE SETTING   In the initiation phase, the steering committee has set the procedures for communications. When structuring the project work, the project manager should also take the communication tasks into account. Communication activities include developing reports and presentations, organizing and preparing meetings, having meetings, compiling meeting minutes, and taking follow-on actions that may result from these meetings.

TYPES OF COMMUNICATIONS   We can distinguish between four different types of communications for the consultants:

1. The project manager regularly communicates with the partner.
2. The project manager regularly meets with the project team. We would distinguish between meetings that include the client team members and those that only include the consultants.
3. The project manager meets with the steering committee.

4. The consultants meet with broader audiences of stakeholders. In a problem solving project, the consultants may have to present their recommended solution to the stakeholders. In an implementation project, the consultants may have to present the implementation plan to the stakeholders.

Plan the project stages

THE PROJECT TASKS   The project tasks at the lowest level of the work breakdown structure serve as the basis for the project planning. The project manager needs to assess the duration of each of these lowest-level tasks in hours, days, weeks, or a relevant unit of time. We would acknowledge that the duration of tasks partially depends on the number and skills of individuals assigned to the project. These individuals are consultants and in some cases also employees of the client. Some clients will assign a number of their own employees to the consultancy project.

RESOURCES   If the number of individuals – consultants and client employees – is predefined in the project contract, then the project manager takes these resources as a starting point for assessing the duration of tasks. However, if the project deadline is predefined in the contract, then the alternative approach would be to determine how many resources are needed to complete this deadline.

Once the project manager has assessed the duration of each task, they need to identify the logical relationships between these tasks. These relationships typically take the form of dependencies. One task is dependent on another task. For instance, for the valuation of a takeover candidate firm, a consultant wants to make a prognosis of future cash flows for that firm. The consultant first needs to make a prognosis of that firm's revenues and costs.

DEPENDENCIES   We can distinguish between internal and external dependencies. Internal dependencies refer to dependencies of the project tasks on other project tasks that are conducted by the project team: the so-called internal tasks. In contrast, external dependencies refer to dependencies of internal activities on project tasks that have been outsourced: the so-called external tasks. An example of an external task is outsourced market research. Large consultancy firms typically have their own research departments, but the project manager may decide for some reason to outsource this particular piece of market research to a third party.

BUILDING FLEXIBILITY   The steering committee needs to determine the points at which the progress and quality of the project have to be reviewed (monitoring). The project manager has to take these reviews into account when planning the project. They should also build flexibility into the project planning. There should be some allowance for some unforeseen slippage. If possible, the project manager should plan a so-called 'week zero' for the consultancy team. This week can be used for briefing the consultants, and if necessary for training in methods, tools, and techniques, as well as getting familiar with the client business.

PLANNING THE ACTIVITIES   Once the duration of project activities as well as their dependencies has been assessed, then the project manager can plan the activities in the right sequence to meet the required completion data. The project manager needs to take into account the constraints of the project. Examples of such constraints are limited staff and limited access to data. The project manager needs to be very practical. For instance, if one analysis is a financial benchmark of various competitors, and another analysis is an operational benchmark of the same competitors, then the project manager may divide these competitors among the consultants. Each consultant should collect from 'their' competitors both the financial and the operational data. This saves time and costs.

The project manager also needs to explicitly state the planning assumptions about uncertainties regarding the project. Examples of uncertainties surrounding a consultancy project may be the response of stakeholders to the project or unforeseen developments within the client's industry.

PLANNING TECHNIQUES   Project managers may use various planning techniques such as the Gantt chart to develop a plan or schedule for the project activities. For large and complex projects, management consultants may even use planning software. Figure 11.3 on the next page provides a simplified example of a Gantt chart for the planning of a problem solving project, involving the testing of a hypothesis (see Figure 11.2). The chart not only plots the tasks in time, but also points out who is responsible for each task. Furthermore, the figure includes the milestones. These are meetings with the steering committee when the project manager needs to present the interim or final deliverables.

Allocate the project resources

THE PROJECT RESOURCES   Once the project planning is complete, the project manager needs to allocate the project resources to the planned tasks. The resources of the management consultancy project comprise the time and skills of people and the infrastructure, as well as a budget for expenditure. The project manager needs a budget for the project-related expenses, such as travel and lodging, as well as a budget for outsourcing certain project activities. The project manager may decide to outsource some of the project activities, such as market research, to sub-contractors.

STRUCTURE OF A PROJECT ORGANIZATION   These resources should allow the project manager to execute the project work in the scheduled

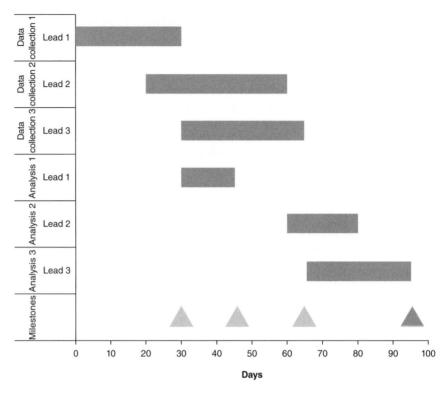

FIGURE 11.3 *Planning the consultancy project tasks with a Gantt chart*

Notes: the triangles indicate the milestone meetings with the steering committee. 'Lead' refers to a consultant with responsibility for particular project tasks (see also Figure 11.4)

time frame. Figure 11.4 presents an example of the structure of a consultancy project organization. The project team may include client employees. The selection of client employees is a delicate matter and we will discuss this at a later stage. In our example, the project manager has broken down the work into three work streams, and allocated each stream to a sub-team consisting of consultants and client employees. In addition to the three work streams, the project manager works with a consultant who is an industry specialist – for instance, in banking – and a consultant who is a functional specialist – for instance, a specialist in mergers and acquisitions. This specialist is part of the consultancy firm but is not part of the project team. The consultants may also outsource the expertise tasks. For instance, the outsourced specialist for research may be a third party, such as Evalueserve. Besides the consultancy staff, the project also needs support staff, such as information and research specialists for data collection, communications specialists for PowerPoint presentations and reports, and last but not least, secretaries for general administrative support.

SUPPORT STAFF   Figure 11.4 distinguishes between three types of support staff. First, the team has an information and research specialist. This person collects data through desk research – for instance by searching databases – for the work streams. Second, the project manager has assigned a communications specialist to the project. This person works with the consultants to produce the (PowerPoint) presentations, the reports, and other project documentation. Chapter 14 will elaborate on the communications function. Third, the project manager has a secretary for administrative support.

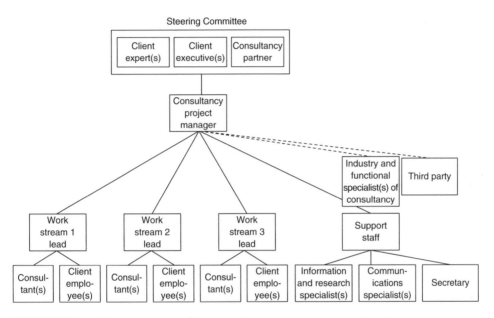

FIGURE 11.4   *The structure of a consultancy project organization*

The infrastructure for the project consists of computers and access to a computer network (internet). The project team also needs furnished office space to work in, the so-called 'team room'.

FIXED RESOURCES   We have described a project design where the project manager first makes a plan of the work, and subsequently determines how much resources are needed. Often the project manager will have fixed resources available. These resources are derived from the terms and conditions of the contract. The project manager may find that the required resources exceed the resources they have available. You may ask: how should the project manager deal with this challenge? First, the project manager has to try to get the most from the available resources. This means that the consultants may be stretched to increase their productivity. If stretching the team and other resources is not sufficient to get the work done in time, then the project manager needs to make suggestions to the steering committee for decisions on the trade-offs between quality, scope of work, time, and costs. For instance, the committee may decide to reduce the scope of the project – for instance, save on the 'nice-to-have' deliverables and focus on the 'need-to-have' ones – or extend the project deadline, which means allowing a certain delay.

Develop a project risk plan

RISK ASSESSMENT   The project manager needs to assess and analyse the risks associated with the project. Risks are in particular relevant for implementation projects (see Chapter 15). The project manager needs to identify the likely risks. Then they need to estimate the likelihood of each individual risk. How likely is this to happen? Next, the project manager needs to estimate the impact of each risk on the quality, time, cost, and scope of the project. Questions to be asked include: if this risk event is going to happen, how much will it reduce the quality of the project deliverables? How will it increase the amount of a work, and the required time and cost to do the additional work? The estimates of the likelihood and impact of risk events help the project manager to prioritize the risks.

RISK MANAGEMENT   After having prioritized the project risks, the project manager develops a plan for managing these risks. A formal risk plan is usually reserved for (large and complex) implementation projects. In problem solving projects, the project manager takes an informal approach. Then, the project manager's experience is often sufficient to assess the risks, and deal with them. In a politically laden project, the project manager needs a well-developed antenna to sense the (political) risks in a timely fashion.

ANTICIPATING AND COUNTERING RISKS   In the formal approach to risk management, the project manager needs to select the appropriate measures for each risk. We can distinguish between preventive measures and countermeasures. Preventive measures aim to prevent the risk from happening, or at least reduce its likelihood and impact. The countermeasures include a contingency plan to reduce the impact of the risk event. The contingency plan is an outline of measures that need to be taken if the risk occurs. The project manager plans the preventive measures and countermeasures for the project risks and assesses the required resources for these measures. To anticipate the risks, the project manager needs to identify the lead indicators of these risks. These indicators become the so-called 'trigger metrics'. They trigger the measures. The project manager uses these metrics as part of project control. The project manager needs the steering committee's approval for the risk management plan.

PHASE 3: EXECUTION

Work of consultants

After the project manager has designed the project, and the steering committee has approved this design, then the execution phase can start. The execution of the project is about the implementation of the design plan. It is about carrying out the tasks at the lowest level of the work breakdown structure (see Figure 11.2). Carrying out these tasks is the work of the consultants on the project. In some cases, client employees may work with the consultants in the project team. But even if there are no client employees in the project team, the consultants will aim to keep the client involved in the project. Management consultancy is a service. In services, the client is often involved in the production process because the production and consumption of services are difficult to separate. If the consultancy project includes the consultants' assistance with the implementation of advice, then the involvement of the client will be even larger.

Communication with the steering committee

Alongside the (technical) work on the client's problem, the consultants need to communicate with the steering committee on a regular basis. At regular intervals, the project manager will meet with the steering committee to present and discuss the project's progress. The client may also invite sounding board members to participate in the discussion. The consultants may also meet with other stakeholders inside and outside the client organization.

PHASE 4: CONTROL

Responsibility of the steering committee

The execution of the project needs to be controlled in order to enhance the chances of meeting the project objectives. This project control is a responsibility of the steering committee. The control process comprises three steps. First, the steering committee determines the project's key performance indicators (KPIs). Second, these KPIs need to be monitored. The committee typically delegates the measuring to the project manager. The project manager reports the measurements to the steering committee. Third, the committee needs to take corrective and adaptive measures if the KPIs deviate from the objectives.

Determine the project KPIs

The KPIs of the project are typically formulated in terms of the project's quality, scope (quantity), time, and cost. The project's quality refers to the degree to which the deliverables of the project meet the client's requirements. The project's scope points to the contractually agreed upon work. The scope defines what tasks belong to the project. Time refers to the duration of project tasks. In complex (problem solving) projects, the KPIs are typically limited to the process, such as the timing. In such cases, the KPIs do not cover the content. The steering committee evaluates the content themselves. Cost is about three categories:

1. The costs of the people – both consultants and client employees on the project.
2. The project expenses.
3. The cost of the project infrastructure.

If the project is fixed fee or performance-based fee, then cost control is a concern of the consultants. What the client pays is not related to the consultants' costs. Only if changes in the project's scope cause overruns of the project budget will the consultants seek to renegotiate the budget with the client.

Monitor the KPIs

The project manager regularly, at least at the project milestones, measures the KPIs. If the KPI measurements deviate from the objectives, then corrective and adaptive measures may be required. The project manager reports at regular intervals to the steering committee. The reports comprise the KPI results, the project status, and an overview of current issues as well as potential issues. Furthermore, the report gives the budget status (a comparison of actual expenses and budgeted expenses for the report period) and schedule status (tasks completed versus the plan). In addition to the KPIs, the project manager keeps other recordings of the project and maintains a daily log of any notes and actions made during the day, including any important meetings and decisions.

Take corrective and adaptive measures

The steering committee uses the measurements of the KPIs to review the progress against objectives. In case of issues – say the project does not proceed according to plan – corrective and adaptive measures may need to be taken. We can distinguish between two types of issues. One type of issue arises when the project team does not execute the project according to the plan, which has negative consequences, such as insufficient quality, delays, and cost overruns. The steering committee needs to decide on *corrective* measures to address such issues. The type of measures depends on the cause of the issue. The second type of issue occurs if changes inside or outside the client organization imply a change in the objectives or scope of the project. Such changes require *adaptive* measures. The steering committee may need to adapt the plan, the time schedule, and the available resources.

Execution stages

To make the project more controllable, it may be broken down into execution stages. At the end of each stage, the steering committee organizes a so-called 'gate review' (see Figure 11.5). The project manager may proceed to the next stage only if the steering committee authorizes that next stage. If the gate review reveals issues, then the steering committee may decide on corrective and adaptive measures. As such, gate reviews serve as a quality assurance. Gate reviews also enable the steering committee to reduce the project risk. Depending on the outcome of the gate review, the steering committee may decide to opt out of the project. In this case the steering committee stops the project.

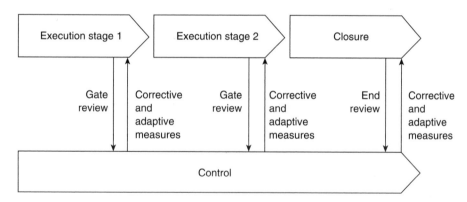

FIGURE 11.5 *Project control*

PHASE 5: CLOSURE

Control of the closure

After the execution phase has been completed, the project enters the closure phase. As with the execution, closure of the project should also be controlled. To control the closure, the project manager prepares the so-called 'end of project report' for the steering committee. This report provides measures of the success of the project. It assesses the project's outcomes against the project's objectives. In the case of a problem solving project, the main question to be answered is: have the consultants developed an effective solution for the client's problem? In the case of an implementation project, the main question to be answered is: have the consultants implemented the solution effectively, in time, and within budget?

The end of project report

The end of project report also includes the impact of changes on the project. Furthermore, the report specifies the time used, costs, and resources. The steering committee needs to verify and confirm that the project's objectives have been achieved (the so-called 'end review' in Figure 11.5). If the client accepts the project deliverables and confirms that the objectives have been achieved, then the steering committee may decommission the project. The project file is then closed. The project manager hands over the project documentation to the client. The steering committee formally ends the project.

Project evaluation

The committee may evaluate the project for the purpose of learning. In such a case, the committee develops a so-called 'lessons learned report'. Such a report typically documents all elements – both successes and mistakes – that can be useful for future projects. Furthermore, for any loose ends, the management consultancy firm – partner and project manager – may give follow-on action recommendations. The consultancy and the client may also plan a post-project review.

Client relationship management

The closure of the project implies the disbandment of the project team. Typically the steering committee will organize a celebration of the project completion. The steering committee then acknowledges – and rewards – the contributions of the team members: the project manager, the consultants, and the client employees. After the withdrawal of the consultants, the partner in the consultancy firm maintains the relationship with the client. The partner monitors the client's progress and does follow-ups to maintain a good relationship with the client executive. The project manager will maintain a relationship with his or her counterpart at the client organization. This is important for future business development for the consultancy firm. Over time, the project manager may get promoted to partner. His or her counterpart at the client organization may become executive. Then the newly promoted partner will already have a network at the executive level.

To summarize, Figure 11.6 provides a brief overview of the roles of the various stakeholders – the client, the partner in the consultancy firm, the project manager, and the consultants on the team – during each of the five project phases.

Project phases	Initiation	Design	Execution	Control	Closure
Client	Owns a problem. Commissions the project.	Approves the design and the selection of the team members.	May act as sounding board. Where necessary, makes decisions.	Decides corrective and adaptive actions. Evaluates and accepts deliverables.	Accepts the solution. Evaluates and decommissions the project.
Consultancy partner	Supervises the development of the proposal. Acquires the project.	Supervises the development of the design by project leader. Communicates with the client.	Supervises the project leader. Communicates with the client.	Evaluates the deliverables, and supervises the project leader. Communicates with the client.	Evaluates the project, and maintains the relationship with the client.
Consultancy manager (project leader)	Develops the proposal.	Develops the design. Forms the team.	Supervises the project team. Coaches individual consultants. Communicates with client counterpart(s).	Evaluates the deliverables, takes corrective and adaptive actions, and supervises the project team.	Evaluates the project, Disbands the team.
Consultants (project team members)	Collect the data and conduct data analysis for the proposal.	Train – when necessary – the client employees on the team.	Execute the project. Communicate with client counterpart(s).	Execute the corrective and adaptive actions.	Handover project documentation to client.

FIGURE 11.6 *Project phases and stakeholders' roles*

CASE STUDY

Client team members

Working with client employees

A retailing organization, named OldRetail, has hired Acme Consulting for a strategy implementation project. Acme has assigned Jacqueline as project manager. She is a rapidly rising star in the Acme hierarchy. She has already been appointed as manager after only three years. The implementation project for OldRetail will be her first project as a manager. Jacqueline has been preparing the project thoroughly. Everything went well except for one thing. During the contract negotiations, Acme's partner Ron and the executive at OldRetail had agreed that three employees of OldRetail would strengthen the project team. To be precise, OldRetail had promised to supply three seniors from the control department, HR, and from corporate planning, to work on the project for three days per week for the entire six month duration of the project.

Identifying the client employees

Jacqueline had approached her counterpart at OldRetail, a manager named James, several times to get the names of these employees. Again and again James would come up with a pretext. Finally, Jacqueline decided to use Ron, Acme's partner on the project, to induce the executive at OldRetail to come up with the promised employees for the team. Two weeks before the planned kick-off of the project, Jacqueline's counterpart James finally hands her the CVs and contact details for three employees: Jill, Daniel, and Fred.

Unpleasant surprises

When Jacqueline reads through the CVs, and subsequently interviews the people, she is unpleasantly surprised. Jill is a trainee at the control department who only started working for OldRetail two months ago. Daniel is with R&D and is close to retirement. He is very cynical about the new strategy. According to Daniel it looks similar to a previous consultancy attempt a decade ago that did not work. Finally,

Jacqueline meets Fred. He is a senior in corporate planning. However, Fred turns out to be in an outplacement trajectory. He has to leave the firm within half a year because of underperformance. Fred is frustrated and makes it clear to Jacqueline that she should not have high expectations of his contribution. After Fred has left the interview room, Jacqueline stares out of the window. What should she do with these three people?

Reflective questions

1. Does Jacqueline have a problem? Why? Why not? Explain your answer.

2. What does this case tell you about the attitude of this particular client towards the project and towards its consultants? Elaborate on your answer.

3. If you were in Jacqueline's position, what options would you consider? What are the pros and cons of each option? Evaluating these pros and cons, what would you do? Explain your answer.

ORGANIZING THE MANAGEMENT CONSULTANCY PROJECT

The consultancy project team selection

Selecting the members of the project team is an important decision. Often, the management consultancy firm will have already suggested a team of consultants during the proposal phase. The project team needs to have all the required competences on board. Together the consultants in the project team should have the required set of skills, knowledge, and experience to realize the project objectives. The client is given the opportunity to judge this proposed team. Clients, in particular the sophisticated ones, may demand changes to the team if they are not satisfied with the proposed team. Remember that the quality of individual consultants within a consultancy firm may vary (recall the performance appraisal scores that range from 1 to 5). The client should not settle for a so-called 'B-team' – staffed with average or below-average performers (3–5 performance) – but instead demand one of the firm's A-teams, which are staffed with the firm's top performers (1–2 performance).

Client employees

CLIENT MOTIVATIONS   The client and the consultancy partner may decide to include some client employees in the project team. The client may want some of its employees on the project to learn from the consultants. One motivation for the client is to develop new competences. Another motivation for clients on the project is that they gain knowledge about the solution and keep this knowledge within the organization after the consultants have left. Keeping the knowledge about the solution is important for the subsequent implementation of that solution. The client may also want to use their own employees on the project to save on the money spent on consultants. The client employees then substitute, partly, for consultants on the project. Because of the use of client employees, there are fewer consultants needed on the project team. As a result, the project fee will be lower.

CONSULTANT MOTIVATIONS   Not only the client but also the consultancy partner may want client employees on the project team, for instance if the consultancy firm lacks specific knowledge and skills with respect to the client organization and sector. Client employees on the project may be important to obtain access to knowledge in the client organization and to get support for the solution. Client participation in solution development enhances the chances of successful implementation of that solution. The input from client employees may enable consultants to develop solutions that are more feasible to implement. Moreover, client participation in solution development may give the client organization the feeling that they have created the solution themselves. This ownership of the solution increases acceptance by the stakeholders.

SELECTION OF EMPLOYEES   The consultancy partner should never let the client unilaterally decide which employees will be assigned to the project team. The partner should set clear expectations concerning the profile of project team members. The project objectives cannot be achieved with the wrong skills, knowledge, or attitudes on board. The consultant should therefore be selective about the candidates proposed by the client. The usual selection criteria for client employees on the project team will include problem solving skills, interpersonal skills, and technical (functional) skills. Client employees must also be flexible (recall that consultancy is an extreme job), and committed to the project cause (remember that stakeholders with a conflict of interest might sabotage the project). But most important for the consultant are the client employee's organizational skills and organizational network.

ADVANTAGES OF CLIENT EMPLOYEES   As insiders, these employees understand the client organization, the culture, and the politics. It is critical for the project's success that the client employees on the project team know how to communicate and with whom to communicate in other departments of the client organization. Involvement of client employees in the project team is important for communications with the client. Client employees may be used to explain the project to the client organization. As stated before, participation by client employees in the project is also important for the client organization's acceptance of the consultant's recommendations. It helps to fight the not-invented-here syndrome. Moreover, client employees' participation may ease the implementation of these recommendations.

Team development

COMMITMENT   The commitment of all members of the project team is critical for the success of the project. To enhance commitment, the project objectives should be made clear to all. Moreover, all project members need to own the shared objectives. The members should identify with the objectives. Mutual accountability is another critical success factor. All project members are accountable (for their own work). The members should identify with the team. It should be 'we' and 'us' instead of 'you' and 'they'. Individual objectives and rewards for team members should be aligned with the project objectives. If they contribute to the project's success, they will benefit. Under-performers will be removed from the team.

COMPOSITION   A project team should be more than the sum of its individual members. The project manager should strive for synergy between members, while minimizing conflict and tension within the team. The team should have a complementary mix of competences and styles to fulfil the necessary roles for the project. Moreover, all project team members should be aligned to work in the direction of the project objectives. There should be cohesion between the members to work as a team. The project manager should check for personality issues that may undermine cohesion of the team. The project manager not only needs cohesion, they also need diversity in the team. Diversity is required for creativity and innovation. Moreover, the different roles and tasks in a team require diversity in that team.

DYNAMICS   Teams will typically develop according to a specific pattern. They will move through distinct phases of development. Figure 11.7 shows five common phases of team development (Tuckman, 1965). For each phase, we sketch the team dynamics in terms of the behaviour of the team members. Moreover, we outline how the project manager should deal with the challenges presented by these team dynamics.

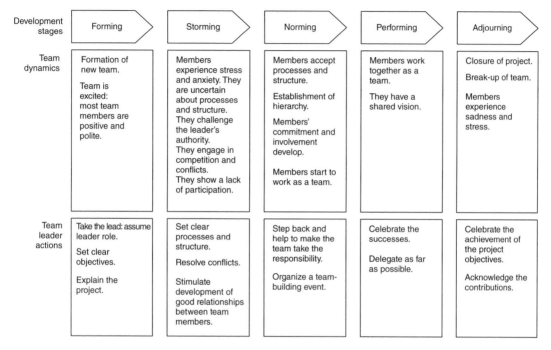

FIGURE 11.7 *Five stages of team development*

Source: based on Tuckman (1965)

THE CONSULTANCY PROJECT MANAGER

The project manager has three main responsibilities: to manage the project, to manage the client relationship, and last but not least, to manage the project team.

Project management

PROJECT DELIVERY   The project manager needs to keep the project on track. They have to manage the delivery of the project. The project manager is responsible for achieving the project objectives in terms of quality, scope, and time. Therefore, they need to manage use of the consultants and other project staff. The project manager also has to keep the expenses within budget. Moreover, they need to maintain the project records, including a project book.

REPORTING TO THE PARTNER   The manager reports to the partner. The project manager needs to communicate regularly with the consultancy firm's partner. The project manager keeps their superior up to date about the status of the project. The partner is typically involved in multiple projects and will therefore have less information about the operations of this specific project than the manager. As a member of the steering committee, the partner receives updates from the project manager. But the one-on-one reporting by the project manager is more frequent and provides richer information than is exchanged with the client in the steering committee meetings. For instance, if there are issues with employees or stakeholders of the client, then the project manager will discuss these first with the partner only.

MANAGING THE PARTNER   The project manager may also use the partner as a sounding board and ask for advice. The partner maintains relations with (high-level) stakeholders inside the client organization that are beyond the reach of the project manager. By providing information to the partner, the project manager may influence the communication between the partner and these stakeholders. The project manager not only manages the team of consultants, they also 'manage' the partner.

PREPARING THE PARTNER   The project manager has to make sure that the partner is fully prepared for meetings with the client. The project manager has to prepare the reports and presentations that the partner wants to use in meetings with the client. The partner provides feedback to the manager. During the project and after the closure of the project, the partner evaluates the project manager. The partner's evaluation is important input for the project manager's performance appraisal.

Client management

The project manager is responsible for communicating with the client in the steering committee. They should set the expectations of the client. The project manager needs to make clear what they need from the client, and what they will provide for the client. Furthermore, the project manager needs to make the client understand how they would like to work with the client. The project manager should not accept any client requests for changes in the project scope, unless these are approved by the steering committee.

Team management

CREATING THE TEAM The project manager is responsible for creating an effective team. Figure 11.7 outlines the role of the project manager during the five stages of team development. The project manager has to manage the team dynamics and resolve conflicts between team members. In particular, outcasts or black sheep will require the attention of the project manager.

MOTIVATING THE TEAM The project manager should ensure the motivation of the team. Figure 11.7 shows how the morale of the team typically changes during the stages of team development. Even within the performing stage morale may fluctuate. It is inevitable that the team will be confronted with setbacks, for instance if the consultants cannot get the data they need for their diagnosis, on the consultants' efforts to implement a recommendation fail because of resistance from client employees.

TEAM MORALE Disappointment and frustration lower consultant morale. But even if the project goes according to plan, morale may still deteriorate. Recall that management consultancy is an extreme job. The stress and long hours can have a negative impact on the consultants' morale. The project manager should make efforts to restore team morale when it is low. The manager may give the team a pep talk, or may organize a sports event for the team, such as a small squash tournament after office hours. These are just two examples of measures that a project manager may take. If the team achieves success then the project manager should celebrate it with the team because success should be reinforced. The project manager may organize a team event to celebrate the success, for example, a team dinner in a good restaurant.

LOGISTICS The project manager is also responsible for the logistics of the project team and for the support infrastructure. Logistics of the project team is about (international) travel and lodging. If the client site is a large distance from the consultancy firm's office, then the project team stays at a hotel during the project. The support infrastructure of the project refers to secretarial support, communications support (e.g. PowerPoint production), and the office and ICT-infrastructure (computers and internet access) for the project team.

COACHING OF CONSULTANTS The relationship between the project manager and the consultants on the team is vital for the success of the project.

Understanding the consultants. The project manager should develop a full understanding of the consultants. The manager should learn not only about each consultant's experience and competences but also about their personalities. Does the consultant need a lot of structure or will they prefer freedom? How does the consultant react under pressure? Consultancy firms may use psychological tests to develop a profile of their consultants. This also helps the consultants to understand themselves better. Such information enables the project manager to coach the consultant better.

Discussing expectations. Before the start of the project, the project manager typically has a personal meeting with each consultant on the team. The manager and the consultant will discuss the consultant's expectations and the consultant's wishes for personal professional development. The project manager needs to set consultant expectations and should make sure that all team members understand the project, the objectives, and the tasks. The project manager should stretch the objectives for the individual consultants, but the objectives should still be manageable. The project manager should look after the development needs of the consultants on the team. Consultants may have a need to build specific skills, knowledge, and attitudes for their career development. The project manager should take into account the consultants' wishes when allocating tasks and giving feedback.

Coaching and evaluating. During the project, the project manager operates as a personal coach for each individual consultant. Moreover, the project manager needs to set the consultants' expectations about the client relationship. The project manager should instruct the consultants how to approach and deal with the client. During the project and after the closure of the project, the project manager evaluates each individual consultant. The manager's evaluation is important input for the consultant's performance appraisal.

THE CONSULTANCY PROJECT TEAM MEMBER

Junior versus senior consultant

SENIOR CONSULTANT   We can distinguish between junior and senior consultants on the project. Seniors are consultants with a couple years work experience. In larger projects, the project manager may delegate parts of the project work to senior consultants. The senior is responsible for the so-called 'work stream' (see Figure 11.4). Two examples of a work stream are the valuation of a takeover target company and the analysis of the cost structure of the client organization. As a work stream leader, the senior consultant coordinates a small sub-team of junior consultants and in some cases also client employees.

JUNIOR CONSULTANT   The junior consultant typically has little or no (consultancy) working experience. They report to the project manager, or – if the project work is broken down into work streams – to a work stream leader. The junior has to execute the tasks at the bottom of the work breakdown structure (see Figure 11.2). The tasks of the junior are predefined in the project work plan. Typically, a junior consultant collects data and analyses these data. For instance, the junior may have to assess opportunities for a cost reduction of a takeover candidate company's operations. The junior consultant receives instructions from the project leader, or work stream leader, about which cost items to analyse, which data from the takeover candidate to use, which benchmark to use, and where to collect the data.

DELEGATION OF WORK   Usually, the project manager hands over a slide template of the desired output to the junior. The junior has to enter the analysis results into the slide in order to complete this slide. If the project team includes a communications specialist, then the consultant hands over the analysis results to the specialist. The specialist then creates the PowerPoint slide from the analysis results. The more experienced the junior is, the less detailed the instructions need to be from the project manager. The project manager develops the junior for a senior position by giving them increasing responsibilities. Coaching is critical for this development process. The project manager should watch the consultant carefully to see when they are ready for larger responsibilities.

EXPECTED TO CONTRIBUTE   In consultancy firms that are a meritocracy, all consultants are expected to contribute to the discussion during team meetings. Even the most junior consultants should speak their mind. For instance, if they dissent, and have good arguments for their dissent, then they are expected – if not required – to speak up. In a meritocracy, it is the power of ideas and arguments that counts, not the seniority or rank of the individual.

PERSONAL PLAN   To progress to a next level position, the consultant makes a personal plan. If the consultant has a mentor, then the mentor helps the consultant with the preparation of this plan. Otherwise, the HR staff of the consultancy firm provide assistance with the preparation of the plan. The personal plan is based on the past performance of the consultant and indicates what personal development is necessary to attain the next level, that is project manager (or the in-between position of work stream leader). The personal plan gives insight into the strengths and weaknesses of the consultant. It points to the areas where the consultant has to improve, for instance, financial modelling or interviewing. The project manager will take these areas for improvement into account when allocating the tasks among the consultants on the project team. Moreover, the project manager may provide additional guidance to the consultant to improve their performance in a weak area.

EXTREME JOB   The junior consultant has to deal with the challenges that the extreme job of consultancy poses. For young people just out business school the transition from a relatively carefree student life to a hectic consultancy life can be testing. The junior has to adapt to their new responsibilities, the unpredictable work load, and the long hours. However, young people typically have relatively high staying power and energy. Moreover, the opportunity costs of the consultancy life – unpredictable work and long hours – are lower for juniors as they probably will not yet have families of their own. Moreover, the responsibilities of the junior are small compared to those of the project manager, and even more so the partner. Typically, the junior is shielded by the project manager – and the partner – from any big political issues in the relationship with a client and other stakeholders. However, the junior may still face political issues within the project team and, on a small scale, with the client.

TENSIONS BETWEEN CONSULTANTS   Tensions between consultants in a team are not unusual. These may result from a lack of chemistry between individuals. Moreover, the up-or-out policy may cause rivalry between colleagues. Recall that not all consultants in the firm get promoted. Up-or-out pressures may induce unethical behaviour. Colleagues may use each others' ideas or work without giving them credit. Even though team work is part of the evaluation, each consultant wants to enhance their promotion chances by excelling. The ideal from the firm's perspective is to have consultants excel at their assigned tasks *and* help their colleagues. The consultant should make sure that their contributions to others' work are visible in order to get credit from the project manager.

CLIENT POLITICS   In the execution of tasks, the consultant may also be confronted with client politics on a micro-scale. For instance, the junior consultant may need sales data from one of the client's sales managers to make an analysis. This manager may feel threatened by the consultancy project and may therefore use all kinds of evasions in order not to give the requested data to the junior. If the junior cannot solve this problem, then they cannot do the analysis. As a consequence, they will not be successful. Management consultancy, even at a junior level, is not just about technical skills.

SUMMARY

PHASES OF A PROJECT   The consultancy project is a heterogeneous concept. Projects vary with the type of consultancy. They also differ in scope. Nevertheless, projects typically follow five phases.

The first phase is *initiation*: the organization and the procedures for the project are established. The second phase is *design* of the project. The project work is broken down into increasingly smaller pieces: the so-called work breakdown structure. The next stage is *execution* of the project. This is the phase of the actual consultancy work: diagnosing problems, developing solutions, and – if applicable – assisting with the implementation of the solution. Parallel to the execution phase runs the *control* phase. Project control is about monitoring the project's progress and when necessary taking corrective and adaptive actions. The final stage is *closure* of the project. The project needs to be formally closed down, following predefined procedures to make sure that the project objectives are met and accepted by the client.

PROJECT STRUCTURE   The project organization structure consists of the steering committee and the project team. The client and the consultancy partner take part in the steering committee. The project team consists of the consultants – and in some cases client employees – and the project manager. The project manager allocates the work among the consultants and provides guidance and feedback. They have to guide the team through the stages of team development: forming, storming, norming, performing, and adjourning. The project manager's evaluation of the consultant is important input for the performance appraisal of the consultant. Junior consultants get predefined tasks that typically consist of data collection and data analysis. The challenges of the extreme job of consulting may be a huge shock for juniors who are used to college life. The micro-politics of the consultancy team and interfacing with the client make clear why it is not sufficient for consultants to excel in the execution of their technical tasks.

REFLECTIVE QUESTIONS

1. Reflect on the role of the client during each phase of the project life cycle. What are the most critical actions in the distinct phases that the client may take to ensure the project's success? Explain your answer.

2. During the execution phase of a project for LargeManufacturer, the client – the general manager of LargeManufacturer – has to go on sick leave. He is not expected to return before the deadline for the project. His replacement wants to change the project scope. This will lead to more work and higher costs for Macintosh & Company, the consultancy firm. His replacement has not indicated any willingness to renegotiate the project fee. What should the partner from Macintosh do? Provide argumentation for your answer.

3. Describe the tension for the consultant between the need to be a team player and the pressure of the up-or-out policy. Assume you have a colleague on the team who wants to make a good impression on the project manager, at the expense of you and the other consultants on the project. How would you deal with this situation? Explain your answer.

Internal versus external consultants – who is in the lead?

Internal and external consultants

Marcel is a project manager with Pyramid Consultancy. He is assigned to a project for BigAutomotive, which is a large producer of passenger cars and trucks. BigAutomotive has hired Pyramid to conduct a cost study. The client is no longer cost competitive and therefore it wants Pyramid to reduce costs. Pyramid has done several very successful cost reduction projects for other automotive companies and is therefore nicknamed the 'cost slasher'. The client executive at BigAutomotive has demanded that the Pyramid consultants work together with the client's internal consultants. BigAutomotive has recently set up an internal consultancy department. Most of the internal consultants have come from external consultancy firms. However, none of them is a Pyramid alumnus.

Two captains on the ship

Pyramid has assumed that they will manage the consultancy project. In fact, the Pyramid partner has assigned Marcel as project manager. The Pyramid partner has presumed that BigAutomotive will supply internal consultants for the various work streams. However, during the preliminary meetings, Marcel speaks to his counterpart Fritz at BigAutomotive's internal consultancy department. Fritz has been told by the executive that he will also be project manager. Together with Marcel, he is supposed to lead the consultancy project. Fritz was a manager with the prestigious consultancy firm the Crimson Consultancy Group. He makes clear that he absolutely does not want to work under the supervision of Pyramid Consulting.

Off the record

The next day, when Marcel is at the client's premises, one of Fritz's colleagues approaches Marcel. This colleague informs Marcel – off the record – that the internal consultants of BigAutomotive will not cooperate with Pyramid unless Fritz gets an equal position in the project management. Marcel discusses the issue with the Pyramid partner. They conclude that the cooperation of the client is a critical factor for the success of the project.

Questions

1 Is cooperation between the external consultants of Pyramid and the internal consultants of BigAutomotive really a critical success factor? Explain your answer.

2 What are the advantages and disadvantages for Pyramid of sharing project management responsibility with the internal consultants of BigAutomotive?

3 What would you recommend to the partner and project manager of Pyramid? Elaborate on your answer.

FURTHER READING

Friga, P. (2009) *The McKinsey Engagement: A Powerful Toolkit For More Efficient and Effective Team Problem Solving*. New York: McGraw-Hill.

REFERENCES

Maister, D. (1993) *Managing the Professional Services Firm*. New York: The Free Press.

Minto, B. (1987). *The Pyramid Principle: Logic in Writing and Thinking* (revised 3rd edn). London: Minto International Inc.

Schein, E.H. (1987) *Process Consultation II: Lessons for Managers and Consultants*. Reading, MA: Addison-Wesley.

Tuckman, B. (1965) 'Developmental sequence in small groups', *Psychological Bulletin*, 63 (6): 384–399.

12

STRUCTURED PROBLEM DIAGNOSIS

INTRODUCTION

The *formal* hiring reasons for management consultants concern solving the client's problem. The question arises: how do consultants solve problems? Different consultants may use different problem solving methods. The structured problem solving method is the hallmark of the world's top tier management consultancy firms, such as McKinsey & Company, the Boston Consulting Group, Bain & Company, Booz & Co, Roland Berger Strategy Consultants, and A.T. Kearney. This Chapter 12 and Chapter 13 are indicative of the problem solving approach as used by these top tier firms. These chapters provide a step-by-step guide to the structured problem solving method. We illustrate the method with two running cases. Structured problem solving consists of problem diagnosing and solution development. Problem diagnosis (Chapter 12) translates a client problem into a single question. Solution development (Chapter 13) is about answering that question. Consultants have to communicate their recommended solution to the client in order to get a decision to implement this solution (Chapter 14). Finally, consultants may assist the client with implementation of the solution to help the client achieve the desired result (Chapter 15). Figure 12.1 outlines this process, which runs from problem to result. This chapter closes with a summary, reflective questions, a running case study, suggestions for further reading, and references.

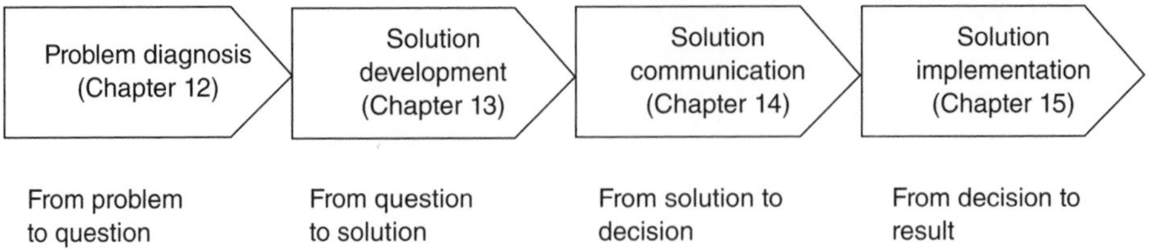

Problem diagnosis (Chapter 12)	Solution development (Chapter 13)	Solution communication (Chapter 14)	Solution implementation (Chapter 15)
From problem to question	From question to solution	From solution to decision	From decision to result

FIGURE 12.1 *An overview*

Main learning objectives

- Understand the reasons for structured problem solving.
- Understand the differences between analysing problems and analysing opportunities.
- Understand the result gap concept.
- Understand the principles of logical structuring.
- Know how to decompose a result gap in driver gaps.
- Know how to segment a result gap.
- Know how to structure the possible causes of a result gap.
- Understand abductive reasoning.
- Know how to test a possible cause.
- Know how to formulate a key question in the consultancy project.
- Know how to develop a problem statement.

THE PEOPLE SIDE OF PROBLEM SOLVING

This book explains structured problem solving as practiced by the top consultants. Its focus is on the method and the techniques. Real life problem solving on a consultancy project, however, is not just about methods and techniques. It is not like solving a case in business school. You do not receive a case pack with all the facts you need. There is no (friendly) professor who leads the case discussion in class. It is not cracking the case in a job interview for a consultancy firm either.

Dropped behind enemy lines

Consultants doing problem solving in real life projects are more likely to resemble elite troops operating behind enemy lines. Elite soldiers are dropped in hostile territory to execute a difficult mission under high time pressure. Management consultants are also parachuted into an unfamiliar environment. They are outsiders in the client organization. The consultants all of a sudden then invade the territory of the client organization members. As a consultant you should not expect that you will be received with open arms by the client members. Some client employees have good reasons to fear the arrival of consultants. In particular, if the client top management want the consultants to increase cost competitiveness, read 'reduce employment'. In such projects, client members may be uncooperative or even hostile. Some might even try to (secretly) sabotage the consultants' activities.

More than problem solving

Even if the instruction to the consultants is not about cost reduction, client members may still be reserved and uncommunicative towards the consultants. Consultancy projects are typically associated with uncertainty. Even client members that may expect to benefit from the arrival of consultants do not know for sure what outcome the consultancy project may lead to. Problem solving in a consultancy setting is not only about the problem but also about the people. Consultants not only have to be good at problem solving, they also have to be sensitive to people issues and possess good interpersonal skills. They have to be very good at communication. Moreover, consultants need mental toughness to deal with the stress and frustration that these people issues may cause.

APPROACHES TO PROBLEM SOLVING

Structured problem solving as practiced by the world's top tier management consultants is a systematic approach that requires a fair amount of discipline, as this book will make clear. You may ask yourself: why do the world's top tier consultants make the effort? What is wrong with other approaches to problem solving? We distinguish between three extreme alternatives (see Figure 12.2).

Guessing

One extreme option is what we call 'guessing'. This type of problem solving is solely based on creativity. It lacks analysis. It is an intuitive approach based on gut feeling. There is no testing of ideas. Solutions are implemented without testing them, which makes this a risky form of problem solving.

Analysing

A second extreme option is the complete opposite of guessing. This type of problem solving relies only on analysis. There is no place for creativity. It is driven by frameworks instead of focusing on the problem. The problem solver wants to use as many (text book) frameworks as possible. Analysis is an end instead of a means to an end (which should be problem solving). Therefore, this option is like 'boiling the ocean'.

Experience

The third extreme is experience-based problem solving. This method is neither based on creativity nor on analytical frameworks. Instead the solution is based on the problem solver's experience. The problem solver has seen the problem, or at least that is what they think. They have solved the problem before and already know the solution. The risk inherent to this approach is that the problem solver may err on the problem identification. They think that they have defined the problem correctly, but this problem may not be the real problem. They may focus on the wrong problem because they are relying on experience rather than on analysis of the problem at hand.

Advantages of structured problem solving

Figure 12.2 positions structured problem solving vis-à-vis the three extreme alternatives. Structured problem solving combines the best of all worlds. The structured problem solving method always focuses on the problem, not on analytical frameworks, thereby avoiding 'boiling the ocean'. Structured problem solving verifies the problem, thus avoiding a focus on the wrong problem. It uses creativity and experience to develop hypotheses about possible solutions. However, the structured problem solving method prescribes that all hypotheses are tested (that is the underlying assumptions of the hypothesis are analysed) before the solutions are recommended.

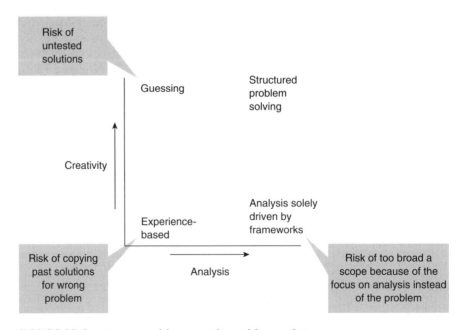

FIGURE 12.2 *Some problems with problem solving*

WHAT IS A PROBLEM?

Defining the client's problem

What is the client's problem? Many people may consider it a superfluous question. The client has already defined their problem. 'We have a cost problem'. Or 'Our culture has become a problem'. Or 'We need a new strategy'. In cases where the client has not yet defined the problem, then it may be obvious to the consultants what the client's problem is. 'This is a restructuring problem'. Or 'The client lacks competitiveness'. Or 'Productivity is a problem'.

Such definitions are not good enough for the world's top tier consultants. These statements are too vague to form a foundation for a top tier consultancy project. Moreover, if clients have defined the problem, how do the consultants whether know this definition is correct? Consultants should not take the client's definition of the problem for granted. The client may be unaware of the real problem, or they may have an interest to hide the real problem from the consultants (see Chapter 10 concerning clients' hidden agendas).

Why is it a problem?

For many people, determining the client's problem seems to be a non-problem. However, these same people may find it problematic to give a definition of what constitutes a problem in general. Ask yourself: what is a problem? Some people may define problems as questions and they would be right to do so. The structured problem solving approach formulates problems in a question format. However, it is not very insightful to say that a problem is a question. Other people may define problems in categories, such as cultural problems, strategic problems, and organizational problems. You may ask: why is culture a problem? This question forces you to look at the consequences. These consequences are the basis of the definition used in the structured problem solving method of the world's top tier consultants. Considering the consequences helps you to determine whether you have identified the right problem, instead of the wrong one.

THE RESULT GAP

The problem-owner

According to the structured problem solving method, a problem is a gap perceived by the problem-owner between the achieved result and the result that is desired by the problem-owner. A problem does not exist in a vacuum. A problem cannot exist independent of an actor, that is, a person or a group of persons, such as a management team. This actor is the so-called 'problem-owner'. For example, the manager has achieved a profit of US$5 million, whereas the desired profit is US$6 million. Therefore, the manager faces a profit gap of $1 million. The existence of this gap represents a problem for the actor because that gap implies that the owner does not have the result that they desire.

Closing the gap

How do we define problem solving? If we define a problem as the gap between the achieved result and the desired result of the problem-owner, then we may define problem solving as closing that result gap. The solution to the problem is a proposed action to increase the problem-owner's result from its achieved level to the desired level.

The result

EXTERNAL PROBLEM SOLVERS   Management consultancy depends on the fact that some problem-owners prefer to hire external experts to solve their problems. We would acknowledge that management consultants may do more than problem solve. They may also help clients to seize opportunities. This chapter also pays attention to diagnosing opportunities.

PROBLEM-OWNERS   Management consultants usually work for organizations, not individuals. Therefore, we shall only look at problem-owners which are organizations, typically represented by (higher) management of such organizations. Consultants may work both for (profit) companies and non-profit organizations.

DESIRED RESULTS   The desired results of these organizations typically vary. Companies usually define their desired results in profits or in company value (publicly listed companies typically focus on shareholder value). Non-profit organizations form a highly heterogeneous population with wide-ranging desired results. For instance, hospitals may formulate results in terms of the quality and volume of their cures, while schools may define results by the percentage of graduates and how high their grades are.

Two types of result gaps

DIFFERENT REASONS   We define a problem in terms of its impact on the problem-owner's result. The problem is defined as the result gap, which is the gap between the owner's achieved result and the desired result. If the owner is a company, then the result gap may be defined as the difference between the company's achieved profit and that company's desired profit. Because a result gap is the difference between the achieved result and the desired result, a gap may arise for different reasons.

DECREASING ACHIEVED RESULT   First, a result gap may arise because the achieved result has declined (see the example in the left-hand graph in Figure 12.3). Let us assume the desired result of the company in our example is $20 million. The company used to have a profit of $20 million but the profit has declined to the current (achieved) level of $9 million. The declining result is responsible for the result gap which is $11 million (20 – 19 = 11).

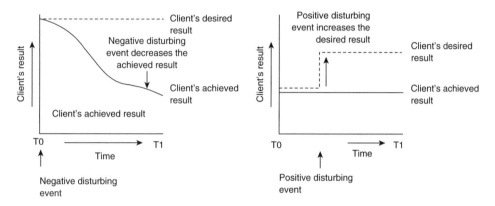

FIGURE 12.3   *Two different developments of result gaps*

Notes: T0 = time in the past. T1 = present time.

INCREASING DESIRED RESULT   Second, a result gap may arise because the company raises its desired result (see the right-hand graph in Figure 12.3). Let us assume that the company in our example used to have a desired result of $20 million and that the company achieved an actual result of $20 million. Over time, the company has raised its desired result from $20 million to $28 million. However, the actual achieved result remained at $20 million. As a consequence, the company has created a result gap of $8 million (28 – 20 = 8).

Causes of result gaps

THE DISTURBING EVENT   You might ask: why did the company's achieved result decrease (left-hand graph), or why did the desired result increase (right-hand graph)? At the starting point, time 'T0', the company's achieved result equalled its desired result. At that time, no result gap existed. Then something happened that caused the achieved result to decrease (left-hand graph). Or something else happened that caused the desired result to increase (right-hand graph). This 'something' is what we term the 'disturbing event'. We call this event disturbing because the event disturbs the balance between the achieved result and the desired result.

TWO TYPES OF DISTURBING EVENTS We may distinguish between two types of disturbing events. On the one hand, we have the negative disturbing events which cause the achieved result to decrease. On the other hand, we have the positive disturbing events which cause the desired result to increase. The negative disturbing events affect the achieved result. The positive disturbing events affect the desired result.

In this chapter we will discuss consultancy projects in which clients face a negative disturbing event and projects in which clients face a positive disturbing event. The distinction is relevant because the consultants' diagnostic approach varies with the nature of the disturbing event.

Existing and expected result gaps

Thus far we have discussed the result gaps that already exist. At present, the client has a gap between its present achieved result and its present desired result. Consultants may also work on expected result gaps. The client may expect a result gap to arise in the future and so hires the management consultants to help develop a solution for the expected gap. The expected gap may arise for two reasons. Either the achieved result is expected to decline, or the desired result is expected to increase. Both developments will cause a result gap in the future.

The benefits of a result focus

By defining the client's problem in terms of the result gap, the consultants make sure that they focus on the client's desired result. This result focus ensures the effectiveness of problem solving. The diagnosis of the problem will concentrate on explaining the result gap (this chapter). The solution development will concentrate on solutions that will close the result gap (Chapter 13). The result focus will prevent analysis for the sake of analysis (the trap of the approach that solely focuses on analysis: see Figure 12.3).

STRUCTURED PROBLEM DIAGNOSIS

Preparatory steps

We first explore how consultants diagnose a client's result gap that is caused by a decrease in the client's achieved result. A negative disturbing event caused a decrease in the achieved result. The client's desired result did not change.

How to approach this problem, that is: how to close the result gap? A natural inclination may be to start collecting and analysing data. We may begin with a SWOT analysis or another popular analytical technique. However, this is not the most efficient and effective approach. The top tier consultants withstand the temptation to immediately jump into all types of analyses and thereby risk boiling the ocean. Before these consultants start analysing, they will take a couple of preparatory steps. They will lose time while taking these steps, however they will recoup this time later because their analysis in the next stage will be much more focused than that of people who dive into analysis right away.

THREE STEPS   The structured problem diagnosis method of the top consultants distinguishes between three steps (see Figure 12.4):

1. What is the problem?
2. Where is the problem?
3. Why does the problem exist?

These three questions are based on 'sequential analysis' (Holland, 1972, cited in Minto, 1987). First, the consultants identify the result gap. This gap identification ensures that the consultants work on a real problem. Second, the consultants determine the distribution of the result gap across segments. An uneven distribution informs the consultants about where to focus their diagnosis. Third, the consultants determine the root cause(s) of the result gap. They investigate the negative disturbing event in-depth and analyse how precisely the negative disturbing event caused the result gap. If the gap is unevenly distributed across segments, then the consultants investigate the causes by segment gap. They focus on the segments with the largest result gaps.

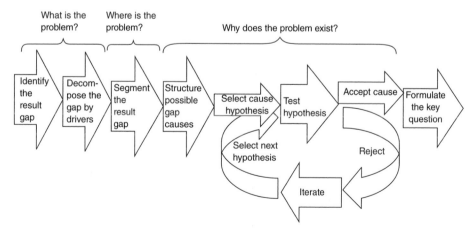

FIGURE 12.4   *The structured approach for diagnosing a problem*

Identify the result gap

DETERMINE THE CLIENT'S RELEVANT RESULT   Ideally, the consultants will identify the result gap *before* the start of the consultancy project. During the initial meetings with the client, the consultants should already develop an idea of the result gap (see Chapter 10). They will develop their proposal on the basis of the result gap. The consultants need to determine the client's relevant result. What result does the client (top manager) perceive as the most relevant result? Does the client focus rest on quality, brand image, costs, revenues, market share, profit, shareholders' value, sustainability, customer satisfaction, employee satisfaction, or something else?

TAKE A CRITICAL STANCE   The consultants should take a critical stance against the client's result. They should ask the client why they think this particular result is the most relevant. For instance, the client perceives market share to be the most relevant result. The consultants may ask the client why they perceive market share to be the most relevant result.

- Is market share the ultimate objective of the client?
- Why is it so important to have a high market share?
- Is market share an end in itself, or is market share a means to a higher end?

If the client answers that market share is most relevant because it leads to profit, then the consultants have achieved two things. First, they have uncovered a hidden assumption of the client, namely that market share leads to profit. Second, the consultants have uncovered an even more relevant result, namely profit. Profit is the most relevant result.

UNCOVER HIDDEN ASSUMPTIONS   Market share is only relevant (to achieve profit) if it leads to profit. We would acknowledge that in general market share leads to profit. However, *developing* a higher market share does *not always* lead to a higher profit. First, developing a higher market share may be costly. The client may have to invest (heavily) in, for instance, product innovation, production facilities, and marketing. Second, the client's market may be unattractive as a result of which the client will not be able to recoup their investments. For instance, rivalry may be intense and both buyers and suppliers may be powerful. Consultants should therefore critically evaluate the relevant result that the client comes up with.

DISTINGUISH MULTIPLE RESULTS   Clients may indicate more than one relevant result. Instead of a single result, they may want to achieve multiple results. In this case, consultants should investigate whether these results are related to each other in some way. Consultants need to be attentive to hierarchical relationships between results. The previous example illustrates the hierarchical relation between market share and profit. Market share may drive profit. Therefore, market share is hierarchically subordinate to profit. If the client indicates multiple results that are hierarchically related, then the consultants should focus on the hierarchically highest result.

DEVELOP A RESULT HIERARCHY   In our example, the hierarchically highest result is profit. Another example of a hierarchical relation is the relation between brand image and profit. The client may indicate that the results are defined in terms of brand image and profit. The consultants may point out that brand image is subordinate to profit. The brand image is a means not an end. Brand image is a desired result insofar as brand image contributes to profit. If investments in brand image do not result in profit increases, then brand image should not be a desired result. Instead of having two results, brand image and profit, the consultants should advise the client to concentrate on the hierarchically highest result, which is profit.

UNRELATED RESULTS   Clients may have multiple results which are not hierarchically related. Consultants should investigate whether these results are related in some other – non-hierarchical – way. If the results are unrelated, then gaps for each of these results will present distinct problems. For instance, a company may want to combine profit and non-profit objectives. Examples of the latter category are corporate social responsibility projects. If the company has a gap in its profit and a gap in its non-profit and these gaps are unrelated in terms of disturbing events, then the consultants may suggest defining separate projects.

RELATED RESULTS   Clients' multiple results may also be related. In this case, the consultants should approach the corresponding result gaps in an integral way. Because the results are related, the consultants cannot develop a solution for an individual result gap without considering the other result gaps. The consultants should develop solutions for all result gaps. For instance, a university indicates that quality of education and quality of research are the relevant results. Education and research relate to each other via the university faculty. The faculty is responsible for both education and research. Solutions to improve the quality of the university's education should take into account the quality of the university's research, and vice versa.

INTEGRATIVE DIAGNOSIS   The consultants should diagnose the education and research gaps as an integrated client problem. Instead of a one-dimensional result gap, the client has a two-dimensional result gap, with each result representing a different dimension. Figure 12.5 visualizes a two-dimensional result gap. The client has two related results, which are X and Y. The desired results are Xd and Yd. The achieved results are Xa and Ya. The result gap for X is $Xd–Xa$. For Y the result gap amounts to $Yd–Ya$. The client currently is in position A, which represents the client's achieved results along the two dimensions. The desired end position is D, which represents the client's desired results along the two dimensions.

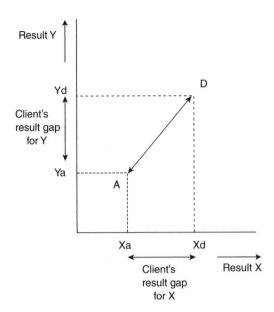

FIGURE 12.5 *A two-dimensional result gap*

Decompose the result gap by result drivers

The consultants focus on the client's hierarchically highest result in order to ensure the effectiveness of their solution. The consultants' proposed solution will address the client's highest, or ultimate, result. Consultants must avoid the trap of developing solutions for means rather than ends. Recall the example of increasing market share in an unattractive market. Solutions for increasing market share will not always increase the profit for the client. Determining the result gap at the highest level has advantages for solution development. However, it also has its drawbacks. The higher the level of the result, the more complex it becomes to diagnose the result gap. Therefore, consultants must first determine the result gap at the highest level, but subsequently decompose the result gap into a hierarchy of lower level gaps. This decomposition to lower levels makes diagnosis easier. Moreover, decomposition of the result gap provides insight into possible centres of gravity. Such centres become focus areas for the consultants.

FOCUS ATTENTION   Figure 12.6 provides an example of such decomposition. CandyCorp is a producer of candy bars. The company has hired consultants to solve its profit problem. The consultants decompose the result gap by result driver. Which driver is responsible for what share of the gap? The consultants not only look at the present result gap and its decomposition. They also consider the development of the gap over time. At what point in time did the gap emerge? How has the gap evolved since then? The

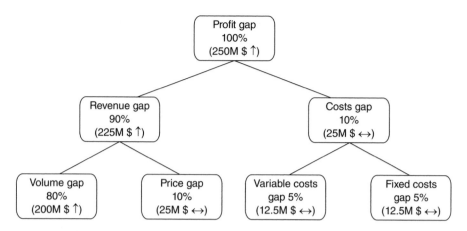

FIGURE 12.6 *Decompose a result gap in result driver gaps*

Notes: ↑ = increasing; ↔ = stable; M = million
Percentage of a low-level gap indicates what part of the profit gap is explained by that low-level gap
Revenue gap = Pd × Qd – Pa × Qa = (Pd – Pa) × Qd + (Qd-Qa) × Pa = price gap + volume gap
(P = price; Q = quantity or volume; d = desired; a = achieved)

consultants must also look at the development of the gaps per driver. Are these gaps increasing, stable, or decreasing?

Analyse the gap

COLLECT THE DATA   Figure 12.6 is a relatively simple structure. In real life consultancy projects, the consultants may have to decompose the result into even lower level drivers. For instance, they may need to decompose costs into smaller cost items. Developing the structure is one thing, collecting the data is another. The consultants need to get the data about the various result drivers from the client organization. They have to request the data from client organizational members who 'own' the data, such as the controller or financial director.

Getting the data may not be easy. The client members may be reluctant to share the data with the consultants. The data owners or other stakeholders may fear what the consultants will do with the data. The analyses of the consultants may also have unfavourable consequences for these stakeholders. Therefore, consultants may have a difficult time obtaining all the data for their result driver structure. Chapter 13 elaborates on data collection.

CHECK THE DATA   Even if the consultants receive the data, they should be careful. Consultants should never accept client data without verifying them because the data may be incorrect for various reasons. First, the client members may consciously supply misleading data to put the consultants on the wrong track. They may do so because they have their own agenda.

Second, client members may supply faulty data without being aware of the errors. The data may be polluted. For instance, there may be errors in a database. For instance, by accident the wrong data may have been entered into a file. It is easy to make a typo in a spreadsheet. Furthermore, the client may have wrongly calculated data. For instance, the client may use a flawed cost allocation system. Therefore, the supplied cost data do not represent the real costs. The consultants should critically review the received data. Can these data be true? Preferably, consultants must have multiple sources of data, which allow them to compare data from different sources.

EXAMPLE   The top tier consultants always strive to visualize such decomposition structures. Our example, CandyCorp (see Figure 12.6), has a profit gap, which means that the firm's achieved profit is smaller than its desired profit. As profit equals revenues minus costs, the consultants decompose the profit gap into a revenue gap and a costs gap. The consultants may find that the revenues gap for the largest part (90 per cent in Figure 12.6) explains the profit gap. The achieved costs are more or less in line with the desired costs. These findings allow the consultants to focus their attention on the revenues side. This focus will increase the efficiency and speed of the problem diagnosis process. However, the consultants may also find that the costs gap largely or fully explains the profit gap. In this case, the consultants will focus on the cost side. If the revenue gap and the costs gap are equally important to the profit gap, then the consultants need to diagnose both revenues and costs. The idea is that the consultants focus their attention in line with the importance that a lower-level gap has for the high-level result gap.

DEVELOP MORE FINE-GRAINED INSIGHTS   The consultants may continue to decompose result gaps into lower-level gaps. The further decomposition may provide more fine-grained insights, which consultants may use to sharpen their focus. For instance, the consultants may decompose the revenue gap into a volume gap and a price gap. The volume gap is the difference between the number of products or services actually sold by the client and the desired number. The price gap is the difference between the achieved price and the desired price per product or service. Again, the relative importance of the result gaps determines the amount of attention that consultants should give to each gap.

BUILD A MODEL   The decomposition of the result into its drivers is not only valuable for analysing the result gap. The consultants may use the structure of result drivers to build in an Excel spreadsheet an economic model of the client's business. This spreadsheet model shows how the client achieves its result. The consultants may use this model to calculate how much a possible cause contributes to the client's result gap and how much a possible solution to the problem contributes to the client's result. To what extent does this particular cause explain the result gap? Does this particular solution really close the result gap?

The consultants may also use the model to calculate how different scenarios may affect the solution's contribution to the client's result. Such calculations can help the consultants to answer the question: how sensitive is the solution to uncertainties? Before the consultants may use the model to run possible solutions, they should first calibrate their model. They should run the model on historical data. To assure the model's quality, consultants may have their model verified by (financial) experts within the client organization, such as the controller or chief financial officer. The consultants create a transparent model. They write down all formulas and assumptions. Clear documentation of the model is critical when the consultants hand over that model to the client on completion of the project.

CONSIDER INTERDEPENDENCIES BETWEEN RESULT DRIVERS Decomposing the result into drivers helps to reduce the complexity of analysis. The consultants divide the complex high-level result metric into increasingly simple lower-level metrics. This 'divide and conquer' strategy simplifies the analysis. However, consultants should be aware of the risk of oversimplification. Oversimplification lurks because (some) result drivers may be related. Reducing the high-level result into a series of low-level results may overlook interdependencies between these low-level results. For instance, consider the decomposition of the profit gap into a revenue gap and a cost gap. The client may have a surplus of revenue and a negative cost gap. The too high cost, however, may be the reason for the revenue surplus. For instance, high quality may lead to high volume but also to high cost. Similarly, a volume gap may be related to a price gap. Because the price is too high, the volume is too low. Consultants should therefore not analyse a result gap in isolation. Instead they should consider the interdependencies between the sub gaps when exploring the causes of the overall result gap.

CASE STUDY

AcStrat Consulting – identify and decompose the result gap

The problem-owner

AcStrat Consulting is a small but prestigious management consultancy firm which focuses on board level strategy advice. The consultancy works for the CEOs of (very) large multinational companies, mostly Fortune Global 500 members, across all industry sectors. AcStrat is organized into twenty industry practices, such as Energy, Financial Services, and Telecommunications. AcStrat only provides advice on strategy development. It refrains from strategy implementation.

The firm is privately held by its ninety partners. AcStrat employs about 630 consultants and 360 support staff. The consultancy operates from fifteen offices, which are located in nine countries, mostly in Western Europe and North America, but also some in Asia and the Middle East. Last year, the firm generated US$525 million in revenues.

Identify the result gap

What is the result gap? During the past few years, AcStrat Consulting has faced decreasing profits. Last year, the firm suffered its first loss in its thirty year history. The result gap is the difference between the current loss and the desired profit.

AcStrat's managing partners decided to initiate an internal study to investigate the cause(s) of this loss and develop a solution.

An internal taskforce decomposes the profit gap in a logical structure (see Figure 12.7). They find that a decreasing volume of work (in terms of billable hours) explains most of the profit gap. Increasing indirect costs explain most of the remainder of the gap. AcStrat has held its consultancy capacity constant. Therefore, the decreasing volume of work causes a decreasing utilization of AcStrat's consultancy capacity.

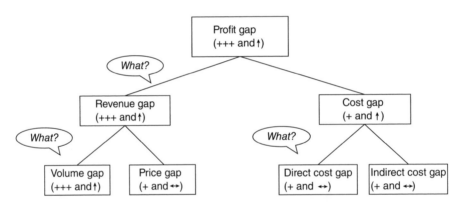

FIGURE 12.7 *Decomposing the profit gap in profit driver gaps*

Notes: The plus signs (+) indicate the size of the gap; ↑ = increasing; ↔ = stable

Segment the result gap

WHERE IS THE GAP?   By now, the consultants have determined the client's result gap. We would acknowledge the co-existence of multiple result gaps (see Figure 12.5), but for clarity, we will only speak of a single result gap. The consultants have decomposed the result gap into increasingly low-level result driver gaps. Therefore, they have gained insight into the contribution of the various low-level driver gaps to the high-level gap. The question arises: how to proceed?

We may be tempted to start investigating the cause of the most important low-level result gap. We would admit the urge to develop an explanation of that result gap. However, at this stage it is not efficient to start developing such explanations. Why is this the case?

CREATE A FOCUS   Diagnosing a low-level result gap may prove voluminous. The amount of diagnostic work increases with the scope of the client's activities. This scope may be measured in terms of the number of segments where the client is active. Examples of segments are products, markets, distribution channels, countries. The more segments, the more diagnostic work consultants have to do. The example of CandyCorp (see Figure 12.6) may illustrate how it works. Assume that the volume gap explains 90 per cent of the firm's profit gap. Therefore, the consultants will first investigate this particular gap. Recall that the volume gap is the difference between the achieved volume of products and the desired volume. Assume that CandyCorp has one product, which it sells in three different countries. Let us call these countries A, B, and C. In each country, CandyCorp sells its products through four different distribution channels: supermarkets, petrol stations, the hospitality channel (restaurants, hotels, bars), and vending machines. Both the countries and the channels are segments.

DETERMINE PRIORITIES   The consultants want to know how the volume gap is distributed over the countries and channels. Insight in the distribution of the gap enables the consultants to determine how to focus their attention. Figure 12.8 shows how they decompose the volume gap, first by country and second by channel. The first-level decomposition, by country, shows a very uneven distribution of the volume gap. The volume gap in country A explains 70 per cent of CandyCorp's overall volume gap (the overall volume gap is 100 per cent). Therefore, the consultants first investigate country A further. They decompose country A's volume gap by channel. This decomposition also reveals an uneven distribution. The supermarkets channel explains 57 per cent (40/70) of country A's volume gap and 40 per cent of the overall volume gap. Based on these insights, the consultants determine that the supermarkets in country A are a priority for further diagnosis. To further pinpoint the area where the result gap concentrates, the consultants may decompose the volume gap of supermarkets in country A. We do not show this decomposition in Figure 12.8 on the next page.

THE '80/20 RULE' (THE PARETO PRINCIPLE)   The purpose of decomposition is to identify an uneven distribution of the result gap. This unevenness points to the Pareto Principle. This is the so-called '80/20 rule'. In many cases, 20 per cent of the explanatory factors will explain 80 per cent of the result. For instance, 20 per cent of customers account for 80 per cent of the revenues. The consultants want to identify the unevenness in a minimum number of

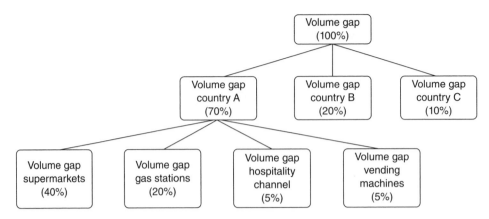

FIGURE 12.8 *Determine the distribution of the result gap across segments*

decompositions. When creating decomposition structures, as in Figure 12.8, they will begin with the segmentation criterion that is most differentiating. In the example, the consultants may choose from two segmentation criteria: country and distribution channel. They chose the country as the first criterion because it is a stronger differentiator than the channel. The unevenness of the distribution over countries is larger than the unevenness over channels. Therefore, the consultants begin with the decomposition by country and subsequently decompose by channel.

AVOID THE TRAP OF THE AVERAGE   Uncovering the distribution of the overall result gap over the different segments of the client's scope (such as products, channels, and countries) enables the consultants to avoid the trap of the average. What do we mean by that trap? The average does not indicate the distribution. Relying on the average alone is based on the hidden assumption that there is no distribution. For instance, a client company with two product divisions A and B has an average result gap of 5 per cent (the gap expressed as a percentage of the desired result). You may be tempted to conclude that both product divisions A and B have a gap of 5 per cent. However, consultants decompose the overall result gap into the gaps of the individual segments. Such decomposition may reveal that division A has a positive result gap of 5 per cent (its achieved result exceeds its desired result), while division B has a negative gap of 10 per cent (its desired result exceeds its achieved result).

UNCOVER THE HIDDEN GAP   In the example of CandyCorp, you may be tempted to focus solely on country A because of its large volume gap (see Figure 12.8). However, there may be large gaps at lower levels in the structure that are hidden at the higher level. For instance, country B has a much lower gap than A. However, the lower overall gap for B may be the result of a very large negative gap (achieved volume below desired volume) in country B's supermarkets that is partially compensated for by positive gaps (achieved volume above desired volume) in country B's petrol stations and hospitality channel. The gap in country B's supermarkets may even exceed country A's supermarket gap. Therefore, consultants will also decompose the other segments to uncover possible hidden gaps at lower levels.

CONSIDER INTERDEPENDENCIES BETWEEN SEGMENTS Decomposition of the result gap into segments increases the focus of the diagnosis. This is a benefit. Consultants reduce the complexity of a client's result gap by breaking it down into increasingly low-level segment gaps. Subsequently, they focus on those low-level gaps that contribute most to the overall gap. Exclusive focusing on the largest low-level gaps implies a hidden assumption that the segments are independent of each other. For example, a client company may have a large negative result gap in country X and a positive gap in country Y. However, these results may be interlinked via the client's transfer pricing system. The client's subsidiary in country X produces for the subsidiary in country Y. Because country X has a higher corporate tax rate than Y, the client applies a relatively low transfer price. The low transfer price reduces the result of the subsidiary in country X while increasing the result of the subsidiary in country Y. The result gaps of country X and Y are interdependent because of the transfer pricing. Consultants decompose the result gap into segments, but they also consider the interdependencies between these segments.

MINI CASE STUDY

AcStrat Consulting: segment the result gap

Where is the result gap?

AcStrat's internal taskforce segments the volume gap (see Figure 12.9). The consultants develop a logical structure of segments and segment the volume gap by geography. They compare the volume gap by segment. All segments show a gap, but the largest gaps are in Western Europe and North America. Subsequently, the consultants segment the volume gap by office, partner, and industry sector. However, these segmentations only reveal minor differences between segments.

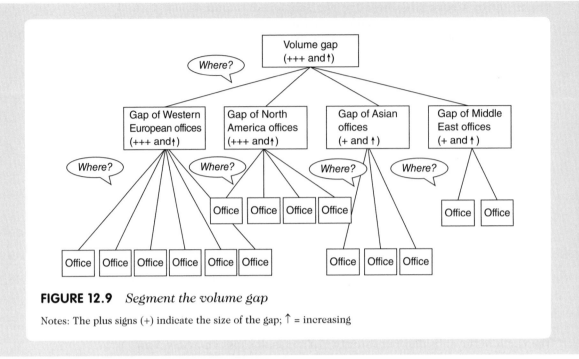

FIGURE 12.9 *Segment the volume gap*

Notes: The plus signs (+) indicate the size of the gap; ↑ = increasing

Structure possible causes of the result gap

The example about the interdependencies between segments takes a step towards explaining the result gap. The next step in the structured problem diagnosis is explaining the result gap, or more precisely, explaining the low-level gap that contributes most to the overall gap. The consultants have to answer the question: why does the negative result gap exist? Consultants need to know since when the result gap has existed, to identify and investigate the negative disturbing event.

STRUCTURING THE POSSIBLE CAUSES OF THE RESULT GAP   After having collected these possible explanations of the result gap, the consultants create a logical structure for the possibilities. Figure 12.10 provides an example of a logical structure of possible explanations for CandyCorp's volume gap in the supermarket channel. These explanations are about the causes of the firm's result gap. The volume gap may have three possible causes. First, only a small number of supermarkets have CandyCorp's product in their assortment. Second, the supermarkets that sell the client's product have a relatively low sales volume in the product category to which the CandyCorp's product belongs. The third possible explanation for low volume is that the client product has a small share of the product category sales volume of the supermarkets where the product is sold.

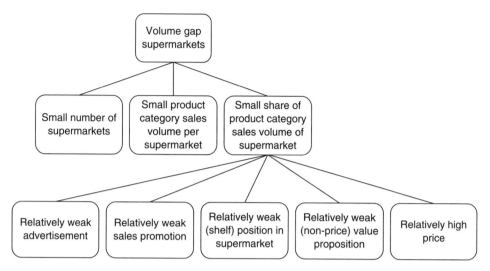

FIGURE 12.10 *A logical structure of possible causes of a volume gap*

Note: This figure only shows the possible explanations for 'small share of product category sales'. It does not show the possible explanations for 'small number of supermarkets' and 'small product category sales volumes'.

Logical structuring

MECE   Consultants want to develop structures of possible explanations that are logical. The question arises: what constitutes a logical structure? The top tier consultants develop structures whose members are MECE. MECE is an acronym coined by McKinsey alumna Barbara Minto when she worked for that firm. MECE is an abbreviation of Mutually Exclusive, Collectively Exhaustive (Minto, 1987). The members of the structure should be mutually exclusive, that is there must be no overlap of members. The structure should also be collectively exhaustive, namely having no missing members.

Although Barbara Minto coined the acronym MECE, the underlying knowledge is much older. It can be traced back to the philosopher-theologian John Dun Scotus (1266–1308). Scotus published three requirements of a clear division. First, all members resulting from the division are part of the subject matter that is divided. Second, the division has a mutually exclusive character. Third, the division exhausts the subject matter to be divided. Figure 12.11 on the next page visualizes these three requirements of a logical structure.

PART OF THE SUBJECT MATTER   Let us illustrate the three requirements of a clear structure. First, all members are part of the subject matter. Assume the subject matter is the client's profit. The consultants divide profit into revenues, costs, and reputation. Revenues and costs are members of the profit equation (profit equals revenues minus costs). However, reputation is not a member of profit. Reputation can be a determinant of profit. Therefore,

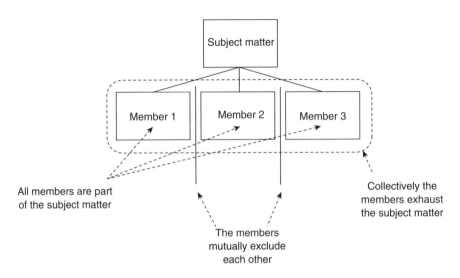

FIGURE 12.11 *Three requirements of a logical structure*

Source: Scotus (1982)

it may be a member of a division of profit determinants. But reputation is not a member of the division of profit.

MUTUALLY EXCLUSIVE   Second, the division of the subject matter has a mutually exclusive character. In terms of Minto: the members are mutually exclusive. Assume the consultants have to structure the possible explanations for the client's high product costs. They come up with three possible explanations which are low production scale, high product quality, and high product differentiation. Scale is mutually exclusive with product quality and with product differentiation. However, product quality and product differentiation are not mutually exclusive. Quality can be a differentiator.

COLLECTIVELY EXHAUSTIVE   Third, the division exhausts the subject matter to be divided. In Minto's terminology: the members are collectively exhaustive. Assume the consultants need to explain the client's decreasing sales. The client operates in a couple of customer segments within a particular product market. The consultants structure the possible explanations for the client's sales decline. They distinguish between declining market demand and the client's decreasing share of the segments it operates in. These explanations are mutually exclusive, though not collectively exhaustive. A third explanation may be the decline of the client's segment shares of the total market. The market as a whole may be stable. The client's shares of its segments may be stable. However, if the client's segments decrease (their share of the total market decreases), then their sales will decrease. Figure 12.12 provides a visualization of a flawed structure. This structure violates each of the three requirements of a clear structure.

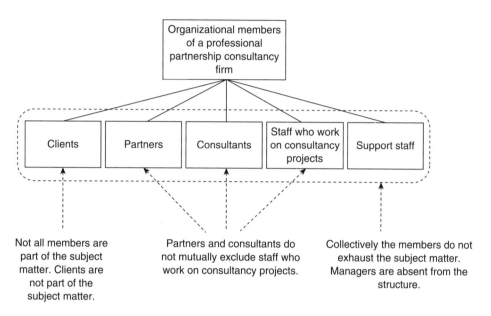

Not all members are part of the subject matter. Clients are not part of the subject matter.

Partners and consultants do not mutually exclude staff who work on consultancy projects.

Collectively the members do not exhaust the subject matter. Managers are absent from the structure.

FIGURE 12.12 *An example of a structure that does **not** meet the three requirements*

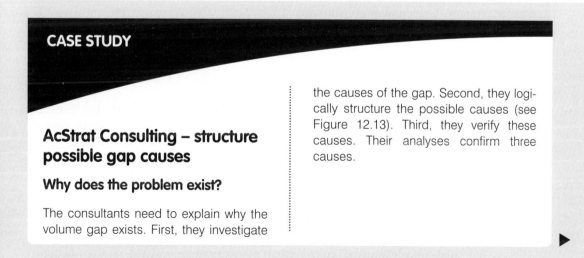

CASE STUDY

AcStrat Consulting – structure possible gap causes

Why does the problem exist?

The consultants need to explain why the volume gap exists. First, they investigate the causes of the gap. Second, they logically structure the possible causes (see Figure 12.13). Third, they verify these causes. Their analyses confirm three causes.

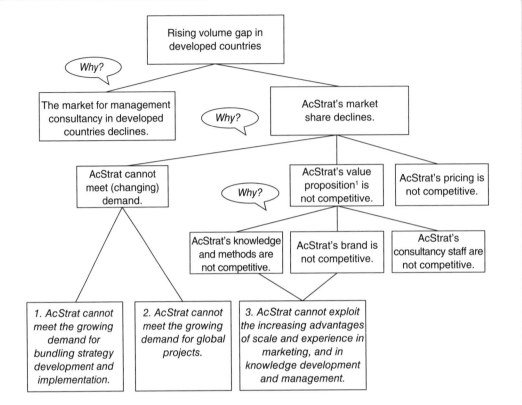

FIGURE 12.13 *Structure the possible gap causes*

Note: Outcome of analyses confirms three causes (italicized text). (1): Value proposition for strategy development consultancy.

Select a hypothesis about a possible cause

IDENTIFYING THE BEST POSSIBLE EXPLANATION To identify the cause of the result gap, the consultants use a technique called 'abductive reasoning'. Abductive reasoning is inferencing to the best possible explanation of a given result. The American philosopher Charles Sanders Peirce (1839–1914) introduced the term as 'guessing'. Given an observed result, the consultants identify what they think is the best possible explanation of the result gap. For instance, the client company has too high a cost per unit of product. The consultants consider alternative explanations and conclude that a scale disadvantage in production may best explain the client's high cost. If the scale disadvantage were true, then a high product cost is a matter of course. This possible, because it is untested, explanation serves as a hypothesis. The consultants subsequently test their hypothesis. Is it true that the client has a scale disadvantage? If the test of the hypothesis leads to an acceptance of the hypothesis, then the consultants have verified their explanation of the gap.

HYPOTHESIS REJECTION They have identified the cause of the result gap. This cause explains the gap. However, if the test of the hypothesis leads to a rejection of the hypothesis, then the consultants need to identify an alternative possible explanation for the result gap. The alternative explanation becomes the next hypothesis. The consultants continue formulating and testing hypotheses about the causes of the result gap, until they have a verified cause.

PARTIAL EXPLANATION In some projects, a single verified cause may not explain the whole result gap. For instance, the scale disadvantage only explains half of the cost gap. The consultants have to formulate and test hypotheses about additional causes, until the verified causes together explain the whole cost gap. Because additional hypothesis formulation and testing are time consuming and expensive, consultants may not continue this work until they can explain 100 per cent of the result gap. If 20 per cent of the consultants' time is sufficient to explain 80 per cent of the result gap, then the consultants will not spend an extra 80 per cent of their time to explain the remaining 20 per cent of the gap. However, the client may demand a 100 per cent explanation and accept the time and costs.

THREE TYPES OF INFERENCING Deductive and inductive inferencing are relatively well known compared to abductive inferencing (see Figure 12.14).

Deductive inferencing. Deductive inferencing moves from a general rule to a specific result. The general rule forms the precondition (high market share leads to a high profit). This is the first premise. Based on the general rule a specific case is identified (client has a high market share). This is the second premise. If both premises are true than the conclusion must be true (client has a high profit).

Inductive inferencing. In contrast, inductive referencing moves from specific cases and specific results to a probable general rule. It is a form of probabilistic reasoning. If the premises about the specific cases and specific results are true then the conclusion is probably true. For instance, the consultants identify ten companies with a high market share. In all ten cases, the companies also have a high profit. Therefore, it is probable that a high market share leads to a high profit.

Abductive inferencing. The third type of inferencing, abduction, aims to explain a specific result. Abductive reasoning, as presented by Peirce in his 1903 Harvard lectures on pragmatism, is about seeking a hypothesis to account for this specific result. The consultants observe that the client has a high profit. One hypothesis to account for a high profit is: a high market share leads to a high profit. Therefore, there is reason to suspect that the client has a high market share. The consultant should verify whether the client has a high market share.

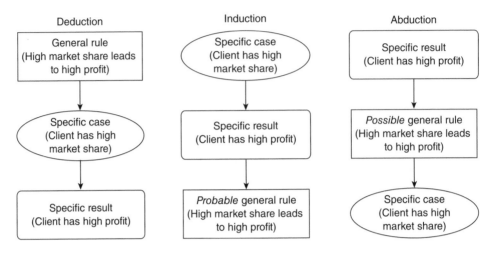

FIGURE 12.14 *Three types of inferencing*

GENERATE IDEAS ABOUT THE POSSIBLE CAUSES OF THE RESULT GAP The consultants use abductive reasoning to explain the result gap. They seek a hypothesis about an explanation. The hypothesis is what the consultants think is the best possible explanation of the result gap. The consultants select the hypothesis from the range of possible explanations of the result gap. They create an overview of the possible explanations. They should make sure that they do not overlook explanations as they do not want to hear from the steering committee: 'Why have not you considered [the overlooked explanation]?' Often, the consultants will have done similar consultancy projects. They will have experience with this type of problem or they will be aware of analogies. That is a reason why the client has hired them. These consultants may use this experience to create overviews of possible explanations. If they lack such experience, they may organize brain storming sessions with knowledgeable clients and other stakeholders to collect ideas about possible explanations.

Test a hypothesis about a possible cause

TEST THE POSSIBLE CAUSE Based on their own insights and/or those of knowledgeable clients and other stakeholders, the consultants conclude that a small share of the category sales of the supermarkets that sell the client's product is the most probable cause of the low volume of CandyCorp's product in the supermarket channel (see Figure 12.10). This is an untested hypothesis.

To verify their hypothesis, the consultants investigate the client's share of the category sales. They find that CandyCorp has a low share which explains the volume gap. The analysis confirms the consultants' hypothesis that the small share explains the volume gap. Now they know that the small share of the client's product is the cause of the volume gap.

DIG DEEPER   However, a new question arises: why does CandyCorp's product have a small share? Therefore, the consultants investigate the possible causes of this small share. Figure 12.10 distinguishes between five alternatives that the consultants have come up with (see the lowest level of the structure). Based on their own insights and/or those of knowledgeable clients and other stakeholders, the consultants conclude that a relatively weak (non-price) value proposition is the most probable cause of the client product's small share of the category sales. This is again an untested hypothesis which the consultants need to investigate. Assume that the investigations confirm the hypothesis. Now the consultants know that the weak value proposition explains the small share.

TEST THE ROOT CAUSE   However, the diagnosis is not yet complete. The consultants need to find out why the value proposition is weak. We will not discuss these next steps but the consultants will continue their diagnosis until they have developed a fundamental understanding of the problem. They will search for the root cause of the result gap. This rich insight enables the consultants to develop very effective solutions that are superior to those developed by others who lack an in-depth understanding of the problem.

COLLECT DATA   To verify the hypotheses about possible causes, the consultants need to collect data (see Chapter 13 for an overview of data collection techniques). They should not collect data because of the data. Data collection is a means not an end. The purpose is to verify a possible cause. Therefore they should not collect more data than are necessary for this verification. This data collection may be more difficult than the one required for the result decomposition. The consultants may need data about all kinds of subjects, both within and outside the client organization. Consultants will not receive a pack containing all the data needed to solve the problem. They will have to find the data themselves. Some data will be quantitative while other data will be qualitative.

INTERACT WITH PEOPLE   Some data may be codified while other data may be tacit. Consultants have to visit the client's premises and if necessary other places, such as customers, suppliers, distributors, and competitors. They need to talk to people, both inside and outside the client organization. In particular people on the front line are valuable sources of information. They know the operations. They know the customers and suppliers. The consultants may also have to observe people: how do they work and how do they behave? Studying people is also important in order to understand their attitude towards the consultants, the project, and towards possible solutions. Better understanding of the stakeholders is critical for understanding the feasibility of implementing particular solutions. Will this organization be able to implement those solutions? Furthermore, interaction with people inside and outside the client organization is important for creating understanding and support. The stakeholders may have a negative attitude about the consultants and the project. Through communication, the consultants may try to improve the stakeholders' attitude.

Accept, reject and iterate

ACCEPT THE CAUSE   The consultants use the analysis to test the possible cause of the result gap. The analysis of a possible cause may lead to one of two outcomes. Either the analysis confirms the cause and leads to an acceptance of this cause, or the analysis leads to a rejection of the possible cause. The confirmed cause forms (a part of) the explanation of the result gap.

REJECT THE POSSIBLE CAUSE   If the consultants have to reject the possible cause on the basis of the analysis, then they have to identify an alternative possible cause. Subsequently, they will have to test this alternative cause. The consultants continue to test possible causes until they have a sufficient explanation of the result gap. By sufficient we mean that the consultants can explain most of the result gap. The explanation does not necessarily have to cover 100 per cent of the result gap. The steering committee decides what is 'sufficient'.

MEASURE THE EXTENT OF THE EXPLANATION   When the consultants have confirmed a cause for the result gap, then they will measure the impact of this specific cause on the result gap and will do this with the help of the economic model of the client's business that they have built. To what extent does this specific cause explain the result gap? Does this specific cause explain the whole result gap or does it explain (only) a part of it? If the specific cause explains the whole gap, then the consultants have a complete explanation of the result gap. They are ready to formulate the key question.

ACCEPT AND ITERATE   In the example of CandyCorp, the consultants may analyse the relatively high price as a possible cause of the client's small share of product category sales. The analysis may identify a relationship between price and sales. The consultants may analyse that the client's high price cannot fully explain the low sales. Assume the desired sales are one hundred and the achieved sales are seventy. The result gap is then thirty. Based on the price–sales relationship, the high price is expected to generate sales of eighty. The high price explains two thirds of the result gap (twenty of the thirty). The price differential cannot explain the remaining one third of the result gap. There must be at least one additional cause for the low sales.

ITERATE TO EXTEND THE EXPLANATION   If the confirmed cause only explains part of the gap, then the consultants need to identify one (or more) other possible causes of the result gap until they have extended the explanation sufficiently. The consultants need to analyse these causes. They will continue identifying and analysing possible causes until they can explain a sufficient part of the gap. As stated before, a 100 per cent explanation of the gap may neither be feasible nor desirable.

DECIDE ON THE TRADE-OFF   The Pareto Principle or the '80/20 rule' may apply here. For example, the consultants have confirmed two causes that together explain 80 per cent of the client's result gap. The data collection and the analyses required to explain the remaining 20 per cent are expected to take at least four times as much time and effort as the analysis of the two afore-mentioned causes. The steering committee has to decide on the trade-off between the marginal benefits of explaining the 20 per cent and the marginal costs of the additional data collection and analyses. The time opportunity costs of consultants are usually high because consultancy projects in general have a fixed duration. Time spent on additional analyses of possible causes of the result gap cannot be spent on developing solutions to close that gap.

Both in the case of a rejected cause and in the case of a confirmed cause that only explains a part of the result gap, the consultants have to iterate. They have to repeat the process of identifying and testing a possible cause.

Formulate the key question

Based on the three steps of problem diagnosis, the top tier consultants formulate the problem as one single question. This question ensures the focus for the consultants and guides them in the solution development. The question has the following form: *how should the client respond to the root cause of the result gap to close this?* Closing the profit gap means achieving the desired result. Therefore, we may formulate the key question as: *how should the client respond to the root cause of the result gap to achieve the desired result?* In a real project, the question incorporates the specific desired result: x millions of client's currency before a specific date. We illustrate the process of question formulation with our example.

Summary: from gap to question

IDENTIFY AND DECOMPOSE THE RESULT GAP   The first step of the problem diagnosis is about identifying the result gap. CandyCorp in our example had a profit gap of $250 million (see Figure 12.6). By decomposing the profit gap, the consultants discovered that the volume gap explained most of the profit gap. Therefore, the consultants turned their attention to the volume gap.

SEGMENT THE RESULT GAP   In the second step, the consultants investigated where CandyCorp's volume gap was largest. The consultants segmented the volume gap and found out that the supermarket channel in country A accounted for the largest part of the volume gap (see Figure 12.8). Therefore, the consultants further narrowed their focus to the volume gap of the supermarket channel in country A.

STRUCTURE THE POSSIBLE CAUSES OF THE GAP AND TESTING THESE CAUSES   In the third step, the consultants investigated why the volume gap in country A's supermarket channel existed. The consultants structured the possible explanations for this volume gap (see Figure 12.10). They used the structure to seek a hypothesis to explain the gap. Assume that the small share in the supermarkets' category sales have been caused by a relatively high price and a relatively weak shelf position in the supermarkets. Both causes are due to the introduction by the supermarkets of retail brands in the CandyCorp's product category. Assume that this retail brand introduction took place in all three countries where CandyCorp operates and that it caused volume gaps in the client's supermarket sales in all countries. The introduction of retail brands is therefore the root cause of the volume gap in the supermarket channel and thereby the root cause of the largest segment of the client's profit gap.

FORMULATE THE KEY QUESTION   Based on this root cause, the consultants formulate CandyCorp's problem as a question. How should CandyCorp respond to the introduction of retail brands by supermarkets in order to close its profit gap? Closing the profit gap means achieving the desired result. In a real project, the question incorporates the specific result. Assume CandyCorp's desired result is a profit of $500 million within two years. Now the consultants can formulate the key question as follows: *how should CandyCorp respond to the introduction of retail brands by supermarkets in order to achieve a profit of $500 million within two years?*

Define the problem statement

INVESTIGATE THE CONTEXT FOR SOLUTION DEVELOPMENT   Top tier consultants always create a problem statement. This statement outlines the problem diagnosis and provides a context for solution development (see Figure 12.15 on the next page). The problem diagnosis consists of a description of the negative disturbing event and the result gap which arose because of the negative disturbing event (the root cause of the gap). The negative disturbing event and the result gap are the two components of the key question that in its turn summarizes the client's problem.

INVESTIGATE THE STAKEHOLDERS   Next, the consultants investigate the context for the solution development. By the context we mean the factors

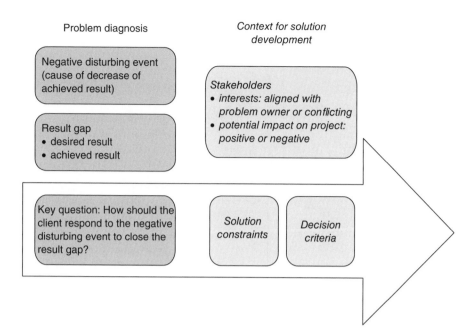

Problem diagnosis

Context for solution development

Negative disturbing event (cause of decrease of achieved result)

Result gap
• desired result
• achieved result

Stakeholders
• *interests: aligned with problem owner or conflicting*
• *potential impact on project: positive or negative*

Key question: How should the client respond to the negative disturbing event to close the result gap?

Solution constraints

Decision criteria

FIGURE 12.15 *The problem statement*

that consultants should take into account when developing a solution to the problem or an answer to the key question. First of all, the consultants need to analyse the stakeholders (see also Chapter 10). The consultants should also identify the main stakeholders. The main stakeholders are those that are probably affected by the problem solving project and by the solution, and/or may influence the project and the solution. Figure 12.16 on the next page visualizes how consultants may map the main stakeholders. The figure plots the stakeholders along two dimensions. Horizontally, we position stakeholders on the basis of their impact on the project and the solution. The vertical axis indicates the interests of the stakeholders, which may reflect the nature of the impact of the project and solution on these stakeholders. The resulting quadrants represent four categories of stakeholders.

IDENTIFY THE CONSTRAINTS   Before consultants start developing solutions for the client's problem, they should identify the constraints if any that limit the solution space. Not all solutions that the consultants may develop will be feasible or acceptable for the client and the stakeholders. The constraints reduce the theoretical solution space (see Figure 12.17). They are also absolute. This means that the client will reject any solution that violates a constraint. In Figure 12.17, the two constraints reduce the theoretical solution space to the smaller blue box. By knowing upfront the remaining solution space, the consultants will not waste time developing solutions outside this space.

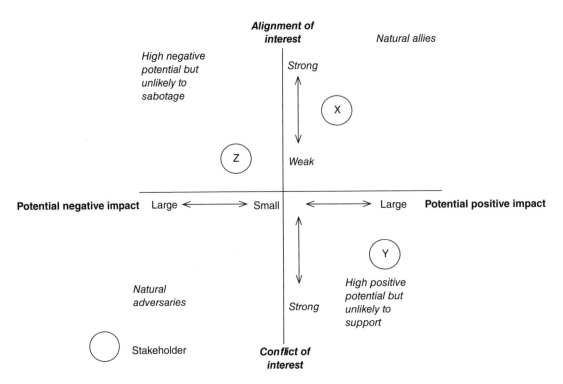

FIGURE 12.16 *Map the stakeholders*

IDENTIFY THE CRITERIA   The consultants should also know beforehand what decision criteria the client will apply. How will the client decide upon the proposed solution(s) by the consultants? The criteria come into play after the constraints. First, the constraints reduce the solution space. The client will not consider solutions outside the reduced solution space. Second, the criteria rank the remaining solutions within the reduced solution space. The client uses the criteria to evaluate the solutions within the solution space (see Figure 12.17 on the next page). By knowing the criteria, the consultants will also know how to evaluate possible solutions. When possible, the consultants will only select solutions that meet the client's criteria.

INVESTIGATE THE EXPECTATIONS   In addition to the criteria and constraints, the consultants should know what other factors influence the client's satisfaction with the recommended solution and the consultancy project. The consultants should know upfront: when will the client be satisfied with our recommendation and with the project? What does the client expect from the recommendation and from us? Knowing these expectations may guide the consultants. However, if the consultants find out that the client holds unrealistic expectations, then they may try to convince the client to adjust their expectations.

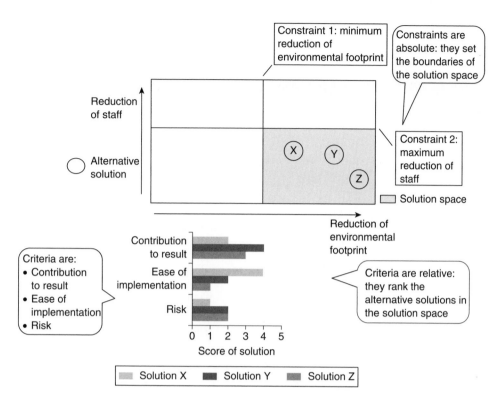

FIGURE 12.17 *Constraints and criteria*

AcStrat Consulting – formulate the key question and define the problem statement

The consultants have – through analysis – verified that changing demand as well as increasing scale and experience advantages explain AcStrat's profit gap. The consultants have interviewed the managing partners and other main stakeholders to get insights into the decision criteria and constraints. They have also conducted a stakeholder analysis. Based on these activities, the consultants are able to complete the problem statement. Figure 12.18 presents this statement.

TABLE 12.1 *Problem statement*

Problem statement	AcStrat
Achieved result	A loss of X USD
Disturbing events	Changing demand and increasing scale and experience advantages
Desired result	Within one year reach a breakeven result, and within three years realize a profit per partner of Y USD
Key question	How should AcStrat Consulting respond to the changing demand and increasing scale and experience advantages to realize a profit per partner of Y USD within three years?
Stakeholders	AcStrats partners, consultants, support staff, clients, and alumni
Constraints to the solution	• No financial reserves for absorbing further losses (no time) • No room for investment
Decision criteria	• Profit per partner • Maintaining the partnership base intact • Speed of implementation • Ease of implementation

STRUCTURED OPPORTUNITY DIAGNOSIS

A positive disturbing event

A positive disturbing event for the client allows that client to increase its desired result. The idea is that the positive disturbing event allows the client to achieve a higher desired result. Therefore, the client can raise its objective, that is, its desired result. The positive disturbing event creates an opportunity for the client.

PERCEPTION   Client and/or consultants perceive an opportunity for the client. We may distinguish between two alternative points of departure. One point of departure is when the client believes there is an opportunity and hires a consultant to develop advice which allows the client to seize that opportunity. The alternative point of departure is when consultants believe there is an opportunity for a client or prospect. The consultants approach the client or prospect with a proposal for seizing the opportunity. Consultants explore client opportunities to sell projects.

MEASUREMENT OF THE RESULT GAP   In the case of a problem, the consultants can directly measure the result gap. In the case of a perceived opportunity, the consultants cannot measure the result gap immediately. They may measure the client's achieved result but they cannot yet measure the increase in the desired result. First, the consultants need to develop a better understanding of the opportunity, in particular the monetary value of that opportunity, before they may assess the new (increased) desired result for their client. The sequence of steps in an opportunity diagnosis differs from the sequence in a problem diagnosis (see Figure 12.18).

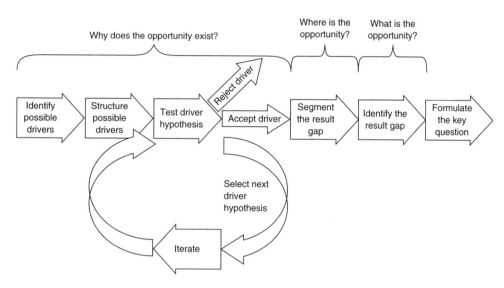

FIGURE 12.18   *The structured approach for diagnosing an opportunity*

Identify the possible opportunity drivers

POSSIBILITIES   The opportunity drivers are the answer to the question: why does the opportunity exist? To assess a client's opportunity, the consultants have to know the drivers of that opportunity. The first step for the consultants is to identify the possible drivers of the client's opportunity. Please note the use of the adjective 'possible'. At this stage, the consultants have not yet verified the drivers. Therefore, they cannot be sure the identified factors are the real drivers of the opportunity.

CONSULTANTS' EXPERIENCE   The consultants may have had experience with the particular opportunity. They may have conducted previous consultancy projects on comparable opportunities. These projects may have taken place in the same sector as the current project or in other sectors. The consultants may exploit their knowledge about similar opportunities, or even the same opportunity, to identify the drivers of the opportunity. If the consultants' knowledge is insufficient, then they may turn to the client or to external experts.

OTHER EXPERTISE   Inside the client organization, the consultants may find individuals, managers or professionals, with relevant knowledge about the opportunity. Moreover, the consultants may approach experts outside the client organization who have knowledge about the opportunity.

Consultants may use interviews with client organizational members and external experts to collect information about possible drivers. Consultants may also organize a workshop with these people to brainstorm about possible opportunity drivers. The idea of the workshop is to stimulate divergent thinking. The workshop participants should be free to introduce their suggestions for what may drive the opportunity.

Structure the possible opportunity drivers

After the consultants have generated the possible drivers, they will develop a logical structure for the possible drivers. This logical structuring allows the consultants to create oversight, to eliminate the overlap between drivers, and to identify omissions, if applicable. The resulting structure is a hypothetical model of the opportunity. Figure 12.19 on the next page provides an example of an opportunity based on a new product to increase profit. The opportunity of the new product depends on three drivers:

1. The willingness of customers to pay for the product.
2. Relatively low switching costs for customers.
3. The ability of customers to pay for the product.

The willingness to pay for the product depends on the relative value proposition of the product, which is the product's value relative to existing products and substitutes, and on the relative price, that is the price of the product compared to those for existing products and substitutes.

Test the hypotheses about possible drivers

TEST ALL POSSIBLE DRIVERS   The possible drivers are just that: possibilities. The consultants have to verify all drivers. They are the consultants' hypotheses and they need to be tested. For the test, the consultants need to design analyses. For instance, they need to analyse the relative technical performance of the new product. The consultants need to benchmark the

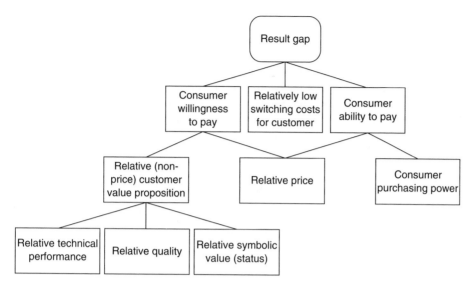

FIGURE 12.19 *A hypothetical model of the opportunity*

technical performance of the new product with the performance of alternative products. The analysis may verify a hypothesis (driver). The consultants accept the verified driver. However, the analysis may also lead to a rejection of the hypothesis (driver).

ANALYSE DRIVER STRENGTH   The consultants need to analyse the strength of the verified, accepted drivers. The strength of a driver influences the size of the opportunity. Take the example of Figure 12.19. If the relative technical performance of the new product is high and if the customers attach a high weight to technical performance, then the opportunity will be large compared to the situation where the relative performance is lower and/or the weight of performance is lower.

Accept, reject, and iterate

SIZE OF THE OPPORTUNITY   After all the analyses have been done, the consultants are able to separate the accepted drivers from the rejected drivers. The consultants continue the opportunity diagnosis with the accepted drivers. They have to estimate the size of the opportunity. The size of this opportunity depends on the number of drivers and the strength of each individual driver. We can distinguish between two extreme situations.

CLEAR ACCEPTANCE   In one extreme, the consultants' analyses will lead to the acceptance of all possible drivers and the analyses will indicate that all the drivers are strong. This extreme situation presents a big opportunity. Therefore, the consultants should continue with the opportunity diagnosis.

CLEAR REJECTION In the other extreme, the analyses lead to the rejection of all possible drivers, or all the verified drivers appear to be (very) weak. Rejection of all drivers means there is no opportunity. There is no reason to continue the opportunity diagnosis. Weak drivers imply that the opportunity is small. The steering committee will typically decide to stop the opportunity diagnosis.

AMBIGUOUS SITUATIONS The in-between situations are ambiguous. There are few drivers and they have moderate strength. The steering committee has to judge whether it is worthwhile to continue the opportunity diagnosis in these in-between situations.

Segment the result gap

For a more fine-grained insight into the opportunity, the consultants will divide the opportunity into segments. For instance, the consultants may segment the opportunity according to customer type, geography, or distribution channel. The choice of segmentation criterion depends on the client context and the nature of the opportunity. Consultants want to know how the opportunity is distributed over the various segments. We may conceptualize a spectrum of options. One extreme of the spectrum is an opportunity that is evenly spread over all segments. The opposite extreme is an opportunity that is fully concentrated in one single segment. The consultants have to assess the strength of the verified opportunity drivers in the various segments to get a better idea of the distribution of the opportunity. The consultants have already assessed the strength of drivers in the previous step. But this was an assessment in a general way. The consultants did not distinguish between segments. This insight into the opportunity distribution will allow consultants to concentrate on the most important segments and develop a solution that in any case targets these segments. Figure 12.20 on the next page visualizes the segmentation of buyers for the new product. The consultants evaluate the strength of the three opportunity drivers for each segment.

Identify the result gap

ASSESS THE SIZE OF THE OPPORTUNITY Based on the verified opportunity drivers and the segments, the consultants may assess the size of the result gap. Knowledge of the distribution across segments enables the consultants to prioritize this assessment tasks. The consultants will first work on and put most effort into estimating the size of the largest segments.

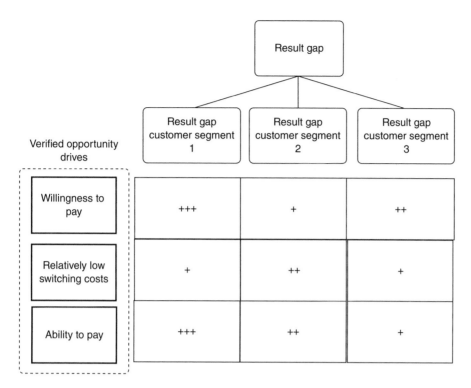

FIGURE 12.20 *Segment the result gap*

Figure 12.21 on the next page shows how the opportunity drivers determine the size of the opportunity in profit terms. The consultants quantify the size of the opportunity for the segments with the use of these drivers.

DECIDE ON THE DESIRED RESULT   Given the opportunity size, the client has to decide what increase of its desired result is appropriate. Assume the opportunity of the new product in terms of profit is $250 million. The client thinks that it is realistic to assume that the company can get a 40 per cent share of that profit opportunity. The increase in the client's desired result is $100 million. The consultants cannot determine the client's desired result. Setting the desired result is the responsibility of the client. Of course, the consultants may, if asked by the client, give a recommendation for the desired result.

Formulate the key question

Based on the consultants' assessment of the opportunity size, the client has determined what new desired result is appropriate. Based on the adapted desired result, the consultants formulate the following question: *how should the client respond to the opportunity to achieve the increased desired result?*

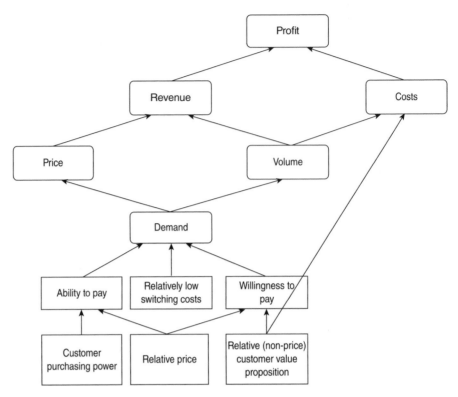

FIGURE 12.21 *Identify the opportunity (in terms of profit)*

SUMMARY

Problem diagnosis

This chapter is an interpretation of the structured problem diagnosis method of the world's top tier management consulting firms. We distinguished between five steps in problem diagnosing. The problem is defined as a gap between the achieved result and the desired result of the client. The consultants first identify what is the gap. Second, they decompose the gap by drivers. Third, they investigate where the gap is. Fourth, they explain why the gap exists. Then, they formulate the problem in the form of a key question: how should the client respond to the root cause of the result gap to achieve the desired result? Figure 12.22 on the next page summarizes the process of structured problem diagnosis.

Opportunity diagnosis

Consultants also help clients seize opportunities. The structure for diagnosis opportunities differs from that for problem diagnosis. The consultants

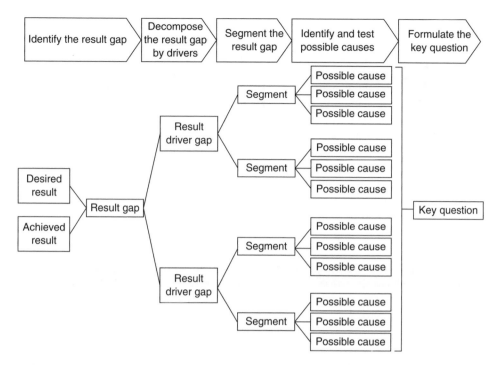

FIGURE 12.22 *The process of structured problem diagnosis*

first verify why the opportunity exists (identify the opportunity drivers). Second, they analyse where the opportunity exists (segments). Third, they estimate the size of the opportunity.

Ivy Business School

Introduction to the client

Ivy Business School is a top-ranked private non-profit graduate business school, which is located in the United States. Its mission is to develop global business leaders. Ivy is consistently ranked among the global top three in the most important business school rankings.

The school has a single campus from which it offers a portfolio of degree programmes (MBA, DBA, and PhD) and executive education programmes (about seventy open enrolment and seventy custom programmes). Last year, about 2,000 degree students (of which one third are international), and 10,000 executive students (of which two thirds are international) participated in these programmes. The degree programmes together generated $100 million in tuition and the executive programmes generated $180 million. Ivy also has a publishing division which produces business school cases (selling 10 million copies annually), business books (both textbooks and professional books, in total 2 million copies annually), and a business magazine (a circulation of 300,000 and 4 million article reprints annually). The publishing activities generate $180 million in revenues. Moreover, Ivy receives about $100 million in annual endowments from its 100,000-plus alumni network. Table 12.2 provides an overview of the organization. Ivy has about 250 faculty members, among which are several internationally renowned, 'star' professors. The school employs about 1,250 support staff members.

TABLE 12.2 *An overview of the organization*

	Education division	**Publishing division**
Offerings	Degree and executive programmes	Cases, books, and magazine subscriptions and reprints
Knowledge	Premier	Premier
Immersion	Rich interaction in class and on campus	No interactive content
Target markets	Selectivity is key: focus on tier 1 students (high position, high potential, high budget for education)	Broader scope: both tier 1 and tier 2 students
Volume	Low (12,000 students)	High (10 million cases, 4 million article reprints, 2 million books, magazine circulation of 300,000)
Pricing	High premium	Low premium
Revenues	$280 million	$180 million
Reputation	Prestigious certification of global top 3 school	Prestigious brand of global top 3 school

The disturbing event: the development of online learning technologies

Online learning

Digital technologies for online learning are becoming increasingly powerful. As a result, online learning is improving in terms of its quality, richness, and sophistication. Moreover, student access to online education is growing due to the spread of broad band technology, which allows for high-bandwidth connections. Various mid-ranked and lower-ranked business schools and online learning companies have already started offering online learning. There are also 'online-only schools'.

Towards real time interaction

The first online learning offerings, including web-based videos, cases, and exercises, were 'asynchronous' in the sense that they did not provide real time interaction with instructors and fellow students. Massive open online courses (MOOCs) are an example of such asynchronous offerings. Massive multiplayer online role playing games (MMORPGs) are an example of synchronous online applications.

More recent online learning offerings are synchronous. Synchronous online learning is about real time, live, interactive sessions, so-called virtual classrooms, with online instructors and online communities of fellow students.

Residential learning

At the same time, residential learning in business schools is becoming increasingly expensive. To illustrate this trend: the tuition fee of an MBA has risen faster than the starting salaries of graduates. These increasing costs have contributed to a diminishing enrolment in residential programmes.

Is online learning an opportunity?

Increase the share of global talent

Online learning technologies may allow Ivy Business School to increase its share of the global population of talented students. Online learning has an unlimited geographical reach. Ivy may be able to extend its (geographic) reach and thereby increase international participation rates.

Overcome capacity constraints

The school faces supply constraints. Currently, Ivy's capacity to offer educational programmes is limited by the capacity of its academic faculty. Adding high quality staff is difficult and expensive. Moreover, Ivy's supply is constrained by the capacity of its campus. This campus does not allow for expansion.

Serve alumni better

Online technologies may also allow Ivy to strengthen its ties with its alumni and support the school's ambition of lifelong learning. Ivy wants to stimulate its alumni to regularly attend new programmes at the school to prepare for the next stage of their career.

Or is it a problem?

Most demanding students

Various mid- and lower-ranked business schools have already started with online learning initiatives. As a top ranked school, Ivy serves the most demanding students: the so-called tier 1 students. At present, the online learning technologies do not meet the requirement of these most demanding students. But in the future, online learning may develop into an acceptable alternative for Ivy's students.

Immersion quality

Although Ivy acknowledges the increasing performance of online learning technologies, the school has concerns about the programme quality. Even the most sophisticated online learning offerings are still no match for the quality of the

▶

immersion of Ivy's residential learning. However, can Ivy afford to wait until the technologies are perfect? By then it may be too late because Ivy missed out on first mover advantages.

Premium pricing

Moreover, as a top ranked school with premium pricing, Ivy has much to lose because online learning will drive tuition fees down.

Selectivity versus scale

Online learning will relieve Ivy's capacity constraints in terms of faculty and campus facilities. However, part of Ivy's proposition is selectivity in student admission. The school's profile of exclusivity does not go together with massive online learning. Ivy fears a dilution of its certification if it offers massive online programmes. However, it also dreads that its star professors may set up their own online shop or be lured away by online learning players. Some stars have already participated in video lectures by online players.

Publishing activities

Ivy's publishing products are paper-based or in a non-interactive, electronic form. Real time interactive online offerings may disrupt Ivy's traditional publishing business.

The consultancy project

Ivy's board are divided about their response to online learning. Some board members want to hold back with introducing online learning until the performance of online learning technologies has become good enough to match the demand of Ivy's tier 1 students. Other board members, including the head of publishing, say that it will then be too late for Ivy to enter the online learning arena. They urge that Ivy enters online learning right now. The dean asks himself: *what should Ivy do?*

The dean has invited the managing director and founder of Acme Consulting, who is an MBA-alumnus, to help Ivy find out how to respond to the challenge of online learning. Out of gratitude towards his alma mater, this alumnus has offered to do this consultancy project pro bono.

Identify and structure the possible opportunity drivers

Why do we expect that the opportunity exists? The consultants first identify the possible drivers of the online learning opportunity. They use desk research and interviews with knowledgeable stakeholders inside and outside the Ivy Business School. Subsequently, the consultants structure these drivers in a logical order (see Figure 12.23).

Test the possible drivers

The consultants test the possible opportunity drivers. They analyse each of the individual drivers at the lowest level of the structure (see Figure 12.24). The analyses confirm all drivers in the structure. All drivers are substantial. Therefore, the consultants accept the opportunity. The analyses confirm that the opportunity exists.

Segment the result gap

Where is the opportunity? Or more precisely: how is the opportunity distributed

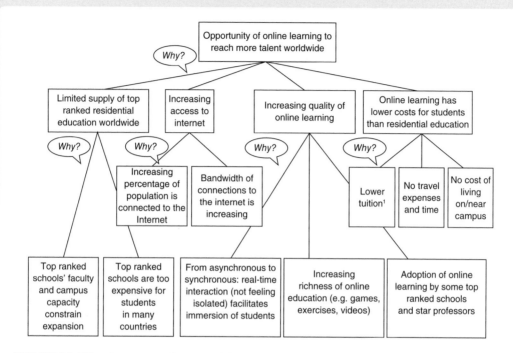

FIGURE 12.23 *Structure the possible opportunity drivers*

Notes: (1) Development costs are five times the costs of development for residential education. Delivery cost (non-interactive) is 1/10,000 of residential. Delivery costs with interaction are 1/10 of residential.

over the various segments? The consultants segment the opportunity for the education activities. They create a logical structure of segments. The consultants also use the drivers to assess the opportunity per segment. How is the opportunity distributed across segments?

Identify the result gap

What is the opportunity? How large is it? The consultants estimate the size of the opportunity (in terms of number of students) by segment. They sum up the segments to arrive at the total opportunity. If cannibalization of residential programmes is expected, then the consultants will subtract the loss in residential programmes from the gain in online programmes. Figure 12.25 provides an illustration of only *one segment*.

Determine the desired result

The consultants estimate the size of the segment opportunity. Figure 12.26 conceptually presents the opportunity in terms of a shifting share of residential and online learning. Online learning gains a share at the expense of residential learning.

The client, the board of the Ivy Business School, determines what the new desired result is on the basis of the consultants' estimate of the opportunity size. The board decides that the school should aim to

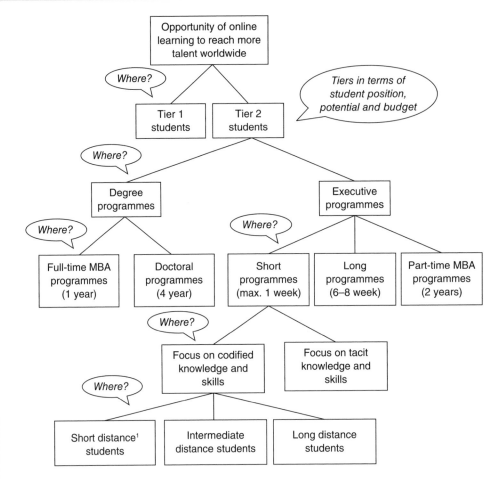

FIGURE 12.24 *Segment the opportunity gap*

Note: (1) Distance to campus

reach 5 per cent of the global higher education market within ten years.

Formulate the key question

The consultants are able to formulate the key question: how should Ivy respond to the development of online learning technologies (the positive disturbing event) to reach a 5 per cent share of the global higher education market within ten years? Next, the consultants complete the opportunity statement. Table 12.3 displays this statement.

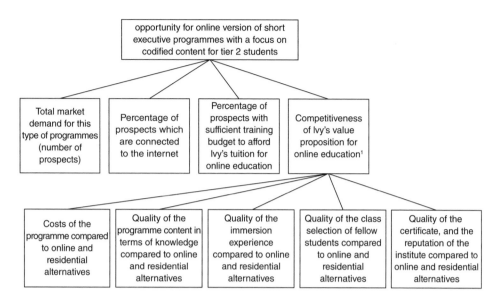

FIGURE 12.25 *Identify the segment opportunity*

Note: (1) Costs are author's addition. The other dimensions of competitiveness of educational propositions are based on Laseter (2012)

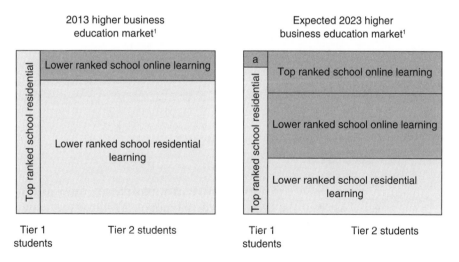

FIGURE 12.26 *The opportunity of online learning*

Note: (1) The surface indicates the share of a market segment; these are fictitious charts: they are not based on empirical evidence; a = top ranked school online learning

TABLE 12.3 *The opportunity statement*

Problem statement	Ivy Business School
Achieved result	Ivy has less than a 1 % share of the global higher business education market (degree and executive education).
Disturbing event	The development of online learning technologies
Desired result	Within 10 years, a 5 % share of the global higher business education market (*based on an estimation of the size of opportunity*)
Key question	How should Ivy respond to the development of online learning technologies to reach a 5 % share of the global higher business education market within 10 years?
Stakeholders	Ivy's board, faculty (in particular the star professors), support staff, students, and alumni
Constraints on the solution	• Maintain a high quality of education and publishing (premier knowledge) • Maintain high level admission standards • Alignment of (star) faculty
Decision criteria	• Quality of education and publishing • Quality, international composition, and volume of student intake • Ease of implementation • Risks • Financial results

EXERCISES

1. A management consulting firm, LargeConsultancy, faces a revenue gap. Last year the firm realized an amount of billings (revenues) that was below the desired level. Preliminary analysis reveals that there is no volume gap. The number of billed hours roughly equals the desired number. Therefore, a gap in billings per hour should explain the billings gap. Structure the possible drivers of this gap in billings per hour. The structure should have one level of maximally seven drivers. The drivers should be MECE.

2. A small manufacturer of sports cars, DriveFun, occupies a strong position in the high-end sports car segment of the automotive market. In the 1990s, DriveFun traded down by adding a cheaper model, The

Rookie. DriveFun used to be highly profitable. Since the early 2000s, its profitability has deteriorated because the sports car market segment, in which DriveFun operates, became saturated, while competition within the segment increased. DriveFun's CEO is becoming increasingly worried. The company cannot trade down any further (adding even cheaper models) without eroding its high-end reputation. What should the CEO do? Assume the CEO has hired you as the consultant to solve the company's problem. Formulate the key question for the consultancy project.

3. A small trading company, InternationalTrading, sells four products (Products 1–4) in five countries (A, B, C, D, and E). InternationalTrading has a profit problem and it has hired you as a consultant to solve this problem. You have identified that the company's $2 million revenue gap explains most of the profit gap. Next, you want to segment this revenue gap. InternationalTrading's financial manager has produced a data table (see Table 12.4). How should you structure the data to segment the revenue gap in the most meaningful way? Use the data table to calculate the relevant segment sizes.

TABLE 12.4 *Data table*

Revenue gap	Product 1	Product 2	Product 3	Product 4
Country A	40	70	60	30
Country B	40	70	60	30
Country C	280	490	420	210
Country D	20	35	30	15
Country E	20	35	30	15

Note: revenue gaps are in thousands of US dollars

REFLECTIVE QUESTIONS

1. What do you consider to be the strengths of the structured problem diagnosing approach? Explain your answer.

2. What are its weaknesses? How might these weaknesses be overcome? Explain your answer.

3. For what type of consultancy projects is this structured approach most appropriate? For what type is it less appropriate? Explain your answer.

FURTHER READING

Minto, B. (1987) *The Pyramid Principle: Logic in Writing and Thinking* (revised 3rd edn). London: Minto International Inc.

REFERENCES

Holland, B.R. (1972) *Sequential Analysis*. London: McKinsey & Company.

Laseter, T. (2012) 'The university's dilemma', *Strategy + Business*, 27 November 2012. Available at: www.strategy-business.com/article/00147?gko=da535 (accessed 6 April 2013).

Minto, B. (1987) *The Pyramid Principle: Logic in Writing and Thinking* (revised 3rd edn). London: Minto International Inc.

Scotus, J. D. (1982) *A Treatise on God as First Principle* (revised 2nd edn). Chicago: Franciscan Herald Press.

449

13

STRUCTURED SOLUTION DEVELOPMENT

INTRODUCTION

Structured problem solving is a two-stage process. Chapter 12 introduced the first stage, which is the structured problem diagnosis. This chapter presents the second stage, structured solution development, which is indicative of the approach used by the top tier management consultants, such as McKinsey & Company, the Boston Consulting Group, and Bain & Company. We provide a step-by-step guide to developing solutions in a structured way. We illustrate the process with the running case study about AcStrat Consulting. The chapter closes with a summary, the running mini case study about the Ivy Business School, reflective questions, exercises, suggestions for further reading, and references.

Main learning objectives

- Understand the reasons for structured solution development.
- Understand the relevance of identifying the client's decision points.
- Know how to develop possible solutions.
- Know how to structure possible solutions.
- Know how to evaluate possible solutions.

- Know how to formulate a hypothesis.
- Know how to identify the assumptions of a hypothesis.
- Know how to structure the assumptions of a hypothesis.
- Know how to design analyses for testing the assumptions.
- Know how to collect data for the analyses.
- Know how to model the impact of a solution on the client's result.
- Understand the implications of uncertainty on solution development.
- Understand how to evaluate solutions under uncertainty.
- Understand how to make decisions about alternative solutions.

WHY USE A STRUCTURED APPROACH?

Why do consultants use the method of structured solution development? Because they want to recommend solutions that are effective, that is: solutions that close the client's result gap. The structured method forces consultants to identify and test the underlying assumptions of their solutions. Without the structured approach to solution development, some or all assumptions may remain hidden and will not be put to the test. An untested solution is a leap of faith.

The structured approach is also efficient. Through its use of hypotheses, the method avoids 'boiling the ocean'. Instead of investigating all possible solutions to the problem, the consultants will prioritize the options and take the most promising one as their initial hypothesis.

The structured solution development process

The solution is the answer to the key question: how to respond to the disturbing event to close the result gap or achieve the desired result? Figure 13.1 on the next page outlines the steps of the structured approach to solution development as used by the world's top tier consultants. Structured solution development is based on hypothesis generation and testing. If the consultants have to reject a hypothesis, they have to develop an alternative hypothesis. The solution development can therefore be an iterative process.

IDENTIFY THE DECISIONS

When consultants think about solutions they first think about the decisions their client may take. Solutions should close the client's result gap. Solutions should also imply decisions by the client. These decisions should

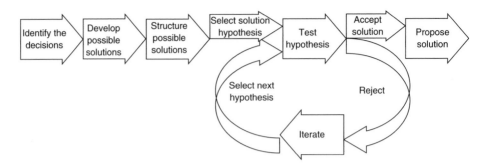

FIGURE 13.1 *The structured solution development process*

imply actions. These actions should lead to closure of the result gap. Without actions no closure of the result gap occurs. When thinking about possible solutions, the consultants should identify what decisions the client may take. These decisions provide a foundation on which to generate ideas for solutions. As an illustration, Figure 13.2 gives a structure of decisions related to a new strategy.

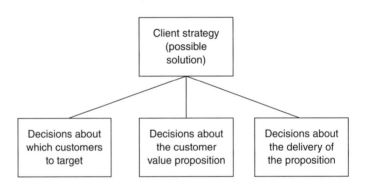

FIGURE 13.2 *Identify the decisions related to a new strategy*

Identify the decision outcomes

The set of decisions may lead to numerous options. For instance, assume the client may take three decisions. Let us call these decisions A, B, and C. Assume further that each decision is binary, which means that there are only two outcomes for each decision. This set of three binary decisions creates eight different outcomes. Figure 13.3 visualizes the corresponding decision tree. In real life the number of decisions may easily exceed three, while the number of outcomes may be higher than two. Imagine how the number of possible outcomes increases.

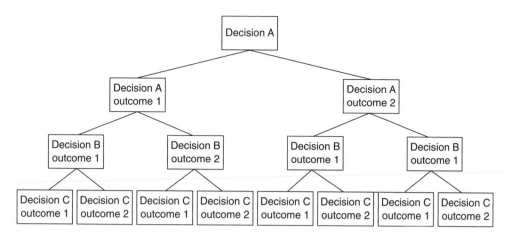

FIGURE 13.3 *Identify the set of decision outcomes*

Anticipate opposition

It is important to consider the tree of possible decision outcomes (see Figure 13.3). It provides a complete overview of all possible solutions. Although the client will ultimately choose one solution, the knowledge of all alternatives is valuable. During the final presentation of their recommended solution, but maybe also during interim presentations, the consultants may face opposition from the client or other stakeholders. They may be interested in alternative solutions. They could say: 'Haven't you thought of that solution?' or 'Why did not you consider that solution?' By having the complete structure of possible solutions (as visualized in the tree in Figure 13.3), the consultants may anticipate what alternative solutions the opposition may come up with.

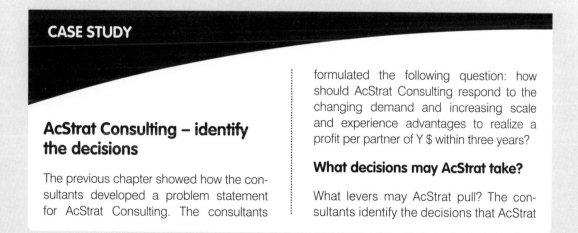

CASE STUDY

AcStrat Consulting – identify the decisions

The previous chapter showed how the consultants developed a problem statement for AcStrat Consulting. The consultants

formulated the following question: how should AcStrat Consulting respond to the changing demand and increasing scale and experience advantages to realize a profit per partner of Y $ within three years?

What decisions may AcStrat take?

What levers may AcStrat pull? The consultants identify the decisions that AcStrat may take to solve the problem. First, the consultants identify the key decision areas (see Table 13.1). Second, they identify for each decision area what options AcStrat has. These are the alternative decision outcomes.

TABLE 13.1 *Identify the decision areas and alternative outcomes*

Decision area	Alternative decision outcomes

Target clients (what clients to work for)	• Client industries
	  o Maintain (currently, 20 industry practices)
	  o Focus (reduce number of practices)
	• Client geographic scope
	  o Maintain (currently, mainly Fortune Global 500 multinationals)
	  o Shift to smaller and less internationalized companies

Scope of services (what services to offer)	o Maintain (currently, only strategy development advice) o Expand, in particular the inclusion of strategy implementation o Narrow down

Scale	• Maintain (currently, a relatively small player in terms of scale of operations)
	• Grow
	  o Autonomous growth
	  o Mergers
	  o Alliances
	• Shrink

Cost	• Reduce costs
	  o Indirect costs (currently, relatively high indirect costs)
	  o Direct costs

DEVELOP POSSIBLE SOLUTIONS

Structure the solution development

It is not feasible, and certainly not efficient, to analyse all possible decision outcomes. Instead of 'boiling the ocean' of possible decision outcomes, the consultants will develop a selection of possible solutions. We can distinguish three ways in which consultants develop possible solutions:

1. Exploit the consultancy firm's collective experience.
2. Exploit the public domain knowledge.
3. Explore new solutions.

Exploit the firm's collective experience

KNOWLEDGE ACCUMULATION   Most consultants, in particular the large firms, will first consider their accumulated experience. Have the consultants seen this problem (or opportunity) before, or have they seen a similar or somewhat related problem? The problem may be new to the client. It may even be new to the client sector. However, the problem may not be new to the consultancy. Large consulting firms undertake large numbers of projects each year. Assume a consultancy firm with 10,000 consultancy staff. An average project team consists of three consultants and a project manager. Assume that a consultant is assigned to an average of four projects a year. The same applies to a manager. Such a firm will conduct 10,000 projects annually. Imagine how their knowledge from projects accumulates over the years. In a decade, this firm will have accumulated experience of 100,000 projects! Such a firm has probably seen all types of problems and opportunities in all kinds of organizations and all types of sectors or industries.

KNOWLEDGE MANAGEMENT   Whether the consultancy can exploit its collective knowledge depends on how well the firm has organized its knowledge management. If the consultancy has a sophisticated knowledge management system, then the consultants will have access to this accumulated knowledge. IT systems may offer the codified knowledge, whereas the organization of the firm's experts (the functional and industry practice groups) may supply the tacit knowledge. Codified knowledge may refer to a procedure type consultancy, while tacit knowledge may refer to a grey hair type of consultancy. The knowledge system may offer structures for possible solutions for all types of client problems and opportunities. Probably, such systems will have solutions organized by client sector. For each type of problem, they will have solutions differentiated by client sector. These solutions are not generic but client sector-specific. Imagine the efficiency benefits that such knowledge brings to the consultancy project. Firms with such knowledge management are able to deliver their projects faster and at lower costs than firms that lack such knowledge.

Exploit the public domain knowledge

CUSTOMIZE STANDARD FRAMEWORKS   The collective experience of a particular consultancy firm as embodied in its knowledge management system is private domain knowledge. It is proprietary knowledge of that specific consultancy firm. Some proprietary knowledge diffuses into the public domain. The public domain knowledge is available to all. This knowledge is distributed over business school curricula, print media (articles, books, and reports), and the internet. The consultants may tap into this public domain knowledge to develop possible solutions. The consultants may choose standard analytical frameworks from the public domain. These standard frameworks are by definition generic. Consultants may use these frameworks as a starting point. They may customize these frameworks to make them fit the specific situation of their client.

EXAMPLES OF FRAMEWORKS Take for instance solutions for strategy problems and opportunities. The strategy map by Kaplan and Norton is a framework for developing such solutions (Kaplan and Norton, 2004). Porter's competitive forces framework may also be a starting point for solution development (Porter, 1985), while the Blue Ocean strategy canvas is a framework for (marketing) strategy development (Kim and Mauborgne, 2005). The 4Ps of the marketing mix are another framework for marketing strategy development. Ohmae's 3-C framework may also be useful for solution development (Ohmae, 1991). Ansoff's growth strategies provide a valuable structure for developing growth options (Ansoff, 1957). The BCG matrix and the GE-McKinsey matrix may be helpful for generating solutions about a corporate portfolio strategy. Consultants may use Porter's value chain concept to develop solutions for processes (Porter, 1985). The McKinsey 7-S model may be valuable to develop solutions that involve the organizations. This is not an exhaustive list but a selection of examples.

Explore new solutions

NEW PROBLEMS The client's problem (or opportunity) may be new to the world. Sometimes, new problems and opportunities will emerge that are new to the client and the consultants. An example was the rise of the new economy in the 1990s as a result of the internet. The internet made new business models possible. Depending on the client's perspective, these models were new opportunities or new problems. Consultants did not have experience with these problems. Therefore, they needed to explore new solutions. Exploiting existing knowledge refers to a procedure type and grey hair type of consultancy. Exploring new knowledge fits with a brain type of consultancy.

Exploring solutions is necessary for the consultant if the problem is new to that consultant. If they do not have experience with a particular problem, and if there is no public domain knowledge available about that problem, then they need to explore a solution to that problem.

STRUCTURED BRAINSTORMING   Consultants may use divergent thinking to explore new solutions. Brainstorming is an obvious technique for idea generation. The consultants may invite knowledgeable stakeholders from inside and outside the client organization, with different perspectives. The consultants create a setting which stimulates divergent thinking about solutions for the problem. Such brainstorming may take the form of a workshop. Consultants typically limit divergence to a certain extent. It is not brainstorming in the sense of generating ideas at random. The consultants apply structure to the development of possible solutions in the following ways. First, the point of departure for idea generation is the key question. All ideas should answer this question. Second, ideas should take into account the possible decision areas that the client has to consider.

STRUCTURE POSSIBLE SOLUTIONS

Mutually exclusive

After generating ideas for possible solutions, the consultants will want to create an overview. They will filter the ideas. Not all ideas pass the constraints and criteria imposed by the clients (see the problem statement). Next, the consultants will divide the remaining solutions into a logical structure. Most important is to ensure that these solutions are mutually exclusive. Consultants want to avoid overlap of possible solutions because in the next stage they want to investigate those solutions. If different consultants in parallel investigate solutions which are overlapping, then the consultants' investigations will imply duplicate work. In the chapter about problem diagnosis we emphasized the importance of logical structuring of a subject into elements which are both mutually exclusive and collectively exhaustive.

Not collectively exhaustive

In solution development, creating a collectively exhaustive set of possible solutions is not an end but a means. It ensures that the consultants do not overlook any possible solution. However, in practice it may be too unwieldy. Therefore, consultants have to create a balance between costs and benefits. There is a trade-off between, on the one hand, the time opportunity costs of trying to exhaust the number of solutions, and on the other hand, the value of the additional solutions. At some point, the consultants will have included the most relevant solutions. They may use the steering committee and other knowledgeable stakeholders inside and outside the client organization as a sounding board to verify whether they have identified the most relevant solutions. The remaining solutions – not included in the structure – may only have theoretical value. But they are less relevant compared to the solutions already included. It is more important to have the most relevant solutions in the structure, than to have all the (theoretically possible) solutions in the structure. The consultants do not strive towards a collectively exhaustive structure of possible solutions.

SELECT A HYPOTHESIS ABOUT A POSSIBLE SOLUTION

The problem statement

How do consultants select a possible solution from the solution structure to use as their initial hypothesis? The consultants may use the problem statement as a guide. The problem statement contains the client's decision criteria. How does the client compare and evaluate alternative solutions? What does the client consider most important? Is the client only interested in the solution's contribution to the result, or do other factors play an important role as well? Other factors may include the ease of implementation of a solution or the level of risk involved in a solution. The consultants need to know what solution characteristics determine client satisfaction. With what type of solution will the client be satisfied? Of course, it is difficult for consultants to evaluate a possible solution before they have investigated it. Selecting the hypothesis to a large extent depends on the consultants' judgement. The experience of the consultants plays an important role here. If they have done similar projects in the past, then they may use these analogies to judge the possible solutions. The consultants may also solicit feedback from knowledgeable stakeholders inside or outside the client organization.

Initial hypothesis

The consultants select the possible solution that seems most promising in terms of the client's decision criteria. Subsequently, the consultants formulate their initial hypothesis. Recall that the hypothesis is a possible answer to the key question. Therefore, the consultants formulate the hypothesis as an answer to that question. Typically, the hypothesis takes the following form: if the client does [the solution], then the client closes the result gap. Or in short: the [solution] creates the desired result.

AcStrat Consulting – select a hypothesis

The consultants explore the most probable solutions and put them in a structure (see Figure 13.4). Next, they select the candidate solution to serve as the initial hypothesis. This hypothesis consists of two sub-hypotheses at different levels of the structure (see the boxes with italic text).

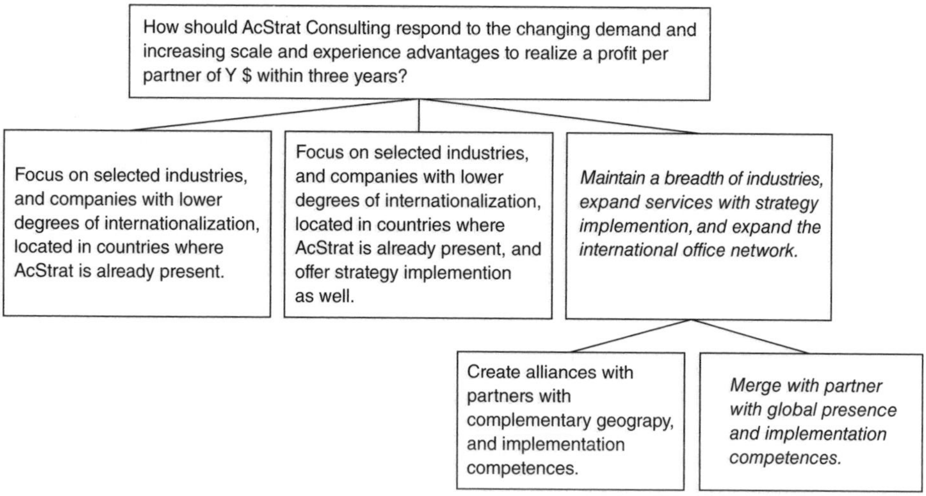

How should AcStrat Consulting respond to the changing demand and increasing scale and experience advantages to realize a profit per partner of Y $ within three years?

Focus on selected industries, and companies with lower degrees of internationalization, located in countries where AcStrat is already present.

Focus on selected industries, and companies with lower degrees of internationalization, located in countries where AcStrat is already present, and offer strategy implemention as well.

Maintain a breadth of industries, expand services with strategy implemention, and expand the international office network.

Create alliances with partners with complementary geograpy, and implementation competences.

Merge with partner with global presence and implementation competences.

FIGURE 13.4   *Select a hypothesis*

TEST A HYPOTHESIS

Forms of inferencing

Before the consultants can recommend a solution to the client, they need to verify this solution. The consultants' hypothesis is an untested solution. The consultants have to test their hypothesis. How do consultants test a hypothesis about a solution? This hypothesis testing differs from hypotheses about possible causes of the result gap. In the problem diagnosis, we discussed abductive inferencing. Abduction is appropriate for seeking explanations for a given result. However, for testing a solution, the consultants will use other forms of inferencing. The preferred option is deduction. If deduction is not feasible, then consultants may resort to induction (see Figure 13.5).

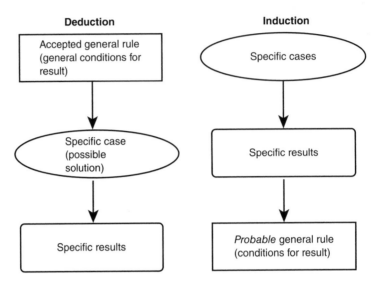

FIGURE 13.5 *Two types of inferencing for solution testing*

Deductive inferencing

Deduction moves from the general to the specific. The point of departure is the general rule. For deductive inferencing about solutions, the consultants need to determine the generally accepted conditions for the results of a solution. Under what circumstances will the implementation of the solution deliver the desired result? The consultants need to identify and structure these assumptions. When structuring the assumptions, it is essential that these are mutually exclusive and collectively exhaustive. Completeness is important because all assumptions need to be satisfied for the solution to be effective. Consultants may use the management literature to identify the general conditions of a solution. For instance, if the solution is a strategy, then the consultants may consider using the 3-C framework by Ohmae (1991). According to this framework, the three critical success factors of a strategy refer to customers, competitors, and the company. The solution should include a value proposition that focuses on the specific needs of selected customers. The proposition should meet not only today's customer needs but also future needs. The proposition should contain an advantage over competitors. The proposed proposition should beat both the existing as well as future propositions by both incumbent players and new entrants. Finally, the company should be able (have the competences or be able to develop the competences) to deliver the proposition in a cost effective manner. We may interpret each success factor as a condition for a result, or as an assumption for the hypothesis about the solution. If the consultants use deductive referencing, then they have to test the assumptions of their hypothesis. The assumptions in Figure 13.6 are the general conditions for a price reduction to generate the desired result.

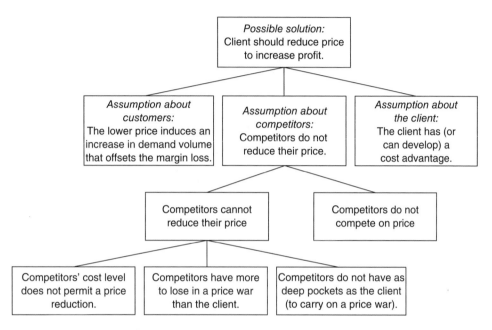

FIGURE 13.6 *Identify and structure the assumptions for a price reduction*

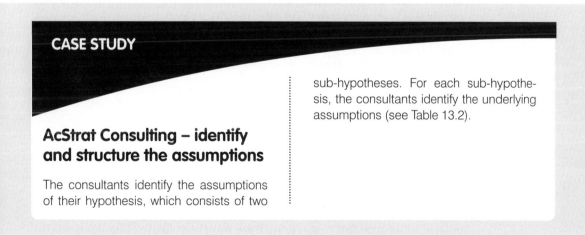

CASE STUDY

AcStrat Consulting – identify and structure the assumptions

The consultants identify the assumptions of their hypothesis, which consists of two sub-hypotheses. For each sub-hypothesis, the consultants identify the underlying assumptions (see Table 13.2).

TABLE 13.2 *Identify and structure the assumptions*

Sub-hypothesis	Underlying assumptions
Maintain targeting of current markets but increase international presence and add strategy implementation.	• Current target markets offer opportunities for seizing scale advantages. • International presence allows an opportunity to seize the increased demand for global projects. • Including implementation services meets the increased demand for bundling strategy development and implementation.
Merge with partner with global presence and implementation competences.	• There is a partner with global presence and implementation competences interested in a merger with a strategy consulting firm. • A merger between AcStrat and the partner offers attractive synergies. • It is possible to integrate the two organizations. • There are no alliance partners with complementary office networks and implementation competences. • In a declining market, a merger is more attractive than autonomous growth. • AcStrat does not have the financial resources to invest in international expansion and the development of implementation competences for autonomous growth.

Inductive inferencing

An alternative to deductive inferencing is inductive inferencing. The consultants do not test the general conditions but investigate specific cases about other firms. Figure 13.7 on the next page illustrates inductive inferencing. If the sample of cases is representative and substantial (for clarity reasons, the figure only shows three cases), then the consultants will infer that a price reduction will probably lead to a profit increase. Based on that conclusion the consultants may recommend that the client reduces its price to increase its profit.

Create the first draft of the final presentation

After formulating the initial hypothesis and structuring the underlying assumptions of that hypothesis, the consultants will already create the first draft of their final PowerPoint presentation to the client. The consultants will create an overall structure for this presentation (see Chapter 14). Moreover, they will design the individual PowerPoint slides for this presentation. Because the consultants have not yet collected and analysed the

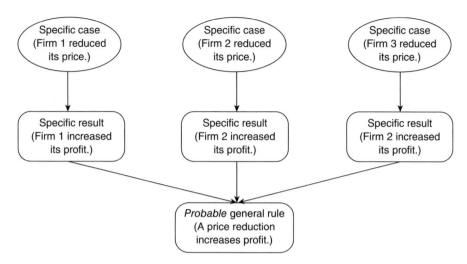

FIGURE 13.7 *Inductive inferencing*

data, they will use the expected outcomes in their slides. After the analyses, the consultants will replace the expected outcomes of analyses with the actual outcomes. If they have to reject their initial hypothesis, and refer to an alternative hypothesis, then the consultants will adapt their draft of the final presentation accordingly. Chapter 14 will elaborate on the structuring of presentations and the design of slides.

DESIGN THE ANALYSIS

Standard versus custom analyses

The test of a hypothesis means tests of each assumption underlying the hypothesis. To test an assumption, the consultants may use standard, off-the-shelf, analytical frameworks, or they may design or use a customized framework. Some examples of standard frameworks are Porter's competitive forces framework, the value chain framework, and the McKinsey 7-S model. However, the standard frameworks may not suffice for all assumptions. In such cases, consultants may design analyses for the specific purpose of analysing that particular assumption. The archetype designs for consultants' custom analyses are the driver analysis and the benchmark analysis.

Driver analysis

LOWER THE LEVEL OF ABSTRACTION One popular analytical design is the driver analysis. Consultants measure a subject through its drivers.

Measurement of a subject requires facts. Some subjects are too abstract to measure directly. The idea is to focus on the subject's drivers because they are more concrete then the subject. The subject may be the volume of market demand, the price of a product, or the cost of manufacturing a product.

AN EXAMPLE OF A DRIVER ANALYSIS   For example, the client is a manufacturer of cat food and faces stagnating demand in its home country, which results in decreasing profits. The consultants have formulated a hypothesis about entering a new host country to increase profits. The consultants need to verify the assumptions underlying their hypothesis. One assumption is that the new host country provides sufficient demand for cat food. The question arises: what drives the volume of demand for cat food in that country? Figure 13.8 gives an example of the drivers of the demand for cat food. It is essential that the drivers form a logical structure: the drivers are mutually exclusive and collectively exhaustive. They should be measurable. The consultants can find facts for three out of five drivers in Figure 13.8:

1. The number of households in the country.
2. The share of households with one or more cats.
3. The average number of cats per household with one or more cats.

Some drivers may be too abstract to measure directly. In the example, the remaining drivers are too abstract: 'share of households that feed their cats with cat food' (some households may give their cats the leftovers of human food), and the average consumption per cat. The consultants have to identify the drivers of these abstract drivers to arrive at a lower the level of abstraction. Consultants will continue identifying drivers of drivers until they arrive at a low enough abstraction level, where they can find the facts to measure the drivers.

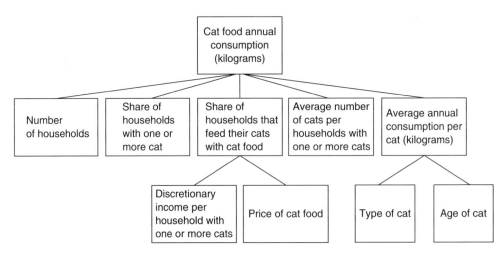

FIGURE 13.8   *Structure of the drivers*

Benchmark analysis

COMPARE SUBJECTS Benchmarking is another popular analysis design among consultants. Benchmarking is comparing subjects. For competitive analysis in particular, consultants may use benchmarking. For instance, consultants may benchmark the costs of the client and its main competitors. They may also compare the value propositions of the client and its competitors. For example, how do the product quality, performance, and price of the client's product compare to those of the competition?

Combine driver and benchmark analysis

Consultants may combine a driver analysis and a benchmark analysis. They may also compare drivers. In the cat food example, the consultants may use a comparison of drivers in the home country and drivers in the host country. Such a comparison may, for instance, help to assess the host country's share of households that feed their cats with cat food. Assume that the consultants have data about the level of discretionary income and the level of cat food prices in both countries. The comparison (see Figure 13.9) shows that the drivers are more favourable for the host country. Therefore, they may assume that the host country's share of households that feed their cats with cat food will probably be at least as high as in the home country. This is a highly simplified example. If the consultants have data about a large number of countries, then they can use statistical analysis to assess the host country's share of households that feed their cats with cat food.

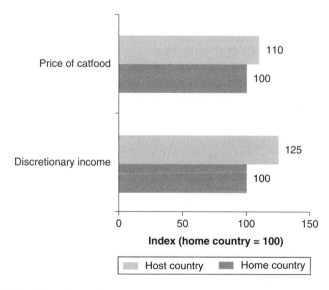

FIGURE 13.9 *Benchmark*

AcStrat Consulting – design the analysis

Two years ago, a consultancy firm named Delta Consulting showed interest in a merger with AcStrat. At that time, AcStrat refused to discuss a merger. However, at present, AcStrat is interested. Delta is still willing to discuss a merger between the two firms.

As an example, we focus on one of the assumptions for the merger: 'A merger between AcStrat and the partner offers attractive synergies'. This is a relatively high-level assumption. To analyse it we need to lower the level of abstraction (see Figure 13.10). We consider one of the lower-level assumptions underlying the high-level assumption: 'AcStrat and Delta can increase sales and/or decrease costs by aligning their market positions'. Subsequently, we consider an even lower level of abstraction. We focus on one of the underlying assumptions of the low-level assumption. This lower-level assumption is: 'AcStrat and Delta can cross sell their services'. Cross-selling means that the two firms can sell their services to each other's clients. This assumption is concrete enough to be tested by means of analysing it.

Based on the assumption 'There are opportunities for cross-selling', the consultants' design uses the following analyses:

- driver analysis of cross-selling opportunities
- benchmark analysis of cross-selling opportunities in other mergers

The consultants identify the data requirements of their analyses. They need data about the clients of AcStrat and Delta.

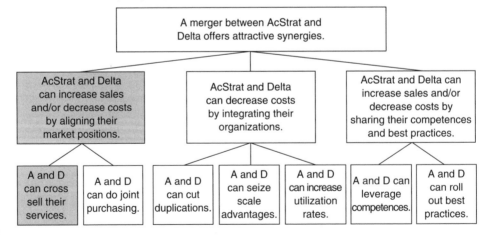

FIGURE 13.10 *Structure of assumptions at different levels*

Notes: A refers to AcStrat, D refers to Delta.

COLLECT THE DATA

Hypothesis-driven data collection

Consultants have to collect the data to test the assumptions in their hypothesis. What data do the consultants need? The hypothesis determines the data needs. Without a hypothesis, the consultants may be tempted to try to 'boil the ocean'. All data may seem relevant. With their hypothesis, consultants will know exactly what data they need to test the hypothesis. Figure 13.11 visualizes the relationship between the hypothesis and the data.

Without data, consultants cannot test their hypothesis. Without tests, the consultants lack the strength of fact-based argumentation to convince the client of the value of their recommended solution. Therefore, the structured solution development method relies on data collection. The data should be representative of the subject to be analysed. Consultants should refrain from biased testing. They have to resist the temptation to filter the data that support their hypothesis. This is the so-called 'confirmation bias'.

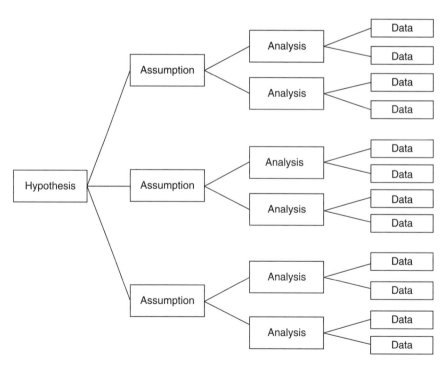

FIGURE 13.11 *From hypothesis to data*

Note: The number of assumptions, analyses, and data may vary by hypothesis.

Data sources

The consultants have defined the data requirements. The next question is: where to collect the data? Figure 13.12 distinguishes between desk research and field research. Desk research is about data that are already available and stored inside or outside the consultancy firm. Field research is about collecting new data that do not yet exist. Consultants have to go out (in the field) to collect these via one or more techniques: interviews, observations, surveys, and experiments. Consultants start with the easiest sources, and if these sources do not provide all the required data, then consultants will move to increasingly difficult sources. Typically, consultants begin with desk research and after exhausting this source they initiate field research to collect the remaining data.

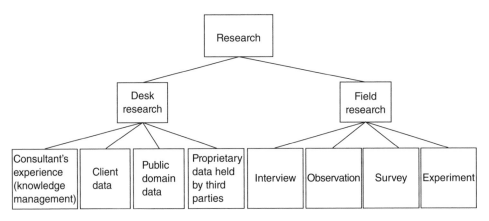

FIGURE 13.12   *Research by consultants*

Desk research

CONSULTANCY KNOWLEDGE   Consultants always start with the data they already possess. They look inside the consultancy firm for the accumulated knowledge. Large firms typically have knowledge management systems where consultants may look up information by industry practice and functional practice. Consultancy firms not only have information stored in IT systems. The people in the firms are also carriers of (tacit) knowledge. Consultants that search for data should therefore not just check the databases of the firm's knowledge management system, they should also consult colleagues with relevant experience and expertise. To facilitate such consultation, consultancy firms may have an overview of experts by subject. For each expert the overview provides the contact details.

PUBLIC DOMAIN DATA   After having exhausted their internal data sources, the consultants will look outside the consultancy firm for the further data they need for their analyses. The consultants may explore the public domain sources. For instance, they may use official statistics and other publications by governments and industry associations, but also the (digital) news media may provide relevant data for the consultants.

CLIENT DATA   A third important data source is the client. The client may have relevant data ready for the consultants. Besides the external (financial) reporting, the client may have all types of internal data which the consultants may need for their analyses. The internal audit department may be a rich source. But other departments, such as HR and corporate planning, may also provide valuable data.

Although the client may have a lot of data, this does not always mean that those data will be readily available to the consultants. Not all client organizational members may be open to the consultants. Some may fear the consultants may use the data against them. They may want to cover up their mistakes and weaknesses. Such people may become defensive and they may even sabotage the consultants' attempts to collect data. Consultants may therefore have a hard time obtaining the required data from the client organization.

PROPRIETARY DATA FROM THIRD PARTIES   A fourth and final source of already available data that may be collected through desk research is proprietary data held by third parties, other than the consultants and the client. These third parties may be research agencies or other consultancies. They will have collected data which they have not make public. They may share their data for a fee. For instance, research agencies sell their research reports or sell access to their databases for a fee. If consultants cannot find such data elsewhere they may buy the data from these third parties (typically they will have negotiated with the client that the client will reimburse the expenses).

Field research

GIVING UP IS NOT AN OPTION   If desk research does not offer a solution, then consultants have to turn to field research. We already mentioned that collecting data from some client members may be difficult. However, field research can be especially hard work. One of the reasons why clients may hire consultants is that consultants persevere more in data collection. They are prepared to go further and dig deeper to uncover the data required.

On a consultancy project, junior consultants typically have to collect the data. However, the challenge of data collection may in some cases prove to be too much for them. They may therefore be tempted to give up and go back to their project manager to explain that the data task is impossible. 'I am sorry, but it is impossible to get that data'. Although understandable (from the point of view of the consultant), such an attitude is not acceptable to the project manager (and the consultancy firm). The consultant will not get away with this.

CREATIVITY AND HARD WORK   When confronted with difficulties in collecting the data, the consultants should try harder and be creative in order to obtain the necessary data. For instance, a consultant needs to estimate the expenditures on advertising by a client's competitor. What if the competitor does not publish that kind of information? The consultant may count the number of commercials in the media. Next, the consultant may multiply this number by the usual fee to arrive at an estimate of the advertising expenditures. Another example is where a consultant needs to estimate a competitor's overhead. The competitor is privately held and therefore does have to report detailed financial results. The consultant may resort to more creative ways of data collection. They may for instance take a closer look at the competitor's office building. They may collect information about the office space (number of square meters) and deduce from that space how many staff the competitor employs. In another example, a consultant needs to estimate the production volume of a competitor's manufacturing plant. The consultant may position themself at the gate of that plant and count the number of incoming and outgoing trucks. This seems monkish work but it may give the consultant (and the client) valuable data.

COMPETITIVE INTELLIGENCE   Gathering data about the competition is one of the most difficult challenges. In many cases, the hypotheses of consultants will contain assumptions about the competitors of the client. For example, in the case of a solution for a client's problem, the consultants have to make assumptions about whether and how the client's competitors may respond to the client's solution. Another example here is the opportunity for the client. The consultants have to make assumptions about whether and how the client's competitors may seize this opportunity. Therefore, the consultants need to gather data about the client's competitors. Figure 13.13 visualizes some main sources of competitive intelligence.

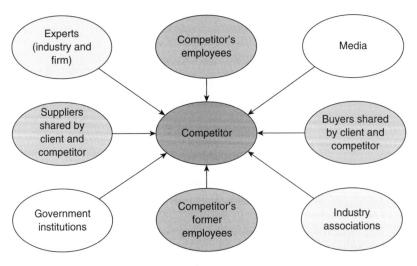

FIGURE 13.13   *Some main sources of data about a competitor*

GREY AREAS   Desk research is in most cases insufficient for competitive intelligence. Data published by the competitor (such as websites and annual reports), the media, and reports by governments and industry associations may be helpful but not sufficient. Therefore, consultants will need to do field research on the client's competitors. Of course, their data gathering activities should not break any law. Moreover, the consultants should refrain from entering grey areas in terms of ethics. How ethical is it to interrogate people covertly (where the interviewee is not aware of the real purpose of the interview) about a competitor?

EXPERTS   The publicly shared knowledge – through, for example, reports and websites – by experts within industry associations and government institutes may only provide a part of their knowledge. Consultants may probe the privately held knowledge of experts through interviews with these individuals. They may then do the same with other firm experts and industry experts, such as investment analysts and specialized journalists. These experts may be willing to share more insights in a personal interview. It helps if the consultants can share some interesting data with the experts, thereby creating a 'win-win situation'.

SHARED BUYERS AND SUPPLIERS   One step further in terms of ethics is to interview the buyers of the client who also buy from the particular competitor that the consultants need to investigate. Some consultants may interview the so-called 'shared' buyers. Some consultants may do the same with suppliers of the client who also supply to that particular competitor, the so-called 'shared' suppliers.

FORMER EMPLOYEES   Taking another step further in terms of ethics, some consultants might interview former employees of that competitor. Some former personnel of that competitor may now be employees of the client.

COMPETITIVE INTELLIGENCE FIRMS   There are specialist competitive intelligence firms – *not* management consultancy firms – that would go further and covertly interrogate former employees and even current employees of the competitor. These competitive intelligence firms work for clients not for consultants. We would like to emphasize that such intelligence practices are unethical and that these intelligence practices do not belong to management consultancy. Such competitive intelligence firms may use former state intelligence officers.

These intelligence firms may seek out former employees of the competitor that are currently active elsewhere. Social media are very helpful in this respect. These intelligence firms may covertly interrogate these people, carefully hiding their real purpose, which is collecting competitive intelligence. Finally, some intelligence firms may even approach current employees of that competitor. The intelligence firms may come into contact with these employees via various routes, among which are trade shows, conferences, networking events, or an informal setting, such as Friday afternoon drinks in a local bar near the competitor's office.

Precisely because such competitive intelligence constitutes a grey area, some clients may want to outsource this to intelligence firms. Management consultants will refrain from such practices.

ANALYSE THE ASSUMPTIONS

The work plan

The project manager of the consultancy firm typically develops a work plan (see Chapter 11). The plan is the basis for delegating the tasks to the project team members. The project manager uses the plan to divide the work among the team members. The work plan should give detailed and concrete instructions to the team members and may cover one or more hypotheses. For each hypothesis, the work plan elaborates all assumptions. Table 13.3 provides a simplified elaboration of one assumption of a hypothesis.

TABLE 13.3 *Plan the work for a hypothesis test*

Assumption	Sub-assumption	Analysis	Data	Data sources	Deliverable	Consultant	Deadline
Assumption 1: Country X is an attractive market.	Market is large.	Driver analysis	Households; cats per household; consumption per cat	Government statistics; market research reports; client data	Bar chart comparison of market in country X and other countries	Jim	June 1
	Market growth is high.	...	...	...	...	...
	Profitability of incumbents is high.					
Assumption ...	...	...	...	...	...	...

AcStrat Consulting – analyse the assumptions

Analysis: current combined revenues

The consultants collect data about clients of AcStrat and Delta and the revenues for these clients. Based on the data, the consultants identify three areas for cross-selling (see Table 13.4).

Analysis: expected cross-selling opportunities

The consultants calculate the ratios between the revenues of the three service categories for the overlapping clients (strategy development : strategy implementation : other services = 1 : 5 : 10). Let us assume that these ratios may be applied to the other (non-overlapping) clients as well. Based on this assumption, they calculate the cross-selling opportunities (see Table 13.5). We would acknowledge that this assumption may be an oversimplification. The non-overlapping client bases of AcStrat and Delta probably differ from the overlapping clients. As a consequence, the revenue ratios may differ from those of the overlapping clients. However, this assumption is beyond our simplified example.

TABLE 13.4 *Identify the areas for cross-selling*

Revenues (mln USD)	Strategy development	Strategy implementation	Other services provided by Delta	Total
Overlapping clients	125	625	1250	2000
AcStrat only clients	400	X sell opportunity	X sell opportunity	400
Delta only clients	X sell opportunity	4000	8000	12000
Total	525	4625	9250	14400

Note: 'X sell' refers to cross sell; 'overlapping clients' refers to organizations that are both clients of AcStrat and clients of Delta

TABLE 13.5 *Analyse the cross-selling opportunities*

Revenues (mln USD)	Strategy development	Strategy implementation	Other services provided by Delta	Total
Overlapping clients	125	1250	2500	3875
AcStrat only clients	400	2000	4000	6400
Delta only clients	800	4200	8400	13400
Total	1325	7450	14900	23675

UNCERTAINTY

Future solutions

There are limits to what data collection may contribute to hypothesis testing. Data are by definition about the past. There are no facts about what will happen in the future. Only if one assumes that the future will be like the past, can one extrapolate historical facts. However, this is a dangerous assumption.

The consultants' recommended solution is always about the future. The client has not yet implemented the solution. First, the client needs to adopt the consultants' recommended solution. Then the client needs to implement the solution. Implementation takes time. Therefore, we may conclude that solutions are about the future.

As solutions are about the future, and because there are no facts about the future, consultants cannot test a hypothesis about a solution before that solution has been implemented. Therefore, the consultants cannot guarantee certainty when they recommend a solution to their client. At best, the consultants' analyses of the assumptions underlying the hypothesis may indicate the likelihood that the solution will generate the predicted result. Of course, the level of uncertainty may vary by the type of client problem or opportunity. For instance, compare a consultant's recommended solution for a cost reduction in the client's operations with a recommendation to enter an industry that is completely new to the client.

Chart the key uncertainties

DEVELOP SCENARIOS   We will discuss two techniques that consultants may use for dealing with uncertainty. First, consultants may chart the key uncertainties that face the client. The consultants may identify what are the main drivers of uncertainty. Based on these drivers, the consultants may develop alternative scenarios for the future. For instance, the client is the European airplane manufacturer World Aircraft Corporation (WAC). WAC faces increasing competition from manufacturers in the emerging markets, which reduces its profit. The firm has hired management consultants to provide advice about how WAC should respond to this competition in order to return to its original profit before the increase in competition. Which solution may work best for WAC depends among other things on how the global airplane market develops. The consultants identify some main drivers of uncertainty in this market, among which are the price of jet fuel and the degree of regulation of markets (see Figure 13.14 on the next page). The fuel price influences the volume of air transportation, and thus the number of airplanes required, as well as what type of airplanes will be most in demand. The degree of market regulation also influences how the volume for air transportation will develop, and consequently it influences the demand for airplanes, both the number of planes and the mix of types.

FIGURE 13.14 *Develop scenarios*

DRAW DECISION TREES   In the project for the airplane manufacturer WAC, the consultants may develop a hypothesis about a price reduction. The hypothesis says: reducing the prices enables WAC to return to its original profit level under the increasing competition from emerging market competitors. A price reduction is effective in securing profit if the following conditions are met: either the price reduction leads to increased demand (implying a high price elasticity of demand), or the competitors cannot or will not match the client's price reductions. These conditions represent the assumptions. In this case both assumptions need to be verified to accept the hypothesis. The consultants build a financial model (in Excel) to calculate the client's profit under the different values in these two assumptions. Based on these calculations, the consultants may draw a decision tree to chart the uncertainties (see Figure 13.15 on the next page).

Conduct a sensitivity analysis

ASSESS THE IMPACT OF UNCERTAINTY   In the second technique for dealing with uncertainty, the consultants may assess the impact of uncertainty on their solution. How will uncertainty affect the result of the solution? The sensitivity of a solution to uncertainties determines the value of that solution. Assume that in the project for WAC the consultants identify in total three main drivers of uncertainty: fuel price, market regulation, and economic

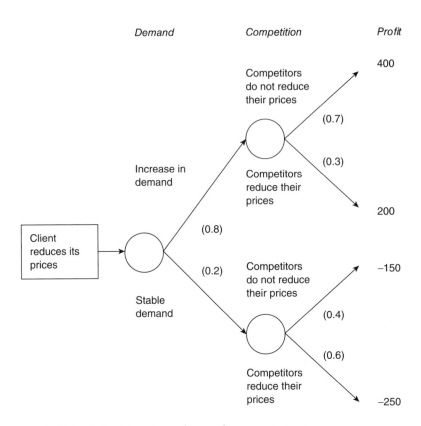

Demand   Competition   Profit

400

Competitors
do not reduce
their prices

(0.7)

Increase in
demand

(0.3)

Competitors
reduce their
prices

200

Client
reduces its
prices

(0.8)

(0.2)

Competitors
do not reduce
their prices

−150

Stable
demand

(0.4)

(0.6)

Competitors
reduce their
prices

−250

FIGURE 13.15 *A decision tree charts the uncertainties*

Note: The number between brackets indicates the probability of an event occurring.

growth. For each driver the consultants may estimate how the different values of drivers create different profit levels for their client. The consultants use their financial model to calculate the profits under the different values of these drivers. Figure 13.16 on the next page visualizes the impact of the different drivers on the client's result. The consultants rank the drivers by the spread between the lowest result and the highest result. The driver which creates the largest spread has the largest impact on the result. The result is most sensitive to that driver. The consultants rank the drivers in descending order of their spread, or in descending impact on the result. Because the bars in Figure 13.16 resemble a tornado, the figure is called a tornado diagram.

Uncertainty and communication

When the consultants present their recommendation (the recommended solution), it should be clear to the client what the level of certainty is for this recommendation. For the client's decision making it is critical to know

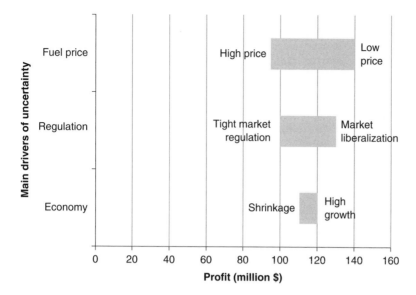

FIGURE 13.16 *A tornado diagram visualizes the sensitivity of solutions*

how certain it is that the recommended solution will generate the desired result. Consultants should therefore indicate the level of certainty of their recommendation. Consultants may use the so-called Harvey balls[1] to indicate that certainty (see Figure 13.17). For instance, the consultants may recommend to WAC to enter country X. The market for airplanes in that country seems attractive. However, country X has a high degree of corruption and organized crime. These factors may undermine WAC's profit in that country and lower the level of certainty of the solution's result.

FIGURE 13.17 *Harvey balls indicating the degree of certainty*

Solutions that deal with uncertainty

CONTINGENCY PLANNING   Given the uncertainty about the effectiveness of their 'best' solution, what should consultants do? Consultants may consider several options to deal with uncertainty. First, they may develop

---

[1]Named after Harvey Popel. He was a consultant with the consultancy firm Booz Allen & Hamilton. Popel introduced this use of the symbol in the 1970s.

multiple solutions for different futures. They may develop a (limited) number of scenarios. For different scenarios they may develop different solutions. They will recommend a solution for the most probable scenario. The other solutions are then back-ups. When (at a later stage) it becomes clear that an alternative scenario will emerge, then the client may switch to the alternative solution, which the consultants have developed for that particular scenario. This is contingency planning.

HEDGING   Second, the consultants may develop one solution that is robust enough to deliver acceptable results for the client under different scenarios. Of course there is a trade-off between results and the robustness of a solution. A 'specialist' solution that is fine-tuned to a specific scenario will outperform the generalist solution if that particular scenario evolves. However, if an alternative scenario evolves then the generalist solution will still produce an acceptable result, while the specialist solution may fail completely. An example to increase robustness is hedging. For instance, for an airliner the fuel price is the main driver of uncertainty. The consultants may bet on a low fuel price and develop a recommendation that fits a low price scenario. However, the consultants may make their solution more robust by including hedging against price increases. Of course, such hedging costs money. However, it reduces the downward risk for the client. It is an insurance premium.

STAGE GATES   Third, the consultants may manage the risk to the client by developing a solution that postpones commitment until uncertainty diminishes to an acceptable level. An example is the stage gate approach to innovation projects. Consultants may recommend to the client to invest in a new technology as it seems an attractive opportunity. However, the new technology is surrounded by high uncertainties. The consultants may recommend a limited initial investment in a first stage development of the technology. If the client successfully completes this stage, then the consultants will recommend that the client increases its commitment to the new technology. This increasing commitment means a larger investment in the next stage. However, if the stage is not successful, then the client can withdraw with relatively small costs incurred.

REAL OPTIONS   Fourth, a variation on the postponement strategy is the real option. Consultants may advise the client to purchase a real option. For instance, the client faces a possible opportunity in a new technology or a new market. However, uncertainty is still high. Therefore, the client is reluctant to commit large resources in the early (and uncertain) stage. The client wants to wait and see what will happen: will the opportunity evolve or not? However, the client wants to avoid missing the boat. If it becomes clear that the opportunity will evolve, the client may be too late to seize the opportunity. The consultants may advise the client to purchase a real option, which is a right to play in the new game (of the opportunity). As an example of a real option, the client may purchase (an equity stake in) a company that is betting on the new opportunity. Alternatively, the client may set up a relatively small business unit that will bet on the opportunity. This unit is another real option. If the opportunity takes off, then the client may use its real option (its stake in the external company or its own business unit) as a launcher to scale up its commitment and seize the full benefits of the opportunity.

Evaluate solution options

Under uncertainty, the consultants may end up with multiple solutions. Each one of these solutions has been analysed and accepted. The assumptions of these solutions have been accepted. But due to uncertainty, the consultants may not have been able to verify each assumption with facts. The effect of a solution may depend on some circumstances, which are uncertain. There may not be a single solution that outperforms the other solutions under all circumstances (scenarios). The relative performance of individual solutions varies with the circumstances. Take the example of the airplane manufacturer WAC. The consultants have identified three alternative solutions (X, Y, and Z). They use their financial model to calculate the profit of each solution under each of the four scenarios. Figure 13.18 visualizes the outcomes of these calculations.

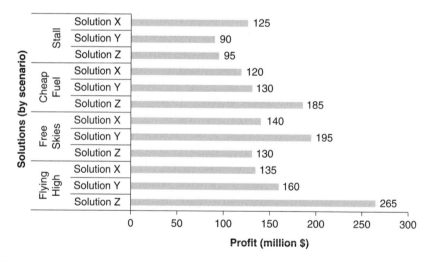

FIGURE 13.18 *Profit under different scenarios*

The consultants may attach a probability to each of the four scenarios. Based on these probabilities, the consultants may calculate the expected profit of each solution under the four scenarios (see Figure 13.19). The expected profit is the weighted average of the profits of that solution in the four scenarios. The probabilities determine the weights of the individual scenarios.

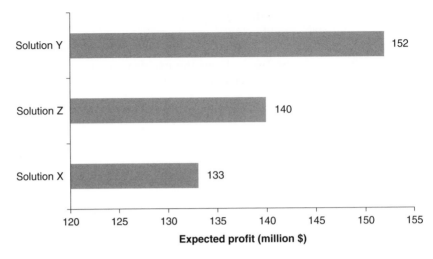

FIGURE 13.19 *The expected profit for alternative solutions*

MAKE DECISIONS ABOUT THE SOLUTION

Competing solutions

SINGLE BEST SOLUTION   The consultants recommend the solution but the client decides on the solution. Regarding the recommendations to the client, we may distinguish two situations. First, the consultants have identified a single best solution. By this we mean that one solution outperforms any alternative solution on each one of the client's selection criteria (as specified upfront in the problem statement). In this situation it is easy for the consultants to make a recommendation because all of the client's criteria point in the same direction, meaning the same solution. If that solution satisfies all of the client's criteria in a superior way, then the decision for the client is also easy. The client should adopt the consultants' recommended solution.

NO CLEAR WINNER   However, in the second situation the consultants have identified alternative solutions without a clear winner. There is no single solution that is always better than the others. Different solutions will win according to different criteria of the client. Even on a single criterion, different solutions may win in different scenarios (for instance, see Figure 13.18). In such situations, consultants may be better off refraining from recommending any single solution. Instead of making the selection for their client, the consultants should present alternative solutions to the client. In this situation, selecting a solution involves trade-offs between the advantages of individual solutions. Deciding on these trade-offs is the responsibility of the client. The consultants may only facilitate the client's decision making.

AN INTRODUCTION TO MANAGEMENT CONSULTANCY

They may do so by making the decision alternatives and the trade-offs as transparent as possible. Table 13.6 provides an example of what consultants may do. The consultants know upfront which criteria the client will use to select a solution. In fact, the consultants will have specified the client's decision criteria in the problem statement (see Chapter 12).

TABLE 13.6 *Evaluate alternative solutions*

	Contribution to result	Ease of implementation	Risk	Overall
Solution X	◗	●	◣	◗
Solution Y	●	◗	◗	◕
Solution Z	◕	◣	◗	◗

Note: The Harvey balls indicate the score for a solution on a criterion

EVALUATE SOLUTIONS   Assume that the client has defined three decision criteria: contribution to result, ease of implementation, and risk. The ease of implementation refers to the complexity and the amount of work, and the required resources to execute the solution. Risk refers to the probability that the solution may not create the desired result. This risk has got to do with the probability that the client cannot implement the solution, as well as the probability that the client can implement the solution but the solution does not work. The consultants evaluate each solution on each criterion and subsequently calculate a weighted average (the overall score).

If the client prioritizes the solution's contribution to the result then the client should adopt solution Y. However, if ease of implementation is most important to the client, then they should choose solution X.

THE CONTRIBUTION OF THE SOLUTION   Assume the client decides to adopt solution Y. Figure 13.20 on the next page visualizes how this solution contributes to the client's profit. After all, the solution is about closing the client's result gap. This figure shows what result the client will achieve when they implement the solution.

Non-competing solutions

MAP COMPLEMENTARY SOLUTIONS   Not all solutions are alternatives, meaning that the client needs to choose between them: 'either A or C'. Some solutions are non-competing and may be combined: 'both B and C'. Sometimes the solutions will have to be combined to achieve the desired

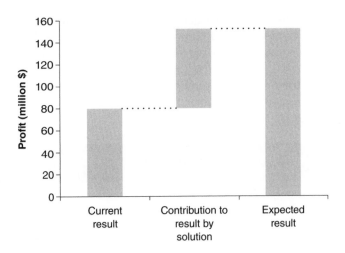

FIGURE 13.20 *The contribution to the result by the solution*

result (see Figure 13.22). For instance, no single solution is able to close the client's result gap. The client needs to combine several (non-competing) solutions to close the gap. Assume that the client has only two criteria for decision making about solutions: the contribution of the solution to the result and the ease of implementation of the solutions. Figure 13.21 provides a map for plotting the solutions. For instance, the client has a profit gap. The consultants

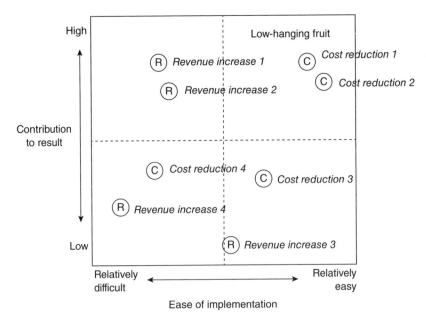

FIGURE 13.21 *Map of complementary solutions*

AN INTRODUCTION TO MANAGEMENT CONSULTANCY

have come up with several non-competing solutions to increase revenues (in the figure labelled as: 'Revenue increase #'). But they have also identified various non-competing solutions to reduce costs (labelled as: 'Cost reduction #').

CHOOSE A SEQUENCE   The consultants may divide the map into four quadrants. The top right quadrant represents the 'low-hanging fruit solutions': these solutions provide a relatively high contribution to the client's result while they are relatively easy to implement. The client will probably focus first on the solutions in this quadrant. The bottom left quadrant contains the least attractive solutions because these promise a relatively low result contribution, while they are relatively difficult to implement. The solutions in this quadrant are the lowest priority for the client. Assume that the client selects five non-competing solutions: three solutions for a cost reduction (1, 2, and 3), and two solutions for a revenue increase (1 and 2). Figure 13.22 shows how these five non-competing solutions together will allow the client to close the result gap.

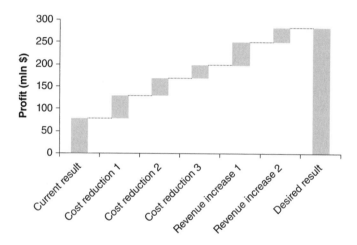

FIGURE 13.22   *Multiple complementary solutions to close the result gap*

PLAN FOR IMPLEMENTATION

Lower the level of abstraction

The client has adopted a solution. The solution prescribes how the client should close the result gap: 'If you do this, then you achieve that'. It promises a result improvement. The solution holds the potential for a result improvement. To realize this result improvement, the client needs to implement the solution. Implementation of the solution means actions. To achieve results, the actions should be concrete. Actions take place at the level of the individual actors inside or outside the client organization. However, the solution typically demands a high level of abstraction (for instance, the client should acquire a competitor with complementary competences to achieve the desired result). To realize the result, the individual actors need concrete instructions, which are actions defined at a low level of abstraction. The high-level solution therefore needs to be translated into low-level actions for individual actors.

Prepare for implementation

The consultants may increase their value to the client by making this translation. Implementation is a new project, after the problem solving project. The translation into actions is a work breakdown structure (see Chapter 11). The more hierarchical the client organization, the more translations to lower levels the consultants need to make. Figure 13.23 gives a stylized example. The client organization consists of a number of units. Each unit consists of sub-units. Each sub-unit consists of a number of individual actors. The consultants may first translate the solution to the level of the client's units. The consultants may break up the solution into high-level actions for each unit. Next, the consultants (together with the unit manager) may translate the high-level actions into lower-level actions for sub-units. Finally, the consultants translate the actions for sub-units into concrete actions for

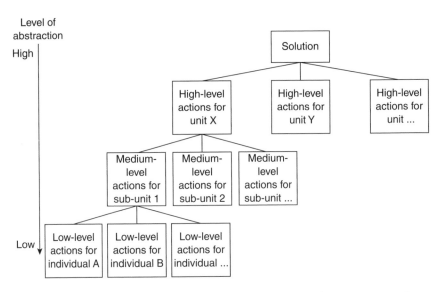

FIGURE 13.23 *Translate the solution into increasingly concrete actions*

Note: To keep this figure clear, it only shows the breakdown for unit X. However, in a complete action plan, the consultants break down the high-level actions for unit Y and Z to the level of actions for individual actors.

individual employees with these sub-units. As implementation is a project, the resources have to be allocated and a time plan needs to be made. Chapter 15 will elaborate on implementation.

SUMMARY

The structured solution development process consists of a series of steps (see Figure 13.24).

1. The consultants identify what are the key decisions that the client may take to solve the problem.
2. The consultants generate ideas for possible solutions to the problem based on these decisions. They develop a logical structure for these possible solutions.
3. They select the seemingly best solution from the structure of possible solutions. This will become their initial hypothesis.
4. They identify and structure the assumptions of this hypothesis.
5. For each assumption, the consultants design and execute an analysis. If all assumptions are verified then the consultants have a solution.
6. If they have to reject one or more assumptions, then the consultants have to select another hypothesis from the structure of possible solutions. Hypothesis selection and testing can therefore be an iterative process.
7. The consultants break down the solution into actions to facilitate implementation.

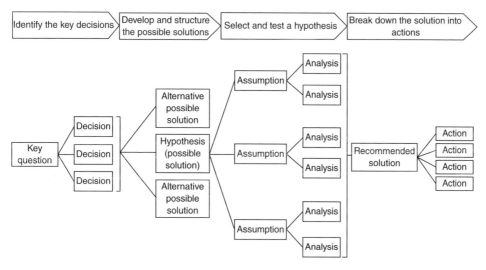

FIGURE 13.24 *The structured solution development process*

Ivy Business School

The previous chapter illustrated how the consultants developed an opportunity statement for the Ivy Business School. They formulated the following key question: how should Ivy respond to the development of online learning technologies to reach a 5 per cent share of the global higher business education market within ten years?

Identify the decisions

What levers may the Ivy Business School pull? The consultants identify the decisions that Ivy may take to solve the problem. The consultants identify the key decision areas (see Table 13.7).

Develop possible solutions

The consultants identify what options Ivy has for each decision area. These options are the alternative decision outcomes.

TABLE 13.7 *Identify decision areas and alternative outcomes*

Decision area	Alternative decision outcomes
Target clients	• Tier 1 students • Tier 2 students
Timing of entry into online learning	• Enter now • Wait until online learning technologies meet requirements of tier 1 students.
Programmes for online learning	• All programmes • A selection of programmes
Value proposition for online learning	• Immersion (pure online or a blended offering of online and residential learning) • Selectivity (admission standards) • Certification and branding (same as residential or differentiated) • Knowledge (same content as residential or differentiated) • Tuition
Development and delivery infrastructure for online learning • Programme development • Online delivery platform • Network of satellite campuses (for blended offering)	• In-house • Outsourcing • Alliance

Structure possible solutions and select an initial hypothesis

The consultants explore the most probable solutions and put them in a structure (see Figure 13.25). Next, they select the best candidate solution to serve as their initial hypothesis. This hypothesis consists of four sub-hypotheses, existing at different levels of the structure (see the highlighted boxes in Figure 13.25).

Identify and structure the assumptions of the initial hypothesis

The consultants identify the assumptions for each sub-hypothesis. Table 13.8

presents the sub-hypotheses and their underlying assumptions.

Design the analyses of the assumptions

The consultants need to verify the assumptions underlying the hypothesis. As an illustration, we focus on the following assumptions of the sub-hypothesis to target tier 2 students:

- Tier 2 students prefer top ranked school online learning over lower ranked school residential learning.
- Tier 1 students prefer top ranked school residential learning over top ranked school online learning.

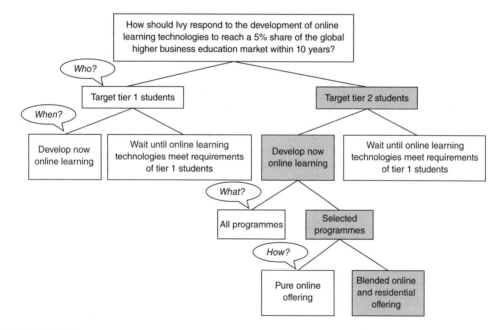

FIGURE 13.25 *Structure possible solutions and select the hypothesis*

TABLE 13.8 *Identify and structure the underlying assumptions*

Decision	Sub-hypothesis	Underlying assumptions
Who?	Target tier 2 students	• Tier 2 students prefer top ranked school online learning over lower ranked school residential learning. • Tier 1 students prefer top ranked school residential learning over top ranked school online learning.

When?	Develop now online learning	• Online learning disrupts lower ranked school residential learning now.
		• There are first mover advantages for top ranked schools.
		• Ivy has the resources and capabilities to develop online learning for tier 2 students:
		  o Ivy Publishing has experience with marketing to tier 2 students.
		  o Ivy Publishing has the resources and capabilities for product development.
		  o Ivy Business School has sufficient financial reserves for investments in the development of online learning content and infrastructure.

What?	Selected programmes	• Online learning technologies do not (yet) meet the content requirements of all programmes. • Benefits of online learning vary across programmes.
How?	Blended online & residential offering	• Tier 2 students prefer blended over pure online offerings. • Blended offering enables Ivy to differentiate by using its core strength of immersion.

The consultants have to analyse the key drivers of the students' purchasing decision regarding higher business education. The consultants decide to conduct focus interviews and a survey to identify the key purchasing decision criteria for both tiers of students.

Next, the consultants decide to benchmark the Ivy residential offering against the Ivy blended offering and lower ranked schools' residential offerings. The consultants intend to use a survey for this benchmark.

The consultants develop a driver analysis of the purchasing decisions of tier 1 and tier 2 students. To identify the drivers, the consultants first do a round of focus interviews with students to develop an idea of the key purchasing decision criteria and their relative importance (weight in students' decision making). Subsequently, the consultants set up a survey to validate the

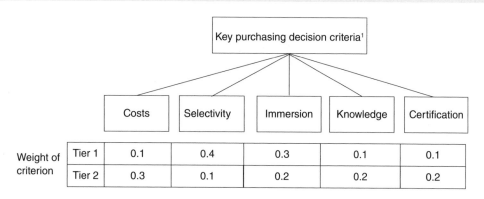

FIGURE 13.26 *Identify the drivers*

Note: (1) Costs are the author's addition. Other criteria are based on Laseter (2012). The weights of the criteria are fictitious numbers.

interview results. Figure 13.26 presents the results of the research: the key purchasing criteria used by students. The weights that students attach to the individual criteria vary by tier of students.

Analyse the assumptions

How does Ivy Blended compare with alternatives regarding the key purchasing decision criteria of tier 1 and tier 2 stu-

TABLE 13.9 *Analyse the preferences of tier 1 students*

Tier 1 students		Unweighted score			Weighted score		
Criterion	Weight	Tier 2 school Residential	Ivy Blended	Ivy Residential	Tier 2 School Residential	Ivy Blended	Ivy Residential
Tuition (0.1)	0.1	5	3	1	0.5	0.3	0.1
Selectivity (0.4)	0.4	1	3	5	0.4	1.2	2
Immersion (0.3)	0.3	4	3	5	1.2	0.9	1.5
Knowledge (0.1)	0.1	2	4	5	0.2	0.4	0.5
Certification (0.1)	0.1	1	4	5	0.1	0.4	0.5
Total (1.0)	1				2.4	3.2	4.6

TABLE 13.10 *Analyse the preferences of tier 2 students*

Tier 2 students		Unweighted score			Weighted score		
Criterion	Weight	Tier 2 school Residential	Ivy Blended	Ivy Residential	Tier 2 School Residential	Ivy Blended	Ivy Residential
Tuition (0.3)	0.3	5	3	1	1.5	0.9	0.3
Selectivity (0.1)	0.1	1	3	5	0.1	0.3	0.5
Immersion (0.2)	0.2	4	3	5	0.8	0.6	1
Knowledge (0.2)	0.2	2	4	5	0.4	0.8	1
Certification (0.2)	0.2	1	4	5	0.2	0.8	1
Total (1.0)	1				3	3.4	3.8

dents? The consultants develop a benchmark analysis of these key purchasing decision criteria. They identify the relevant benchmark, which is a selection of schools, and use the survey to collect the data. The score per criterion ranges from 1 (lowest) to 5 (highest). Tables 13.9 and 13.10 show the results of the analysis.

Interpret the results of the analyses

The results of the analyses confirm the assumptions.

- All students prefer top ranked school residential learning over top ranked school online learning.

- All students prefer top ranked school online learning over lower ranked school residential learning.

Tier 1 students can afford top ranked school residential learning and will therefore not consider top ranked school online learning. In contrast, tier 2 students cannot afford top ranked school residential learning. Those tier 2 students who can afford top ranked school online learning will prefer this offering over lower ranked school residential learning.

Based on the results of the analyses, the consultants develop the output charts (see Figure 13.27) and present these charts to the steering committee.

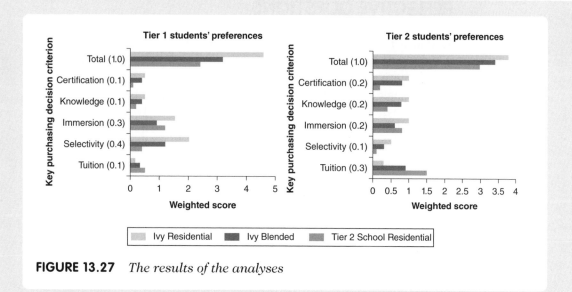

FIGURE 13.27 *The results of the analyses*

EXERCISES

1. The partners of Acme Consulting think that online consultancy may be an opportunity. Online consultancy is offering web-based services (diagnostic software, data sets, and advice), which clients may use to solve their problems (and seize opportunities). The firm has set up a task force to explore this opportunity. As a partner of Acme's taskforce you have to estimate how much revenue there is to be made with online consultancy worldwide in the coming five years. Design a two-level driver analysis for estimating this revenue opportunity. Each level should contain no more than seven drivers. The structure should be insightful, actionable, and MECE.

2. Assume the size of the online consultancy opportunity is $X billion. Acme wants to realize a 10 per cent share of this opportunity. Formulate the key question for Acme. Explain your answer.

3. What decisions may Acme take with regard to the online consultancy opportunity? Identify the key decision areas.

4. Building on the decision areas, formulate a hypothesis and create a structure of assumptions for this hypothesis (one level of assumptions, maximally seven).

REFLECTIVE QUESTIONS

1. Management consultants formulate and test hypotheses about possible solutions. How can management consultants develop higher quality hypotheses? Explain your answer.

2. Management consultants create draft presentations based on their initial hypothesis *before* they collect and analyse the data to test this hypothesis. Isn't this inefficient because they may have to reject their initial hypothesis? Why do they do this? Elaborate on your answer.

3. Management consultants strive for fact-based analysis to support their solution development. What should they do if the required data are not available? Explain your answer.

FURTHER READING

Courtney, H. (2001) *20/20 Foresight: Crafting Strategy in an Uncertain World*. Boston, MA: Harvard Business School Publishing.

Gottfredson, M. and Schaubert, S. (2008) *The Breakthrough Imperative: How the Best Managers Get Outstanding Results*. New York: HarperCollins.

Kaplan, R.S. and Norton, D.P. (2004) *Strategy Maps: Converting Intangible Assets into Tangible Outcomes*. Boston, MA: Harvard Business School Publishing.

Koller, T., Goedhart, M. and Wessels, D. (2005) *Valuation: Measuring and Managing the Value of Companies* (4th edn). Hoboken, NJ: Wiley.

Minto, B. (1987) *The Pyramid Principle: Logic in Writing and Thinking* (revised 3rd edn). London: Minto International Inc.

Ohmae, K. (1991) *The Mind of the Strategist: The Art of Japanese Business*. New York: McGraw-Hill.

REFERENCES

Ansoff, I. (1957) 'Strategies for diversification', *Harvard Business Review*, 35 (5): 113–124.

Kaplan, R.S. and Norton, D.P. (2004) *Strategy Maps: Converting Intangible Assets into Tangible Outcomes*. Boston, MA: Harvard Business School Publishing.

Kim, W. and Mauborgne, R. (2005) *Blue Ocean Strategy: How to Create Uncontested Market Space and Make the Competition Irrelevant*. Boston, MA: Harvard Business School Press.

Laseter, T. (2012) 'The university's dilemma', *Strategy + Business*, 27 November 2012. Available at: www.strategy-business.com/article/00147?gko=da535 (accessed 6 April 2013).

Ohmae, K. (1991) *The Mind of the Strategist: The Art of Japanese Business*. New York: McGraw-Hill.

Porter, M.E. (1985) *Competitive Advantage: Creating and Sustaining Superior Performance*. New York: The Free Press.

14

STRUCTURED COMMUNICATIONS

INTRODUCTION

Top tier consultancy approach

This chapter focuses on the development of a well-structured communication of the recommended solution. It is indicative of some of the methods and techniques used by the top tier management consultants, such as McKinsey & Company, the Boston Consulting Group, and Bain & Company. An important work in this respect is Barbara Minto's *The Pyramid Principle: Logic in Writing and Thinking* (1987).

From solution to decision

This chapter focuses on PowerPoint presentations as they are a very important medium for consultancy presentations. However, the methods and techniques may also be applied to presentations using other software and to written reports. The purpose of the presentation is to introduce the solution and get the client to progress from solution to decision. We address the question: how to structure a client presentation to increase its effectiveness? Structuring creates presentations that are easier to understand, are more convincing, and take less time and fewer slides.

Develop the presentation before data analysis

We have located this chapter about communication after the chapters on structured diagnosis and solution development and before the chapter about implementation. However, we would acknowledge and emphasize that communication takes place at *all* stages of the consultancy project. What is more, top tier consultants design their first draft of the final presentation after they have developed their initial hypothesis and before they begin with data collection and analysis.

Focus on key message

This chapter explains the top tier consultants' method for structuring client presentations. This method concentrates on the key message to the client and the underlying argumentation. The consultants translate the presentation structure into a sequence of PowerPoint slides, whereby each slide carries a message. This chapter also explains how to design an effective slide. We illustrate the method with the running case study about AcStrat Consulting. The chapter ends with a summary, the running mini case study about the Ivy Business School, exercises, reflective questions, and suggested further reading.

Main learning objectives

- Understand the importance and the role of presentations in consultancy projects.
- Know how to structure a (final and interim) presentation.
- Know how to select the appropriate structure for a particular audience.
- Know how to develop the argumentation.
- Know how to develop a story board.
- Understand the concept of horizontal flow.
- Know how to develop a slide title.
- Understand the concept of vertical flow.
- Know how to develop a slide body.

COMMUNICATIONS DURING THE PROJECT

All forms of communication

This chapter is about the structured approach to communications as used by top tier management consultants. The methods and techniques of structured communication are applicable to all forms of communication such as PowerPoint presentations, written (text) reports, email, and verbal communication. We illustrate the approach with the PowerPoint presentations that these consultants often use. We use PowerPoint presentations as an example of structured communication because they lend themselves very well to illustration, and because PowerPoint is very popular in top tier consultancy. Top tier consultants may call a presentation a 'deck' (of PowerPoint slides).

Use of presentations

Consultants will use presentations during the entire consultancy cycle. The use of presentation starts before the project. Consultants may use PowerPoint presentations of their project proposal to convince the client and sell the project. During the preparation for the project, the project manager may use presentations to inform the steering committee and the project team members about the planned approach. During the problem solving project and also during the solution implementation project consultants will use presentations in various settings.

PRESENTATIONS FOR TEAM MEETINGS   First, the project team uses presentations in their team meetings. The project manager uses presentations to delegate the work. The team members use PowerPoint presentations to present their results to the project manager and the other team members. PowerPoint presentations are the means by which to share ideas, exchange information, and align activities.

PRESENTATIONS FOR STEERING COMMITTEE MEETINGS   Second, the project manager uses presentations for meetings with the steering committee. The presentation is about the progress of the team. It contains the results that the project team has achieved. The presentation may also include topics on which the committee has to decide or provide feedback. The steering committee uses the presentations by the project manager as a control mechanism. After the consultants have developed their solution, they will use presentations to convince the client. The purpose of such presentations is to get the client to decide to adopt the solution.

PRESENTATIONS FOR STAKEHOLDERS' MEETINGS   Third, during the problem solving project, the consultants may give presentations to other stakeholders, beyond the client members in the steering committee. Consultants may organize meetings with stakeholders in the client organization. The consultants present information about the purpose and progress of the project. These presentations serve various goals. By informing the stakeholders, the consultants strive to induce a positive attitude among the stakeholders. Consultants will need the cooperation of (some) stakeholders in order to conduct the project successfully. Consultants may use presentations to solicit feedback from the stakeholders. The presentations also serve to create support among stakeholders. Support for the solution is important for the implementation of that solution. When the consultants implement their solution, communicating with stakeholders is even more important. Consultants may use this communication to create a sense of urgency among stakeholders that implementation of the solution is necessary. Chapter 15 elaborates on the role of communication during implementation.

DEVELOPING THE FINAL PRESENTATION

Develop the argumentation

The final presentation to the client is to show not what the consultants have done ('We have done so many and such complex data collection and analyses') but rather what the client should do ('You should implement the recommended solution'). This section focuses on the final presentation to the client.

We can distinguish between interim presentations and the final presentation of the project. During the interim presentations (to the steering committee) the consultants present their progress. The final presentation takes place at the end of the project. The consultants have developed a solution for the client. In the final presentation they present their recommendation to the client. The purpose is to explain the solution and get the client to adopt the solution. Recall that it is the client that makes the decision. The only thing that consultants can do is to induce the client to accept their solution. The presentation should therefore be clear and convincing. The argumentation for the solution is critical. This argumentation should be strong. Therefore, the top tier consultants will use a structured approach. The structure is about the argumentation.

Develop the structure

Developing the structure for the final presentation does not begin only after the solution has been developed. At the start of the solution development phase, the top tier consultants already begin developing the final presentation. After they have formulated their initial hypothesis, the consultants develop a first draft of their final presentation (see Figure 14.1). This draft is based on the expected solution (their initial hypothesis). They may create a draft structure for that presentation. Of course, consultants may have to adapt their structure during the project if they have to reject their hypothesis or if unforeseen developments occur. The creation of a presentation may be an iterative process. By creating a draft of the final presentation, the consultants know what to focus on. They have already defined their end product. They can now work with that end product in mind.

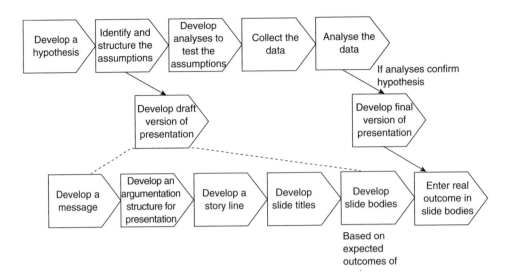

FIGURE 14.1 *Develop the first draft before the analyses*

Understand the audience for the final presentation

The consultants adapt their presentation to the audience. The purpose of the presentation is to convince the client to adopt the solution. The consultants should understand the client's decision making process. In the problem statement they have already identified the client's decision criteria and constraints. They have also identified the key stakeholders. For the final presentation, the consultants need to know who is in the audience. Which stakeholders are in the audience for the final presentation? For the preparation of the final presentation, the consultants focus on three characteristics of the stakeholders in the audience.

LACK OF KNOWLEDGE   First, the consultants have to take into account the stakeholders' prior knowledge about the subject of the presentation. How much do the stakeholders already know about the problem and the solution? The audience may include client managers who are not part of the steering committee and other members of the client organization. They will typically lack (detailed) knowledge about the project. The less the audience knows, the more the consultants have to explain.

NEGATIVE STANCE TOWARDS THE SOLUTION   Moreover, the consultants need to take into consideration the attitude of the stakeholders towards the presentation's subject. If the stakeholders deny the problem, than the consultants need to provide arguments for the problem's existence. If the stakeholders take a negative stance towards the consultants' recommended solution, than the consultants have to pay more attention to the defence of their solution.

NEGATIVE STANCE TOWARDS CONSULTANTS Finally, the consultants have to consider the attitude of the stakeholders towards consultants. Some may have a negative stance towards consultants. Even if these stakeholders acknowledge the problem and appreciate the solution, they may still object because it is consultants who propose the solution. The consultants should then anticipate even opposition against a well-argued recommendation.

Develop the long version of the final presentation

ADAPT TO THE AUDIENCE Depending on the characteristics of the audience (knowledge about the subject, attitude towards the subject, and attitude towards the consultants), the consultants will choose either a long or short presentation. They will have to choose a long presentation if the audience (or members of it) has a lack of knowledge, or a negative attitude towards the subject or towards the consultants. Each of these conditions – knowledge about subject, attitude towards subject, and attitude towards consultants – is sufficient to choose a long presentation. To deal with the lack of stakeholders' knowledge, the consultants need to explain more. To deal with the negative attitude of stakeholders also takes time and effort. The consultants may choose a short presentation if all members of the audience possess sufficient knowledge, and have a positive, or at least a neutral, attitude towards both the subject and the consultants. In this section we will discuss the long version for a client problem (see Figure 14.2). Hereafter, we

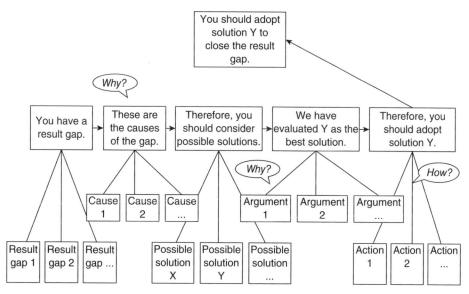

FIGURE 14.2 *Develop a long version of a solution to a problem for uninformed and unfriendly audiences*

present the long version for a solution to a client opportunity. Subsequently we present the short version.

PRESENT THE RESULT GAP   If the project is about a problem, then the consultants will start their presentation with this problem (in Figure 14.2 see the box entitled: 'You have a result gap'). The audience may deny the existence of a problem or they may play it down. Therefore, the consultants should first make the audience acknowledge the problem. The consultants have to show the result gap. They may present the result gap by segment if there are substantial differences between the segments (in Figure 14.2 see the structure of lower-level boxes: result gap 1, result gap 2, result gap ...).

The consultants should make clear to the audience that the result gap is structural. The gap will not go away by itself. To support this message, the consultants may show the historical development of the gap and a prognosis of the future result gap under a 'business-as-usual' scenario. The message is: if the client does not take action, then the result gap will grow.

Of course, all the data presented by the consultants need to be verified in advance by the consultants. If members of the audience can shoot a hole in the gap analysis, the consultants can forget about the rest of their presentation. In particular, members with a negative stance towards the consultants or towards their solution will certainly try to question the consultants' analysis of the client's result gap. Therefore, the gap analysis should be bullet proof. A solid gap analysis forces the audience to acknowledge the existence of the result gap, and hence the problem. Even the most negative members will have to admit the gap. They can no longer deny the problem. Now, they must consider the consultants' solution. The audience may ask: 'Why does the result gap exist?' The consultants will answer this question in the next step of their presentation.

PRESENT THE CAUSES OF THE RESULT GAP   Subsequently, the consultants will explain why the problem exists (in Figure 14.2 see the box entitled: 'These are the causes'). This explanation is important for the audience's understanding of the problem. Showing their understanding of the causes also builds the credibility of the consultants in the eyes of the audience. Furthermore, an understanding of the causes underlies the solution development. Solutions should address the causes. However, presenting the causes may be confrontational and sensitive. If the (main) causes are internal (causes inside the client organization are responsible for the result gap), then it may be interpreted as an accusation (the client organization is to blame). If those accountable for causing the problem are in the audience, then the consultants should anticipate resistance from them. All data and analyses necessary for explaining the problem causes need to be thoroughly verified (check, double check). Opponents should not be able to breach the consultants' argumentation. The consultants can proceed with their conclusion only if the audience accepts the consultants' explanation of the problem (the indicated causes).

If the project is about an opportunity for the client, then the sequence of the presentation is different. The consultants begin with explaining why an opportunity exists. They show the opportunity drivers. The message is: 'These drivers create an opportunity for you'. Next, the consultants show the implications of the drivers: 'Therefore you have a result gap.'

PRESENT THE POSSIBLE SOLUTIONS   Now the audience is ready for the consultants' conclusion. The consultants present the implication of the result gap (in Figure 14.2 see the box entitled: 'Therefore you have to consider possible solutions'). Because of the gap, the client should take action. The consultants may put forward the key question: how should the client respond to the causes to achieve the desired result? This stimulates the audience to think about possible solutions. Subsequently, the consultants present the solutions they have considered. The solution set is not collectively exhaustive because that is not feasible (see Chapter 13). The consultants may use the client's decision criteria and constraints (as described in the problem statement) to justify their choice. Members of the audience might come up with different solutions which are not presented by the consultants. The consultants should be able to explain why they have not included these solutions. Therefore it is important to consider a broad set of decisions and solutions at the beginning of the solution development phase. Such a broad set allows the consultants to anticipate possible opposition by the steering committee or by other audience members during the interim and final presentations.

PRESENT THE EVALUATION OF THE SOLUTIONS   After the consultants have settled any objections against the proposed set of possible solutions, they may present their evaluation of these solutions (in Figure 14.2 see the box entitled: 'We have evaluated Y as the best solution').

Evaluation based on the client's criteria. If the consultants begin with presenting their best solution, the audience may ask themselves: why is it the best solution? Therefore, the consultants should address this 'why' question in advance. First, they present the evaluation criteria. Second, they present the outcome of their evaluation. Based on the outcome, they introduce their recommended solution. They show how implementation of the recommended solution will close the result gap.

Inconclusive evaluation. We would acknowledge that in some projects the evaluation of alternative solutions may be inconclusive: different criteria may point to different solutions. If at all possible, consultants should solve this issue before a final presentation to a broad audience. If the evaluation is inconclusive, then the consultants should put it forward to the steering committee.

Ideally, the steering committee (in a small circle of other influential stakeholders, if any) makes the trade-off between the alternative solutions. In this case, the consultants present the steering committee's choice in the final presentation.

Criticism. Again, opponents may criticize the consultants' solution. They may disapprove of the criteria and constraints. However, these criteria and constraints are the responsibility of the client. The opponents may also question the evaluation techniques and data used by the consultants. The challengers may also criticize the expected contribution of the solution to the client's result. They may doubt the assumptions underlying this prognosis of the result. Consultants should be prepared for such critique. They have to be able to defend any data source, any assumption, and any technique they have used in the evaluation. To support their defence the consultants may prepare backup material to present just in case.

PRESENT THE SOLUTION TO BE ADOPTED If the audience accepts that Y is the best solution given the evaluation criteria, then they may ask: how will the solution work? Now the consultants can make their recommendation (see the box in Figure 14.2 titled: 'Therefore, you should adopt solution Y.'). The consultants explain how the solution may work. They translate the (abstract) solution into concrete actions.

DEVELOPING A PRESENTATION FOR AN OPPORTUNITY Figure 14.2 shows the structure of a presentation of a solution to a problem. Consultants will take a slightly different approach when they present a solution for an opportunity (see Figure 14.3 on the next page). They first have to present the opportunity drivers before they can introduce the opportunity. They need to convince the audience why it may expect an opportunity to exist for the client. After the audience accepts the consultants' explanation, it is ready to learn about the size of the opportunity. The size of the opportunity determines the result gap.

DEVELOP ARGUMENTATION FOR THE SOLUTION We can distinguish between three complementary ways by which consultants provide argumentation for their recommended solution.

Client's criteria In the first approach the consultants explicitly use the client's criteria. Figure 14.4 provides an example. Assume that the client has defined three criteria:

1. Contribution to result.
2. Ease of implementation.
3. Risk.

For each criterion the consultants display how they have evaluated the solution. For each criterion, they benchmark the solution against alternative solutions. The outcomes of these benchmarks are the arguments for the recommended solution. Figure 14.4 only provides qualitative arguments. However, the consultants will strive for (quantitative) fact-based argumentation, to quantify the argumentation whenever possible. For instance, instead of the 'highest contribution to the result' the consultants will give an estimate of this contribution, for instance, $100 million. They may demonstrate ease of implementation by, for example, specifying the required implementation time (for instance, in terms of months), and the required

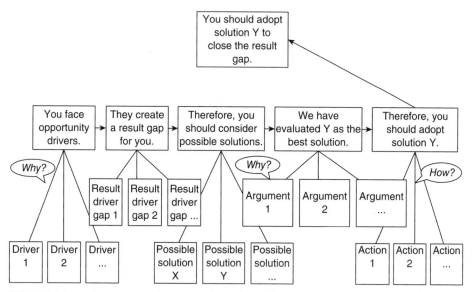

FIGURE 14.3 *Develop a long version of a solution to an opportunity for uninformed and unfriendly audiences*

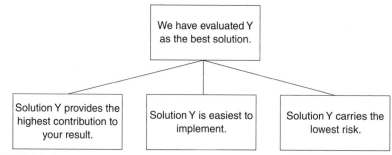

FIGURE 14.4 *Base argumentation on the client's evaluation criteria*

investments in human resources and capital. They may demonstrate the risk of a solution by showing the outcomes of a sensitivity analysis (for instance, a tornado diagram; see Chapter 13).

Deductive arguments   In the second approach for argumentation, the consultants may use the verified assumptions underlying the solution as arguments for justifying their recommendation. In the solution development stage, the consultants formulated a hypothesis about the solution. Subsequently, they defined the underlying assumptions of the hypothesis. They have tested these assumptions and the test results led to verification of the assumptions. These verified assumptions are arguments in favour of the solution. If the hypothesis assumptions are general conditions, then this argumentation is deductive. The consultants move from general conditions to the specific case of the client.

Figure 14.5 provides an example of argumentation that is based on verified assumptions. In the previous chapter, we showed the assumptions underlying a hypothesis about a price reduction. We have used these arguments to build an argumentation for the solution. In Figure 14.5 we do not include quantification. As stated before, consultants will strive for (quantitative) fact-based argumentation.

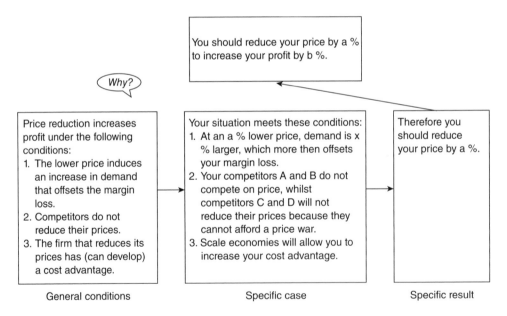

FIGURE 14.5   *Base argumentation on deductive arguments*

Inductive arguments   In the third approach for argumentation, the consultants will use inductive arguments for justifying their recommendation.

In the solution development stage, the consultants may have used induction to test their hypothesis. The consultants use the outcomes of the inductive test as the arguments for the solution (see Figure 14.6).

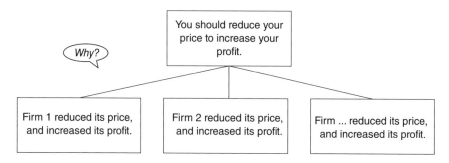

FIGURE 14.6 *Base argumentation on inductive arguments*

ELABORATE THE SOLUTION   If the consultants have offset any objections against the recommended solution, then they may continue with elaborating the solution. They may set out what decisions and actions the client needs to make to implement the recommendation. This exposition may be an introduction to a subsequent discussion about the implementation of the solution.

CASE STUDY

AcStrat Consulting – develop a long version of a presentation

The previous chapter showed how the consultants analysed the assumptions underlying their initial hypothesis about a merger of AcStrat and Delta. Assume that the consultants have analysed all assumptions of their hypothesis.

All assumptions have been verified. Therefore, the consultants accept the hypothesis. The consultants recommend that AcStrat merges with Delta to close its profit gap. The consultants have to present their recommendation to the steering committee of AcStrat. Because the consultants expect some resistance from certain committee members, they develop a long structure to present their solution (see Figure 14.7).

▶

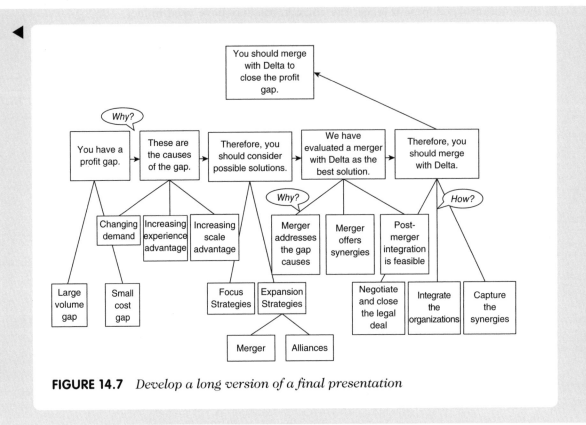

FIGURE 14.7 *Develop a long version of a final presentation*

Develop the short version of a final presentation

UNDERSTANDING THE AUDIENCE The characteristics of the audience influence the choice between a long and a short version of the presentation. Recall that consultants look at the audience members' prior knowledge about the subject, their attitude towards the subject, and their attitude towards consultants. A short version of the final presentation is appropriate under three conditions.

Knowledge. First, the attending stakeholders have a certain level of knowledge about the project. Therefore, the consultants do not have to elaborate on the problem solving. The audience may include client managers who are not part of the steering committee. Though they are not directly involved in the consultancy project, they may still have sufficient knowledge about it.

Attitude towards the solution. Second, the attending stakeholders are expected to have a positive attitude towards the solution. The attendants are unlikely to oppose the proposed solution.

The consultants may have already checked the attitude of the attendants. They may have met the attendants on an individual basis. The consultants may even have tested their recommendation with these attendants to find out how they will react. Alternatively, the consultants may have consulted with their allies in the client organization, who are members with aligned interests who are willing to cooperate with the consultants. These allies of the consultants may provide insights on the attendants' attitude.

Attitude towards the consultants. Third, the attending stakeholders are expected to have a positive attitude towards the consultants. These people do not have negative feelings about the particular consultants or about consultants in general. The consultants may therefore expect a friendly audience.

If these conditions are favourable to the consultants, the final presentation will be relatively easy and therefore the consultants do not need to make a long presentation. A relatively short presentation may suffice. This leaves more time for discussing the next steps in implementing the solution. Of course, the consultants should be prepared for the unexpected.

FALL-BACK PLAN   There is always a chance that the audience, or one or a few members, may respond negatively to the consultants' recommendation. Therefore, the consultants should have a long version of the presentation ready, just in case. If the audience opposes the recommendation and the argumentation, then the consultants should have back-up slides ready to elaborate on their proposed solution and the underlying argumentation. Thus, the consultants still develop a long version, but they do not expect to have to show the long version. If the audience responds as expected then the short version will be enough.

STRUCTURE OF THE SHORT VERSION   Figure 14.8 illustrates the structure of a short version. There is no difference between a presentation about a problem and a presentation about an opportunity. The structure reads from top to bottom and from left to right. The consultants start with the message in the top box. The recommendation ('You should adopt solution Y to close the result gap') raises the question: how will solution Y close the result gap? The consultants then explain that their solution consists of a couple of actions (action 1, action 2, and so on). The audience may ask why this action may work. In this case, the consultants give the arguments for the particular action. Figure 14.8 shows how the three different types of argumentation may be used in the presentation. In practice however, consultants may use only one or two types.

WHY AND HOW   Please note the difference between the long version and the short version. In the long version the consultants first elaborate on the 'why' question' (why is it a good solution?), before the audience is ready to

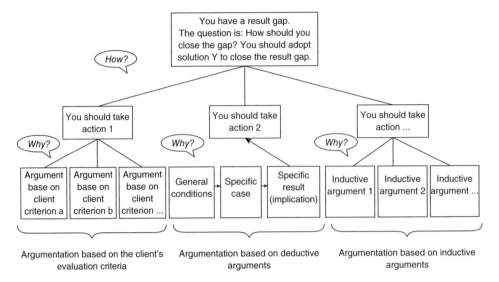

FIGURE 14.8 *Develop a short version for informed and friendly audiences*

discuss the 'how' question (how will this solution work?). In the short version, the consultants begin with answering the 'how' question. Afterwards, they answer the 'why' question. However, the consultants may also leave out the justification of their solution if their audience is not interested in the 'why' question. The audience may have sufficient confidence in the consultants (or in the work of their colleagues on the executive committee) that they will want to pass over the justification and move to a more detailed elaboration of the recommended solution (see Figure 14.9).

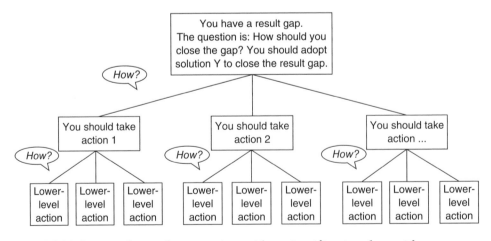

FIGURE 14.9 *Develop a short version without justification, but with an elaboration of actions*

AN INTRODUCTION TO MANAGEMENT CONSULTANCY

DEVELOPING THE INTERIM PRESENTATION

Relatively simple situations

Before the final presentation, the consultants present a series of interim presentations to the steering committee. The exact number varies with the scope and complexity of the project. The interim presentation to the steering committee may serve various purposes: monitoring, soliciting feedback, and facilitating decision making. Figure 14.10 provides an illustration of an interim presentation to facilitate a decision by the steering committee. The consultants have tested a hypothesis about a possible solution Y. These test results are positive. The presentation begins with stating the client's decision criteria (as defined in the problem statement). The client's criteria are the point of departure for solution development. Subsequently, the consultants present their evaluation of their solution based on the client's criteria. This evaluation justifies their solution. The solution meets all criteria. Therefore, the consultants recommend their solution. They set out the individual actions to implement the solution.

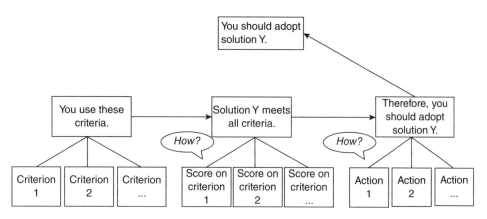

FIGURE 14.10 *Develop a structure for an interim presentation*

More complex situations

The previous example is relatively simple. The evaluation results are unambiguous. All criteria are positive for the solution. In other cases, the evaluation of solutions may produce unequivocal outcomes. Different decision criteria may point to different solutions. For instance, criterion 1 favours solution X, while criterion 2 suggests solution Y. Figure 14.11 provides an illustration. In this case, the client cannot have it all. The

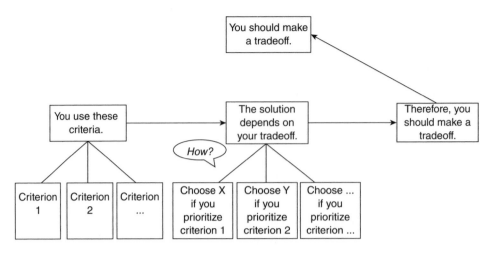

FIGURE 14.11 *Develop a structure for a trade-off decision*

client has to make a trade-off between criteria. The consultants do not have the responsibility to take the decision. However, they can help the client by structuring the decision. They can point out under which conditions the client should choose what solution. Trade-offs may occur because alternative solutions have different strengths. There is no clear winner. Uncertainty may aggravate the ambiguity of the evaluation. If the level of uncertainty is high, then the consultants will not be able to test all the assumptions underlying their hypotheses. The consultants may only work with probabilities. To facilitate decision making, the consultants may set out these probabilities. For instance, if you (the client) think that scenario A will occur, then X is the best solution. However, for scenario B, Y will be the best solution.

DEVELOPING A STORY LINE

The horizontal flow

So far, the consultants have structured their presentation with horizontal and vertical relations between the presentation elements (such as the arrows and lines between the boxes shown in Figure 14.11). However, the PowerPoint presentation has a linear form: a sequence of slides. The consultants present the PowerPoint slides one after another. Therefore they have to transform the structure of horizontal and vertical relations between presentation elements into a horizontal sequence of slides. This sequential structure should be a story line. The presentation needs to be a story. Each individual slide contributes a piece to the story. Together the slides should constitute the story.

The story board

The consultants take the elements of the presentation (such as Figure 14.11) and put them in a sequence. Consultants may use Post-It notes to do this. They write on Post-It notes what the presentation element is about. Then they post the notes on a board. In this way they create a story board. The use of Post-It notes is handy because it provides flexibility. Consultants can easily make corrective changes to individual notes or to their sequence. Creating a story board may be an iterative process of learning. Ideally, the messages on the Post-It notes should read like a story. The consultants term the sequence of slide messages the 'horizontal flow' of the presentation. In Figure 14.12 we provide an example of sequencing the elements of a presentation with the help of a story board. This sequence is based on the structure in Figure 14.2.

1. You have a result gap of $80 m	2. The largest result gap is in segment X	3. These are the causes of the result gap	4. You have various options to close the result gap	5. These are your criteria for evaluating options
6. Y is the best option to close the result gap	7. Customer arguments support option Y	8. Competitor arguments support option Y	9. Organization arguments support option Y	10. Implementation of option Y raises your result by $100 m
11. These are the actions for implementing option Y	12. These are the resources required for implementing option y	13. This is the time line for implementing option Y	14. This is the project organization for implementing option Y	15. These are the next steps

FIGURE 14.12 *A story board shows the story line*

Duration of the presentation

The presentation should not be long. The span of attention of most people is maximally forty minutes. A shorter presentation is even better: the shorter the better. Twenty to thirty minutes may be a reasonable amount of time. The consultants should not try to cram in too many slides in the twenty minute slot. One slide each minute is probably too much, it is better to reserve two to three minutes per slide. The consultants should not exhaust their audience and lose them halfway through the presentation. There should also be room for questions about the presentation and a discussion about the next steps.

DESIGNING A PRESENTATION SLIDE

Slide design before data collection

Top tier consultants design their slides before they start collecting data and analysing those data. They design their slides on the basis of the expected insight from their analysis. They use the expected (fictitious) outcomes of their analysis as the content for their slides. After the analysis, they enter the real data onto the slides.

Message versus data

Junior consultants may be so proud of all the analyses they have done that they will want to show all the analytical results on 'their' slides. However, a slide should not just show off the number and complexity of analyses the consultants have done, but also should demonstrate the relevant insight for the clients. The question arises: how to design slides?

Some people may try to cram in as much information as possible in a slide. Reducing the font size is helpful in this respect. Others may try to impress (or intimidate) the audience by creating complex three-dimensional graphs. Some people may think that the presentation should be entertaining and they may resort to moving objects, colours, and sound effects.

Top tier consultants think about slides as building blocks in their presentation. Each slide should have a function. Each slide should be relevant to the presentation. The purpose of the presentation is to introduce the solution and get the client to progress from the solution to a decision. Every slide should be a stepping stone towards that decision. Because of the fewer the better, consultants cannot afford to have irrelevant slides or slides without a function.

CASE STUDY

AcStrat Consulting – design a presentation slide

One of the junior consultants on the task-force had to make a benchmark analysis of the profitability of AcStrat and the main competitors. Table 14.1 presents the outcomes of the benchmark. The consultant has to create a PowerPoint slide for the team meeting. What type of slide should he make? What should it look like?

TABLE 14.1 *The data table*

Firm	Revenues	Profit	Profitability
Acstrat	2.2	−0.06	−3%
B	0.2	0.04	20%
C	0.3	0.06	20%
D	0.4	0.075	19%
E	0.5	0.09	18%
F	1.6	−0.01	−1%
G	1.5	0.01	1%
H	3	−0.01	0%
1	5.8	0.3	5%
J	7	1.1	16%
K	8	1.65	21%
L	6	0.6	10%
M	7.5	1.4	19%

Notes: Revenues and profit in billion $. Profitability = profit / revenues

Develop the slide title

TITLE WITH A MESSAGE   Some people create slides without titles. These people may think titles are not necessary or they may not know what titles would be appropriate. They will leave it to the audience to figure it out. Other people do use titles. They may create headings such as: 'Revenues', 'Profits', or 'Benchmark'. Such titles are better than no title. However, they will still leave the audience in the dark. Why does the presenter have a slide about the 'Revenues'? So what?

Top tier consultants put a title on each slide. Their titles always contain a message. The message answers the 'So what?' question. Some consultants may use a second title at the bottom of the chart. This is the so-called kicker. The kicker answers the 'so what?' of the slide body.

ONE MESSAGE PER SLIDE   Top tier consultants formulate the message before they design the slides. The messages are defined during the structuring phase of the presentation. The storyline is a logical sequence of messages. The messages together constitute the horizontal flow of the presentation. Each message gets a slide. The slide is just the carrier of the message. Each slide has a message. Consultants do not design slides without a message. However, they refrain from slides with more than one message. Consultants discipline themselves to communicate one message per slide.

FORM OF THE TITLE   The slide title has to convey a message. Therefore, a title consisting of nouns only will not suffice. Take for example: 'Profitability'. Consultants not only use nouns but also verbs. With nouns and verbs together the consultants create titles that are short sentences. The title should be relatively simple and short. The title should be maximally two lines. These short sentences communicate the message. For example: 'AcStrat is at the bottom of the profitability curve' or 'E-commerce offers a growth opportunity'. By reading the title, the audience should be able to understand the meaning of the slide. The audience then better understands why the consultants have presented that particular slide.

Develop the vertical flow

TOP-DOWN DESIGN   Top tier consultants begin slide design with the title. After they have formulated the title, they start working on the so-called 'slide body' (see Figure 14.13). Consultants therefore design their slides in a top-down fashion. Starting from the top (the slide title) they move to the centre (the slide body). The slide title (the message of the slide) determines the slide body.

SUPPORT FUNCTION   The sole purpose of the slide body is to support the slide title. Recall that the function of the slide is to convey a message. The message is in the title. The function of the slide body is to support the message. The top down relation between slide title and slide body is the 'vertical flow'. The slide body flows from the slide title. The slide titles together constitute the horizontal flow, while each slide title has a vertical flow to its slide body. These two flows (horizontal and vertical) constitute the logic of the presentation. The horizontal flow creates the presentation logic. The vertical flow makes the slide logical.

JUSTIFICATION   Below the slide body, the consultants put the justification for the slide. The justification answers three questions the audience may have. First, what sample of data is the slide body about? Second, where do the data come from (source)? Third, what type of analysis did the consultants use? The slide justification is critical because opponents in the audience will typically attack the slide body, in particular the data and the analysis.

AcStrat Consulting – design a presentation slide (continued)

The junior consultant has benchmarked the profitability of AcStrat and its main competitors (see Table 14.1). This analysis may be used to explain the profit gap. The consultant has created a PowerPoint slide for the team meeting (see Figure 14.13).

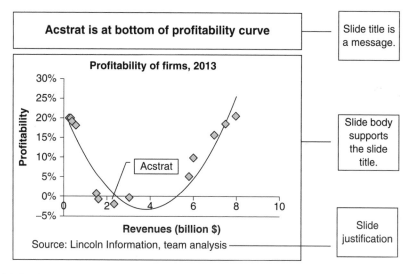

FIGURE 14.13 *The slide body supports the slide title*

Develop the slide body

ARGUMENTATION Top tier consultants do not put a message in the slide title without supporting arguments in the slide body. The slide body always supports the message of the slide. But it should do no more than that. Consultants do not put data in the slide body if these data are not necessary for the message in the title. *No conclusions in the slide title without arguments in the slide body. No arguments in the slide body without conclusions in the slide title.* The latter rule helps consultants to make their slide body lighter.

LEAN SLIDE BODY Consultants do not put ballast in the slide body. When they have designed a slide body, the consultants scrutinize every element of the slide body. Does this element contribute to the slide message? If not, then the consultants remove that element from the slide body, even if the production of that element took up a lot of effort. Consultants will not present data just because they spent so much time and effort in collecting and analysing those data. What matters is the data's relevance to the decision at hand. They must avoid being side tracked.

FACT-BASED SLIDE BODY Whenever possible, consultants will put facts in the slide body. They will refrain from purely conceptual slide bodies. Consultants will not draw a slide body about the conceptual relationship between the scale of production and the costs of production (conceptual boxes and arrows). Instead, consultants will show empirical evidence for such a relationship. It is more convincing to show the actual relationship with facts than telling the audience that such a relationship exists without providing evidence. *Don't tell but show.* Empirical proof is more convincing than conceptual argumentation. To convince the audience, it is critical that the presented facts are correct. Consultants should verify each fact before they put it in the slide.

USING VISUALIZATIONS

Visualization of quantitative facts

Top tier consultants use visualizations whenever possible. Visuals are easier to understand than (high density) text blocks and numerical tables. Imagine a slide filled with bullet lists of sentences in a small font size. Imagine a slide with a screen view from an Excel spreadsheet ... Therefore, consultants avoid text slides and numerical table slides as much as possible.

Choosing chart types

If top tier consultants want to use numerical quantitative facts in a slide body, they prefer to present the facts in a chart. Consultants use Excel to create charts (such as bar, column, line, pie, scatter, bubble, and radar charts). Consultants are disciplined in the choice of chart because not every chart type is appropriate for every type of quantitative fact. Different chart types fit different types of quantitative facts. The consultants will want to convey the message as effectively as possible. Therefore, it is important to choose the most suitable form for presenting the data. Table 14.2 outlines for different messages what is the appropriate chart type. Resist the temptation to use 3D charts. These may be fun to create, but generally they are hard to read.

TABLE 14.2 *Choose the chart type for messages based on quantitative data*

Message is about:	Comment	Chart type
Comparisons	In general	Bar chart
	Industry cost curve	Column chart
Components	In general	Pie chart
	Combination with comparison	Stacked bar chart
	Segmenting the result gap	Bar waterfall chart
Relations	In general	Scatter plot (2 variables), Bubble chart (3 variables)
	Portfolio	2 by 2 matrix (or variant, e.g. 3 by 3)
Time series	In general	Column chart or line chart
	Combination with comparison	Stacked column chart
	Contribution of solution to result	Column waterfall chart

Comparisons

For benchmarks, and comparisons in general, consultants will choose bar charts (see Figure 14.14 on the next page). They do not use column charts for benchmarks because audiences typically associate columns with time logic. Excel offers all types of bar charts. Resist the temptation of 3-D charts. Keep the chart as simple as possible. Remember, do not show facts that are not necessary for the slide message. If possible, consultants will rank the bars: from largest to smallest. Put the largest bars on top. Ranking makes it easier to understand the message. If the subject has components then consultants use the stacked bar. For instance, consultants want to benchmark the sales of the client and its main rivals. Company sales are coming from different geographic markets. These markets are the components of the company sales. To guide the audience, the consultants may connect the components through dotted lines.

ORGANIZATION OF THE DATA   If the consultants benchmark multiple subjects, then consultants organize the bars in such a way that they support the message. Figure 14.14 shows two different types of organization for the same data. The right-hand chart organization better supports the slide message ('Client has a competitive advantage in quality but lags in design and price') than the left-hand chart. If the message is only about the quality ('Client has a competitive advantage in quality'), then the consultants will leave out the data about design and price. The consultants only show facts that are necessary to support the slide message. They want to keep the slide as simple as possible to convey the message.

Client has a competitive advantage in quality but lags in design and price

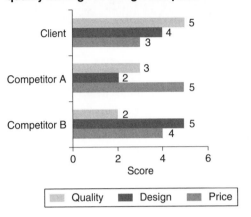

Client has a competitive advantage in quality but lags in design and price

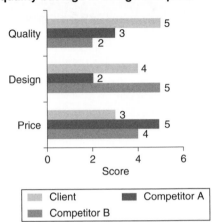

FIGURE 14.14 *Organize the bar chart to support the slide message*

INDUSTRY COST CURVE   Consultants usually do not use column charts for displaying comparisons or benchmarks. However, there are exceptions. A popular chart to show economies of scale is the industry cost curve. This curve uses columns (see Figure 14.15). Each column represents a different firm (in Figure 14.15, the letter in the column refers to the firm). The width of the column refers to the firm's volume of production. The height of the column represents the firm's production cost of one product. The consultants rank the firms according to their production volume. They begin with the largest volume. The rising columns indicate the scale effects in production. The consultants may use statistical analyses to determine the exact scale effect.

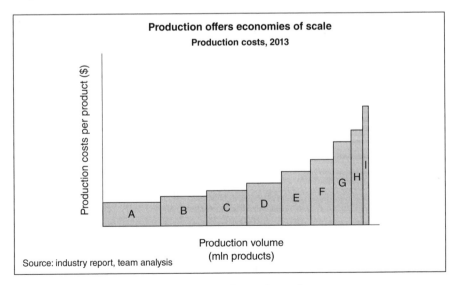

FIGURE 14.15 *A column chart visualizes the industry cost curve*

AN INTRODUCTION TO MANAGEMENT CONSULTANCY

Components

Consultants use a pie chart to show the components of a subject. An example is the shares of a market. If the consultants want to show a benchmark of components, then they use a stacked bar chart.

SEGMENT THE RESULT GAP   The bar waterfall chart is a special bar chart, which is popular with top tier consultants. It is not a standard option in Excel. Consultants may use the bar waterfall to visualize the distribution of the client's result gap (see Figure 14.16). The chart shows how the segments of the result gap compare. You can create it by choosing a stacked bar chart and selecting 'no fill' and 'no line' for one of the two data series.

Relations between variables

Consultants may use scatter plot charts to visualize the relation between two variables. For instance, the consultants investigate whether there are scale effects in the client's production activities. Figure 14.17 on the next page plots the cost per unit against the volume of production (in units). The scatter plot chart visualizes the scale effects. The consultants may use statistical analyses to determine the exact scale effect.

RELATION BETWEEN THREE VARIABLES   Consultants may want to show relations between more than two variables. They may use bubble charts to present three variables. The size of the bubble indicates a third variable,

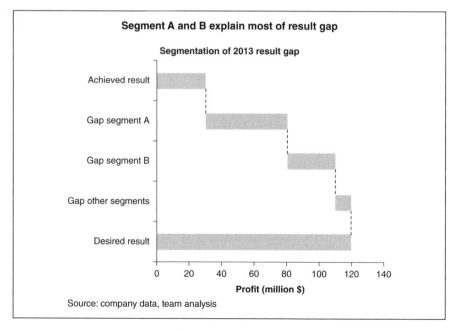

FIGURE 14.16   *A bar waterfall visualizes the segmentation of the result gap*

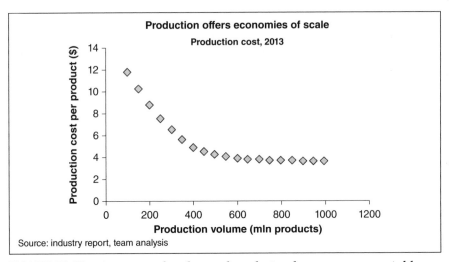

FIGURE 14.17 *A scatter plot shows the relation between two variables*

in addition to the two variables measured along the two axes. Figure 14.18 provides an example.

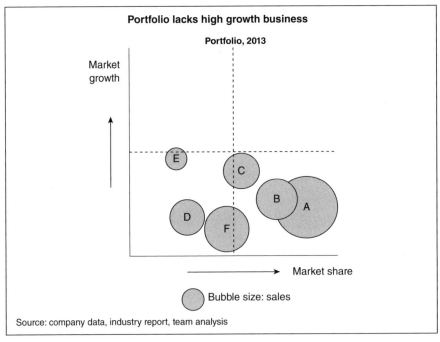

FIGURE 14.18 *A bubble chart shows the relation between three variables*

Time series

If the data are longitudinal, then the consultants may use a column chart or a line graph. Figure 14.19 visualizes the growth of the client's sales over a period of time. To give a further indication of growth, the consultants may add to the chart a 'compound average growth rate' (abbreviated as CAGR). The note to Figure 14.19 presents the formula for calculating a CAGR.

CONTRIBUTION OF SOLUTION TO THE RESULT   Top tier consultants typically show the expected contribution of their solution to the client's result. To visualize this effect, consultants will use a column waterfall chart. This is a special type of stacked columns not found in Excel (but you can create

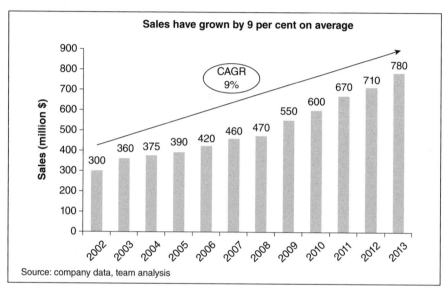

FIGURE 14.19   *A column chart visualizes developments over time*

Notes: CAGR = Compound Average Growth Rate. Sales 2012= S_{2012}
Formula: CAGR = $((S_{2013} / S_{2002}) \wedge (1/11)) - 1$. Other form: $S_{2013} = S_{2002} \times (1 + CAGR) \wedge 11$

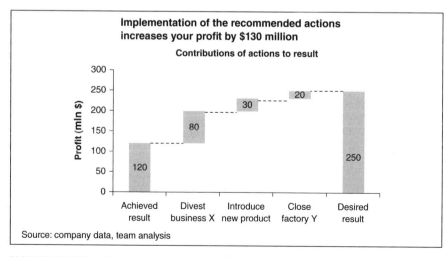

FIGURE 14.20   *The column waterfall shows the contribution to the result*

AcStrat Consulting – design a presentation slide (continued)

One of the arguments for the recommended solution (merge with Delta) is 'Merger offers synergies'. The consultants develop the following slide to support this argument (see Figure 14.21). The slide shows how the solution contributes to the client's result.

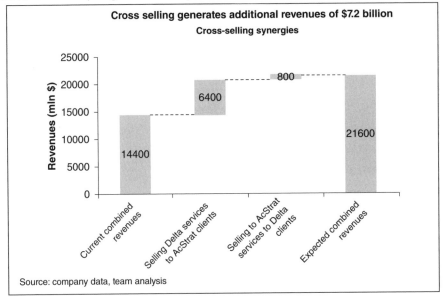

FIGURE 14.21 *Presentation slide shows the contribution to the result*

it: select from one of the two series: 'no fill' and 'no line'). Figure 14.20 on the previous page provides an example. The solution in this example consists of three actions.

Visualization of qualitative facts

AVOID WORDY SLIDES Quantitative facts lend themselves to charts. The top tier consultants try to quantify as much as possible. However, some qualitative facts do not lend themselves to quantification. Therefore, consultants also have to present qualitative facts. But consultants avoid text slides that resemble book pages (see Figure 14.22).

Recommendations

- You have to do this, and this and this.
- You also have to do these three things: (a) this, (b) this, and (c) this
- Furthermore, it is necessary that you do this and this
- In addition, you have to consider this and that
- We also recommend that you do this and this
- You need to do that also
- For the implementation phase, you have to do this, this and this
- In case of this, you need to do these things: a, b and c
- You have to do this, and this and this.
- You also have to do these three things: (a) this, (b) this, and (c) this
- Furthermore, it is necessary that you do this and this
- In addition, you have to consider this and that
- We also recommend that you do this and this
- You need to do that also
- For the implementation phase, you have to do this, this and this
- In case of this, you need to do these things: a, b and c

FIGURE 14.22 *A slide should not resemble a book page*

USE SHAPES TO VISUALIZE TEXT Consultants try to make qualitative slides visually attractive. Consultants use all kinds of shapes to visualize text. Nowadays PowerPoint provides many templates for processes, lists, hierarchies, cycles, pyramids, and other types of relationships. In this section we provide some examples of forms that consultants use.

Process To show processes consultants use arrows, both horizontal and vertical ones. Figure 14.23 shows an example of horizontal arrows with text blocks underneath.

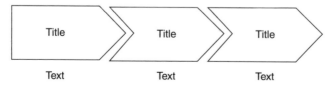

FIGURE 14.23 *Arrows visualize a process*

Action plan

Consultants may use a variation on the arrow theme to outline an action plan (see Figure 14.24).

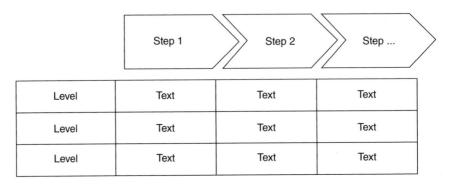

Level	Text	Text	Text
Level	Text	Text	Text
Level	Text	Text	Text

FIGURE 14.24 *Arrows visualize an action plan*

Categories   Consultants may use a matrix to present categories of data and show how the categories relate (see Figure 14.25).

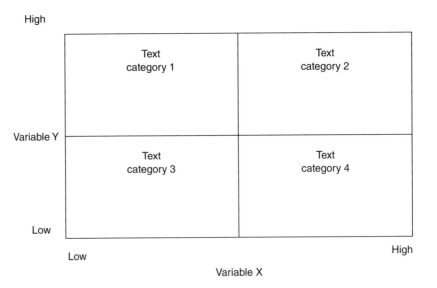

FIGURE 14.25 *A matrix shows relations between categories*

Text boxes   Consultants may create all kinds of text boxes to organize qualitative data in a slide (see some examples in Figure 14.26).

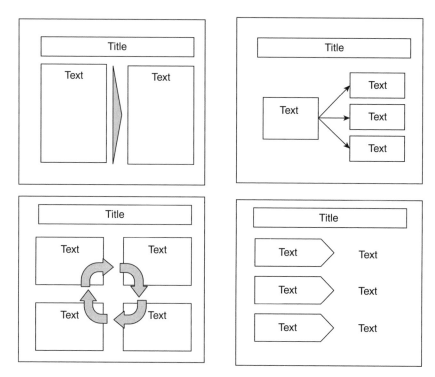

FIGURE 14.26   *Text boxes organize qualitative data*

Showing the presentation structure

THE MOVING BOX AGENDA   If the presentation is relatively long, then the audience may lose their way. Even if the consultants have structured their presentation very well, the audience may ask themselves: where are we? Where does the slide fit in the bigger picture? To help the audience understand the position of a slide in the presentation, and to help the audience navigate their way through the presentation, consultants may use two techniques. One technique is a slide with the agenda of the presentation (see left-hand slide in Figure 14.27). Each bullet on the agenda slide represents a section of the presentation. After each section, the consultants repeat the agenda slide. However, each time they move the box to the bullet that indicates the next section. This moving box explains to the audience where they are in the presentation.

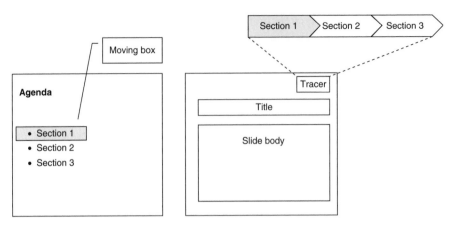

FIGURE 14.27 *Moving box and tracer show the presentation structure*

THE TRACER   An alternative navigation technique is the so-called 'tracer' (also called the tracker or leader). The tracer is a small visualization or text in the top right (or left) corner of each slide (see the right-hand slide in Figure 14.27). The tracer indicates where the slide fits in the bigger picture of the presentation. The tracer may be a visual with different components, whereby each component represents a section of the presentation. In the tracer of a particular slide, the consultants highlight the component to which that slide belongs. Consultants may use a single agenda slide at the beginning of their presentation. In this slide they introduce the tracer. When using the tracer on the subsequent slides, they do not need to use subsequent 'moving box' agenda slides. That would be a duplication.

SUMMARY

The purpose of a client presentation is to convince the client to accept the recommended solution. Top tier consultants develop a logical structure of argumentation to make their presentations more convincing. They develop the first draft of their presentation after they have developed their hypothesis about the solution and before they begin their hypothesis testing (see Figure 14.28). Consultants adapt the presentation structure to the audience, in particular their knowledge and their attitude towards the solution and consultants. Consultants translate the argumentation structure into a story line. The story line is a sequence of messages (the horizontal flow). Each message is converted into a slide. Consultants design their slides from the top down: from slide title to slide body (the vertical flow). The argumentation in the body supports the message in the title. No argumentation without a message and no message without argumentation.

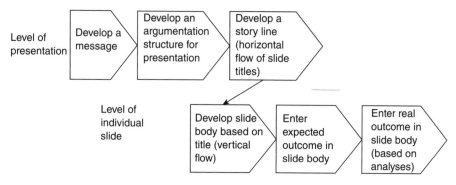

FIGURE 14.28 *Create a horizontal flow for the presentation and a vertical flow for each slide*

Ivy Business School – develop the presentation

In Chapter 13, the consultants developed a solution for the Ivy Business School. The consultants recommended that Ivy should adopt a phased approach, beginning with a blended offering of selected programmes for tier 2 students.

Develop the short version of the final presentation

The consultants develop a structure to present their recommended solution to Ivy's board (see Figure 14.29).

Develop a presentation slide (1)

The consultants develop a presentation slide for one argument for the recommendation 'Blend residential and online learning'. Figure 14.30 presents this slide.

Develop a presentation slide (2)

The consultants develop a presentation slide for another argument for the recommendation 'Blend residential and online learning'. Figure 14.31 presents this slide.

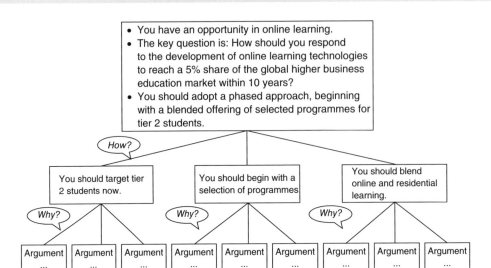

FIGURE 14.29 *Develop the short version of the final presentation*

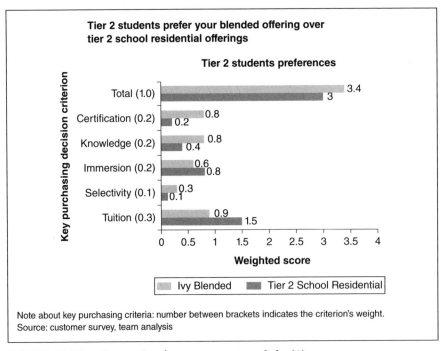

FIGURE 14.30 *Example of a presentation slide (1)*

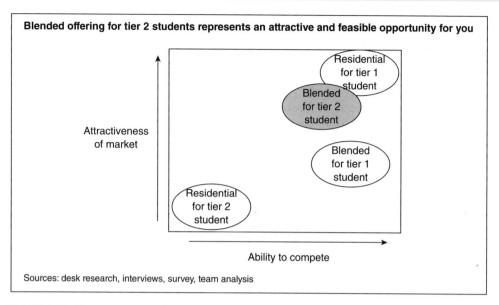

FIGURE 14.31 *Example of a presentation slide (2)*

EXERCISES

1. GlobalJet is one of the largest manufacturers of commercial jet airplanes. The company has hired the prestigious consulting firm Macintosh & Company to develop a strategy for a promising project that GlobalJet's R&D department is working on: the SpaceBus. The SpaceBus is a passenger-carrying space vehicle. The vehicle has a capacity for fifty passengers and flies in the higher reaches of the stratosphere, around 50 kilometres. The jet airplanes of GlobalJet and other manufacturers fly in the lower reaches of the stratosphere, at about 9 to 12 kilometres. On intercontinental flights, the SpaceBus is expected to fly four times as fast as a normal jet. The consultants at Macintosh have done some research. They have concluded that consumers will regard the SpaceBus as a highly prestigious means of intercontinental travel. Macintosh expects that the class of wealthy consumers around the world would be able and willing to pay the cost of travel with the SpaceBus. The consultants have compared two alternative approaches to commercializing the SpaceBus, namely GlobalJet developing the vehicle alone or with an alliance partner. Because of the huge investment, and because GlobalJet does not possess all the critical competences, Macintosh advises an alliance with the World Aircraft Corporation (WAC). The consultants have developed an action plan for setting up the alliance, which includes the setting up of the joint

venture, the allocation of resources to the venture, and the development of the first prototype. Assume you are the partner at Macintosh who has to give the final presentation to GlobalJet's steering committee. You have decided to develop a long structure for the presentation. Design this structure on the basis of the information provided.

2. As part of a strategy consulting project for a client, you have to analyse the attractiveness of three markets (X, Y, and Z). You have collected and analysed the data (see Table 14.3). Based on these data you have to design a complete slide that can be presented to the steering committee. You may assume that the profit margins are stable.

TABLE 14.3   *Data table*

	Current size	Expected annual growth	Current profit margin
Market X	4500	13%	24%
Market Y	2500	24%	18%
Market Z	1100	19%	37%

Notes: Current market size in thousands of US dollars. Expected annual market growth refers to a five year period. Current profit margin refers to the profit margin for key firms operating in that market.

3. The small trading company named InternationalTrading (see exercise in Chapter 12) has a revenue gap. The desired revenues are US$7.5 million but the achieved revenues amount to US$5.5 million. As a consultant you have segmented this revenue gap. For the interim presentation to the steering committee you have to produce a PowerPoint slide. Based on the data table (see Table 14.4) create a complete slide that is ready to be presented to the committee.

TABLE 14.4   *Data table*

Revenue gap	Product 1	Product 2	Product 3	Product 4	Total
Country A	40	70	60	30	200
Country B	40	70	60	30	200
Country C	280	490	420	210	1400
Country D	20	35	30	15	100
Country E	20	35	30	15	100
Total	400	700	600	300	2,000

Note: amounts in thousands of US dollars

REFLECTIVE QUESTIONS

1. This chapter distinguishes between long and short presentation structures. When does it make sense for management consultants to develop a long structure? Explain your answer.

2. What are the advantages and disadvantages of using PowerPoint? How do these advantages and disadvantages compare? Elaborate on your answer.

3. Assume you are a partner at Acme Consulting, and you are about to begin your final presentation for an audience of client executives. Then, one of the executives – not a member of the steering committee – stands up and says: 'I don't like this ritual dance! We all know what is coming. During the next forty minutes, you are going to bury us under thirty-something slides crammed with quantitative data that are new to us. Your team has toiled for three months on the analyses and we have to grasp it within forty minutes? I want a level playing field. Let us have a real discussion about our issue without your slides'. What would you do? Explain your answer.

FURTHER READING

Minto, B. (1987) *The Pyramid Principle: Logic in Writing and Thinking* (revised 3rd edn). London: Minto International Inc.

Zelazny, G. (2007) *The Say It With Charts Complete Toolkit*. New York: McGraw-Hill.

15

STRUCTURED IMPLEMENTATION

INTRODUCTION

In Chapters 12 and 13 we discussed how management consultants may use a structured approach to solve the problems of clients and develop solutions. The current chapter is about how consultants may use a structured approach to assist a client with implementing a solution.

Implementation implies change. We begin with discussing the relationship between consultants and change. Next, we discuss the relationship between the client and change. Subsequently, we outline how consultants may structure an implementation project. Implementation projects may fail for various reasons. We explore the main causes of failure and discuss possible approaches to lower the chances of failure. After implementation of the solution, the client and/or consultants may evaluate the implementation. We briefly talk about the challenges of such evaluations. The chapter ends with a summary, reflective questions, a mini case study, suggested further reading, and references.

Main learning objectives

- Understand why consultants and client organizations have different attitudes towards change.

- Distinguish between the different roles for management consultants in change projects.
- Distinguish between the interests of client top management regarding change and the interests of lower-level management and professionals.
- Understand the relationship between the development of a solution and its implementation.
- Distinguish between the stages of a structured implementation project.
- Critically reflect upon the performance of management consultants in implementation projects.
- Distinguish between the main causes of failure of implementation projects.
- Know the benefits and difficulties of evaluating implementation projects for clients and consultants.

CONSULTANTS AND CHANGE

Agents of change

CONSULTANCY'S REASON FOR EXISTENCE Without the client's need for change, there is no reason for management consultancy. Management consultancy's reason for existence is helping a client to change, whether through advice on change (a narrow definition of management consultancy) or through advice and implementation (a broad definition). The advice, or recommendation, of management consultants is about change for clients. Almost always, the consultants will recommend changing something at the client organization, for example the client's strategy, structure, or a process. Clients might receive a consultant's recommendation to keep everything as it is with suspicion. Clients expect consultants to recommend change. They hire consultants to induce some kind of change. A critical success factor for the consultants' advice is the feasibility of the implementation of that advice. First, the client should accept the solution and support its implementation. Second, the client should have the resources and capabilities to implement the solution.

RECOMMEND AND IMPLEMENT CHANGE In our narrow definition of management consultancy, the consultants recommend a certain change and the client implements this recommendation. The consultants only point out what needs to be changed and why. In addition, the consultants may specify – typically at a high level of abstraction – how the client should implement the change. This is the so-called action plan. The consultants produce a report and provide a final presentation to the client. They do not decide on the recommended change. It is the client who decides whether the solution will be implemented, that is whether the recommended change will take place. Management consultants that only generate advice, and then leave without implementation, may still be perceived as agents of change because their advice aims at change. Management consultants in the broad definition definitely are agents of change because they assist clients with the management of the solution implementation.

The execution of change

MANAGEMENT TASKS   According to our broad definition of management consultancy, management consultants may, in addition to developing recommendations, assist their client with the *management* tasks for implementing the solution. We can distinguish between the management and the execution of an implementation. The first is about design, planning, and control of the implementation work, while the latter is about the actual work that needs to be done to implement the solution. Our definition of management consultancy excludes the actual execution of the change as a result of the implementation of the recommendation. Some examples of execution are the development of new (IT) systems, the off-shoring of value-adding activities, and the retraining of staff.

TYPES OF CONSULTANCY   Client top management may delegate the execution of the change to their lower management and employees. Alternatively, the client may hire the same consultancy firm that developed the solution to implement the advice. However, solution development and solution implementation are distinct activities, with different economics and different success factors. In particular, if the solution developer is a brain type of consultancy firm, then this consultancy is a less suitable candidate for implementation. First, brain type consultants are relatively expensive. Second, their competences are in the area of complex problem solving, not in implementation. Third, these brain type consultancies typically lack the capacity, in terms of the number of people, for (large-scale) implementation projects. Clients may therefore hire procedure type of consultancies or professional services firms that are specialized in the implementation of solutions.

ASSISTANCE WITH THE MANAGEMENT OF IMPLEMENTATION   Client top management is responsible for managing implementation. Management consultants may assist client top management with managing the implementation. The consultants may facilitate the implementation process. They may provide a process for implementation and assist client management in using this process. However, management consultants do not take decisions regarding implementation. Decision making is the responsibility of client top management. Management consultants may only advise on the implementation decisions.

Different types of change

DIFFERENT SUBJECTS Not all changes are alike. Changes may vary along different dimensions, such as the subject of change, the scope of change, and the timing of change. The subject of change can be many things. The McKinsey 7-S framework provides an overview of the interconnected elements of organizational change: the strategy, the structure (organization), the style (management style and culture), the shared values (guiding principles), the staff, the skills (of key people), and the systems (routine processes). An integral change project comprises all seven S's. Figure 15.1 presents the framework.

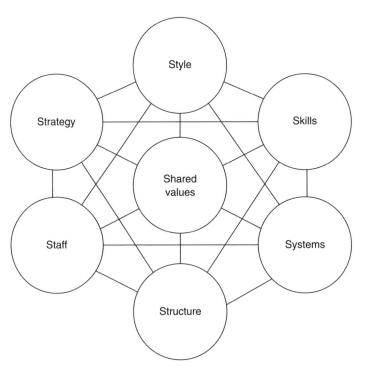

FIGURE 15.1 *The McKinsey 7-S framework provides an overview of the interconnected elements of organizational change*

DIFFERENT SCOPES The scope of change may vary as well. This scope may range from narrow to wide. An example of a narrow scope is the change of a single department, a single location, or a single system within the client organization. In contrast, wide scopes of change refer to many departments, many locations, and many systems in the client organization.

We also may distinguish different timings for client changes. Some clients hire consultants to help implement change to prevent future problems. This is called *anticipatory change*. Other clients only decide to call in consultants for a change project when the client organization is already in crisis. This is termed *responsive change*.

FROM RECOMMENDATION TO IMPLEMENTATION

RECOMMENDATION ONLY   In the past, most clients used to hire management consultants to provide advice only. At that time, consultants developed recommendations that were typically packaged in an impressive text report or a PowerPoint presentation. The clients would then implement the advice themselves. However, over time, clients learned that a recommendation is no guarantee for results (see our first case about the bank on p. 544). A sound recommendation is a necessary but not a sufficient condition for the desired result. To achieve the desired result, the client needs to implement the recommendation. Implementation means change and change is difficult. Implementation of a recommendation is therefore difficult. Implementation may fail to produce the desired result because the recommendation is flawed or because of difficulties in the implementation of the recommendation. We shall come back to this later in the chapter.

IMPLEMENTATION INCLUDED   There are several reasons why a client might hire consultants to implement a solution.

> *Results instead of reports*. Clients are not interested in consultants' reports and presentations of recommendations. Reports are a means not an end. Clients want results. To ensure results, clients increasingly hire management consultants not just to develop a recommendation, but also to implement that recommendation. However, implementation by management consultants may be relatively expensive for clients. Hiring consultants to implement a solution makes sense if the client lacks an understanding of the implementation process or if the client lacks the resources and capabilities to implement the solution.
>
> *Blaming each other*. It may be convenient to have the same consultants develop a recommendation and implement it. As the same consultants are responsible for both recommendation and implementation, clients avoid the blaming game. Blaming games may result after an implementation fails. Solution developers and solution implementers may blame each other. Blaming may arise if the causes of the implementation failure are unclear. Is the failure due to a flawed recommendation or a flawed implementation? If the same consultants are responsible for the recommendation as well as the implementation, then only one party is to blame. The same consultants are accountable. Moreover, by putting the development of the recommendation and its implementation in the same hands, the client eliminates the risk of

miscommunication and misunderstanding during the handover of the recommendation by the developers to the implementers.

Switching consultants. However, in some cases the clients have good reasons to hire different consultants for the development of the recommendation and for the implementation. Clients will hire a specialist consultant for development, then another specialist consultant for implementation. This resembles the saying: different horses for different courses. This may be a good decision if specialist consultants (either development or implementation) are better than consultants who combine development and implementation. Moreover, the generalist consultants (who do both development and implementation) may be too expensive compared to specialist consultants.

ROLES OF MANAGEMENT CONSULTANTS DURING IMPLEMENTATION

CRITICAL VERSUS FUNCTIONALIST VIEWS We may distinguish between different roles for management consultants in the implementation of solutions. Table 15.1 on the next page compares the critical view of consultancy with functionalist views on three different types of consultancy.

The rhetorician. In the critical view, the consultant is a rhetorician with a doubtful role in the implementation process. The three functionalist views distinguish between the expert type of consultancy, doctor-patient consultancy, and process consultancy.

The expert. The expert consultant may provide specific pieces of expertise in the area of implementation. For instance, a client may hire the expert consultant to design a plan for a large-scale transformation process. Alternatively, the client may hire a specialist consultant for their communication or motivation expertise.

The doctor. The doctor-type of consultant covers a much broader span of activities regarding implementation. The doctor consultant may diagnose the client's readiness for change, subsequently design a change plan for the client, and finally implement the plan as well.

The facilitator. The process consultant only enables the process of implementation. The process consultant possesses competences in this process. Such a consultant transfers their process expertise to the client by educating, guiding, and coaching the client. The process consultant facilitates the process, while the client diagnoses the organization's readiness for change, designs a change plan, and implements that plan.

DIFFERENT WAYS OF ADDING VALUE During an implementation project, consultants may add value to clients in different ways. Consultants may

TABLE 15.1 *Views on consultancy and implementation differ*

Consultancy type	Consultancy by rhetorics (critical view)	Expert consultancy	Doctor-patient consultancy	Process consultancy
Consultant's role	Consultant sells management fashion, creates impressions that clients receive value	Consultant provides expertise for implementation	Consultant implements the solution that was developed in previous stage	Consultant helps client to implement solution by providing a process
Client's role	Client is passive, and is manipulated	Client implements and uses consultants' expertise as input in the process	Client is passive and undergoes the implementation	Client implements with the help of consultant (co-creation)
Consultant-client relationship	Powerful, persuasive consultant	Powerful client, consultant respected for expertise	Powerful consultant respected for competences	Equal relationship

Source: based on Nikolova and Devinney (2012)

help to prepare the client organization for change. To prepare the organization for change, consultants may conduct several activities, including assessing the client's readiness for change, advising on changes to the client's seven S's, communicating with the client employees and other stakeholders, training the employees, and coaching the management. Consultants may also help client management to identify and overcome resistance to change. Furthermore, consultants may help client top management with interpersonal issues and conflict resolution as a result of the implementation.

CLIENT DELEGATES   We may envision a spectrum of alternative divisions of roles and responsibilities between clients and consultants during implementation. At one extreme of the spectrum, the client delegates the implementation of a solution to management consultants. In such a case, consultants take the lead in the implementation process. They have to inspire and motivate the client employees and they fulfil all the tasks outlined in the structured implementation process described hereafter. Such services qualify as outsourcing rather than management consultancy.

CLIENT TAKES OWNERSHIP   At the other extreme of the spectrum, the client takes ownership of the implementation process. The client hires consultants to provide some specific expertise – the expert consultants – or they use the consultants as a process consultant. Depending on the division of roles, the level of emotional involvement of the consultants and the level of client–consultancy intimacy may vary. Often the project will use a phased model. Initially, the consultants are in the lead. But over time, the client employees take over the responsibilities step-by-step.

Imposed versus participative change

PROCESS VERSUS PACKAGED SOLUTION   Management consultants may follow different routes to implement solutions at client organizations. They may design a change programme (a *packaged solution*). However, consultants may also stimulate and support a process of discovery and learning by the client (*process consultation*). The packaged solution implies change that is imposed on the client. In contrast, process consultation means participative change. The latter approach typically takes longer but is probably more long lasting. Because the client employees participate in the process, it is more likely that they will accept and adopt the solution. Participation therefore helps to institutionalize the change. Participation is not necessarily limited to internal stakeholders (client employees) but may also include external ones, such as the client's customers and suppliers, whose cooperation is required for the implementation.

DIFFERENT HORSES FOR DIFFERENT COURSES   We do not posit that participative change is always a better choice than imposed change. It is a situational choice. If time is critical, there is no room for participative change. For example, if the client faces a liquidity crisis, then there is no time for democratic consensus building to arrive at a solution. Under high time pressure, the client needs to turnaround fast. Because imposed change is faster, it may better fit that particular situation. The old saying goes: different horses for different courses. Different situations require different approaches to change.

CLIENTS AND CHANGE

Why clients hire consultants for change

OVERT REASONS   There are many reasons why clients may want to change. We can distinguish between clients' overt and covert reasons for change. Overt reasons for change have to do with result gaps for the client organization as a whole, which is the difference between the client's desired result and the actual or expected result. Chapter 12 examines all kinds of causes for result gaps. These causes refer to overt reasons for client organizations to change. The causes of result gaps may lie inside and outside the client organization. To close their result gap, clients need to change. The solution for closing the result gap determines what type of change the client needs to make.

COVERT REASONS   Besides the overt reasons, we also acknowledge covert reasons why clients may want to change. Such reasons are usually based on the personal agendas of client top managements and organizational politics. For instance, a client (top) manager may have a pet project that they want to implement even though it is not in the interests of the client organization as a whole. The client manager may hire a consultant to manage the implementation of the pet project. Another example of a covert reason is a client manager who wants to change the organization structure to weaken the position of rival colleagues within the client organization. Consultants are hired to help implement the new organization structure. Chapter 10 discussed the various reasons for hiring consultants. Consultants should always try to discover the real reason why clients want to hire them. If the client's stated problem is not really a problem, or if the client insists on a solution that is not (really) a solution to the client's problem, then the consultants should not accept the project.

Why clients find implementation difficult

DISLIKE OF CHANGE   Most clients find it difficult to implement change irrespective of whether or not the change is recommended by management consultants. This difficulty mainly concerns the fact that implementation means change. Most client organizations are not good at change. Client organizations are typically not designed for change but rather for efficiently performing a given set of value-adding activities. Moreover, client employees may resist change even more when that change is proposed by consultants. The client employees perceive consultants as outsiders and their negative attitude may be based on the not-invented-here syndrome.

REINFORCEMENT   Most client organizations are not good at change because the organizations are built on stability and routine. We would acknowledge the existence of organizations that are designed for change: the so-called agile, flexible, and resilient organizations. However, most client organizations are typically good at running their *current* business. Clients have developed routines for their current business activities. By repetition they accumulate experience and become increasingly good at what they already do. They follow the learning curve and increase their performance over time. Moreover, success reinforces the existing routines. Success is a confirmation that a client does the right thing. Success also makes clients more risk averse. Clients do not like to change a successful business because of the risk of losing that success. The old saying is: never change a winning team. Similarly, it is hard to change a successful business. However, even if the current business is not that successful, (most) clients may be reluctant to change because of a general negative attitude towards change. The question arises: why do (most) people dislike change?

Why people at the client organization may dislike change

RISK   People at the client organization – internal as well as external stake-holders – may not like the change proposed by management consultants because change implies the risk that the consultants' recommendation may not work or that it may be wrongly implemented. Change may also imply that some stakeholders inside or outside the client organization may suffer even if the change is successful (from the perspective of the client organization). For instance, a reorganization of a client organization may imply that some client employees and supplier employees lose their jobs.

EFFORT   Moreover, some client managers may end up with fewer employ-ees and assets under their control. Even if the stakeholders do not lose their resources or their position, people do not like change because change entails effort. As a result of the change, people may need to unlearn old behaviour and learn new behaviour instead. People may need to acquire new knowledge and develop new skills to function in the changed environment.

Within the client organization appetites for change may vary

TOP MANAGEMENT VERSUS OTHER STAKEHOLDERS   Consultants should not perceive the client as a single entity. The client consists of different factions with different interests, such as top management, middle man-agement, and professionals. Their interest in change, and their interest in management consultants, may vary across these factions. Therefore, consultants need to distinguish between these different factions within the client organization.

How may interest differ across factions? For instance, top management in the client organization may have an interest in changing the organiza-tion. An example is a newly appointed top manager who is eager to make their mark in 'the first hundred days in office' and wants to meet share-holders expectations. The new manager may be hired for change, or sim-ply wants to make a difference.

TOP MANAGEMENT PRESSURES AND INCENTIVES   Typically, top managers are under pressure from the company's shareholders and other stakehold-ers to prove their worth. Moreover, top managers typically have financial incentives – stock options and other bonus schemes – that stimulate change in the business in order to improve its success. They may want to prove their worth and create shareholder value by creating change in the organi-zation. In general, new top managers do not like to watch the store, even if it is a successful store. To summarize, most top managers have a tendency to create change. Because the rest of the organization does not share their appetite, they may hire consultants to support them.

MIDDLE MANAGEMENT AND PROFESSIONALS MAY NOT BE INVOLVED   Two other factions in the client organization, the client's middle management and professionals, may have a different attitude to change and to consultants. Top managers may develop plans for change without involving other stakeholders in their organization, or may delegate the task of developing a change plan to management consultants. In such cases, top management may fail to consult or inform middle management and professionals. The top management simply drops the plan into the organization.

MIDDLE MANAGEMENT AND PROFESSIONALS MAY BE VICTIMS OF CHANGE   Middle managers and professionals are typically the subjects or victims if you like of such change plans. Usually it is the middle managers and professionals of the client that will have to change. Middle managers and professionals have to put in the effort and they may see their positions weaken or even at risk as a result of the intended change. The client's middle managers and professionals have to learn new behaviour and may need to acquire new knowledge and skills to survive the change. Therefore, these factions may resist change, as well as resist consultants as agents of change. A remedy is to involve the stakeholders who are crucial for implementation in the development of the solution or change plan.

MIDDLE MANAGEMENT AND PROFESSIONALS MAY BE TIRED OF CHANGE   In some client organizations, top managers want to change too much and to do this too often. As a result, the other people in the client organization – middle managers and professionals – may get tired of change. Their morale declines and the best people will abandon ship (because they find better opportunities outside the organization). Given the fact that new top managers have a tendency to introduce change, and given the decreasing tenure of top managers, the rate of change for organizations is likely to increase, which may be good business for consultants.

CONSULTANTS AS AGENTS OF CHANGE FOR OTHERS   Management consultants like change because it is their business. Not for nothing are they the agents of change. You may ask: are management consultants a different species from client managers and employees? A consultant is certainly not a different species. We need to nuance our statement. Management consultants like to change *clients*. Consultants do not necessarily like to undergo change. If their own (consultancy) organization is subject to change, their response is similar to the client managers and professionals. Changing others is different from being changed by others. Consultants are agents of change *for others*, to be precise, a change for their clients.

From solution development to implementation

Hiring a consultancy

MidSizeBank was confronted with a strongly changing market. The bank's top management struggled with the question of how to respond to its changing environment. Therefore, MidSizeBank hired a management consultancy firm, The Waterfall Consultancy Group, to develop a new strategy for the bank. During a short but intensive project, a team of Waterfall consultants collected a huge amount of data and conducted many sophisticated analyses with these data. The hard work by the Waterfall consultants resulted into an ambitious strategy that would allow MidSizeBank to achieve high growth in the changing banking environment.

The brilliant recommendation

The Waterfall partner convinced MidSizeBank's top management with an impressive presentation. According to Waterfall the bank has large opportunities for growth. The Waterfall analyses led to the discovery of some very attractive opportunities for MidSizeBank in current and new markets. Waterfall recommended that MidSizeBank develop some new financial services and enter new distribution channels to seize these opportunities. After the client's acceptance of the recommendation, the Waterfall consultants handed the project documentation over to the client. MidSizeBank received many computer files filled with PowerPoint presentations and back-up materials.

The implementation attempt

After the consultants from Waterfall had left, the bank's top management team together with the bank's top twenty-five managers attempted to develop an implementation plan for the new strategy. The presentation of the strategy had been convincing. The strategy was logical and well-argued. MidSizeBank's management therefore expected that translating the new strategy into actions would be relatively easy. However, when the client managers went one step further than the twenty-slide PowerPoint presentation of the Waterfall partner, the bank's managers could not agree upon the interpretation of the strategy. Different managers had different and conflicting interpretations. For instance, what precisely was meant by 'differentiation'? At a high level of abstraction, the strategy still made sense. Trying to lower the level of abstraction led to ambiguity. The managers could not solve the ambiguity in the recommended strategy. Cascading the high-level strategy abstraction to implementable tasks proved to be mission impossible. What should the client do?

Hiring another consultancy

MidSizeBank decided not to invite Waterfall back to make the translation of the strategy to implementation. MidSizeBank did not consider that operationalizing a strategy was Waterfall's strength. Therefore, MidSizeBank turned to another management consultancy named ActionConsult. ActionConsult's flagship product is their strategy roadmap. This is a pragmatic method to make strategy concrete and operational. ActionConsult does not develop an implementation plan but only provides a process for operationalization. The firm's process consultants use their roadmap method to help MidSizeBank develop an implementation plan based on the client's new strategy. MidSizeBank's top management team takes the role of the steering committee. The top twenty-five managers apply the roadmap method to Waterfall's strategy while the consultants of ActionConsult give guidance and feedback on the work of the bank's managers.

Questions

1 Reflect upon the strategy development project by Waterfall. Do you consider their project successful? Explain your answer.

2 Compare the types of consultancy offered by Waterfall and ActionConsult. What are the main differences?

3 How do you assess the chances of success of the approach by ActionConsult? Elaborate on your answer.

RELATION BETWEEN SOLUTION DEVELOPMENT AND IMPLEMENTATION

Sequential approach with the separation of developers and implementers

Traditionally, client top management with the help of management consultants or the assistance of the client's staff functions formulate a change (see Figure 15.2 on the next page). They design a desired new state, which can be many things, such as a new strategy, a new organization, or a new process. If top management hire a consultant, then the consultants may formulate a solution and leave. Subsequently, top management delegate to middle management and professionals the task of implementing the consultants' recommendation. They have to execute the change and they are often subject to that change. The development and implementation of a solution are done in a sequence, one after the other. Moreover, development and implementation are done by different parties, respectively the developers and the implementers.

Sequential but integrated approach

DEVELOPERS INTEGRATE IMPLEMENTATION IN THE SOLUTION Instead of the traditional approach of separating the roles of development and

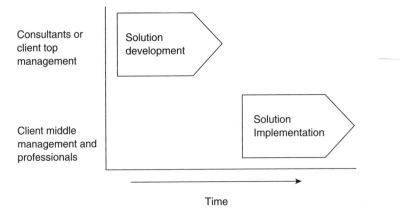

FIGURE 15.2 *Keep solution development and implementation separate*

implementation of solutions, more sophisticated approaches may try to integrate development and implementation. The client and the consultants document the approach in the project plan. We distinguish between two such approaches (see Figure 15.3). In the first approach, developers take implementation into account when developing a solution. The people who develop a solution may be different from the group who need to implement a solution. But the developers consider implementation when developing a solution. For instance, management consultants may take explicitly into account which individuals will be affected and in what way by the solution (the stakeholder analysis: see Chapter 10). The consultants anticipate what specific obstacles may arise during implementation. When choosing a solution, they take into consideration the feasibility of implementation.

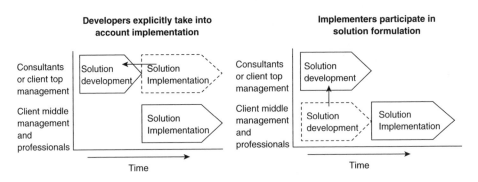

FIGURE 15.3 *Integrate solution development and implementation*

IMPLEMENTERS PARTICIPATE IN SOLUTION DEVELOPMENT In the second approach, the implementers, the people who are involved in implementation, participate in the development process. Involving the implementers increases the chances of a successful solution implementation. Even better is to involve the people who are subject to the change. Involving these stakeholders in development may lead to better quality solutions *and* increase the acceptance and support for the solution. Inclusion of these people creates ownership of the solution and helps to fight against the 'not-invented-here syndrome'.

Involving those who are subject to the change and those who have to implement the change does not mean that these people will make the ultimate decision about a solution. Development does not necessarily become a democratic process. These people may provide valuable ideas and suggestions for the solution. However, client top management will decide. Consultants may involve implementers and other stakeholders in the problem solving phase to enhance the chances of successful implementation of their solutions.

Iterative approach

In situations with high levels of uncertainty, even the most sophisticated sequential approaches of solution development and implementation may fail. If the development of a solution has a very low certainty, then an iterative approach with small steps may work better (see Figure 15.4). The development and implementation of a possible (uncertain) solution may be interpreted as an experiment. The client and the consultants implement a possible small-step solution, and evaluate its effect. This is a trial-and-error approach. The client and the consultants learn by doing. Such learning by doing may be the only feasible approach in highly uncertain situations. Under high uncertainty, it is not realistic to assume that a solution can be found in one single attempt, which is one single sequence of development and implementation.

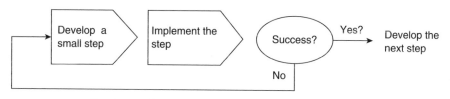

FIGURE 15.4 *Iterate small solution steps*

STRUCTURED IMPLEMENTATION

Plans and people

We would acknowledge situations of high uncertainty where only an iterative approach of experimentation may work. Having said that, we now discuss how consultants may use a structured, sequential approach to change. Before we discuss the details of this approach, we would emphasize that change always has two components: the plan and the people. Consultants may design a plan for the implementation of a solution. However, even the best plan will fail if it does not consider the human dimension.

Implementation of a solution always has an impact on (at least some) people. Stakeholders inside or outside the client organization will be affected by the implementation. The effect of change is not necessarily positive for all involved. Consultants should therefore always take the human side into account when preparing an implementation project.

A sequential approach

How should management consultants change a client? Let us assume a sequential process is feasible, that is, the level of uncertainty is not prohibitive. There are numerous approaches to change. We sketch a structured approach that incorporates elements of Lewin's (1951) change model, as well as some elements of Kotter's (1996) model of organizational transformation. Figure 15.5 on the next page outlines the seven steps in this change process. We assume that the consultants have already developed a solution and that the client has accepted the consultants' recommendation (see Chapters 12 and 13).

Step 1: Form a team for implementation

START AT THE TOP   Implementation of a solution needs the involvement of those to be changed. The consultants may need to involve people at all hierarchical levels of the client organization as well as external stakeholders whose cooperation is required for the implementation. However, the change should start at the top of the client organization. Having been confronted with the need for change, all people in the client organization will typically look to top management for guidance and support. Consultants must ensure that the top of the client organization acts as a role model for change. The top management should show commitment to the implementation project, inspire and give confidence.

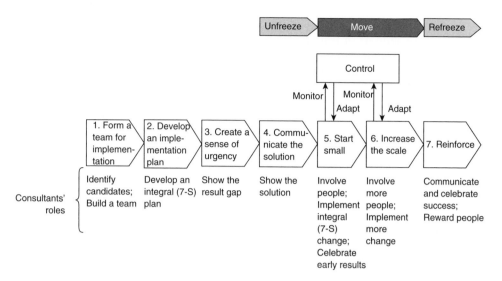

FIGURE 15.5 *Develop a structured approach to implementation*

Notes: 7-S refers to the McKinsey 7-S framework
Sources: based on Lewin (1951) and Kotter (1996)

INVOLVE ALL LEVELS   Involving client people at all levels is good for three reasons.

1. Such involvement may give consultants better knowledge of and insight into the client organization, which may enable them to achieve a better implementation.
2. Involvement of lower levels enhances the capability of the client organization for implementation of the solution.
3. Involvement is necessary for generating support and commitment by the client organization.

Recall that consultants are outsiders. You may ask: why should clients hire outsiders? In some cases, the client organization may lack the people with the required capabilities for implementing the change. The client may then outsource the implementation tasks to consultants or to third party service providers, such as interim managers. Client top management may also prefer outsiders so employees can blame these outsiders (the scapegoat role of management consultants).

AVOID TOP-DOWN RULE   Management consultants need to engage stakeholders inside and possibly also outside the client organization. The consultants form a capable coalition of client organizational members and other stakeholders to lead the implementation. Neither client top management nor the management consultants can bring about the transformation without the support of the client organizational members and other stakeholders. Implementation cannot be imposed from the top (management) or from the outside (management consultants). Even if the change can be forced upon the organization, it will not stick. So-called institutionalization of the change will not take place. People do not like to be overruled. Therefore, top-down rule will not deliver lasting results. Force applied by managers or consultants will not lead to acceptance of the change, it will only lead to (temporary) toleration. Therefore, the consultants need to forge a coalition of client organizational members and other stakeholders.

FORM A COALITION   The consultants' capacity to transform the client organization depends on the quality of the participants in their coalition. Consultants need to recruit participants with sufficient hierarchical power, which is the power to get things done in the client organization. The coalition partners should get people to act. Therefore, consultants like to have client managers with adequate authority in the coalition. The coalition should also have the necessary competences on board for the implementation tasks. The consultants have to engage people inside, and perhaps outside, the client organization with the right skills, knowledge, and experience for the implementation tasks. Additionally, credibility of participants in the coalition is an important selection criterion that consultants use. The coalition needs to be accepted by the client organizational members and other stakeholders. The client top management may also be interested in the consultants' evaluation of the client employees in the coalition. The consultants' judgment of the employee's performance on the project may help the client top managers when deciding whether to give this employee more responsibilities.

REPLACE TOP MANAGEMENT   Management consultants work with the coalition to manage the implementation. The coalition does the actual implementation work (recall that management consultancy is assisting client top management with the managerial tasks of implementation). Even though the consultants may actually manage the implementation, client top management remain responsible. However, in some situations top management are the problem. First, the top managers are responsible for causing the crisis, or the bad situation in general, that necessitated a change in the client organization. Second, the top managers are unable or unwilling to support the required change in the client organization. In both cases, consultants should first attempt to help client management perform better, for instance through personal coaching. If the client top managers are unwilling or unable to improve their performance, then only one option is left, that is replacement. The replacement of client top management is not the responsibility of consultants. Non-executive directors are responsible for replacing failing top managers. Consultants may only advise these non-executive directors.

CASCADE THE CHANGE   The coalition acts as a catalyst to spark change in the client organization. The consultants use the coalition as a lever to get the organization in motion. In (very) large and hierarchical client organizations, management consultants may use a cascade model, or a multi-stage model, to mobilize the organization. Figure 15.6 visualizes a cascade of three stages. Cascading goes hand in hand with communication. In the first stage of the cascade, the consultants create a coalition at the top of the client organization. If the client is a corporation then the top consists of the members of the executive management team, such as the chief executive officer, the chief financial officer, and the executive vice presidents of the client's divisions. In the second stage of the cascade, the consultants form a coalition of the top fifty leaders of the client organization. This typically includes the middle managers. In the third stage of the cascade, the consultants forge a coalition of the top 250 leaders, including lower management. Finally, the plan is cascaded to the level of all employees of the client organization.

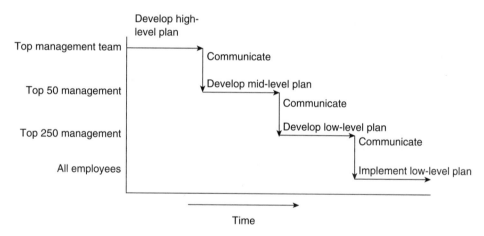

FIGURE 15.6   *Cascade the implementation to mobilize the client organization*

Step 2: Develop an implementation plan

We have assumed that the consultants have already developed a solution (see Chapters 12 and 13). The coalition needs to be convinced that the consultants' solution is the best option for the client organization. Getting the coalition to accept a solution may be difficult if the coalition was not involved in the development of that solution. We would acknowledge that developing a solution together with the client coalition helps to ensure client ownership of the solution. The consultants thereby avoid the not-invented-here syndrome.

Assuming that the solution has already been developed, the consultants only have to develop an implementation plan together with the coalition. The implementation plan is a co-creation of the consultants and the client coalition. The consultants may provide the process for developing an implementation plan, while the client members add their (tacit) knowledge of the client organization. An integral implementation plan deals with all elements of the client organization, as represented by the McKinsey 7-S framework (strategy, structure, staff, skills, style, systems, and shared values).

Step 3: Create a sense of urgency

ASSESS READINESS FOR CHANGE   If the client – in the form of an individual top manager – and its management consultants are ready for change, they should not assume that the rest of the organization and other stakeholders whose cooperation is required are also ready. Even all members of the client top management team may not be ready. The team may be divided. The management consultants may analyse the readiness for change of the client organization and the other stakeholders. The consultants' analysis may reveal that the client organization and the other stakeholders are not even aware of a need for change.

CREATE AWARENESS   Without awareness of the need for change, any attempt to launch a change plan will meet resistance from the client organization and the other stakeholders. These people will certainly question the need for change. Therefore, the management consultants first have to create awareness of the need for change among the members of the client organization and the other stakeholders. We have mentioned before that people generally do not like to change. They need to be convinced of the necessity for change. The literature talks about the need for 'unfreezing' (Lewin, 1951).

NEVER WASTE A GOOD CRISIS   Consultants should arouse anxiety and dissatisfaction among the client organization and other stakeholders as a precondition for change. Consultants need to confront these people with the problem (that needs to be solved by the change) to make the case for change. The consultants need to create 'a burning platform' to raise awareness of the need for change. A crisis is therefore welcome for consultants and client top managers who want to implement change. 'Never waste a good crisis' was coined in politics but it is applicable to management consultancy as well.

SHOW THE RESULT GAP   If consultants want to disturb the status quo, they need to show the result gap. The message should be specific and concrete. Do not tell but rather show the facts. Consultants show the client employees what will happen if their organization continues with business as usual. We may distinguish different situations for the client. The client may already face a crisis and performance is negative. Then it will be relatively easy to create awareness. Most difficult situations are when client performance is good, but the consultants anticipate a future problem for the client organization. Having a successful client organization change in order to seize an opportunity is also challenging. In particular in difficult situations, repeated communication is necessary. Consultants have to communicate again and again to let the message sink in.

PRESENT THE BAD NEWS   Sometimes it is better if management consultants as outsiders bring the bad news message. They may be perceived as objective and independent. Additionally, client top management may use the consultants as the 'bad guys', reserving the role of the 'good guys' for themselves. Figure 15.7 visualizes how most people commonly respond to bad news. People typically go through different emotional states. The exact pattern depends on the severity of the negative consequences for the individual and on the degree of control that the individual may have over the problem. Denial is a common response to bad news. Client employees and other stakeholders may have blind spots. To enable change, these people need to be convinced that the bad news is true.

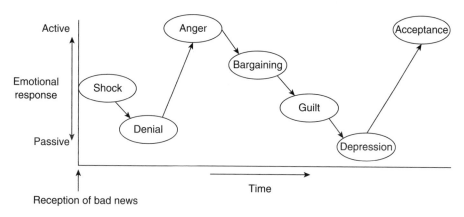

FIGURE 15.7   *How most people commonly respond to bad news*

CHANGE THE MIND SET   All people, including client employees and other stakeholders, may have certain reference frames that filter the bad news. Consultants have to change the mind set of these people. People may also have become subject to group think. Consultants should uncover any hidden but wrong assumptions that client employees and other stakeholders may have about the organization and the environment. These assumptions may have become outdated. As a result, their reference frames have become obsolete. Here is an added value for management consultants: identifying the blind spots of the client organization.

UNFREEZE ATTITUDES   After the consultants have created awareness, the client employees and other stakeholders are open to change. They have been 'unfrozen' and are ready to accept change. The consultants should not only confront the client's people with the need for change. They also have to communicate that both the client organization and the leadership are capable – they can develop and implement a plan for the required change. The client employees and other stakeholders should become aware of the need for change but they should not be talked into a depression and despair. Therefore, it is critical to provide as soon as possible a vision of how the client organization should deal with the bad news.

Step 4: Communicate the solution

INFORM UPFRONT   People typically do not like unpleasant surprises. Therefore, the client employees and other stakeholders need to be informed upfront about the implementation. The communication may be both focused internally, such as town hall meetings, and externally, that is to the (mass) media and specific external shareholders groups.

The consultants design the communication of the solution and its implementation plan. The actual communication may be done by the client top management or by the consultants.

DELEGATE TO CONSULTANTS   In some cases, client top management delegate the communication to consultants. If the solution is sensitive – for instance, it includes a headcount reduction, off-shoring, outsourcing, plant closure, and downsizing – then the client may let the consultants do all the communication. The case for delegation to consultants becomes stronger if informal hiring reasons play a role, that is if the consultants are hired to legitimate client decisions that have already been made (before hiring the consultants), or to fulfil the scapegoat role. Delegating the communication to consultants is not without its drawbacks. It increases the distance between client management and employees. Client management should decide on this trade-off.

COMMUNICATE THE VISION   In their communications, the consultants should provide guidance and motivation to the client organization and stakeholders. The consultants communicate the solution to the client organization and other stakeholders to create interest. A shared vision across the client members is essential for a successful implementation. Consultants should put in huge efforts to communicate the vision for the client organization. The message should be easy to understand for everyone involved in the implementation project. The message should be addressed to the individual client employee and stakeholder. The work council and the unions are important stakeholders in implementation projects. If they accept and support the implementation, then the chances of success will increase considerably.

COMMUNICATE TO THE INDIVIDUAL   Ultimately, change takes place at the level of the individual. The individual needs to know how they personally will be affected by the change and what they specifically need to do. Each individual needs to be informed about the required new behaviour, new knowledge, new skills, new values, new incentives, new rewards, new sanctions, etc.

The consultants may use various communication channels, such as town hall meetings, video messages, the client intranet, and small group meetings. The consultants communicate the desired results, the benefits, plus the plan to achieve them. The implementation requires the support of the people whom it concerns. Therefore the communication should be inspiring and energizing, and create enthusiasm.

OVERCOME SCEPTICISM   Client organizational members and other stakeholders may have negative feelings about the intended change. Change implies disturbance in the on-going operations. They do not like the related uncertainty. Client employees and other stakeholders may have worries about their job security and future job requirements. They may also be puzzled: can I meet the new demands? Remember, not everyone may win as a result of the implementation of the consultants' solution. Some client employees and other stakeholders may face a deterioration of their position or even a job loss. These people will be highly sceptical about the solution. A typical reaction to the communication of the solution is: we have tried this before and it did not work. If the management consultants have implemented the solution elsewhere, then the best practices can be used to try to convince client employees and other stakeholders about what the benefits of the solution are and that implementation is feasible. However, some people may remain sceptical: this solution might work in other organizations but we are different. People at the client organization may have a lack of respect or trust in change agents, in particular if the management consultants are external to the client. In such situations, client top management may need to support the consultants.

ORGANIZE WORKSHOPS   How can management consultants achieve the client organization's acceptance, commitment, and ownership of the solution? A common tool used by consultants is workshops with client employees. Workshops allow for two-way communication, which is more effective than one-way. Client organizational members should have the opportunity to raise questions and receive answers. Consultants may solicit suggestions and feedback from client members. Workshops also offer an opportunity for people to vent their objections to change. The literature distinguishes between so-called sharpeners and levellers (Kubr, 2002). Sharpeners ask very specific and detailed questions. They have a genuine interest and want to be convinced that the solution and the implementation are right. In contrast, levellers generalize and broaden the issue. Often, they are more interested in the form of their objections than in the content of their objections. These people are difficult to convince.

COMMUNICATE, COMMUNICATE, COMMUNICATE   Repeated communication is a critical success factor. The message should not be communicated once but several times to sink in. Communication remains critical during the subsequent steps of the implementation processes. Because of the emotions and interests of client members and other stakeholders, these people need to be kept informed. Consultants continue the communications during the subsequent steps of change. They need to keep all involved and affected stakeholders up to date. Consultants should show progress, whenever possible, in order to motivate. The process should be as transparent as possible because transparency helps acceptance and increases the feeling of being involved. Consultants cannot communicate too much. Implementation is about communication, communication, and communication.

Step 5: Start small

REDUCE RISK AND CREATE SHORT-TERM GAINS   The consultants may start the implementation on a small scale. Starting small may give some benefits. This small-scale change may serve as a pilot test for the organization-wide implementation. The pilot may reduce the risk for the client. Moreover, a small-scale start enables an opportunity to create short-term gains.

EMPOWER PEOPLE   Consultants need to involve the client organization members. After all, change takes place at the level of the individual. To empower the individuals for implementing the change, the consultants may have to take an integral approach, changing all seven S's (strategy, structure, staff, skills, style, systems, and shared values). For instance, the consultants may have to change the client organization structure to enable new behaviour by client organizational members. The consultants may adapt the client's reporting structure and other organizational relationships. To empower the client people, the consultants may have to design new roles and suggest that top management assign new responsibilities to particular client employees. The client members should get the opportunity to make decisions and take actions (to implement the solution).

DEVELOP PEOPLE   For their new roles and responsibilities, client organizational members may need new knowledge and skills. Management consultants may help with client learning. The consultant as an educator may facilitate the development of new skills and provide coaching to enable the new behaviour. Client top management may stimulate learning by permitting failure. People are allowed to make mistake if they learn from these, but repeating the same mistake is unacceptable. A tolerance of failure also encourages risk taking. Consultants may also propose new performance indicators and rewards to align client people's behaviour with the intended change.

CONTROL THE PROJECT   Implementation is a project which needs to be controlled. Consultants may monitor the progress of the implementation project by gathering and analysing data. Often, the consultants will develop a dashboard with which they can monitor the status of the key performance indicators. If the implementation deviates from the planning, then consultants will advise the client about adaptive and corrective measures, depending on the situation.

GENERATE SHORT-TERM GAINS   Change typically takes a long time to materialize, while the emotions of involved stakeholders during a change project show strong movements. Stakeholders need early benefits for motivation. The dynamics of stakeholders' emotions are to some extent similar to those of project teams (see Chapter 11 for the stages of team development). Figure 15.8 visualizes the dynamics which draw the analogy with a rollercoaster. To dampen the downswing in the emotional state, it is important to generate gains in the short term. By starting the implementation on a small scale, the client members may be able to realize results sooner than when starting on large scale. Short-term gains may infuse hope and confidence in the stakeholders. As a result, these gains reinforce implementation. Consultants recognize and reward people who achieve early wins.

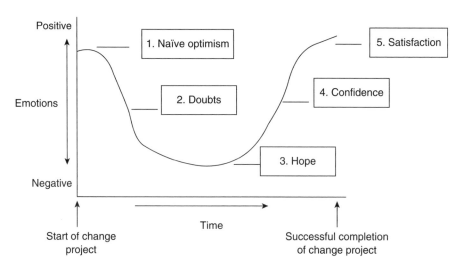

FIGURE 15.8   *A change project may resemble an emotional rollercoaster*

CELEBRATE SMALL WINS   For the purpose of motivation, consultants may also break large implementation processes in bite-size, digestible chunks. Instead of a marathon, consultants create a series of short races. The consultants define a series of small, including short-term, wins, instead of one big but long-term win. Completing a small piece of the implementation is an achievement, which consultants use as an excuse to celebrate. Consultants should not overdo these celebrations. They need to avoid the trap of creating the illusion that enough has been achieved already, which would signal that no more effort is needed.

Step 6: Increase scale

MAKE ADDITIONAL CHANGES   After the first (small) change has been realized, consultants may increase the scale and scope of the changes. They may spread the change to other business units and departments of the client organization. Additionally, consultants may make additional changes to any of the client's seven S's (strategy, structure, staff, skills, style, systems, and shared values).

MANAGE CONFLICTS   Implementation may lead to conflicts. Conflicts may arise for several reasons. Some main reasons include:

1. Client members' resistance to change.
2. Disagreement about the planned implementation objectives and methods.
3. Competition for scarce resources.
4. Personal clashes between client members, or between client members and consultants.

The best approach to manage conflicts is confrontation. Consultants may use a structured problem solving process to address the conflict (treat the conflict as a problem to be solved), and let the conflicting parties work out their disagreement. An alternative approach to conflicts is 'forcing', that is adopting one side at the expense of the others. However, forcing is least effective. Consultants may also use the approach of compromising, which is developing a solution that is acceptable to all parties. Alternatively, consultants may apply 'smoothing', that is emphasizing common interests, while de-emphasizing disagreements. Finally, consultants may opt for withdrawal, which means a retreat from the conflict situation.

Step 7: Reinforce

REFREEZE NEW BEHAVIOUR   Consultants need to reinforce the new behaviour by client members. This new behaviour needs 'refreezing' (Lewin, 1951). Management consultants may refreeze the new behaviour in formal structures, systems, and processes. Furthermore, the consultants need to institutionalize the transformed behaviour of client organizational members. The new behaviour needs to become part of the client's (new) culture. The client members must accept the new behaviour, not just tolerate it. Members accept the new behaviour only if they are convinced that it is better.

CHANGE THE CLIENT STAFF   Consultants should communicate to the client members the benefits of the new behaviour to reinforce this behaviour. Consultants need to communicate how the new behaviour contributes to the client's organizational performance. Consultants should introduce rewards and advise top management on promotions that enable the institutionalization of the desired behaviour. Client members who behave in the intended way receive a reward and recognition. The consultants will first warn and then take sanctions against client members who resist the change. Finally, changing staff, through the hiring and firing of people, may help to make the desired behaviour part of the new culture. The consultants may advise client top management to hire people who fit the new culture or can be moulded to that culture. Additionally, the consultants may advise the client top management to take their leave of existing client members who will not or cannot adopt their behaviour.

WHY SOME IMPLEMENTATION PROJECTS MAY FAIL

The outcome of an implementation project may be conceptualized as a continuum ranging from perfect implementation to complete disaster. In real life, the outcome will be somewhere in between these extremes. We may distinguish between two possible reasons why a consultant's implementation fails to (fully) achieve the desired results for the client (see Figure 15.9 on the next page).

Flawed solution

The first possible reason is a flawed solution. The implementation may have been perfect but the consultant's solution cannot create the desired results. The analysis underlying the solution may be incomplete or incorrect. The consultant may have drawn the wrong conclusions from the analysis results. The critical view on consulting would blame consultants' rhetoric – consultants promote ineffective products. The solution may also have been overtaken by reality. Unforeseen changes may have made the solution obsolete or outdated. Alternatively, the solution may not address the real problem. A flawed solution may be a consequence of the client manipulating the consultants to work on the wrong problem (see Chapter 10), or manipulation by factions within the client organization with a different agenda may undermine the problem solving by the consultants.

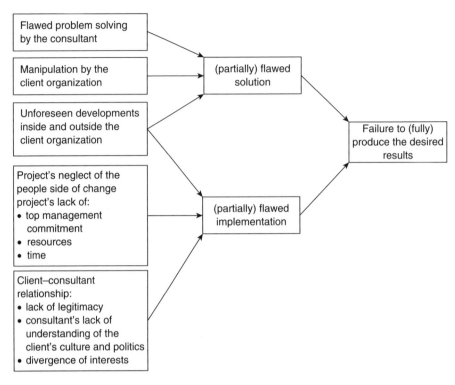

FIGURE 15.9 *Why some implementation projects may fail to (fully) produce the desired results for clients*

Flawed implementation

The second possible reason is a (partially) flawed implementation process. The consultants have made one or more mistakes in any of the steps of the implementation process (see Figure 15.5). We distinguish between three main categories of reasons for flawed implementation:

1. Unforeseen developments.
2. Neglect of the people side of change.
3. The client–consultant relationship.

UNFORESEEN DEVELOPMENTS   Implementation failure is not always due to flaws in the implementation, which could have been anticipated and prevented by the consultants. Unforeseen developments inside or outside the client organization may also cause a failed implementation. Implementation plans may be overtaken by reality. For instance, external shocks to the implementation such as an economic crisis may make a solution obsolete or outdated. Other unforeseen developments may include changes inside the client organization. Examples of internal shocks to the implementation are a turnover of people at the (top of the) client, and a (related) change of the top management's agenda. The client's interests and objectives may change, which may have negative consequences for the implementation project. Of course, we may debate to what extent consultants should build in flexibility and develop contingency plans to accommodate external and internal shocks.

NEGLECT OF THE PEOPLE SIDE   An implementation plan may also fail because it neglects the people side of change. Implementation is not a mechanical process but a social process. We have already discussed people issues. Here, we emphasize several people issues.

Resistance to change. First, client organizational members may resist the intended change because the consultants have not (effectively) dealt with the issues of client members' awareness, willingness, and ability to change. The client members may not be aware of the need for change. They may not be willing to change. They may also not be able to change. Client members may resist consultants in general because they are seen as outsiders and because of their conflicting interests (see Chapter 10). Another major source of resistance is risk aversion by client members. The consultants' implementation project induces the risk of failure of the client's current business. The stakes rise with the success of the client's current business. The more successful the client, the higher the risk (of performance decline) that change may entail, and the higher the resistance to change. If the consultants insufficiently communicate their risk management, then resistance may undermine the implementation.

Organizational power and politics. The second people issue is about organizational power and politics. The change intended by the consultants may shift power, resources, and status across client factions and individual actors. Some people at the client organization risk losing control and they may even risk losing their position. Consultants may have neglected these people or their attempts to develop solutions for them may have failed. Such failure may also be due to a lack of commitment from client top management.

Client culture. The third people issue is about the client's culture. Culture may explain resistance and seemingly irrational and dysfunctional processes in the client organization. Culture may also be (part of) the cause of the client's problem. At the deepest level, culture is about the client's values and beliefs. Culture also includes client members' attitudes, norms, and taboos. Culture may express itself via symbols (such as jargon, gestures, and objects such as cars), rituals and heroes, dress codes, handling forms, and the level of formality. Culture is even more important in international consulting projects.

Consultancy projects spanning multiple countries not only face issues of organizational culture but also face differences between national cultures. Management consultants need to understand the client culture in order to adequately deal with it.

Lack of top management commitment. Implementation may fail because of a lack of commitment from client top management. For instance, the client may be reluctant or will even refuse to be visible in the change process. The client top management may refuse to deal with sabotage by client organizational members and external stakeholders. The client top team may be divided about the implementation. Some members may be committed to the implementation, while others may have reservations or even resist the implementation plan. Moreover (some members of) the client top management may have a hidden agenda that is not (fully) aligned with the implementation plan. Finally, client top management may lack the guts to commit to the implementation plan. They may, for instance, fear (powerful) stakeholders, such as work councils, unions, and shareholders.

Lack of resources. Other causes of implementation failure are a lack of resources, a lack of skills and experience, and a lack of time. For instance, the client and/or the consultancy firm do not assign the right people to the change coalition. People are appointed on the basis of availability instead of quality. The consultancy firm may put a B-team on the project. The consultants' and the client's top talent may be too busy with other (higher priority) business. Moreover, the assigned people may not be properly prepared for the change. They may, for instance, lack information and training.

Lack of time. A too tight time schedule may also undermine implementation. An implementation may fail because of a lack of time. For instance, the consultants did not reserve (sufficient) time for preparing the client organization and for dealing with the inevitable setbacks. In particular, projects involving external consultants face time constraints. These consultants are relatively expensive. Hiring external consultants implies an out-of-pocket expense. Clients will therefore minimize the duration of consultancy projects. They will want to minimize the amount of time they need to pay consultants. Because of the high cost, consultancy projects have a relatively short duration. However, change in an organization typically has a long-term trajectory.

THE CLIENT–CONSULTANT RELATIONSHIP   The third category of reasons for flawed implementation is based on the relationship between the client and the consultant. We can distinguish between three reasons:

1. The consultants' lack of legitimacy.
2. The consultants' lack of understanding of the client.
3. The divergence of client and consultant interests.

Lack of legitimacy. Implementation may fail due to differences between the client and the consultants. The consultants are outsiders to the client organization. They may lack legitimacy in the client organization. The client top management may consider the consultants as legitimate, but the lower levels of the organization may not. The people at the lower levels of the client organization may see the consultants as agents of client top management. Consultants are perceived as implementers of change which is desired by the top management. The client organizational members dislike the change and prefer continuity. Because of this conflict of interests between consultants and the lower level client members, and because of the consultants' lack of legitimacy, these client members will not (voluntarily) give their support to the consultants. Even worse, these client organizational members will not even accept the consultants.

Lack of understanding of client politics. Consultants typically have limited or no access to the tacit knowledge inside the client organization. Consequently, consultants lack an (in-depth) understanding of the client's culture and politics. Therefore, consultants cannot – or can only insufficiently – take the client's culture and politics (fully) into account. Consultants are constrained to follow a rationalistic approach rather than a socio-political approach to the implementation. However, this approach comes at a price. A disregard of the client's culture and politics undermines the success of consultants. Consultants have to take into account client culture and politics. They should know:

- What change is acceptable to the client?
- What pace of change is feasible?
- Who are the informal leaders inside the client organization?
- What arguments have to be used?

Lack of understanding of client culture. We have already discussed the *client's* culture. However, we should not forget that consultants also have a culture. Some consultancy firms may even have very strong cultures. As a result, the consultancy project may imply a confrontation between two (very) different cultures. Consultants have to overcome this cultural distance between them and the client to successfully implement the solution. Consultants may (at least partially) overcome the lack of tacit knowledge of the client context by developing a long-term relationship with the client. Through their continued involvement with the client, via a series of projects, consultants may gradually become a sort of insider to the client organization. Consultants may also overcome the lack of understanding client politics and culture by working closely with the client, for instance, the consultants may include client employees in their project team.

Divergence of interests of client top management and other client stakeholders. Divergence in interests, and to a higher extent, conflicts of interests between client and consultants may cause the failure of the implementation. We have already discussed conflict of interests between client top management on the one hand, and the other client organizational members on the other hand. Now, we focus on the position of consultants vis-à-vis the client. Client top management hire and pay the consultants. The consultants work for the top management, not for the rest of organization. In the case of divergent interests of top management and the other client members (lower management and professionals), management consultants may be drawn into intra-organizational politics. Consultants should not make the mistake of assuming a neutral, arbiter position. They should remember they are hired by top management to represent interests at the top. A conflict of interest between client top management and the rest may undermine implementation of the solution if lower management and employees refuse to cooperate or resist implementation. Beforehand, the consultants should investigate possible conflicts of interests. Consultants need to understand who will benefit from the implementation and who will stand to lose (see Chapter 10).

Divergence of interests of client top management and consultants. However, the interests of the consultants and the client top management may not always run in parallel either. Consultants might want to sell a standardized solution rather than customize their solution to the specific needs of the client. Standardized solutions are more efficient than customization. Efficiency of implementation is in the interests of consultants, but clients are interested in the effectiveness of the solution. Client top management may therefore demand a customized solution. Another source of divergence of interests between client top management and the management consultants is the hidden agenda that some clients may have. We have discussed before that clients may have informal reasons for hiring consultants. Such clients may manipulate consultants to implement their hidden agenda. Implementation may be the formal reason to hire the consultants, but the real reason may be something else. For instance, the top manager may want to get rid of a rival, or may want to shift the balance of power. In such cases, the client top management may have little or no interest in the success of the implementation, as long as the hidden objective is achieved. This lack of top management commitment may undermine the implementation project.

EVALUATE THE IMPLEMENTATION

During the project

Evaluation of the implementation project takes place at several moments in time during the execution of the project. Management consultants and/or the client monitor the progress of the project. This project evaluation is part of the control process. An important purpose of project evaluation is quality

AN INTRODUCTION TO MANAGEMENT CONSULTANCY

assurance. Based on the periodic evaluation of the project, the consultant and the client may take adaptive and corrective measures. Therefore, the evaluation should not be postponed until the end of the project.

Evaluate the project outcome

After the completion of the project, client and consultants may evaluate the success of the implementation. Has the project achieved its objectives? It may be impossible to fully evaluate the success of the project because some effects of the implementation may need a long time to materialize. For example, an organizational change may take a long time to become institutionalized. Typically there is a long time lag between the implementation of a new strategy and the impact on the client's performance, in terms of profitability and growth. Evaluating the long-term effects of a project cannot take place immediately after completion of the project.

Evaluate the consultants

Evaluation of the project's success may serve other purposes besides quality assurance.

Determining the fee. An evaluation after the completion of the project may be used to determine the consultants' fee, where a performance-based fee was agreed upon. Then the level of the project's success determines the amount of the consultancy fee.

The contribution of consultants. Client and consultant may not only evaluate the success of the project but also the effect or contribution of the consultants to this success. How did the consultants contribute to the project results and what was their added value to the project?

Performance appraisals. Management consultancy firms may use project evaluation in the performance appraisal of individual consultants, managers, and partners. The rewards and career prospects of the individuals will depend (at least to a large extent) on the evaluation of their behaviour and performance during projects.

References. Management consultancy firms also like to use project evaluations to prove their success. Positive project evaluations, in particular if signed by the client, constitute a powerful reference for the marketing of the consultancy firm's services. Positive project evaluations enable the consultancy firm to build a reputation.

Evaluate the process

Evaluation is typically not limited to the success of the project, in terms of its impact on the client's results. Evaluation may also include other aspects, such as time and costs. Did the consultants complete the project in time and within budget?

In addition, evaluation may consider the process of implementation. Did the consultants implement the solution properly? Furthermore, evaluation may assess how ethically consultants and others involved in the project have behaved. Finally, client and consultants may evaluate the cooperation between client and consultants during the project. How well did the client and consultants work together in the implementation project?

Lessons learned

Client and consultants may also evaluate a project to learn from the experience. Based on the evaluation, each may draw lessons from the project. The experience may help both client and consultants to be more effective and efficient in subsequent projects. Management consultants systematically archive their project experiences in knowledge management systems. If the knowledge is only in the heads of people, then the firm loses the knowledge when the individuals leave the firm.

Difficulty of evaluating consultants

It is difficult to evaluate the specific contribution of the management consultants to the implementation. You need to isolate this particular factor from the other factors influencing the outcome of an implementation project. Not only do the activities of the management consultants have an impact on the implementation, but so do the activities of employees and other stakeholders inside and outside the client organization. Moreover, industry developments and macro-environmental developments may affect the outcome of an implementation project. An implementation project may fail notwithstanding the high-quality work by consultants. Alternatively, an implementation may succeed despite the low-quality work of consultants.

Evaluate the success of an implementation

MEASURE THE IMPACT ON CLIENT RESULT   The most relevant success criterion for evaluating an implementation project is the contribution to the client's objectives. Clients would like to measure the project's impact on their desired result. For instance, how does the project contribute to the client's profit? Clients may also like to assess the impact of the project on their revenues and costs. For instance, how much does a growth strategy project increase the client's revenues? Similarly, how much does a restructuring project reduce the client's costs?

Cost reductions are easier to relate to an implementation project than revenue increases. The relationship between consultants' recommendations and cost reductions is more direct than the relation between recommendations and revenue growth. For instance, it is relatively easy to measure the cost reduction as a result of the downsizing of the client's operations.

MEASURE DELIVERABLES   Besides measuring improvements in the client's output (such as profits, revenues, and costs), we may also consider other project's deliverables, such as reorganization or the implementation of a new organizational process. Measurement of the deliverables is based on the assumption that the deliverables lead to higher outputs. If we cannot measure outputs then we may still measure deliverables.

For instance, an implementation project may result in a new organization structure for the client. The consultants may not be able to measure the impact of the new organization structure on the client's performance, but they can measure to what extent the new structure is properly implemented. Another example is the development of new systems and processes for the client. Even if the performance improvement is difficult to measure, the consultants may measure the extent to which the systems and processes have been appropriately implemented.

How to evaluate

DECIDE UPFRONT ON CRITERIA   It is essential that before the start of the project, the client and the consultant agree upon the set of evaluation criteria. Determining the evaluation criteria after completion of the project may give the impression of opportunism.

HARD DATA   Whenever possible, project evaluations should be based on verifiable (quantified) facts, instead of opinions. Evaluation of the project's success should, whenever possible, use quantified facts about the client's performance improvement, such as a cost reduction or a revenue increase.

SOFT DATA   If hard data (facts) are not available and data gathering is not (economically) feasible, then the project evaluation should be based on soft data. Soft data include opinions and perceptions from different stakeholders. For instance, the consultants may evaluate how satisfied client employees have become after the implementation of the recommended solution.

COLLECT DATA   The evaluation data may be collected in various ways. The client's control department may have data about the client's performance. The consultants may use surveys and interviews to solicit the opinions of employees, customers, suppliers, and other stakeholders. Typically, the consultants will put the outcomes of the evaluation in a report, which they will subsequently present to the client.

Terminate the project

After the evaluation of the project, the consultants have to handle any loose ends from the project that still exist. Typically, the consultants will produce a closing report for the client. Subsequently, the consultants will hand over the project documentation to the client. The consultants should remain committed until the official end of the project. This may be difficult, in particular if a new client project is waiting.

SUMMARY

A structured approach to implementation

Implementation of the solution recommended by the management consultants implies change for the client organization. Management consultants do not conduct the actual implementation work but they do assist client (top) management with management of the implementation.

This chapter outlined a structured process of implementation, and indicated the possible roles of management consultants in that implementation process. The literature distinguished between a critical view and a functionalist view on the consultants' role in implementation.

Why some projects may fail

We also discussed why some consultancy implementation projects may fail to produce the desired results. We distinguished between failure due to flawed solutions and failure as a result of a flawed implementation. Flawed implementation may be due to various reasons, such a project's lack of commitment, resources, time, legitimacy, a neglect of the people side of change, a consultant's lack of understanding of the client culture and politics, unforeseen developments, a divergence of interests among client stakeholders, and a divergence of interests between clients and consultants.

Evaluation

Evaluation takes place during and after the project. Such evaluation may focus on different things, including the project outcome, the contribution of management consultancy, the process of implementation, and cooperation between client and consultant. We discuss how to evaluate. We acknowledge the difficulties of evaluation, in particular, the outcome of a consultancy project, and the contribution of the consultants to this outcome.

The merger of AcStrat and Delta

The merger decision

AcStrat and Delta have agreed to merge. However, there is a huge difference between the two firms (see Table 15.2).

AcStrat is a fraction of Delta's size. In fact, it is an acquisition. AcStrat becomes the new strategy development practice area within Delta. AcStrat's ninety partners exchange their shares in AcStrat for shares in Delta. All AcStrat partners become Delta partners. All AcStrat consultants get an offer from Delta. However, two thirds of AcStrat's support staff are made redundant.

TABLE 15.2 *Compare the two firms*

	AcStrat	Delta	%
Partners	90	2100	4.3%
Consultants	630	42000	1.5%
Total consulting staff	720	44100	1.6%
Leverage	7	20	35.0%
Revenues	525	13875	3.8%
Revenues per consultant	729	315	231.8%
Revenues per partner	5833	6607	88.3%
Offices	15	90	16.7%
Consultants per office	48	490	9.8%

Note: The percentage refers to the ratio of AcStrat to Delta

The post-merger integration plan

A taskforce, consisting of some senior partners of Delta and AcStrat, develops a post-merger integration plan. They structure the integration with the help of Maister's framework of the balanced firm. The taskforce takes into account the four elements of the framework: talent, economics, organization, and clients. Table 15.3 presents the diagnosis and the recommendation for each element.

▶

TABLE 15.3 *Recommended integration of AcStrat and Delta*

	AcStrat (before merger)	Delta (before merger)	Recommended integration of AcStrat and Delta
Talent	• Top talent • High compensation • Premium employer • Big career opportunities (but up-or-out)	• Modal workforce • Medium compensation • Middle of the road employer • Medium opportunities	• Keep separate recruitment • Keep higher compensation for Acstrat • Employer reputation of Acstrat diluted • Lowering of career opportunities for Acstrat
Economics	• High billing rates • Small project teams	• Medium billing rates • Large project teams	• Keep high billing rates for AcStrat • Keep small project teams for AcStrat
Organization	• Low leverage • Small offices • 15 offices	• High leverage • Large offices • 90 offices	• Keep low leverage for AcStrat • Share the large Delta offices • Spread AcStrat over more offices in different countries
Clients	• Board level of Fortune Global 500 clients • Mainly Western markets	• All levels of management and all sizes of clients • Truly global	• AcStrat trades down to lower-level clients • Create global scope for AcStrat

Reaction to the plan

Resistance

The partners of the merged firms agree with this integration plan. But the communication of the plan causes unrest among the AcStrat consultants and managers. There is resistance to the forced spreading of staff over Delta offices in different countries, mostly in fast-growing countries in Asia and South America. In particular, AcStrat people with (young) families, mostly managers, do not want to relocate to a foreign Delta office. Moreover, the AcStrat people consider it unattractive to work for smaller clients. They prefer to work for Fortune Global 500 companies. The consultants also fear the erosion of AcStrat's traditionally strong reputation. AcStrat will become a sub-brand of the much less prestigious Delta organization.

Voluntary turnover

The AcStrat consultants are afraid that their CVs will become less valuable. Many consultants start to look for opportunities elsewhere. The best consultants have the best opportunities and leave the organization. Consultants who have no external option stay in the merged firm but their motivation has dropped considerably.

Clash of consultant types

Moreover, the two types of AcStrat and Delta consultants do not seem to match. The AcStrat consultants look down upon their new colleagues. They feel superior to the Delta consultants. The Delta consultants are not happy with the newcomers. The news about keeping high compensation for the AcStrat consultants has led to envy and animosity among the Delta consultants. The Delta people feel discriminated against. They feel they have become second-class citizen in their own organization.

Questions

1 To what extent is this merger likely to realize the intended synergies, that is: cross-selling, joint purchasing, cost reductions, leveraging competences, and rolling out best practices? Explain your answer.

2 What should the taskforce do now to improve the performance of this merger? Elaborate on your answer.

3 Was the merger a good solution? Take the perspective of the AcStrat partners. Explain your answer.

REFLECTIVE QUESTIONS

1. Smart & Company is a brain type of consulting firm. Traditionally, the firm only offered advice (our narrow definition of consultancy). Because of the increasing demand of their clients for results rather than reports, Smart considers adding implementation to its service offerings. To what extent is it desirable and feasible for Smart to enter implementation consulting? Explain your answer.

2. When should a client organization hire external management consultants to assist with implementation of a solution, and when should the client do the implementation without external consultants? Explain your answer.

3. The chapter discusses a possible divide between the interests of client top management on the one hand, and lower management and professionals on the other hand, when it comes to implementation of a solution. Assume you are a management consultant who is hired to implement a reorganization plan at a particular client company. You

find out that the top management behave opportunistically and want to disregard the justified concerns of lower management and professionals against this reorganization, in order to obtain a huge bonus. What should you do? Explain your answer.

FURTHER READING

Keller, S. and Price, C. (2011) *Beyond Performance: How Great Organizations Build Ultimate Competitive Advantage*. Hoboken, NJ: John Wiley.

Kipping, M. and Clark, T. (eds) (2012) *The Oxford Handbook of Management Consulting*. Oxford: Oxford University Press.

Kotter, J. (1996) *Leading Change*. Boston, MA: Harvard Business School Press.

REFERENCES

Kotter, J. (1996) *Leading Change.* Boston, MA: Harvard Business School Press.

Kubr, M. (ed.) (2002) *Management Consulting: A Guide to the Profession*. Geneva: International Labour Organization.

Lewin, K. (1951) *Field Theory in Social Science*. New York: Harper & Row.

Nikolova, N. and Devinney, T. (2012) 'The nature of client-consultant interaction: a critical review', in M. Kipping and T. Clark (eds), *The Oxford Handbook of Management Consulting*. Oxford: Oxford University Press, 389–410.

INDEX

grey hair consultancy *cont.*
  people in, 277
  personalization strategy and, *225*
  profit per partner and, 263, *264*
guessing, 422

Hammer, M., 189
Harvey balls, 477, *477*
hedging, 478
Henderson, B., 52, 248
human resource management (HRM), 227–228

Iacocca: An Autobiography (Iacocca), 194–195
Iacocca, L., 194–195
IBM, 53–54, 184
IBM Consulting Group
  competition and, 148, 156
  history of, 55, 69, 162
  organizational structure of, 246
  scale of, 125
identity, 253
implementation assistance
  overview, 16–17, 222–223, 323, 535
  recommendation vs., 537–538
  roles of management consultants and, 538–540, **539**
  solution development and, 545–547, *546–547*
  See also structured implementation
In Search of Excellence (Peters and Waterman), 61, 68,
    87–88, 198, 199
indirect procurement, 357–360, *357*
induction
  hypothesis testing and, 460, *460*, 462, *463*
  overview, 423, *424*
  presentations and, 504–505, *505*
industrial engineers, 47
industrial revolution, 45
industry convergence, 166–167, *167*
industry cost curve, 518, *518*
Information Consulting Group (ICG), 61
information technology, *167*, 168–170, 184, 234
information technology (IT) consultancy
  business models of, 63–65
  corporations and, 155–156
  effect of, **89**, 90
  history of, 53–55, 62–63, 67–68, 183–184, 185
*An Inquiry into the Nature and Causes of the Wealth of
    Nations* (Smith), 47
intellectual abilities, 287–288
intellectual property, 192, 356
inter-personal interaction qualities, 288
interim management, 23
interim presentations, 497, 509–510, *509–510*
internal combustion engine, 183
internal consultancy, 255
internal management consultancy
  vs. external management consultancy, 31–32, **32**,
    92–96, **93**, *96*
  overview, 25
internal studies, 225–226

International Council of Management Consulting
    Institutes (ICMCI), 13, 34, 35, **36**
internet, 184, 185–187, 218, 456
interpersonal fit, 335
interviews, 224, 279–286
investor capitalism, 58
involuntary turnover, 305–306
isomorphism, 97–98

junior consultants, 392–393, 469
junior partners
  client's perspective on, 333
  overview, 292, **292**, *293*, *294*

Kaplan, R., 189, 194, 456
Kennedy Information, 118
key performance indicators (KPIs), 381–383
Kipping, M., 259
knowledge
  accumulation of, 140, *140*, 455
  development of, 324
  effects of, 86–88, *86*, *87*
  exploration and exploitation of, 139–144, *140*
  public domain and, 455–456
  risks and, 98–99
knowledge management, 225–227, 229, *229*, 455
knowledge management systems, 226
Kotter, J., 548
KPMG, 124–125, 156

labour specialization, 47
leaders (tracers, trackers), 526, *526*
leadership
  business models and, 241–245, *241*
  control and, 248–250, 252
  culture and, 250–253
  economics and, 259–268
  legal forms and, 253–255
  organizational structure and, 245–247, *245*, *247*,
    248, *248*
  overview, 228
legal advice, 23–24
leverage
  client's perspective on, 333
  growth and, 267, *267*
  overview, 257–258, *258*, 301
  profit per partner and, 263
  pyramid structure and, 291
Lewin, K., 548
liability, 356
Little, A.D., 46
  See also Arthur D. Little (consultancy firm)

M-form, 51–52
Maister, D.H., 259
managed professional business (MPB)
  career structure of, 292
  overview, 245, 246–247, *247*
  vs. professional partnerships, 251

mini-MBA, 295
Minto, B., 419
Monitor Group, 24
monitoring, 249
moving box, 525, *526*
multiple office consultancy firms, 246

negative disturbing events, 406
neo-liberalism, 200–201
networking, 217–218, 295
new entrants
    competition and, 151, *151*, 162–165, **163**, 168–169
    disaggregation of the value chain and, 235–236
Norton, D., 189, 194, 456

Ohmae, K., 456, 460
oil, 183
one-firm model, 246
online consultancy, 170
operational excellence, 144, 145
operations, 215–216
operations consultancy
    business models and, 63–65
    effect of, 89, **89**
    history of, 45–49, 62–63
operations–sales sequence, 215
opportunism, 98
opportunity
    diagnosis and, 432–437, *433, 435, 437–438*
    presentations and, 502, *503*
organization and strategy consultancy
    business models of, 63–65, 66
    effect of, **89**, 90
    history of, 49–53, 62–63, 66–68
    See also organization consultancy; strategy
        consultancy
organization consultancy
    effect of, 90
    history of, 51–52, 183
out-consultants, 309
outsourcing, 169, 230–231, 237
overdependence, 96–97

P2-architecture. *See* professional partnerships
Pareto principle (80/20 rule), 221, 415–416, 427
partners
    capacity planning and, 264–265
    interviews and, 284
    overview, 292, **292**, *293, 294*
    project managers and, 390
    promotion to, 301–303, *303*, 312–314
    responsibilities of, 257, 301
    sales leads and, 327
    steering committees and, 390
    See also junior partners; profit per partner; senior
        partners
Peirce, C.S., 422
penicillin, 183
performance appraisals, 296, 298–303, **299**, **300**, 565

Perot, R., 54
personal coaching, 24, 295
personality, 288
personalization strategy, 225
Peters, T.J., 24, 68
    See also *In Search of Excellence* (Peters and
        Waterman)
pharmaceutical discoveries, 183
plastics, 183
Popel, H., 477n1
Porras, J., 199
Porter, M.
    competitive forces framework and, 151, *151*, 221, 456
    on competitive strategies, 144, 146
    on competitors, 153
    as management guru, 24, 194
positive disturbing events, 406, 432–433
presentations
    interim presentations, 497, 509–510, *509–510*
    during the project, 495–496
    See also final presentations
PriceWaterhouseCoopers Consulting, 69
The Principles of Scientific Management (Taylor), 48
pro-bono projects, 12, 325
problem solving
    approaches to, 401–402, *402*
    people and, 400–401
problem statements, 428–430, *429*, **432**, 458
problems
    definition of, 403
    result gaps and, 403–406, *405*
procedure consultancy
    codified knowledge and, 225
    compared to brain and grey hair consultancy,
        142–143, *143*
    implementation and, 535
    knowledge exploitation and, 456
    leverage and, 259
    organizational structure and, 247
    overview, 141–142, 173, 195–196
    people in, 277
    profit per partner and, 263, *264*
    training and, 294
    See also software-based consultancy
process consultation, 27
procurement, 216, 356–360
product leadership, 144–145
productivity, 263–264
professional managers, 56
professional partnerships
    career structure of, 292
    legal form of, 254
    vs. managed professional business, 251
    overview, 245–246, *245*
professional procurement, 358
professional services
    categories of, 21–25, **22**
    See also consultancy services
professionalism, 251, 252